CITIES UNDER STRESS

LIST OF CONTRIBUTORS:

Thomas J. Anton
Roy W. Bahl
Kenneth P. Ballard
William J. Baumol
W. Patrick Beaton
Robert W. Burchell
Stephen C. Casey
Jerry P. Cawley
Margaret A. Corwin
Edward Duensing
Glenn W. Fisher
Judith Getzels
David Greytak
Richard D. Gustely
James W. Hughes
Franklin J. James
Kevin L. Kramer
Helen F. Ladd
David Listokin
Katharine C. Lyall

Ann R. Markusen
Astrid E. Merget
Lennox L. Moak
John H. Mollenkopf
Thomas Muller
Richard P. Nathan
Dick Netzer
George Palumbo
John E. Petersen
George E. Peterson
Robert Ross
Seymour Sacks
Annalee Saxenian
Larry Schroeder
John Shannon
Donald Shepard
George Sternlieb
Bruce Wallin
Marc A. Weiss

CITIES UNDER STRESS

the fiscal crises of urban america

edited by
robert w. burchell and david listokin

THE CENTER FOR URBAN POLICY RESEARCH
RUTGERS, THE STATE UNIVERSITY OF NEW JERSEY
P.O. BOX 489
PISCATAWAY, NEW JERSEY 08854

CENTER
FOR URBAN
POLICY RESEARCH

Published in the United States of America
by the Center for Urban Policy Research
Building 4051—Kilmer Campus
New Brunswick, New Jersey   08903

Library of Congress Cataloging in Publication Data
Main entry under title:

Cities under stress.

  Bibliography: p.
  1. Municipal finance—United States—Addresses,
essays, lectures. 2. Intergovernmental fiscal
relations—United States—Addresses, essays, lectures.
I. Burchell, Robert W. II. Listokin, David.
HJ9145.C48   352.1'0973   80-21214
ISBN 0-88285-064-4

Cover Design by Francis G. Mullen

About the Contributors

Thomas J. Anton is Professor of Political Science and Director of the Intergovernmental Fiscal Analysis Project, University of Michigan.

Roy W. Bahl is Professor of Economics and Director, Metropolitan Studies Program, Maxwell School, Syracuse University.

Kenneth P. Ballard is Economist, Regional Economic Analysis Division, Bureau of Economic Analysis, U.S. Department of Commerce.

William J. Baumol is Professor of Economics, Department of Economics, Princeton University.

W. Patrick Beaton is Associate Research Professor, Center for Urban Policy Research, Rutgers University.

Robert W. Burchell is Research Professor, Center for Urban Policy Research, Rutgers University.

Stephen C. Casey is Research Associate, Center for Urban Policy Research, Rutgers University.

Jerry P. Cawley is Research Associate, the Intergovernmental Fiscal Analysis Project, University of Michigan.

Margaret A. Corwin is Associate at Romanek-Golub, a Chicago real estate firm.

Edward Duensing is Librarian, Center for Urban Policy Research, Rutgers University.

Glenn W. Fischer is Regents Professor of Urban Affairs, Political Science Department, Wichita State University.

Judith Getzels is Principal Research Associate, American Planning Association.

David Greytak is Professor of Economics and Associate Director, Metropolitan Studies Program, Maxwell School, Syracuse University.

Richard D. Gustely is Chief of Analysis Branch, Regional Economic Analysis Division, Bureau of Economic Analysis, U.S. Department of Commerce.

James W. Hughes is Professor of Urban Planning and Policy Development, Livingston College, Rutgers University.

Franklin J. James is Director, Urban Policy Staff, U.S. Department of Housing and Urban Development.

Kevin L. Kramer is Research Associate, the Intergovernmental Fiscal Analysis Project, University of Michigan.

Helen F. Ladd is Assistant Professor, Department of City and Regional Planning, Harvard University.

David Listokin is Associate Research Professor, Center for Urban Policy Research, Rutgers University.

Katharine C. Lyall is Professor, Center for Metropolitan Planning and Research, Johns Hopkins University.

Ann R. Markusen is Assistant Professor, Department of City and Regional Planning, University of California, Berkeley.

Astrid E. Merget is Associate Professor of Public Administration, Public Administration Department, George Washington University.

Lennox L. Moak is consultant to Blyth Eastman Dillon and Company and Senior Lecturer, School of Urban and Public Policy, University of Pennsylvania.

John H. Mollenkopf is Director, Program on Urban Studies, Stanford University.

Thomas Muller is Principal Research Associate, The Urban Institute.

Richard P. Nathan is Director, Princeton Urban and Regional Research, Woodrow Wilson School, Princeton University.

Dick Netzer is Dean, Graduate School of Public Administration, New York University.

George Palumbo is Assistant Professor of Economics, Canisius University.

John E. Petersen is Director, Government Finance Research Center, Municipal Finance Officers Association.

George E. Peterson is Director, Public Finance Group, The Urban Institute.

Robert Ross is Assistant Professor of Economics, Siena College.

Seymour Sacks is Professor of Economics, Economics Department, Syracuse University.

Annalee Saxenian is a doctoral candidate, Department of City and Regional Planning, University of California, Berkeley.

Larry Schroeder is Associate Professor, Metropolitan Studies Program, Maxwell School, Syracuse University.

John Shannon is Assistant Director, U.S. Advisory Commission on Intergovernmental Relations.

Donald Shepard is Research Associate, Metropolitan Studies Program, Syracuse University.

George Sternlieb is Director, Center for Urban Policy Research, Rutgers University.

Bruce Wallin is Analyst, Taxation and Finance Section, U.S. Advisory Commission on Intergovernmental Relations.

Marc A. Weiss is a doctoral candidate, Department of City and Regional Planning, University of California, Berkeley.

CONTENTS

SECTION V. THE NEW DOMINANCE OF INTERGOVERN-MENTAL TRANSFERS

BIBLIOGRAPHY

INTRODUCTION

Robert W. Burchell and David Listokin - ISSUES IN CITY FINANCE: OVERVIEW AND SUMMARY

INTRODUCTION

Cities Under Stress: The Fiscal Crises of Urban America is a collection of invited essays about cities in the United States and the problems they face in delivering adequate and regular public services to their resident populations. *Cities Under Stress* are those declining, and in some cases, rapidly growing, political subdivisions which cannot adequately meet current public service demands. *The Fiscal Crises of Urban America* are the specific inabilities of many of these jurisdictions to: (1) provide regular operating funds to support threshold levels of basic services—police, fire, public works, tax assessment/collection, recreation/culture, etc.; (2) regularly and fully fund capital facilities or pension and benefit systems; (3) maintain an adequate and sound financial position in the public bond markets; (4) critically evaluate necessary services/expenditures and shape a public service system that reflects these needs; and, (5) maximize the mix of and emphasis on local revenues and intergovernmental transfers such that local businesses and residents are not overburdened and federal/state dependency is not incurred.

The introduction which follows is divided into two parts. *Part I*, traces the growth of the field of municipal finance and, within its development and maturation, isolates several recurring issues or themes. *Part II*, structures and summarizes the various contributions to this volume according to these identified issues.

PART I
THE GROWTH OF MUNICIPAL FINANCE:
ISSUES OF EMPHASIS OF THE FIELD

BACKGROUND—THE STUDY OF PUBLIC FINANCE

The study of public finance in the United States dates from the late nineteenth century when the justification, nature and impact of the public fisc was first analyzed. In 1879, Henry George criticized the existing tax structure and advocated a single value tax.[1] Shortly afterwards, H.C. Adams discussed the nature and burden of taxation in *Public Debts* (1887) and the *Science of Finance* (1898).[2] These pioneers laid the conceptual foundation for successor analyses in the first half of the twentieth century including Seligman's *Studies in Public Finance* (1925)[3] and other monographs by Fagan (1935), Hansen and Perloff (1944) and Pigou (1949).[4]

This first half century of public finance literature was characterized by the following themes.[5] Attention focused on *public revenues* as opposed to *public expenditures/services.* While there were some exceptions, such as Herbert Simon's study of local services in the San Francisco Bay Area (1943),[6] prior to the 1950s public finance was appropriately referred to as the "economics of taxation."[7] Typically, significant public revenues, such as property taxes, would be described and then analyzed as to their: *incidence*—who paid the tax; *efficiency*—how fruitful was the revenue after adminstrative costs were considered; *stability*—what fluctuations in revenue producing capacity could be expected; and *burden*—how did public taxation influence the private sector.

REFINEMENTS IN THE PUBLIC FINANCE ANALYSIS OF REVENUES AND EXPENDITURES

Beginning in the 1950s, the public finance literature burgeoned in number and expanded in scope. The analysis of revenues took into account newly important income sources such as sales and income taxes and applied the then emerging econometric techniques to examine them. More important was the maturation of study to include significant attention to the other half of the public finance equation—*public outputs/expenditures.* As discussed by Haveman and Margolis:[8]

> Since the mid-1950s. . .the economics literature reflect(s) a concern with the effect of public *expenditures* on the size and composition of the nation's output, the allocation of its resources, and the distribution of its income. Similarly, the practice of governmental budgeting and decisionmaking has begun to recognize the importance of applying analysis to *expenditure* decisions. The economic analysis of taxation policy has become supplemented by serious efforts to evaluate and appraise public *expenditure* alternatives (emphasis added).

Pioneer work in public output/expenditure analysis was done by Richard Musgrave (1959)[9] and Charles Tiebout (1956, 1961).[10] The former considered the *role* or *function* of the public service sector, while the latter studied *variations in the delivery or choice of public outputs* and how and why these variations occurred.

In *The Theory of Public Finance*[11], Musgrave posited a tripartite view of public output/expenditures—these served the roles of: (1) *resource allocation;* (2) *income distribution;* and (3) *stabilization of the economy.*[12] Tiebout elaborated on the allocation dynamic and discussed a decentralized choice process for public goods/expenditures, namely that mobile consumers would choose to reside in those communities providing their desired public service amenities at their desired level of taxed cost.[13] Tiebout thus conceptualized the allocation process in market terms—"the consumer may be visualized as walking to a private market place to buy his goods. . .to a community where the prices (taxes) of community services are set."[14] He further argued that this process was efficient—in contrast with Paul Samuelson's allegations that a decentralized choice for public goods increased their cost.[15]

The Musgrave-Tiebout analyses in the 1950s, sparked a new generation of public finance studies in the 1960s and 1970s. These considered both revenues and expenditures as well as the historical issues/themes of allocation, incidence, equity, efficiency, stabilization, etc.[16]

EMERGENCE AND THEMES OF MUNICIPAL FINANCE
IN THE 1960s AND 1970s

Another indication of the growing breadth of public finance[17] was the increasing attention paid to important subsectors such as the subnational level—state and local finance. This paper focuses on the latter or *municipal* sector. Municipal finance was traditionally largely ignored except as an object of derision by muckrakers or the subject for remediation by the "scientific government" writers of the 1920s to 1940s.[18] By the late 1950s - early 1960s, this situation changed and municipal finance moved to the forefront of interest. As discussed by Harvey Brazer in 1967:[19]

> State and local finance is more than an institutional subdivision of public finance. It is concerned with taxation, expenditures, debt issue and management, and intergovernmental fiscal relations in the context of a multiplicity of open economies. This distnctive feature will offer a peculiarly inviting and challenging opportunity for study.

Brazer's prediction proved prophetic as the 1960s and 1970s saw an outpouring of municipal finance literature by economists, planners and political scientists. In the 1960s, landmark monographs were published by Netzer (1966), Campbell and Sacks (1967), Bahl (1969), and others.[20] The literature of this period considered both sides of municipal finance equation, i.e., costs as well as revenues. On the *cost* or *expenditure* side, the literature focused on *consumption* or *output* based determinants—the reasons *why* expenditures occurred, such as changes in population size or growth rate of the residential sector and the basic nature and composition of the nonresidential sector. The focus on revenue was on the primary revenue source of the times—property taxes.

The 1970s saw important works by Margolis(1970), Baumol (1973), Peterson (1976), Bahl (1976) and others.[21] The literature in this period also analyzed both expenditures and revenues but with a growing breadth and sophistication. In terms of *expenditures* it considered not only *consumption factors*—why expenditures occurred, but also: (1) *production elements*—the *inputs* (land, labor and physical infrastructure) needed to provide services; and (2) *production throughput*—the *process* including bureaucratic, political and other factors entailed in the delivery of public services. Examples include: Stanley's analysis of the impacts of municipal employee unionization (1972), Newton's examination of the politics of public services (1975) and Bahl's study of police service production inputs

(1978).[22] For *revenues*, the 1970s literature continued to emphasize the property tax, especially such topics as the effect of this revenue on urban redevelopment and the necessary reform of the property tax including regional tax base sharing and various tax limitation strategies. And for the first time local *nonproperty tax revenues,* such as user charges, miscellaneous revenues and state and federal *intergovernmental transfers* were analyzed in-depth.

The 1970s also saw increasing reference to the *crisis* nature of municipal finance. The 1973 ACIR review, *City Financial Emergencies,*[23] was followed by others depicting and measuring the growing level of urban fiscal "hardship", "distress" or "burden." Examples include: Pettengill's, *Can Cities Survive—The Fiscal Plight of American Cities*(1974); Stanley's, *Cities in Trouble* (1976); Nathan and Adam's *Understanding Central City Hardship* (1976); Meyer and Quigley's *Local Public Finance and the Fiscal Squeeze* (1977) and Bahl's *The Fiscal Outlook for Cities* (1978).[24]

These themes are elaborated subsequently, yet this condensed review reveals that from a relatively minor subject of public finance twenty years ago, municipal finance has blossomed into a largely independent discipline. With this change, the municipal finance literature has grown in magnitude, expanded in breadth, matured in its use of analytical tools, and in recent years, begun to consider the origins and nature of urban fiscal stress.

THE NURTURING OF MUNICIPAL FINANCE DURING THE 1960s AND 1970s

The ascendancy of municipal finance in the 1960s and 1970s was due to several factors including: 1) *a general increase in public expenditures*; and growing interest in 2) *metropolitan dynamics; 3) the nature and causes of urban crisis;* 4) *issues of public service equity;* and 5) *the effects and spread of fiscal federalism.*

THE GROWTH OF EXPENDITURES

The sheer growth of expenditures by local units of government has flagged attention to municipal finance. In 1967, Brazer commented that the "resurgent interest in . . .local finance stems not only from the wide array of conceptual issues. . .but also from the growing recognition of the importance of [this] sector in the national economy."[25] A decade later municipal finance continued in growth and economic significance. As noted by Petersen and Spain:[26]

The state and local sector have become highly significant economic topics. In the last three decades, state and local expenditures have increased dramatically as a percentage of the gross national product, growing from 10 percent in 1950 to 17 percent in 1978. . .Also, employment in the state-local sector has grown faster than in any other major part of the economy during the last twenty years, moving from 4 million full time employees in 1955 to 12 million fully employed by 1978.

INTEREST IN METROPOLITAN DYNAMICS

The 1960s and 1970s witnessed increasing attention to such metropolitan concerns as city-suburb relationships, the development of metropolitan and local land use policies and the dynamics of industrial location. Publications by Vernon and Hoover (1959), Bollens and Schmandt, (1965), Chinitz (1964), Forrester (1969), Campbell and Sacks (1967), Kain (1969) and the Committee for Economic Development (1970)[27] considered such issues as economic shifts between city, suburb and non-metropolitan areas; the pressure promoting exclusionary zoning by outer ring communities; and the locational decisions of industries across metropolitan and regional lines. *Study of the metropolitan dynamic has fostered interest in municipal finance. The way in which communities provide services and impose taxes to pay for public services are deemed essential factors influencing many characteristics of and changes in the metropolitan area.* To illustrate, from the early 1960s (Carroll and Sacks [1961], Pickard [1962] and Beck [1963]) to the late 1970s (Meyer and Quigley [1977]),[29] analysts examining industrial location decisions have emphasized the local property tax burden and quality of local services as important influences. The property tax and interlocal variations in this levy are also viewed as contributory factors influencing the housing search patterns in metropolitan areas. As aptly stated by Norman Williams in *American Planning Law:*[30]

> The dominant role of the local real property tax system in American land use controls must be clearly understood. . .Fiscal considerations have come to dominate land use controls. . .The demand for those services now financed locally has been increasing and the financial pressure on local governments has necessarily been increasing along with it. Moreover, more and more such governments have discovered that land use controls can be used effectively to improve the municipality's fiscal position. Specifically, zoning can be used to encourage "good ratables" and also to discourage "bad ratables".

Municipal finance in general, and property tax in particular, are deemed to influence metropolitan development in other ways as well. The low taxation of land, based on the value of current use, is charged as a factor encouraging the speculative holding of *undeveloped* land in the path of urban development.[31] Conversely, the property tax's reassessment provisions have been viewed as discouraging the rehabilitation of *deteriorated* urban properties.[32]

THE URBAN CRISIS *(See also 100-200 Series Bibliography)*

The problems of the cities came to the fore in the 1960s and 1970s. Urban disturbances were followed by national task forces i.e., Kaiser (1976), Douglas, (1968), and HUD (1975),[33] and enactment of scores of social and housing programs. The commissions and programs were designed to identify and remedy the causes of the urban crisis. These included social and physical factors as well as fiscal origins of both a demand and supply nature. In the words of the National Advisory Commission on Civil Disorders: "the decay of the central city continues—its revenue base eroded. . .its budget and tax rate inflated by rising costs and increasing numbers of dependent citizens."[34]

The nexus between urban and fiscal is seen in a rich literature in the 1960s and 1970s including: Brazer (1959), Heilbrun (1966), Bahl (1969, 1975, 1978), Netzer (1970), Margolis (1971), Hirsch (1971), Neenan (1972), Fisher (1973), and Muller (1975).[35]

The worsening urban financial problems in the late 1970s reinforced the study of urban municipal finance. New York City serves as a prime example. This economically distressed city, already the subject of numerous economic analyses from the 1960s to the mid 1970s[36] as its economic fortunes wavered,* became a central topic of the municipal finance literature in the late 1970s when the City faced financial bankruptcy.[37] These studies referred to New York's experience as a harbinger of the problems that would confront other

---

* So many studies were conducted that a "Study of the Studies" was compiled in December 1971. See City of New York Commission on State-City Relations, *A Study of the Studies: An Analysis of the Work and Recommendations of a Generation of Task Forces on New York City's Fiscal Crisis* (New York: December 1971).

urban areas; adopted New York as the case study to examine the dynamics of decline; and used New York's financial records as benchmarks for gauging the fiscal solvency of other central cities.[38]

ISSUES OF EQUITY

The 1960s and 1970s witnessed growing sensitivity to issues of equity[39] including equal access to jobs, educational opportunities, public services, voting rights, etc. Federal and state courts issued landmark decisions such as *Shaw, Serrano* and *Robinson*[40] placing the force of law to further the promise of equity in American society
Sensitivity to equity is another factor encouraging the study of municipal finance and services. At times this linkage is *explicit* such as *Shaw* guaranteeing that blacks and whites should benefit equally from the provision of local services[41] or *Robinson v. Cahill* mandating that public education could not be funded solely from the local property tax as this levy yielded uneven local resources.[42] The advocacy of regional tax base sharing to replace interlocal inequities in property tax wealth has a similar theme.[43]
More frequent, however, is the *implicit* theme of equity in many municipal finance concerns. The analysis of a tax's *incidence* is fired by the objective that the *burden* of taxation should be fairly allocated.[44] The more than decade long ACIR study of metropolitan disparities and the tax capacity of jurisdictions[45] is also, in part, motivated by concerns of equity, namely that metropolitan fiscal disparities be reduced and that the tax burden of states and localities be related to their individual economic capacities.

FISCAL FEDERALISM

The last two decades have seen *fiscal federalism*[46] —the provision of revenues/expenditures/services across the federal, state and local levels of government—become a central issue to social scientists as well as an explicit federal strategy under the Nixon, Ford and Carter administrations.[47] This period has seen some changes in the *administrative* responsibility of providing services, (i.e., state rather than local assumption for public transportation) and has witnessed sweeping shifts in the *funding* burden as states and especially, the federal government have enacted major assistance programs for municipalities and school districts.
Fiscal federalism is *directly* linked to the concerns of municipal finance such as the provision and financing of public services. It is

also related to many of the 1960-1970 themes which have been described as *indirectly* fostering interest in municipal finance. The growth of subnational expenditures has, in part, been realized by the growing federal largesse. Concern over some of the shortfalls of the existing metropolitan system (i.e., periodic disfunctional placement of industry and a growing suburban exclusionary ring), is one of the reasons generating interest in fiscal federalism, especially the search for more equitable division of governmental responsibilities in metropolitan areas. Similarly, the urban crisis is inexorably linked to fiscal federalism, both in its *causes* (i.e., central cities often must shoulder an unfair tax burden), and its *remediation* (i.e., federal or state governments should fund a larger share of central city welfare and other social service expenditures). Finally, issues of equity are often synonymous with fiscal federalim. A potentially inequitable system of funding schools from the local property tax is altered through greater state financial assumption. Financial inequities faced by central cities are addressed by increased state and federal spending, etc.

The close relationship between fiscal federalism, municipal finance and the multiple related concerns fostering the study of municipal finance and fiscal federalism is evidenced from the titles of numerous publications such as: *Fiscal Balance in the American Federal System* (1976), *Fiscal Issues in the Future of Federalism* (1968), "Federalism and Intergovernmental Problems of Urban Finance" (1973), and "Social Equity and Fiscal Federalism" (1974).[48]

In summary, municipal finance emerged as a separate area of study only twenty years ago. Though a young discipline, it has received significant attention in the 1960s and 1970s because it has touched upon many of the central issues associated with these decades.

RELATIONSHIP OF MUNICIPAL AND PUBLIC FINANCE

Municipal finance, having significant roots in public finance, shares many similarities with its progenitor, including: 1) *themes,* 2) *conceptual frameworks,* and 3) *functional distinctions.* Similar *themes* include the focusing on the incidence, burden and equity of public revenues. Discussion of these characteristics is found in the classical European public finance literature including works by Pareto and Pigou; figures prominently in the writings of significant early American public finance theorists such as Seligman and Musgrave; continued in the pioneer municipal finance literature by Netzer and Burkehead; and still remains of central concern in the more current municipal finance writings by Mieszkowski and others.

Municipal finance also continues the more important *conceptual ideas and frameworks* found in the public finance literature. Musgrave's tripartite schema of government activities serving the goals of resource allocation, income distribution and stabilization of the economy has been used as a framework to consider the appropriate functions of local government.[49] Tiebout's concepts have also been incorporated in considering many municipal finance topics. One example is the evaluation of the effects of intergovernmental transfers on public choice and governmental efficiency—do such transfers prolong the life of inefficient local governmental units that without such aid would be "voted out" by residents deciding to leave because of high taxes/poor services. Tiebout's concepts have also been used in studying the municipal finance conerns of capitalization of the property tax and suburban exploitation, namely that high city property taxes are capitalized to lower urban property values, thereby encouraging urban residents to "vote with their feet" and move to the suburbs.

Municipal finance also shares with public finance the characteristic that studies often are divided along the *functional lines of public expenditures* or *public revenues.* This distinction is followed in the discussion below which examines public finance themes in the areas of municipal expenditures, traditional municipal revenues, and emerging municipal revenues.

SIGNIFICANT THEMES IN THE MUNICIPAL FINANCE LITERATURE

MUNICIPAL EXPENDITURES

The municipal finance literature has examined the *input, output and throughput* of public expenditures. The earliest and most significant attention was given to the *consumption or output* of local government, namely what social/economic determinants influence the level/type of municipal outlays. In 1959, Harvey Brazer authored one of the earliest determinants studies.[50] After considering the expenditure patterns of hundreds of cities, he concluded that municipal size, growth rate and degree of urbanism all were significantly correlated with variations in local costs. The Brazer analysis was followed by a rich determinants literature in the 1960s and 1970s.

In the 1960s, Hirsch (1960) examined the effects of population size and growth; Baumol (1963) considered the influence of governmental size and complexity; Kee (1964) studied the influence of intrametropolitan and intercity fragmentation; Sacks (1964) analyzed the impact of intergovernmental grants; and Osman (1966) considered the effect of categorical grants.[51] The 1960s determinants literature grew so rich and complex that there developed a separate strain *summarizing* the extant literature. Examples include: Miner (1963), Jurnow (1963), Bahl and Saunder(1965), and Bahl (1968).[52]

Determinants analysis was pursued vigorously in the 1970s. Weicher (1970), Sunley (1971), Gabler (1971), Booms (1971) Sternlieb (1974), Pattie (1974) and Beaton (1975) considered the influence of such "classical" factors as population size and growth rate.[53] (The "literature of the literature" also continued; see Barro [1974] and Gramlich [1976]).[54] "New" determinants were also analyzed including the composition of a community's tax base (Ladd, 1974), and the size/nature of a community's nonresidential work force (Beaton, 1978).[55]

While study of the determinants of the *consumption* or *output* stage of public expenditures has dominated the municipal finance literature, in recent years attention has also turned to the *supply* or *input* as well as the *throughput* or *process* of municipal services. The supply side was historically considered mainly by planners/ regional scientists interested in the physical infrastructure demands of growth. Early examples include the Wheaton and Schussheim (1955) and Isard and Coughlin (1957) projections of the capital facilities (i.e., roads, sewers, street lights, etc.) required by suburban subdivisions.[56] In the late 1960s - early 1970s economists joined this group in studying service input. Bahl's 1978 analysis of police service production elements—manpower, and operating and capital components—typifies this new level of scrutiny.[57]

The 1970s also saw analysis of municipal expenditure *throughput - the process* affecting the delivery of services. This *process* is clearly complex and includes many elements. Stanley (1972), Peterson (1976) and others have examined how unionization, bargaining for fringe benefits and other factors affect the *labor* input to providing public services.[58] Political scientists have studied the influence of the *bureaucracy* on service delivery and have also searched for more efficient *management tools* such as PPBS, cost-benefit analysis, and zero base budgeting.[59] The service delivery process also has a *political* imprint and this important aspect of throughput has been considered by Lineberry and Fowler, Davis and others.[60]

An associated change in the 1970s municipal finance *expenditure* literature is the increasing attention to important *cost subsectors.* One example, discussed already, is the *public service labor market* and the associated issues of pension costs, public/private salary comparisons, etc. Another is the topic of *public capital needs, outlays and financing mechanisms* including such issues as bond rating systems, the security of public issues and the effect of rising interest rates. The ACIR, (1970), Bahl and Greytak (1976) and Peterson (1978) represent just a small sampling of the subsector-specific literature contributors.[61]

MUNICIPAL REVENUES - PROPERTY TAX
(See also 400 Series Bibliography)

The study of municipal finance traditionally focused on the *property tax*—the most significant revenue for most local units of government. While early public finance writers such as Seligman had "scathing denunciation" for this revenue,[62] municipal finance literature in the 1960s questioned many of the traditional accusations. Seminal works by Burkhead (1963) and Netzer (1966),[63] arguing that the property tax's advantages outweighed its demerits, have been followed by numerous studies, in part supporting and in part questioning, the Burkehead - Netzer conclusions. Examples include publications by the U.S. Advisory Commission on Intergovernmental Relations, Lindholm (1968, 1977), Mieszkowski (1972), Aaron (1975), and Hamilton (1975).[64]

The 1970s literature is also characterized by consideration of *reforms* designed to address the property's tax's believed harmful effects on certain group or areas. These reforms include the introduction of circuit breakers to alleviate the property tax burden on the elderly; adoption of regional tax base sharing mechanisms to reduce interlocal revenue disparities; revision of property tax statutes to remove disincentives to inner-city rehabilitation; introduction of property tax abatement/deferment programs to provide an incentive to urban renovation; adoption of a classified property tax system to encourage growth of desired real estate sectors; and improvement in the equity and efficiency of property tax assessment and administration.[65]

In numerous respects these studies have set the conceptual base for evaluation of Proposition 13 generation reforms limiting either 1) property taxes that can be imposed or 2) increases in public expenditures funded from the property tax. These measures have been studied by Harriss (1973), Ladd (1978), Peterson (1978), and others.[66]

NONTRADITIONAL MUNICIPAL REVENUES
(See also 500-600 Series Bibliography)

While the property tax has clearly dominated municipal finance revenue studies, the increasing significance of new sources, such as local nonproperty taxes (i.e., user charges) and state and federal intergovernmental assistance has sparked interest in these revenues. To illustrate, the literature has considered many facets of intergovernmental transfers. Some studies examined *trends* - how has the funding/emphasis of intergovernmental assistance changed, especially in urban areas. Examples include: Nathan (1968), Herbert (1975), Maxwell (1975), Peterson (1976), and Break (1978).[67] Another topic is the *impact* of intergovernmental assistance. Several analysts have considered the *price/substitution effect* of intergovernmental grants - how extralocal assistance affects the local price of services and consequently the local desirability to increase the level of services.[68] Early work in this area by Scott (1952) has been followed by a rich literature including: Sacks (1964), Gramlich (1969), Oates (1972), Weicher (1977), and the ACIR (1977).[69] The related *income* effect of intergovernmental assistance has also been studied, namely how extralocal aid can result in added local income for private/public expenditures. As discussed by George Break:[70]

> By increasing the fungible resources available to the recipient government, most grants generate income effects. These can be observed most clearly when the grants are completely general and completely unrestricted, and the establishment of general revenue sharing in 1972 greatly expanded research opportunities in this area.

In addition to considering the *trends* and *impact* of intergovernmetal assistance, the municipal finance literature has also analyzed *the extent to which aid is allocated to those communities with the greatest fiscal and other needs.* This analysis typically entails measurement of a community's fiscal capacity, a topic which although not new has recently assumed considerable significance. The measuring of local capacity was a topic of early concern to those involved in school aid. Classical studies include Cubberly's *School Funds and Their Apportionment* (1905), Strayer and Haig's *The Financing of Education in the State of New York* (1923) and Newcomber's *An Index of the Tax Paying Ability of State and Local Governments.* (1935).[71] As intergovernmental assistance expanded to include additional non-educational activities so did interest in measuring local capacity. In 1937, for example, the Social Security

Board examined the use of income as a fiscal capacity measure[72] and similar studies were continued by Studenski and Landreth in the 1940s and 1950s.[73]

The introduction and growth of scores of intergovernmental aids in the 1960s and 1970s, such as Revenue Sharing and Community Development Block Grants, further encouraged study of local capacity and the targeting of aid to municipalities. The ACIR authored numerous influential monographs on this topic (1962, 1971) as did Reischauer (1974), the National Science Foundation (1957), and Nathan (1976).[74] In a similar fashion, the introduction of multiple programs in the late 1970s designed to alleviate urban distress, further catalyzed interest in measuring city fiscal and other characteristics. Important urban hardship measurement studies were conducted by Nathan (1976), Peterson, (1978), and the U.S. Departments of the Treasury (1978) and Housing and Urban Development (1979).[75]

PART II
SUMMARY OF *CITIES UNDER STRESS* ACCORDING TO IDENTIFIED MUNICIPAL FINANCE ISSUES

INTRODUCTION

Cities Under Stress: The Fiscal Crises of Urban America views the reaction to urban fiscal difficulties as taking very characteristic forms:

(1) a questioning of the city's role—are urban agglomerations dinosaurs of the metropolitan area and, as such are their observed fiscal problems the precursor of "going out of business?"

(2) an analysis and comparison of the city and its structure to other cities as a way of forecasting the extent/duration of current ills.

(3) a search for the roots of expenditure increases while altering or controlling service demand.

(4) a scrutiny and rethinking of traditional local revenue sources to emphasize revenue productivity and de-emphasize revenue burden.

(5) an embracing of intergovernmental financial assistance yet a rejection of concommitant intergovernmental influence.

These reactions to fiscal stress by cities represent both the themes and basic partitions of this book. The volume contains five or six essays in each of the following subject areas:

I. *The City in Stress - Does it Have the Economic Functions to Support Its Service Base?*
II. *Fiscal Profiles of Cities in Stress*
III. *Municipal Expenditures - Cause and Control*
IV. *Historic Municipal Revenues - Reworked and Retooled*
V. *The New Dominance of Intergovernmental Transfers*

The essays, which are summarized in the following pages, have been carefully chosen to present balance in coverage, point of view, and methodological approaches to the identified issues.

THE CITY IN STRESS - DOES IT HAVE THE ECONOMIC FUNCTIONS TO SUPPORT ITS SERVICE BASE?
(See also 100-200 Series Bibliography)

The first collection of essays begins with a description of the city in stress. Does the city have currently viable or future alternative economic functions to support its public service base? The section begins with two classic views of the future of the city. The first is that the city, in any form, is no longer able to support its economic base; various indicators are used to show its lack of capacity as an ongoing entity. The other is that the city is indeed capable of withstanding change, will adjust to its external environment and while, in the short term, may be somewhat distressed and resource poor, it will emerge as a renewed entity streamlined and attuned to a new set of demands.

THE CITY RESISTANT TO CHANGE

The traditional view of cities and their capacities is expressed in the paper by William Baumol - *Technological Change and Urban Equilibrium* - in which he discusses the growth of cities historically as : (1) outgrowths of the need for transportation centers; (2) aggregations of facilities desiring quick and easy communications; and finally, (3) critical geographic locations for manufacturers relative to resources for the product that was being produced. These were the classic reasons for city formation and for a significant node developing within selected geographic areas.

As Baumol explains it, cities now undergoing change have had to alter their form and consequently, new types of cities are developing. Cities have grown peripherally outward because there is currently available auto/truck transportation and an interstate sytem that minimizes the cost and time of product distribution. In addition, we now employ the telephone, remote computer terminal, telex and other forms of communication which permit the separation of administration and production functions. Finally, most industries employ a continuous production process which encourages larger, typically peripheral, locations.

A critical mass of complementary activities as evidenced in a metropolitan node—the unique city advantage—has been eroded by each of these technological advancements. Baumol notes that, most probably, a large share of the labor force will follow economic entities to the periphery of metropolitan areas and current central cities will be much smaller and poorer. Over the short-run, central cities will experience population thinning, housing abandonment and commercial /industrial decline. Cities initially will react to change in terms of increasing welfare-dependent populations, civil unrest, higher than average crime rates, etc. There is, however, an historic role for cities. In the long term they will serve as home for historic metropolitan needs: the cultural activities found in theaters, libraries and museums, retain specialty shops and restaurants of various varieties and scales.

Continuing this view of central city is the paper by Franklin James - *Economic Distress in Central Cities.* James notes that the key to understanding central cities is to analyze their employment trends i.e., the direction and magnitude of job growth. Cities which are experiencing negative job growth will also likely experience population losses, reductions in per capita income, higher-than-average unemployment rates, drops in property valuation per capita and clearly burdensome per capita tax rates. James notes that fully one-third of the major cities in the United States have lost significant segments of their job base over the previous decade. While most of this took place in the Northeast and North Central regions of the country, and particularly so in the manufacturing sectors of these areas, loss was not totally contained within these regions. Manufacturing growth in the South and West as a whole, has barely held its own. Franklin James is careful to point out that substantial growth in Southern and Western high technology industries as well as in their service sectors have contributed to the difference in job growth that is normally associated with the Sunbelt/Frostbelt, boom/bust phenomenon. Further, according to James, the trends that we have observed in the past are likely to continue into the future. He notes that of those cities whose job base *declined* during the 1960s, the large majority of them repeated this trend during the 1970s. The repetitive sequence for job *growth* locations also seems to be true.

James points out four key factors affecting the viability of central cities:

1. The suburbanization and decentralization of population and jobs;

2. General recessions;

3. Regional shifts of employment from Frostbelt to Sunbelt; and

4. The failure by older central cities to attract the growth industries of electronics and ordinance.

In the first case, suburbanization and decentralization, James points to the historic cheaper land and better access of the suburbs. As to general recessions, cities and the people who live in them are much more dependent upon a generally healthy national economy than is the case of suburban locations and their residents. City dwellers are the first to be hit by short and long term unemployment and have the fewest options for subsequent employment. Regional economic shifts have also been very hard on the central city. Not only have primary industries shifted from the North to the South and West but indeed they have taken with them secondary and tertiary industries which, in the aggregate, prove to be significant losses. Finally, the failure to attract the growth segment of economic development - the high technology industries as well as office space - has contributed significantly to the decline of the central city. In conclusion, James notes that what must be done to revitalize central cities is to *target* investment tax credits, accelerated depreciation, and investment development bonds directly to these locations.

In the following article by George Sternlieb and James W. Hughes - *New Dimensions of the Urban Crisis* - the decline of the central city is related to another index of change—population and population-related income. Sternlieb and Hughes point to the fact that for the past decade (1970-1980), four-in-ten cities of over 25,000 in population have lost population. If one views the family structure associated with this population loss, it is evident that the central city has lost traditional male-headed households which have been replaced by untraditional households, i.e. those headed by unrelated individuals or by females. On average, male-headed households tended to be wealthier than those of their replacements and this has had an effect on the economic base of cities. Sternlieb and Hughes note, that related to these household shifts, over the period 1970 to 1977, there has been a loss of personal income in core areas of 64.8 billion dollars. If one assumes that rent payments approach 25 percent of household income, the central cities have lost 16 billion dollars in rent paying capacity. If it is further assumed that 20 percent - or thirteen of the 64.8 billion dollars - would go to the purchase of food staples, at $200 per square foot to support a store and at an average of 20,000 square feet for each food facility, another way of viewing the decline in household income of central cities is that this loss could have resulted in the closing of 3,000 urban supermarkets over the last decade. Finally, Sternlieb and Hughes point to the fact that, while poverty in the United States is declining, in central cities it continues to increase. The authors believe that this is largely true because male-headed households are climbing out of poverty and into the suburbs while female-headed families and unrelated individuals - more often city dwellers - remain subject to all of poverty's limitations and sensitivities.

THE CITY ENCOMPASSING CHANGE

The other side of the central city picture is probably best represented by an article appearing in *Harper's* by T.D. Allman, under the title "The Urban Crisis Leaves Town."[76] In his survey of central city conditions, Allman notes that the World Trade Center in Manhattan is fully occupied, New York's Citicorp Tower, the eighth highest structure in the world, is also at-or-near full occupancy. In Boerum-Hill in Brooklyn, and Capital Hill in the District of Columbia, the issue is not neighborhood abandonment but rather the displacement of resident blacks by whites who desire to live in these neighborhoods. Further, there is selective revitalization in downtowns across the United States of considerable magnitude. The infusion of American capital to central cities is being matched by international investment by the Japanese, the mid-Easterners, Canadians, and the Germans. Allman points out, for instance, that over the period 1976 to 1978, New York City added 100,000 jobs to its employment base—

the equivalent of one-half the current employment base of the City of Atlanta. Chicago has had in recent times a lower unemployment rate than Los Angeles, and Baltimore and St. Louis have had lower unemployment rates than El Paso, Texas. Allman concludes that generally, our traditional central cities are strong and, if there have been economic shifts from the Northeast to the Southwest, the national economy can absorb these shifts, thus negating the scenario that one region is directly taking from the other. The rationale behind Allman's position is that central cities are now almost exclusive beneficiaries of a service sector explosion which now is the biggest single employer in many areas.

The themes of Allman's popularized article dominate the papers that are presented in the remaining portion of this section. In the article by Touche-Ross, Inc. and the First Bank of Boston - *Urban Fiscal Stress: A Comparative Analysis* - this belief in the resurgence of the central city is manifest in the view of the city's future fiscal resources. Prevailing wisdom has always been that older, declining cities are those most likely to have high tax burdens and expenditure ratios, and as such, those most fiscally stressed. According to the Touche-Ross study this may not be the case. Some older industrial cities are financially stronger than many of the newer cities that are emerging throughout the United States. Pittsburgh and Trenton, N.J. for example, may be much better off in terms of fiscal capacity, bonding ratings, etc. than the cities of Atlanta and Denver, whose expenditures are increasing at far greater rates than are their tax bases. The Touche-Ross study emphasizes that fiscal stress is not inevitable nor is it a constant in older, aging, manufacturing-dominated cities. Fiscal and financial equilibrium can be achieved in places with low economic resources. Further, cities with potentially-high economic resources are not immune from fiscal strain. The study concludes that the best indicators of fiscal stress may not be socio-economic indicators but rather those which gear much more closely to specific measures of fiscal capacity. The latter include: revenue diversity, tax burden per capita, property valuation per capita, etc.

The essay by John Mollenkopf - *The Post Industrial Service City* - hews closely to the general theme of urban resiliency and indicates that to better understand cities we must develop a new model of the forces that make cities grow. Cities of the future must be looked upon as the new beneficiaries of service versus manufacturing jobs, public versus private employment and political rather than economic patronage. Under this model there undoubtedly will be some larger cities that will have frail capacities yet there also will be smaller towns moving very quickly into full city status in every sense of the word. The former group of frail cities will not decline to the point of extinction but instead will assume a level of support that reflects the need for their services within the region. Mollenkopf further analyzes the supposed "temperate" city or Sunbelt advantages. He asks: Are wages really lower in the South? Is there any indication that more capital facilities per capita are being constructed there? Finally, are unions less entrenched in these locations such that workers may be found at cheaper rates? According to the author, there are no indications that any of these statements are true. Wages for skilled workers are not much different in the North than they are in the South; the value added or capital facilities per wage dollar are relatively equal; and levels of unionization are not significantly different when standardized per basic industry job. And while welfare dependency and Aid-For-Dependent-Children is higher in the North, the basic poverty level of workers and their families is far higher in the South. Mollenkopf concludes that the agglomeration of advanced services and headquarters are concentrated in a handful of cities across the nation; the Northeast and North Central regions of the country are heavy beneficiaries of these concentrations and likely to remain so in the future. Middle class, professional demand for urban realty has increased dramatically—cities across the United States will inherit this renewed demand more or less regardless of geographic location.

FISCAL PROFILES OF CITIES IN STRESS
(See also 100-200 Series Bibliography)

The second session of invited essays deals with economic profiles of cities in stress. This section views the classic indicators of central city decline and their ability to predict a city's future capacity to fund public services. This section differs from the first in that we move from the general policy considerations of whether or not the city in its current form has a future, to an analysis of the specific measures which evaluate a city's short term economic response capacity and the relationship of these measures to the ability of the city to finance its public services.

The first paper, by members of the Center for Urban Policy Research staff - *Measuring Urban Distress* - analyzes the several indices of urban hardship, i.e., the procedures used by federal agencies to rank cities in terms of need as a prerequisite to the distribution of their intergovernmental revenue transfers. This article surveys, in broad fashion, the various classification systems used to specify urban distress by fifteen agencies and research institutions throughout the United States.

The need indices or hardship ranking systems are grouped into three general areas. The first, *Programmatic Area Eligibility,* are those indices which serve as a first-cut, pass-fail system for jurisdictional funding eligiblity—i.e., does a city qualify for federal assistance or not. These would contain most of the HUD Urban Development Action Grant and Economic Development Administration programs. A second category of hardship measures is termed *Relative Distress/Need Indices* and ranks cities in terms of need for potential revenue allocations above a particular threshold. For instance, Newark, Chicago and Denver may be ranked 1, 10, and 30th respectively, according to economic distress—all cities with a ranking of 10 or higher will receive funding in proportion to severity of distress. This group of rankings is typically produced by research organizations or oversight committees such as: The Brookings Institution, The Congressional Budget Office, The General Accounting Office, and the Institute for the Future.

A third category of hardship measure is *Resource Allocation Systems.* Need designation systems under this grouping distribute revenues to already-qualified jurisidictions on the basis of hardship. Typical of these allocation procedures are those mechanisms associated with the Community Development Block Grant and General Revenue Sharing programs.

After viewing the various classification systems, grouped by the three allocation mechanisms discussed above, the conclusion drawn by the Center for Urban Policy Research team is that classification systems for specific purposes, i.e., for the isolation of locations of social, economic and/or fiscal distress, because they employ similar variables, almost always derive similar cities in a reasonably similar rank order. This finding implies from a policy perspective that given certain variable constructs, cities and particularly large cities can, with relative regularity, be ranked in terms of urban distress. Not only can they be so classified, but given a definite objective, i.e. the specification of economic, social, physical or fiscal distress, most classification systems will produce the same results. Notwithstanding technical difficulties and political grandfathering of one type or another, intergovernmental transfers potentially can be targeted to those locations most in need of revenue assistance.

In the article which follows by John E. Petersen - *Big City Borrowing Costs and Credit Quality* - Peterson notes that the various urban hardship indices developed by different public agencies have a definite equivalent in the private sector. This equivalent is the city bond ratings developed by private bond rating agencies throughout the country. Petersen looks at several of the measures found within the more common urban hardship indices and observes that both the inclusive measures and derivative rankings are replicated by the direction and alphabetical scale of the city bond ratings. Petersen further notes that there is a "Catch 22" position between the public and private urban distress rating systems that may allow financially frail cities a new life at the credit tables. City hardship indices specify locations of urban hardship/need, to which intergovernmental transfers, once directed, may improve the bond ratings of the cities that are involved (i.e., they improve the city's fiscal solvency). Once bond ratings have been upgraded, the city is then able to incur a new wave of financial obligation. As increased debt is incurred, the city is rendered increasingly vulnerable should the federal government's revenue support be diminished for any one of several reasons. Petersen begins his essay by noting that there have been significant changes in the way that cities finance their obligations over the past decade. Despite declining populations and resident incomes, the largest 45 cities in the United States have found diverse avenues to fund increasing local expenditures. Petersen notes that expenditures grew 12 percent annually over the period 1967 to 1977: 7.5 percent due to inflation; 4.5 percent in real growth. On the other side of the equation, while revenues grew to meet the expenditure demand, it was the revenue category of intergovernmental transfers that grew the fastest (three times that of own-source revenues) in attempting to meet the funding demands of increased expenditures. Petersen notes, that in 1967, three-quarters of the funds that were used to pay for local public obligations came from own-source revenues; a decade later this figure was well below 60 percent. In 1967 the federal government financed 5 percent of local expenditures; in 1977 the figure was over 20 percent.

Petersen is quick to point out that as a result of these changes in revenue emphasis the fiscal fortunes of local municipalities are clearly intertwined with that of the federal government. The final observation that John E. Petersen makes is that the greatest area of current and future municipal fiscal uncertainty is their unfunded employer pension liabilities.

This latter topic is the subject of George E. Peterson's essay - *Funding Capital Expenditures and Pension Systems* - in which he discusses both pensions and capital facilities as troublesome fiscal issues. Peterson notes that both for pension funding and for capital facilities development, cities are being shortsighted about future costs and this myopic view will mean either tremendous unanticipated costs associated with future funding or a future expenditure obligation that cannot be met. Cities are skimping on the provision of capital facilities and funding pensions to ease the financial burden of current taxpayers. This will have significant negative impacts as we move into the future. George E. Peterson indicates that there has been a recent bulge in both the number of public employees at the state and local level as well as the wages paid to these employees. This means that there will be a growing number of pensions and greater pension levels to fund once current employees retire from public service. Pension costs in major cities now equal all other debt service costs combined, and in the near future, will significantly exceed current debt service costs. Peterson concludes with a warning that pension funds pose significant liability for local governnments due to: (1) their scale, (2) the magnitude of the required government contribution, and (3) the timing or discharge of these obligations.

The article by Tom Muller - *Service Patterns of Stressed Cities* - takes Peterson's position on capital facilities and extends the same kind of logic to the muncipal operational outlays of primary and secondary education and public safety. Muller indicates that two prime requirments of families brought back to the central city are to: (1) publicly educate their children, and (2) live in an environment free from harm. Insufficient funding of public services so that these desires remain unmet may have a multiplier effect in terms of future families' decision to move to the city. Muller cites the out-migration of traditional middle class famiilies and initial replacement by specialized families (childless couples, unrelated individuals) and singles as a reaction to the inadequacies of the public service system. Further, the remaining large number of dependent traditional families will make it exceedingly difficult to fund the necessary future operational outlays for both public safety and education. As these trends continue and as there is less reason to particpate in a deteriorating public educational system, there will be less and less of an active constituency for this portion of the system's continuous upgrading.

The final article of this section - *Fiscal Adjustments in Declining States* - deals with the necessary actions that cities, unable to support their service base, must take. Roy Bahl and Larry Schroeder point to the fact that despite significant cutbacks by the former, cities of the Northeast as opposed to those of the South, are spending as much per capita for the public services which they provide. Southern, sunbelt cities exhibit powerful population, income, and ratable base growth while Northeastern cities lag considerably in all categories. Yet, public service expenditures per capita continue to be comparable. The inference made by Bahl and Schroeder is that, in the midst of stagnant tax base growth, Northern cities are continuing to spend money for public services at an alarming rate. The authors feel this course of action is fiscal suicide. Rather, a strategy must be developed to increase productivity and to decrease local services. This hopefully will lead to slower growing local tax rates and more stable local tax bases. In the long run, the federal government must assume at least a portion of the costs of public welfare to relieve the larger cities of this burden and additionally, provide regional development subsidies to specific locations which no longer are competitive.

MUNICIPAL EXPENDITURES - CAUSE AND CONTROL
(See also 300 Series Bibliography)

For several decades there have been attempts by both practitioners and academics to isolate the basic causes of municipal expenditures and to control their growth. Due largely to the findings that have occurred, i.e., that the magnitude and growth of municipal expenditures are more related to local population/population change characteristics and/or land use mix than to specific spending patterns, budgetary modes, or to the capacity of supervisory personnel, cause and control have proceeded on largely individual fronts. The *cause* literature, principally determinants analyses, has focused on multivariate analysis of municipal population, economic, locational and financial characteristics in an attempt to associate expenditure change with other static or dynamic characteristics of cities. The *control* literature has sought improvements in productivity, information systems, budgetary process or legislated spending power as a means to limit or to direct spending.

The first article of this section by Helen F. Ladd - *Municipal Expenditures and Population Change* - builds on earlier work by the same author and views the effect of population change on municipal expenditures. Ladd deals with non-school expenditures in Massachusetts' cities and towns and concludes that per capita local expenditures vary with the direction and pace of population change. Expenditure levels are "U" shaped functions of the rate of population change: highest in cities which are rapidly growing or declining; lowest in cities which exhibit moderate rates of positive growth.

The policy implications of Ladd's findings are obvious: the most critical points of cities' fiscal imbalance appropriate for intergovernmental intervention come at the birth and decline of their service systems.

Seymour Sacks *et al.* employ a cross-sectional model to evaluate the impact of intergovernmental aid on local expenditures in their paper - *Intergovernmental Transfers and Expenditure Determinants.* Sacks and his collegues attempt to sort out the impact of various categories of aid, i.e., direct federal, pass-through and own state aid on educational and non-educational expenditures of localities aggregated by state.

Sacks *et al.* conclude that educational expenditures are more directly related to the income of a locality, and non-educational expenditures to its tax base than they are to levels of intergovernmental assistance. All of the intergovernmental aid variables show modest but positive associations with educational and noneducational expenditures, however. Thus the principal determinants of school and non-school expenditures continue to be district wealth variables, i.e. per capita income and per capita tax base, respectively. When the various types of intergovernmental transfers are teased-out separately, they also are associated with local expenditure increases, although at much lower levels.

David Greytak and Donald Shepard in their essay - *Tax Limits and Local Expenditure Levels* - view the effects of legislated expenditure limitations or "caps" on local expenditure patterns. Greytak and Shepard, using U.S. Census data for local jurisdictions, conclude:

(1) limits restrict expenditure growth, i.e. absent explicit restraints, local expenditures grow independent of constituent demands;

(2) second generation limiting techniques (levy limits) are more effective expenditure controls than first generation techniques (rate limits); and

(3) the presence of limits cultivates non-property tax revenue sources

Greytak and Shepard note that, while their analysis tentatively suports the potential effectiveness of expenditure limitations, effects may differ according to the direction and rate of population change as well as by other structural characteristics of the community.

Margaret Corwin's and Judith Getzels' article on *Capital Expenditures: Causes and Controls,* uses survey research to associate different capital expenditure profiles with growing and declining cities. Growing communities are faced with demand for more capital facilities than their tax base and resultant revenue stream can support; declining communities confront an underutilized but deteriorating capital plant that likewise cannot be supported by the existing tax base and regularly accruing revenues. It is for these two development scenarios, i.e. start-up and decline, that capital facility provision is most difficult, both from a financial perspective as well as from problems arising from local political, technical and legal limitations.

Corwin and Getzels conclude that, in most cases, even the existence of a plan does little to make the start-up or decline, capital facilities planning/funding phase more rational. Local governments are hard-pressed in both cases and seem unable to exact adequate intergovernmental technical, legal or financial assistance to get them through these periods.

The final article of this section by Astrid Merget - *Public Service Equity During Fiscal Constraint* - moves from the general theme of identifying and measuring expenditure causes or monitoring expenditure controls to the effect of expenditure constraints (planned or unplanned) on different segments of the resident population. Merget indicates that fiscal emergencies are felt disproportionately by the poor/disadvantaged and, as such, there is latent discrimination in the access of a city's population to available public services. In much the same fashion as Ann R. Markusen and Glenn Fisher, Merget argues for more of a political/behavioral than economic approach to the allocation of, and thus access to, public services.

TRADITIONAL MUNICIPAL REVENUES - REWORKED AND RETOOLED
(See also 400 Series Bibliography)

The purpose of the following section is to detail classic alternative revenue resources as well as creative approaches to maximize their contribution while minimizing their deleterious effects. Discussed are: (1) the ideal revenue balance, (2) historic revenues - property tax, user charges, miscellaneous revenues, etc., and (3) the potentials and limitations of revenue raising through tax base sharing.

Glenn Fisher in his article - *What is an Ideal Revenue Balance?* - considers the criteria which economists typically use to rate a revenue system: productivity, economy, efficiency, administrative ease, flexibility, equity, etc. He notes that while these criteria are important, a proper revenue balance can be achieved only if greater attention is given to political as well as economic critera. Fisher specifically recommends the addition of: (1) the effect of a revenue source on the structure of government; and (2) the acceptability of a revenue source to the tithed population, as revenue selection criteria. These additional criteria are critical to correctly view the political system as being affected by rather than affecting the revenue raising system. According to Fisher, Proposition 13 and tax base sharing endeavors definitely affect the relationships between both governments at various levels and between government and the public. The formulation and institutionalization of these types of fiscal controlling mechanisms must be viewed with a great deal of care. Shifting to specific revenue selection, Fisher sees more emphasis on sale/income type taxes and grants-in-aid, and less on the real property tax as contributing toward a more ideal revenue system.

Dick Netzer's essay - *The Property Tax in the New Environment* - discusses the future role of the property tax in a nation characterized by:

1. slower than previous growth in taxable real property value;

2. geographically uneven growth rates;

3. growth of the state-local government financial aggregate slower than the GNP; and

4. replacement of informal and extra-legal adjustments in individual property tax burdens by legislated solutions and class actions.

Netzer notes that while empirical data on changes in the market value of taxable property are sketchy and unreliable, the property tax base of a city *should* be affected by long-term economic changes specific to that city. What can be gleaned from the limited empirical evidence available is that one may forecast for declining cities decreasing property tax yields and stable tax rates and for growing cities, slowly increasing tax yields with decreasing effective tax rates.

With this the case, Netzer suggests that if own-source revenues are continued to be emphasized in older urban areas, one set of theories would allow these revenues to rely on a system of local revenue raising mechanisms which includes both taxation of land values and a wide array of user charges. This system, while it would minimize immediate, significant revenue losses, would not change the fact that in the long run, declining cities will continue to have relatively weak tax bases.

Lennox Moak in his article *Non-Tax Revenues - The Growth of User Charges* - agrees with Netzer on the vitality and potential for user charges as a revenue resource in urban areas. He notes that for the support of local expenditures, as of 1977, non-tax revenues were on a par with intergovernmental transfers and both narrowly trailed local taxation as the most important source of local government revenues. User charges for sewer, water, electricity, and gas are steady and reliable; those for airports and hospitals are the most lucrative.

In addition to user charges, municipal finance directors are also turning towards cash mangement of idle monies (reserves, uncommitted revenues, etc.) and revenues from retirement systems as growing sources of municipal income. The growth of non-tax revenues, in excess of the growth in local taxes, offers significant potential for the shifting of considerable amounts of costs from the local taxpayer to the service charge mechanism. It is primarily through this vehicle that public willingness to pay affects the scope of basic services which are delivered. For urban areas, this additionally shifts some of the revenue financing burden to those who daily commute to the city, use that city's services while there, but contribute primary tax revenues to suburban jurisdictions.

Katharine C. Lyall and W. Patrick Beaton in their papers on *Tax Base Sharing* present classically optimistic and pessimistic appraisals of the concept's formulation and institutionalization. Lyall discusses the purposes of tax base sharing as:

1. reducing fiscal disparities among jurisdictions;

2. providing fiscal incentives for more rational land use planning;

3. rendering a favorable environment for business development; and

4. adding stability to the community life cycle of cities and suburbs.

She concludes that, at least according to the results of the Twin Cities experiment, tax base sharing accomplishes most of the above-listed objectives. Tax base sharing does not, however, provide significant fiscal relief to central cities (there is not enough to go around) nor does it reduce the tax burden of either the poor or near poor (little correlation between fiscal capacity of jurisdiction and personal income of residents). Further, there may be significant problems in the various distribution formulae designed to implement the revenue sharing mechanism.

This is the issue on which the article by W. Patrick Beaton focusses—i.e., what are the examples of mechanisms to implement tax base sharing and what are their effects? Beaton uses both the Twin Cities (Minnesota) and the Maryland formulae to examine the effects of these tax sharing schemes on 18 declining New Jersey cities. His analysis indicates that tax base sharing renders one-half to two-thirds of the 18 declining cities in an inferior fiscal position. Beaton therefore concludes that while the objectives of tax base sharing may be laudible, careful attention must be paid to the procedures of implementation.

THE NEW DOMINANCE
OF INTERGOVERNMENTAL TRANSFERS
(See also 500-600 Series Bibliography)

The purpose of this section of the volume is to discuss the growing influence of intergovernmental transfers on the municipal fisc. Basic questions addressed in this section are: Do intergovernmental transfers accomplish their preconceived objective? Via which data sources can we measure their impact? Are they being distributed according to need? What is their impact in terms of: (1) future economic stability, and (2) revenue dependency of the areas to which they are applied?

The first essay by Richard P. Nathan - *Federal Grants - How Are They Working* - deals with the structure, growth and distribution of intergovernmental transfers by prescribing answers to "seven myths" of grants-in-aid:

(1) There is unremitting growth in the specificity and narrowness of federal grants.

(2) Federal grants are increasing in both size and number.

(3) Federal grants are slotted to the large central cities while the rest of the metropolitan area is slighted.

(4) Federal grants are directed and controlled by knowledgeable and highly skilled bureaucrats.

(5) The urban crisis as we have known it is a thing of the past.

(6)   State and local government's annual surplus could easily balance the federal government's shortfalls.

(7)   Nothing works at the federal level - the governmental system is in chaos.

Nathan indicates that intergovernmental transfers are, for the most part, having their projected impact and the system is in control, although the annual stipend for recurring grants is decreasing and the system monitoring their impact is far from perfect. He further notes that: (1) the deployment of federal grants is much more broadbased and regionally distributed than is popularly believed; (2) their continued employment is necessary given the fiscal plight of most older cities and the limited revenues of state and county governments which host these jurisdictions; and (3) while grants appear to be having postitive impacts, the data which are available on their use and accomplishments are far from complete.

Thomas J. Anton *et al.* in their article - *Federal Spending in States and Regions* - go to great length to detail the paucity of data monitoring the geographical recipients and magnitudes of intergovernmental transfers. They further indicate that results of analyses of "who gets what" largely relate to which data are used, how they are aggregated and the type of analysis employed. Anton and his colleagues attempt to lay a foundation for intergovernmental revenue distributive analysis in which current Census data (U.S. Census of Governments) and other data available from the U.S. Department of Treasury (Federal Aid to States) and the Office of Management and Budget (Federal Aid to State and Local Governments) are employed in conjunction with Federal Outlays Data (Geographical Distribution of Federal Funds) from the Community Services Administration. The authors champion this last data source as having enough breadth, depth and history to obtain a handhold on federal-to-state and federal-to-local revenue transfers.

After carefully reviewing the data sources, Anton *et al.* discuss the regional distribution of outlays, types of outlays, and the specific patterns of both agency and program federal monies. They draw the following conclusions:

(1)   There appears to be no major shift in the state or regional distribution of total outlays.

(2)   Project grants are increasing in importance of total outlays; formula grants are decreasing.

(3) Major federal departments concentrate expenditures in a few states but this concentration varies from year to year.

(4) Program outlays by states are unstable due to changing definitions and federal department emphases.

(5) There is little support for a regional bias in grant distribution.

Ann R. Markusen *et al.* in their article - *Who Benefits from Intergovernmental Transfers?* - pay close attention to the warnings of Anton and embark on a discussion of the beneficiaries of intergovernmental aid according to three criteria: (1) spatial (regional revenue concentrations); (2) temporal (change in concentrations over time; and (3) functional (importance of categories and types of expenditures). After distinguishing aid from outlays, Markusen and her colleagues note that the concentration of *federal* aid per capita is highest in the Northeast, second in the West and South and lags considerably in the North Central region. Larger and older central cities tend to get more *federal* aid than do newer and smaller cities. *State* aid per capita to cities almost directly parallels their size whereas city/suburb aid concentrations appear to be mixed.

Markusen's analysis highlights that there is a large unknown as to who should and who does receive intergovernmental transfers. Even though current grantsmanship is more "computer politics" than political "pork-barrelling", the question of whether those who need intergovernmental assistance really get it, (i.e., the people themselves rather than the statistical aggregates of municipality or region), is probably answered in the negative.

The authors point out that no simple geographic correspondence exists between needy populations and specific political subdivisions. Even if it did, given the discretionary behavior of local governments, there is no guarantee that those who are poor would ultimately evidence real income gains as a result of the impact of federal-to-local dollar transfers.

As an alternative to the technocracy of grant allocation through city-need designation schemes, the authors attempt a behavioral explanation. They point out that congressional committees and agencies within the federal government have spatial affinities and ties to constituents which shape the distribution of their expenditures. Further, economists rather than be mesmerized by one or another city hardship index, might well spend their time analyzing the various power relationships between government agencies and levels of government and between the public and private sectors as factors affecting the expenditure patterns of cities.

John Shannon and Bruce Wallin in their essay - *Fiscal Imbalance in the Federal System* - discuss the growth and trials of General Revenue Sharing as an intergovernmental transfer. They note that at its initiation and at its request for renewal two different moods prevailed in the nation (1) initially, a view of the federal government as a superior benefactor; and (2) subsequently, a view of this same level of government as inept and wasteful. Further, at the initiation of General Revenue Sharing a fiscal imbalance in the revenue allocation system was presumed—the federal government had more progressive revenue raising mechanisms than did locals. This system, through sophisticated allocation schemes, was capable of balancing existing regional fiscal inequities. Finally, Revenue Sharing took the regular grantsmanship burden from local officials and allowed them broader discretion in the use of acquired funding.

Currently, a new view of the fiscal interelationships of the federal and state-local governments prevails. The federal government is viewed as increasingly strapped while a considerable number of state governments exhibit recurring surpluses.

This has led to a growing recognition on the part of locals that: (a) there will be a general slow-down of direct federal-to-local funds; and (b) the *state* will become an increasingly-frequent intergovernmental transfer partner. While the federal fiscal system may be more progressive than that of the states, the states have more intimate knowledge of areal or jurisdiction disparities than the federal government. General Revenue Sharing, in a reconstructed format, could potentially serve as a blending mechanism for federal distributional superiority and state intimacy with local fiscal problems. This, according to the authors, is the role that Revenue Sharing, in particular, and intergovernmental transfers, in general, should play.

The final article of this section by Richard D. Gustely and Kenneth Ballard concerns the *Regional Impact of Federal Grants*. Gustely and Ballard use the National Regional Impact Evaluation System (NRIES) to answer first: to what extent do grants have different regional stimulative effects? and second: to what extent do the distributive effects of grants reallocate income regionally? In answer to the first question, the authors conclude that federal grants-in-aid do have (1) significant, (2) long-term and (3) differing stimulative effects. In answer to the second, although there are significant and regionally different distributive effects of the current grants-in-aid system, the existing sytem does not produce any significant changes in per capita income distribution than would be produced by an alternative personal income based formula. Thus, the current system, at first blush, appears to have stimulative economic effects, yet not unplanned-for, income distributional effects.

CONCLUSION

Most cities in the 1980s will be characterized by a continued diminishment of revenues relative to the costs of providing public services. The imbalance between public service appetite and public service provision must be minimized. Yet at the same time, the city must remain a safe and clean place to dwell, a competent educator of its residents' children, a source of recreation and cultural opportunity, and a provider of public transportation and other services. In short, while the city must be fiscally trim—it also must work.This is the dilemma of city administrators, finance directors, planners and program heads as we enter the decade of the 1980s.

At the local level there must be continued evaluation of revenue potential versus impact on residents/workers, as well as, a prioritizing and selective paring back of municipal services. Locals must look to other governments - local, state, federal- for a sharing of necessary service obligations as well as minimization of the provision of duplicative services. Cities must also be cognizant of their levels of financial impaction vis à vis other cities so that necessary decisions regarding participation in federal and state intergovernmental transfers may be made.

Cities Under Stress - The Fiscal Crises of Urban America - provides a basic foundation for the understanding of the cause and nature of the financial problems that face cities. The essays which follow represent the leading edge of thought in both the conceptual and technical issues of municipal finance.

NOTES

1. Henry George, *Progress and Poverty* (1879). See discussion in Harold Groves, *Financing Government* (New York: Henry Holt, 1946).
2. H.C.Adams, *Public Debts* (1887); *Science of Finance* (1898).
3. Edwin R.A. Seligman, *Studies in Public Finance* (New York: Macmillan, (1925).
4. Elmer Fagan and C. Ward Macy, *Public Finance* (London: Longmans Green and Co., 1935); Alvin H. Hansen and Harvey S. Perloff, *State and Local Finance in the National Economy* (New York: W.W. Norton, 1944); A.C. Pigou, *A Study in Public Finance* (London: Macmillan, 1949).

5. See Groves, *Financing Government.*

6. Herbert A. Simon, *Fiscal Aspects of Metropolitan Consolidation* (Berkeley: Unversity of California Bureau of Public Administration, 1943).

7. Robert H. Haveman and Julius Margolis, *Public Expenditures and Policy Analysis* (Chicago: Markham, 1970), p. 2.

8. Haveman and Margolis, *Public Expenditures and Policy Analysis,* p. 3.

9. Richard A. Musgrave, *The Theory of Public Finance* (New York: McGraw Hill, 1959).

10. Charles M. Tiebout, "A Pure Theory of Local Expenditures," *Journal of Political Economy* (October 1956), pp. 461-424; Charles Tiebout, "An Economic Theory of Fiscal Decentralization," in *Public Finance Needs, Sources and Utilization* (Princeton: Princeton University Press, 1961).

11. Musgrave, *The Theory of Public Finance.*

12. Charles E. Mclure Jr., "Revenue Sharing: Alternative to Rational Fiscal Federalism" *Public Policy* (Summer 1971), pp. 467-478.

13. Wallace E. Oates, *The Political Economy of Fiscal Federalism* (Lexington, Mass.: Lexington Books, 1977).

14. Tiebout, "A Pure Theory of Local Expenditures," p. 422. Cited in Oates, *The Political Economy of Fiscal Federalism,* p. 7.

15. See Oates, *The Political Economy of Fiscal Federalism,* p. 7.

16. See for example, James M. Buchanan, *Fiscal Theory and Political Economy* (Chapel Hill: University of North Carolina Press, 1960); James M. Buchanan, *Public Finance in Democratic Process* (Chapel Hill: University of North Carolina Press, 1967) and William J. Baumol, *Welfare Economics and the Theory of the State* (London: Bell and Sons, 1965).

17. For a review of the shift in the scope of the public finance literature, see Haveman and Margolis, *Public Expenditures and Policy Analysis,* Introduction.

18. See Clarence E. Ridley, *Measuring Municipal Government* (New York: Municipal Administration Service, 1967); Mabel Walker, *Municipal Expenditures* (Baltimore, Johns Hopkins Press, 1930). Cited in Alan K. Campbell and Seymour Sacks, *Metropolitan America: Fiscal Patterns and Governmental Systems* (New York: Free Press, 1967), pp. 35-37.

19. Harvey E. Brazer, (editor), *Essays in State and Local Finance* (Ann Arbor: University of Michigan Institute of Public Administration, 1967) pp. 1-3.

20. Ruth Mace, *Municipal Cost Revenue Research in the United States* (Chapel Hill: University of North Carolina, 1961); Dick Netzer, *The Economics of the Property Tax* (Washington, D.C.: Brookings Institution, 1966); Alan K. Campbell and Seymour Sacks, *Metropolitan America: Fiscal Patterns and Governmental Systems* (New York: Free Press, 1960); Roy W. Bahl, *Metropolitan City Expenditures: A Comparative Analysis* (Louisville: University of Kentucky Press, 1969).

21. Margolis and Haveman, *Public Expenditures and Policy Analysis;* George E. Peterson, "Finance" in William Gorham and Nathan Glazer (editors), *The Urban Predicament* (Washington, D.C.: Urban Institute, 1976); Jesse Burkhead and Jerry Miner, *Public Expenditures* (New York: Aldine - Atherton, 1971); John P. Crecine, *Financing the Metropolis* (Beverly Hills, California: Sage Publications, 1970).

22. David T. Stanley, *Managing Local Government Under Union Pressure* (Washington, D.C.: Urban Institute, 1972) Kenneth Newton, "American Urban Politics, Social Class, Political Structure and Public Goods" *Urban Affairs Quarterly*, Vol. 11 (1975).

23. U.S. Advisory Commission on Intergovernmental Relations, *City Financial Emergencies* (Washington, D.C.: ACIR, 1973).

24. Robert B. Pettengill and Jogindar S. Uppl, *Can Cities Survive - The Fiscal Plight of American Cities* (New York: St. Martins Press, 1974); David Stanley, *Cities in Trouble* (Columbus, Ohio: Academy for Contemporary Problems, 1976); Richard P Nathan and Charles Adams, Jr. "Understanding Central City Hardship" *Political Science Quarterly*, Vol. 91, No. 1 (Spring, 1976); John R. Meyer and John M. Quigley, (editors), *Local Public Finance and the Fiscal Squeeze: A Case Study* (Cambridge: Ballinger, 1977); Roy Bahl, (editor), *The Fiscal Outlook for Cities - Implications of a National Urban Policy* (Syracuse: Syracuse University Press, 1978),

25. Brazer, "Introduction - *Essays in State and Local Finance*, pp. 3-4.

26. John E. Petersen and Catherine Lavigne Spain, (editors), *Essays in Public Finance and Financial Management* (Chatham, New Jersey: Chathan House, 1980), p. ix. This monograph was originally published by the Municipal Finance Officers Association in 1978. See John E. Petersen et al., *State and Local Government Finance and Financial Management* (Washington, D.C.: Municipal Finance Officers Association, 1978).

27. Edgar M. Hoover and Raymond Vernon, *Anatomy of a Metropolis* (Cambridge: Harvard University Press 1959); John C. Bollens and Henry J. Schmandt, *The Metropolis: Its People, Politics and Economic Life* (New York: Harper, 1965); Benjamin Chinitz (editor), *City and Suburb: The Economics of Metropolitan Growth* (Englewood Cliffs, New Jersey: Prentice Hall, 1964); Jay W. Forrester, *Urban Dynamics* (Cambridge: M.I.T. Press, 1969), Campbell and Sacks, *Metropolitan America;* John Kain, "Theories of Residential Location and Realities of Race" Harvard University Program on Regional and Urban Economics (1969). Discussion paper no. 47. Committee for Economic Development, *Reshaping Metropolitan Government* (New York: CED, 1970).

28. See, for example, Harvey E. Brazer, "Some Fiscal Implications of Metropolitanism" in Guthrie S. Burkhead (editor), *Metropolitan Issues: Social, Governmental, Fiscal* (Syracuse: Syracuse University Press, 1962), pp. 61-82.

29. J.J. Carroll and S. Sacks, "Influence of Industry on the Property Tax Base and the Pattern of Local Government Expenditures." Paper presented at Conference of Regional Science Association, December 27, 1961; Alan K. Campbell, "Taxes and Industrial Location in the New York Metropolitan Region," *National Tax Journal*, Vol. 11 (September, 1958); Jerome P. Pickard, *Changing Land Uses as Affected by Taxation* (Washington, D.C.: Urban Land Institute, 1962), Research Monograph No. 6; Morris Beck, *Property Taxation of Urban Land Use, Northeastern New Jersey* (Washington, D.C.: Urban Land Institute, 1963), Research Monograph No. 7; John R. Meyer and John M. Quigley, "Fiscal Influences Upon Local Patterns," in Meyer and Quigley (editors), *Local Public Finance and the Fiscal Squeeze: A Case Study*, pp. 1-18.

30. Norman Williams, Jr., *American Planning Law: Land Use and the Police Power* (Chicago: Callaghan, 1974), Vol. 1, pp. 293-294.

31. Congressional Research Service, *Property Taxation: Effects on Land Use and Local Government Revenues*, Background Study for the Subcommittee on Intergovernmental Relations of the Committee on Government Operations, United States Senate (Washington, D.C.: Government Printing Office, 1971), p. 54.

32. See discussion later in this essay.

33. U.S. Commission on Urban Problems, *Building the American City* (Washington, D.C.: Government Printing Office, 1968); U.S. Department of Housing and Urban Development, *Housing in the Seventies* (Washington, D.C.: Government Printing Office, 1975).

34. National Advisory Commission on Civil Disorders, *Report*, (New York: Bantam, 1968), p. 283.

35. Brazer, *City Expenditures in the United States*; James Heilbrun, *Real Estate Taxes and Urban Housing* (New York: Columbia University Press, 1966); Roy W. Bahl, *Metropolitan City Expenditures: A Comparative Analysis* (Lexington: University of Kentucky Press, 1969); Dick Netzer, *Economics and the Urban Problem* (New York: Basic Books, 1970); Julius Margolis, "Urban Fiscal Problems," *Wharton Quarterly* Vol. 5, No. 3 (Spring 1979); William B. Neenan, *The Political Economy of Urban Areas* (Chicago: Markham, 1972); Glenn W. Fisher, "Problems of Financing Local Government in the United States of America" *Local Finance* (September 1973), pp. 8-19; Roy W. Bahl and Walter Vogt, *Fiscal Centralization and Tax Burdens* (Cambridge: Ballinger 1975); Bahl, *The Fiscal Outlook for Cities*; Werner Z. Hirsch et al., *Fiscal Pressures on the Central City* (New York: Irvington, 1971); Thomas Muller, *Growing and Declining Urban Areas: A Fiscal Comparison* (Washington, D.C.: Urban Institute, 1975).

36. See Temporary Commission on City Finance, City of New York, *Toward Fiscal Strength: Overcoming New York's Financial Dilemma* (New York: November 1965); *Study of the Studies: An Analysis of the Work and Recommendations of a Generation of Task Forces on New York City's Fiscal Crisis* (New York: December 1971).

37. Roy W. Bahl, *Taxes, Expenditures and the Economic Base: A Case Study of New York City* (Syracuse, NY: Syracuse University, Maxwell School of Citizenship and Public Affairs, 1974); John Berenyi, "Causes and Effects of The New York Financial Crisis," *Local Finance* Vol. 7, No. 2 (April 1978), pp. 3-11; Benjamin Chinitz, *The Decline of New York in the 1970's: A Demographic Economic and Fiscal Analysis* (Springfield: VA: NTIS, 1977); Terry Nicholas Clark, *How Many New Yorks? The New York Fiscal Crisis in Comparative Perspective* (Chicago: University of Chicago, 1976).

38. Philadelphia Economy League, *How Philadelphia Can Avoid Following in the Steps of New York City: Findings, Conclusions, and Recommendations* (Philadelphia: Pennsylvania Economy League (Eastern Division), 1976).

39. See John Rawls, *The Theory of Justice* (Cambridge: Harvard University Press, 1971).

40. *Hawkins v. Town of Shaw* (437 F. 2d 1268 [5th Cir. 1971]). *Serrano v. Priest* 487 P 2d 1241 (1972); *Robinson v. Cahill* 67 N.J. 473, 303A 2d 273.

41. Peter B. Block, *Equality of Distribution of Police Services: A Case Study of Washington, D.C.* (Washington, D.C.: Urban Institute, 1974); Robert Lineberry, "Equality, Public Policy, and Public Services: The Underclass Hypothesis and the Limits to Equality," *Politics and Policy*, Vol. 4 (December 1975); Astrid D. Merget, "Equalizing Municipal Services: Issues for Policy Analysis, "*Policy Studies Journal* (Spring 1976).

42. Joel S. Berke, *Answers to Inequity: An Analysis of the New School Finance* (Berkeley, CA: McCutchan Publishing Corporation, 1974); Mark Haskall, "Toward Equality of Educational Opportunity," *Urban Education*, Vol. 21, No. 3 (October 1977), pp. 313-236; Richard W. Linkholm, (ed.) *Property Taxation and the Finance of Education* (Madison, University of Wisconsin Press, 1974); J.F. Murphy, "Fiscal Problems of Big City School Systems: Changing Patterns of State and Federal Aid," *Urban Review*, Vol. 1, No. 4 (Winter 1978), pp. 251-265; Robert L. Bish, "Fiscal Equalization Through Court Decisions: Policy-Making Without Evidence," in Elinor Ostrom (ed.) *The Delivery of Urban Services: Outcomes of Change* (Beverly Hills, CA: Sage, 1976), pp. 75-102; Phillip E. Vincent, "School Finance Reforms and Big City Fiscal Problems," paper prepared for the United States Committee on Taxation, Resources, and Economic Development Conference, Cambridge, MA, October 1977.

43. Roy Bahl, and David Puryera. "Regional Tax Base Sharing: Possibilities and Implications," *National Tax Journal* Vol. 29, No. 3 (September 1976), pp. 328-335; William Fischel, "An Evaluation of Proposals for Metropolitan Sharing of Commercial and Industrial Property Tax Base," *Journal of Urban Economics* Vo. 3 (1976), pp. 253-263; Katherine C. Lyall, "Tax Base Sharing: A Fiscal Aid Towards More Rational Land Use Planning," *Journal of the American Institute of Planners* Vol. 41, No. 2 (March 1975), pp. 90-100; Andrew Reschovsky, and Eugene Knaff. "Tax Base Sharing: An Assessment of the Minnesota Experience," *Journal of the American Institute of Planners*, Vol. 43, No. 4 (October 1977) pp. 361-370; Margaret Simms, *Metropolitan Tax Base Sharing: Is It the Solution to Municipal Fiscal Problems?* (Washington, D.C.: Urban Institute, 1977).

44. For examples of incidence studies see Herbert A. Simon, "The Incidence of a Tax on Urban Real Property" *Quarterly Journal of Economics* Vol. 57 (May 1943); John G. Cragg, et al, "Empirical Evidence on the Incidence of the Coporation Income Tax." *Journal of Political Economy* Vol. 75 (December, 1967), p. 811; Charles E. McLure, Jr. "The Interregional Incidence of General Regional Taxes," *Public Finance*, Vol. 24 (1969), p. 457; Peter Mieszkowski, "Tax Incidence Theory: The Effects of Taxes on the Distribution of Income," *Journal of Economic Literature* Vol. 7 (December, 1969), p. 1103; John Heinberg, and Wallace E. Oates, "The Incidence of Differential Property Taxes on Urban Housing: A Comment and Some Further Evidence," *National Tax Journal*, Vol. 23 (March, 1970), p. 92.

45. See, for example, U.S. Advisory Commission in Intergovernmental Relations, *Fiscal Balance in the American Federal System - Metropolitan Fiscal*

Disparities (Washington, D.C.: ACIR, 1967); U.S. Advisory Commission on Intergovernmental Relations, Measuring the Fiscal Capacity and Effort of State and Local Areas (Washington, D.C.: ACIR, 1971).

46. Fiscal federalism has long been a topic of consideration by economists, political scientists, etc. See for example, George Break, Intergovernmental Fiscal Relations in the U.S. (Washington, D.C.: Brookings Institution, 1967); Cl. Lowell Harriss, "Federal-State-Local Fiscal Relationships: Historical Background," in Tax Institute of America (editor), Federal-State-Local Fiscal Relationships (Princeton: Tax Institute of America, 1968); Committe for Economic Development, Fiscal Issues in the Future of Federalism (New York: CED, 1968), Supplementary Paper No. 23.

47. See, for example, C. Chester Johnson, "The Carter Administration's Fiscal Federalism," in Proceedings of the Seventieth Annual Conference on Taxation (1977) - National Association Tax Institute of America, pp. 101.

48. A.H. Bish, Federalism, Finance and Social Legislation in Canada, Australia and the United States (Oxford: Clarendon, 1955); U.S. Advisory Commission on Intergovernmental Relations, Fiscal Balance in the American Federal System (Washington, D.C.: ACIR, 1976); Committee on Economic Development, Fiscal Issues in the Future of Federalism (New York: CED, May 1968), CED Supplement Paper #23, Richard E. Wagner, The Fiscal Organization of American Federalism (Chicago: Markham, 1971); D. Boes, "Federalism and Intergovernmental Problems of Urban Finance" Public Finance, Vol. 28, (1973), pp. 56-81; David O. Porter and Teddie Wood Porter, "Social Equity and Fiscal Federalism" Public Administration Review, Vol. 34, No. 1 (January /February 1974), pp. 36.

49. E. McLure, "Revenue Sharing: Alternative to Rational Fiscal Federalism," pp. 467-478.

50. Brazer, City Expenditures in the United States.

51. William J. Baumol, "Urban Services: Interactions of Public and Private Decisions," in Howard Schaller (editor), Public Expenditure Decisions in the Urban Community (Washington, D.C.: Resources for the Future, 1963); Woo Sik Kee, "Central City Expenditures and Metropolitan Areas" National Tax Journal Vol. 18 (1965), p. 337; Seymour Sacks and Robert Harris "The Determinants of State and Local Government Expenditures and Inter-Governmental Flow of Funds," National Tax Journal Vol. 17 (1964), p. 75; Jack Osman, "The Dual Impact of Federal Aid on State and Local Government Expenditures," National Tax Journal Vol. 19 (December, 1966), pp. 362-372.

52. Ernest Kurnow, "Determinants of State and Local Expenditures, Re-Examined," National Tax Journal, Vol. 16 (1963), pp. 252-255; Seymour Sacks, and Robert Harris. "The Determinants of State and Local Government Expenditures and Inter-Governmental Flow of Funds," National Tax Journal, Vol. 17 (1964), pp. 75-85.

53. John C. Weicher, "Determinants of Central City Expenditures: Some Overlooked Factors and Problems," National Tax Journal Vol. 23 (1970), pp. 379-396; Emile M. Sunley, Jr., "Some Determinants of Government Expenditures Within Metropolitan Areas," The American Journal of Economics and Sociology Vol. 30 (1971), pp. 345-64; Teh-wei Hu, and Bernard Booms, "A

Simultaneous Equation Model of Public Expenditure Decisions in Large Cities," *The Annals of Regional Science* Vol. 5 (1971), pp. 73-85; L.R. Gabler, "Population Size as a Determinant of City Expenditure and Employment: Some Further Evidence," *Land Economics* Vol. 47 No. 2 (May 1971), pp. 130-138; George Sternlieb, et al. *Housing Development and Municipal Costs* (New Brunswick, NJ: Rutgers University, Center for Urban Policy Research, 1972); Patrick Beaton, "The Determinants of Police Protection Expenditure," *National Tax Journal* Vol. 29 (1975), pp. 328-335.

54. See paper by Sacks et al. in this monograph.

55. Helen F. Ladd, *Local Public Expenditures and the Composition of the Tax Base*. Unpublished Ph.D. Dissertation, June, 1974 Harvard University; see Patrick Beaton analysis in Robert W. Burchell and David Listokin *The Fiscal Impact Handbook* (New Brunswick: Rutgers University Center for Urban Policy Research, 1978).

56. William L. Wheaton, and Morton J. Schussheim, *The Cost of Municipal Services in Residential Areas* (Washington, D.C.: G.P.O., 1955); Walter Isard, and Robert Coughlin. *Municipal Costs and Revenues Resulting from Community Growth* (Wellesley, MA: Chandler-Davis, 1957).

57. Roy W. Bahl, "The Determinants of Local Government Police Expenditures: A Public Employment Approach," *National Tax Journal*, Vol. 31 (March 1978) p. 67.

58. Stanley, *Managing Local Government Under Union Pressure;* Peterson, "Finance" in *The Urban Predicament*, p. 109.

59. Fremont J. Lyden and Ernest G. Miller, *Planning Programming Budgeting: A Systems Approach to Management* (Chicago: Markham, 1970).

60. Robert L. Lineberry and Edmund P. Fowler, "Reformism and Public Policies in American Cities" *The American Political Science Review*, Vol. 61 (Sept. 1967), p. 701; Newton, "American Urban Politics.::

61. U.S. Advisory Commission on Intergovernmental Relations, *Financing Capital Needs* (Washington, D.C.: ACIR, 1970); Ray W. Bahl and David Greytak, "The Response of CIty Government Revenues to Changes in Employment Structure" *Land Economics* Vol. 52 (November 1976); George E. Peterson, "Capital Spending and Capital Obsolescence: The Outlook for Cities" in Bahl, *The Fiscal Outlook for Cities* p. 49. See also U.S. Congress, Joint Economic Committee, *Changing Conditions in the Market for State and Local Government Debt* (Washington, D.C.: Government Printing Office, 1976); U.S. Advisory Commission on Intergovernmental Relations, *Understanding the Market for State and Local Debt* (Washington, D.C.: ACTR 1976).

62. Seligman, *Essays in Taxation*.

63. Jesse Burkhead, *State and Local Taxes for Public Education* (Syracuse: Syracuse University Press, 1963); Netzer, *Economics of the Property Tax*.

64. See for example, U.S. Advisory Commission on Intergovernmental Relations, *Financing Schools and Property Tax Relief* (Washington, D.C.: ACIR, 1973); Richard W. Lindholm, *Property Taxation USA* (Madison: University of Wisconsin Press, 1967); Arthur D. Lynn, Jr. (editor), *Property Taxation: Land Use and Public Policy* (Madison: University of Wisconsin Press, 1976);

Peter Mieszkowski, "The Property Tax: An Excise or Profits Tax" *Journal of Public Economics* (April 1972), pp. 73-96; Henry J. Aaron, *Who Pays the Property Tax: A New View* (Washington, D.C.: Brookings Institution, 1975); Bruce W. Hamilton, "Zoning and Property Taxation in a System of Local Governments" *Urban Studies* (June 1975); Richard M. Lindholm (editor), *Property Tax Reform* (Cambridge: Lincoln Institute of Policy, 1977).

65. See, for example, ABT Associates, *Property Tax Relief Programs for the Elderly.* Report prepared for the U.S. Department of Housing and Urban Development (Washington, D.C.: Government Printing Office, 1975), 3 Vols.; Advisory Commission on Intergovernmental Relations, *Property Tax Circuit Breakers: Current Statutes and Policy Issues.* (Washington, D.C.: Government Printing Office, 1975).

66. C. Lowell Harris,"Property Taxation After the California Vote" *Tax Review,* Vol. 39 (August 1978); Helen J. Ladd, "An Economic Evaluation of State Limitations on Local Taxing and Spending Powers" *National Tax Journal,* Vol. 31 (March 1978), pp. 1-18.

67. Richard P. Nathan, "The Tax Sharing Approach" in Tax Institute of America, *Federal-State-Local Fiscal Relationships,* p. 107; George E. Peterson, "Finance," *The Urban Predicament;* George F. Break, "Intergovernmental Finance" in Petersen and Spain, *Essays in Public Finance,* p. 95.

68. See Break, "Intergovernmental Finance," *The Urban Predicatment,* p. 96.

69. A.D. Scott, "The Evaluation of Federal Grants" *Econometrica,* Vol. 19 (1952), pp. 377-394; J. Henderson, "Local Government Expenditures: A Social Welfare Analysis" *Review of Economics and Statistics,* Vol. 50 (1960), pp. 156-163; Seymour Sacks and Robert Harris," The Determinants of State and Local Government Expenditures and Intergovernmental Flows of Funds" *National Tax Journal* (March, 1964); E.M. Gramlich, "The Effect of Federal Grants on State-Local Expenditures: A Review of the Econometric Literature" *National Tax Association Papers and Proceedings 1969,* pp. 569-593; W.E. Oates, *Fiscal Federalism* (New York: Harcourt Brace Jovanovich, 1972); J. Weicher, "Aid Expenditures and Local Government Structures" *National Tax Journal,* Vol. 25 (1972) pp. 573-584: Advisory Commission on Intergovernmental Relations, *Federal Grants: Their Effects on State-Local Expenditure, Employment Levels, Wage Rates* (Washington, D.C.: ACIR, 1977).

70. Break, "Intergovernmental Finance" *The Urban Predicament* p. 97.

71. E.P. Cubberly, *School Funds and Their Apportionment* (New York: Teachers College of Columbia University, 1905); G.D. Strayer and R.M. Haig, *The Financing of Education in the State of New York* (New York: Macmillan, 1923); Mabel Newcomber, *An Index of the Tax Paying Ability of State and Local Goverments* (New York: Teachers College of Columbia University, 1935).

72. P.H. Wieller, *Fiscal Capacity of the States: A Source Book* (Washington, D.C.: Social Security Board, Bureau of Research and Statistics, 1937) cited in J.S. Askin, *Estimation of Local Fiscal Capacity.* Unpublished Ph.D. dissertation, University of Michigan 1971.

73. Paul Studenski, *Measurement of Variations in State Economic and Fiscal Capacity* (Washington, D.C.: The Social Security Board, 1943); Harry Landreth, *The Measurement of Local Fiscal Capacity* (unpublished Ph.D. Dissertation, Harvard University, 1959).

74. U.S. Advisory Commission on Intergovernmental Relations, *Measures of State and Local Fiscal Capacity and Tax Effort: A Staff Report* (Washington. D.C.:ACIR, 1962); U.S. Advisory Commission on Intergovernmental Relations, *Measuring the Fiscal Capacity and Effort of State and Local Areas* (Washington, D.C.: ACIR, 1971); Robert D. Reischauer, *Rich Governments - Poor Governments: Determining the Fiscal Capacity and Revenue Requirements of State and Local Government* Brookings Institution, Staff Paper, December 1974; National Science Foundation, *General Revenue Sharing* (Washington, D.C.: National Science Foundation, 1975); Nathan et al., *Monitoring Revenue Sharing* (Washington, D.C.: Brookings Institution, 1975); Nathan et al., *Revenue Sharing: Second Round* (Washington, D.C.: Brookings Institution, 1977).

75. Nathan and Adams, "Understanding Central City Harship"; U.S. Department of the Treasury, Office of the State and Local Finance, *Report on the Fiscal Impact of the Economic Stimulus Package on 48 Large Urban Governments* (Washington, D.C.: Treasury, January 1978); George E. Petersen. . .(et al.) *Urban Fiscal Monitoring* (Washington, D.C.: Urban Institute, 1978); Harold L. Bunce and Robert L. Goldberg, *City Need and Community Development Funding* (Washington, D.C.: Government Printing Office, January 1979), U.S. Department of Housing and Urban Development, Office of Policy Development and Research, Division of Evaluation. See also Harold Bunce, *An Evaluation of the Community Development Block Grant Program* (Washington, D.C.: U.S. Department of Housing and Urban Development, 1976).

76. T.D. Allman, "The Urban Crisis Leaves Town," *Harper's* (December, 1978).

SECTION I

*The City In Stress - Does It Have
the Economic Functions to Support
Its Service Base?*

William J. Baumol - TECHNOLOGICAL CHANGE AND THE NEW URBAN EQUILIBRIUM

This paper discusses a hypothesis about the economics of the city which is not entirely unfamiliar. It is the view that technical change has deprived the city of many of its former advantages as a location for production and that, consequently, the equilibrium size of the city is now much smaller than it was a half century ago. I will suggest that the transition to the new equilibrium is inherently a slow, lengthy process, and that many of the ills that now beset cities are manifestations of this transition process. The prognosis that follows from this hypothesis offers considerable hope for the long run, but is rather less encouraging for the short run. I will also suggest some implications for public policy.

THE CITY'S HISTORICAL ADVANTAGES IN PRODUCTION

From the late Middle Ages to the beginning of the twentieth century, cities possessed at least three attributes that gave them an absolute advantage in manufacturing. First, they were ideal transportation terminals, earlier offering port facilities for ships[1] and, later central railroad depots. Second, cities were the best location for

I am grateful to the Sloan Foundation whose support greatly facilitated the preparation of this paper. I have also benefited significantly from comments by Daniel Baumol.

economic activities in which easy and rapid communication is of great importance. Third, cities were the only places that could sustain indivisible services with large output capacities. Let us briefly consider each of these advantages in turn to see just how recent technological change has eroded them all.

Both water and rail transportation techniques favor the central terminus. With rare exceptions, neither of them offers door-to-door service, and many of the exceptions are cases in which the shipper has placed himself next to the terminus rather than the terminus being brought to the shipper. There are several reasons for this pattern. First, ships and trains are frequently most economical when their capacity is very large.[2] It therefore does not pay to bring the entire vehicle to the door of a shipper of modest size even when that is physically possible. Second, extension of the route of a railroad requires costly construction and this is at least equally true of the construction of artificial waterways. Where, in addition, loading and unloading require expensive plant and equipment, the advantages of bringing freight to a few central points become clear. So long as there was no efficient means of transportation by which freight could be transferred economically for distribution over a wide geographic area it meant that economic activity which required extensive use of the transportation network secured a substantial advantage from a location close to a terminal. When enough economic activity lay close to a terminal and, for lack of cheap and rapid transportation, the labor force also resided nearby, that place automatically became a city.

Activities which require quick and easy communication also used to need proximity. Banks, stock exchanges and other financial institutions, government agencies and other service organizations whose work is substantially handicapped by long delays in the communication process found it essential to locate cheek by jowl, and they too found their proximity requirements satisfied only within the confines of a city.

Finally, the city's economy benefitted from being the only viable location for many indivisible service institutions. Only in cities could one find shops large enough to offer a very great selection to customers. The non-city resident could meet day to day requirements from local distributors, but customers who desired more than staples had to go to the city for specialized and unusual items, for a large selection from which to choose or for items which offered unusual quality or style. Cultural activities congregated in cities for the same reason. Small towns cannot support a house which provides grand opera or symphony orchestras.

Without any pretense at being exhaustive, one can ascribe to these three elements much of the attraction of the city as a locus of economic activity. Their presence stimulated the growth of our cities in the 19th and early twentieth centuries, with population following the growing economic opportunities. No doubt there were lags in the adjustment process but there seems no reason to believe that the sizes of the populations in the nation's cities were much out of proportion to the available employment.

TECHNOLOGICAL CHANGES AND THE CITY'S LOST ADVANTAGES

At least four developments over the course of the last century have substantially eroded these advantages of the city as a location for productive activity. The first of these was the invention of the telephone and its widespread adoption. This reduced the need for proximity as a means to speed and facilitate communication. I will suggest later that the effect of this innovation upon the city's economy has probably been considerably less drastic than those of the other three changes. The second of our four changes is, of course, the invention of the motor vehicle driven by an internal combustion engine. The automobile has permitted dispersion of the labor force, making it possible for workers to live considerable distances from their work. The truck has played at least as important a role in permitting dispersal of factory sites. No longer was it necessary for a factory to be built close to a central terminal. Indeed, a central location for the factory became a net disadvantage as congestion of urban traffic increased the time and delay involved in getting goods from the terminal to the urban factory even if the distance between the two was relatively small.[3]

This second development brought its full consequences only with the appearance of the third, the construction of the interstate highway system. The network of superhighways permitted rapid road transportation among many localities which before had been all but isolated from one another.

Though they did help to connect the cities to one another, the highway system on balance served to reduce or eliminate what was left of the ancient transportation advantage of the city and also destroyed some portion of the scale economies it offered. The new roads permitted residents of many sparsely settled areas to meet easily at central locations thereby assembling the volume of demand necessary for the viability of enterprises which previously could survive only in a city. Shopping centers began to boast department stores which soon undermined some of the most venerable shops in central cities. Cultural centers were constructed near convenient superhighway exits, where they were surrounded by rural landscapes and no other activities that one could consider urban in character.

The last of the four significant developments to be mentioned here is the emergence of continuous production processes, probably beginning with the assembly line. The relevant feature of this innovation in productive processes is that it tends to favor single storied factories which occupy more acreage than the old fashioned multi-story plants. This too, has reduced the attractiveness of an urban location for industry, not only because of the higher rents on urban land,[4] but also because in a city it is not easy to assemble continguous parcels of land which together are sufficient for the construction of a large one-story factory.

All of these changes produced the predictable consequences. Industries have closed down urban factories as they were depreciated by age and obsolescence. Their successors were placed in suburban locations, sometimes relatively close to the cities which housed them before, sometimes in distant parts of the country to which they were attracted by lower wages and other economic advantages. In sum, the argument leads us to expect a reduction in the equilibrium volume of economic activity within the city, and the facts seem to fit in with this prognosis.

It should be emphasized that none of this is meant to imply that *all* urban economic activity is destined to depart. Neither the previous nor the prospective equilibrium point is a pure polar case. Even when the city's economic advantages were at their peak a number of economic activities were nevertheless best located in the countryside, agriculture being only the most obvious example. Similarly, the new equilibrium, as I will argue later, will still leave the city as the preferred location for a variety of activities. The change is just a matter of degree. The issue is not whether or not all activity will leave the city, but rather how much will remain there under the new equilibrium and what sorts of activities it will involve. But if the prospective change is limited in scope, its implications for the structure of the city are nevertheless profound.

EFFECTS ON THE URBAN POPULATION

One natural consequence is that the labor force will follow industry out of the city. If the number of jobs available in the city under the new equilibrium is half what it was under the old we should expect that ultimately the size of the urban population will fall correspondingly. Thus, this analysis leads us to expect that future cities will be very much smaller than they are today, both in volume of economic activity and in sheer size of population.

As we all know, in the postwar period there has in fact been a considerable exodus from the cities, at least by the middle income groups. Much of this migration has probably occurred for reasons other than the cities' lost economic advantages.[5] Until recently, however, the net effect on the overall size of the urban population has been rather modest. The wealthier migrants were replaced by an initial influx of poor from elsewhere in the country. This, too, is partly ascribable to causes other than the process discussed in this paper. But I will argue next that such a temporary inward migration is in fact to be expected during the transition between our two equilibria. Indeed, I will suggest that many of the urban problems of our time can be ascribed to the character of the transition.

LAGS IN THE EQUILIBRIUM PROCESS

Economic adjustments vary enormously in speed. Some can occur in weeks or even days. Money flows, for example, can be redirected with great rapidity, because money is not nailed to any geographic point. The greater the share of the objects destined for relocation which are immobile, the slower will be the adjustment process. Partly this reflects the higher cost of greater rapidity in a process of change. Construction of new facilities requires time and beyond some point hastening of the process is always expensive. But there is a second reason which is important for our analysis. Physical plant is a sunk cost which, when the facility is not to be replaced, essentially becomes a free good. So long as it still can produce output the net value of which is positive, it will continue to be used, even if the net value of the output has been reduced by some change such as the technological developments with which we are concerned. The optimal replacement date will still normally lie in the future when the old plant has deteriorated sufficiently. The move will take the form of construction of the replacement plant at the location which is optimal in the new equilibrium. The optimal replacement date will be that at which the present value of the excess in marginal net output at the new location over that in the old location is equal to the marginal capital cost incurred by earlier plant construction at the new site. Here the margins, of course, refer to a small change in the date of replacement rather than to a small change in output level.

The reason which makes it pay to continue to use industrial plant long after an urban location for a productive process has ceased to be optimal also dictates continued use of the city's excess housing stock. It becomes a free good, a heritage from the past, which can generate a flow of housing services at lower social cost than newly constructed residences despite the latter's superior location.

There is then a parallel reason which dictates both for firms and residents substantial lags in the process of readjustment toward the new equilibrium. In both cases we can expect the transition process to be substantial. But there is also a significant difference between the two adjustment processes. The most striking difference between the standard models of the firm and the consumer is that the latter's maximization process is taken to be circumscribed by budget constraints while the former is not. Business firms have readier access to the capital market, which supplies the resources needed for any outlay that promises to be profitable. Consumers simply do not have equally flexible sources of funds. The presence of the budget constraint which limits the options available to a consumer suggests strongly that consumers, and particularly poor consumers, will have to delay their relocation longer than a firm. That is, their budget constraints will tend to induce them to delay their exodus from the city if earlier departure is costly.[6]

STYLIZED HISTORY OF THE ADJUSTMENT PROCESS

The preceding remarks about the comparative timing of the departure of firms and residents from the city is rather abstract. A description that is a bit more concrete can add flesh to the model. Let us therefore try to summarize what seems to be a "natural" sequence of events in the adjustment of the city to a new equilibrium involving a reduced level of economic activity and a reduced population. This stylized description will, of course, not accord completely with the observed history because the latter is affected by what, for our purposes, may be considered fortuitous developments such as differences in generosity of welfare payments at different locations and other variations in pertinent public policy.

The sequence of events which our discussion should lead us to expect may run somewhat as follows. First, innovation erodes the advantages of the city as a location for production. As a result, with some lag, firms begin gradually to withdraw from it, with earlier departures in those industries which are most heavily affected by the technological changes and whose plant depreciates most rapidly.

One would expect this to single out industries for which truck transportation is particularly well suited, for which transportation cost constitutes a large proportion of value added, and whose plant is not highly durable.

As economic activity begins to withdraw, residences of those able to afford the move can also be expected to change, also with some lag.[7] The departure of these more affluent residents leaves behind it a stock of vacant housing which, essentially, becomes a free economic good, its market value and, consequently, the market value of its rents reflecting this redundancy.[8]

This low cost housing immediately becomes a magnet for the poor who find the city providing them with cheaper places to live. In other words, the transition process disturbs the previous equilibrium in the housing market for the poor and makes the city more attractive on that score than it was previously. True, there is a scarcity of jobs to go along with the low price of housing, but since the exodus of industry is not yet completed, the seriousness of the unemployment problem has not yet reached its peak. Moreover, those who happen already to be unemployed outside the city have nothing to lose on that score by moving into an urban residence. Thus, the stock of housing abandoned by the middle class becomes, in effect, a collection of warehouses in which society stores its impecunious members.

This housing stock is scheduled to deteriorate "naturally," as part of the process of transition to the new urban equilibrium. Since from the long-run point of view it is redundant, it does not pay any private owners to invest heavily in repair and maintenance, let alone, improvement.

But the transition process involves more than this. As the job market for the poor immigrants grows increasingly tight it produces an explosive situation in which the prospect of unemployment for the indefinite future becomes a stimulus to frustration and rage. I shall not indulge myself in an attempt at amateur social psychology, but surely there are grounds for association of high crime rates, violence and destruction of property with this frustration.

Two consequences follow. First, the induced violence hastens the deterioration of the housing stock. The burning of the slums by their residents is, from this viewpoint, no historical accident, but part of the sequence of events in the adjustment toward the new urban equilibrium.

The second consequence is that the induced violence serves to make the city even less attractive than it would have become other- wise to both firms and more affluent residents. The numbers who are induced to leave exceed the quantities required for adjustment to the new equilibrium. But that is only a temporary phenomenon.

As the housing stock of the poor continues to deteriorate and even to disappear, as jobs fail to materialize and tend to become scarcer, net migration of even the poor can be expected. Those who came into the city will be induced to leave and they will be accompanied by still others who once had a place in the city's economy. This must be so, if the new equilibrium involves a smaller number of unskilled and semi-skilled jobs than the old and therefore calls for a smaller number of impecunious inhabitants. Their equilibrium number will not drop to zero—probably it will be far from that. But it will be significantly smaller than it was before.

This analysis suggests that long-run equilibrium also will require the return of some firms and some of the more affluent workers who have left the city. For as the size of the population of the poor adjusts to the new volume of job opportunities, unemployment will fall correspondingly and with it, the frustrations that lead to the urban violence of recent decades. And as the housing stock declines to its new equilibrium level the deterioration of buildings and neighborhoods will be reduced or eliminated.[9] These changes can be expected to increase the attractiveness of the cities and to bring back marginal emigrants who were induced to leave by the deterioration of social conditions rather than by lack of economic opportunities.[10]

The long-run prognosis, then, is relatively encouraging. After a painful transition process cities will emerge significantly smaller but economically viable and even prosperous, with a more even balance of the different income groups in its resident population. The social ills that have escalated in recent years can be expected to abate. Economic activity will consist far more heavily than before of service and administrative activities and manufacturing will play a considerably smaller role.

This sanguine forecast, unfortunately, does not imply that the new equilibrium is just around the corner. Our cities still have a long way to go in the painful adjustment process, and much of the public urban policy can be expected to protract this period rather than facilitate the transition. I will return to these issues. But first one must examine the grounds for optimism about the viability of a smaller urban economy under the new technological circumstances.

RESIDUAL ECONOMIC ADVANTAGES OF THE CITY

The main thing to be recognized in seeking to determine what economic advantages the city still offers is that technical change has eroded but not destroyed most of the advantages the city offered before. Specifically, today and for the indefinite future it still offers benefits in ease of communication and in a market sufficiently large to permit the provision of services which cannot survive without it.

While the telephone has reduced some of the benefits of proximity, many types of activity still require frequent face to face communication. This is, for example, true of members of the top management of large corporations who often meet with each other, with lawyers, with representatives of government agencies, etc. When all the parties have their home bases in the same city this advantage is obvious. But even if the people involved have widely separated home bases, the proximity to airports which the city offers is an overwhelming advantage. When travelling to New York to meet with someone from Washington, I often arrive later than the person from Washington even though I have only the 50-mile journey from Princeton. Firms have quickly learned the potency of this advantage. I know of one major corporation which announced some years ago, with considerable fanfare, that it was moving its headquarters from a major city into the countryside some 50 miles away. Today its legal headquarters indeed remains the shiny new edifice outside the city. But it has not given up the urban building which once served as its headquarters, and it is there that the president, the chairman of the board and a preponderance of its vice presidents go everyday.

The city also remains the location par excellence for variety retailing. Paradoxically, it is no longer the giant department stores but the small specialty shops congregate in central cities. Wide selections of unusual electronic components, rare tropical woods, unusual food products can be obtained quickly only in urban centers. But other activities which depend upon ready availability of a wide choice of unusual items also benefit by being nearby.

The dispersal of cultural activities which was mentioned earlier has made the arts and entertainment more accessible to suburban and rural areas but it has not robbed the city of its role as focal point for cultural institutions. Theaters, museums and opera houses continue to be found preponderantly in the major cities, and there is little reason to expect any radical change in this pattern in the foreseeable future.

The variety in retailing including the wide range of services such as restaurants along with the supply of cultural activities in turn serves to reattract some middle and upper income groups, which can become the focus of the rehabilitation of the smaller city of the future. These individuals bring not only themselves and improvements in their neighborhoods. They attract renewed and expanded service activities which are supported by their business. More than that, firms which are on the lookout for this sort of personnel are apt to be drawn to the city whose amenities and cultural activities can make it easier to hire engineers, scientists, technicians, lawyers and management personnel.

The list of attractions of the city in the new equilibrium, like all the attribute lists in this paper, is necessarily incomplete. But that is unimportant for our purposes. For our argument only requires some evidence that while technological change has imposed an economic handicap upon the cities, it has not driven them from the economic race. There is every reason, then, to expect the future city to be a very viable economic entity[11] albeit one which is very much smaller than it once had been.

POLICY IMPLICATIONS

The relatively sanguine view of the city's future is not meant to imply that the concern of policymakers over urban problems is unjustified. While a transition problem is by definition a short-run phenomenon, short-runs have a way of growing distressingly long, and this seems particularly likely to hold for the transition of the cities to their new equilibrium. Thus, policy measures which ameliorate these temporary problems are entirely appropriate, indeed, they are undoubtedly urgent. At stake is the welfare of generations of city dwellers, particularly in the neighborhoods which can be expected to abandon their present form in the next few decades.

But what the analysis suggests is that attempts to rehabilitate and improve these areas to any substantial extent will be disappointing at best. Such measures may serve as palliatives which bring temporary relief. But the reconstruction of housing in a devastated area which, even when rebuilt, cannot be expected to attract jobs for its residents must ultimately prove to be a cruel gift, even if it yields transitory political benefits, and perhaps initially, some benefits for its inhabitants.

But such programs are to be questioned not only because they are wasteful and their benefits destined to be short lived but, more important, because they actually serve to stretch out the unhappy period of transition and impede the readjustment toward the new and more desirable equilibrium. A rebuilt South Bronx can only lure the jobless into remaining longer where they have no economic prospects. One can be fairly confident that the reconstructed homes will be transformed into slums soon enough, and that the torch will be back at the task of destroying them soon enough.

Rather, the analysis suggests that rational policy should emphasize several measures of a different sort: a) improvements in that housing stock which still survives, which offer low costs *at the expense of durability*. For in areas with no long-term economic future there is little justification for investments which are designed to last; b) provision of inducements for emigration from the city, perhaps including subsidies to help cover costs of moving and housing outside the city[12]; c) special training programs for jobs located in areas of relative labor shortage; d) design of reconstruction plans for devastated areas whose purpose is *not* to restore those areas to anything like their former density, but which instead hasten and cushion the transition to their next stage.

Once more, this list is intended to be illustrative and suggestive, not exhaustive. The basic point is that at least some historical forces cannot be resisted for long. Attempts to undo their effects are not only bound to be fruitless but may well make things worse. This does not mean that we are powerless to influence the course of events. Understanding of the underlying forces offers us knowledge of the constraints which circumscribe our policy options. It is within the limits imposed by these constraints that we are free to act in a way that contributes to social welfare. The preceding policy discussion is meant as a first step suggesting how this can perhaps be done.

CONCLUDING COMMENT

There is probably little in this paper that has not been said before. Certainly, its empirical observations such as the effects of transportation changes upon the urban economy, the devastation of ghetto areas and, more recently, the return of some more affluent residents and "gentrification" of the centers of cities are commonplace observations.

If anything is new here it is the implicit treatment of the subject as an informal exercise in comparative statics—the replacement of one equilibrium by another and, simultaneously, in terms of the time path of the transition process. Viewed in this way, the analysis becomes less of an exercise in casual forecasting than it may at first appear. Rather, it is an attempt to pull together various well known strands of theoretical analysis and empirical observation. The purpose is to distinguish the degree to which we are faced by what may be described somewhat pompously as "historical inevitabilities" and the degree to which there remains room for maneuver and for choice of effective policies.

If the argument is correct it can account for a number of developments which otherwise may seem almost fortuitous and rather puzzling, such as the burning of the slums and their resistance to policy countermeasures, in sharp contrast to the preliminary signs of success of efforts to reattract less impecunious residents to the city. The analysis also suggests that a number of policy proposals emerging from the highest quarters and attracting considerable popular support are seriously misguided and threaten to exacerbate the problem they are intended to control.

**APPENDIX: BUDGET CONSTRAINT AND
SPEED OF TRANSITION**

In the text it was suggested that tightening of the budget constraint reasonably can be expected to lead to postponement of migration decisions because postponement reduces the cost of the move. However, it was asserted in a footnote that this cannot be proved on the normal premises of comparative statics. This appendix shows briefly why the result cannot be proved from those premises, and indicates some assumptions that can be used to support this inference.

For this purpose let

y represent a vector of dated quantities of goods and services consumed (which may itself be a continuous function of time)

t = the date of emigration from the city

r = the discount rate

$U(y,t)$ = the utility (profit) function giving the present value of expected future benefits

$C(t,r)$ = the cost of moving at date t

By the Hicksian rule, since we shall be holding all prices constant, it is completely legitimate to treat y as a single variable. Then the standard model of the individual decisionmaker's choice process requires him to

maximize $U(y,t)$
subject to the budget constraint

$py + C(t,r) = b$.

The decision-maker is taken to select those values of y and t which maximize U and the objective is to determine the effect of a change in budget, b, upon optimal timing, t, of the move, i.e., to determine the sign of $\partial t / \partial b$.

Once the problem is posed in this way two things immediately become clear: first, that $\partial t / \partial b$ is a garden-variety income effect the mathematical properties of which are unaffected by the happenstance that the pertinent decision variable is a (utility affecting) choice of moving date rather than a quantity of consumption; second, it becomes obvious that for the usual reasons, the sign of $\partial t / \partial b$ is indeterminate using maximization premises alone because the numerator for the derivative is a non principal minor whose sign, therefore, is not fixed by the second-order conditions. However, a rather crude alternative argument is possible.

By going through the tedious exercise of solving the maximization problem it is readily shown that

$$(1) \quad dt \quad = \quad \begin{vmatrix} O & U_{ty} & -C_t \\ O & U_{yy} & -p \\ -db & -p & O \end{vmatrix} / D,$$

where subscripts denote partial differentiation, and where D, the determinant of system of total differential equations, is positive, by the second order conditions. The numerator of (1) is

$$(1) \quad -db \begin{vmatrix} U_{ty} & -C_t \\ U_{yy} & -p \end{vmatrix} \quad = \quad db\,(pU_{ty} - C_t U_{yy}).$$

Here U_{yy} is negative if we can assume that there is declining marginal utility of consumption;

C_t,   the marginal cost of postponement of moving, can also be assumed to be negative and

U_{ty}, the effect of postponed migration upon marginal utility of y, can be assumed negative on the argument that, in this model, the city is a less desirable place in which to live and consume, i.e., that both the total and marginal utility of a given amount of consumption are higher in the new location.

Hence, each term in brackets on the RHS of (1) is negative, yielding the expected result, $\partial t / \partial b < 0$.

NOTES

1. Technological change in the late 18th century already profoundly affected the character of acceptable port facilities. It is not widely recognized today that a ship's crew had no way of determining its latitude until John Harrison invented the first accurate ship's clock in the middle of the 18th century and, following him, Arnold and Earnshaw produced the first relatively inexpensive ship's chronometers toward the end of the century. Before that, wherever possible, ships avoided ports with dangerous areas nearby since miscalculations about location were all too easy. There are records of ships not making for ports with treacherous areas nearby and travelling many additional days to safer habors, even though members of of the crew were dying of scurvy daily.

2. Of course, there are exceptions. Thus, canal boats are, typically, relatively small.

3. In the long-run equilibrium such handicaps are equalized at the margin. But, as we will see, the bulk of our concern will relate to the long period of transition toward a new equilibrium which, like all equilibria, probably will never quite be attained.

4. As industry is driven from the city relative land costs are, of course, depressed and this serves as a partial offset to the comparative static effect of the change in productive techniques. Where an equilibrium is stable, a shift in one of the relationships generally can be expected to induce a cushioning in price. However, except perhaps where the relevant relationships are "pathological," a shift in such an economic relationship cannot be expected to cause a price change sufficient to leave equilibrium quantities totally unaffected.

5. Elsewhere I have offered a dynamic model which describes this exodus as a cumulative process. To set it off one merely needs a change, such as the construction of superhighways, which induces some of the city's more affluent residents to move to the suburbs even if they then commute to work in the city. It therefore induces deterioration and aggravates other problems associated with a lower overall economic status. Simultaneously, it tends to raise the per capita tax burden of the remaining residents. Thus the first wave of emigration reduces the attractiveness of the city to those

who stay behind and sets off a second wave of outward movement. By the same process, that in turn induces a third and then a fourth wave, each step in this sequence setting the stage for its successor. If the analysis is correct, the cumulative character of this process helps to account for the transitoriness of the effects of many of the urban programs that have been undertaken in recent decades.

6. I deliberately avoid an unqualified statement because, as is shown in the Appendix, a comparative statics analysis of this issue does not give us a categorical answer about the relation between optimal date of relocation and tightness of the budget constraint (where we can interpret the absence of any constraint as the extreme case of a loosened constraint). The reason for the ambiguity is that we are dealing with an income rather than a substitution effect and, as we know, the usual assumptions of comparative statics are insufficient to determine the sign of the income effect.

7. Here is an example of a possible divergence between our stylized history and the actual facts. As already noted, innovation in transportation also independently encouraged suburbanization of residences and may have inaugurated a cumulative process of departure from the city by residents with middle and upper income levels. Thus, in fact, this exodus need not have lagged behind that of industry. Indeed, it may have stimulated the moves of some firms which were induced to follow their key personnel into the suburbs.

8. Apparently, there has been an increase in the ratio of number of households to size of population which has somewhat offset the effect of emigration from the city upon the demand for its housing stock.

9. Here again the conclusion is qualified because other influences are likely to intervene. For example, rent control laws can continue to discourage maintenance expenditures.

10. Other influences, which were more accidental, have also played a role in this. Rising fuel prices and the trend toward several jobs per family have, for example, increased the cost of commuting from the suburbs.

11. I do not mean to imply that all of our cities can be expected to survive. I should not be surprised if a number of middle sized metropolises were to become ghost towns in, say, the next half century.

12. The new housing should presumably be more dispersed than the old to avoid the creation of new centers of unemployment.

Franklin J. James - ECONOMIC DISTRESS IN CENTRAL CITIES

INTRODUCTION

During the 70s, economic change in central cities has been both rapid and complex. Some cities have experienced accelerating growth. The economies of other cities have slipped from growth to decline. Some cities experiencing economic decline during the 60s have suffered from snowballing job loss in the 70s. *These rapid, often unanticipated developments have altered virtually every index of the attractiveness or viablity of central cities, including city fiscal balance.*

In large part, the forces undercutting city economies are beyond the control of cities, states, or the Federal government, resting as they do on basic technological realities, popular preferences, and national and international economic shocks. However, available evidence also shows that government policies have had an important

The author wishes to acknowledge the comments and editorial assistance of Judith V. May and Avis Vidal. The opinions and conclusions expressed in this paper are those of the author alone, and need not reflect those of the U. S. Department of Housing and Urban Development.

19

role in undercutting city economies and in speeding up the pace of their economic decline. By altering these policies, the pace of city economic decline could be reduced giving cities and their residents more time to adapt to new economic roles and opportunities.

The Federal government has begun to respond, through increases in direct federal investments in the economic development of rapidly declining, distressed cities. The Urban Development Action Grant Program and the expanded Economic Development Administrations will offer more than $1 billion in grants for economic development in F.Y. 1980. Moreover, the Federal government is making determined efforts to take into account the impacts of major projects or programs on urban economies prior to making funding decisions, thus constricting the availability of federal assistance for activities weakening the economies of distressed cities. For example, federal environmental impact review now covers the urban impacts of projects.

Understanding the dimensions of central city economic change during the 70s, the impacts of change, and the forces guiding it is necessary for the further development of intelligent federal economic development policy. This paper will focus on providing insight into these issues.

THE PACE AND DIMENSIONS OF ECONOMIC CHANGE

The enormous diversity of city economic performance during the 70s challenges our ability to understand city economic performance and to cope with economic problems.

MEASURES OF CITY ECONOMIC DIVERSITY

Employment trends are basic indicators of the strength and diversity of city economies. Job changes experienced by major cities during the first half of the 70s ranged from growth rates exceeding 40 percent, to losses of up to one-third of the job base.[1]

However, strong patterns underlie this diversity. Estimates of overall employment trends during the 60s and the first half of the 70s are available for 79 major central cities. As a group, these large cities experienced much the same average annual rate of job growth between 1970 and 1977 as they had between 1960 and 1970 (see Exhibit 1). Examined city by city, the data show a remarkable pattern of accelerating growth during the 70s in cities which had grown previously and accelerating job loss in cities which lost jobs during the 60s.

Economic Distress

EXHIBIT 1

Employment Trends in 79 Major Central Cities: 1960-1977

City Type	Number of Cities	Average Annual Percent Change in Employment (unweighted)	
		1960-1970	1970-1977
Cities Losing Jobs, 1960-1970	23	−0.8	−1.8
Losing Jobs 1970-1975	21	−0.8	−2.2
Gaining Jobs 1970-1975	2	−0.3	2.2
Cities Gaining Jobs, 1960-1970	56	2.1	2.4
Losing Jobs 1970-1975	11	0.9	−0.8
Gaining Jobs 1970-1975	45	2.4	3.2
TOTAL	79	1.3	1.2

Source: Employment estimates provided by Seymour Sacks

Altogether, 23 of the 79 cities experienced job losses during the 60s. Nineteen of these 23 cities are older central cities of northeastern or midwestern metropolitan areas. All but two of these cities suffered from a higher pace of job loss in the 70s than they had experienced in the 60s.

By contrast, the 56 large cities which enjoyed job growth in the 60s saw their average rate of employment growth accelerate during the 70s. The pattern did not hold in all cases. For example, 11 cities which had experienced job growth during the 60s began to lose jobs during the 70s, and an additional 18 cities experienced lower rates of job growth during the 70s than in the 60s. However, 27 of the 56 cities which had grown during the 60s experienced accelerated growth during the 70s. 23 of these growing cities are newer cities in the South and West.

CHANGING INDUSTRIAL STRUCTURE

As importantly, declining cities are experiencing rapid changes in their industrial structure and the types of jobs available for resident workers.

The manufacturing sector and the blue-collar jobs offered by this sector are accounting for much of the overall job loss in declining cities. These changes are displacing workers from jobs and occupations in which they are experienced, forcing them to seek alternative employment in economies offering shrinking opportunities.

For many years, central city economies have been shifting away from goods production industries, such as manufacturing to service industries and white collar work. The loss of blue-collar jobs has been particularly marked in cities experiencing overall economic decline. Exhibit 2 presents separate figures on the industrial composition of private sector job changes between 1967 and 1972 in selected declining cities and growing cities. Overall, job growth in growing cities included in the exhibit was relatively balanced among manufacturing, retail trade, wholesale trade and selected services. Employment in each sector grew by between 20,000 and 85,000 jobs during the five-year period. By contrast, the manufacturing sector absorbed over two-thirds of the overall job loss in the declining cities. Growth in the service sectors of these declining economies was extremely limited, replacing less than one-fifth of the lost manufacturing jobs.

Available evidence suggests that manufacturing job loss in declining cities has been especially rapid in industries offering lower paying jobs within reach of lower skilled workers. A recent study of employment trends in Baltimore divided Baltimore's manufacturing industries into two groups: (1) those that paid relatively high wages and offered mostly full-time, permanent jobs; and (2) low-wage industries offering substantial numbers of temporary or part-time jobs. Approximately 18 percent of the city's manufacturing employment fell into the low-wage or part-time sector in 1962. This figure was substantially the same in 1970. By 1974, it had fallen to 14 percent. Put another way, the low-wage or part-time manufacturing sector absorbed half of the overall manufacturing job loss in Baltimore between 1962 and 1974, despite the fact that it accounted for less than one-fifth of manufacturing jobs at the start of the period.[2] More recent data show that the decline of low-wage or part-time manufacturing jobs persisted in Baltimore through 1976, accounting in that year for only 12 percent of manufacturing jobs.[3]

EXHIBIT 2

Industrial Composition of Employment Changes in 28 Major Growing
and Declining Central Cities: 1967-1972

	Fourteen Selected Cities Experiencing Employment Growth		Fourteen Selected Cities Experiencing Employment Loss	
	Absolute Job Changes 000s	Percent of Total Job Loss or Gain	Absolute Job Changes 000s	Percent of Total Job Loss or Gain
Manufacturing	39.1	16.9	−281.0	78.6
Retail Trade	76.8	33.2	− 55.0	15.6
Wholesale Trade	30.6	13.2	− 67.9	19.0
Selected Service	84.5	36.6	+ 47.0	−13.0
TOTAL of above	231.0	100.0	−357.0	100.0

Source: Harvey A. Garn and Larry C. Dedebur, "Metropolitan Prospects in the Context
of the Changing Distribution of Industry and Jobs" (Washington, D.C.: The
Urban Institute, Working Paper 5111-4, November 10, 1978).

By contrast, the industrial composition of jobs in cities with growing economies appears to have been much more stable during the
70s. In Denver, for example, private sector employment grew by
one-third between 1962 and 1974, while the proportion of city
jobs in manufacturing hardly changed (22 percent of jobs were in
manufacturing industries in 1962; by 1976, this had fallen to 20
percent). Moreover, the proportion of Denver's manufacturing jobs
in low-wage or part-time industries was low but constant during
the period.[4]

IMPACTS ON CITIES

The loss of economic vitality in declining cities has had widespread impacts on the well-being of these cities and their residents.
One important impact has been a dimunition of the tax base of
cities. One recent study (summarized in Exhibit 3) reported that
overall capital investment per production worker by manufacturers
was an average of $8,910 in central cities between 1970 and 1975,
and $12,064 in surrounding suburbs, a difference of 35 percent.
Job loss also can cut into the occupancy of and demand for existing commercial and industrial plants diminishing their value and their
contribution to the local tax base.

EXHIBIT 3

Capital Investment in Manufacturing Industries Per Production Employee
By Region: 1970-1975

Region	Central City	Balance of Urban County	Percent Differences
New England	$ 5467	$ 6952	27%
Middle Atlantic	6197	11480	85%
North Central	9796	14528	49%
South Atlantic	11626	9594	-18%
South Central	12206	32043	163%
West	8395	11774	40%
Average, U.S.	8910	12064	35%

Source: Thomas Muller, "Central City Business Retention: Jobs, Taxes and Investment
Trends," paper prepared for the Department of Commerce Urban Roundtable
February 1978.

More importantly, city job loss in declining cities has been associated with generally poor economic performance in terms of a wide variety of other economic indicators.

Another recent study of economic indicators in 147 central cities establishes that cities losing jobs also have performed poorly in terms of several indicators of basic economic strength. In Exhibit 4, the 147 cities have been classified into three groups: (1) those experiencing seriously adverse job losses during the first half of the 70s (i.e., these cities showed very rapid employment declines); (2) those experiencing adverse job losses (i.e., significant job losses); and (3) cities experiencing relatively good job performance. Four other measures of economic well-being of city residents have also been classified as seriously adverse, adverse, or good in this exhibit.

As can be seen, every city experiencing seriously adverse job loss also showed adverse or seriously adverse performance in terms of income level among residents, growth in income, unemployment, and unemployment change. By contrast, most cities enjoying strong employment growth also enjoyed high levels of income, rapid income growth, low unemployment rates, and slow growth in unemployment rates during the period.

EXHIBIT 4

Relationships Between City Employment Change and Other Indicators of
Economic Performance for 147 Large Central Cities

Other Economic Indicators	Changes in City Employment: 1970-1975 (figures are numbers of cities)				
	Seriously Adverse	Adverse	Good	Very Good	Total
Income Level					
Seriously Adverse	2	0	0	3	5
Adverse	12	29	21	20	82
Good or Very Good	0	16	44	0	60
					(147)
Income Growth					
Seriously Adverse	2	17	0	0	19
Adverse	12	12	38	0	62
Good or Very Good	0	16	27	23	66
					(147)
Unemployment Rate					
Seriously Adverse	2	4	8	0	14
Adverse	12	29	5	3	49
Good or Very Good	0	12	52	20	84
					(147)
Unemployment Rate Change					
Seriously Adverse	14	0	0	0	14
Adverse	0	39	8	3	50
Good or Very Good	0	6	57	20	83
TOTAL, ALL CITIES	14	45	65	23	147

Source: Harvey A. Garn and Larry C. Ledebur, "Metropolitan Prospects in the Context of the Changing Distribution of Industry and Jobs" (Washington, D.C.: The Urban Institute, Working Paper S111-4, November 10, 1978).

FACTORS INFLUENCING EMPLOYMENT CHANGES IN CITIES

The rapid pace of job loss in older declining cities is not the result of any single force. Rather, it appears to be due to several factors. Historic patterns of urban economic development left many older cities with marginal economic bases as the cities entered the 70s. Tough economic environments which have prevailed during the decade expose the underlying economic vulnerabilities of older cities.

Suburbanization and Decentralization

Suburbanization of jobs is by far the most significant long-term force sapping the economic strength of distressed central cities. Jobs have been thinning out in metropolitan areas for many years, growing less rapidly in the urban core and more rapidly on the metropolitan periphery.

Two of the more important reasons for employment decentralization have been the plentiful supplies of comparatively cheap, vacant land in suburbs, and transportation and communication innovations such as the truck, automobile and telephone. Vacant land made new development and growth in suburbs easier and cheaper compared to new development in densely built-up older areas. Transportation and communication innovations enabled business establishments to take advantage of suburban land with less sacrifice in access and information than would have occurred if conversion still required personal meetings and transportation still required horses, trains, trolleys or waterways.[5]

Different sectors of the urban economy have been subject to different decentralization forces. In manufacturing, for example, changes in production technology and transportation needs have hastened suburbanization. The growing use of the truck for inter-city as well as local transport has made location near interstate highways one of the most important determinants of the accessibility of a plant to markets or suppliers.[6] Congestion on city streets has reduced the attractiveness of central city locations. By locating in suburbs, manufacturers also have more opportunity to build or occupy modern single-story production facilities, consistent with today's continuous production techniques which rely on the horizontal movement of work-in-process to achieve production economies. Older production space in cities is often housed in multistory buildings, effectively precluding the economic use of these horizontal operations.[7]

In retailing, central city employers have been exposed to competition from regional shopping malls. Largely a post-war invention, these malls are generally located close to the intersection of major highways and built with the latest customer amenities. Thus, they combine easy automobile access, protection from inclement weather, and variety of selection which historically were the exclusive prerogative of the city.

In a similar fashion, wholesaling has been decentralized in part as a result of the increasing use of the truck for inter-regional travel;

in part, because warehouse space is relatively cheap in suburbs; and, in part, because of the suburbanization of industry and retailing.

Suburbanization and decentralization during the 50s and 60s set the stage for the rapid job loss in older cities with older businesses, older infrastructure and older stocks of business and industrial facilities.

RECESSION AND CITY ECONOMIC PERFORMANCE

The twin recession of the 70s quickly uncovered the economic weaknesses of the economies of older cities, and resulted in very sudden and substantial job losses. Exhibit 5 presents measures of private sector employment in eight major cities for the period 1962-1976.[8] As can be seen, private employment peaked in 1970, following a decade of steady employment and expansion. Employment fell in these cities by 3.7 percent between 1970 and 1971, as the first of the recession of the 70s hit. Over 119,000 jobs were lost in a single year by the eight cities. Employment levels recovered slowly through 1973 and 1974. When the second more severe recession of the decade hit in 1975, the cities lost 177,000 or 5.8 percent of their private sector jobs. Recovery had hardly begun in 1976, the most recent year for which such data are available.

Debate has long waged over how recessions affect the economies of central cities. The focus of the debate has been the question of whether or not the amplitude of recessionary impacts is more severe in central cities than in suburban or nonmetropolitan areas. The evidence on this question remains contradictory and unclear.[9] As can be seen in Exhibit 5, suburban as well as central city economies were damaged by the recessions, and, as a group, experienced job losses in both 1971 and 1975; but older, declining central cities recovered more slowly than newer, still growing cities. Exhibit 6 presents annual employment measures for each of eight cities for which such data are available. Four of the eight are declining cities in the Northeast or Midwest: Baltimore, Boston, Philadelphia and St. Louis. Recession resulted in rapid, sudden job losses in each of these four cities. For example, Philadelphia lost 43,000 jobs between 1970 and 1971, and another 49,000 between 1974 and 1975. As significantly, city employment showed only weak signs of recovery between these two recessions, and the beginnings of national economic recovery in 1976 were not reflected in job growth in Philadelphia. This same pattern is also apparent in the data for St. Louis and Boston.

EXHIBIT 5

Employment Trends in Eight Central Cities and Their Suburbs 1962-1976[a]

A. Employment Levels

	1962	1967	1968	1969	1970	1971	1972	1973	1974[c]	1975[c]	1976[c]
Cities											
Number[b]	2858	3113	3134	3173	3193	3074	3093	3161	3040	2869	2872
Percent of SMSA	55.6	51.4	50.2	49.5	48.9	48.5	47.6	46.5	43.0	42.2	41.6
Suburbs											
Number[b]	2278	2942	3104	3243	3334	3269	3404	3634	4024	3928	4047
Percent of SMSA	44.4	48.6	49.8	50.5	51.1	51.5	52.4	53.5	57.0	57.8	58.5

B. Employment Changes

	Average Annual Change 1962-1967	1967-1968	1968-1969	1969-1970	1970-1971	1971-1972	1972-1973	1974-1975	1975-1976
Cities									
Absolute Change[b]	51	21	39	20	–119	19	68	–177	11
Percent Change	1.8	0.7	1.2	0.6	–3.7	0.6	2.2	–5.8	0.4
Suburbs									
Absolute Change[b]	133	162	139	91	–65	135	230	–95	101
Percent Change	5.8	5.5	4.5	2.8	–2.0	4.1	6.8	–2.4	2.6

a Only private wage and salary jobs covered under Social Security are included. Employment levels are measured in March of each year. The eight areas considered are Baltimore, Boston, Denver, New Orleans, Philadelphia, St. Louis, San Francisco and Washington, D.C.

b Thousands of jobs

c Due to changes in definitions of employment location these data are not directly comparable to data from earlier years.

Source: U.S. Bureau of the Census, *County Business Patterns.*

The remaining four cities are from the South and West, with generally stronger economies: Washington, D.C., Denver, New Orleans and San Francisco. These cities have hardly proved immune to recessions. For example, San Francisco also gained jobs as the national economy recovered from both recessions. A similar pattern prevails in other stable or growing cities.

It appears that in distressed cities, employment declines during recessions have long-run impacts. Existing, marginal businesses cut back or shut down, and the investment opportunities foregone cannot be counted on to reappear when business conditions improve. By contrast, in growing cities, business retrenchment during recessions means that businesses defer taking advantage of investment opportunities, but when the economy improves, they again take advantage of them.

REGIONAL SHIFTS IN ECONOMIC ACTIVITY

Shifts of employment from the North to the South and West took place during the 70s on a very large scale, further undercutting the economies of older cities in declining regions.

Exhibit 7 displays the nature and magnitude of regional and industrial shifts which have occurred during the 70s. Between 1970 and 1977, overall employment growth largely stopped in the Northeast. In 1970, the economy of this region provided almost 19 million jobs. Between 1970 and 1977, this figure grew by only 500,000. During these years, the number of jobs in the nation grew by over 1 million. A less dramatic but similar pattern prevailed in the North Central region, where employment growth slowed markedly during the 70s. By contrast, between 1970 and 1977 almost three-fourths of overall national job growth took place in the South and West.

The exhibit also indicates that manufacturing industries have played a major role in these regional shifts. Since 1960, virtually all new manufacturing jobs have been created in the South and West. During the 1960s, the Vietnam War and other factors buoyed national manufacturing activity by almost three million new jobs, with the result that no region of the nation experienced an absolute decline in manufacturing jobs. During the 1970s, recessions, the end of the War, and other factors stymied national growth in manufacturing employment, and, for the first time since the end of World War II, the Northeast and North Central regions experienced protracted losses of manufacturing jobs.

EXHIBIT 6

Private Employment in Central Cities and Suburbs of Eight SMSAs: 1962-1976[a]

	1962	1967	1968	1969	1970	1971	1972	1973	1974[d]	1975[d]	1976
Baltimore Number[b]											
City	340	367	363	369	367	363	360	366	329	310	301
Suburb	157	216	226	232	238	238	243	261	313	303	311
City Share[c]	68.4	63.0	61.6	61.4	60.7	60.3	59.7	58.4	51.2	50.6	49.2
Boston Number[b]											
City	422	441	448	454	467	443	449	451	423	399	391
Suburb	618	723	757	771	798	759	774	814	869	823	822
City Share[c]	40.6	37.9	37.2	37.1	36.9	36.9	36.7	35.7	32.7	32.7	32.2
Denver Number[b]											
City	199	221	231	243	254	256	275	297	275	262	267
Suburb	77	94	107	120	125	133	153	175	219	216	228
City Share[c]	72.1	70.2	68.3	66.9	67.0	65.8	64.3	62.9	55.7	54.8	53.9
New Orleans Number[b]											
City	184	230	230	224	226	223	237	242	217	208	213
Suburb	44	70	75	77	84	85	90	97	131	131	140
City Share[c]	80.7	76.7	75.4	74.4	72.9	72.4	72.5	71.4	62.4	61.4	60.3
Philadelphia Number[b]											
City	737	773	771	778	775	732	720	727	698	649	639
Suburb	582	658	695	723	740	716	733	776	872	849	867
City Share[c]	58.1	54.0	52.6	51.8	51.2	50.6	49.6	48.4	44.5	43.2	42.4
St. Louis Number[b]											
City	356	377	381	383	376	254	351	357	331	300	293
Suburb	252	266	278	400	394	382	399	426	464	461	494
City Share[c]	58.6	50.7	50.2	48.9	48.8	48.1	46.8	45.6	41.6	39.4	37.2
San Francisco Number[b]											
City	343	382	387	398	402	387	388	397	457	434	450
Suburb	410	408	534	557	576	563	583	599	631	625	647
City Share[c]	45.6	42.9	42.0	41.7	41.1	40.7	40.0	39.9	42.0	41.0	41.0
Washington, D.C. Number[b]											
City	282	322	323	324	326	317	313	324	310	307	316
Suburb	192	307	323	363	379	393	429	486	525	520	538
City Share[c]	59.5	51.2	49.3	47.2	46.2	44.6	42.2	40.0	37.1	37.1	37.0

a. Only private wage and salary jobs covered under Social Security are included. Employment levels are measured in March of each year.

b. Thousands of jobs

c. Percent of jobs in central city

d. Definitions changed; data not comparable

EXHIBIT 7

Regional Levels of Manufacturing and Non-Manufacturing Employment,
1960-1977

Region	Employment Levels (000s)			Employment Levels (000s)	
	1960	1970	1977	1960-1970	1970-1977
A. Manufacturing Employment					
Northeast	5,573	5,611	4,961	38	−650
North Central	5,456	6,265	6,242	809	−23
South	3,690	5,126	5,710	1,436	584
West	1,957	2,377	2,673	420	296
U.S. TOTAL	16,676	19,379	19,586	2,703	207
B. Non-Manufacturing Employment					
Northeast	10,043	13,044	14,187	3,001	1,143
North Central	10,381	13,655	16,271	3,276	2,616
South	10,556	15,156	19,801	4,599	4,646
West	6,379	9,450	12,375	3,071	2,925
U.S. TOTAL	37,359	51,305	62,634	13,946	11,329
C. Total Employment					
Northeast	15,616	18,655	19,148	3,039	493
North Central	15,837	19,920	22,513	4,085	2,593
South	14,246	20,282	25,511	6,035	5,230
West	8,336	11,827	15,048	3,491	3,221
U.S. TOTAL	54,035	70,684	82,220	16,649	11,536

Source: U.S. Bureau of Labor Statistics: *Employment and Earnings for States and Areas.*

The manufacturing trends have greatly affected central city economies in both growing and declining regions. As shown in Exhibit 8,
between 1970 and 1975, central cities in New England, the Middle
Atlantic, and the North Central regions lost a substantial proportion
of their manufacturing jobs (ranging from 18 percent in the East
North Central region to 27 percent in the Middle Atlantic region),
and these cities continued to lose jobs, but at a slower rate in the
period 1975 to 1976. Central cities in the South also lost manufacturing jobs between 1970 and 1975, due in large part to national
recession, but they lost a lower proportion of jobs (ranging from 6

percent in the South Atlantic region to 10 percent in the South East region) and their losses were halted or reversed during the period 1975 to 1976 with the beginning of national economic recovery. (Northeastern and midwestern suburbs also lost manufacturing jobs between 1970 and 1975, while southern suburbs, on balance, gained jobs.)

Even more significant than these trends may be the changes that occurred in the 70s in the characteristics of the manufacturing jobs that are growing in the South. Analysts have long assumed that much of the manufacturing job growth in the South took place in industries needing low-skilled, low-wage workers. As shown in Exhibit 9, it now appears that average manufacturing wages have converged among regions in both central cities and suburbs.

Strikingly, average wages paid in 1975 by central city manufact-urers were lowest in New England. Moreover, manufacturing workers in central cities in New England and the Middle Atlantic regions appear to have been less productive in 1975 than were central city workers in any other region of the nation, when productivity is measured in terms of value added per worker.[10] Low wages are not necessarily attractive to employers when productivity is also low, and consequently, they may not spur increased investment in north-ern cities. It appears that some cities of the once-dominant "manu-facturing belt" of the nation now may have among the most back-ward manufacturing economies in the nation.

THE FAILURE TO ATTRACT GROWTH INDUSTRIES

Cities losing older businesses and industries due to recession and regional shifts have proven unable to replace them with newer activities. Large cities historically have been centers of economic innovation. Firms doing businesses in large cities often specialized in producing new products or services which required skilled manage-ment and craft labor and which embodied technological advances. Cities also have been the sites of major headquarters and financial centers supporting and directing innovation throughout the nation. As new products or services become standardized, their production is shifted to areas where production is less expensive or to areas where expanding markets demand them.[11] To maintain the vitality of their economies, large cities must be able to generate new services, products and businesses. Many declining cities have not been able to do so.

The Manufacturing Sector A close look at the manufacturing sectors of growing and declining cities suggest why many older,

EXHIBIT 8

Manufacturing Employment in Central Cities and Urban Counties by Region

Region	Number of Cities	City Total Employment (in thousands)			Number of Counties	Balance of Urban County[a] Total Employment (in thousands)		
		1975	1976	Percent Change 1970-1975		1975	1970-1975	Percent Change 1975-1976
New England	5	160	157	−21%	5	242	−10%	−2%
Middle Atlantic	10	1092	1066	−27%	8	379	− 4%	−2%
East North Central	19	1396	1398	−10%	19	890	− 1%	0
West North Central	6	325	305	−19%	5	69	−12%	−6%
South Atlantic	10	338	336	− 6%	9	104	−11%	0
South East	5	199	199	−10%	5	73	4%	0
South West	8	431	447	− 2%	7	107	15%	4%
West	12	716	724	5%	10	630	1%	1%
All Cities/Urban Counties	75	4657	4632	−17%	60	2463	− 1%	1%

a   Balance of urban county is urban county less its central city. For example, Cook County less Chicago, or Wayne County less Detroit.

Source: Thomas Muller, "Central City Business Retention: Jobs, Taxes and Investment Trends," paper prepared for the Department of Commerce Urban Roundtable, February 1978.

EXHIBIT 9

Change in City and Balance of County Manufacturing Payroll by Region, 1970-1975

Region	Hourly Wage Per Prod. Employee 1975	Annual Payroll Per Employee 1975	Percent Change in Payroll Per Employee 1970-1975	Hourly Wage Per Prod. Employee 1975	Annual Payroll Per Employee	Percent Change in Payroll Per Employee 1970-1975
New England	$4.55	$10,463	40%	$4.41	$11,004	50%
Middle Atlantic	4.81	12,013	46%	5.67	12,644	49%
East North Central	6.12	13,404	47%	6.34	14,118	47%
West North Central	5.63	12,400	41%	5.51	12,479	56%
South Atlantic	4.60	10,464	31%	4.18	10,354	44%
South East	5.00	11,060	52%	5.73	11,849	44%
South West	4.69	11,559	47%	5.24	12,196	42%
West	5.30	12,940	43%	5.29	12,020	44%
Average	5.32	12,363	43%	5.61	12,902	46%

Source: Thomas Muller, "Central City Business Retention: Jobs, Taxes, and Investment Trends," paper prepared for the Department of Commerce Urban Roundtable, February 1978.

declining cities have failed to attract or generate new, growing industries. To a large extent, they have declined because they have continued to rely on old manufacturing industries which appear to have limited potential for future growth, and which have proved vulnerable to economic setbacks in the 70s. In 1970, for example, Pittsburgh and Buffalo's largest manufacturers produced iron and steel. New York City's major manufacturers were apparel producers and printers. Cleveland's largest manufacturing employers were in fabricated metals and nonelectrical machinery.[12]

By contrast, many new cities of the South and West are established centers of production in relatively newer, high technology industries. For example, the largest manufacturing employers in Los Angeles, Dallas/Fort Worth, and San Diego were in aircraft and electronics. The largest employers in San Jose and Tucson were in electronics and ordnance. These newer industries have certainly not insulated cities from losses of employment.[13] However, available evidence suggests that these industries have generated high levels of technological innovation in recent years,[14] and there is little doubt that they provide a base for economic expansion during the 70s and beyond.

Many declining central cities have had only limited success in inducing new manufacturing firms or establishments to locate in their jurisdictions. This is important because a recent study found that young business establishments during their first four years produce a substantial percentage (approximately 80 percent) of all new jobs in city economies.[15] A number of recent studies have examined the kinds of business decisions affecting industrial location. With substantial uniformity, these studies have found that the most important decisions accounting for overall differences in manufacturing employment growth are the location choices of new business establishments and decisions regarding the expansion or contraction of employment in existing businesses. Business relocation within central cities or from central cities to suburbs has not been found to be a major contributor to employment loss in cities, and business relocation among regions has been found to be relatively rare.[16]

Exhibit 10 presents recent data on rates of new business formation within metropolitan areas. As can be seen, rates of new business formation were lowest by a substantial margin in central counties (counties containing central cities of metropolitan areas) of the North. Rates of new business formation were half as high in central counties of metropolitan areas of the Middle Atlantic region as they were in comparable counties of the South and West.

EXHIBIT 10

New Manufacturing Establishments Formed Between 1969 and 1975
as a Percent of Total Manufacturing Establishments in 1969

Region	Metropolitan Areas	Core Counties	Suburban Counties
New England	24.9	24.1	29.1
Middle Atlantic	19.3	16.9	26.2
East North Central	24.1	21.1	33.1
West North Central	26.3	23.5	40.4
South Atlantic	36.8	39.3	32.8
Southeast	23.4		23.4
Southwest	37.9	37.3	43.0
Mountain	41.7	32.1	61.3
Pacific	40.1	39.7	45.1

Source: See Exhibit 2.

Exhibit 11 summarizes data on net changes in manufacturing employment in central counties by region, and the contribution to these changes made by three factors: net business inmigration, net business expansion, and employment in new businesses minus employment in dying businesses. Rates of new business formation in major central counties in New England and the Middle Atlantic regions were so low that employment loss between 1969 and 1975, due to the difference between the employment in new businesses and dying businesses, amounted to almost 19 percent of the total manufacturing employment base in the counties in 1969. By contrast, higher rates of new business formation in the South more closely balanced employment losses due to business closures; and net employment expansion of existing businesses (including recently formed business) was very substantial.

The forces which account for the low rates of new business formation in many central cities are complex. One reason why cities are failing to attract new businesses is that the rapid economic development of suburbs has enabled suburbs to better compete for new business. Markets for products and suppliers of inputs needed by manufacturers are much more evenly spread within metropolitan areas than was true in the past. Business services and rentable production space which were once concentrated in central cities are today available in many suburbs.[17]

EXHIBIT 11

Components of Employment Growth in Selected Central Counties
of Major Metropolitan Areas: 1969-1975

Region	Percent Employment Change 1969-1975	Employment in New Businesses Minus Employment in Dying Businesses	Net Expansion of Employment in Existing Businesses	Net In-migration in Businesses
New England	−18.0	−18.5	−1.1	−0.5
Middle Atlantic	−22.1	−18.9	−0.4	−2.8
East North Central	− 5.4	−13.8	9.7	−1.3
West North Central	8.1	−12.6	22.0	−1.2
South Atlantic	4.0	−12.4	12.0	4.4
Southeast	NA	NA	NA	NA
Southwest	12.1	− 3.3	18.1	−2.7
Mountain	− 9.3	−11.1	3.7	−1.9
Pacific	− 2.3	− 5.7	3.3	0.1

Source: See Exhibit 2.

At the same time, available evidence, though limited, implies that the availability of financing plays a role. New business establishments are commonly small and rely heavily on long-term debt and equity financing. A number of experts report that small new businesses generally face greater difficulties in obtaining needed financing than do larger, established ones and that these difficulties are greatest for businesses choosing locations in cities.[18]

The Office Sector Many declining cities also have failed to attract firms in another basic and expanding sector of the national economy, the office industry. Since 1950, virtually all net national employment growth has occurred in so-called "tertiary" industries: services, trade, finance and government. Office jobs now comprise about one-half of all white-collar jobs in office work, and more than one-half of office jobs are located in detached office buildings.[19]

Historically, the office industry has been disproportionately concentrated in the central business districts of major metropolitan areas. Such locations long offered superior transportation facilities and extensive support services such as legal firms, accounting and management services, and job printers. Most importantly, central business districts were attractive to offices because so many other offices were located there. This facilitated face-to-face communication among decisionmakers in private industry or government.

Many declining cities with established office industries have
proved unable to capitalize effectively on the growing importance
of office work. Newer metropolitan office centers have emerged
in the South and West. This is indicated by growth in the number
of jobs in central administrative and auxiliary units. Sixty percent
of the nation's employment in such units is concentrated in 18 major
urban areas. Between 1954 and 1972, employment in these establishments grew most rapidly in Houston, Atlanta, Denver, Washington, D.C., Los Angeles and Boston.[20] Of the eleven metropolitan
areas centered around declining central cities for which data are
available, only three experienced higher than average rates of growth
of central office employment: Boston, Cincinnati and Minneapolis-
St. Paul.[21] Employment in the major national office centers—New
York and Chicago—grew significantly less rapidly in percentage
terms than in the nation as a whole. Of course, due to their large
size, absolute office growth in these two cities exceeded growth in
any of the other metropolitan areas. However, in relative terms, the
two areas lost some of their dominance.[22]

The relatively slow growth of office employment in older declining cities is not attributable to rapid suburbanization of this
industry. Some observers have argued that technological advances
ranging from the computer to telephone and photocopying machines
have diminished the ties of central offices to central business districts.
However, this is not reflected in actual headquarters location decisions. Much of the suburbanization of headquarters offices has
occurred in the New York region. The scale of the New York region
and the intense level of urbanization of its "suburbs" make New
York unique. What appears, in fact, to have occurred is that advances
in communication and data processing have enabled more businesses
to separate office, sales and production functions into separate
plants, enabling the businesses to fine-tune the location of each of
their establishments. Headquarters functions remain solidly concentrated in central business districts.

Historic patterns of industrial specialization account in part for
the eroding position of northern office centers. Much of the office
industry in declining northern cities grew up around the headquarters
of the major industrial firms of the region. Detroit, Cleveland and
Pittsburgh are prime examples. Recent growth in headquarters office
employment has been most rapid in trade and service industries.
Employment in central administrative and auxiliary units of non-
manufacturing firms grew 56 percent between 1963 and 1972. The
comparable figure for manufacturing industries is only 40 percent.
Growing cities of the South and West have been disproportionately

successful in attracting the headquarters establishments of these relatively new and dynamic industries. Offices of these industries were most substantial in Atlanta, Dallas, Los Angeles, San Francisco and Washington, D.C. In contrast, a number of declining northern cities missed out almost entirely in attracting new jobs in the headquarters of service and trade firms. Examples are Philadelphia, Pittsburgh, Detroit and Cincinnati.[23]

BARRIERS TO ECONOMIC DEVELOPMENT IN DECLINING CITIES

In part, patterns of urban growth and decline signal secular adjustments to changed technology and altered roles for cities in the national economy. It is unlikely that older central cities could ever again reclaim a dominant role in national manufacturing. Even were this possible, it could be undesirable unless the cities would provide efficient locations for these industries.

But, the current rapid pace of job loss in cities cannot simply be assumed to be an efficient reaction to economic forces. The costs of providing physical infrastructure in new places and of adjusting the physical infrastructure and land use patterns of currently developed areas to the needs of new industries and technology are substantial. These costs are borne publicly and are therefore not adequately taken into account by private businesses when they select their locations. Environmental sensitivities and inflation in financing and land costs have pushed up the costs of new development and infrastructure to very high levels in recent years.[24] Furthermore, changes in the location and character of employment opportunities mean that individuals who wish to be productively employed must adjust their work-related skills, their locations, or both. Substantial segments of the population have a restricted ability to make such adjustments because of low skills, low incomes, discrimination, or family obligations. The costs of enabling them to participate fully in the changing economy, or of providing for their basic survival needs if they cannot participate, are likewise not borne directly by individual businesses making locational choices.

In addition, economic development in distressed cities has been hampered by federal and state policies which have undercut the competitiveness of the cities. Unfortunately, not enough is known about the types of public action which most effectively accomplish economic development goals in cities with a declining job base. Some recent evidence offers insight into specific deterrents to central city economic development whose ill effects might be ameliorated though public policy. The evidence has two basic implications. The first is that the basic economic disadvantages of cities compared to their suburbs are not very great. In many instances they can be neutralized by shallow subsidies of the magnitudes which several federal economic development programs currently have in operation. Thus, urban economic development is a feasible option in central cities. Second, the evidence suggests a number of local and national policies which have undercut the economies of declining cities and which, if reversed, could support efforts to strengthen city economies.

THE COST DISADVANTAGES OF CITIES

Many experts have pointed out that technological changes and other economic forces have weakened the ability of cities to compete with smaller suburban or nonmetropolitan communities. For example, land is relatively scarce in central cities and is typically divided into small parcels under separate ownership. As a result, assembling a site large enough for a major single-story plant is difficult, time-consuming, expensive and risky. On these grounds alone, many businesses prefer to build in industrial parks or sparsely settled areas where parcels of suitable size are readily available.

In addition to the difficulty of acquiring land, firms may incur higher monetary costs if they locate in central cities rather than in suburbs. The limited available evidence suggests that expenditures for plant or offices, for land, and taxes tend to be higher in the central city.[25]

Two studies have developed profiles comparing building and operating costs for prototypical manufacturing establishments in central city and suburban locations. The first study analyzed the costs of buying land and constructing a new manufacturing facility at three locations in Boston: one in the central city, one on the major circumferential highway roughly dividing the inner and outer ring suburbs and one on a circumferential highway well beyond the currently developed metropolitan area. The study found that land prices in the central city averaged three to four times as much as land on the fringe, and that building the most attractive type of centrally located plant (including land and building) was about 25 percent more costly than the best-choice suburban plant.[26] While it is likely that these cost differences are decreasing over time, as prime suburban land becomes scarcer and hence more costly and as densities in central cities fall, the cost differences that exist continue to favor suburban locations. The second study developed a profile of overall operating costs for a typical manufacturing establishment in the city of Atlanta and in its suburbs. Exhibit 12 presents three quantitative estimates of the annual costs and income per employee in three alternative types of locations: (1) in an existing 20-to-30 year old plant in Atlanta; (2) in a new plant in Atlanta; and (3) in a new plant in Atlanta's suburbs. Overall costs are shown to be highest for manufacturers in a new plant in the central city and lowest for a new plant in the suburbs. Differences in land and building costs are reflected in the modest variation in capital costs and debt service. Most of the differences in operating costs at different locations are attributable to differences in local taxes. Overall, annual costs vary by as much as $800 per employer per year. This differential amounts to 2 percent of total annual income and costs per worker. From another perspective it amounts to 30 percent of the estimated net before-tax income which might be received in a suburban location.

EXHIBIT 12

Annual Costs and Income of a Specified Manufacturing Plant in Alternative Locations Within the Atlanta Metropolitan Areas: 1977[a]

Annual Costs and Income Per Employee	Establishment Locations		
	New Plant in Suburbs	New Plant in Central City	Existing Plant in Central City
Annual Sales	$40,000	$40,000	$40,000
Annual Costs			
Payroll	10,000	10,000	10,000
Materials	16,800	16,800	16,800
Capital Costs and Debt Service[b]	3,300	3,400	3,200
Local Taxes[c]	600	1,300	1,250
Other Operating Costs	6,900	6,900	6,900
Net Annual Income Before State and Federal Taxes	2,400	1,600	1,850

a   The establishment used to determine these figures manufactures paper box products in a one-story plant employing 200 persons, of whom 80 percent are production workers. Machinery and equipment costs are assumed to be $16,000 per square feet. All types are rounded to the nearest $100.

b   Capital costs assume that debt comprises 75 percent of the costs of buildings, land, machinery and equipment. The estimates further assume that mortgages on plant and buildings carry a 25-year term and 9½ percent interest rates. Debt on machinery and equipment is assumed to carry a 7-year term and an 8 percent interest rate.

c   Estimates assume an effective property tax rate in Atlanta City of 2.4 percent, and 1.2 percent for a typical rate in the Atlanta suburbs, metropolitan area. In addition, annual inventory taxes were assumed to comprise $60 per employee in Atlanta City per year, and $30 in suburbs.

Since financing subsidies are one principal form in which public economic development assistance is delivered to private business, the magnitude of interest rate subsidies required to neutralize cost differences is an especially useful indicator of the size of cost differences. Such data are presented in Exhibit 13. Conventional interest rates in the table are those prevailing in Atlanta in 1977: i.e., 9.5 percent on financing for building and land, and 8 percent for machinery and equipment. The exhibit illustrates that subsidies reducing these interest rates to 6.0 percent for city locations would have neutralized three-fourths of the cost disadvantages of an existing city plant. Three-percent financing would have made a central city location more attractive in economic terms. Interest rate subsidies of this magnitude are well within the range of financing incentives offered by a number of federal economic development programs in effect or proposed, including the National Development Bank proposed by the Carter Administration in 1978. The financing authorities proposed for the banks are being implemented by the Economic Development Administration and the Department of Housing and Urban Development.

EXHIBIT 13

Net Annual Income of a Specified Manufacturing Plant in the Atlanta
Metropolitan Area, Assuming Various Levels of Financing Subsidies
are Available to Plants in the City

Interest Rates on Business Financing for Land, Building and Equipment		Establishment Location		
Land and Building	Machinery and Equipment	New Plant in Suburbs	New Plant in Central City	Existing Plant in Central City
Conventional Financing				
9.5%	8%	$ 2,400	$ 1,600	$ 1,850
Subsidized for City Establishments				
6.0	6.0	2,400	2,100	2,250
3.0	3.0	2,400	2,500	2,750

Source: Andrew M. Hamer, "The Impact of Federal Subsidies on Industrial Location Behavior: Preliminary Conclusions from a Case Study" (Atlanta, Georgia: Georgia State University, October 11, 1977).

LOCAL GOVERNMENT'S EFFECT ON THE ATTRACTIVENESS OF
CENTRAL CITIES

Some evidence suggests that local government policies and resources are sometimes major barriers to economic growth. Exhibit
14 summarizes a recent survey of businessmen in which they reported on the factors which most strongly influence their location
choices. The figures in the exhibit are the percentage of respondents
rating the factor as important or very important in their location
choices. The most important factor was found to be city attitudes
toward business.

The fact that local government services and behavior influence
investment decisions is revealed by the importance that the businessmen attached to crime, the adequacy of public facilities, public
services and public schools.

The same study also found that the businessmen's perceptions of
business climates were related to the strength of the cities' economies
in recent years. Businessmen rated business climates in 10 major
central cities as follows:

Highly Favorable Business Climates (More than 80% favorable)	Somewhat Favorable (50 to 80% favorable)	Least Favorable (Less than 50% favorable)
Dallas	Pittsburgh	Detroit
Seattle	St. Louis	New York City
Phoenix	Minneapolis	
Atlanta	Los Angeles	

Source: Joint Economic Committee of the Congress, "Central City
Businesses–Plans and Problems" (Washington, D.C.: U.S. Government Printing Office, January 14, 1979).

Overall, the results suggest that business climates are perceived by
businessmen to be worse in declining cities.

Local government regulatory and tax structures may directly
affect the ease and profitability of doing business in a city. One
study shows that declining cities are more likely than growing
cities to have payroll or income taxes, types of tax which many
businessmen find objectionable.[27] Another study suggests that
businesses undertaking major plant modernization or expansions
are more likely than others to move out of a city, because they

EXHIBIT 14

City Characteristics Reported to be of Most Importance to Businessmen

City Characteristics	Percent of Businessmen Reporting the Factor Strongly Affects their Locational Choice
1. City government attitudes toward business	88.5%
2. Crime Level	88.0
3. Adequacy of public facilities	85.9
4. Market demand for produce or service	85.1
5. Adequacy of public services	82.8
6. Quality of city's schools	82.2
7. Cultural attractions	80.6
8. Cost of Energy	80.0

Source: Joint Economic Committe of the Congress, "Central City Businesses—Plans and Problems" (Washington, D.C.: U.S. Government Printing Office, January 14, 1979).

fear bureaucratic delays in obtaining zoning and building permits required by major plant changes.[28] Public actions may directly cause business relocation out of cities. It appears that 13-to-14 percent of manufacturing plants relocating in the Cincinnati and New England regions were forced to move by public construction projects or other public actions.[29]

It appears that cities can influence actions affecting their local communities. It also appears that some declining cities have been unable or unwilling to respond efficiently to the needs of the business sector.

EFFECT OF FEDERAL POLICY ON THE ATTRACTIVENESS OF CENTRAL CITIES

Federal policies can impede as well as promote economic development in declining central cities. Some efforts to assist city economies have been so poorly designed or administered as to be ineffective. Some federal programs aimed at other goals have inadvertently hurt city economies. The federal actions have accelerated the pace of employment shifts and made it more difficult for cities and their residents to adjust to change.

Federal Tax Policy The federal tax code has offered, and is continuing to offer, a number of investment incentives damaging to city economies. These incentives do not directly encourage business investment in growing areas rather than declining cities. Typically, they encourage investment in new plant and equipment and discourage reinvestment or improvements in existing facilities. In combination with other factors discouraging the location of new facilities in declining cities, these elements of the tax code have had a powerful negative influence on city economies. Among the most harmful features of the present tax code for cities are the following:

- Investment tax credits. The investment tax credit offers over $10 billion in annual savings to businesses undertaking new investments in equipment and machinery. It was instituted to encourage business investment, and studies have shown it to be fairly effective in meeting this goal. Tax aid is concentrated on growing businesses and thus on growing areas. The businesses in declining cities which are most likely to receive investment tax credits are those which are relocating outside the city as part of plant modernization or expansion efforts.[30]

- Accelerated depreciation for new industrial or commercial plants. Owners of new commercial or industrial plants are permitted to claim more rapid depreciation than owners of existing properties. This tax provision is meant to encourage investment in new structures; like the investment tax credit it favors growing areas rather than already developed ones.[31]

- Industrial Development Bonds. The Federal tax code permits states and localities to issue tax exempt bonds financing private businesses which, like regular financing, are backed up by the creditworthiness of the private borrowers and the facility being financed. While available evidence is limited, tax exemption on IDBs results in considerable losses of federal tax revenues, yet the bonds are not targeted effectively to encourage economic development in declining or distressed cities, nor are the bonds targeted on private projects needing public subsidy. Often, the bonds are used in ways which damage the economies of distressed cities by encouraging new and relocating businesses to build new plant offices in growing areas.[32]

Transportation and Highways Federal transportation spending and investments also have accelerated the pace of job loss in many declining cities. Unlike tax policy, federal transportation policies sometimes have worked to create additional, direct incentives for investment and jobs to move away from declining cities. For example, beltway construction in urban areas has greatly increased the ease of travel for work or shopping within and among suburban areas. As a result, beltways have increased the degree to which suburban businesses and commercial centers can compete with cities for suburban workers and have thereby diminished the attractiveness of potential commercial and office revitalization efforts in cities.[33]

Sometimes, federal transportation policies have worked to the disadvantage of city economies by affecting the costs and quality of various transportation modes to users. Federal subsidies of highways encourage travel by private automobile, a mode of travel more effective in suburbs and in rural areas, where traffic congestion is less severe than in cities and land for parking facilities is available at lower cost and in greater quantity. Moreover, federal policies curtail the ability of cities to limit congestion and improve services on federally-assisted highways through the imposition of appropriate user changes. This has meant lower quality automobile and truck transportation in cities.

A final way in which federal transport policy has influenced the economies of older cities is through past policies which have offered far greater federal subsidies for new construction compared to the maintenance of existing facilities. Subsidies of new transport facilities accrue disproportionately to growing areas requiring new facilities. The past low level of assistance for maintenance and improvements to existing facilities has meant that built-up areas with established transport systems have had to bear a higher proportion of the costs of their transportation. It also may mean that existing systems in these areas have been under-maintained. Declining central cities are prominent victims of this bias. The collapse of New York City's West Side Highway indicates the potential costliness of this bias to both cities and the nation.[34]

Direct Federal Business Assistance Programs Federal business assistance programs are often poorly targeted to aiding businesses in distressed or declining cities. Small Business Administration programs, for example are not targeted geographically at all. Business grants and loan assistance from the Economic Development Administration are designed to be available only in distressed communities, yet in 1978, over three-fourths of the nation's people lived in communities formally eligible for EDA assistance. Administrative practices targeted EDA assistance to more distressed communities, but only to a degree.[35]

CONCLUSIONS

Employment loss in older central cities is not undesirable per se. It is in part, a signal that the national economy is adjusting to new technological and economic realities, and thus increasing the nations productive power. However, both communities and people require time to adapt to change. The evidence imples that neither people nor communities have been able to cope with the accelerated pace of economic change which has prevailed in cities in the 70s. As employment has declined so has the economic welfare of distressed central cities and their residents.

If declining cities are to have a healthy economic future they must generate and build on new industries, activities, and functions. This will require intensive effort at the local level to improve business climates and to build modern infrastructure and facilities required by business today. In some cases, it will require direct public assistance to business to neutralize the cost disadvantages of cities, particularly land and local tax costs. At present, few older, declining cities have the resources to mount such efforts. Cities will need aid from their states and from the federal government. As importantly, cities need time in which to adjust to change.

If distress is to be ameliorated in cities, then one important objective for public policy is to slow down the pace of economic shifts so as to provide cities with declining economies greater time and opportunity to adapt. As has been seen, full employment and national economic stability would relieve one important cause of the rapid pace of city employment loss. More relevant, given the limited control of the nation over the national economy, a number of federal policies in the tax code and elsewhere have quickened the pace of change in the past and if reversed, could slow it in the future.

NOTES

1. Harvey A. Garn and Larry C. Ledebur, "Metropolitan Prospects in the Context of the Changing Distribution of Industry and Jobs" (Washington, D.C.: The Urban Institute Working Paper 5111-4, November 10, 1978).

2. Bennett Harrison and Edward Hill, "The Changing Structure of Jobs in Older and Younger Cities" (Cambridge, Massachusetts: Harvard-MIT Joint Center for Urban Studies, New England Political Economy Working Paper No. 2, October 1978).

3. U.S. Bureau of the Census, *County Business Patterns.*

4. Bennett Harrison and Edward Hill, *op. cit.*

5. Franklin J. James, ed., *Models of Urban Land Use* (New Brunswick, N.J.: Rutgers University Center for Urban Policy Research, 1973).

6. Ibid.

7. Ibid.

8. The U.S. Bureau of the Census made important definitional changes in 1974 in the data series on which the Exhibit is based. Employment data in 1974 and after are not exactly comparable to those of earlier years.

9. See Roger J. Vaughn, *The Urban Impacts of Federal Policies:* Volume 2, *Economic Development* (Santa Monica, California: The Rand Corporation, June 1977), p. 16.

10. Thomas Muller, "Central City Business Retention: Jobs, Taxes and Investment Trends," (paper prepared for the Department of Commerce Urban Round Table, February 1978).

11. John Rees, "Technological Change and Regional Shifts in American Manufacturing," *The Professional Geographer,* Vol. 31, No. 1 (February 1979).

12. John H. Mollenkopf, "Paths Toward the Post-Industrial Service City: The Northeast and the Southwest," paper prepared for conference on "Municipal Fiscal Stress—Problems and Potential," Rutgers University Center for Urban Policy Research and U.S. Department of Housing and Urban Development, March 8-9, 1979.

13. Ibid.

14. Rees, *op. cit.*

15. David L. Birch, "The Processes Causing Economic Change in Cities," paper prepared for a Department of Commerce Roundtable on Business Retention and Expansion, February 22, 1978; revised on September 1978.

16. Some studies have found that establishments relocating from central cities to suburbs are, as a result, on average, expanding their employment and production and need larger or higher quality facilities. Thus, these firms are a vital element of the economic bases of cities. However, the direct loss of jobs to central cities or to declining regions which results from relocation is small. See Roger Schmenner, *The Manufacturing Location Decision: Evidence from Cincinnati and New England* (Cambridge, Mass.: The Harvard-MIT Joint Center for Urban Studies, March 1979).

17. Raymond S. Struyk and Franklin J. James, *Intrametropolitan Industrial Location: The Pattern and Process of Change* (Lexington, Mass.: Lexington Books, 1975).

18. See, for example, Beldon Daniels and Michael Kieschnick, *Theory and Practice in the Design of Development Finance Innovations* (Cambridge, Mass.: Harvard University Department of City and Regional Planning, November 1978).

19. Regina Armstrong, "National Trends in Office Construction, Employment and Headquarters Location in U.S. Metropolitan Areas," mimeo. (New York: Regional Plan Association, March 1, 1977).

20. Ibid.
21. Ibid.
22. Ibid.
23. Ibid.
24. Robert A. Leone and John R. Meyer, "The Economics of U-Shaped Costs" (Cambridge, Mass.: Harvard University Graduate School of Business Administration, undated).
25. Intra-metropolitan differences in the costs of material, equipment and financing can be assumed to be very small or negligible. No available evidence suggests that there are systematic tendencies for labor costs to be higher in central cities. The ability and willingness of higher-wage workers to commute sometimes long distances to jobs means that employers often compete for workers in metropolitan-wide labor markets. Collective bargaining agreements often dictate common wage levels within a city or metropolitan area. With some exceptions, the most important geographic variation in labor costs are found among regions or types of metropolitan areas, not within individual urban areas. Exceptions which occasionally are important apply to particular types of workers. For example, employers of clerical labor may find educated working wives from middle-income households to be especially productive workers. Such women are typically found in largest numbers in suburban areas, and working women have been shown to be unwilling, on average, to travel as far to jobs as are men. Suburban locations can offer labor costs advantages for clerical employers, such as the data processing or record-keeping elements of the office industry.
26. Andrew M. Hamer, "The Impact of Federal Subsidies on Industrial Location Behavior: Preliminary Conclusions from a Case Study" (Atlanta, Georgia: Georgia State University, October 11, 1977).
27. Thomas Muller, "Central City Business Retention: Jobs, Taxes, and Investment Trends," paper prepared for the Department of Commerce Urban Roundtable, February 22, 1978; revised June 1978.
28. Roger W. Schmenner, *The Manufacturing Location Decision: Evidence from Cincinnati and New England* (Cambridge, Mass.: The Harvard-MIT Joint Center for Urban Studies, March 1978).
29. Ibid.
30. George Peterson, Franklin James and George Reigeluth, *Federal Tax Policy and Urban Development* (Washington, D.C.: The Urban Institute, forthcoming).
31. Ibid.
32. The Legislative and Urban Policy Staff, "Industrial Development Bonds" (Washington, D.C.: U.S. Department of Housing and Urban Development, Working paper, 1979).
33. Thomas Muller, et al, *The Impact of Beltways on Central Business District: A Case Study on Richmond* (Washington, D.C.: The Urban Institute, April 1978).
34. David A. Grossman, *The Future of New York City's Capital Plant* (Washington, D.C.: The Urban Institute, 1979).
35. Reid Ewing, "Barriers to Central City Economic Development" (Washington, D.C.: U.S. Congressional Budget Office, 1978).

George Sternlieb and James W. Hughes -
NEW DIMENSIONS OF THE URBAN CRISIS

INTRODUCTION

The central cities of the United States are increasingly a focal point for the unfortunates of our society. The expanding concentration of improverished, socially disabled households in urban areas has gained momentum through the 1970s. The resultant impact on the fiscal operating statement—which is merely one of the several indicators—is all too clearcut: the poor cost more; the broken family is much more subject to the disease of juvenile delinquency, of the requirements for intensive social and protective services, than is the case for the more fortunate.

On the other side of the ledger is the decline of buying power and incomes, which in turn is reflected by increased difficulties in maintaining the level of municipally-derived revenues. Abandoned housing, which increasingly characterizes so many of our central cities, is now joined by equivalently ravaged commercial and industrial facilities. Central cities are becoming—and increasingly, must become—wards of the state and federal governments. This is not the result merely of fiscal maladministration, but rather of basic demographic tides.

In the brief analyses which follow, the first element to be examined will be summary data on the impact of selected migration on the incomes of central city residents. The latter, in turn, are the essential dynamos which historically have driven and maintained the independent capacity of cities to support themselves and their human requirements. As is all too evident from the analyses shown, this is a wasting resource. After these summary elements are presented, attention will be directed to underlying dynamics and building blocks, focusing particularly on a key barometer of social unhealth and fiscal disability—the marked rise of the low incomed, female-headed family in central cities. In an inflationary era in which increasingly not only the good life, but its minimum requirements depends on the dual income household, the growth of single-spouse families—complicated very frequently with all the problems of youthful dependents—is both the mirror of the cities' trauma—and in very large parts accounts for it.

RESIDENT INCOME DECLINE AND SELECTIVE MIGRATION FROM THE CENTRAL CITY

There are more people and households moving out of central cities than are moving into them: those that move out have higher incomes than their replacements. It is the revenue side of municipal operations and the lag therein which increasingly underlies the fiscal traumas that are surfacing. While much attention has been riveted on the expenditure side of the ledger, which has provided innumerable anecdotes on measures of waste and fiscal irresponsibilities, these are largely excuses and rationalizations which obscure the basic central city problem.

In Exhibit I, data are shown indicating the personal income loss in central cities due to net migration from 1970 to 1974 and 1975 to 1977. Whether it is families or unrelated individuals, the pattern is similar.[1] The more affluent are leaving, the newcomers are fiscally less well endowed. From 1970 to 1974 there was a reduction in aggregate resident income within central cities of $29.6 billion due to migration. In the two years from 1975 to 1977, the equivalent figure was a loss of $18 billion.

In Exhibit 2, these data have been converted into constant dollars (interpolating for 1974 to 1975, for which data are not available). This indicates an average annual net change (between 1970 and 1977) in 1976 dollars of $9.3 billion. Since these data are cumulative, by 1977 there has been a loss, in 1976 dollars, of $64.8 billion.

EXHIBIT 1

Income Losses In Central Cities Due to Net Migration:
1970 to 1974 and 1975 to 1977
(1970 metropolitan definition)

Income in 1973 of Families and Unrelated Individuals 14 Years Old and Over Who Migrated to and From Central Cities Between 1970 and 1974.

Subject	Living in Cities in 1970	Moved Out of Cities Between 1970 and 1974	Moved to Cities Between 1970 and 1974	Net Change Between 1970 and 1974
Families (thousands)	16,823	3,363	1,563	− 1,800
Mean Income (Dollars)	$13,349	$14,169	$12,864	−$1,305[1]
Aggregate Income (billions of dollars)	$ 224.6	$ 47.7	$ 20.1	− 27.6
Unrelated Individuals (thousands)	6,975	1,066	926	− 140
Mean Income (dollars)	$ 6,143	$ 7,099	$ 6,092	−$1,007[1]
Aggregate Income (billions of dollars)	$ 42.8	$ 7.6	$ 5.6	−$ 2.0

Income in 1976 of Families and Unrelated Individuals 14 Years Old and Over Who Migrated to and From Central Cities Between 1975 and 1977.

Subject	Living in Cities in 1970	Moved Out of Cities Between 1970 and 1974	Moved to Cities Between 1970 and 1974	Net Change Between 1970 and 1974
Families (thousands)	16,359	2,003	985	− 1,018
Mean Income (dollars)	$16,120	$15,986	$14,992	−$ 994[1]
Aggregate Income (billions of dollars)	$ 263.7	$ 32.0	$ 14.8	−$ 17.2
Unrelated Individuals (thousands)	8,812	994	940	− 54
Mean Income (dollars)	$ 7,388	$ 8,055	$ 7,612	−$ 443[1]
Aggregate Income (billions of dollars)	$ 65.1	$ 8.0	$ 7.2	−$ 0.8

Note: 1. Simple unweighted difference.

Sources: U.S. Department of Commerce, Bureau of the Census, *Current Population Reports*, Special Studies P-23, No. 55, "Social and Economic Characteristics of the Metropolitan and Nonmetropolitan Population: 1974 and 1970," September 1975.

U.S. Department of Commerce, Bureau of the Census, *Current Population Reports*, Special Studies, P-23, No. 75, "Social and Economic Characteristics of the Metropolitan and Nonmetropolitan Population: 1977 and 1970," November 1978.

EXHIBIT 2

Derivation of Income Losses (1976 Dollars) in Central Cities
Due to Migration: 1970 to 1977
(1970 metropolitan definition)

Average Annual Net Change, 1970 to 1974:	−7.4 billion (1973 dollars)[1]
Ratio of 1976 to 1973 Consumer Price Index:	$\frac{170.5}{133.1} = 1.28$ [2]
Average Annual Net Change, 1970 to 1974	−$9.4 billion (1976 dollars)[3]
Average Annual Net Change, 1975 to 1977	−$9.0 billion (1976 dollars)[4]
Net Change, 1974 to 1975	−$9.2 billion (1976 dollars)[5]
Total Change: 1970 to 1977	−$64.8 billion (1976 dollars)[6]
Average Annual Net Change: 1970 to 1977	−$9.3 billion (1976 dollars)[7]

Notes: 1. Derived from Exhibit 1.
              2. U.S. Bureau of Labor Statistics, *Monthly Labor Review.*
              3. 1.28 x $7.4 billion = $9.4 billion.
              4. Derived from Exhibit 1.
              5. Mean of annual averages of two periods.
              6. Sum of annual averages of all periods.
              7. −$64.8 billion ÷ 7 years = −$9.3 billion.

Source: Center for Urban Policy Research analysis

So in the latter year, if no migration had occurred, $64.8 billion more in annual incomes would have accrued to central city households than was actually received.

The ramifications of these losses are of very significant magnitude. If we were to use the conventional rule-of-thumb of 25 percent of income alloted to rent, this represents a departure in excess of $16 billion. If we were to further view this decline in rent-paying capacity in terms of its impact on housing values, the results are evident. Assume that an efficient, well-managed apartment house sells for five times its gross rent roll; the loss of $16 billion in rent-paying capacity translates into a $80 billion reduction in residential real estate values—and with it a proportionate decline in municipal income derived from real property taxation. There are equivalent implications, which need little elaboration, on basic retailing and service industries as well. The pattern of empty stores, of old, fading central business districts, and of vacated downtown department stores, is a reflection of this declining residential income base.

As best as we can analyze the data, this has been a sustained dynamic process with little sign of abatement. While much has been made of the relatively few cases of middle-class stabilization and/or return to the city—i.e., the "Capital Hill" phenomena and the like—as yet these are relatively trivial. A witness to the phenomenon is the accompanying data in Exhibit 3 on the median annual income of families and individuals (in constant dollars) for renter households in the boroughs of New York City. The decline since 1969 in all cases has been most substantial, with the overall city median declining from $6,500 to $4,800 over the 1969-to-1977 period. This pattern was largely paralleled from 1974 to 1977, with losses of one-seventh of total income in the brief three-year period. The only exception is a relatively minor 1.9 percent increase (again in constant dollars) in Manhattan. A new town may be evolving intown— the gentrified neighborhood—but it is a relatively slender ray of light, much too limited to support and bring back with it the aging entities that we call central cities.

THE UNDERLYING DEMOGRAPHIC REALITIES

Underlying the ominous situation depicted above is a complex chain of demographic shifts.[2] It is a consequence not only of population losses, but a sustained shift in household and family configurations which has seen a rapid growth in those particular family formats of apparently minimal economic viability. Before the more detailed elaborations of the basic phenomena are presented, it is useful to briefly summarize the broader parameters.

1. While the total population of all central cities declined by 4.6 percent (2.9 million persons) from 1970 to 1977, the total number of households increased by 6.3 percent or 1.3 million.

   a) The population losses were the result of a decline of almost 4.0 million whites (-8.1 percent) and an increase of 542,000 blacks (4.2 percent).

   b) The household gains were the province both of whites (458,000 or 2.7 percent) and blacks (773,000 or 19.1 percent).[3]

2. The increase in the number of households while population is declining is caused by shrinking household sizes. The latter, in turn, is a consequence partly of declining fertility and smaller families.

EXHIBIT 3

Median Annual Income of Families and Individuals, By Borough, In Constant (1967) Dollars,
For Renter Households, New York City, 1964, 1967, 1969, 1974 and 1977

Characteristics	1964	1967	1969	1974	1977	Percent Change 1974 to 1977
Total New York City	$5,900	$6,000	$6,500	$5,400	$4,800	−11.1%
Borough						
Bronx	$5,600	$5,700	$6,000	$4,700	$4,000	−14.9%
Brooklyn	5,800	5,800	6,000	4,900	4,200	−14.3
Manhattan	5,500	5,600	6,100	5,400	5,500	+ 1.9
Queens	7,100	7,500	8,100	7,000	5,800	−17.1
Richmond	7,100	6,800	7,700	7,100	6,100	−14.1

Source: Peter Marcuse: *Rental Housing in the City of New York* (New York: Housing and Development Administration, 1979).

a) The average family size in central cities has declined from 3.47 persons in 1970 to 3.30 in 1977.

b) The large urban family, the traditional focus of the "urban housing dilemma," is declining markedly. A decline of over 34 percent in the number of seven-person-or-more-families has occurred from 1970 to 1977; the losses for six-person and five-person families totaled 23.1 and 13.5 percent, respectively.

3. If the latter occurrence was solely the result of the decline in the birth rate, there would be cause to be sanguine. However, it is also a function of increasing family fragmentation.

 a) While the number of primary individual households in central cities increased by 30.7 percent, primary families decreased by 2.4 percent. The latter, however, is the residual of a sharp decline in husband-wife families (-7.6 percent) in the context of the rapid growth of female-headed (no husband present) families (30.7 percent).

 b) By 1977, only 51.8 percent of all households in central cities comprised husband-wife families. Female-headed (no husband present) families accounted for 13.9 percent of all households, while primary-individual households accounted for 32.1 percent.

4. Partitioning the central city households by race isolates somewhat similar patterns of evolution, but the magnitudes vary significantly.

 a) The number of white-primary families declined by 6.3 percent, the result of an 8.8 percent decrease in husband-wife families and a 15.5 percent increase of female-headed families.

 b) While black husband-wife families decreased by 7.8 percent, the female-headed equivalents expanded by 48.5 percent. As a result, there was an actual increase (10.1 percent) in primary families.

 c) By 1977, only 38.2 percent of black, central city households comprised husband-wife families. Female-headed families accounted for 29.0 percent of all households.

5. The rise of female-headed families in central cities is accentuated if they are considered as a proportion of total primary families rather than total households.

a) 15.2 percent of all central city white families were headed by females in 1977.

b) In contrast, over 41 percent of black families are headed by females in the nation's central cities in 1977. This compares to slightly over 30 percent in 1970.

6. The examination of the incomes attendant to the various family configurations brings to light the scale of the emerging problem.

a) All families in central cities (both white and black) had a median income of $13,952 in 1977. Their counterparts in suburbia had a median income of $17,101. While both experienced absolute declines in real income over the 1970-to-1977 period, the gap between the two has widened.

b) Female-headed families in central cities had a 1977 median income of $6,658. The median of their suburban counterparts stood at $8,985. Again the gap has widened over time.

c) Black female-headed families in central cities had a median income of only $5,135 in 1977. The suburban equivalent stood at $5,789.

d) Consequently, there are not only sharp urban-suburban income discontinuites, but also a faltering in the level of income accruing to female-headed families. And the problem is even more accentuated for black, female-headed families. The family configuration showing the most dynamic growth in the central city is that with the most severely lagging income.

7. The detailing of the poverty status of individuals by family status over the 1970-to-1977 period indicates the harsh results of these trendlines.

a) For the nation as a whole, the number of individuals below the poverty level declined by 2.2 million people or 8.2 percent. At the same time, there was an increase of 710,000 female heads of families (38.7 percent) under the poverty level. In 1977, 33.0 percent of all female family heads were in poverty.

b) In contrast, the number of individuals below the poverty level in central cities increased by 235,000 individuals or 2.5 percent. There was an increase of 370,000 female heads (44.7 percent) below the poverty level. In 1977, 37.1 percent of all female family heads were in poverty.

c) Most ominous is the economic situation of black central city residents. The number of individuals below the poverty level increased by 441,000 people or 11.8 percent. Female heads of family in poverty expanded by 57.1 percent; by 1977, 51.1 percent of all female family heads fell below the poverty level.

The evolution and linkage of incomes and household configurations, as well as select migration, has as its ultimate consequence the central city personal income losses and their attendant negative implications as depicted earlier. A more detailed examination of these critical elements comprise the remaining analyses of this presentation.

POPULATION LOSSES

The central cities of the United States are losing population; in this retrenchment, it is the very largest of them—those central cities in metropolitan areas with a million or more population—which are the heaviest losers. As shown in Exhibit 4, while the total population of the United States from 1970 to 1977 grew by 6.4 percent, the central cities in total lost 4.6 percent of their residents. The experience of the central cities in the largest metropolitan areas was a decline of 7.1 percent. In the central cities of smaller metropolitan areas, losses of 1.6 percent were evidenced.

RACIAL POPULATION SHIFT

The overall data mask significant shifts in racial character. Central cities as a whole, in the seven-year period under consideration, lost nearly one in twelve of their whites (-8.1 percent). Indeed, in the large metropolitan areas, the central city equivalent was nearly a one in eight (-12.3 percent). But gains in black population only partially offset these losses, thus creating the absolute decline. For example, in central cities in metropolitan areas of one million or more, the increase in the number of blacks was only 2.3 percent. The latter resulted from the enormous level of out-migration of central city blacks to suburbia. Current census data indicate, for example, that in the last two years for which data are available (1976 to 1978), this amounted to a net out-migration of some 400,000 people. This process is mirrored by the fully one third (33.9 percent) increase of blacks in suburban areas of our SMSAs.

EXHIBIT 4

Population By Type of Residence: 1970 and 1977
(numbers in thousands; 1970 metropolitan definition)

	TOTAL (ALL RACES)		Change: 1970 to 1977		WHITE		Change: 1970 to 1977		BLACK		Change: 1970 to 1977	
	1970	1977	Number	Percent	1970	1977	Number	Percent	1970	1977	Number	Percent
U.S. Total	199,819	212,566	12,747	6.4	175,276	184,335	9,059	5.2	22,056	24,474	2,418	11.0
Metropolitan Areas	137,058	143,107	6,049	4.4	118,938	122,177	3,239	2.7	16,342	18,048	1,706	10.4
Central Cities	62,876	59,993	– 2,883	– 4.6	48,909	44,951	–3,958	– 8.1	12,909	13,451	542	4.2
Suburban Areas	74,182	83,144	8,932	12.0	70,029	77,226	7,197	10.3	3,433	4,596	1,163	33.9
Central Cities in Metro-politan Areas of 1 Million or More	34,322	31,898	– 2,424	– 7.1	25,007	21,939	–3,068	–12.3	8,664	8,863	199	2.3
Central Cities in Metro-politan Areas of Less than 1 Million	28,554	28,095	– 459	– 1.6	23,903	23,012	– 891	– 3.7	4,245	4,588	343	8.1

Source: Center for Urban Policy Research Analysis of Data Presented in: U.S. Department of Commerce, Bureau of the Census, *Current Population Reports*, Special Studies P-23, No. 55, "Social and Economic Characteristics of the Metropolitan and Nonmetropolitan Population: 1977 and 1970," November 1978.

HOUSEHOLD SHIFTS

Yet within this pattern of population decline there is remarkably little equivalent shrinkage in the need for housing, at least as measured by total units. As shown in Exhibit 5, the number of households has continued to grow even in the central cities most characterized by absolute population losses. It is particularly striking in this context to note the 15.2 percent increase in the number of black households within the central cities of larger metropolitan areas. This is seven times the increase (2.3 percent) in absolute population growth of this group. As we will note, this represents both a very positive tribute to upgrading in housing and also a far-less salubrious fragmentation of households.

Part of the process of household growth in the context of population stability and decline is the actual shrinking size of families, as shown in Exhibit 6. So very much of the housing trauma of the post-World War II era involved the difficulties of housing large-scale families that it is now particularly heartening to see the diminishing need shown in Exhibit 6, both in the average size of families and most significantly, in those families in central cities with five persons of more.

But this is not merely a consequence of a declining birth rate, it is also the drastic change in the configuration of households, most importantly, that of the single-spouse family. In Exhibit 7 are shown data on this point for the nation as a whole, all central cities and central cities in metropolitan areas of one million or more people. Primary families as a group in central cities are shrinking both relatively and in absolute numbers. The case is most strikingly evident in terms of the decline (-965,000 or -7.6 percent) of husband-wife families for all central cities over the 1970-1977 period. For central cities in the larger metropolitan areas, a decline of 12.0 percent or 813,000 families was experienced. In the latter case, husband-wife families have now (1977) achieved minority status, with only 48.8 percent of households in this configuration.

Fully one out of seven (14.8 percent) of all households in the central cities in major metropolitan areas are female headed (no husband present); moreover, the configuration is the dynamic growth element, with an increase of 22.9 percent in such incidence from 1970 to 1977. Indeed, if we were to sum primary individual households headed by females with families headed by the equivalent sex, they would represent virtually one in three of all central city households.

EXHIBIT 5

Households By Type of Residence: 1970 and 1977
(numbers in thousands; 1970 metropolitan definition)

	TOTAL (ALL RACES)				WHITE				BLACK			
			Change: 1970 to 1977				Change: 1970 to 1977				Change: 1970 to 1977	
	1970	1977	Number	Percent	1970	1977	Number	Percent	1970	1977	Number	Percent
U.S. Total	63,447	74,142	10,695	16.9	56,609	65,353	8,744	15.4	6,178	7,776	1,598	25.9
Metropolitan Areas	43,851	50,414	6,563	15.0	38,622	43,646	5,027	13.0	4,733	5,981	1,248	26.4
Central Cities	21,401	22,741	1,340	6.3	17,254	17,712	458	2.7	3,833	4,566	733	19.1
Suburban Areas	22,450	27,672	5,222	23.3	21,368	25,937	4,569	21.4	900	1,415	515	57.2
Central Cities in Metropolitan Areas of 1 Million or More	12,056	12,246	190	1.6	9,230	8,914	−316	−3.4	2,625	3,025	400	15.2
Central Cities in Metropolitan Areas of Less than 1 Million	9,344	10,494	1,150	12.3	8,024	8,798	774	9.6	1,207	1,541	334	27.7

Source: Center for Urban Policy Research Analysis of Data Presented in: U.S. Department of Commerce, Bureau of the Census, *Current Population Reports,* Special Studies P-23, No. 55, "Social and Economic Characteristics of the Metropolitan and Nonmetropolitan Population: 1977 and 1970," November 1978.

EXHIBIT 6

Families By Size and Type of Residence: 1970 and 1977
(numbers in thousands; 1970 metropolitan definition)

| | U.S. Total | | | | All Central Cities | | | | Central Cities in Metropolitan Areas of 1,000,000 or People | | | |
| | | | Change: 1970-1977 | | | | Change: 1970-1977 | | | | Change: 1970-1977 | |
	1970	1977¹	Number	Percent	1970	1977¹	Number	Percent	1970	1977¹	Number	Percent
TOTAL FAMILIES	50,967	56,710	5,743	11.3	15,816	15,529	−287	−1.8	8,621	8,144	−477	−5.5
2 persons	18,139	21,530	3,391	18.7	6,033	6,334	301	5.0	3,362	3,336	−26	−0.7
3 persons	10,618	12,472	1,854	17.5	3,407	3,497	90	2.6	1,866	1,837	−29	−1.6
4 persons	9,649	11,483	1,834	19.0	2,798	2,888	90	3.2	1,498	1,468	−30	−2.0
5 persons	6,107	6,209	102	1.7	1,700	1,471	−229	−13.5	897	762	−135	−15.1
6 persons	3,328	2,800	−528	−15.9	936	720	−216	−23.1	497	387	−110	−22.1
7 persons or more	3,126	2,216	−910	−29.1	943	619	−324	−34.4	502	353	−149	−29.7
Average Size of Family	3.57	3.38			3.47	3.30			3.44	3.31		

Note: 1. 1977 family data include a relatively small number of secondary family heads who are not household heads.
2. Numbers may not add due to rounding.

Source: Center for Urban Policy Research Analysis of Data Presented in: U.S. Department of Commerce, Bureau of the Census, *Current Population Reports*, Special Studies P-23, No. 55, "Social and Economic Characteristics of the Metropolitan and Nonmetropolitan Population: 1977 and 1970," November 1978.

EXHIBIT 7

Households By Type and Residence: 1970 and 1977
(numbers in thousands 1970 metropolitan definition)

	U.S. Total				All Central Cities				Central Cities in Metropolitan Areas of 1,000,000 or more people			
			Change: 1970-1977				Change: 1970-1977				Change: 1970-1977	
	1970	1977	Number	Percent	1970	1977	Number	Percent	1970	1977	Number	Percent
TOTAL	63,447	74,142	10,695	16.9	21,401	22,741	1,340	6.3	12,056	12,246	190	1.6
Primary Families	50,967	56,472	5,505	10.8	15,816	15,444	− 372	− 2.4	8,621	8,092	−529	− 6.1
Husband-Wife Family	43,717	57,471	3,754	8.6	12,748	11,783	− 965	− 7.6	6,783	5,970	−813	−12.0
Male Head (No Wife Present)	1,621	1,461	−160	− 9.9	587	499	− 88	−15.0	360	304	− 56	−15.6
Female Head (No Husband Present)	5,629	7,540	1,911	33.9	2,480	3,161	681	27.5	1,478	1,817	339	22.9
Primary Individuals	12,480	17,669	5,189	41.6	5,584	7,298	1,714	30.7	3,435	4,155	720	21.0
Male	4,597	6,971	2,374	51.6	2,139	2,971	832	38.9	1,376	1,747	371	27.0
Female	7,883	10,698	2,815	35.7	3,445	4,327	882	25.6	2,059	2,408	349	16.9

	U.S. Total		All Central Cities		Central Cities in Metropolitan Areas of 1,000,000 or more people	
	1970	1977	1970	1977	1970	1977
TOTAL	100.0	100.0	100.0	100.0	100.0	100.0
Primary Families	80.3	76.2	73.9	67.9	71.5	66.1
Husband-Wife Family	68.9	64.2	59.6	51.8	56.3	48.8
Male Head (No Wife Present)	2.6	2.0	2.7	2.2	3.0	2.5
Female Head (No Husband Present)	8.9	10.2	11.6	13.9	12.3	14.8
Primary Individuals	19.7	23.8	26.1	32.1	28.5	33.9
Male	7.2	9.4	10.0	13.1	11.4	14.3
Female	12.4	14.4	16.1	19.0	17.1	19.7

Source: Center for Urban Policy Research Analysis of Data Presented in: U.S. Department of Commerce, Bureau of the Census, *Current Population Reports*, Special Studies P-23, No. 55, "Social and Economic Characteristics of the Metropolitan and Nonmetropolitan Population: 1977 and 1970," November 1978.

Central city populations, then, are increasingly dominated by household types which, as will be shown subsequently, are characterized by relatively low incomes, a major problem which cuts across racial partitions.

RACE AND HOUSEHOLD CONFIGURATION

The decline in primary families is largely a white phenomenon, undoubtedly in part as a function of select migration. The whites who are increasing in number and proportion in the central city are largely in primary individual households. Indeed, husband-wife families declined both among whites and blacks in central cities with the former showing a loss of nearly a million, the latter approximately 150,000 (Exhibit 8). The only family type expanding in number within central cities among whites was female-headed (no husband present), with an increase slightly under 250,000. The faster growing incidence of this phenomenon among blacks, however, is indicated by the 432,000 increase in black female-headed (no husband present) families. Nearly 60 percent of the total growth of black households over the 1970-to-1977 period was in this format.

Thus, the white population of central cities is decreasingly that of primary families, increasingly that of single individuals. The sum of these produce a relatively minor increase in total household numbers. Among blacks there is an equivalent decline of husband-wife families to a level where they represent only 38.2 percent of total households—and are nearly matched by a female-headed (no husband present) 29 percent incidence—nearly triple that of white central city households. One out of three (33.0 percent) white households now is in the primary individual sector. The incidence among blacks is nearly as high at the three in ten level (29.7 percent).

The vigor of the shift in household formation in terms of the percentage of primary families headed by females is emphasized by Exhibit 9, which shows the ratios of such households in 1977 versus 1970. There is significant growth both for whites and for blacks; the level of absolute gain, however, in the latter group is nearly double that of the former. Indeed, in all central cities, the growth ratio for the seven years under consideration among blacks is at the 1.34-1.35 level.

By 1977, more than four in ten of all black primary families in central cities were headed by a female.

EXHIBIT 8

Central City Household Type By Race: 1970 and 1977
(numbers in thousands; 1970 metropolitan definition)

	WHITE				BLACK			
			Change: 1970 to 1977				Change: 1970 to 1977	
	1970	1977	Number	Percent	1970	1977	Number	Percent
TOTAL	17,254	17,712	458	2.7	3,833	4,566	733	19.1
Primary Families	12,665	11,870	−795	− 6.3	2,917	3,212	295	10.1
Husband-Wife Family	10,667	9,730	−937	− 8.8	1,891	1,744	−147	− 7.8
Male-Head (No Wife Present)	439	340	− 99	−22.6	136	146	10	7.4
Female Head (No Husband Present)	1,559	1,800	241	15.5	890	1,322	432	48.5
Primary Individuals	4,589	5,842	1,253	27.3	916	1,354	438	47.8
Male	1,688	2,289	601	35.6	409	631	222	54.3
Female	2,901	3,533	652	22.5	507	723	216	42.6
TOTAL	100.0	100.0			100.0	100.0		
Primary Families	73.4	67.0			76.1	70.3		
Husband-Wife Family	61.8	54.9			49.3	38.2		
Male Head (No Wife Present)	2.5	1.9			3.5	3.2		
Female Head (No Husband Present)	9.0	10.2			23.2	29.0		
Primary Individuals	26.6	33.0			23.9	29.7		
Male	9.8	12.9			10.7	13.8		
Female	16.8	20.1			13.2	15.8		

Source: Center for Urban Policy Research Analysis of Data Presented in: U.S. Department of Commerce, Bureau of the Census, *Current Population Reports*, Special Studies P-23, No. 55, "Social and Economic Characteristics of the Metropolitan and Nonmetropolitan Population: 1977 and 1978," November 1978.

EXHIBIT 9

Percentage of Primary Families Headed By Females, By Race and Type of Residence: 1970 and 1977

(1970 metropolitan definition)

TYPE OF RESIDENCE	TOTAL (ALL RACES)			WHITE			BLACK		
	1970	1977	Ratio 1970-1977	1970	1977	Ratio 1970-1977	1970	1977	Ratio 1970-1977
U.S. Total	11.0	13.4	1.22	9.2	10.7	1.16	28.0	36.8	1.31
Metropolitan Areas	11.7	14.6	1.26	9.7	11.6	1.21	28.9	37.7	1.30
Central Cities	15.7	20.5	1.31	12.3	15.2	1.24	30.5	41.2	1.35
Suburban Areas	8.4	10.6	1.26	7.9	9.6	1.21	22.2	27.9	1.26
Central Cities in Metropolitan Areas of 1 million or more	17.1	22.5	1.32	13.1	16.0	1.22	30.8	41.7	1.35
Central Cities in Metropolitan Areas of less than 1 million	13.9	18.3	1.32	11.5	14.4	1.25	30.0	40.1	1.34

Note: Ratios computed from unrounded percentages.

Source: Center for Urban Policy Research Analysis of Data Presented in: U. S. Department of Commerce, Bureau of the Census, *Current Population Reports*, Special Studies P-23, No. 55, "Social and Economic Characteristics of the Metropolitan and Nonmetropolitan Population: 1977 and 1970," November 1978.

INCOME AND FAMILY CONFIGURATIONS

There appears to be a significant relationship between low incomes and female-headed households. This holds true both for whites as well as blacks, but is much more compelling for the latter group. As shown in Exhibit 10, for example, all families in central cities in 1977 had money incomes of slightly under $14,000. Families with female heads, however, had incomes of less than half that, $6,658. For white families with female heads total money income was $7,914. For blacks it was an abysmally low $5,125. And these ratios are degenerating over time, when contrasted with equivalent data for suburban areas.

For every category shown, the ratio between central city and suburban incomes from 1970 to 1977 has declined sharply. All central city families, regardless of their configuration, have incomes which are not keeping pace with equivalent configurations in suburbia and are declining in absolute dollars over time as well.

Female-headed households in central cities have shown the most marked decline in real incomes over time. The selective migration of blacks to suburbia undoubtedly underlies, at least in part, the one substantial increment (and again these are data in constant dollars) of income accruing to families from 1970 to 1977: total black families in suburbia experienced an income gain of almost $1,300 from $10,745 in 1970 to $12,037 in 1977. The black income decline in central city is clearly linked with the selective migration of husband-wife families and the residual dominance of female-headed households.

THE INCREASING TRAUMA OF RENTAL HOUSING

In another context, reference has been made to the increasing problem of rental housing in central cities—the issues of mortgage delinquency and foreclosure, particularly in HUD-held guaranteed mortgages.[4] Within this context, it is important to focus on the data shown in Exhibit 11, which shows median incomes of household types in central cities by race and tenure for 1973 and 1976. (These are not constant dollars.)

Certainly there has been much more vigor of income growth among owners than holds true of renters, with the level of growth in the former triple that of the latter. And this holds true for blacks as well, but is much more extreme. Among the two-or-more-person black households who are owners, incomes increased 21.2 percent. Despite the declining value of the dollar over time, black renters experienced only a 1.5 percent increase.

EXHIBIT 10

Total Money Income in 1969 and 1976—Families By Sex, Race,
And Type of Residence
(in constant 1976 dollars, Families as of March 1967 and April 1970)

	Central Cities	Suburban Areas	Ratio of Central City to Suburban
Total All Races			
All Families			
1970	$14,566	$17,160	.85
1977	13,952	17,101	.82
Families with Female Head			
1970	7,586	9,351	.81
1977	6,658	8,539	.78
White			
All Families			
1970	15,601	17,413	.90
1977	15,069	17,371	.87
Families with Female Head			
1970	9,014	9,842	.92
1977	7,914	8,985	.88
Black			
All Families			
1970	10,188	10,745	.95
1977	9,361	12,037	.78
Families with Female Head			
1970	5,494	5,425	1.01
1977	5,125	5,789	.89

Note: 1970 Metropolitan definition.

Source: Center for Urban Policy Research Analysis of Data Presented in: U.S. Department of Commerce, Bureau of the Census, *Current Population Reports*, Special Studies P-23, No. 55, "Social and Economic Characteristics of the Metropolitan and Nonmetropolitan Population: 1977 and 1970," November 1978.

The latter ratio was very largely the result of a declining real income among renter families headed by females. For this category there was an absolute decline of 11.3 percent in incomes. And this obviously would be the more accentuated if it were in constant dollars.

Increasingly, the central city is the focal point of the poor. Selective migration and limited economic opportunities for advancement have produced this result.[5] It is mirrored in the next set of data to be presented here—that on poverty status.

EXHIBIT 11

Median Income of Household Types in Central Cities By Race: 1973 and 1976
(1970 metropolitan definition)

	TOTAL (ALL RACES)				BLACK			
			Change: 1973-76				Change: 1973-1976	
	1973	1976	Number	Percent	1973	1976	Number	Percent
Owner Occupied								
2-or-More-Person Households	$12,900	$15,800	$2,900	22.5	$10,400	$12,600	$2,200	21.2
Male Head, Wife Present	13,600	17,000	3,400	25.6	11,700	14,700	3,000	25.6
Other Male Head	12,800	14,000	1,200	9.4	11,300	11,000	–300	– 2.7
Female Head	8,000	9,200	1,200	15.0	7,000	7,200	200	2.9
1-Person Households	4,400	5,900	1,500	34.1	3,900	4,100	200	5.1
Renter Occupied								
2-or-More Person Households	$ 8,300	$ 8,800	$ 500	6.0	$ 6,500	$ 6,600	$ 100	1.5
Male Head, Wife Present	9,600	11,500	1,900	19.8	8,400	10,400	2,000	23.8
Other Male Head	8,300	8,200	–100	– 1.2	5,900	7,900	2,000	33.9
Female Head	5,800	5,300	–500	– 8.6	5,300	4,700	–600	–11.3
1-Person Households	4,600	5,500	900	19.6	3,500	4,400	900	25.7

Notes: 1. 1976 income is that received in 1975.
2. 1973 income is that received in 1972.

Source: U.S. Department of Commerce, Bureau of the Census, *Annual Housing Survey*, 1973, 1976.

POVERTY STATUS

Nationally, poverty is declining in incidence. In the 1970-to-1977 period under consideration, there was a decline of 2.2 million persons who met the poverty criteria. Exhibit 12 presents the data on individuals by family status who fell below the poverty level.

Every category was reduced except for females who were heads of families; in this group there was an absolute increase of 710,000 individuals, nearly 40 percent. Indeed almost a third of all females who head families fall into the poverty category.

The basic problem is much more clearly focused when the analysis is limited to central cities as shown in Exhibit 13. Unlike the national pattern, there is an *absolute* increase in the number of persons in central cities who fall below the poverty line. While the total central city population declined by 4.6 percent, those in poverty status increased by 2.5 percent. This occurred despite a decline in poverty status among males who headed families and their wives. This gain was completely obliterated—and practically all of the total loss accounted for—by the increase in females who headed families—and their children as well. In central cities female family heads who were under the poverty line increased by 44.7 percent over the seven-year period. By 1977, 37.1 percent of such individuals were below the poverty line.

Male-headed families and wives are climbing out of poverty. Female-headed families increasingly are subjected to all of its limitations and strictures.

The incidence of such groups, in turn, has strikingly impacted the fiscal vigor of central cities—while increasing the stress on the social services provided to them. And, this is increasingly a problem which is impacting the black citizens of central cities. As shown in Exhibit 14, the number of black persons in families in poverty status in central cities grew by more than one in nine (10.9 percent) from 1970 to 1977. Among unrelated individuals, there was an increase of one in six (17.7 percent). While there was a significant reduction of male heads and wives in poverty, it was more than overcome by the single largest poverty status growth group, that of female heads of families, which increased by nearly a quarter of a million (57.1 percent).

By 1977 more than half (51.1 percent) of the black females who headed households were below the poverty line. In turn, they substantially accounted for the 42.1 percent of all black related children under 18 years within families who also met the poverty designation.

EXHIBIT 12

Poverty Status in 1976 and 1969, Persons By Family Status, U.S. Total All Races[1]

(numbers in thousands)

Family Status	1970	1977	Change: 1970 to 1977		Percent Below Poverty Level	
			Number	Percent	1970	1977
All Persons	27,204	24,975	-2,229	- 8.2	13.8	11.8
In Families	21,250	19,632	-1,618	- 7.6	11.7	10.3
Head	5,500	5,311	- 189	- 3.4	10.8	9.4
Male	3,667	2,768	- 899	-24.9	8.1	5.6
Female	1,833	2,543	710			
Wives	3,438	2,606	832	-24.2	7.9	5.5
Related Children under 18 years	10,560	10,081	- 479	- 4.5	15.3	15.8
Other Family Members	1,752	1,634	- 118	- 6.7	9.8	7.1
Unrelated Individuals	5,954	5,344	- 610	-10.2	37.1	24.9
Male	1,913	1,787	- 126	- 6.6	29.9	19.7
Female	4,041	3,557	- 484	-12.0	41.9	28.7

Notes: 1. Families and unrelated individuals as of March 1977 and April 1970. Excludes unrelated individuals under 14 years old, members of the Armed Forces living in barracks and college students in dormitories.

Source: Center for Urban Policy Research Analysis of Data Presented in: U.S. Department of Commerce, Bureau of the Census, *Current Population Reports*, Special Studies, P-23, No. 55, "Social and Economic Characteristics of the Metropolitan and Nonmetropolitan Population: 1977 and 1970," November 1978.

EXHIBIT 13

Poverty Status in 1976 and 1969, Persons By Family Status, Central Cities, All Races[1]

(numbers in thousands)

Family Status	1970	1977	Change: 1970 to 1977		Percent Below Poverty Level	
			Number	Percent	1970	1977
All Persons	9,247	9,482	235	2.5	14.9	15.8
In Families	6,852	7,302	450	6.6	12.5	14.3
Head	1,755	1,961	206	11.7	11.1	12.6
Male	928	764	−164	−17.6	7.0	6.2
Female	827	1,197	370	44.7	33.5	37.1
Wives	861	718	−143	−16.6	6.7	6.1
Related Children under 18 years	3,692	4,017	325	8.8	18.4	23.9
Other Family Members	544	606	62	11.4	8.7	8.8
Unrelated Individuals	2,396	2,180	−216	− 9.0	33.1	24.6
Male	801	796	5	− 0.6	27.1	20.6
Female	1,594	1,384	−210	−13.2	37.3	27.7

Notes: 1. Families and unrelated individuals as of March 1977 and April 1970. Excludes unrelated individuals under 14 years old, members of the Armed Forces living in barracks and college students in dormitories.

Source: Center for Urban Policy Research Analysis of Data Presented in: U.S. Department of Commerce, Bureau of the Census, *Current Population Reports*, Special Studies, P-23, No. 55, "Social and Economic Characteristics of the Metropolitan and Nonmetropolitan Population: 1977 and 1970," November 1978.

EXHIBIT 14

Poverty Status in 1976 and 1969, Persons By Family Status, Central Cities, Blacks[1]
(numbers in thousands)

Family Status	1970	1977	Change: 1970 to 1977		Percent Below Poverty Level	
			Number	Percent	1970	1977
All Persons	3,726	4,167	441	11.8	29.1	31.0
In Families	3,196	3,543	347	10.9	27.7	30.2
Head	725	908	183	25.2	24.9	28.0
Male	290	223	− 67	−23.1	14.3	11.7
Female	436	685	249	57.1	49.1	51.1
Wives	260	194	− 66	−25.3	13.9	11.3
Related Children under 18 years	1,940	2,081	141	7.3	36.5	42.1
Other Family Members	271	360	89	32.8	18.9	19.8
Unrelated Individuals	530	624	94	17.7	41.7	36.4
Male	197	274	77	39.1	32.6	31.6
Female	333	350	17	5.1	50.0	41.4

Notes: 1. Families and unrelated individuals as of March 1977 and April 1970. Excludes unrelated individuals under 14 years old, members of the Armed Forces living in barracks and college students in dormitories.

Source: Center for Urban Policy Research Analysis of Data Presented in: U.S. Department of Commerce, Bureau of the Census, *Current Population Reports*, Special Studies, P-23, No. 55, "Social and Economic Characteristics of the Metropolitan and Nonmetropolitan Population: 1977 and 1970," November 1978.

The urban crisis is not over—it is rather entering on its most fearful challenge. The demographic shifts within our society have left major urban areas increasingly the focal point for the distressed—not merely the impoverished, but the increasingly inpoverished. A thin facade of office structures, of new, swinging singles groups, distracts the eye from the functional reality.

NOTES

1. Households are generally of two types: primary families and primary individuals. Primary families comprise two or more related individuals and are usually subdivided into three types—husband-wife families, male head (no wife present) and female head (no husband present). Primary individual households comprise either a single person living alone or two or more unrelated individuals. They are usually subdivided into male and female headed sectors. The Census Bureau, however, plans to replace the term "head" with "householder."

2. For a more comprehensive summary of population trends, see: George Sternlieb and James W. Hughes, *Current Population Trends in the United States* (New Brunswick, N.J.: Rutgers University, Center for Urban Policy Research, 1978).

3. Other races have not been included in the analysis; consequnetly the black and white components do not add to the total.

4. See George Sternlieb and Robert W. Burchell, "Multifamily Housing Demand: 1975-2000 " A Study prepared for the use of the Subcommittee on Priorities and Economy in Government of the Joint Economic Committee, Congress of the United States (U.S. Government Printing Office, Washington, D.C., 1978).

5. See analysis in: George Sternlieb and James W. Hughes, "The Wilting of the Metropolis," Hearings before the Committee on Banking, Currency, and Housing, U.S. House of Representatives, *Toward a National Urban Policy* (U.S. Government Printing Office, Washington, D.C., 1977).

John H. Mollenkopf - PATHS TOWARD THE POST INDUSTRIAL SERVICE CITY: THE NORTHEAST AND THE SOUTHWEST

THOUGHTS

"The city puts a premium upon innovation and progress and is able, through the collective power of great masses, to achieve fundamental changes in the existing order. Cities have traditionally been regarded as the home of inventions and revolutions. They secularize the sacred beliefs, practices, and institutions; they democratize knowledge, fashions, and tastes, and consequently generate wants and stimulate unrest. . . This may aid in understanding both the achievement and the disorder characteristic of cities. The grandeur of the city is capable of stirring men's souls and rousing their imagination. It is not merely the magnificent size of the structures, the hum of the traffic, the display of culture and wealth side by side the most abject poverty and degradation, but it is also the imposing demonstration of human ingenuity, the sense of personal emancipation amidst a variegated cultural life that stires the city man to thought and action, and gives urban existence its zest. In modern civilization it is the city that becomes the scene where the ultimate struggle between contending forces is waged and decided."

National Resources Committee,
Our Cities, June, 1937

77

CITY IN STRESS

"I am delighted to be here, flattered, and slightly melancholy at the reason for it. . . You are an urban organization and I am not really an urban expert. I am a financial surgeon. I try to put the pieces back together without leaving too many scars and without spilling too much blood. It is probably symptomatic of the times and of urban problems today that somebody of my discipline is here as opposed to a real urban expert. . . We have practiced probably the most brutal kind of deflation ever put into practice by any large governmental entity in the world. As a result, we have probably institutionalized recession in our economy for some time to come. Our actions were absolutely inevitable. . . every one of us who participated in these decisions would do it all over again."

MAC Chairman Felix G. Rohatyn, speaking
to the San Francisco Planning and Urban
Research Association, April 14, 1978

INTRODUCTION

In the last ten years, U.S. cities have apparently passed a high water mark in their development pattern. The largest cities, which had inexorably gained population from decade to decade, not only ceased to grow, but actually began to lose population. The New York metropolitan area gained population every decade between 1790 and 1970, but lost 3.4% of its population between 1970 and 1974, causing many second thoughts about its historical role as first among equals in the system of cities. This remarkable change produced such headlines as "the end of the metropolitan era," (Alonso), "the death of the cities," (William Bauer in the *Public Interest*), and "the end of empire and the last days of New York," (*Society*) among academic analysts and journalists alike.

The emergence of cities which had been backwater towns before World War II into front-rank status has been equally striking, if subject to far less attention. Cities like Phoenix, San Jose and San Diego bounded upward in the urban rankings past cities which had seemed secure in their position.

These two developments—decline among the biggest cities and rapid growth within an emerging group of newer, smaller cities—run counter to accepted ideas about why and how cities grow. The traditional approach used by economists draws an analogy between cities and nations and emphasizes "export" activities as the basis for metropolitan growth. Drawing on modernization theory, this approach has tended to posit a "take-off" stage leading to long-term, sustained mature development. Neither the sharp reversals experienced by the large cities nor the new cities' rapid rise in the rankings sit well with this theory. Indeed, recent literature reviews have concluded that this entire component of economic analysis has a long way to go. Jackson and Soloman report that available studies are "limited to manufacturing," "static" and "nonpredictive." (Jackson and Soloman, 1977.) With characteristic understatement, the Rand Corporation's Roger Vaughan has observed that "further theoretical research and the improvement of urban data bases are necessary before the factors that affect the process of urban development can be properly understood." (Vaughan, 1977, p. 46.)

This paper is offered as a tentative and exploratory contribution to that effort. It challenges a number of the dominant perceptions among economists about why the largest cities have declined and the newer ones have grown so rapidly, and it offers an alternative analysis. The traditional approach argues that factor costs and agglomeration diseconomies within the largest cities have altered individual firm location decisions in such a way as to put the largest cities at a competitive disadvantage with alternative locations. In this approach, key variables are to be found in economics, particularly input costs and the manufacturing decision calculus. By contrast, this paper will argue that such differences, where they exist, are not sufficiently large to have caused such basic changes in the system of cities. Moreover, by looking carefully at the rapidly growing cities as well as the declining ones, this paper will point out some anomalies which the economists' traditional approach does not explain.

Having criticized the way economists have approached this problem, an alternative model will be offered. To preview the argument to come, three factors appear to determine the rate, timing and composition of urban development: 1) the role a particular city plays in the entire network which makes up the city system, 2) the particular characteristics of the economic "wave" upon which the city initially rose to prominence within the system of cities, and 3) the relative political strength of growth-oriented coalitions in determining development policy vis-a-vis alternative contenders for political influence. In contrast to the approach traditionally taken by economists, this alternative model stresses services rather than manufacturing, public sector decisions rather than individual firm decisions, and politics rather than economics as the key determinants of the urban trajectory. Cities which play a key nodal role, which have an advanced services rather than an industrial base, and which have not experienced extensive conflict over the distribution of the costs and benefits of economic change have grown most rapidly—the Southwestern cities typify this path toward the post-industrial city. Cities which have not stressed or enhanced their role as a nodal point in the economy, which have retained their specialization in basic goods production, and which have experienced significant political turmoil over urban growth—such as Detroit or Newark—have fared most poorly.

The looseness of our conceptual grip on the urban development process has not prevented leading analysts from bringing sometimes draconian conclusions to the attention of policymakers. This paper will conclude by following its predecessors into the realms where wiser heads might fear to tred.

In order to overcome the "old city" parochialism which characterizes the urban development literature, this paper contrasts the experience of the ten largest Northeastern cities with that of the eleven largest Southwestern cities. This latter group constitutes a polar opposite to the older cities; any good theory about urban development has to account for the experiences of both.[1] These two groups include all but nine cities having a 1970 central city population over 500,000 and maximize the difference in founding dates and periods of rapid expansion which have been hypothesized to be important. Each of these groups of cities has considerable internal variation in size, population make-up, etc. In a few quite telling dimensions, however, the Southwestern cities commonly differ from those in the Northeast.

Exhibit 1 presents a clear picture of the phenomena that need explaining. All the large Northeastern central cities declined in population between 1960 and 1973. More recently, the *metropolitan* population declined in New York, Chicago, Philadelphia, Cleveland, Pittsburgh and Buffalo. In contrast, population surged upward in both central city and metropolitan areas of the Southwest. Central city growth rates between 1960 and 1973 range from a low of 9.5% for Denver to a high of 156% for San Jose.[2] While Northeastern metropolitan areas gained an average of 9% between 1960 and 1973, the Southwestern SMSA's grew on average in excess of 45%. (In order to avoid the artificial differences which local boundary-drawing can introduce into the Northeastern/Southwestern comparisons, all subsequent references will be based on metropolitan area numbers unless stated otherwise.)

Southwestern employment also has grown considerably in comparison to the Northeast. Northeastern SMSA employment increases between 1960 and 1970 ranged from 4.7% for Pittsburgh to 26.0%

EXHIBIT 1

Northeast and Southwest Urban Population Changes

City	Central City Population 1960[a]	1970[a]	1973[a]	1960-73 CC change	1960-73 SMSA change	1970-73 SMSA change	1970 CC rank
New York	7,782	7,895	7,645	−1.8	2.8	−3.4	1
Chicago	3,550	3,369	3,173	−10.6	13.6	−0.1	2
Philadelphia	2,003	1,949	1,862	−7.0	12.0	−0.3	4
Detroit	1,670	1,514	1,387	−16.9	13.4	0.0	5
Baltimore	939	906	878	−6.5	19.3	3.3	7
Cleveland	876	751	679	−22.5	5.3	−3.9	10
Milwaukee	741	717	691	−6.9	13.0	0.8	12
Boston	697	641	618	−11.3	10.0	1.8	16
Pittsburgh	667	604	520	−23.2	−1.2	−2.8	24
Buffalo	533	463	425	−20.3	3.5	−1.4	28
10 City average	1,946	1,831	1,787	–	–	–	–
Los Angeles	2,479	2,812	2,747	10.8	16.7	−1.6	3
Dallas/Ft. Worth	1,036	1,237	1,175	13.4	44.0	5.1	8/33
Houston	938	1,234	1,320	40.9	54.1	11.2	6
San Diego	573	697	757	32.1	43.4	11.8	14
San Antonio	588	708	756	28.6	33.0	10.3	15
Phoenix	439	587	637	45.1	75.3	20.9	19
Denver	494	515	541	9.5	51.0	12.2	22
San Jose	204	483	523	156.0	–	10.9	31
El Paso	277	322	353	27.1	–	22.0	45
Tucson	213	263	308	45.3	–	23.3	53
Albuquerque	201	244	273	36.1	–	13.7	58
11 City average	677	828	854	–	–	–	–

for Baltimore, but in the Southwest increases ranged from 8.1% in Los Angeles to a whopping 79% in San Jose. The Southwestern average is three times that of the Northeast. (See Exhibit 5, last column.) More recently, some metropolitan areas in the Northeast, notably New York, have actually lost jobs. (Among the more recent studies on this subject, see Carlaw, 1976, Sternlieb and Hughes, 1975, and Vaughan, 1977.)

What explains this contrasting picture of decline and growth? Why has the trend line reached monotonically upward in the Southwest while evidently inflecting downward for the Northeast some time around 1970? What factors truly distinguish the experience of these two sets of cities and what do they imply in terms of our conceptual model of urban development?

THE ORTHODOX MARKET MODEL

Economics has generated a voluminous but inconclusive mono-graphic literature on these questions. For the sake of simplicity, the recent volume edited by George Sternlieb and James Hughes may be taken as a representative example of this literature. (Sternlieb and Hughes, 1975.) In this approach, the market choices of two types of actors—producers and consumers—play a central role. Both engage in a simple utility calculation: producers look at how labor, land, capital and other input costs vary across different locations, factor in marketing costs, and choose the location which optimizes profits. Consumers weigh the amenities of different locations against such costs as housing, job availability, commute time, etc. and also pick a location which optimizes their satisfaction. The basic argument offered by this approach is that the cities which have declined must have agglomeration diseconomies which have made them somehow less attractive to producers and consumers over the last decade or so.

Sternlieb and Hughes offer a number of variations on this theme. According to them, the Northeastern cities have suffered from "a lack of [immigrant] demand as well as deterioration in physical amenities," (p. 2), "production methods and approaches which are no longer competitive," (p. 2), "high levels of unionization" which "reduces the flexibility of the region to service new demands," (p. 2), "automation and routinization" of formerly labor-intensive industries, (p. 3), "high levels of dependency," (p. 3), "new areas of competition" from rural areas and the Third World (p. 3), loss of a monopoly over a "critical mass of consumers such as to provide a unique demand for specialized services and goods," (p. 4) and high operating costs resulting from an overly complex, uncoordinated system of production (p. 40).

It is not easy to distill empirically verifiable propositions out of such claims. Indeed, all market explanations have a solipsist quality: consumer preferences produce market outcomes, but market outcomes shape consumer preferences. Nevertheless, certain basic assumptions and arguments can be identified:

1. Aggregate population and employment figures provide the best indicators of "health."

2. Manufacturing employment and the provision of new manufacturing enterprises to supplant those which have matured and diffused away from their original locations are, in Sternlieb's words, "at the crux."

3. Individual cities compete to attract such jobs along economic lines—cities offering the lowest wages, land costs, etc., will win the competition.

4. In this context, the older cities have conditions (not yet specified) which make them "not competitive" with respect to alternative locations, in this case the Southwestern cities.

5. Similar factors operate with respect to population migration, though employment possibilities probably lead, shape and constrain individual choices.

When looked at from the Northeastern point of view, these notions have a certain surface plausibility. But does the data really bear them out? Only a comparative analysis of the two groups of cities can decide the question one way or the other. But before we can turn to the evidence, certain conceptual problems with these five assumptions must be resolved.

CRITIQUE OF THE ORTHODOX MARKET MODEL

While aggregate figures for population and employment certainly reveal something important about what is happening to a metropolitan area, they also conceal as much as they reveal. It is quite possible, as Paul Porter and Roger Starr have argued, that "fewer might be better" if the poor depart while the middle class remains. (Porter, 1976, Starr, 1976.) If uncompetitive forms of production are driven under, or firms are forced to trim workers to compete more effectively, remaining producers may be all the more profitable and productive. In short, aggregate figures say nothing about distribution or the possibility that a small aggregate change hides large but opposing changes in component parts. As we shall see, this conceptual problem is also an important factual point in the analysis of urban growth.

Secondly, simply because manufacturing jobs may be disappearing from the Northeast does not mean that they are reappearing anywhere else. Indeed, as we shall see, manufacturing accounts only for a minority of the employment growth in the Southwestern cities, and even then is of a qualitatively different nature from that which has disappeared from the Northeast. Finally, even where manufacturing employment has initially located in the Southwest in preference to the Northeast, it cannot be said that workers willing to accept lower wages or cheaper land supplies or closer proximity to the market accounts for that choice. After all, how could the substantial migrations which have taken place have been possible at all if there were not a need to import a trained labor force to the Southwest for the jobs being developed there? In fact, some Southwestern political voices sharply criticize growing firms which import employees rather than give hiring preference to long-time local residents, particularly the Chicano community. The presence of a certain type of labor force cannot be posited as the cause of a development if that labor force is recruited only subsequent to the development.

Thirdly, while the analogy between cities and firms or cities and nations in international trade may have some merits, it obscures forces that operate across cities and create interdependence among them. Cities are decreasingly independent observations, operating on their own. Rather, they have become enmeshed in a complex network in which, to use Alan Pred's term, "multilocational organizations" have come to predominate. (Pred, 1977, Chapter 1.) Acts which in earlier times were coordinated by impersonal market exchanges have been internalized into multilocational organizations, particularly large corporations and the federal government. A good case can be made that much of the economy has come to be organized by the large corporations, while large parts of the polity remain fragmented and uncoordinated.[3] Indeed, it will be argued below that these developments have created a curious reversal of nineteenth century capitalism in which unified economic actors benefit from the competition among entrepreneurial governments each seeking to entice economic growth with the most favorable political climate.[4]

Because of its insistence that cities are independent observations, the orthodox market model tends to miss the quite simple point that cities like New York may benefit in a variety of ways from the growth of cities like Phoenix. This takes us back to the first point of criticism, since the growth of Phoenix may help only some of New York's citizens while causing problems for others.

With regard to the fourth claim, namely that Northeastern cities suffer from "agglomeration diseconomies," care must be taken that this term does not simply become a fudge factor dressed up in fancy language. The exact nature of the diseconomy must be specified and studied comparatively. While it is manifestly true that life in New York has its brutish qualities, we cannot infer from this fact that Phoenix is nicer because it is growing more rapidly. It can be unbearably hot and dry in Phoenix, and in years to come a fixed water supply may be every bit as difficult as New England's heating oil situation. And for every one of Phoenix's amenities, diehard New Yorkers could undoubtedly name several of their own.

DOES THE EVIDENCE SUBSTANTIATE THE ORTHODOX MARKET MODEL?

Exhibit 2 presents some admittedly crude efforts to test some of the market model's claims with respect to the economic determinants of shifting patterns of urban growth. No one disputes that shifts have taken place. The issue is what has caused them, and whether or not the factors adduced by the market model—inter-city differences in the costs and benefits facing firms and secondarily consumers—appear to be the culprit.

George Peterson has pointed out in a number of important papers that public sector capital investments have been declining in real terms over the last decade and that we appear to be on the verge of wasting a tremendously important public asset. (Peterson, 1978.) According to Sternlieb, regional variation in the quality of the public infrastructure and its poor quality within the Northeast, account for the shift in economic growth to the Southwest. The assessment of how "adequate" public infrastructure is can be a difficult issue. The Northeast possesses a much larger amount of such infrastructure, and its replacement value is undoubtedly many times higher than that of the Southwest. On the whole, Southwestern infrastructure is considerably newer and therefore not nearly so far advanced along the maintenance cost curve. But since growth has been so much more rapid, the timing of new investments can be difficult. In many instances costly infrastructure has been put in place (and paid for by the taxpayers) before development has filled the demand for it. In other cases, infrastructure supply lags considerably behind the demand for it. The most important infrastructure in the Southwest is its massively expensive water supply, which has been financed in the past with no-interest and low-interest federal loans. Recent changes in federal policy have sent consumer charges for this infrastructure climbing rapidly, as in the case of Phoenix's Salt River Project. Exhibit 2 indicates that while private construction for all purposes has been larger in per capita and absolute terms for the Southwest, Northeasterners spent far more on a per capita and absolute basis to pay for public infrastructure. (The Northeastern mean is $503 per capita, the Southwestern - $380.) If aggregate size and current maintenance spending on infrastructure are the relevant measures, then this evidence does not support Sternlieb.[5]

EXHIBIT 2
Crude Measures for Sternlieb Hypotheses

City	All 1976 construction ($ millions)	1970 SMA public works $/cap.	Value added/pay-roll $, 1967 SMSA manufacturing	Class A secretary 1975 weekly earnings	1974 cost of living % nat urb av.	1975 state union membership rate	1975 retail sales market size	1972 SMSA AFDC caseload	1969 SMSA percent income ≤ $3,000	1973 SMSA employment	Percent services	Percent government	Percent mfg.
New York	$345	$894	$3.48	$240.50	114	35.7	$46.4	1,037,808	8.7	4,433	42	15	19
Chicago	381	478	3.23	218.50	105	35.8	23.8	517,368	6.3	3,111	32	13	29
Philadelphia	432	495	3.31	217.00	103	37.2	15.9	399,699	7.0	1,939	32	16	26
Detroit	474	474	2.74	227.00	101	39.8	13.3	281,258	6.4	1,750	27	13	35
Baltimore	<150	638	3.15	192.50	99	25.1	5.5	147,216	7.8	882	31	23	19
Cleveland	<150	512	2.92	223.00	101	36.4	8.0	140,069	7.1	894	29	13	32
Milwaukee	<150	562	2.97	207.00	105	31.5	4.7	66,741	6.0	635	28	12	33
Boston	<150	531	3.47	212.50	117	25.1	11.3	n.a.	6.1	1,550	35	15	22
Pittsburgh	<150	450	2.84	231.00	97	27.2	6.1	126,212	7.6	904	30	13	29
Buffalo	150	528	2.93	209.00	105	35.7	4.0	66,078	7.1	515	27	16	31
10 city mean			(3.10)						(8.7)		(31)	(15)	(28)
Los Angeles	$970	$624	$3.20	$233.50	99	30.8	$31.6	640,721	7.7	3,149	33	14	26
Dallas/FW	601	352	3.35	193.50	90	14.4	8.3	87,384	7.8	1,108	32	13	22
Houston	751	305	4.90	214.00	90	14.4	8.9	76,095	8.5	948	35	12	17
San Diego	444	484	2.73	199.00	97	30.8	<4.0	69,860	8.5	574	26	37	12
San Antonio	164	252	3.19	153.00	n.a.	14.4	<4.0	50,546	12.8	378	26	36	10
Phoenix	200	462	3.39	n.a.	94	17.5	4.2	29,515	8.5	466	31	17	18
Denver	<150	502	3.48	204.50	96	20.5	<4.0	56,201	6.6	636	32	19	16
San Jose	275	462	4.58	228.50	104	30.8	<4.0	73,069	5.2	449	39	15	31
El Paso	<150	401	3.19	n.a.	86	14.4	<4.0	11,448	12.7	126	34	37	17
Tucson	<150	414	2.13	n.a.	n.a.	17.5	<4.0	10,322	8.8	127	50	22	08
Albuquerque	170	381	3.50	n.a.	n.a.	14.7	<4.0	17,881	10.8	116	56	19	08
11 City mean			(3.42; 3.13 minus Houston, San Jose)						(8.9)		(36)	(22)	(17)

Wages, while lower on the average for the Southwest in comparison to the Northeast, are closing with national norms, particularly when one controls for occupation and cost of living. Janitors and porters earn $2.30 an hour in Phoenix and Houston compared to $4.10 in Chicago. But skilled service workers, like Class A secretaries, earn $5.28 hourly in the two Southwestern cities while they get $6.10 and $5.85 in Chicago and San Francisco. (Arizona Republic and Gazette, 1977.) Exhibit 2 gives data on the weekly earnings for these secretaries. The Northeastern pay averages $218, the Southwestern $204. When one factors in a 10% difference in the cost of living, one gets a good reason for secretaries to migrate but not a good reason for firms to locate in the Southwest. Similar figures hold for skilled manufacturing occupations. The lower Southwestern average wage derives partly from the greater prevalence of low-skilled, labor intensive work and partly from the greater number of relatively poor people willing to work at such jobs. No one wants a cut-rate brain surgeon, however, and the supply of low-wage labor is attractive only to certain types of industry. As we shall see, the types of industry which have most contributed to Southwestern industrial employment require above-average amounts of skilled technical and professional people, who they typically import, often at considerable cost, from outside the region.

The value added/wage bill figures given in Exhibit 2 bear out this point. Wages by themselves are not so important as what they buy. While the overall value added per wage dollar is higher in the Southwest for 1967, if one substracts the two special cases of Houston (oil) and San Jose (military hardware), the averages are quite similar: 3.10 for the Northeast as against 3.13 for the Southwest.[6] As with the earlier case of public infrastructure, these figures do not bear out the market model's claims. If employment is moving to the Southwest (or new employment starts are more typically originated there), then wages do not appear to be the reason.

The figures on unionization also support this point. While the Northeastern rates are somewhat higher, this reflects the substantially greater prevalence of basic industry jobs which have long eration and aerospace—have been completely organized from the sectors of the Southwest—for example, mining, electric power generation, and aerospace—have been completely organized from the outset. The *Wall Street Journal* has reported instances of Southern cities rejecting proposed plants because of the unions they would bring along and describes "a little-known but widespread attitude in the South; fearful of unions and competition for local labor, community leaders in many areas have quietly been spurning

Northern companies eager to move operations into the Sunbelt" (*Wall Street Journal*, February 10, 1978, p. 1). Unionization rates, we may conclude, probably have not caused the kind of basic changes depicted in Exhibit 1.

As for Sternlieb's claim that the Northeast has lost its grip over "a critical mass of consumers," Column 7 of Exhibit 2 raises considerable doubt. The only Southwestern market which would look truly substantial by comparison with the Northeast is the Los Angeles SMSA. Southwestern retail markets are much smaller and much more widely separated by vast expanses of empty countryside. Closeness to the consumer is a locational factor of primary importance; in this case it suggests the continued importance of locating in the Northeast, not the Southwest.

Sternlieb also cites "dependency" as a blemish on the Northeastern economic picture, and indeed Column 8 of Exhibit 2 shows that the older cities have far larger AFDC caseloads both in absolute terms and as a percentage of the population as a whole. (Northeastern cities hover around 20% while the Southwestern cities average less than 10%.) Interestingly, however, Column 9 of Exhibit 2 shows that poverty (defined as the percentage of families with incomes lower than $3,000 per year) is substantially more widespread in the Southwest. Even if one factors in differences in the cost of living, many more people are—in theory—eligible for AFDC in the Southwest than in the Northeast. The difference, clearly, is the political philosophy under which AFDC is administered and not the extent of need. In fact, the Northeast has done a better job in providing higher wages and broader public support for its less well-to-do citizens, at the cost of higher unemployment, while the Southwest provides more extensive poverty and subemployment (but less unemployment). (See Watkins, 1977, for more evidence on this point.) It will be argued below that the key distinction between the regions lies in the differences of political culture which these figures reflect and not in different economic costs which somehow change employment location decisions. (Firms do not pay AFDC costs—taxpayers do.)

In a way, the last three columns of Exhibit 2 are the most important, for they undermine the orthodox market model's entire reliance on manufacturing employment as "the crux." In fact, Southwestern cities rely much more heavily on service and government employment[7] than do the Northeastern cities. They in turn have substantially more manufacturing employment. Since the latter have declined, a more reasonable conclusion might be that manufacturing is an albatross for the Northeast. The Northeastern

cities have two leaders in service provision—New York and Boston—
but these cities also have substantial manufacturing employment.
The other cities are even more heavily industrial, and the metropolitan areas which have suffered the largest population declines
(Detroit, Cleveland, Pittsburgh) have among the highest industrial
components. By contrast, only San Jose among the Southwestern
cities approximates the industrial workforce common within the
Northeast. San Diego, San Antonio and El Paso are all military
centers with high rates of government employment and little industry. The other Southwestern cities, particularly some of the
smaller ones, have quite high rates of service employment. Overall,
the Southwestern mean service employment is 36% in comparison
to the Northeast's 31%. Industry may be the key to Northeastern
declines, but it is clearly an incomplete statement, for services have
been the key to Southwestern growth. Exhibits 3 and 4 present a
more detailed picture of the industries common to each area.

These two Exhibits show for each city how the two largest industrial sectors within the SMSA changed between 1960 and 1970 and
how their occupational structure looked in 1970. The Northeast
presents a picture of basic industry, heavily reliant on skilled blue
collar labor, experiencing decline. New York SMSA lost a third of
its garment industry, Baltimore 30% of its steel industry (the same
was true of Pittsburgh and Buffalo), and Pittsburgh and Buffalo
lost substantial amounts of their electrical machinery work. Elsewhere, production of the nation's basic capital and durable goods
required slightly rising amounts of labor. In general, the proportion
of professional, technical and kindred labor (PTK) required in these
industries was quite low.

The Southwest presents a different picture. As in the Northeast,
some industries with low PTK levels did not fare well in this decade.
Food products (1.3-5.6% PTK) lost employment in Denver, El Paso
and San Antonio. The border cities of San Antonio and El Paso
evidently picked up some of the sweatshop employment in apparel
which New York lost. But the distinctive element in this picture is
the extremely large employment increases within high-PTK, high
technology, new industries, particularly aircraft, electronics, electrical
machinery and ordnance. The PTK rates for these industries average
well above 20% (the Northeast averaged less, even in the identical
industry categories). San Jose stands out with two industries which
are one-third and one-half composed of professional and technical
employment and which grew several times over during the decade.
Within the region, Los Angeles and San Diego appeared to have lost
some ground to Dallas/Ft. Worth over aircraft, and Los Angeles may

EXHIBIT 3
NORTHEAST
2 Largest Manufacturers, Δ, Occupational Structure

CITY	INDUSTRY	1970 Emplmt.	60-70 Δ	PTK	M & A	Sales	Clerical	Craftsmen & Operatives
							1970 Occupational Structure	
New York	apparel	173,304	-31.9	3.5	7.2	4.9	10.9	71.5
	printing/publishing	128,700	-6.1	17.8	8.8	6.6	29.3	33.9
Chicago	electrical machinery	141,720	0.2	14.6	5.0	1.4	16.0	58.8
	non-electrical mach.	118,793	5.5	11.5	6.7	2.8	16.3	58.9
Philadelphia	electrical machinery	66,768	-1.9	21.1	6.5	1.6	16.6	49.7
	non-electrical mach.	56,350	15.1	17.0	7.4	2.6	15.5	54.5
Detroit	motor vehicles	266,369	8.1	14.1	2.5	0.4	11.9	64.2
	non-electrical mach.	89,813	11.9	11.7	6.0	1.7	11.3	65.5
Baltimore	electrical machinery	26,483	36.4	27.7	5.2	1.0	15.9	46.2
	primary ferrous	24,797	-29.2	5.7	1.3	0.4	10.8	65.6
Cleveland	non-electrical mach.	48,108	14.9	12.4	6.6	2.4	14.8	50.3
	fabricated metals	35,096	19.0	7.3	6.5	2.0	15.0	64.3
Milwaukee	non-electrical mach.	52,755	23.1	11.9	4.4	1.3	14.7	60.6
	electrical machinery	30,963	-7.1	20.4	4.2	0.9	15.7	54.1
Boston	electrical machinery	46,970	-27.2	26.7	8.5	1.5	15.5	44.6
	non-electrical mach.	31,112	31.8	22.7	8.6	2.2	16.8	46.1
Pittsburgh	primary ferrous	94,220	-23.8	8.9	2.3	0.5	12.7	58.5
	electrical machinery	27,553	-7.4	18.8	4.7	1.3	16.2	52.3
Buffalo	primary ferrous	25,076	-21.9	4.6	1.6	0.3	9.3	65.0
	motor vehicles	23,338	0.1	5.2	1.9	0.4	5.7	75.2

EXHIBIT 4
SOUTHWEST
2 Largest Manufacturers, Δ, Occupational Structure

CITY	INDUSTRY	1970 Emplmt	60-70 Δ	1970 Occupational Structure				
				PTK	M & A	Sales	Clerical	Craftsmen & Operatives
Los Angeles	aircraft	118,413	−22.8	26.7	5.8	0.5	18.5	45.5
	electronics	83,772	−19.0	22.5	8.2	1.9	15.9	48.6
Dallas/Ft. Worth	aircraft	58,206	75.3	26.5	3.8	0.4	16.5	48.3
	electronics	39,420	149.5	29.8	5.9	1.3	13.7	46.1
Houston	petrochemicals	24,788	108.8	21.6	6.5	3.0	11.5	49.3
	machinery	24,298	32.6	13.0	5.7	4.0	13.6	59.4
San Diego	aircraft	17,207	−4.2	24.7	3.1	0.6	17.9	51.7
	electrical machinery	9,883	232.9	28.7	7.8	2.0	13.6	46.4
San Antonio	food products	6,452	−7.7	2.7	6.3	5.0	8.9	66.1
	apparel	4,147	64.7	1.1	1.4	1.7	6.9	86.6
Phoenix	electronics	21,412	465.2	24.5	4.6	0.6	12.5	54.6
	machinery	13,341	179.5	29.4	7.4	15.1	15.3	44.2
Denver	machinery	8,850	71.9	23.2	8.7	3.3	14.5	48.1
	food & kindreds	9,746	−15.2	5.6	8.0	4.3	9.7	61.2
San Jose	electronics	40,542	282.3	34.7	7.8	1.0	15.8	38.3
	ordnance	19,243	— —	46.2	7.8	0.4	17.6	25.0
El Paso	apparel	8,695	175.4	2.0	1.3	0.3	7.7	84.2
	food & kindreds	1,519	−31.4	1.3	7.8	6.8	8.0	62.1
Tucson	ordnance	2,576	— —	35.3	5.2	0.2	12.9	43.0
	electrical machinery	1,271	286.3	27.2	8.4	2.4	13.7	44.9
Albuqerque	food products	1,056	−38.2	4.3	11.7	9.7	12.2	52.7
	printing/publishing	1,016	−25.1	17.2	8.9	15.5	20.8	36.3
San Francisco	food & kindreds	23,486	−37.9	7.0	8.5	3.6	15.1	57.2
	electrical machinery	22,365	23.4	23.7	7.4	2.0	17.0	47.0

have lost some electronics employment to such cities as Dallas, San Diego or San Jose. But the overall picture is one of high-technology, new industries oriented to aerospace, defense and computer industry applications. (Houston distinguishes itself in petrochemicals.)

Three interesting conclusions which require a substantial modification of the orthodox market model may be drawn from this data. First, services (themselves often PTK-intense) have played a stronger role in the development of both the Northeast and the Southwest, and particularly the latter, than the model allows. Secondly, the industries which are disappearing from the Northeast are not reappearing, with one or two exceptions, in the Southwest. Rather something generic is happening within the lifecycle of the basic goods production process. Thirdly, in contrast with the low-PTK nature of Northeastern industry, the rapidly growing industries of the Southwest rely much more heavily on white collar professional people. Highly educated labor is a key input for this growth. (And, one might note, highly educated labor is a key product in many Northeastern cities.) Indeed, this technical production process produces goods which are typically consumed not by industry but by service organizations: aircraft for the transportation service industry and the defense service industry, electronics for defense and information processing service applications, and computers for all those who move data around. Services thus take on a dual importance: they are the largest and most rapidly growing employment sector, and they also strongly influence the rhythm of industrial production.

These facts lead to an even more startling conclusion, to which we will return later: since services are so important, and since many Northeastern cities command substantial, even critical service resources, and since much of the manufacturing which was there to leave has left, and since what remains has become more technical and more productive as less technical jobs get displaced or engineered out of existence, perhaps Snowbelt cities' future is not so bad after all!

To sum up, the evidence outlined in Exhibits 2-4 throws considerable doubt on the basic claims made by the orthodox market model. The interregional differences in wages, productivity, unionization, market size, poverty, etc. are simply not large enough to have accounted for the shifts which have taken place. The market model assumes that decisions made by individual firms and consumers examining alternative locations in the Northeast or Southwest aggregate to the changes observed; yet the evidence shows that the

Southwest has not "won" the competition for those who have struck their Northeastern tents and stolen away in the dark. Rather a totally new, regionally-specialized group of services and industries has boosted Southwestern urban rankings. Something more profound than fairly narrow wage rate differences must have influenced the calculations of each industrial segment, whether rising or declining. Finally, the market model fails to give adequate account to service employment increases which have been occurring in the Northeast as well as the Southwest.[8]

These empirical difficulties stem from the conceptual weaknesses which have been pointed out in the market model—the failure to consider interdependence among cities, the changing nature of the service economy, and the role of politics and public sector actors. Given these problems with the market model, what alternative might be more satisfactory?

AN ALTERNATIVE MODEL

Let us begin with the basic notion that cities are enmeshed in a network of interdependencies which more often than not take place within formal organizations such as large corporations and government agencies. If true, a city's particular role in the hierarchical network which binds together all cities will greatly influence that city's fate. Without going into the literature in great detail, there is much reason to believe that organizationally-encased interdependencies have become the dominant element in inter-city relationships. Let us begin with the modern corporation.

Alfred Chandler, in his magisterial work on the business corporation, *The Visible Hand*, concludes "modern business enterprise took the place of market mechanisms in coordinating the activities of the economy and allocating its resources." (Chandler, 1977, p. 1.) He shows how, with rapidly improving production and transportation technologies and consequently widening markets, administrative coordination became more profitable than market coordination. The multi-unit enterprise administered by salaried middle and top managers rose to capitalize on this potential, and eventually it reshaped the organization—and one might add the geography—of the economy. Central administrative units at the top make strategic decisions about overall resource allocations; middle managers located at the center or out in the field oversee and coordinate the way specific operating units work; and dispersed operating units actually produce. This hierarchical organization can coordinate a highly complex production process aimed at world-scale markets.

The consequences of the "managerial revolution" and the rise of the modern business enterprise have been enormous. Charles Lindblom has described some of the power implications: "people enter one set of markets—consumer markets—to exchange that money for desired goods and services. Because in each of these two sets of markets they face a business enterprise, the enterprise sits astride the whole market system, a momentous development in social organization the implications of which are not yet wholly revealed" (Lindblom, 1977, p. 37).

Changing relations between cities is one such implication. Central coordinating units in one city (corporate headquarters, banking institutions) coordinate a wide range of activities taking place in subordinate cities. (See Pred, 1977, Chapter 1 for a path-breaking analysis of such inter-city patterns.) The predominant pattern which has developed since World War II within the largest U.S. cities has been characterized by a steady centralization of command and control and information processing activities simultaneously with a steady decentralization (even expatriation) of subordinate production units.

Hymer adapted Chandler's organizational distinctions about corporate levels to the city system and argued that world cities concentrated strategic planning headquarters, national cities, which contain diverse and interrelated production, and regional cities, which are based on one or two types of absentee-owned, branch plant activities (Hymer, 1971). Robert Cohen has undertaken statistical studies which demonstrate the appropriateness of this conceptualization. (Cohen, 1977.) In an important unpublished study, Cohen has added an important modification to Chandler's basic observations about the corporation. Since World War II, Cohen argues, high level business services organized outside the corporate boundary (such as investment banking, corporate law, management consulting and information processing) have come to play a central economic role. "Since their specialization involves concentration and geographic economies of scale," Cohen argues, "it has resulted in the agglomeration of advanced services and corporate headquarters in but a few of the largest cities in the nation." (Cohen, 1978, Chapter 9.) Cohen goes on to show that, while corporate headquarters are much more concentrated in the biggest cities than is production as a whole, high level business services are even more concentrated than corporate headquarters. The prevalence of advanced corporate services and corporate headquarters give these cities a grip over their economic future which cities down the hierarchy could never hope to gain.[9]

In addition to the corporate headquarters/corporate services activities discussed by Hymer and Cohen, the "third sector" also plays a strong role in nodal cities. Non-profit organizations of all types, but particularly those concerned with education, research and managing information in general provide critical training and backup to the private economy. In addition, the health and hospital service sector, the culture and leisure service industry round out the picture. They both depend upon and reinforce corporate service activities.

The second key factor in an alternative model of urban growth stems to some degree from the first: the nature of the "economic wave" which a particular city rides into the hierarchy of cities, and the resulting mix of industrial and service activities which characterizes it. There have been three such waves, and each has created a peculiar geographic division of labor which has overlapped and interacted with its predecessor. The pre-industrial commercial expansion which took place before the Civil War made the port cities of Boston, New York and Philadelphia into important places. The late 19th century urban industrial boom influenced these cities, but also created giant cities in Pittsburgh, Cleveland, Chicago, Detroit and elsewhere in the American Ruhr. This urban/industrial revolution created staggering social conflict, but it also planted (as Chandler shows) the organizational seeds of the third wave of urban economic development. This last wave has been characterized by the decentralization of industrial production outside the conflict-ridden industrial cities, the rise of the service sector, and the growth of high-technology industry (including the military-industrial complex). These new industries located in patterns quite different from 19th century industrialization, in concert with the "ruralization" of 19th century industrial production. This last wave modified the earlier urban hierarchy by undermining the standing of some cities, adding other cities (particularly the Southwestern cities) to the standings and reinforcing the position of still others (including the leading cities of the Northeast).

The third key factor grows out of the first two: the scope and orientation of local and national government, and the extent of overt local political challenge to conservative, growth-oriented local government. It will be argued that a key reason corporate decisionmakers relocated 19th century productive activities outside the large industrial cities was their desire to escape a hostile and threatening political environment. A relatively unified private sector sought to encourage a competitive dynamic among fragmented local political jurisdictions which would reward favorable local jurisdictions and punish the hostile. If this competitive dynamic could be encouraged, then business would not need to intervene in, or even participate directly in, local politics. The rules of the game themselves would produce the desired outcome.

Decisionmakers at the top of the urban hierarchy thus chose to relocate industrial activities outside the central cities in the years after the Depression and to locate them in the most favorable areas. At the same time, these decision-makers sought to reshape the social and infrastructural geographies of the higher-level cities to facilitate their new roles as command and control/information processing centers. While these decisionmakers largely succeeded in this effort, they triggered in some cities a new round of urban political conflict over land use and urban development which also influenced the inter-city allocation and reallocation of high level service activities. In some cities, like St. Louis and Detroit, where central city black populations appeared to be too large and threatening to tame, whole new "central business districts" were constructed in the suburbs.

In contrast to the market model's stress solely on economics, the alternative model asserts that politics and government count. They count in two ways: the third wave of metropolitan development could not have been constructed without extensive government intervention on a variety of fronts (including defense production siting, infrastructural support for suburbanization and urban renewal). Its path thus has been strongly influenced by the degree to which government policy favoring the private sector has been secure from political challenge.

To sum up, in contrast to the market model, the proposed alternative model claims that three factors have influenced urban growth trends over the last four decades. They are: (1) the particular city's role in the hierarchical network of cities, (2) the mix of industrial and service activities which a particular city has inherited from the timing of the "wave" upon which it rode into the network of cities, and (3) the degree to which political conflict has attended its development. According to this model, a city's fate correlates positively with occupying a nodal point, negatively with its having been a 19th century industrial newcomer (but positively with newer service and high-technology activities and negatively with political challenges to pro-growth politics).

DOES THE EVIDENCE SUBSTANTIATE
THE ALTERNATIVE MODEL?

Exhibits 5 through 8 provide some initial data by which the adequacy of this alternative model can be tested. Exhibit 5 shows some basic measures of network centrality. Exhibit 5 shows that the Northeastern cities have 219 of the *Fortune* 500's headquarters, while the Southwestern cities have only 48. (Though some of these headquarters have moved from central cities to suburbs, recent studies have shown that the distribution has remained remarkably stable, on a net basis, across SMSA's. See Vaughan, 1977, p. 19.) The banking resources of New York alone far exceed the combined capacity of all Southwestern cities. Even among the Southwestern cities, the influence of Los Angeles, Dallas and Houston over the others is clear. 30% of total *Fortune* 500 sales, 40% of *Fortune* 500 foreign sales and 70% of the auditing done for *Fortune* 500 firms take place within firms headquartered in the New York SMSA. Rather than view economic activities taking place in the Southwest as competing with those of New York, it might be more accurate to say that they frequently benefit New York. The same can be said for the other Northeastern cities possessing corporate head-quarters, large banking resources and plentiful advanced corporate services. Exhibit 5 also shows that New York, Chicago, Philadelphia, Cleveland, Boston, Detroit and Baltimore contain 56.8% of all large law firms (50+ members) while Los Angeles and Houston are the only Southwestern cities to have such firms at all (10.1%).

Absentee ownership is widespread in the Southwest. Major em-ployers in the smaller cities tend to be branch plants, repatriating profits to higher level cities elsewhere for reinvestment. The largest home-based firms tend to be utilities, banks and smaller oil com-panies, while the biggest employers are aerospace, mining, oil and electronics branch plant operations. As such, local influence over firm decisionmaking and firm commitment to local operations can be quite limited. (In 1977 alone, Phoenix lost 13,000 electronics jobs in an industry down-turn.)

The first factor—nodal centrality—thus favors some of the North-eastern cities and some of the Southwestern ones. Philadelphia, Boston, New York and similar advanced service cities have experi-enced job gains which have resulted from their "sitting astride" important market linkages. So, too, have such Southwestern cities as Houston and Dallas. Cities in both groups that fall lower down in the urban hierarchy have not benefitted so much.

EXHIBIT 5

Role in the Urban Hierarchy

City	No. 1976 *Fortune* 500 HQ'S	Total 1975 bank deposits ($ billions)	Percentage of all 50+ law firms 1973	Percentage of all lawyers (1972 Census)	Percentage of all 1973 Am. Institute of CPA members
New York	112	177.5	21.2	12.3	10.5
Chicago	34	39.3	13.6	4.9	5.2
Philadelphia	11	17.0	7.6	2.4	3.2
Detroit	10	15.6	2.5	2.0	2.5
Baltimore	1	4.9	2.5	1.2	1.0
Cleveland	15	9.5	4.2	1.4	1.5
Milwaukee	10	4.6	0.9	0.8	0.9
Boston	10	13.1	4.2	1.4	1.5
Pittsburgh	15	11.8	0.9	1.0	1.2
Buffalo	1	11.8	0.0	0.7	–
Los Angeles	21	32.3	5.9	4.5	5.1
Dallas/Ft. Worth	7	10.5	0.0	1.1	1.8
Houston	10	9.7	4.2	1.3	2.3
San Diego	3	0.8	0.0	0.5	–
San Antonio	0	0.7	0.0	–	–
Phoenix	3	3.2	0.0	–	–
Denver	4	3.4	3.4	1.8	–
San Jose	0	–	0.0	–	–
El Paso	0	–	0.0	–	–
Tucson	0	–	0.0	–	–
Albuquerque	0	–	0.0	–	–

The second factor—industrial mix and service/industrial balance—has already been discussed above. Cities in which 19th century industrial activities have predominated, and where no nodal service activities offset them, have fared the worst. Pittsburgh seems to provide the arch case of this effect; the other large Northeastern cities, as Exhibit 6 shows, have had rises in service employment to offset manufacturing declines (e.g., New York, Chicago, Philadelphia, Boston and even Buffalo.) In the Southwest as a whole, with no 19th century manufacturing to kill off, both services and new industry grew, but services grew much more rapidly.

Indeed, Exhibit 6 demonstrates quite thoroughly that services provided the primary fuel of overall urban employment growth. While in each case Southwestern rates of increase exceeded those of the Northeast, they began from smaller base numbers. In each group of cities the absolute numbers of jobs gained have been truly remarkable.

Services are arrayed along Exhibit 6 in decreasing order of their PTK content, and it is interesting to note that gains were greater in the more PTK-intense "third sector" services than in the less PTK-intense business services. In particular, professional services (ranging from architecture to lawyers and therapists) increased dramatically in all Northeastern cities except Milwaukee and in all Southwestern cities.

Exhibit 6 also shows that service increases followed the same basic pattern for the Southwest as for the Northeast, but at higher rates. Not shown in Exhibit 6, but equally true, is the predominance among Southwestern cities of service employment by comparison to industrial employment. On average, almost twice as many people work in services as in industry in these cities.

From these figures we can conclude that in cities where a post-industrial economy had to be constructed by first demolishing the 19th century industrial base, gains have been only modest. But, as in the Southwestern cities, where no such obstacle existed, but rather a post-industrial economy could be fashioned *de novo,* growth has been most rapid.

This brings us to the third and final factor: political conflict and the organization of the local public sector. High-level business decisionmakers have deflected investment away from contested zones and towards more favorable climates. Business readily admits this point. In an article entitled "Business Loves the Sunbelt (And Vice Versa)," *Fortune* magazine points out:

EXHIBIT 6

Percentage Changes in 1960-1970 SMSA Service Employment

City	Education (60% PTK)	Health/hosp. (60% PTK)	Professional services (60% PTK)	Non-profits (40% PTK)	Business services (25% PTK)	Communications (15% PTK)	Public Administration (15% PTK)	Finance, admin-istration, R.E. (10% PTK)	Change in total ser-vice employment	Change in total manu-facturing employment	Percent manufacturing in PTK class	Total change in SMSA employment
New York	85.7	38.3	96.9	35.6	31.5	27.0	25.0	29.2	34.4	-15.5	11.1	5.4
Chicago	67.1	47.1	110.1	14.7	44.6	7.8	20.2	27.5	41.3	-5.8	10.1	5.0
Philadelphia	83.8	58.1	190.7	17.9	67.2	12.7	34.4	37.4	139.2	-1.6	11.9	14.2
Detroit	32.4	67.5	135.6	30.7	56.1	23.5	28.0	44.2	24.3	8.6	11.5	18.2
Baltimore	102.7	68.2	215.6	66.4	137.9	40.9	78.9	40.5	63.4	5.0	9.8	26.0
Cleveland	80.0	56.7	137.3	27.6	61.4	54.2	25.0	40.1	29.1	6.7	10.4	19.0
Milwaukee	112.0	96.5	165.0	27.4	49.8	11.5	20.2	45.0	35.6	5.5	10.9	21.8
Boston	68.0	54.8	233.3	37.0	53.6	25.4	18.0	36.0	29.5	-13.5	15.6	11.0
Pittsburgh	10.3	-0.6	19.8	21.6	19.1	7.5	-20.4	-25.2	-13.2	-10.5	11.7	4.7
Buffalo	88.9	52.6	127.6	34.0	46.6	-0.1	15.9	22.4	37.9	-5.9	9.4	7.0
10 City mean	73.1	53.9	143.2	31.3	56.8	21.0	24.5	29.7	42.1	-2.6	11.2	13.2
Los Angeles	51.9	51.4	115.5	53.7	39.5	20.7	18.7	27.7	31.3	-3.6	14.2	8.1
Dallas/F.W.	114.1	102.2	215.8	32.9	146.7	38.8	43.7	71.5	65.5	64.1	15.9	49.1
Houston	141.5	122.4	223.3	69.3	210.4	88.5	106.1	87.3	93.4	60.3	14.9	69.5
San Diego	123.9	107.9	229.3	85.2	87.3	49.7	33.6	28.2	62.9	4.5	20.6	38.0
San Antonio	116.9	105.8	168.4	43.9	72.9	51.2	27.2	57.6	49.0	43.7	5.5*	34.4
Phoenix	112.9	74.5	119.8	94.0	142.0	50.5	51.9	74.5	48.2	101.4	18.2	55.0
Denver	111.8	88.7	155.9	60.1	126.8	36.6	28.5	58.3	59.0	24.1	17.6	39.6
San Jose	122.2	128.0	182.6	112.1	206.4	134.2	87.4	100.2	107.9	85.4	28.7	79.3
El Paso	86.3	80.8	182.4	40.7	85.0	1.9	35.1	28.3	39.2	30.0	5.9*	23.0
Tucson	111.3	92.4	171.7	79.3	76.1	29.0	48.4	61.7	61.3	-3.1	18.5	36.0
Albuquerque	109.0	66.5	133.7	117.2	5.3	12.2	18.2	47.8	40.4	-0.5	12.0	25.9
11 City Mean	109.2	92.8	172.6	71.7	108.9	46.7	45.3	58.5	59.9	36.9	15.6	39.5

(PTK = professional, technical and kindred workers)

(Minus El Paso and San Antonio* 17.8)

(Employment primarily in apparel*)

Passing over the decay, crime, social turmoil, and high costs that help drive jobs and people from their big cities, (Northerners) complain that the Sunbelt is pirating away business and industry with cheap, docile labor and unfair tax concessions. The complaint suggests that a lot of those Northerners are missing a key point about the Sunbelt's boom. It's booming in great part because of it's pro-business—and Northern cities by and large aren't. Much of the region is a repository of traditional American values—patriotism, self reliance, respect for authority—and both racial disorders and street crime are relatively rare. . .It is also true than many Sunbelt states solicit new business with zeal and skill. . .the most effective form of aggressive behavior. . .is the joining together of politicians and businessmen to shape state laws that favor business.

(Brecker, 1977, pp. 134-136.)

Implicit in this statement are three planes which influence the typical investor's location decision: a) the structure and composition of local budgets, particularly in terms of a social service versus business development orientation; b) the broader political culture, in terms of political values, the degree of intergroup conflict and mobilization of opposition, and the differential access to government by different interests; and c) the stability of hierarchy within the overall social structure. According to the business viewpoint, the Northeast strikes out on each count, while the Southwest solidly connects. Exhibits 7 and 8 suggest that on each of these planes the two groups do indeed stand at opposite extremes.

THE COMPOSITION OF LOCAL POLICIES

In the Northeast, the years after World War II saw the rise of pro-growth coalitions which utilized urban renewal funds to help transform cities which had been developed on the basis of 19th century manufacturing into modern corporate headquarters cities. (Mollenkopf, 1975, Gordon, 1977). Friedland has shown that the presence of corporate elites strongly influence the amount of money raised for, and spent on, this transformation (Friedland, 1976, Chapter 2).

The highly destructive consequences of urban renewal triggered tremendous social turmoil, both in terms of community mobilization against the land use transformation under way and in terms of rioting and a generalized breakdown of urban political authority (Mollenkopf, 1975 and 1977a, Friedland, 1977). This turmoil

EXHIBIT 7

Government and Racial Characteristics

City	Form of government	Bond rating	Non-ed. city workers/1000	1970 CC gov't exp./cap	CC Pct. Black	CC Pct. Spanish	1950-70 Land area increase via annexation	CC assessed valuation subject to tax, 1975
New York	M	BA	31.9	$894	21.1%	10.3%	0%	$39.4B
Chicago	M	AA	14.3	478	32.7	7.4	8	24.2
Philadelphia	M	A	19.8	495	33.6	1.4	0	5.8
Detroit	M	BAA	19.2	474	43.7	1.8	0	5.8
Baltimore	M	A	26.3	638	49.7	0.9	0	3.2
Cleveland	M	A	18.6	512	38.3	1.9	0	1.5
Milwaukee	M	AAA	13.1	562	14.6	2.2	0	2.0
Boston	M	A	27.8	531	16.4	2.8	0	1.8
Pittsburgh	M	A1	11.8	450	20.2	0.1	0	5.8
Buffalo	M	BAA	16.7	528	20.4	0.8	0	1.0
10 City Average	M	–	20.0	556	–	–	1	$9.0B
Los Angeles	M	AAA	15.5	624	17.9	18.4	3%	$8.5
Dallas/Ft. Worth	CM	AAA	15.8	352	24.9	4.4	128	5.0
Houston	M	AAA	8.7	305	25.7	12.1	250	5.8
San Diego	CM	AA	12.0	484	7.6	12.7	241	5.1
San Antonio	CM	AA	12.4	252	7.6	52.2	281	1.2
Phoenix	CM	AA	9.7	462	4.8	14.0	16,000	2.7
Denver	M	AA	17.3	502	9.2	16.8	40	1.9
San Jose	CM	AA	7.9	462	2.4	21.9	8,000	1.6
El Paso	CM	A1	9.7	401	2.3	58.1	4,050	0.5
Tucson	CM	A1	11.7	414	3.5	23.9	308	1.2
Albuquerque	CM	A1	13.2	381	2.3	34.9	112	0.9
11 City Average	CM	–	12.3	422	–	–	2,674	3.1

EXHIBIT 8

Political Conflict and Compensatory Spending

City	Extent of neighborhood organization[a]	Neighborhood organizational militance[a]	Extent of organizational coalitions[a]	Community Action Program expenditures 1965-1969[a]	Urban Renewal Program expenditures 1949-1969[b]	Model Cities Program expenditures 1966-1969[a]	Spilerman riot intensity index[a]	Gini index of metropolitan income inequality 1970[c]
Philadelphia	high	med	med	$44.8	$274	25.5	28	.338
Detroit	med	high	high	44.6	77	20.2	1049	.326
Baltimore	med	high	high	58.8	90	10.8	858	.337
Cleveland	high	high	high	59.3	49	8.0	29	.335
Boston	high	high	high	107.0	133	15.6	33	.347
Pittsburgh	med	med	med	98.2	111	6.3	150	.329
Buffalo	high	high	high	26.0	23	5.6	32	.318
Seven N.E. City Average	high−	high−	high−	$62.7	$108	13.1	311	.333
Los Angeles	high	med	med	$78.9	$40	$8.9	19	.361
Ft. Worth	low	low	med	18.8	2	0.0	00	.331
Houston	low	low	med	106.7	0	13.6	53	.350
Phoenix	low	low	low	27.3	0	0.0	26	.356
Denver	high	high	high	69.0	29	11.6	08	.350
San Jose	high	med	med	35.0	9	0.2	00	.316
Tucson	low	med	med	22.9	6	3.3	06	.369
Seven S.W. City Average	med−	low+	med	$51.2	$12	$5.4	16	.348

Sources: a. Barss, Reitzel and Associates, *Community Action and Urban Change* (Cambridge: Barss, Reitzel, 1969)

b. Department of Housing and Urban Development, *Urban Renewal Directory* (Washington, D.C.: Government Printing Office, 1970)

c. Department of Commerce, Bureau of the Census, *1970 Census of Population* (Washington, D.C.: Government Printing Office, 1971) undermined the stability of the pro-growth coalition and required the construction of a Northeastern urban welfare state in order to restore some degree of political legitimacy which reshaped the size and composition of these cities' budgets. Affirmative action hiring, new programs such as the Community Action and Model Cities Programs expanded public employment, rapidly increasing public sector wages, and formal incorporation of community groups and public sector into the local political process resulted from this process of coopting and incorporating dissent.

The Southwestern cities, being largely built on a clean slate, did not require the massive redistribution of land and employment under way in the Northeast during the 1950's and 1960's. Indeed, Southwestern society remained so racially segmented and politically underdeveloped that little need be spent on the resident population to assure political stability. (This was the era in which the Parr organization in Duval County, Texas, could assure that Lyndon Johnson got "enough" votes from the district's Chicanos.) Growth was so vigorous in Southwestern cities that it provided ample funds to fuel local politicians ready to act favorably where necessary. Shady land developments with political overtones were apparently common in the area (Investigative Reporters and Editors, 1977).

Exhibits 7 and 8 show the large differences in government composition and spending patterns these two courses of urban development generated. Northeastern cities average 20.0 public employees per thousand population, while the Southwest averages only 13.1 (Exhibit 7). New York ranks first and Massachusetts fifth in terms of per capita state and local tax collections, while New Mexico is thirty-third, Arizona nineteenth, Colorado twenty-fourth, Utah forty-third and Texas forty-first. Seven Northeastern cities spent an average of $108 million each on urban renewal between 1949 and 1969, while seven Southwestern cities spent only $12 million on the average. O.E.O. spent an average of $5.12 million in Southwestern cities (only $3.45 if Los Angeles and Houston are subtracted), while spending an average of $6.27 million in the Northeastern cities. The Model Cities differential is even greater: $5.4 million in the Southwest, $13.1 in the Northeast (Exhibit 8). The public sector is clearly smaller, less of a tax burden and less oriented towards social cohesion in the Southwest.

POLITICAL CULTURE

This spending pattern reflects not only different development histories, but strongly different structural patterns of political influence. With the exception of Houston and Denver, the major Southwestern cities are governed through a city manager form of government. With the additional exception of Tucson, they are non-partisan and at-large (Goodall, 1967). As numerous studies have shown, this type of government structure reduces government's responsiveness to working class voters, limits political participation and favors business-oriented policy outputs. (Gordon, 1975, collects a number of such studies.)

In this organizational environment for politics, business elites have have striking influence over the electoral process. In Phoenix, Dallas, Albuquerque, Fort Worth and San Antonio, among other Southwestern cities, business elites have organized slate-designating and fund-raising bodies which have virtually monopolized electoral outcomes. The Phoenix Charter Government movement, for example, has lost only one city council race in twenty years (*New Times*, July 27, 1977, p. 7). As a result, far fewer Blacks, Chicano's and Indians have been elected than either their numbers or recent minority electoral experience in the Northeast might suggest.[10] According to one observer of San Diego, "The business community has a virtual monopoly in deliberation on solutions to civic problems" (Goodall, 1967, p. 159).

While political leaders in Northeastern cities rarely made decisions which threaten core interests of their business communities, one of the consequences of the 1960's is that fewer decisions can be made behind closed doors, more diverse voices must be consulted and community interests must be balanced against business desires. Why suffer under such Northeastern constraints, many businessmen must ask themselves, when the Southwest can provide such a relatively cost-free, unencumbered political environment? In short, the Southwest offers an arena for reconstructing the pro-growth coaltions so severely damaged by political conflict in the Northeast.

Exhibit 4 gives data on the degree of neighborhood mobilization and conflict that characterized the two sets of cities during the late 1960's. The data on the former are drawn from a 100-city survey of the Community Action Program's impact. In each city, a randomly selected poverty area was examined to determine the number of groups active, their goals and strategies, and the level of militance (Barss, Reitzel, 1970). The seven Northeastern cities nearly always had extensive and militant organizations, working to a large extent in coalition. In the Southwest, one the other hand, except for Denver and to a lesser extent Los Angeles and San Jose (which experienced Chicano activism during this period), the level of activity was modest to nonexistent. The overall averages were distinctly lower than in the Northeast. Data on the intensity of riot activity draws the difference even more sharply: Northeastern cities experienced wrenching and violent challenges to prevalent authority patterns, while the Southwest experienced either no such conflict or only modest conflicts.

SOCIAL STRUCTURE

Exhibit 8 also shows that the Gini inequality index for Northeastern metropolitan areas is substantially less than in the Southwest. The range of variance across all cities lies between about .300 and .380, so the difference between the two averages, .333 and .348, takes on particular significance. The gap between rich and poor in Southwestern cities has been perpetuated by economic as well as political discrimination, particularly against Chicanos and Indians, but also against Blacks (Mollenkopf, 1977b).

A pamphlet issued by Tucson's Development Authority for Tucson's Economy unwittingly illustrates the plight of minority workers and government attitudes toward it. Responding to a rhetorical question about the availability of workers, the pamphlet states:

> There are a substantial number of workers actively seeking employment in Tucson. And, Tucson's heritage and proximity to Mexico generate an above average Mexican-American work force. This fact, when coupled with a large underemployed group, and the unemployed American Indian, results in a large number of trainable unskilled workers who qualify for training courses and OFT assistance. Employers who have established plants in Tucson say that our Mexican-Americans are easy to train, will follow instructions, are more loyal, and equal or exceed the productivity of workers in other parts of the country.

(*Arizona Daily Star*, March 26, 1977, p. 1)

Underemployment, exclusion from high-wage occupational categories, employer and union discrimination, lack of bilingual education and similar problems continue to plague the Southwest's minority population, even while business booms for middle-class, white migrants to the area, boosting average per capita earnings figures.

Perhaps even more that the economic differences outlined, these facets of political life distinguish Southwestern from Northeastern cities and provide the basis for rapid economic growth. In the Southwest, the public budget is disproportionately designed to promote capital investment and avoid "wasteful" social spending. The structure of local government and political participation reinforce this pattern of business-oriented outcomes. Unlike the Northeast, even though inequality and exclusion prevail, minority communities have not mobilized, either through community organizations or through violent protest, with sufficient power to challenge these arrangements. Just as the breakdown of political support for growth in the Northeast heralded urban decline, the institutionalization of pro-growth politics in the Southwest has evidently played a central role in its growth. Unlike the market model, this alternative also accounts nicely for the timing of the Northeastern down-turn and, given the chastening political events of the Nixon years and the urban fiscal crisis, its recent turn-around.

In sum, the experience of the two groups of cities which have been subjected to comparative examination can be explained far more effectively by the alternative model proposed than by the orthodox market approach. Conceptually, the alternative model allows us to consider factors—such as the interrelationships among cities and the role of politics and the public sector—which a cost-of-production market model cannot easily handle. In place of the physiocratic assumptions of the market model, the alternative model makes it possible to see how the changing nature of the inter-city relationship, the shifting composition of the economy as a whole and the resulting tension in private sector/local public sector relationships influence the fate of each individual city. In this alternative model, economic growth in one city is not seen to be in economic conflict with another city. Rather, private sector elements in both cities can benefit from the *political* competition among cities to provide the most attractive environment for the private sector. In the final analysis, the political environment, rather than any specific input cost (be it land, labor or capital), casts the final determining ballot.

This alternative model satisfies the basic requirements of a good theory better than the market approach. It shows how outcomes derive from the choices made by higher level economic decision-makers in response to a variety of local conditions (and in turn it shows how local political choices are shaped and constrained by this competitive environment). The alternative approach accounts better not only for the observed aggregate changes but also for the movement of component parts (e.g., the decline of manufacturing compensated by rise of services required by a nodal network position and a world of "visible hands"). Finally, and most importantly, it accounts for timing and sequence more effectively than does the

market model. The long-term manufacturing decline, it has been
argued, was produced by decisionmakers' desire to avoid the political and social overhead costs generated by the "undigested"
experience of 19th century urban industrial conflict. They chose
the more favorable, more conservative political environments of
the Southwest in which to locate new industrial activities, while
simultaneously refashioning both the old and the new cities for
their post-industrial roles. In some places polictical conflict of substantial proportions arose in the 1960's to challenge these development plans. Subsequently, even post-industrial service employment
developments have been channeled away from such areas. In the
final analysis, the older, industrial, politically contested, non-nodal
cities (one thinks of Newark, Gary and similar places) have fared
the worst economically.

CONCLUSION

Where the cities have successfully followed the path towards the
post-industrial service economy—and cities like Boston, New York
and Philadelphia, as well as the Southwestern cities have apparently
done so—they have turned traditional notions of the "urban crisis"
upside-down. Because of the heavy professional component to the
emerging service sectors, middle class professional demand for urban
turf has increased dramatically. The central business districts of
Boston, New York, San Francisco and other "world cities" are
experiencing an unprecedented surge of high-rise office investment.
"Disinvestment," redlining, abandonment and similar standards
of the 1960's urban repertoire have become outmoded. (For one
thoughtful comment on this fact, see Allman, 1978.)
    These shifts in urban reality should cause us to reexamine some of
the basic distinctions which have governed our understanding of the
urban economy. Both the basic (export)/tertiary (domestic consumption) distribution and the productive/unproductive investment
distinction require major modification. Traditional thinking has
emphasized the importance of basic industry and productive investments and has tended to see services and service infrastructure as
"unproductive" activities. Yet these are the very things which
have spurred the growth of our cities—and in fact our whole economy.
Spending on schools, health care, higher education and the like have
come under increasing attack because they are thought to be "wasteful." Yet, upon examination , it appears they have provided the
basic economic infrastructure upon which the post-industrial service

city has been constructed. Reduced spending in such areas may have some nasty, and presently unanticipated, urban effects. Perhaps critics of institutions like the City University of New York ought to think twice.

Moreover, this analysis has suggested that the private sector has benefitted from an invidious political competition it has stimulated among public jurisdictions. The austerity measures taken in the Northeastern cities, as well as the sparsity of public services in the Southwestern cities, has been reinforced and disciplined by this competition. As a result, to use Senator Moynihan's words, "the ethic of collective provision" has been called into question (Moynihan, 1978). With the good Senator, we may question the wisdom of pulling the plug on the welfare state (particularly since the welfare state has provided the technical underpinnings of the emergent post-industrial service city.)

On the basis of the market model, some observers have advocated policies designed to "cut cities' losses" and "make them more competitive." Slashed service spending has been proposed as a means to this end, as have subsidies to capital investment. Ironically, the result has been to reward firms for doing what they would be doing anyway, while ignoring the damage which the growth of the middle class professional big city labor force is doing to inner city ethnic and minority workingpeople's neighborhoods. Indeed, if anything, the major cities have suffered from an excess of competitive success—in terms of trimming social spending, shifting decision initiative from the public to the private sector, displacing politically troublesome minority communities with middle class professionals and reshaping the metropolis in the image of the corporations.

To draw but the barest outline of the policy implications which follow from the alternative mode proposed, would imply finding a way to resolve the antagonism between post-industrial urbanism and democratic city politics. On the one hand, government (both federal and local) might as well facilitate further development within the high level services and headquarters economy now characterizing the major cities. But on the other hand, policy at all levels should do what it can to dampen the Gresham's Law effect local fragmentation and political competition have on the quality of the public sector. One of the main lessons to be had from this comparison of the Northeastern and Southwestern urban experiences is that growth is not an unalloyed good. The Southwest may be growing rapidly because the development process itself is feeding

110 CITY IN STRESS

on unequal stratification, a lack of accountability within local government and projects which maximize private gain without considering the social costs. (See Mollenkopf, 1977b, for a discussion of some of the severe problems which have stemmed from rapid and unplanned Southwestern urban growth.) Luckily, this is an issue which Southwesterners themselves have begun to address without waiting for advice from the policymakers.

The author thanks Tom Brose and other participants in the Conference on the Rise of the Southwest for help in thinking about these issues.

NOTES

1. In addition, an adequate conceptual model should have the following attributes: 1. It should isolate real trends and not artificial products of how boundary lines are drawn or categories defined. 2. It should account for sequence and timing of events. 3. It should show how outcomes result from real actors' choices. 4. It should predict the trajectories of the possibly conflicting components of change as well as their aggregate.

2. Even a comparison of the absolute numbers of jobs gained in the Southwest is impressive; these percentages are not merely an artifact of beginning from a small base.

3. Robert Goodman first suggested this idea to me, and talks with Paul Peterson have sharpened my thinking about it. Peterson has retooled Charles Tiebout's ideas about local governments as market competitors in the provision of public service packages into what he calls a "unitary" theory of local budgeting. See Peterson, 1978.

4. Other multilocational organizations are probably important too, but the modern business enterprise is probably the most significant.

5. The Northeast has many more public services, such as mass transit, than the Southwest. Are these attractive? And to whom? The November 19th, 1978 New York Times reports an amusing illustration of this question. According to the Times American Airlines President and former New York Emergency Financial Control Board member Albert Casey defended his corporations move to Dallas because it would get his workers out of New York traffic jams. Mayor Koch countered it would only put "four or five people at the top closer to their golf courses."

6. Between 1976 and 1972 this gap widens modestly. The Southwestern mean value added/wage dollar ratio rose 7.5%, the Northeastern figure 4.5%. Better Southwestern performance, however, must be interpreted as a result, rather than cause of the shifts taking place since 1960.

7. Usual federal and military, not local government, employment.

8. The market model also fails the basic tests outlined in the first note. It does not account for the sequence and timing of the downward inflection of northeastern growth nor the post World War II southwestern

rise. It is not convincing on actors' choices or the movement of component elements of aggregate changes.

9. Business is not the only network that matters, but it is probably the one that matters most.

10. No comprehensive statistics on municipal elections by party, much less by the candidate's ethnic background, appear to be reported on a systematic basis. The Joint Center for Political Studies, "National Roster of Black Elected Officials," reports a far lower incidence of black elected officials in Los Angeles, Dallas and Houston, where blacks are numerous. than in Northeastern cities like Newark and Detroit, where they are also numerous. Chicago and Boston, on the other hand, are notable holdouts against black electoral inroads. The Chicanos in the Southwest appear to be more completely excluded from local politics than are other ethnic groups, although La Raza Unida party has had some influence in rural parts of Texas and Colarado.

REFERENCES

Alcaly, R. and Mermelstein, D., (1977), The Fiscal Crisis of America's Cities, (New York: Vintage).

Allaman, P. and Birch D., (1975), "Components of Employment Change for Metropolitan and Rural Areas in the United States by Industry Group, 1970-1972 Working Paper No. 8" (Cambridge, Massachusetts: Joint Center for Urban Studies).

Allman, T.D., (1978), "The Urban Crisis Leaves Town" *Harper's* (December), pp. 41-56.

Arizona Republic and Phoenix Gazette, (1977), "Inside Phoenix 1977."

Barss, Reitzel and Associates, (1970), Community Action and Institutional Change (Warrenton, Virginia: Clearinghouse for Scientific and Technical Information).

Carlaw, C., (1976), "Boston and the Flight to the Sunbelt," Research Department, Boston Redevelopment Authority, October, 1976.

Chandler, Alfred D., (1977), The Visible Hand (Cambridge: Belknap Press of Harvard University Press).

Cohen, Robert, (1977), "Urban Effects of the Internationalization of Capital and Labor," unpublished paper, Conservation of Human Resources Program, Columbia University.

————, (1978), The Corporation and the City, unpublished manuscript, The Analytic Sciences Corporation, Arlington, Virginia.

Friedland, R., (1976), Class Power and the Central City, unpublished Ph. D. dissertation. Sociology Department, University of Wisconsin.

Goodall, L. ed., (1967), Urban Politics in the Southwest (Tempe: Arizona State University).

Gordon, D., (1978), "Capitalist Development and the History of American Cities," in L. Sawers and W. Tabb, eds., Marxism and the Megalopolis (New York: Oxford University Press).

Hymer. S., (1971), "The Multinational Corporation and the Law of Uneven Development," pp. 123-132 in J. Bhagvati, ed., Economics and World Order (New York: World Law Fund).

Investigative Reporters and Editors, Inc., (1977), Series of 22 news articles on Don Bolles murder case in Phoenix and related issues.

Jackson, J. and Soloman, A., (1977), "Urban and Regional Development: A Critical View of the Literature," (Joint Center for Urban Studies).

Lindblom, Charles, (1977), Politics and Markets (New York: Basic Books, Inc.).

Mollenkopf, J., (1975), "The Postwar Politics of Urban Development," Politics and Society 5:3.

————. (1977a), "The Fragile Giant: Crisis of the Public Sector in America's Cities," in R. Alcaly and D. Mermelstein (1977).

————. (1977b), The Rise of the Southwest: Problem and Promise, Round-table Conference on the Rise of the Southwest, Phoenix, Arizona.

Moynihan, D.P., (1978), "The Politics and Economics of Regional Growth," The Public Interest, Number 51, pp. 3-21.

Porter, Paul, (1977), Testimony given before the Subcommittee on the City of the Banking, Finance and Urban Affairs Committee of the House of Representatives, 95th Congress, 1st Session.

Pred, A., (1977), Advanced City Systems (New York: John Wiley and Sons).

Starr, Roger, (1977), "Making New York Smaller," The New York Times Magazine, (November 14th), pp. 32ff.

Sternlieb, G. and Hughes, J. eds., (1975), Post-Industrial America: Metropolitan Decline and Inter-Regional Job Shifts (New Brunswick: Center for Urban Policy Research).

Vaughan, Roger, (1977), The Urban Impacts of Federal Policies: Vol. 2, Economic Development. Rand Corporation document R-2028-KF/RC, June.

Watkins, A., (1977), "Job Mobility and the Mobility of Jobs," unpublished paper, Economics Department, New School for Social Research.

The First National Bank of Boston - Touche-Ross & Co. - URBAN FISCAL STRESS: A COMPARATIVE ANALYSIS

INTRODUCTION

In recent years, the fiscal condition of American cities—particularly older industrialized cities—has come under close scrutiny. This growing interest in the financial future of urban America appears to be a direct result of recent shifts in municipal finance:

- From 1960 to 1975, municipal expenditures have risen nearly 350 percent, while nominal Gross National Product rose by only 200 percent.
- Municipal debt outstanding tripled, from $23.2 billion in 1960 to $68.8 billion in 1975.
- Municipal government employment has increased by 49 percent from 1960 to 1975, from 1.7 million to 2.5 million.
- Federal aid to cities has grown from $592 million in 1960 to $10.9 billion in 1975, more than an 18-fold increase. Yet, city expenses have increased only 4.6 times. Moreover, cities throughout the country are demanding additional federal funds.

113

These national developments underscore the compelling need for a more accurate and complete picture of municipal finance.

This study was launched to provide new empirical insights into the financial performance of cities with widely differing economic, social and structural conditions. We reasoned that improving the ability to diagnose a municipality's fiscal condition would be important to policymakers at all levels of government. Mayors want to know where they stand and how much managerial "play in the line" there is in the financial structure of their particular cities. State governments, particularly those that have urban policies, want to develop means of measuring the relative fiscal strengths and weaknesses of their cities. And, there has been a renewed federal commitment to urban fiscal issues, as is evident in the Carter Administration's national urban policy, specifically the proposed Supplementary Fiscal Assistance Act.

Yet, there is a paradox about most of the discussions of municipal fiscal stress; namely, policymakers and researchers alike proceed on the assumption that they can detect stress and determine its relative severity by reference to *socio-economic* indicators (e.g., unemployment rate, age of housing stock, etc.). There appear to be two interrelated reasons why socio-economic variables are used to measure the fiscal condition of cities. First, it is assumed that socio-economic conditions cause fiscal conditions; second, it is assumed that socio-economic variables are accurate indicators of financial viability.

These assumptions seem to have a common sense foundation. After all, no city can escape the reality of its socio-economic conditions. Yet, the assumptions are certainly not a self-evident proposition. Many factors can influence the fiscal performance of cities. The level of federal and state aid as well as state assumption of services can affect a city's financial performance. Moreover, management practices vary widely among cities, as does the municipal commitment to particular levels of service delivery. A rich man can spend himself into insolvency, while the frugal clerk succeeds in making ends meet. Might not the same be true for cities? The findings derived from the Sixty-Six Cities Study—described in the following section—provide new insight into this question.

PRINCIPAL CONCLUSIONS SUMMARIZED

Our analysis revealed seven principal findings that are briefly described below:

Older, industrially aged cities are the ones most likely to have high tax, debt and expense rations and to be fiscally stressed. Cities undergo a basic process of industrial aging. Each phase of this process is marked by changes in economic, social and structural conditions which have a significant impact on municipal financial performance.

Yet some older industrialized cities do not show signs of fiscal strain, while some younger, more rapidly growing cities do. In short, although fiscal strain generally accompanies industrial aging, this is not always the case.

Fiscal stress in not inevitable. Achieving a financial equilibrium between the demand for public services and financial resources appears to be within the grasp of management control of most cities. Out of the sixty-six cities subjected to detailed comparative analysis, only four appear to have pushed their tax, debt and expense rates close to or beyond sustainable limits.

Municipal fiscal stress cannot be described on the basis of economic, social and structural conditions alone. Socio-economic indicators are not valid proxies for the financial performance of cities. Measurement of a city's fiscal performance must include financial indicators.

Combined federal and state grant-in-aid programs are more responsive to the social and structural problems than to the economic and financial problems of cities. However, the results of this study show that fiscal stress appears to result more from economic problems than from social or structural problems.

Industrially mature cities are less effective in leveraging their municipal capital spending in ways to encourage private capital investment. For cities in their early growth stages, municipal capital spending levels are accompanied by increases in private manufacturing capital spending. Yet for older industrialized cities, municipal capital spending rises rapidly and then remains high, despite a fall-off in private capital spending.

Current municipal data collection and financial reporting systems are generally inadequate to understand and effectively manage city operations. Variations in municipal accounting practices produce inconsistencies and data gaps as financial performance data are analyzed across cities.

UNDERTAKING THE ANALYSIS OF
MUNICIPAL FINANCIAL PERFORMANCE

The interaction between social/structural forces and municipal financial performance is crucial to defining and measuring municipal fiscal stress. This definition depends on the ability to isolate the impacts of these forces on municipal financial performance. A brief comment on each of these economic, social and structural forces will be helpful in building a foundation for the subsequent analyses.

Economic conditions describe the resource base in a municipality. These conditions reflect a broad range of exogenous forces, especially manufacturing investment and private sector construction.[1] Other factors include income level and distribution, the occupational structure of the labor market, and the size and age of the resident population.

Private sector capital spending is the driving force that produces economic growth. Whenever a city is young, growing rapidly, creating substantial new jobs, and income is rising, expanding private investments will be evident. Conversely, when industrial maturity is reached, private sector capital formation will slow down. Economic conditions—especially investment—have the most signficant impact on a city's financial performance inasmuch as they determine the city's level of resource capability for providing public services. Yet, economic conditions cannot be judged alone because they are influenced by social and structural conditions.

Social conditions describe the consequences of economic growth. For example, rapid private sector investment in manufacturing may induce a lower unemployment rate and the reduction of poverty among those who were previously unemployed. The condition of a municipality's housing stock, as well as the relative share of minority residents, also describe or reflect the municipality's social conditions. Yet, social conditions also include a wide range of circumstances that are distinct from economic conditions and in themselves can induce change. For example, the deterioration of the housing stock will lead to demands for increased municipal fire expenditures and increases in unemployment put pressure on the city to provide social services. Changes in social conditions can force changes in the level and mix of public services.

Structural conditions describe those factors that define the taxing and spending parameters for a city, as well as its relationship to contiguous cities and higher levels of government. These factors include the number of square miles in the city, annexation constraints and population density. Structural factors are vitally important because the spatial dimensions of economic activity (especially investment) often overlap or fall outside of a municipality's jurisdictional boundaries. Furthermore, investment shifts from one city to another can produce dramatic changes in a municipality's tax base.

Economic, social and structural factors, as described above, have major impacts on municipal resources and the demands on these factors. The variables reflecting these three conditions that were used in this analysis are listed below:

Economic Conditions (Variables)
   Change in population
   Percent change in single-family housing starts
   Manufacturing capital spending
   Change in manufacturing employment ratio
   Percent change in manufacturing capital spending
   Median family income

Social Conditions (Variables)
   Percent minority population
   Percent families below low-income level
   Unemployment rate
   Percent pre-1939 housing stock

Structural Conditions (Variables)
   Population density[2]

The sixty-six cities were classified statiscally into four clusters based on the six economic variables: the resulting four clusters were:

   High investment and income cities
   Above-average investment and income cities
   Average investment and income cities
   Below-average investment and income cities

Then, each of these four clusters was divided between high-low socially-dependent populations as well as between high-low structural characteristics. The resulting framework contained sixteen clusters of cities that represented homogeneous economic, social and structural conditions.

To choose the financial variables, the research team studied more than 100 financial data items. Through various statistical techniques,

EXHIBIT 1

The Short List of Municipal Financial Performance Variables

Financial variables	Mean value	Standard deviation	Lowest value	Highest value
Revenue:				
Ratio of local taxes to personal income (tax effort)	5.65%	2.26%	1.92%	13.42%
Local taxes per capita	$25.02	$106.41	$98.76	$556.36
Intergovernmental revenue as a percent of total local revenue	34.60%	12.24%	5.02%	64.00%
Debt:				
Total debt per capita	$516.86	$268.59	$121.66	$1,193.84
Interest per capita	$23.19	$14.30	$5.32	$89.69
Municipal capital spending per capita, five-year average, 1971-75	$82.73	$48.47	$20.55	$223.25
Expenses:				
Fire expenses per capita	$29.55	$10.32	$9.48	$56.42
Education expenses per capita (total from all sources)	$236.94	$60.24	$120.45	$395.08
Health expenses per capita (total from all sources)	$7.56	$9.07	$0.00*	$47.11
Welfare expenses per capita (total from all sources)	$5.52	$14.81	$0.00*	$92.22
Ratio of city full-time equivalent employment to total local employment	3.98%	2.23%	0.95%	10.58%
Average city employee annual income	$7,746	$1,606	$4,158	$12,319
Current operating expenses per capita	$484.61	$120.27	$270.40	$928.36

* A zero value for health and welfare means that the entire process of these programs are borne by other levels of government.

thirteen of the 100 were selected as the basis for the study. Throughout this analysis, these thirteen variables are called the Short List of Municipal Financial Performance Variables (or the Short List of Financial Variables), indicating that they provide substantive insight into the larger set of data from which they were drawn. Unless otherwise noted, all financial data used in the study are for 1975.[3] The financial variables are listed in Exhibit 1, along with the standard deviation, highest, lowest and average values for each.

Data on these economic, social, structural and financial variables were collected and analyzed for sixty-six medium-to-large cities across the country. All cities with populations over 1,000,000 were excluded from the analysis to avoid distorting the results of the study. It is generally recognized that very large cities possess economic, social and structural conditions that make them unique, thus making comparative analyses with medium-sized cities difficult.

The sixty-six cities analyzed in the study are listed in Exhibit 2.

EXHIBIT 2

The Sixty-Six Cities

1. Mobile AL	34. Boston MA
2. Montgomery AL	35. Cambridge MA
3. Phoenix AZ	36. Springfield MA
4. Tempe AZ	37. Worcester MA
5. Tucson AZ	38. Grand Rapids MI
6. Little Rock AR	39. Bloomington MN
7. Daly City CA	40. Duluth MN
8. Fresno CA	41. Minneapolis MN
9. Long Beach CA	42. Rochester MN
10. Pasadena CA	43. Jackson MS
11. Denver CO	44. Kansas City MO
12. Pueblo CO	45. Lincoln NB
13. Bridgeport CT	46. Omaha NB
14. Hartford CT	47. Trenton NJ
15. New Haven CT	48. Albuquerque NM
16. Stamford CT	49. Buffalo NY
17. Hollywood FL	50. Syracuse NY
18. Jacksonville FL	51. Dayton OH
19. St. Petersburg FL	52. Eugene OR
20. Tampa FL	53. Pittsburgh PA
21. West Palm Beach FL	54. Amarillo TX
22. Atlanta GA	55. Austin TX
23. Savannah GA	56. Fort Worth TX
24. Decatur IL	57. Galveston TX
25. Evanston IL	58. Irving TX

26. Indianapolis IN	59. Port Arthur TX
27. Topeka KS	60. San Angelo TX
28. Wichita KS	61. Salt Lake City UT
29. Louisville KY	62. Richmond VA
30. Baton Rouge LA	63. Seattle WA
31. New Orleans LA	64. Spokane WA
32. Greensboro NC	65. Madison WI
33. Baltimore MD	66. Milwaukee WI

These cities may be characterized briefly as follows. The median population size was approximately 250,000. The largest city analyzed was Baltimore (population 905.8 thousand) while the smallest was Rochester, Minnesota (population 53.8 thousand). The geographical distribution is shown below.

Region	Number of cities in sample
Northeast	12
Midwest	11
South	18
High Plains	5
Southwest	8
West	12
Total	66

Within each of the sixteen clusters, the mean values were calculated for the Short List of Municipal Financial Performance Variables. These data were the basis for analyzing the linkages between various sets of municipal economic, social and structural conditions and financial performance.

The following section summarizes the basis for each of the conclusions.

THE PRINCIPAL CONCLUSIONS IN DETAIL

Older, Industrially Aged Cities are the Ones Most Likely to Have High Tax, Debt and Expense Ratios and to be Fiscally Stressed. As a city passes through its various stages of development, there are important impacts on municipal financial performance. Private sector capital spending—especially in the manufacturing sector—follows a clear pattern. Cities in their early growth stages generally have rapid and extensive private sector investment as well as substantial population growth. As cities pass into the stage of industrial maturity, there is a fall-off in investment and, in turn, a sustained loss of manufacturing employment.

There is a strong correspondence, but not a precise fit, between the four economic clusters and the stages of industrial development. Several factors account for the differences. Those cities just beginning to generate significant levels of private investment and those experiencing declining investment may both have, for a period of time, relatively similar investment levels. Also, a city can "buck" the economic aging process to some extent through successful renewal strategies. In such a case, the city would have been placed in a more favorable investment and income cluster than its stage of growth would warrant. Conversely, an industrially young city may have adopted policies which discourage private sector investment, thus placing it in a lower investment cluster.

The concept of industrial aging was integrated into the methodology of the study by grouping the cities according to two key factors in the aging process—population decline and manufacturing employment decline.

Old Industrialized—Cities in which manufacturing employment has declined in two consecutive periods—1954-67 and 1967-72—in which the rate of decline in manufacturing employment accelerated in the second period, and population declined in two periods—1950-60 and 1960-70. The following nine cities were classified in this category:

Bridgeport	Baltimore	Worcester
Hartford	Boston	Trenton
New Haven	Cambridge	Buffalo

Industrially Maturing—Cities in which manufacturing employment declined in the first and second periods or the second alone; population declined in the period 1960-1970. There was no acceleration in the rate of decline in manufacturing employment. The following thirteen cities were determined to be in this category:

Dayton	Mobile
Pittsburgh	Pasadena
Seattle	Louisville
Spokane	New Orleans
Milwaukee	Springfield
Minneapolis	Duluth
Syracuse	

Young Industrial Growth—Cities in which both manufacturing employment and population were expanding in both of the periods analyzed (forty-four cities).

Our analysis of the impact of industrial aging on municipal financial performance indicate that as cities age industrially:

- Taxes rise.
- Current operating expenses rise.
- The municipal work force increases rapidly.

These conclusions are evident from the municipal financial data shown in Exhibit 3.

Note specifically the increases in tax effort (the ratio of taxes to personal income), taxes per capita and current operating expenses from young to old industrial cities. The decline in the ratio of expenses to taxes is the result of the much faster rise in taxes vis-a-vis expenses: as cities age, the percent of their total revenue from state and federal sources tends to stabilize. As a result, local taxes must increase at a faster rate to cover rising costs. Finally, the sharp rise in the municipal work force is obvious—in the case of old industrialized cities it is more than twice as high as in the young cities.

Cities in the advanced stages of industrial aging are concentrated in the northeastern states. The explanation for this finding is straightforward: the Industrial Revolution started first in the Northeast. Counter-intuitive is that high debt ratios are not limited to northeastern cities; some southern cities also have high debt rates.[4]

Exhibit 4 shows that cities with high cost and tax rates are more prevalent in the Northeast, followed by the Midwest and the West. This reflects the geographic distribution of the cities that are economically the oldest. The tabulation also shows the high level of debt financing by cities in the South and Northeast.

Interpretation of the regional distribution for taxes, debt and expenses shown in the preceeding exhibit requires a brief explanation. Eight percent of the cities in the sample, without respect to regional location, have tax ratios that are 85 percent or more of the highest tax ratio for the sixty-six cities. Yet, among northeastern cities, 42 percent of them fall into the 85 percent or more category, while none does for the remaining five regions. Note the higher average debt ratios for the northeast and southern cities. Moreover, the

EXHIBIT 3

Industrial Aging and Municipal Financial Performance

Stages of industrialization	Ratio of local taxes to personal income	Local taxes per capita	Current operating expenses per capita	Intergovern-mental revenue as a percent of total local revenue	Ratio of city full-time equivalent employment to total local employment	Ratio of current operating expenses per capita to local taxes per capita
Old industrialized (9 cities)	9.50%	$407.26	$603.86	37.99%	8.01%	1.482
Industrially maturing (13 cities)	5.51	254.44	517.73	40.66	4.25	2.035
Young, early phases of industrial growth (44 cities)	4.90	239.20	450.50	32.10	3.07	1.883
Total sample mean (66 cities)	5.65%	$265.02	$484.61	34.60%	3.98%	1.829

EXHIBIT 4

Regional Frequency Distributions for Tax, Debt and
Expenses Expressed As A Percent of Maximum
Value for Sixty-Six Cities*

Percentage distribution	Total sample	Northeast	Midwest	South	High Plains	Southwest	West
For local taxes per capita:							
Less than 25%	11%	–	9%	12%	40%	18%	–
26-50%	52	25%	36	71	40	82	40%
51-75%	27	33	45	18	20	–	50
76-85%	3	–	9	–	–	–	10
More than 85%	8	42	–	–	–	–	–
For total debt per capita:							
Less than 25%	20%	8%	18%	18%	–	27%	40%
26-50%	55	50	55	59	60	55	50
51-75%	12	17	18	6	40	9	–
76-85%	3	8	–	–	–	9	–
More than 85%	11	17	9	18	–	–	10
For current operating expenses per capita:							
Less than 25%	–	–	–	–	–	–	–
26-50%	42%	8%	18%	47%	80%	82%	40%
51-75%	52	83	82	53	20	18	60
76-85%	5	8	–	–	–	–	–
More than 85%	2	–	–	–	–	–	–

*Total may not add to 100% due to rounding.

frequency distribution for northeastern cities in terms of their current operating ratios stands in sharp contrast to the ratios of cities in other regions.

Yet Some Older Industrialized Cities Do Not Show Signs of Fiscal Strain While Some Younger, More Rapidly Growing Cities Do

Some old industrialized cities have "bucked the trend" of high per capita taxes, debt and expenditures that are strongly associated with industrial aging. Conversely, young cities do not necessarily avoid high per capita taxes, debt and expenditures. Several young cities studied have financial patterns that are typical of old industrialized cities. These appear to be "younger variants" of their older counterparts.

Exhibit 5 illustrates the fiscal situation for two cities of each type drawn from the data base. There are other cities that may be classified in either of these two categories, but the financial data for these four illustrate this finding. Pittsburgh and Trenton can be characterized as "trend buckers," while Atlanta and Denver are "younger variants." (The means for each city's economic cluster are also shown in parentheses below the financial performance variables.)

Note that, although Pittsburgh and Trenton are industrially maturing and old industrialized cities, their tax, debt and expenses have been managed or controlled and are either below the total sample mean or are very close to it. Moreover, their tax, debt and operating expense rates are consistently below the means for their economic clusters. This is especially significant because methodologically the clusters group cities with similar underlying economic capacity.[5] That Trenton and Pittsburgh are well below their respective means certainly suggests that—relative to other cities with roughly comparable economic resources—their municipal fincancial performance has been well controlled. Conversely, the figures for Denver and Atlanta are well above the means of their economic cluster, showing that their financial commitments have exceeded those of cities with similar economic capacity.

Thus, contrary to much contemporary thinking, cities can maintain a fundamental equilibrium between economic resources and financial performance—as have Pittsburgh and Trenton—even as they reach the advanced stage of industrial aging. On the other hand, Atlanta and Denver offer insight into industrially younger cities whose financial

EXHIBIT 5

"Trend Buckers and Younger Variants" Among the Sixty-Six Cities

Financial variable	CITY				For total sixty-six cities sample	
	"Trend buckers"		"Younger variants"		Sample mean	Sample standard deviation
	Pittsburgh	Trenton	Atlanta	Denver		
Local taxes per capita	$227.07 (327.95)	$333.64 (360.00)	$ 334.19 (218.73)	$442.14 (283.44)	$265.02	$106.41
Total debt per capita	502.79 (515.95)	283.07 (661.59)	1,072.52 (504.01)	595.13 (430.78)	516.86	268.59
Current operating expenses per capita	438.86 (551.66)	530.31 (618.21)	659.94 (469.79)	615.16 (483.72)	484.61	120.27

spending has grown more rapidly than their economic base, thus pushing their tax, debt and expense ratios more in line with those of older cities. Note especially Denver's high tax ratio, Atlanta's high debt ratio, and the high operating expenses for both cities.

FISCAL STRESS IS NOT INEVITABLE

As the preceeding conclusions indicate, there are some cities that do not fit the expected patterns. Some mature cities have low tax, debt and expense ratios while some younger ones have high ratios. The analysis suggests that the management and political decisionmaking process can hold the growth of services in balance with underlying economic resources to maintain financial equilibrium, even under adverse economic, social and structural conditions. Moreover, no city with high expense rates *per se* should be considered stressed, if it has the underlying economic capacity to fund high rates of spending. In other words, the concept of fiscal stress must take into account the underlying resources—the capacity to support tax, debt or spending.

The cities in each of the sixteen clusters are confronted with very similar external forces. Thus, it was possible to identify cities whose financial response deviated from that of cities with comparable economic capacities. On the other hand, lower-than-expected municipal financial performance could indicate underutilized resource capacity.[6]

To develop a more complete understanding of the linkage between resource capacity and spending rates as well as to refine the concept of stress, all cities which had tax, debt, or expense rates greater than one standard deviation from the cluster means were analyzed further. These are shown in Exhibit 6.

A number of generalizations may be made about the cities classified as outliers in this exhibit:

> Only four cities out of the sixty-six—Stamford, Boston, Hartford and Atlanta—fall outside one standard deviation in terms of their tax, debt and expense ratios within their economic clusters. Eight additional cities—Denver, Bloomington, Seattle, Worcester, Duluth, Long Beach, Richmond and Fresno—are outside one standard deviation in two of the three key financial performance measures. Relative to other cities in their clusters, the tax, debt and expense rates of these cities are high, which suggests that they are near or beyond their underlying resource capacity.

EXHIBIT 6

Fiscal Stress: Cities With Taxing, Debt and Spending Rates Greater Than One Standard Deviation From the Means of Their Economic Clusters

Cluster	Number of cities in cluster	Cities with tax performance greater than one standard deviation above cluster mean	Cities with debt performance greater than one standard deviation above cluster mean	Cities with expense performance greater than one standard deviation above cluster mean
High private investment and income:				
Large dependent population	2		(Insufficient data in cluster)	
Small dependent population	7	Denver	Bloomington Baton Rouge	Denver
High population density	3		(Insufficient data in cluster)	
Low population density	6	Bloomington	Baton Rouge	Bloomington
Above-average private investment and income:				
Large dependent population	6	Evanston Stamford	Kansas City Stamford	None
Small dependent population	6	Stamford	Stamford	Stamford
High population density	6	Evanston Stamford	Seattle Stamford	Seattle
Low population density	6	Stamford	Stamford	Stamford

EXHIBIT 6

Fiscal Stress: Cities With Taxing, Debt and Spending Rates Greater Than One Standard Deviation From the Means of Their Economic Clusters

Average private investment and income:

Large dependent population	13	Boston	Louisville Boston	Pasadena Dayton Boston Duluth Worcester Minneapolis
Small dependent population	13	Cambridge Worcester	Eugene Witchita	
High population density	11	Cambridge Boston	Louisville Minneapolis Boston	Pasadena Dayton Boston Duluth Worcester
Low population density	15	Worcester	Eugene Duluth Wichita	

Below-average private investment and income:

Large dependent population	14	New Haven Hartford Richmond	Hartford Richmond Atlanta	Hartford
Small dependent population	5	Long Beach Hartford	None	Long Beach Hartford Fresno Tampa Atlanta
High population density	5	Fresno Richmond Atlanta		
Low population density	14		Hartford Richmond Atlanta	

The twelve cities are scattered throughout the extreme variations in good and bad economic, social and structural clusters. For the three old industrialized cities—Hartford, Boston and Worcester—this may well imply fiscal stress. Two industrially maturing cities, Duluth and Seattle, are also out of line with their economically grouped city counterparts. The remaining seven cities were classified as young growth in terms of their age of industrialization and provide additional insight into the issue of "younger variants." Yet these high expenses, taxes and debt may not be necessarily a sign of imminent stress in these cities because of their stronger economic base.

Importantly, fifty-four cities—the vast majority—appear to have maintained their tax, debt and expense ratios in line with underlying resource capacity. At the least, it may be argued that their tax, debt and expense rates are relatively close to the individual cluster means. This indicates a generally consistent response to the homogeneous/exogeneous economic, social and structural forces.

Finally, the geographical mix of the stressed cities is shown below:

EXHIBIT 7

Geographical Mix of Fiscally Stressed Cities

Region	Number of cities with 2 or 3 ratios in excess of one standard deviation	Total sample
Northeast	4	12
South	2	18
Southwest	–	8
Midwest	2	11
High Plains	–	5
West	4	12
Total	12	66

The high incidence of northeastern cities was expected. The western and southern cities may well be the "younger variants" of their northeastern counterparts. As stated in an earlier finding, this suggests that these cities may respond in a financial manner characteristic of industrially mature cities, although they have not yet reached that stage of economic development.

MUNICIPAL FISCAL STRESS CANNOT BE DESCRIBED ON THE
BASIS OF ECONOMIC, SOCIAL AND STRUCTURAL CONDITIONS
ALONE

Social, economic and structural variables have been often used to
indicate the fiscal condition of cities. In contrast, this study shows
socio-economic conditions are not necessarily valid proxies for the
financial performance of cities. To describe fiscal condition indirectly, solely on the basis of social, economic and structural variables,
could result in classifying some cities as fiscally stressed when, in fact,
they are not.

To demonstrate this, Exhibit 8 shows six cities that are classified
as fiscally stressed or troubled in six widely used studies that purport to statistically measure municipal stress, along with their comparative rankings. The lower the ranking the greater the degree of
fiscal stress.

The sixty-six cities in our study are not classified in terms of best-to-
worst financial performance. It was felt that comparative municipal
financial performance should be undertaken with reference to a
number of financial performance indicators rather than a single index
number. The thirteen variables in the Short List of Municipal Financial Performance Variables capture a large amount of financial variables across cities. Additional statistical refinement can be achieved
by adding other variables in specific areas.

The relevant financial data from this study for these six cities are
shown in Exhibit 9. Comparison of the various rankings of these six
cities shows widely different results; when ranked according to various socio-economic criteria, some cities are classified as stressed. Yet
these same cities ranked according to financial criteria alone may not
show fiscal stress.

- Note that the tax per capita ratio for five of these cities is below
  the average of the total sample, and the tax ratio for the remaining city lies well inside one standard deviation from the sample
  mean.
- Clearly, there is greater variance in the debt ratios as only three
  cities fall below the sample mean. But again, note that all of
  the remaining debt ratios are roughly equal to or below one
  standard deviation.
- Four of the six cities have total operating ratios roughly equal
  to or below the sample mean, and the remaining two cities fall
  well within one standard deviation.

EXHIBIT 8

Comparative Ranking of Cities
(according to Recent Studies)

City	U.S. Treasury[1]	Brookings Institution Urban conditions[2]	Brookings Institution Hardship index[3]	Clark study[4]	National Planning Association study[5]	Urban Institute study[6]
Buffalo	3	3	9	5	9	14
Fort Worth	17	NA	19	20	37	NA
Indianapolis	24	NA	23	NA	14	NA
Pittsburgh	26	6	15	16	8	13
Baltimore	32	9	6	NA	5	18
Jacksonville	43	NA	NA	8	20	NA
Total cities analyzed	48	489	550	54	40	153

NA = Not analyzed in this investigation.

[1] U.S. Department of Treasury, "Report on the Fiscal Impact of the Economic Stimulus Package on Forty-Eight Large Governments." January 23, 1978, Washington, D.C.

[2] Richard Nathan, "Decentralizing Community Development," Report to the Department of Housing and Urban Development, January 1978, Brookings Institution, Washington, D.C.

[3] Richard Nathan, Charles Adams, "Understanding Central City Hardship," *Political Science Quarterly*, Volume 91, Number 1, Spring 1976, pp. 47-62, Washington, D.C.

[4] Terry Clark, et al. "How Many New Yorks—New York Fiscal Crisis in Comparative Perspective," University of Chicago, July 5, 1976, Chicago.

[5] John Craig and Michael Kolleda, "Outlook for the Municipal Hospital in Major American Cities," National Planning Association, April 1976, Washington, D.C.

[6] Harvey A. Garn, Thomas Muller, et al. "A Framework for National Urban Policy," The Urban Institute, December 15, 1977, Washington, D.C.

Although not shown in the exhibit, it is important also to point out that the tax, debt and operating expense rates for these six cities are well within one standard deviation of the means for each of their respective economic clusters. This is especially relevant because the economic clusters have been designed to capture homogeneous exogenous forces that impact on the cities.

EXHIBIT 9

Key Financial Performance Data For Cities Classified as
"Fiscally Stressed" on the Basis of Socio-Economic Variables

City	Local taxes per capita	Total debt per capita	Current operating expenses per capita
Buffalo	$234.27	$707.56	$595.22
Fort Worth	204.81	474.75	382.87
Indianapolis	197.92	396.99	348.97
Pittsburgh	227.07	502.79	483.86
Baltimore	312.65	553.50	514.18
Jacksonville	164.90	554.41	489.61
Total sample mean	$265.02	$516.86	$484.61
Total standard deviation	$106.41	$268.59	$120.27

The financial performance measures for Forth Worth, Indianapolis, Pittsburgh and Jacksonville do not indicate that these cities are "fiscally stressed" when compared to the average performance of the sixty-six cities. Buffalo and Baltimore present a less clear and convincing picture. Buffalo may have higher-than-average debt and operating expense ratios, but certainly not higher tax rates. This may, in part, be explained by Buffalo's very high rate of intergovernmental transfers. Expenses are high in Baltimore, but this by no means leads one to conclude that Baltimore is fiscally stressed.

This does not mean that socio-economic factors are unimportant. To the contrary, the indicators used in these studies are excellent measures of socio-economic problems which unquestionably affect a city's financial performance. However, the focus of new research is shifting to include municipal fiscal conditions. Therefore, to measure fiscal conditions, financial measures are needed.

COMBINED FEDERAL AND STATE GRANT-IN-AID PROGRAMS ARE MORE RESPONSIVE TO THE SOCIAL AND STRUCTURAL PROBLEMS THAN TO THE ECONOMIC AND FINANCIAL PROBLEMS OF CITIES

While the federal and state grant-in-aid system is responsive to social and structural needs, it frequently fails to target funds to cities with

the greatest economic and financial problems. Generally, large intergovernmental transfer payments go to those cities with adverse social
and structural conditions. In contrast, the percent of transfer payments may, under some conditions, be less to cities with below-
average investments vis-a-vis those with high investments. These
points emerged from the analysis of patterns in intergovernmental
aid across the four principal economic clusters as social conditions
shift from small-to-large dependent population rates and as population densities shift from low-to-high. This shows what happened
to intergovernmental aid under different economic, social and
structural conditions.

In principle, intergovernmental transfers[7] are designed to reduce
income disparities and alleviate social problems across cities with
widely differing conditions (equalization). Historically, these transfers have been largely targeted to improve educational, housing,
health, welfare and other social functions. Among the more than
500 Federal grant-in-aid programs, few are directed specifically at
stimulating economic growth. Thus, while there has been an increasing need for fiscal and economic assistance, this has not yet
been reflected in the transfer allocations. The relevant data for
intergovernmental revenue are contained in the exhibit below:

EXHIBIT 10

Intergovernmental Revenue as a Percent
Of Total Revenue

Social/structural conditions	High investment and income cluster cities	Below-average investment and income cluster cities	Percent swing between economic clusters
Small social dependent population	30.2%	33.3%	+10.3%
Large social dependent population	43.0	37.5	−12.8
Low population density	30.4	35.9	+18.1
High population density	38.3	37.6	− 1.8
Percent swing as social/density conditions worsen:			
Small to large social dependent population	+42.4%	+12.6%	
Low to high population density	+26.0	+ 4.7	

The statistical swing data[8] above show the sensitivity of these income transfers, as economic conditions change across the clusters (social and structural conditions held constant) or as social and structural conditions change (economic conditions held constant). As economic conditions worsen among large social dependent population and high population density cities, the percent of intergovernmental transfer income actually declines somewhat, in contrast to what may be expected. At the same time, among the low service-dependent population and low population density cities these transfers increase somewhat as economic conditions deteriorate. The swings in the large social dependent and high population density cities as economic conditions deteriorate are counter intuitive.

Furthermore, the biggest differences in transfer payments are associated with unfavorable social and structural problems rather than adverse economic conditions. Note that the best economic cities with a large social dependent population get more federal and state funds than cities with poor economies but a relatively small social dependent population. The economically well-off cities with large social problems receive the highest percentage of transfers for the sample. This suggests that cities qualify incrementally for more federal and state funds as social problems become more pronounced, irrespective of their economic conditions.

On the basis of this analysis, the intergovernmental transfer system seems to be somewhat more responsive to unfavorable social and structural conditions than to adverse economic conditions. Increasingly, however, national attention is being focused on municipal stability. Therefore, federal and state officials should be aware that past funding patterns may not alleviate severe fiscal difficulties in cities with a large service-dependent population that experience an economic downturn.

Specifically, the economically troubled city is pressed simultaneously on two fronts: no increase in intergovernmental transfers and, as was described in the first conclusion, a rapid rise in expenses. As intergovernmental fund percentages level off, taxes are driven upward.

Additional support for this finding is the performance of intergovernmental transfers across the twenty-six cities in the average investment and income economic cluster. This cluster is especially interesting because it includes cities in the old industrialized stage of development (five cities), cities in the industrially maturing stage (seven cities), and cities in the young, early phases of their industrialization (fourteen cities). Aside from Baltimore, the remainder of the old industrialized cities in this cluster are receiving a smaller percentage of transfer payments than the industrially maturing cities.

This finding needs additional investigation—specifically on a program-by-program basis—but it is clear that while industrial aging and higher taxes and expenses go together, intergovernmental transfers and industrial aging may not. This relationship is interesting inasmuch as there is a strong need among the old industrialized cities both to keep taxes within manageable levels and to encourage private sector investment.

INDUSTRIALLY MATURE CITIES ARE LESS EFFECTIVE IN LEVERAGING THEIR MUNICIPAL CAPITAL SPENDING IN WAYS TO ENCOURAGE PRIVATE CAPITAL INVESTMENT

The first two conclusions addressed the impact of industrial aging on municipal financial performance. There are also special effects on municipal capital spending for infrastructure and private invest-ment. As cities age industrially, they are less likely to leverage their municipal capital spending in ways to encourage private capital investment. Moreover, the slowdown in the growth of the city's economic base occurs at the same time as the demand for services rises—just when the city can least afford to have its resources stagnate or decline.

The relevant ratios shown in Exhibit 11 tell an important story about industrial aging and municipal financial performance: Reading the data from the bottom, the age of industrialization shifts from the youngest to the oldest. The higher the number in the last column, the greater the leveraging ratio and, presumably, the better off is the city. The municipal ratio is included because of its relationship to municipal capital spending.

Two important conclusions are supported by these figures:
- Municipal debt and capital spending rise, albeit irregularly, as industrial aging takes place. Older cities have higher ratios of capital spending to-debt than younger cities.
- Private sector manufacturing spending peaks in the young stage of industrial aging and then falls off abruptly. This means that younger, faster growth cities "leverage" their municipal capital spending in ways to encourage private capital investment.

EXHIBIT 11

Industrial Aging and Municipal/Private Capital Spending

Economic cluster	Stage of industrialization	Total debt per capita	Municipal capital spending per capita, five-year average, 1971-75	Private manufacturing capital spending per capita, 1972	Ratio of municipal capital spending to municipal debt	Ratio of private to municipal capital spending
Below-average investment/income	Old industrialized	$783.03	$133.39	$ 77.54	.170	.581
Average investment/income	Old industrialized	523.08	143.75	111.88	.275	.778
Average investment/income	Industrially maturing	527.84	91.07	112.08	.172	1.231
Average investment/income	Young industrial growth	437.23	58.67	117.69	.134	2.001
Below average investment/income	Young industrial growth	514.51	80.10	96.04	.156	1.199
Mean of sixty-six cities	—	$516.86	$ 82.73	$106.64	.160	1.289

This flattening in manufacturing capital spending is the result of—and may also contribute to—the disappearance of a cost-effective investment environment in the city vis-a-vis alternative suburban and other regional sites.

CURRENT MUNICIPAL DATA COLLECTION AND FINANCIAL REPORTING SYSTEMS ARE GENERALLY INADEQUATE TO UNDERSTAND AND EFFECTIVELY MANAGE CITY OPERATIONS

The pervasiveness of the municipal data problem is shown by the fact that half the cities originally intended to be studied had to be excluded altogether because too much data were missing. Originally, 120 cities were to be studied. For the cities that were included a generally reliable data base was established. Yet even for these cities, there were problems. A major problem was inconsistency of data: for example, expenses are defined in widely differing ways from one city to another. Other problems included insufficient detail and, once again, lack of the desired information. Specific problems included:

- Lack of information on pension fund liabilities.
- Lack of breakdown by source for taxes. Therefore, for example, the residential versus corporate tax burden could not be evaluated.
- Difficulty in matching capital expenditure items with their revenue source and, conversely, matching long-term debt with the proper expenditure item. Hence, it was virtually impossible to determine what portions of capital expenditures were being financed by current revenue or to evaluate the uses of debt.
- Inability to determine uses of short-term debt, i.e., tax anticipation notes versus bond anticipation notes.
- Inability to determine market value of taxable property. These figures, even when available, are typically understated because industrial property changes hands infrequently.
- Lack of information on the condition of long-term assests.

Some of this information could have been gathered from extensive interviews with city officials. However, this kind of effort was beyond the scope of this project. Importantly, it is also beyond the effort that could be expected by investors or officials on other levels of government.

IMPLICATIONS

What do these conclusions mean? How can they be used by policymakers and researchers? We believe that this study is relevant both to all levels of government and to the private sector.

AT THE FEDERAL LEVEL

These conclusions suggest that if federal policymakers want to aid cities that are now financially troubled and to help prevent fiscal stress in the future, changes in funding patterns and allocation criteria may be most productive.

Federal Aid Designed to Combat Fiscal Stress Should be Distributed on the Basis of Criteria Weighted Strongly Toward Municipal Financial Condition. This study shows clearly that nonfinancial variables do not accurately describe the financial condition of a city. Using financial criteria in the funding formulas is needed to assure that aid to relieve fiscal stress reaches cities that are, in fact, stressed. This is not to suggest that all federal programs should rely on financial funding criteria. Programs to remedy social problems logically should use social indicators in the grant distribution formula or requirements. However, aid to relieve fiscal stress will better reach the cities intended to be served by the program if financial criteria are used instead of non-financial criteria.

Federal Aid Designed to Prevent Fiscal Stress and to Promote Financial Stability in the Long Term Should Be Most Effective If It is Targeted at Strengthening the Economic Base of Cities, Notably by Encouraging Private Investment and Private Sector Job Creation. The study shows that deteriorating economic conditions create the greatest financial pressures on cities. While social and structural problems are important in this respect, they have less impact on a city's financial well-being than do economic problems. Therefore, fiscal stress may be best averted by programs designed to stabilize or enhance economic conditions. Of course, economic stimulus should not be the only objective of federal aid, to the exclusion of social and other goals. However, to the extent that federal policymakers emphasize economic and fiscal problems, careful consideration will have to be given to the trade-offs between meeting current needs and meeting long-range economic needs.

Programs Designed to Remedy Financial and Economic Problems Must Be Accurately Targeted and Appropriately Controlled to

Assure the Intent of Each Program is Fulfilled. The study shows clearly the importance of sound planning and management in avoiding fiscal stress. Such planning and management quality should be encouraged through the design of economic and financial assistance programs. Moreover, targeting of funds to specified purposes, use of performance requirements, development of management incentives and even the formulation of new types of grant programs that combine such targeting, management requirements and incentives with local discretionary authority are the types of tools that can assure productive use of federal aid.

At The State Level

State aid to cities now accounts for approximately one-third of city revenues. Therefore, all the implications described above for federal policymakers apply as well to state officials. At the same time, states have a unique role to play in assisting cities.

There is an emerging interest in developing new ways to monitor municipal fiscal conditions. The states can be central in this regard. The Advisory Council for Intergovernmental Relations completed a study in 1973 entitled "City Financial Emergencies: The Intergovernmental Dimension," which dealt largely with the state role in helping cities avoid and overcome municipal fiscal stress. In this study, the ACIR recommends that "each state designate or establish a single state agency responsible for the improvement of local managment functions such as accounting, auditing, and reporting. The Commission further recommends that the agencies be responsible for early detection of financial problems in order to prevent local financial crises."

An Early Warning System on Fiscal Stress Could Be Developed Based on the Short List of Financial Variables Used in This Study. Such a system would permit detection of fiscal stress while there is still adequate time for constructive resolution of the underlying problems. The federal government could refine the details of such a program and encourage the states to implement the system as part of national urban policy. Alternatively, states might compete for special grant funds to develop such a system on a pilot basis (using, for example, Section 701 funds from the Department of Housing and Urban Development or Section 302 funds from the Economic Development Administration).

AT THE MUNICIPAL LEVEL

The analysis reveals that, while federal and state aid is important, revenues from local sources remain the backbone of most cities' capacity to deliver public services. The data further suggest that there is considerable latitude for changing or increasing operations within the resource limits of most cities. Most operate well below the level of tax and debt ratios that are carried by some of the oldest cities. Thus, many cities can absorb the demands for aging now—their concern is for the future. Yet some industrially mature cities show that financial equilibrium can be achieved late in the aging process, although this often has happened only through difficult program and employment reductions needed to combat severe fiscal problems.

The point is that the success of these older cities, along with the widely differing patterns of fiscal performance by cities with similar economic, social and structural conditions, highlight the importance of management and political decisionmaking in avoiding fiscal stress. Below are key implications for municipal policymakers.

City Officials Must Improve Municipal Budgeting and Planning. City officials should regularly address such key issues as: Where is the city today in terms of its resource base and the segments that require public services? Is the city growing? Maturing? What are the city's objectives? How is the city changing? What public investments and programs will best provide needed services and encourage economic growth or stability?

As has already been indicated, current accounting and reporting practices in cities are inadequate to answer many of these questions. The data base clearly needs to be improved. In addition, capital planning should be integrated into the city's central budgeting and financial management system in those cities where operating and capital budgeting are now separate, unrelated processes.

Another important problem is one of timing: elected and appointed officials are pressed to produce results within a single term of office. Yet major investment projects that could encourage development of the city's economic base require more time. In addition, cities faced with taxpayer revolts may find it increasingly difficult to fund expensive capital projects. Funding, in this instance, is a matter of prioritization which can only be determined by elected officials and the citizenry.

Cities Must Leverage Municipal Capital Spending In Ways That Develop Their Future Resource Base. Maintaining the economic base through private investment is critical to maintaining revenue from local sources. In younger cities, the investment occurs relatively spontaneously. However, maturing and older cities must allocate both capital and services toward maintaining this process. In some cases this may require difficult trade-offs between immediate social services versus long-term job opportunities and tax base growth. But the private/public investment partnership is essential in dealing with potential fiscal stress.

Importantly, all public resources should be used to their most efficient advantage, including federal and state aid. Often in the past, such aid has been directed at and used to expand programs or displace normal operating costs. As a result, these funds have been more a contributor to, than a solution for, fiscal problems. As economic conditions deteriorate, these funds may not grow proportionally. If federal or state allocations change, the city is left to fund particular services on its own. More attention must be given to directing these funds to strengthening the economic base.

Cities Must Strive to Improve Their Structural Conditions to Strengthen Their Economic Bases. Structural factors affecting the cities' costs and revenues are significantly associated with stress. Those cities able to alter their boundaries or revenue base through annexation or other measures were able to prolong the periods of fiscal stability and to moderate increases in debt and taxes. Though these changes do not alter the industrial aging process, they are important in an overall program to manage fiscal stress. Where legal or regulatory barriers to structural reform exist, they should be reviewed for their impact on all jurisdictions and modified as appropriate.

Public Officials Must Adjust Operations and Spending to Match Stabilizing or Declining Resource Bases as Their Cities Age Industrially. Many cities are already taking advantage of opportunities to improve service delivery by streamlining operations instead of increasing costs. However, even such improvements can be made only up to a certain point. After that, many cities face painful budget decisions.

The conclusions suggest that there is more opportunity than is generally realized for cities to operate within their financial resources. Prioritizing city needs can help to adjust spending to a

limited, even declining, resource base while city officials simultaneously attempt to rebuild the economic base. Trenton and Pittsburgh have done just this.

PUBLIC AND PRIVATE SECTORS

Two key recommendations can be carried out effectively by government agencies, quasi-public bodies, private institutions, or a combination of these entities.

*Uniform Municipal Financial Accounting and Reporting Standards
Should be Developed and Adopted.* The first step is to determine
which body or organization is to be responsible for developing and
updating accounting and reporting standards for local government.
Currently, several organizations are working on various aspects of
this problem, but no single entity has yet addressed the entire issue.
We would anticipate a strong and continuing role for the Municipal
Finance Officers Association and the National Council on Governmental Accounting, as well as others, in conjunction with the American Institute of Certified Public Accountants and the Financial
Accounting Standards Board to resolve these issues.

Once the standards are defined, the next step is to ensure their
uniform adoption. Upgrading municipal accounting and reporting
systems will surely be time-consuming and costly at the outset.
However, the potential benefits from such uniform practices present
a compelling case for adopting improved standards. These benefits
include improved management, increased investor confidence, more
accurate bond ratings and more equitable distribution of state and
federal aid. While it could be argued that the first three should be
left to the prerogative of each city, the last benefit, distribution of
intergovernmental aid, cannot. Since state and federal aid now
accounts for nearly half of most municipal budgets, it is in the
interest of all concerned that the information on which this aid is
based accurately reflect the condition of the cities to which it
is directed.

Certainly, voluntary adoption of new accounting and reporting standards is to be hoped for. However, the track record of cities in
adopting even existing standards on accounting, reporting and disclosure has not been encouraging. The importance of the matter is
such that, should voluntary adoption not succeed, legislation or
regulation may be required to achieve nationwise conformance.

Additional Research Should be Undertaken, Targeted to Improving Municipal Financial Management. In the course of this study key additional research topics became apparent that potentially could identify important cause and effect relationships that determine municipal financial patterns. Further study in these areas could produce information that could enhance municipal economic growth or stability in the face of industrial aging.

- Examination of public capital spending and private investment to determine more precisely the cause and effect linkages between the two. This linkage refers, specifically, to the role of municipal "leverage" in encouraging private investment. Such findings could be of great use in assisting cities to strengthen their capital spending to stabilize or enhance their economic base, thus providing a new dimension to the local "boot strapping" of the city economy.

- Analysis of the behavior of municipal finances over longer time periods, including business cycle peaks and troughs to identify how city financial performance is affected by cyclical changes or by longer-run structural shifts. Real economic activity will most certainly have at least some impact on the financial well-being of municipalities whose local economic bases are vulnerable to these swings. Conversely, some municipalities are well protected from business cycle changes, either through judicious management or the fortuitous historical evolution of the industrial mix in the community. Yet despite claims to the contrary, little is actually known about this phenomenon. Further research could perhaps identify whether and how municipal management can successfully offset some of the adverse consequences of the business cycle.

- Examination of the relationship of a city's stage of industrial aging to changes in taxes. The study disclosed that, while expenditures rise as a city matures industrially, taxes rise at a relatively faster rate. To the extent that high taxes hasten stagnation and the exodus of industry from older industrialized cities, this finding is significant and merits more research.

- Application of the sixty-six cities study methodology and approach to data collection and analysis to small cities. Ultimately, improved accounting and reporting standards will greatly facilitate analysis of cities of all sizes. In the interim, it would be extremely useful to provide a data base on small cities which often have very difficult problems that differ from those of larger municipalities. Such a data base would support improved planning and better allocation of intergovernmental aid. Funding for such a project could be provided under Section 113 of the Housing and Community Development Act of the Department of Housing and Urban Development.

NOTES

1. Exogenous forces, such as the cyclical swings in the national economy, will generally be reflected in shifts in industry location, investment expansion and decline, and national and state economic policies.

2. This variable could possibly have been used to provide insight into social conditions in a municipality. However, we chose it as a variable to differentiate cities along structural lines. We were specifically interested in a variable that would reflect variations in the tax base, thus providing insight into the extent to which annexation policies have or have not altered the size of the local economic base.

3. The data were adjusted to make comparison among cities statistically valid; also the data were normalized to account for populatiom and economic differences.

4. High debt may, of course, represent a heavy reliance on industrial bond financing, or high rates of infrastructure development.

5. Trenton's above average ratio of federal and state aid may help to keep local taxes and debt down. However, since many federal/state programs require matching funds, more aid can induce additional local expenses rather than save local revenues. Nonetheless, cities with good grants management programs logically ought to fare better than cities which lack this management capability.

6. Unquestionably, factors other than capacity—i.e., local preferences—may influence municipal financial performance. These factors cannot, however, be quantified for purposes of statistical analysis. To assess the willingness of local citizens to support high taxes, expenses and debt—as contrasted with what they are economically capable of supporting—one must examine local political and attitudinal factors.

7. Intergovernmental transfers in our analysis include both federal and state grant-in-aid programs.

8. Statistical swing provides a convenient measure for quantifying the sensitivity of financial variables to changing circumstances. In this exhibit, statistical swing represents the percent variation as social conditions shift from small-to-large dependent population ratios or as population densities shift from low to high and as economic conditions shift from the best conditions (high investment) to worst conditions (below-average investment). While the percentage change may appear small in some cases, nonetheless the amount of state and federal aid involved is substantial.

U.S. Department of Housing and Urban Development - THE URBAN FISCAL CRISIS: FACT OR FANTASY? (A Reply)

INTRODUCTION

Urban Fiscal Stress, the report done by Touche Ross & Company and the First National Bank of Boston is an inadequate assessment of either city credit worthiness or city fiscal distress. While critics have already characterized it as a "banker's report," it is hard to imagine banking profession judging individual or buisness credit worthiness on such a limited set of budgetary variables. It is even less appropriate to evaluate the broader question of city fiscal distress on such a basis.

According to this report, only four of the 66 cities studied suffered signs of serious fiscal stress. If this finding were correct, and if the cities studied were a representative sample, it would imply that the urban fiscal crisis is over.

The analysis is not correct. The study treats the finances of city as if it were an individual applying for an automobile loan. Just as with an individual, if a city does not spend too much and if it is not too far in debt, then it is judged to be financially healthy enough to qualify for a loan. A city's ability to repay debt is not an appropriate indicator of its overall fiscal health. By itself a city's balance sheet does not measure the economic well-being of the jurisdiction nor does it necessarily indicate the future financial circumstances of the jurisdiction. Unlike the individual or private business, the goal of the city is not to accumulate financial assets nor to maximize its income or profits. Rather it is to provide services to people—a goal which cannot be measured by a city's accounting records alone.

The study fundamentally misunderstands what is going on in U.S. cities. The fact that many American cities have balanced budgets has more to do with state laws and the necessity to maintain access to credit markets than with their real economic health.

More specifically, the study has the following conceptual and methodological weaknesses that makes its findings highly unreliable:

1. *The sample is badly constructed and as a result, the findings can not be generalized.* Many of the country's largest cities which face the greatest fiscal stress are not included in the study, i.e., New York, Chicago, Los Angeles, Detroit and Cleveland. Places such as Long Beach, Phoenix, Pueblo and Austin, however, are included. This curious sample selection explains much of the report's finding that "most of the nation's large cities are not financially pressed."

2. *The narrow definition of fiscal stress produces questionable results.* According to this report, a city is under fiscal stress if its taxes, expenditures, or debts are more than one standard deviation from the mean value of the "cluster" of similar cities in the sample.

This definition has a number of implications: First, stress is defined only in comparison with other similar cities. If all cities in a "cluster" were under fiscal stress, this measure could not detect it. Furthermore, this definition of fiscal stress compares cities to each other and ignores the far more meaningful disparities between central cities and their suburbs.

Second, under this definition of distress, cities which spend very little on their public services are considered fiscally healthy, regardless of their level of public services or service responsibilities. *Indeed, if Cleveland had been included in this study it would have been judged to be in sound fiscal condition.* Low levels of spending on public services can reflect a variety of fiscal conditions, from the low tax capacity and unmet service needs characteristic of many distressed cities to the case of fiscally healthy cities with a low level of service responsibilities because most services are provided by counties, special districts, or the state. Similarly, high spending levels, which imply stress under this definition, may be the result of large intergovernmental aid flows, heavy service responsibilities, or state imposed mandates.

Third, there are important dimensions of a city's fiscal health which are inversely related to this definition of fiscal stress. For example, a city with worn-out capital infrastructure and low debt per capita would be viewed as much healthier under this definition than a city which had gone into debt to improve its capital infrastructure. Similarly, a city with an underfunded pension system would appear fiscally healthier than a city with a fully funded system.

3. *The study ignores both the quantity and quality of the services a city delivers to its residents.* As a matter of fact, it completely ignores people and looks only at balance sheets. Under this study a city delivering large quantities of high-quality public services to its poor residents would almost automatically be classified as fiscally strained.

4. *The study uses only 1975 data.* A one-year snapshot of urban fiscal conditions is an extremely unreliable indicator of the real long-term situation—trends are an essential component of urban fiscal analysis. Had the study examined the fiscal fortunes of cities over a period of time, the volatility of short-term city budgetary conditions would have become clear along with the futility of judging current city financial conditions on the basis of data from 1975, the bottom of the 1973-1975 recession. A one-year analysis also is unable to identify cities which are headed for trouble in the future. This further erodes the usefulness in 1979 of a study based on 1975 data.

THE URBAN FISCAL CRISIS

This report is simply the latest in a series of articles in widely-read publications which seriously mislead the reader about the condition of American cities.

The urban fiscal crisis is not over—the future of our cities still demands the priority attention of government at all levels. The circumstances that have generated long-term urban decline—loss of jobs, people and economic base—have not been significantly altered.

Throughout the country, cities and counties with older physical plants, higher proportions of the poor and elderly and higher crime rates still are experiencing economic decline. The loss of population and jobs is not random. The poor and the low-skilled remain in the urban core, while the richer, upwardly-mobile part of the population continues to move to the suburbs. Attempts by local government to cut services or raise taxes in a fiscal crisis lead to further deterioration of the business climate and an increased impetus for the mobile part of the population to move out. It also places an increasing burden on low-income households who cannot afford to move and who are most likely to be dependent on public services. Thus, as conditions continue to deteriorate, many local governments are increasingly vulnerable to future economic downturns.

While the long-run trends still point toward a continued deterioration of the fiscal health of our urban areas, short-run cyclical improvements in the national economy have relieved some of the fiscal pressure. The fiscal situation of some urban governments has improved in the last two years as the result of both local belt-tightening and rapid national recovery from the 1973-75 recession, but this general improvement may be short-lived if the economy slows significantly.

It is essential to distinguish between long-term trends in urban economic activity and short-term cyclical fluctuations if we are to understand the current fiscal crisis. When the trend and the cycle move in the same direction as they did during the 1973-75 recession, the picture is quite clear. Large cities entered that recession in a relatively strong financial position because of the then recent enactment of General Revenue Sharing. Before the recession was over, however, both the economic base and the financial situation of many major cities deteriorated and they required a massive increase in federal aid. At the other end of the cycle, economic expansion and recovery improves the financial position of many cities, but does not substantially alter the long-term trend. Thus, a number of central cities remain economically depressed.

Fragile fiscal health is not a condition confined to any one type or size of local government. It is an equally serious concern for central cities, for older suburbs, for counties, for townships, and for jurisdictions of all sizes, large and small. The following sections contain data primarily for larger cities because of their availability, but smaller places also face severe fiscal problems as is well documented in HUD's recent report to the Congress, *Development Needs of Small Cities*.

CYCLICAL FLUCTUATIONS

Despite the improved financial position of many major central cities in the last two years, their fiscal stability has deteriorated significantly in recent years. Not only have they become increasingly dependent on outside aid for balancing their budgets, but they are vulnerable to cyclical swings of the national economy. When the national economy grows rapidly, local tax revenues rise. When the national economy slows or enters a recession, local governments lose tax revenues—nearly $5 billion as a result of recession in 1975, according to the Advisory Commission on Intergovernmental Reations. The volatility of local revenues dependent on federal aid and national growth represents a potentially serious problem for federal urban policy.

RECESSION AND RECOVERY IN THE SEVENTIES

The economic recovery since 1975 has *marginally* helped the financial position of many major cities and counties in the U.S. *This improvement, however, has not altered the long-term economic decline in many of these cities.* Because the overall economic improvement is relatively recent and because improvements in the national economy are reflected in local budgets only after a lag, evidence on the improved health of local government finances is still incomplete. Some of the indications of improvement are as follows:

1. *The national economic trends in GNP and employment from 1970 to 1977 show a clear relationship to urban finances.* The slowest growth in GNP occurred in 1974 and 1975, the worst years for the budgets of large cities. National employment also had its slowest growth in these two years. The three trends show the same pattern with only slight deviations in timing. This pattern lends substantial support to the case for standby fiscal relief in the event of another recession.

2. *For the fiscal year ending in 1977 many of the nation's thirty largest cities ended the year with total revenues exceeding total expenditures.* In the twenty-seven of these cities for which data were available, general fund revenues exceeded expenditures by $212 million or 3.2 percent of total expenditures. In both 1975 and 1976, these cities as a group had deficits of $28.3 million and $150.7 million respectively. Fiscal year 1977 was the first year revenues exceeded expenditures for these cities since fiscal year 1974, the first year of the recession. Indeed, the relationship between city budget surpluses and the national economic recovery is quite striking. It is important to note that these budget surpluses are small relative to the level of federal aid received by these twenty-seven cities. For example, they received more than $1.6 billion of federal aid under the Economic Stimulus Program (Local Public Works, Antirecession Fiscal Assistance, and Comprehensive Employment and Training Act), more than seven times their 1977 excess of revenues over

surpluses. Equally important, the surpluses do not reflect the hardship generated in a number of distressed cities by the service cuts needed to realize them.

3. *While budget surpluses are one indicator of better financial health, they tell only a very small part of the fiscal story of local government.* Taken by themselves, they ignore the most basic factor of all in assessing fiscal health: are the needs of the people being met? Balancing local budgets by cutting essential services for example, does not lead to fiscal health, but to further long-term decline. Only in the context of the overall local fiscal situation can these surpluses be interpreted properly. Levels of local public services, levels of tax effort, the condition of public sector infrastructure and the extent of local government service reponsibility are all at least as important in determining local fiscal health as the current budget surplus or deficit. Furthermore, most state and local governments are legally prohibited from deficit spending and therefore tend to under budget so as to err on the surplus side. This tendency has been encouraged by the problems of New York City and their impact on local government bond markets across the nation.

4. *Along with the improvement in the overall economic situation, real (after inflation) city general revenues from own sources have begun to increase.* During fiscal years 1974 and 1975, the period of recession, real own source general revenues for cities first fell by $679 million and then during fiscal year 1975 increased only slightly— by $33 million. Fiscal years 1976 and 1977 have shown improvements in the real revenue collection of cities.

Since the rate of real growth in GNP is expected to slow significantly in 1979, these surpluses are expected to be short-lived. If the slowdown in national economic growth is more severe than expected, cities will be vulnerable once again to the kind of fiscal stress they experienced in 1974 and 1975.

LONG-TERM ECONOMIC TRENDS

The long-term decline of a number of urban areas demonstrates even more dramatically their vulnerability to fiscal pressures. The measures commonly used to assess the health and longer-term prospects of urban areas are those less responsive to cyclical changes in economic activity: population, income and employment.

POPULATION

This is a familiar and often-used measure of community condition. Population loss places a special burden on urban governments, magnifying budgetary strain, because while it rapidly depletes taxable resources, essential public expenditures do not drop proportionally. Furthermore it is the better-educated, higher-income households who are leaving the urban core so the impact on their economies is even greater.

Population change affects all revenue sources, including property taxes—the major revenue source for most cities—as well as sales and income taxes.

The following trends illustrate the situation quite clearly:

1. *The population of central cities as a group declined by 4.6 percent from 1970 to 1977 while the suburban population increased by 12 percent.* Large central cities experienced even greater losses during this period, declining by 7.1 percent as a group.

2. *A number of large central cities which grew between 1960 and 1970, have lost population since 1970.* This group includes Dallas, Denver and Los Angeles, cities in the southern and western regions of the country, indicating that central city decline is a national phenomenon with implications for more than a few crisis areas. Among large cities which have declined steadily since 1960, the most rapidly declining cities are Cleveland, Minneapolis and St. Louis, with Buffalo, Detroit and Pittsburgh close behind. New Orleans and San Francisco are also in the category of cities which have steadily lost population since 1960.

3. *The loss of central city population between 1970 and 1977 is symptomatic of the long-run trend in the loss of central city dominance over SMSAs which extends as far back as 1900 in a number of urban areas.* Washington, D.C., for example, accounted for more than two-thirds of the population in its metropolitan area in 1900, but less than one-fourth of it by 1975. Most other major cities experienced similar declines in relative importance. This is an indication of the extent to which the central city is able to capture the tax base of newer and generally wealthier outlying parts of its metropolitan area. Annexation has enabled a number of central cities to capture portions of their suburban tax base and is reflected in the extent of their dominance of the SMSA. Annexation, however, has been confined almost exclusively to the southern and western

regions of the nation in recent years; a few midwest cities have annexed, but no annexation at all has occurred in the Northeast.

4. *Within the same SMSA, from March 1975 to March 1978, more than twice as many people moved from the central city to the suburbs as from the suburbs to the central city.* The back-to-the-city movement is clearly overwhelmed by the continuing exodus from central cities.

INCOME

The income level of cities is another useful indicator of fiscal condition. It is related to a variety of revenue sources, including local income, sales and property taxes. Trends in central city income are indicated by the following.

1. *From 1969 to 1976 the real dollar median income of families living in central cities fell by $614 while the income of their suburban counterparts fell by only $59.* In 1969, the median suburban family earned $2,594 more than the city dweller. By 1976, the suburban family earned $3,149 more than the city family. Not only did city dwellers lose income, but they also lost relative to families living in the suburbs.

2. *Between 1960 and 1975, the ratio of central city to suburban income per capita declined in 73 of the nation's largest 82 metropolitan areas.* This trend was clear in all four regions of the nation with more than 83 percent of these large cities in the East, 86 percent of those in the Midwest, 88 percent of those in the South and 100 percent of those in the West exhibiting declines in this ratio.

In addition to median levels, another important dimension of incomes in central cities is the fraction of the population with very low incomes. Two measures of this illustrate the extra burden on central cities: percent of the population below the poverty level, and transfer payments as a share of local income.

1. *A larger fraction of the poverty population of the U.S. lived in central cities in 1977 than in 1970.* During this period, both suburban and nonmetropolitan areas experienced reductions in the percentage of their population below the poverty level while this percentage rose in central cities.

2. *Transfer payments constituted a larger share of local income in declining urban counties than in growing urban counties in 1975.* This share also grew faster between 1970 and 1975 in these relatively declining areas. Several growing areas have relatively high percentages (Phoenix, San Antonio and San

Diego), but this is generally attributed to retired people (civilian and military) who represent a lesser drain on public resources. The high percentages in Boston (31.7%), Philadelphia (27.0%), St. Louis (28.0%) and New York (25.0%) highlight an increasing reliance on government programs to sustain the local economy.

EMPLOYMENT

A final indicator of long-term decline and fiscal pressure is city employment. Employment affects virtually all potential tax bases in one way or another. Just how much a particular city will be affected by job loss depends on its tax structure and on the mix of jobs in its economy. One ironic problem facing many older cities is that service sector and public sector jobs replacing manufacturing job losses do not generally produce equivalent tax yields. Roy Bahl, Alan K. Campbell and David Greytak have estimated that New York City requires 1.11 service jobs or 1.61 government jobs to replace a manufacturing job in terms of revenues. The trends in central city employment are indicated by the following:

1. *Employment of central city residents declined by 1.4 percent between 1970 and 1977 while employment of suburban and nonmetropolitan residents increased by 25.7 percent.* The employment of central city females actually increased during this period, but it was more than offset by the decline in male employment.

2. *Unemployment was higher among central city residents in 1970 and rose by a larger amount between 1970 and 1976 than unemployment in suburban or nonmetropolitan areas.*

THE ROLE OF INTERGOVERNMENTAL AID

Until now, the crucial factor in local government's ability to withstand slower growth with substantial layoffs and service reductions has been aid from federal and state governments. The role of intergovernmental aid is even more significant when it is examined in the context of rapid inflation of the 1970s. Recent inflation trends have drastically reduced both the purchasing power of local governments and the real volume of increases in state and federal aid to cities:

1. Cities increased their direct general expenditures on goods and services 55.1 percent between 1972 and 1977. *Inflation reduced the real increase in expenditure to only 5.4 percent over that period, however.* In other words, inflation ate up more than 90 percent of the increase in city expenditures between 1972 and

1977. A two percentage point reduction in the inflation rate would increase the purchasing power of city expenditures by over $483 million in 1979—more than HUD's entire Urban Development Action Grant Program.

2. *Inflation also has drastically reduced the purchasing power of federal grants to cities.* Federal grants to cities increased by more than 31 percent per year between 1972 and 1976, but inflation ate up nearly 40 percent of that revenue increase.

POLICY IMPLICATIONS

The facts presented here have clearly demonstrated the fragile nature of the fiscal health of cities. This vulnerability exists because many urban areas are experiencing long-term economic decline, including losses of people, jobs and tax base. These long-term trends are offset in the short-term in many places by the impact of rapid national economic growth, but once that growth rate slows, they face a far bleaker future than their current budget positions suggest.

This dichotomy between the long-term decline and the short-term cyclical swings affecting local budgets suggests that a purely budgetary approach, especially if applied on a comparative one-year basis such as that used in the study *Urban Fiscal Stress*, is seriously flawed. It also suggests that the Carter Administration urban policies, which are targeted primarily on the basis of underlying economic characteristics, have begun to refocus federal aid on real needs. More specifically, it suggests that the Intergovernmental Fiscal Assistance Amendments of 1979 now being considered by Congress are precisely what is needed. The targeted fiscal assistance provisions provide financial support to those urban places suffering the most severe effects of long-term decline. The antirecession provisions promise the stability needed to withstand future recessions. If authority for this program is granted now, the program will be in place to provide financial relief when it is needed most. This policy would provide a much-needed fiscal "emergency net" and would significantly relieve some of the burdens a recession would otherwise impose on those people most heavily dependent on local public services.

SECTION II

Fiscal Profiles of Cities in Stress

Robert W. Burchell, David Listokin, George Sternlieb, James W. Hughes, Stephen C. Casey - MEASURING URBAN DISTRESS: A SUMMARY OF THE MAJOR URBAN HARDSHIP INDICES AND RESOURCE ALLOCATION SYSTEMS

INTRODUCTION

The last several years have witnessed an outpouring of studies and programs concerned with the deteriorating economic, social and physical conditions of the nation's cities. President Carter's urban policy report, *Cities and People in Distress*,[1] reflected the Administration's concern about worsening urban problems. One of the major urban initiatives of his administration—the Urban Development Action Grant (UDAG)—is specially designed to alleviate chronic urban hardship. Existing general purpose programs, such as Revenue Sharing and Community Development Block Grants, are being reexamined to determine if they distribute assistance to those urban communities with the greatest need. Even the continued financial solvency of central cities is being questioned as fiscal crises have confronted New York, Cleveland, Chicago, Newark and other communities.

This paper examines the *identification and measurement of urban distress—the physical, economic and social hardships encountered by cities*. It is divided into five sections. Section One considers the *historical background of identifying/measuring deteriorated urban*

159

areas. Section Two presents an *organizational framework for analyzing and comparing current efforts at measuring urban distress.* These measures include: (1) *programmatic area eligibility standards,* i.e., local unemployment must exceed a certain rate before a community can apply for job training funds; (2) *resource allocation criteria,* i.e., block grants are granted proportionally to the local poverty rate and age of housing with these measures deemed as indicators of hardship; and (3) *separately developed relative distress/need indices,* i.e., the Brookings Institution Intermetropolitan Hardship Index which ranks the distress of central cities. The three categories of urban distress measures are presented and compared in Section Three of the paper using the organizational framework as the format for analysis. Section Four takes a *closer look at the distress measures and examines the similarities and differences in the individual and groups of variables employed by the distress rankings.* Section Five concludes the analysis by considering the *degree of consistency in city hardship designation*—to what extent do the different rankings yield similar or different results in ordering the relative hardship of a common group of cities. This comparison addresses the question of the level of practical variation in the urban hardship measures.

SECTION ONE—MEASURING URBAN DISTRESS: HISTORICAL BACKGROUND

There has been interest in identifying and dealing with impacted urban areas for many decades. At the turn of the twentieth century, several prominent social reformers focused on the adverse conditions of *"slums."*[2] In the 1930s, considerable attention was paid to both urban *"slums"* and *"blighted areas."* The President's Conference on Home Building and Homeownership (1932) described such locations as:[3]

> . . . areas where due to the lack of either a vitalizing factor or the presence of a devitalizing factor, life has been shaped to such an extent that the areas have become economic liabilities to the community and have lost their power to change to a condition that is economically sound.

Numerous groups in the 1930s discussed the characteristics of depressed urban neighborhoods and examined policy options. The Architects Club of Chicago formed a "Committee on Blighted Areas and Housing."[4] Mabel Walker authored a study entitled *Urban Blight and Slums.*[5] The 1931 President's Conference on Home

Building and Homeownership issued recommendations for alleviating "blighted areas and slums."[6]

The exigencies of World War II limited federal action dealing with impacted urban areas until 1949 when the Urban Renewal program was authorized. Urban Renewal was designed to address slum and blighted conditions by encouraging demolition and redevelopment. By the mid-1950s, Urban Renewal implementation was differentiated by differing degrees of urban deterioration.*[7] Core slum and blighted neighborhoods would be renewed by *demolition* and *new construction*. In contrast, areas of lesser blight—*"grey" neighborhoods*—would receive housing *rehabilitation* assistance.

The 1960s and 1970s saw further attention paid to both "grey" neighborhoods and more impacted slum areas. The Douglas and Kaiser Commissions of the late 1960s[8] and the 1973 HUD task force[9] examined the housing problems of central cities and suggested modifications and extensions to the then existing Urban Renewal[10] and mortgage guarantee-subsidy programs. An arsenal of subsidies was marshalled to improve urban conditions. These included: Urban Renewal demolition and new construction, Section 221 (d) (3), Section 235 (j), Section 236, Section 312 and Section 8, new construction and rehabilitation.

The 1960s and 1970s also saw greater attention paid to urban *socioeconomic distress*. Model Cities, for example, was designed to:[11]

... make a substantial impact on the physical and social problems and to remove or arrest blight and decay in entire sections or neighborhoods; to contribute to the sound development of the entire city; to make marked progress in reducing social and educational disadvantages, ill helath, underemployment and enforced idleness; and to provide educational, health, and social services necessary to serve the poor and disadvantaged.

The 1960s and 1970s were also characterized by a heightened attention paid to *depressed regions*. The Area Development Administration (ARA) was formed to deal with problems of long-term

---

*The gradations between these levels of deterioration and the consequent need for differentiating Urban Renewal action was emphasized by the 1953 Advisory Committee on Government Housing Policies and was incorporated into the Urban Renewal Program by the Housing Act of 1954.

unemployment and underemployment in rural areas. The Economic Development Administration (EDA), the successor to the ARA, continued assistance to depressed regions, first rural, but then increasingly urban.

Urban stress has become a central topic of concern and analysis in the late 1970s. A major urban policy review was entitled *Cities and People in Distress.*[12] Congress, financial analysts, and academicians have studied the common and individual economic problems faced by cities[13] including New York, St. Louis, Cleveland and Newark. An article disputing the thesis of an urban crisis was met by a vigorous rebuttal from HUD and others.[14] Even the popular press has discussed the continued problems of older industrial cities in the Northeast and Midwest in a post-industrial society. While the attention to urban distress continues a tradition of many decades, the current concern has been heightened by the following factors:

1. Diminishing resources and the need for targeting. Social program funding is increasingly limited and has sparked attention to *target* remaining funds to those distressed areas most in need. Examples include: a Congressional Budget Office analysis entitled, *City Need and the Responsiveness of Federal Grants Programs*[15] and numerous studies by the Brookings Institution comparing the sensitivity of the CDBG and Revenue Sharing funding allocation formulae to city distress.[16]

2. Growing recognition of the chronic nature of distress. A common view of the 1960s was that urban problems were limited to a few cities and could be resolved with a quick infusion of public assistance. Today, there is growing recognition that the problems are widespread and often chronic and the solutions are much more doubtful and long term. This change in perspective has prompted several studies analyzing urban distress such as *How Cities Can Grow Old Gracefully,*[17] and *Cities in Trouble.*[18]

3. The New York City financial bankruptcy. The financial problems of the nation's largest city alerted the financial and academic community to the quietly growing fiscal crisis of many of the nation's urban areas. The continued financial problems of Cleveland, Chicago and San Francisco have confirmed the need of ongoing monitoring of the nature and magnitude of urban fiscal distress. This concern has prompted such studies as: George Peterson's *Urban Fiscal Monitoring*[19] and Thomas Muller's *Growing and Declining Urban Areas.*[20]

The *measurement* of urban distress, i.e., what is the level of physical, economic and social hardship encountered by different cities, is a central interest of the burgeoning literature on central city problems. Measurement is a key concern because it draws explicit attention to the components of distress and also serves as an operational device for directing relief to those cities with the greatest hardship. As of 1980, approximately fifteen urban distress measures have been developed including: the area eligibility standards for UDAG and EDA Title I and Title IX assistance; the city ranking systems of the Brookings Institution, HUD, Institute for the Future and the Congressional Budget Office; and the inherent urban distress measures incorporated into such major federal assistance program as Revenue Sharing and Community Development Block Grants. It is important to analyze and compare the assumptions and procedures of these federal allocation measures. To facilitate this task, an organizational framework of urban distress measurement is summarized below.

SECTION TWO—ORGANIZATIONAL FRAMEWORK OF URBAN DISTRESS MEASUREMENT

This section presents a simplified schema for analyzing and comparing current measures of urban distress. (These measures are presented in Section Three.) In addition to providing a format for analysis, the framework also serves to highlight the potential complexities of index development and the range of possible options that arise at important decision making points.

The organizational framework consists of six hierarchal components:

1. *Legislative Intent:* Legislative specification of the problem(s) to be addressed—guidance as to what is to be measured.

2. *Conceptual Indicators:* Major analytical dimensions of the problem to be addressed—broad indicator classification.

3. *Quantifiable Variables:* Operational measures of each of the problem dimensions—quantification of the indicator classes.

4. *Variable Definition:* The format of the variables to be used— static versus dynamic levels/or increments versus rates.

5. *Variable Linkages:* Variable transformation and composite index development—the use of aggregative techniques.

6. *Standards and Eligibility Criteria:* The development of thresholds or "cut-off" points—criteria for establishing program eligibility.

The framework can be illustrated by reference to the following hypothetical resource allocation system. The *legislative intent* of a housing subsidy program may be defined narrowly as those actions necessary to alleviate "physical deterioration." Physical deterioration, in turn, may be judged to be a part of at least two *conceptual indicators:* physical and economic downturn. The *quantifiable variables* may include age of housing and per capita income. These are defined *(variable definitions)* as follows: age of housing—percentage of units constructed prior to 1940; and per capita income—average income per person as of 1970. The *variable linkage* then consists of: (1) transforming (via statistical techniques) the age of housing and per capita income variables to standard deviation units; and (2) summing these standard scores. The *variable standard* then may stipulate, for instance, that only scores *higher* than the *median* for all central cities are counted. Finally, the *eligibility criteria* further require that housing assistance will be given only to those areas with a score above the median for *both* the age of housing and per capita income measures.

The organizational framework provides an analytical approach and common language for presenting and comparing the distress measures. It points to the importance of looking at the differing objectives of the rankings, the inclusion of appropriate variables and the expression and linkage of these variables. This sensitivity is important for avoiding such errors as faulting two rankings for not similarly ordering a common set of cities, where the two rankings have different purposes as reflected in their dissimilar legislative intents and/or conceptual indicators.

SECTION THREE—STATE-OF-THE-ART
URBAN DISTRESS MEASURES

The organizational framework is used here to present and analytically partition a variety of programs and formulations which employ indicators of municipal distress or similar hardship conditions. Three alternative types of measures are considered:

1. *Programmatic Area Eligibility Programs:* Operational indicator "systems" used by federal agencies to establish jurisdictional *eligibility* for program participation.

2. *Relative Distress/Need Indices:* Analytical schemes which establish relative distress/need rankings for evaluative or illustrative purposes (not for formal program eligibility).

3. *Resource Allocation Techniques:* Operational or quantitative formulae used to distribute (allocate) program resources among jurisdictions whose eligibility has already been established.

PROGRAMMATIC AREA ELIGIBILITY PROGRAMS

Examples presented here include area eligibility criteria of the federal programs administered by the Department of Housing and Urban Development (HUD) and the Economic Development Administration (EDA)—the two federal agencies most involved in measuring/ alleviating urban distress. These programs include: UDAG (HUD), Title I (EDA), Title IX (EDA), Pockets of Poverty (HUD) and Special Impact Area (EDA).

Urban Development Action Grant Program.

As indicated in Exhibit 1, the *legislative mandate* of UDAG is the alleviation of physical and economic deterioration of cities and urban counties; there was relatively explicit setting of criteria by the Congress in the language which accompanied the passage of the basic authorization for the UDAG program—Public Law 95-128.[21]

The legislation also provides some detailing on the *conceptual indicators*—physical and economic distress—which in turn generate quantifiable variables. Thus the Secretary of HUD is responsible for setting "minimum standards for determining the level of physical and economic distress of cities . . . ."[22] Further, the variables to be utilized in this process are at least partially spelled out in the legislation . . . , "such as the age and condition of housing stock, including residential abandonment; average income; population out-migration; and stagnating or declining tax base."[23] Out of that requirement have emerged six *quantifiable variables:* age of housing, per capita income, population lag/decline, unemployment, job lag/decline and poverty. These are defined in Exhibit 1. To illustrate, the *variable definition* of age of housing is "the percentage of year-round housing units constructed prior to 1940 based on 1970 U.S. census data."

As operationalized, the UDAG selection procedure involved a "go-no-go" or "pass-fail" *eligibility* approach. There are no *variable linkage* procedures to reduce the variables to a single indicator nor is there an overall relative distress measure. (This characteristic is true of *all* the programmatic area eligibility standards.) The variables are considered separately, with the median of each serving as the *variable standard,* i.e., the median or variable standard for age of housing is "34.15 percent or more of the year-round housing was constructed prior to 1940." The *eligibility criterion* is determined by meeting three out of the six measurement standards for metropolitan cities and urban counties, and a slightly more complex procedure— given the limitations of data availability—for smaller cities (see Exhibit 1).

This "pass-fail" approach, where eligibility is determined by simply meeting a certain number of the specified variables, contrasts with a rank ordering or index of urban distress whereby a higher level of priority is given for those areas which, according to the derived indicators, are in greatest need as against those which may meet the criteria of acceptance but are of lesser need. It is important, however, not to overemphasize this difference because it is often more a difference of form rather than substance. To illustrate, the first "pass-fail" round of UDAG area eligibility is followed by a second round of *project selection.* This second stage entails the evaluation of the applications submitted by UDAG-eligible juris-dictions taking into account such factors as impact on the poor, project feasibility, and multiplier benefits, i.e., job creation and local tax revenue. In addition, project selection also involves con-sideration of the relative distress ranking of cities.[24] In short, the two stage UDAG sifting process involves a first tier "pass-fail" eligibility criterion and a second tier review incorporating, as part of the evaluation, a more precise indexing of urban hardship.

Title I and Title IX Programs.

Close parallels in intent and ultimate goal to UDAG are embodied in the EDA Title I and Title IX Programs. The eligibility mechanisms of the EDA loans/grants are also similar to UDAG—they are charac-terized by an initial "pass-fail" area determination—screening which jurisdictions satisfy a select subset of variable standards—followed a second round of project selection from the pool of qualified applicants.

EXHIBIT 1

Urban Development Action Grants: Programmatic Area Eligibility

LEGISLATIVE INTENT:	Alleviate physical and economic deterioration
CONCEPTUAL INDICATORS:	Urban Distress (Physical and Economic Distress)
QUANTIFIABLE VARIABLES:	Age of Housing, Per Capita Income, Population Lag/Decline, Unemployment, Job Lag/Decline, Poverty
VARIABLE DEFINITION:	*Age of Housing:* Percentage of year-round housing units constructed prior to 1940 based on 1970 U.S. Census data.
	Per Capita Income Growth Lag: New increase in per capita income for the period 1969 to 1974 based on U.S. Census data.
	Population Growth Lag: The percentage rate of population growth (based on corporate boundaries in 1960 and corporate boundaries in 1975) for the period 1960 to 1975, based on U.S. Census data.
	Unemployment: Rate of unemployment for 1977 based on August, 1978 data compiled by Bureau of Labor Statistics (Average Annual Rate).
	Employment Growth Lag: Rate of growth in retail and manufacturing employment for the period 1967 to 1972 based on U.S. Census data. (If data not available for both, either can be used.)
	Poverty: Percentage of population at or below the poverty level based on 1970 U.S. Census data. Note: Variable labels as published in regulations: Age of Housing, Per Capita Income, Population Lag/Decline, Unemployment, Job Lag/Decline, and Poverty.
VARIABLE LINKAGES:	None
VARIABLE STANDARDS:	*Medians of Metropolitan Cities*
	Age of Housing Stock: 34.15 percent or more Unemployment: 6.98 percent or more
	Per Capita Income Growth Lag: $1,424 or less Poverty Rate: 11.24 percent or more
	Population Growth Lag: 15.52 percent or less Employment Growth Lag: 7.08 percent or less

EXHIBIT 1 (CONTINUED)

ELIGIBILITY CRITERIA
(MINIMUM STANDARDS):

Metropolitan Cities & Urban Counties

3 of 6 standards

   a) unless applicant's % of poverty is less than ½ median → must meet 4 of 6.

   b) unless % of poverty is greater than 1½ times median, and an absolute per capita income below median; then it may substitute a "unique distress factor" for one of the other criteria (including poverty).

Small Cities (Nonmetropolitan Cities) under 50,000

Because of limited data availability, small cities are eligible if they make three qualification points:

1. poverty greater than the large city or urban county standard: 1 point
2. net growth of per capita income less than the large city standard: 1 point
3. job growth less than the large city standard: 1 point
4. age of housing greater than the large city standard: 1 point
5. population growth less than the large city standard (modified to include only, 1970-1975): 1 point
6. a bonus point for poverty twice the poverty standard: 1 point
7. a bonus point for age twice the age standard, as long as poverty meets the standard: 1 point
8. a loss of 1 point for poverty less than half the standard.

A city with less than 25,000 population follows the same three point eligibility system except that the job growth standard (No. 3) does not apply.

Source: See U.S. Department of Housing and Urban Development, *Pockets of Poverty An Examination of Needs and Options* (Washington, D.C.: Government Printing Office, 1979). For Urban Development Action Grant regulations, see 43 FR 1602, January 10, 1978; 43FR 13370, March 29, 1978; 43 FR 50668, October 30, 1978; 44 FR 33372, June 8, 1979: 45 FR 10740, February 15, 1980.

The generic EDA program—embodied in Title I, Section 201, Section 202, and other EDA assistance elements—is outlined in Exhibit 2. The *legislative intent* specifies the isolation of areas[25] "suffering substantial and persistent unemployment."[26] This serves as the basic *conceptual indicator* demarcating the major phenomenon to be measured. The *quantifiable variables* utilized in its measurement are much broader, however, than implied by the single dimension of substantial and persistent unemployment. The quantifiable variables include: unemployment, per capita employment decline, sudden rise in unemployment, median family income, loss of population and other measures. In general, the stress is upon chronic problems i.e., 1960-1970 trends, supplemented in terms of measures of abrupt changes, by specific current unemployment, economic and demographic data. To illustrate, the *variable definition* of per capita employment decline is the "loss of per capita employment between 1960 and 1970" with the *variable standard* of such loss set at "a decline of more than 1.2 percentage points between 1960 and 1970" (see Exhibit 2).

While there is a rather substantial similarity in Title I variable definitions and standards with those employed under the UDAG program, the former's *eligibility criteria* are far less restrictive. Essentially a Redevelopment Area is designated as a matter of right if a *single* threshold standard is met (i.e., a community with an unemployment rate of 6 percent or more qualifies) as opposed to a UDAG requirement of meeting *three of six* standards. Consequently, more cities are deemed eligible to apply for EDA Title I assistance than for UDAG grants. The practical effect of this difference is, in part, mitigated by a stringent EDA project selection stage as is discussed below.

The EDA program closest to UDAG in objective and area eligibility is Title IX assistance. There are two components to Title IX: *Long Term Economic Deterioration (Title IX—LTED); and (2) Sudden and Severe Economic Dislocation (Title IX—SSED)*. The *legislative intent* of *Title IX—LTED* is to assist severe and long-term economically depressed communities.[27] Two major dimensions of this concern are evidenced by the *conceptual indicators*—chronic distress and current economic distress (Exhibit 3). Thus two distinct sets of quantifiable variables are formulated, incorporating measures of *chronic* economic deterioration as well as variables gauging more *acute* conditions.[28]

Chronic distress is defined *(variable definition)* as the failure to keep pace with average national economic growth trends as measured

EXHIBIT 2

Programmatic Area Eligibility: Suffering Substantial and Persistent Unemployment-Redevelopment Area

PROGRAM/INDEX/ALLOCATION: Economic Development Administration (Title I, Section 201, Section 202, and other EDA assistance) Redevelopment Area definition

CONCEPTUAL INDICATORS: Suffering Substantial and Persistent Unemployment–Redevelopment Area

QUANTIFIABLE VARIABLES: Unemployment, Per Capita Employment Decline, Sudden Rise in Unemployment, Median Family Income, Loss of Population, Other Variables.

VARIABLE DEFINITION: *Unemployment:* Area has experienced "substantial unemployment rate" above national average for preceding six months as measured by statistics provided by the Bureau of Labor Statistics.
Per Capita Employment Decline: Loss in per capita employment between 1960 and 1970 as measured by Bureau of Labor Statistics.
Sudden Rise in Unemployment: Loss, removal, curtailment or closing of a major source of unemployment has caused (within three years *prior* to application) or will cause (within three years *after* application) an unusual and abrupt rise in employment.
Median Family Income: The 1970 area median family income compared to 1970 national median family income as indicated in the 1970 census.
Loss of Population: Substantial loss in area population due to lack of employment opportunity as measured by Census and Bureau of Labor Statistics.
Other Variables: Redevelopment area designated under Economic Opportunity Act of 1964.

EXHIBIT 2 (CONTINUED)

VARIABLE LINKAGE: None

VARIABLE STANDARDS:

Unemployment: Unemployment rate of 6 percent or more; or (b) where the average rate of unemployment has been at least 50 % above national average for 3 of the preceeding 4 calendar years; 75 percent above the national average for 2 of the preceeding 3 calendar years: or 100 percent above the national average for 1 of the preceeding 2 calendar years.

Per Capita Employment Decline: Decline in per capita employment of more than 1.2 percentage points between 1960 and 1970 and areas which also have net outmigration during this period as measured by the 1970 census.

Sudden Rise in Unemployment: Increase in unemployment of at least 500 persons or increase of 2 percentage points or more in area unemployment rate.

Median Family Income: Area median family income must not exceed 50% of national median family income.

Loss of Population: Currently not considered (implicity evaluated in other standards).

ELIGIBILITY CRITERIA: Any one of the standards shown above.

Note: The description "Suffering Substantial and Persistent Unemployment" is found in the Statement of Purpose of the Public Works and Employment Act of 1965 (42 USC 3121).

Source: Economic Development Administration, "Administrative Regulations for Designation of Areas", 13 CFR 302.

EXHIBIT 3

Programmatic Area Eligibility: Long-Term Economic Deterioration

PROGRAM/INDEX/ALLOCATION:	Economic Development Administration Title IX measure of Long-Term Economic Deterioration (LTED). (See Exhibit 4 for Title IX-SSED)
CONCEPTUAL INDICATORS:	*Chronic Distress* / *Current Economic Distress*
QUANTIFIABLE VARIABLES:	Relative lag in employment, population, and per capita income / Unemployment, Per Capita Income
VARIABLE DEFINITION:	*Chronic Distress:* Failure to keep pace with average national economic growth trends over the last five years as measured by relative employment, population and income characteristics (see below). / *Unemployment: Very high* current annual unemployment rate as measured by Bureau of Labor Statistics. / *Per Capita Income: Low* per capita income relative to the national average according to the most recent Treasury statistics.
VARIABLE LINKAGES:	None

EXHIBIT 3 (CONTINUED)

VARIABLE STANDARDS:

Chronic Distress:

(see note below on computation of national average)

a. Five year *average rate of unemployment* greater than national average.

b. Five year *growth in employment* less than the national average.

c. Five year *growth in population* less than the national average.

d. Five year *absolute change in per capita income* less than the national average.

Unemployment: At least 12 percent annual unemployment rate.

Per Capita Income: 75 percent or less of the current national average per capita income.

Separate national averages are computed for SMSAs and areas outside SMSAs. No community is eligible if the per capita income of its residents exceeds 125 percent of the national average.

ELIGIBILITY CRITERIA:

One of *three* standards (unemployment, per capita income, or Chronic Distress). To qualify on a Chronic Distress standard, area must exhibit three out of the four constitutent standards (see a-d above). Area need is considered in selecting from eligible area project applications. Indications of local need include out-migration and/or decline of industries, erosion of the tax base, physical deterioration of capital stock, and decline of public services and amenities.

Source: Economic Development Administration, "Special Economic Development and Adjustment Assistance", 13 CFR 308, 43 FR 57918, December 11, 1978.

by relative: 1) unemployment; 2) employment; 3) population growth and 4) per capita income. The *variable standards* of the four variables comprising chronic distress are measured by five-year trends (i.e., five-year growth in population less than the national average). There is an additional requirement that to qualify on a chronic distress standard, an area must exhibit *three out of the four* constituent variables.

Current distress has the following *variable definitions and standards:* unemployment (at least 12 percent) and per capita income (75 percent or less of the current national average). An area must meet one of the two measures (unemployment *or* per capita income) in order to establish eligibility under current economic distress.

Consequently, the *eligibility criteria* of Title IX—LTED thus require areas to meet one out of three standards: *chronic distress* (three out of four sub-standards); *unemployment;* or *per capita income* (with the latter two elements defining current economic distress). The structure of this somewhat more complex "pass-fail" approach may reflect an implicit weighting scheme since eligibility requires meeting only one of the two acute distress criteria (current annual unemployment, or current per capita income) while it requires *three out of the four* subsets for acceptance under the "chronic distress" category. The inclusion of the former may well serve to broaden participation in, or to ease qualification for, the program.[29]

The Title IX—SSED Program is capulized in Exhibit 4. This program focuses on a third stage of a continuum reflecting duration of economic distress. The first two, current and chronic distress are addressed by Title IX—LTED. The third, sudden and severe economic dislocation, is addressed by Title IX—SSED. The *conceptual indicator* of Title IX—SSED - sudden and severe economic dislocation - has one *quantifiable variable*—unemployment (job loss) defined *(quantifiable variable)* as shown in Exhibit 4. Title IX—SSED has four *variable standards* of unemployment (job loss), depending upon: 1) whether an area is in or outside an SMSA: and 2) the relative local unemployment rate. To illustrate, for SMSAs with an unemployment rate *exceeding* the national average, the unemployment (job loss) standard is 0.5 percent unemployment or a direct reduction of at least 4,000 jobs (see Exhibit 4).

Title IX—SSED illustrates the range of possible formats—including percentage changes versus absolute changes—measuring and appraising a particular dimension of distress. Although more detailed variable analyses will be made in section three of this paper, it is useful to note that Title IX—SSED is characterized by a *combined* measurement approach. It incorporates within its variable definition not only proportional increases in unemployment but also absolute increments of change. General eligibility is determined by either alternative—for example, a loss of 0.5 percent of the employed population or alternately, an absolute loss of 4,000 direct jobs. Targeted under these standards is attention to immediate issues such as local plant closings, etc.

It is important to stress that the Title I, Title IX—LTED and Title IX—SSED area eligibility standards discussed above represent a first round approval process. The basic eligibility criteria of this first round are relatively generous, thus providing a very high level of inclusion. Given limited resources, the second stage of the procedure— i.e., determining from the wide range of claimants who will secure funding—is an implicit necessity.[30] A two-stage approach, eligibility and then project selection, thus characterizes both UDAG and EDA. The two differ, however, in the degree of sifting at the first round. Compared to UDAG, the EDA programs have broad first-stage admission standards, i.e., a larger proportion of urban areas are deemed qualified to submit applications for funding, in some cases as high as 80 to 90 percent of all jurisdictions. At the second or project selection stage, however, the EDA programs have a higher attrition rate, i.e., relative to UDAG, a higher proportion of program-eligible cities do not have their applications funded.

Submunicipal and Special Impact Area Programs.

Within the broad category of programmatic area eligibility there is a distinct subset of programs designed to extend eligibility to *smaller impacted subareas located within jurisdictions which as a whole fail to achieve eligibility under extant impact criteria.* Major examples include: *UDAG Pockets of Poverty* and *EDA Special Impact Areas.*[31]

The original formulation of the UDAG program embodied, as its conceptual basis, the concept of juridical communities which were faced with a variety of physical and economic distress conditions, a lack of self-help capacity to rectify these problems, and a set of potential projects which, with a federal boost, could be implemented and would yield positive results in rectifying conditions of distress. Subsequently, as a complement to this approach, the concept of "Pockets of Poverty" was introduced. This was an effort to incorporate subareas of municipalities which had specific criteria of distress but which were located within jurisdictional boundaries which in *total* did not meet the distress criteria of the broader UDAG program.

Exhibit 5 shows the measures used in identifying these pockets. The Pockets of Poverty *conceptual indicators* use income and poverty as *quantifiable variables* with income and poverty *(variable definition)*

EXHIBIT 4

Programmatic Area Eligibility: Sudden and Severe Economic Dislocation

PROGRAM/INDEX/ALLOCATION: Economic Development Administration Title IX measure of Sudden and Severe Economic Dislocation (SSED) (see Exhibit 3 for Title IX LTED)

CONCEPTUAL INDICATORS: Sudden and Severe Economic Dislocation

QUANTIFIABLE VARIABLES: *Unemployment* (Job loss)

VARIABLE DEFINITION: *Unemployment* (Job loss): Economic dislocation (see note below) resulting in job loss that is significant both in terms of number of jobs eliminated and the attendant impact upon the employment rate as measured by the Bureau of Labor Statistics. The two basic types of eligible economic dislocation include: (1) job losses due to direct actions of the Federal Government, import competition or disasters; or (2) sudden major economic changes of a magnitude beyond the capacity of an area to respond. Discussion in this exhibit focuses on former dislocation type.

VARIABLE LINKAGES: None

EXHIBIT 4 (CONTINUED)

VARIABLE STANDARDS:

A. *For SMSAs with an unemployment rate exceeding the national average:* unemployment (job loss) amounting to
  a. 0.5 percent of the employed population, or
  b. 4,000 direct jobs

B. *For SMSAs with an unemployment rate equal to or less than the national average:* unemployment (job loss) amounting to
  a. 1 percent of the employed population or
  b. 8,000 direct jobs

C. *For non-SMSA areas with an unemployment rate exceeding the national average:* unemployment (job loss) amounting to
  a. 2 percent of the employed population, or
  b. 500 direct jobs

D. *For non-SMSA areas with an unemployment rate equal to or less than the national average:* unemployment (job loss) amounting to
  a. 4 percent of the employed population or
  b. 1,000 direct jobs

ELIGIBILITY CRITERIA:

Above standards are *minimum* criteria. *Specific Preference Factors* include number of jobs lost, percentage increase in unemployment due to the dislocation, characteristics of the affected work force, composition and status of the area economy/workforce, probable magnitude of the secondary/tertiary impacts on the area and national implications.

Source: Economic Development Administration, "Special Economic Development and Adjustment Assistance," 13 CFR 308; 43 FR 52432, November 9, 1978.

defined by the Census. The *variable standards* are as follows: *income* — at least 70 percent of the residents in the Pocket must have incomes below 80 percent of the jurisdiction's median income; *poverty* — at least 30 percent of the residents in the Pocket must have incomes below the national poverty level (see Exhibit 5 for size and other areal requirements). The *eligibility criteria* require that *both* of these standards (income *and* poverty) be satisfied.

The Economic Development Administration's *Special Impact Area* program is conceptually comparable to UDAG Pockets of Poverty (see Exhibits 5 and 6 respectively). Operationally the two are also similar in considering identical or related variables such as income, poverty and unemployment. There is a difference, however, in the scale of geographic incidence. Pockets of Poverty essentially refers to distressed *neighborhoods* within economically sound *communities,* while a Special Impact Area is a more encompassing "floating distress zone" which can include, for example, an economically impacted municipality within a larger non-distressed county.

The issue of geographical scale has implications not only for what area is being examined but what data are *available* for measuring distress. Income, poverty, unemployment and other common data sets used in measuring distress are often available only for larger geographic areas, i.e., counties rather than cities or only for cities of a certain size such as those above 50,000 population. This limitation adds to the difficulty of small area eligibility determination.

RELATIVE DISTRESS/NEED INDICES

These indices are analytical schemes which establish urban distress/ need rankings for evaluative or illustrative purposes as opposed to the purpose of formal program eligibility. Examples examined here include: the *Intrametropolitan* and *Intercity Hardship Indices* developed by the Brookings Institution, the *Urban Need Index* developed by the Congressional Budget Office, the *Community Need Index* developed by HUD; the *Evaluation Index* developed by the Institute for the Future; and the *Urban Fiscal Strain* and *Composite Fiscal Strain Indices* developed by the U.S. Treasury.

Brookings Institution Intrametropolitan and Intercity Hardship Indices.

Exhibits 7 and 8 detail two of the more commonly cited approaches to rank ordering of municipal distress. The goal of both the

EXHIBIT 5

Programmatic Area Eligibility: Pockets of Poverty

PROGRAM/INDEX ALLOCATION:	Urban Development Action Grant measure of Pockets of Poverty (Severely distressed areas in communities/counties not meeting Action Grant Program distress criteria)
CONCEPTUAL INDICATORS:	Pockets of Poverty
QUANTIFIABLE VARIABLES:	Income, Poverty
VARIABLE DEFINITION:	*Income:* Area (see note below) income below jurisdiction's median income as measured by Census and other sources. *Poverty:* Area (see note below) residents have income below the national poverty level (pursuant to criteria provided by the Office of Management and Budget) as measured by Census and other sources.
VARIABLE LINKAGES:	None
VARIABLE STANDARDS:	*Income:* At least 70 percent of the residents residing in the Pocket of Poverty must have incomes below 80 percent of the jurisdiction's median income. *Poverty:* At least 30 percent of the residents in the Pocket of Poverty must have incomes below the national poverty level.
ELIGIBILITY CRITERIA:	Income and poverty standards must both be satisfied. (See note below for minimum geographical size requirements)
Note:	A Pocket of Poverty is an *area* composed of contiguous census tracts, enumeration districts or block groups. For cities above 50,000 population and urban counties, the pocket must contain at least 10,000 persons or 10 percent of the jurisdiction's population. For cities below 50,000 population, the pocket must contain at least 2,500 persons or 10 percent of the jurisdiction's population whichever is more. (Enumeration districts and block groups with median incomes greater than 120 percent of the median income are excluded.)
Source:	U.S. Department of Housing and Urban Development, "Community Development Block Grants: Modification to Urban Development Action Grant Rules to Accomodate Communities Containing Pockets of Poverty," 45 FR 10740, February 15, 1980.

EXHIBIT 6

Programmatic Area Eligibility: Special Impact Area

PROGRAM/INDEX/ALLOCATION:	Economic Development Administration Special Impact Area.
CONCEPTUAL INDICATOR:	Special Impact Area (Pockets of poverty within an otherwise healthy area economy).
QUANTIFIABLE VARIABLES:	Unemployment, Low Income Persons, Rural areas having substantial out-migration.
VARIABLE DEFINITIONS:	*Unemployment:* Area with an abrupt rise in unemployment (see Exhibit 2) or high unemployment as indicated by data from Bureau of Labor Statistics. *Low-Income Persons:* Concentration of poverty families as defined by the Office of Economic Opportunity. *Rural areas having substantial out-migration:* Large outmigration from 1960 to 1970 as established by Bureau of Census or other data indicating out-migration for a more recent 10 year period.
VARIABLE LINKAGE:	None
VARIABLE STANDARDS:	*Unemployment:* For abrupt rise, see Exhibit 2; for substantial unemployment–annual average unemployment rate of at least 8.5 percent. *Low Income Persons:* Majority of families living in poverty. *Rural areas having substantial out-migration:* 1960-1970 out-migration rate of at least 25 percent.
ELIGIBILITY CRITERIA:	Any one of the standards shown above.

Note: There are numerous types of Special Impact Areas, for example, Redevelopment Areas designated by Title VII of the community Services Act are considered Special Impact Areas.

Source: Economic Development Administration, "EDA Administration Regulations for Designation of Areas," 13 CFR 302.

Intrametropolitan Hardship Index and the *Intercity Hardship Index* is to provide a single index generating summary relative ratings for comparative analysis of the level of "city hardship."³² The Intrametropolitan Index shows city stress compared to surrounding suburbs; the Intercity Index shows the distress of one city compared to all cities.

While the two indices measure hardship from different persepctives, they are almost identical in their variable selection, variable linkage and so on. The Intrametropolitan and Intercity rankings have identical *quantifiable variables* (unemployment, dependency, education, income level, crowded housing and poverty), and *variable definitions* (see Exhibits 7 and 8). Both follow a similar *variable linkage* with each of the variables converted into a standard score. The individual scores are not weighted, i.e., each of the parameters is assessed equally, but rather summed and an overall average standard score then determined. The resulting composite index therefore provides a rank ordering indicating the comparative hardship among the jurisdictions included in the analysis.

While the Brookings classification scheme is not used for eligibility determination, its adoption for such a task would involve setting of a threshold level (elibigility criterion or standard) on the index. The exact specification of such a cut-off point would involve a normative judgement, similar in nature to that of UDAG in requiring three of six standards to be met as the basic eligibility criterion. Thus, the distinction between a "pass-fail" and a "relative distress (hardship or need) gradient" may be overemphasized. The latter approach is ultimately transformed into a "pass-fail" system if a threshold standard of eligibility is established on the composite index.

The Brookings Institution's rankings sparked continued research in the "objective" measurement of urban distress. The rankings developed by Brookings have also been used as individual variables in other ranking systems as is illustrated in the following index.

Congressional Budget Office (CBO) Urban Need Index.

The CBO *Urban Need Index* was determined to consist of three major phenomena: social, economic and fiscal; thus three parallel *conceptual indicator* categories were employed—social need, economic need, and fiscal need.³³ For each of these dimensions of need, different sets of *quantifiable variables* are utilized. To illustrate, the quantifiable variables for the economic need conceptual indicator include employment change, population change, per

EXHIBIT 7

Relative Distress/Need Indices: Intrametropolitan Hardship Index

PROGRAM/INDEX/ALLOCATION: Brookings Institution (1979) Intrametropolitan Hardship Index

CONCEPTUAL INDICATORS: Intrametropolitan Socioeconomic Hardship

QUANTIFIABLE VARIABLES: Unemployment, Dependency, Education, Income Level, Crowded Housing, Poverty

VARIABLE DEFINITION: *Unemployment* (percent of civilian labor force unemployed)
Dependency (persons less than eighteen or over sixty-four years of age as a percent of total population)
Education (percent of persons twenty-five years of age or more with less than twelfth-grade education)
Income level (per capita income)
Crowded housing (percent of occupied housing units with more than one person per room)
Poverty (percent of families below 125 percent of low-income level) (all 1970 Census measurements)

VARIABLE LINKAGES: City-suburban ratios are calculated in each metropolitan area for each measure. For per capita income, where a higher amount is a "desirable" characteristic, the suburban amount in each instance was divided by the city area amount. For each of the other five variables, involving "undesirable characteristics," the city value was divided by the suburban value.

EXHIBIT 7 (CONTINUED)

VARIABLE LINKAGES:

The resulting ratios are standardized to avoid giving undue weight to any of the six characteristics. This was done by assigning a value of 100 to the range of variation in each of the six sets of ratios. For instance, for the crowded-housing ratio, the highest and lowest cities are: Newark 3.40, and Salt Lake City; 0.52. A value of 100 was assigned to 3.40 and a value of 0 to 0.52. The ratios in between these two are assigned values from 0 to 100 using the following formula:

$$X = (\frac{Y \quad - \quad Ymin}{Ymax \quad - \quad Ymin}) \; 100$$

where X = standardized ratio to be created

Y = ratios calculated from data in U.S. Bureau of the Census, *County and City Data Book*, 1972, Tables 3 and 6.

Ymax = maximum value of Y

Ymin = minimum value of Y

To continue with the Newark example: its six separate standardized ratios were calculated with the above formula; the ratios were then summed and the total divided by 6. This yielded the figure of 94.8 (if Newark had scored the highest on all six ratios, this number would have been 100 by definition). This operation was repeated for all of the cities, ending up with a composite index with values ranging from 94.8 for Newark to 9.6 for Greensboro.

For purposes of clarity, however, the index is displayed so that cities could be easily identified as to whether they were worse off or better off than their suburbs. To accomplish this, the composite index was adjusted to a base level of 100. The value, 100, would be in this new set the index of a city whose statistics are the same as its suburbs. On a standardized basis (from 0 to 100), such a city would score 22.44. (This is the mean of the standardized index obtained for a city with a ratio of 1,000 on each of the six separate measures.) The central city disadvantage index of Newark thus becomes the ratio of 94.8 to 22.44 (times 100): 422.

Source: Richard P. Nathan and Charles Adams, "Understanding Central City Hardship," *Political Science Quarterly*, Vol. 91, No. 1 (Spring 1976).

EXHIBIT 8

Related Distress/Need Indices: Intercity, Hardship Index

PROGRAM/INDEX/ALLOCATION: Brookings Institution (1976) Intercity Hardship Index

CONCEPTUAL INDICATORS: Intercity Socioeconomic Hardship

QUANTIFIABLE VARIABLES: Unemployment, Dependency, Education, Income Level, Crowded Housing, Poverty

VARIABLE DEFINITION:
Unemployment (percent of civilian labor force unemployed)
Dependency (persons less than eighteen or over sixty-four years of age as a percent of total population)
Education (percent of persons twenty-five years of age or more with less than twelfth-grade education)
Income level (per capita income) (adjusted)
Crowded Housing (percent of occupied housing units with more than one person per room)
Poverty (percent of families below 125 percent of low-income level) (adjusted) (all 1970 census measurements)

(All 1970 census measurements)

VARIABLE LINKAGES:
The variables are standardized according to the procedures specified in the Intrametropolitan Hardship Index, although ratios are not employed. The six standardized values for each city are then summed and the total divided by 6 to establish an overall average. The overall average was not restandardized to base 100.

The adjustment to the per capita income variable is based on the BLS index of annual budgets at the "intermediate level" of living for a four-person urban family. The family unit around which this budget is constructed consists of an employed husband, aged thirty-eight, a wife not employed outside the home, and two children, ages eight and thirteen. The types of consumption reflected in the budget include food, housing, transportation, clothing, and medical care.

EXHIBIT 8 (Continued)

VARIABLE LINKAGES:

This adjustment was made by dividing the income variable for each city by its specific budget index. (For twenty-five of the cities in the sample, direct budget indexes were available from the BLS compilation. For the remaining thirty cities, estimates of budget indexes were made on the basis of proximity to cities included in the BLS compilation.) As a result, cities with a higher than average budget have their per capita income measure reduced; the opposite occurs for cities with a below-average budget. Comparable adjustments were made to the suburban per capita income variable in computing the intersuburb index. (The underlying assumption is that while differences in city and suburban budget size may exist, differences among suburban areas will correspond closely with differences among cities.)

For the variable percent of families below 125 percent of the low-income level, the BLS index of annual budgets at the "lower level" of living for a four-person urban family was used. There are important differences between the lower and intermediate budget levels in terms of the composition of spending as well as in the level of total spending. For example, families in the lower-level budget group are all assumed to be renters.

Using the lower-level budget index, the percent of low-income families variable was adjusted for both the city and suburban index by multiplying that variable by the lower-level budget index. The result was that cities and suburbs in which the lower consumption standard could be financed at relatively less cost had the percent of low-income families variable reduced, whereas for areas where it cost relatively more, an upward adjustment was made to the percent of low-income families variable.

Source: Richard P. Nathan and Charles Adams, "Understanding Central City Hardship," *Political Science Quarterly,* Vol. 91, No. 1 (Spring, 1976).

capita income change, density and aged housing (see Exhibit 9 for variable definitions).

CBO linked *(variable linkage)* the variables as follows. A composite score for each of the dimensions was derived by converting each of the variables into standard scores and an overall average measure secured for each dimension. Thus, a standardized score for each of the quantifiable variables—for each of the municipalities or areas under consideration—is calculated. These are simply summed and averaged in order to secure a rank order listing—the Urban Need Index—on each dimension/conceptual indicator. The principal difference in this procedure, as compared to the Brookings hardship indices, lies in variable definition and complexity; the quantitative technique of index development is virtually identical (see Exhibits 7 through 9).

While the CBO index does provide an effort to maximize variable inputs, the problems of including composite indices such as those grouped under "hardship" together with additional measures raise some very real questions of double counting. It may embody an implicit overweighting of certain variables at the expense of others which might well be argued to be of equal merit. Additionally, the use of ten "raw data" variables in conjunction with four existing indices (each derived from extensive data sets) may well be overly complicated for general understanding. Nonetheless, the explicit development of indices derived from the major dimensions (conceptual indicators) of urban need is of considerable merit.

Department of Housing and Urban Development: Community Need Index. The *Community Need Index* was developed by HUD in 1979 in part as a response to a congressional mandate for an evaluation of city need and CDBG funding.[34] It illustrates the broad range of parameters which can be utilized in urban distress measurement (see Exhibit 10). The Community Need Index further establishes a greater level of sophistication of index formulation by using a grouping algorithm to provide a simplification of the multiple data elements which are considered. The procedure used takes 20 quantifiable variables (incorporating elements of demography, poverty, economic activity, and various measures of social trauma; see Exhibit 10 for *quantifiable variables and variable definitions*), and reduces them into a smaller number of dimensions by the use of factor analysis. This procedure inductively yields three components, or *conceptual indicators,* of community need: *Age and Decline, Density,* and *Poverty.* (In Exhibit 10, the evaluative structure is somewhat artificial, since the conceptual indicators are the result of the factor analysis of the 20 variables. The variables are not deduced from the conceptual dimensions.) For each of the cities, the procedure produces a score on each of the three indicators (factors). The individual indicator scores are then weighted with the linkage procedure (see Exhibit 10 for *variable linkage*) yielding a single index of community need. This process, while complex, is similar to approaches earlier considered (Exhibits 7 throught 9) in their use of a synthetic index.

Institute for the Future Evaluation Index. The HUD procedure outlined above is paralleled in terms of comprehensiveness by the *Evaluation Index* developed in 1975 by the Institute for the Future.[35] This index was constructed in order to evaluate the distribution of revenue sharing funds. It considers three *conceptual indicators— public service requirements, ability to finance* and *level of tax effort—* which in turn consist of multiple *quantifiable variables.* (Actually, as in the case of the HUD Community Need Index, the quantifiable variables are grouped via factor analysis in order to derive the three conceptual indicators.) A complex set of statistical procedures are followed in a *variable linkage* effort to secure a simple composite measure, the Evaluation Index. The data elements and methodological approach followed by the Institute for the Future in deriving the service requirements, finance ability and tax effort are described in Exhibit 11.

U.S. Department of the Treasury: Urban Fiscal Strain Index. A final relative distress measure is presented in Exhibit 12—*the Urban Fiscal Strain Index* devised by the U.S. Department of the Treasury.[36] "Fiscal Strain" is not explicitly broken down into major components but rather stands as a single *conceptual indicator* with five *quantifiable variables* (population change, per capita income change, own source revenue burden change, long-term debt burden change and property value change), gauging a range of urban fiscal conditions. Most interesting are the relatively sophisticated *variable linkage and standards.* These are shown in Exhibit 12 and are summarized below.

A composite index—*Composite Fiscal Strain Index*—is constructed in a fashion analogous to that of the Congressional Budget Office Urban Need Index (Exhibit 9). First, the five fiscal strain variables are converted into standard deviation units (Z scores) with each of the Z scores individually weighted and summed to obtain a *Total Fiscal Strain Value.* These values themselves serve to rank order the cities under analysis. In addition, a *Composite Fiscal Strain Index* is formulated using the Total Fiscal Strain Value as well as five other

EXHIBIT 9

Relative Distress/Need Indices: Urban Need Index

PROGRAM/INDEX/ALLOCATION:	Congressional Budget Office (1978) Urban Need Index		
CONCEPTUAL INDICATORS:	*SOCIAL NEED*	*ECONOMIC NEED*	*FISCAL NEED*
QUANTIFIABLE VARIABLES:	Hardship (2) (see Exhibits 7 and 8) Unemployment Per Capita Income	Employment Change (2) Population Change Per Capita Income Change Density Aged Housing	Tax Effort Property Tax Base (Re-source Base) Service Needs (2)
VARIABLE DEFINITION:	*Intrametropolitan Hardship Index:* (see Exhibit 7) *Instercity Hardship Index* (see Exhibit 8) *Unemployment:* Rate for 1976 *Per Capita Income:* Level in 1973	*Employment Change:* Percent change in total employment within the metropolitan area between 1970 and 1975; percent change in manufacturing jobs within the city between 1963 and 1972. *Population Change:* Percent change between 1960 and 1973. *Per Capita Income Change:* Percent change between 1960 and 1973. *Density:* Population per square mile in 1970. *Aged Housing:* Proportion of housing stock built prior to 1940 (in 1970).	*Tax Effort:* Taxes as a percent of personal income. *Property Tax Base:* Valuation Per Capita. *Service Needs:* HUD Index No. 1 (see note below) HUD Index No. 2

EXHIBIT 9 (Continued)

VARIABLE LINKAGES: The composite indexes of social, economic and fiscal need were created by combining individual measures (detailed in the text) using a method designed to assign equal importance to each component. First, the individual measures were standardized by assigning a value of 100 to the range of variation among cities using the following formula:

$$x = \frac{y - y_a}{y_b - y_a} \quad \text{where,}$$

x = standardized score to be created for each city

y = value on a specific measure of urban need for each city

y_a = value of y indicating least need

y_b = value of y indicating greatest need

Thus, for each measure, the city with the greatest need (that is, the lowest per capita income, the highest unemployment rate, etc.) was assigned a score of 100 and the city with the lowest need a score of 0. Second, the composite measure of need for each city was determined by calculating the average score received on the standardized component measures.

Note: HUD Index No. 1 and HUD Index No. 2 were formulated in Harold Bunce, *An Evaluation of the Community Development Block Grant Formula* (Washington, D.C.: U.S. Department of Housing and Urban Development, 1976).

Source: Congressional Budget Office, *City Need and the Responsiveness of Federal Grants Programs* (1978). See Subcommittee on the City of the Committee on Banking, Finance and Urban Affairs, House of Representatives, 95th Congress, Second Session, *City Need and the Responsiveness of Federal Grants Programs* (Washington, D.C.: Government Printing Office, 1975).

EXHIBIT 10

Relative Distress/Need Indices: Community Need

PROGRAM/INDEX/ALLOCATION:	HUD analysis (1979) Community Need Index		
CONCEPTUAL INDICATOR:	*Age and Decline*	*Density*	*Poverty*
QUANTIFIABLE VARIABLES/ VARIABLE DEFINITIONS:	CPOP6075, PRE1939H, POPAGE65, CRES6372 CRS6372, CPOP7075, CEMP6772, POPAGE65, NEW H, FEMALEH	CRIME, DENSITY, RENTER CHPNEGRO, NONWHITE UNEMPL, FEMALEH	YOUTHPOV, POVERTY, NONWHITE, OVERCRWD, WOPLUM, FEMALEH, WOHSED

CPOP6075 – percent change in population, 1960-75 (inverse indicator of need)

PRE1939H – pre-1939 Housing

POPAGE65 – percent of the population over 65

CRES6372 – percent change in retail sales establishments, 1963-72 (inverse indicator of need)

CRS6372 – percent change in retail sales, 1963-72 (inverse indicator of need)

CPOP7075 – percent change in population, 1970-75 (inverse indicator of need)

POPAGE65 – percent of the population over 65

CRIME – number of violent crimes per 10,000 of the population, 1976

DENSITY – population per square mile

RENTER – percent of housing units occupied by a renter

CHPNEGRO – change in the percentage Negro, 1960-70

NONWHITE – percent of population nonwhite(Negro and Spanish)

UNEMPL – unemployment rate, defined by giving equal weights to the 1976, 1977 and December 1977 unemployment rates

YOUTHPOV – percent of occupied poor and under 18

POVERTY – percent of population with incomes below the poverty level

NONWHITE – percent of population nonwhite (Negro and Spanish)

OVERCRWD – percent of occupied houses with 1.01 or more persons per room

WOPLUMB – percent of occupied houses without adequate plumbing

FEMALEH – percent of families with a female head

WOHSED – percent of population over 25 with less than a high school education

EXHIBIT 10 (Continued)

QUANTIFIABLE VARIABLES/
VARIABLE DEFINITIONS:

NEWH–new private housing units authorized by building permits in 1975 and 1976 as a percentage of total housing (inverse indicator of need)

FEMALEH–percent of families with a female head

CEMP6772–percent change in retail, wholesale and service employment, 1967-72 (inverse indicator of need)

VARIABLE LINKAGE:

The 20 quantifiable (need) variables were grouped via factor analysis into three sets or dimensions: AGE AND DECLINE, DENSITY, and POVERTY, For each of these three dimensions, factor analysis provided a city index score measuring relative per capita need among cities. A city generally received a high score on the three dimensions if it had a high percentage of most of the variables that defined that factor (positive scores indicate above average per capita need; negative scores below average per capita need). A single or composite index of community need was derived by combining and weighting the three dimensions as follows:

$$\text{NEED} = .40 \ (\text{POVERTY}) + .35 \ (\text{AGE AND DECLINE}) + .35 \ (\text{DENSITY})$$

Source: Harold L. Bunce and Robert L. Goldberg, *City Need and Community Development Funding* (Washington, D.C.: Government Printing Office, January 1979), U.S. Department of Housing and Urban Development, Office of Policy Development and Research, Division of Evaluation.

pre-existing urban stress indices (presented in Exhibit 12) as input variables.

A potentially severe problem of double-counting or over-weighting may be inherent in this approach, since a number of the indices added to the analysis are composed of similar variables. Standards are then established on the composite index so that the ranking of cities can be partitioned into three categories of strain—high, moderate and low. And the setting of the cutoff points is somewhat arbitrary, based on defining the top ten scorers as high, etc. Given the data base requirements of this approach it is limited to major cities.

RESOURCE ALLOCATION PROCEDURE

Sensitivity to urban hardship is also inherent in resource allocation formulae. The objective of these mechanisms is no longer on programmatic area eligibility nor indices of relative distress; assuming that the criteria for entrance into a program are established, their task is the distribution of resources via quantitative procedures. It is the composition and structure of the latter which provide insight into, and are conceptually linked to, measures and criteria of distress, i.e., they are efforts to allocate funds proportionate to some criteria of problem status.

Principal among them and providing a prototype for the genus as a whole is the approach shown in Exhibit 13 for *Community Development Block Grant* resource allocation. In addition to the CDBG approach, the resource allocation formula for federal *Revenue Sharing* is shown in Exhibit 14 and the equivalent for the *Comprehensive Employment and Training Assistance* program (CETA) is detailed in Exhibit 15.[37]

All three programs are characterized by complicated allocation approaches and are only summarized here. The Development Block Grant program considers five *quantifiable variables:* population, poverty, overcrowded housing, growth lag and age of housing. The program's *variable linkage* changed substantially from its initial structure of 1974 shown in Exhibit 13 as Formula 1. Its redefinition in 1977 (Formula 2) provided an alternative to be operationalized if it yielded a larger measure of community assistance for the jurisdictions eligible for the program. A comparison of the two formulae indicates the importance of variable selection in altering the profile of allocation. Cleraly, for example, the age of housing parameter in Formula 2 benefits older, lower growth communities.

The exhibits on Revenue Sharing and CETA show the capacities of equivalent allocation/definitions of need formulae to be utilized

EXHIBIT 11

Relative Distress/Need Indices: Evaluation Index

PROGRAM/INDEX/ALLOCATION: Institute for the Future (1975) Evaluation Index (analysis of needs-based allocation formula for general revenue sharing)

CONCEPTUAL INDICATOR:	*Public Service Requirements*	*Ability to Finance*	*Level of Tax Effort*
QUANTIFIABLE VARIABLES:	Health needs Social service needs Recreation needs Environmental needs Public safety needs Transportation needs	Equalized community property value	Tax effort
VARIABLE DEFINITION:	Health needs indicators (shown as example) –Local suicide rate –Infant mortality rate –Birth rate –Death rate –Families with income below $7,500 –Dwellings with more than 1.01 persons per room –One person households –Population 65 and over –Population less than 5 yrs. old –Population younger than 18 and below poverty level –Population 65 and over and below poverty level	Community assessed value adjusted by equalization ratio	See tax effort definitions for Revenue Sharing (Exhibit 14)

VARIABLE LINKAGE: Need indices for each service category, (i.e., health, public safety, etc.) were derived by factor analysis. A composite public service requirement measure was formed by adding the separate individual service measures with each assigned a weight in proportion to their dollar expenditure. A composite evaluation index was determined as follows:

$$\text{Service Requirement} \times \text{Tax Effort}$$
$$\text{Ability}$$

Source: Gregory Schmid, Hubert Lipinski and Michael Palmer, *An Alternative Approach to General Revenue Sharing: A Needs Based Allocation Formula* (Menlo Park, CA: Institute for the Future, 1975).

EXHIBIT 12

Relative Distress/Need Indices: Urban Fiscal Strain

PROGRAM/INDEX/ALLOCATION:	U.S. Treasury (1978) Urban Fiscal Strain Index for 48 largest cities
CONCEPTUAL INDICATOR:	Urban Fiscal Strain
QUANTIFIABLE VARIABLE:	Population Change, Per Capita Income Change, Own Source Revenue Burden Change, Long Term Debt Burden Change, Property Value Change
VARIABLE DEFINITION:	*Population Change:* Annual average local population change between 1972 and 1976 (based on U.S. Census data).
	Per Capita Income Change: Average change in local per capita income between 1969 and 1974 (based on U.S. Census data) as compared to average change in national per capita income between 1969 and 1974.
	Own-Source Revenue Burden Change: Average change in local per capita own source revenue between 1972 and 1976 (based on Census of Government's data) as compared to average change in local per capita income from 1969 to 1974 (based on U.S. Census data).
	Long-Term Debt Burden Change: Average change in local per capita long-term debt outstanding between 1972 and 1976 (based on Census of Governments' data) as compared to average change in local per capita income from 1969 to 1974 (based on U.S. Census data).
	Property Change: Average change in local full market property value from 1971 to 1976 (based on Census of Governments' data).
VARIABLE LINKAGE:	1. Statistical z scores were developed for each city for each indicator by comparing the value for each city divided by the standard deviation from the mean of the 48 largest cities.
	2. Each of the five fiscal strain z scores were weighted as follows: Population Change, .37; Per Capita Income Change, .27; Own Source Revenue Burden Change, .12; Long Term Debt Burden Change, .12; and Change in Full Market Value, .12.
	3. The weighted z scores were summed for each city to obtain a Total Fiscal Strain Value.
	4. The 48 cities were then ranked according to their Total Fiscal Strain Value.

EXHIBIT 12 (Continued)

VARIABLE LINKAGE:

5. A Composite Fiscal Strain Index was developed by considering the ranking of the 48 cities according to 6 "Urban Strain" indices: (a) Treasury Total Fiscal Strain Value, (b) Brookings' Urban Conditions Index, (c) Brookings' Hardship Index, (d) Terry Clark study, (e) National Planning Association Study, and (f) Urban Institute Derived Index.

VARIABLE STANDARDS:

The 48 cities were grouped into high, moderate and low strain categories by considering their deviation from the average for the 48 cities (in terms of their z scores) as follows:

–the 10 cities whose composite z scores were more than –.675 (75th percentile) were categorized as high strain cities.

–the 10 cities whose composite z scores were more than +.675 were categorized as low strain cities, and

–the remaining 28 cities were categorized as moderate strain.

Source: U.S. Department of the Treasury, Office of State and Local Finance, *Report on the Fiscal Impact of the Economic Stimulus Package on 48 Large Urban Governments* (Washington, D.C.: Government Printing Office, 1978).

in a multi-areal staged distribution formula, one in which a proration is made to larger areas which in turn serve as distribution conduits to their constituent elements. This multiple process is most pronounced with respect to revenue sharing which successfully allocates assistance to states, counties and then local units of government.

Summary—State-of-the-Art Urban Distress Measures: Similarities and Differences in Approach and Structure. The partitioning of the several approaches reveals the following themes and characteristics:

1. *While there are individual variations, there are broad similarities in the overall process of indicator operationalization in both the area eligibility and resource allocation measures. Typically, a standard or threshold is established for each of the quantifiable variables—variable linkages are not attempted with the eligibility criteria usually requiring the relevant jurisdictions meeting one or more of the standards. Thus the processes of eligibility determination do not attempt precise rankings of the severity of distress (or other phenomena).*

2. *It is only within the relative distress/need analyses that composite indices and rank orderings of distress/need among jurisdictions are developed. The approaches range in complexity from averaged standard scores across multiple raw variable sets to more comprehensive attempts via factor analysis.*

3. *The differences cited above between the area eligibility/resource allocation measures and relative distress/need indices often blur in practice. For example, area eligibility often follows a two-tier process characterized by "pass-fail" at the first round and some ranking of distress at the second, project selection stage. Conversely, to operationalize a rank order system for eligibility determination requires the establishment of a cut-off point (threshold or standard) on the ranking index. The latter thus transforms a relative distress/need gradient into a "pass-fail" format.*

4. *The varying distress measures often share a common sensitivity to special needs and characteristics. To illustrate, UDAG and Title IX (especially Title IX—LTED) both attempt to gauge/ address chronic urban distress and the Pockets of Poverty and Special Impact Area Programs both provide an additional dimension of sensitivity to different levels of urban distress.*

SECTION FOUR: VARIABLE COMPOSITION
OF ALTERNATIVE DISTRESS MEASURES

Section Three introduced the current urban distress measures and reviewed their overall structure and emphasis. This section extends the analysis to a more detailed level and examines the array of *individual variables* found in the distress indicators. The variables are grouped by: (1) the three categories of distress measures—*programmatic area eligibility, relative distress/need indices, and resource allocation formulae;* and (2) six broad variable categories—*population, employment, housing, income, social and fiscal criteria.*

This sorting allows the comparison of the variables of one program to those of another. Clearly apparent are the programs which contain employment versus income or fiscal variables, population versus housing or social variables, etc. and within these similar subsets, the programs which use absolute versus relative measures or dynamic versus static gauges. This type of procedure enables general statements to be made on the diversity and sophistication of a program's qualification, ranking or allocation criteria as well as the importance of a particular variable set or sets to program participation.

VARIABLE SETS

Variables of distress-indicating mechanisms may be classified into the substantive groupings of population, employment, income, housing, social and fiscal criteria.

Population variables include population change, absolute population numbers, density, specific population-age cohorts related to dependency, etc.

Employment variables consist of employment change in one sector of the economy or another, number or rates of unemployment or significant/abrupt surges in unemployment.

Income variables include the proportion of the population in poverty, those who are defined as low-income, or average/median income or income change relative to other jurisdictions or the nation as a whole.

Housing variables refer to age of structure, housing quality, crowding, number of housing units built annually or percent of year-round housing which is rental.

EXHIBIT 13

Resource Allocation Formula: Community Development Block Grants

PROGRAM/INDEX/ALLOCATION: Community Development Block Grant Allocation of CDBG assistance to metropolitan cities

CONCEPTUAL INDICATOR: "Relative Community Need"

QUANTIFIABLE VARIABLES: Population, Poverty, Overcrowded Housing, Growth Lag, Poverty, Age of Housing

VARIABLE DEFINITION: *Population:* Total current resident population as reported by the Bureau of the Census (most recent decennial or mid-decade census or the most recent updating of such censuses.)

Poverty: Number of persons whose incomes are below the poverty level based on data compiled by the Census for 1970 and the latest reports of the Office of Management and Budget.

Overcrowded Housing: Number of housing units with 1.01 or more persons per unit based on 1970 census data.

Growth Lag: Growth lag means the number of persons who would have been residents in a metropolitan city in excess of the current population of such metropolitan city, if such metropolitan city had a population growth rate, between 1960 and the date of the most recent population count referable to the same point or period in time, equal to the population growth rate for such period of all metropolitan cities.

Age of Housing: The number of existing year-round housing units constructed in 1939 or earlier based on data reported by the Census and referable to the same point or period of time.

VARIABLE LINKAGE: Each variable is expressed as a *ratio* between the metropolitan city value and the sum of the values for all metropolitan areas. (see Below.) As of 1977, CDBG assistance was distributed according to a "dual formula" approach. The first formula distributed funds by considering population (weighted .25), poverty (weighted .50) and overcrowded housing (weighted .25). The second distributed funds by considering growth lag (weighted .20), poverty (weighted .30) and age of housing (weighted .50). These factors are summed and applied against the overall CDBG dollar allocation for metropolitan areas as follows: (as reported in Bunce and Goldberg study, see below)

EXHIBIT 13 (Continued)

VARIABLE LINKAGE:

*Formula 1 (1974 Formula)

$$\left(.25 \, \frac{POP_j}{POP_{SMSA}} + .50 \, \frac{POV_j}{POV_{SMSA}} + .25 \, \frac{OVERCRWD_j}{OVERCRWD_{SMSA}} \right) \times G_{SMSA}$$

*Formula 2 (added in 1977, growth lag formula)

$$\left(.20 \, \frac{GLAG_j}{GLAG_{MC}} + .30 \, \frac{POV_j}{POV_{SMSA}} + .50 \, \frac{AGE_j}{AGE_{SMSA}} \right) \times G_{SMSA}$$

where,

j	=	indicates jth entitlement or metropolitan city
SMSA	=	indicates that the subscripted variable is defined for all SMSAs
MC	=	indicates that the subscripted variable is defined for all metropolitan cities
G_{SMSA}	=	total CDBG dollar allocation to all SMSAs

POP	=	Population
POV	=	Poverty
OVCRWD	=	Overcrowded Housing
AGE	=	Age of Housing
GLAG	=	Growth Lag

*Aid would be granted according to the formula yielding the *largest* allocation.

Note: Hold-Harmless provisions have been in force from FY 1975 to FY 1980. In FY 1975, FY 1976, and FY 1977, the Hold-Harmless was absolute; in FY 1978, FY 1979 and FY 1980, Hold-Harmless protection was phased out by thirds.

Source: Harold L. Bunce and Robert L. Goldberg, *City Need and Community Development Funding* (Washington, D.C.: Government Printing Office, January 1979), U.S. Department of Housing and Urban Development, Office of Policy Development and Research, Division of Evaluation. U.S. Department of Housing and Urban Development, "Administrative Regulations for Community Development Block Grants."

EXHIBIT 14

Resource Allocation Formulae: Revenue Sharing

PROGRAM/INDEX/ALLOCATION: Allocation of Revenue Sharing (State-Local Fiscal Assistance Act of 1973) funds to local governments

CONCEPTUAL INDICATOR: "Relative Community Need"

QUANTIFIABLE VARIABLES: Population, Tax Effort, Per Capita Income, Intergovernmental Assistance

VARIABLES DEFINITION:
(Indicated time periods
for required data are for
Revenue Sharing Entitlement
Period 11)

Population: Resident population as of July 1, 1977 as determined by the Bureau of the Census (Current Population Reports Series P-25)

Tax Effort: Total taxes of the unit of government in Fiscal Year 1978 excluding taxes for schools and other educational purposes as defined from the General Revenue Sharing Survey and Survey of Local Government Finances conducted by the Bureau of the Census in 1978

Per Capita Income (PCI): Estimated mean of total money income received during calendar year 1975 by all persons residing in a given political jurisdiction as of April 1976. Population data are derived from the Bureau of the Census while income data are derived from the 1970 Census updated to 1975 based on income data from the 1969, 1972, 1974 and 1975 federal income tax returns and state/county/money income estimates prepared by the Bureau of Economic Analysis.

Intergovernmental Transfers: Amounts received by a unit of government from other governments in Fiscal Year 1978 for use either for specific functions or for general financial support. Data derived from the General Revenue Sharing Survey and Survey of Local Government Finances conducted by the Bureau of the Census.

EXHIBIT 14 (Continued)

VARIABLE LINKAGE:

Revenue Sharing allocation for local government determined as follows:

$$\frac{\text{allocation to an individual municipality}}{\text{allocation to all municipalities in the county area}} = \frac{\begin{array}{l}\text{population of the municipality X}\\ \text{its general tax effort factor X}\\ \text{its relative income factor}\end{array}}{\begin{array}{l}\text{the sum of the above products for}\\ \text{all municipalities in the county area}\end{array}}$$

(with income expressed as a relative factor comparing areawide average income to local average income). Intergovernmental assistance interacts in allocation formula only when the "50 percent" rule applies. (This rule limits a government's allocation to 50 percent of the total of its adjusted taxes and intergovernmental transfers.)

VARIABLE STANDARDS: None

ELIGIBILITY CRITERIA: See variable linkage

Note: Revenue Sharing funds are allocated in steps to different levels of government, i.e., county, township, municipalities, etc. Each government competes with all other eligible governments for a portion of the total funds to be distributed. The formula also incorporates various "ceiling" and "floor" provisions. To illustrate, if a local unit of government should by formula receive more than 145% of the county per capita amount, the local unit of government is adjusted to the 145% level.

Source: Department of the Treasury, Office of Revenue Sharing, "The General Revenue Sharing Allocation Process."

EXHIBIT 15

Resource Allocation Formulae: Comprehensive Employment Training Assistance

PROGRAM/INDEX/ALLOCATION:	Comprehensive Employment and Training Assistance (CETA) allocation to local jurisdictions
CONCEPTUAL INDICATORS:	"Relative Community Need"
QUANTIFIABLE VARIABLES:	Unemployed persons, excess number of unemployed persons, area of substantial unemployment, low income families
VARIABLE DEFINITION:	*Unemployed Persons:* Persons who are without jobs and who want and are available for work as measured by the Bureau of Labor Statistics.
	Excess Number of Unemployed Persons: Unemployed persons in excess of a base unemployment rate as measured by the Bureau of Labor Statistics.
	Area of Substantial Unemployment: Area which has a high average rate of unemployment for the most recent 12 months as measured by the Bureau of Labor Statistics.
	Low Income: Low family income as measured by the Census.
VARIABLE LINKAGE:	Each variable is expressed as a local share or ratio (i.e., local unemployed persons compared to the total unemployed persons in the entire state or the relative excess number of unemployed persons who reside within the jurisdictions of the prime sponsor as compared to the total excess of unemployed persons who reside within the jurisdictions of all prime sponsors). The variables are weighted differently for the various CETA Titles. To illustrate, Title II-A assigns a weight of 12.5 percent to Low Income, 37.5 percent to Unemployed Persons, and 50 percent to the level of prior fiscal year funding. Title II-D assigns a weight of 25 percent to Unemployed Persons, 25 percent to Excess Number of Unemployed Persons, 25 percent to Area of Substantial Unemployment and 25 percent to Low Income. Local assistance is equal to the sum of the weighted local ratios multiplied by the pool of available CETA funding (by Title).
VARIABLE STANDARDS:	*Excess Number of Unemployed Persons:* The base unemployment rate is 4.5 percent. The "Excess Number" represents unemployed persons in excess of 4.5 percent of the labor force.
	Low Income: Equivalent to $7,000 annual income in 1969, as adjusted by the Consumer Price Index.

Note: Only one aspect of CETA allocation is described above.

Source: Comprehensive Employment and Training Act Reauthorization, Public Law 95-524, 29 USC 801.

Social variables relate to specific characteristics of the population. Education, female-headed households, percent of the population— minority, percent of the the population—dependent, birth/death/ suicide rates, etc.

Fiscal variables concentrate on measures of municipal solvency; local tax effort fiscal capacity, real property valuation per capita, percent of revenues generated from own-sources, etc.

POPULATION-RELATED VARIABLES (EXHIBIT 16)

Programmatic Area Eligibility (Pass-Fail). Four-of-six of the Programmatic Area Eligibility qualification systems use population as a sifting mechanism for program eligibility. For UDAG (Urban Distress) and EDA (Long-Term Economic Deterioration—Title IX—LTED), a *median (UDAG) or average (EDA) population growth rate* over a stated time period* is established for the nation as a whole and those communities falling below this average are eligible under the population criterion.

For the EDA (Special Impact Area) program in rural areas, *severe population decline* caused by one factor, outmigration, (more than 25 percent loss over a ten-year Census period) is one of three criteria which, by itself, may signal program qualification. For EDA (Redevelopment Area—Title I) a similar *population decline standard* (25 percent population loss over the period 1960-1970) is used for selecting redevelopment neighborhoods (defined according to single or grouped Census tracts) for program participation.

Thus, two-thirds of the Programmatic Area Eligibility Programs surveyed here use a population-related variable as a criterion for program qualification. Further, it is always used in its unrefined, aggregate form (i.e., not converted to household or type-of-household change). In two of the four cases, including UDAG (Urban Distress) there is an explicit standard of comparison, i.e., below a national standard of growth.

Relative Distress/Need Indices (Graded Scores). The six Hardship/ Distress Indices all use population criteria as a component of a city-need indexing system. The Congressional Budget Office's Index of

---

*UDAG (Urban Distress)—15.52 percent population growth or less over the period 1960-1975. EDA (LTED)—five year average growth in population less than the national average.

EXHIBIT 16

Population and Employment Variables Used in Program Eligibility, Distress/Need Indices and Resource Allocation Formulae

VARIABLE GROUPINGS / DISTRESS/ALLOCATION CLASSIFICATIONS	Population-Related Variables				Employment-Related Variables		
	Change	Number	Density	Other Age-Segment	Employment Change	Number/Rate of Unemployment	Abrupt Rise In Unemployment
PROGRAMMATIC AREA ELIGIBILITY							
UDAG-URBAN DISTRESS	X				X	X	
UDAG-POCKETS OF POVERTY							
EDA-LONG TERM ECONOMIC DETERIORATION (TITLE IX-LTED)	X	X			X	X	
EDA-SPECIAL IMPACT AREA	X	X					X
EDA-REDEVELOPMENT AREA (TITLE I)	X					X	X
RELATIVE DISTRESS/NEED INDICES							
BROOKINGS INTERCITY HARDSHIP INDEX				X		X	
BROOKINGS INTRA-METROPOLITAN HARDSHIP INDEX				X		X	
CONGRESSIONAL BUDGET OFFICE-SOCIAL, ECONOMIC. FISCAL NEED	X	X	X		X	X	
HUD (1979)-COMMUNITY NEED INDEX	X	X				X	
INSTITUTE FOR THE FUTURE-EVALUATION INDEX	X			X		X	
TREASURY-URBAN FISCAL STRAIN INDEX	X					X	
RESOURCE ALLOCATION FORMULAE							
COMMUNITY DEVELOPMENT BLOCK GRANT	X						
REVENUE SHARING	X	X					
COMPREHENSIVE EMPLOYMENT TRAINING ACT						X	

Source: Rutgers University, Center for Urban Policy Research, Spring 1980.

Economic Need and HUD's Community Need Index employ *population change over thirteen and fifteen year periods* respectively (1960 to 1973/5), as reverse indices of need. The Treasury Department's Index of Urban Fiscal Strain uses this same measure over a much shorter time period (1972-1976). The Institute for the Future (IFTF) Evaluation Index employs select "dependent" portions of static measure, 1960 population, to grade city distress. Four separate "point-in-time" measures are used:

population 65 + years
population 65 + years below poverty level
population <5 years
population <15 years below poverty level

The two Brookings (Inter-Intra) Metropolitan Indices employ a "dependency" measure which is a *static, population-related index* similar to that of IFTF. Brookings uses *percent of the population under 18 years or over 64 years* to establish the dependency ratio for a community.

Again, population is a criterion for establishing hardship or distress in all of the need/gradient indices. Unrefined population change is used by HUD, CBO and Treasury; static population characteristics are used by the Brookings and IFTF indices.

Resource Allocation Formulae (All Pass). Of the three most popular Resource Allocation Formulae, Revenue Sharing, Community Development Block Grants (CDBG) and the Comprehensive Employment Training Act (CETA), two allocate resources according to population criteria (only CETA does not use a population measure). Revenue Sharing distributes resources according to the *relative size* (population) of need-designated jurisdictions. CDBG uses a population measure in each of two separate allocation formulas. In the first or "1974" Formula, the *absolute population size* of a jurisdiction in an SMSA is compared to the population of the SMSA as a whole for resource allocation purposes; in the second or "1977" Formula, the *growth lag* of a specific municipal jurisdiction is compared to the average growth of all metropolitan cities.*

---

* Either formula can be used; aid is granted according to the formula which yields the *largest* allocation.

Population variables are thus critical to all forms of eligibility designation, hardship classification and resource allocation schemes. The more recent and more complex designation schemes appear to use *relative population change* as an index of need as opposed to either absolute population comparisons or age-specific population characteristics.

The only need designation/allocation systems which omit population as a variable are those that by function are almost exclusively tied to economic indicators, i.e., levels or changes in employment, unemployment rates, etc. These include one of the programmatic eligibility programs of EDA (Sudden and Severe Economic Dislocation—Title IX-SSED), the HUD Pockets of Poverty Program, and one of the resource allocation schemes—CETA.

EMPLOYMENT-RELATED VARIABLES (EXHIBIT 16)

Programmatic Area Eligibility. All of the programs included under this grouping, with the exception of UDAG (Pockets of Poverty), use an employment measure to determine jurisdictional eligibility. UDAG (Urban Distress) uses two employment measures: *(1) rates of growth of retailing and manufacturing employment over the most recent Census-monitored, five-year period compared to a national average; and (2) the most recent annualized unemployment rate also compared to a national average, determined by the Bureau of Labor Statistics.*

Two of three of EDA's (Long-Term Economic Deterioration—Title IX-LTED) eligibility criteria are employment measures:

(1) *Chronic Distress*—determined by (a) five-year average rate of unemployment greater than the national average, as well as, (b) five-year average growth in employment less than the national average.

(2) *Unemployment*—a 12 percent or greater level of unemployment for the most recent annualized period.

The remaining EDA programs—Special Impact Area, Redevelopment Area (Title I) and Sudden and Severe Economic Dislocation (Title IX—SSED) use *abrupt rise in unemployment* as a key criterion. Abrupt rise may be expressed as absolute changes in unemployment levels (500 or over persons unemployed) or a change in the percent unemployed (more than 2 percent, etc.). The Redevelopment Area

Program, to select locations of "substantial and persistent unemployment," uses per capita employment decline (change in average employment per resident) and "substantial unemployment rate" (50 to 100 percent above the national average for 1-3 years) in addition to abrupt rise in unemployment as eligibility criteria.

Relative Distress/Need Indices. All of the Relative Distress/Need Indices use a static economic criterion, *unemployment rate,* to grade distress. In most cases (Brookings, Congressional Budget Office, Institute for the Future) the most recent six-month local unemployment rate is used. The HUD Community Need Index uses the *annual unemployment rates for the two immediately preceding years, as well as the monthly rate of the preceding December.* The Treasury Department Index (Urban Fiscal Strain) uses unemployment as a need-ranking determinant by using several other indices already employing this measure in a single, composite index. None of the Relative Distress/Need Indices use change in unemployment rates, relative change in unemployment rates or "abrupt" unemployment as indices of city hardship.

Resource Allocation Formulae. Of the three Resource Allocation Formulae (Revenue Sharing, CDBG, and CETA) only CETA uses an employment measure to distribute its resources. CETA, by definition, is so tied to local unemployment that it uses three separate forms of this variable—*unemployed persons, excess number of unemployed persons and substantial unemployment rate* to distribute funds. This program employs this variable in all forms as a static, relative comparison.

Employment-related variables are found as primary determinants of both meliorative programmatic eligibility designations as well as city distress/need classifications. They are found less often in the general resource allocation schemes.

The programmatic area eligibility schemes, of which UDAG is a prime example, tend to use more dynamic measures of employment, i.e., relative employment change or change in unemployment rates as eligibility criteria. The relative hardship/need indices use the static measure of comparative unemployment.

HOUSING-RELATED VARIABLES (EXHIBIT 17)

Programmatic Area Eligibility. The only program to employ a housing variable to determine eligibility in this category is the UDAG

Urban Distress program. It uses *proportion of year-round housing built prior to 1940* compared to a national median on the same variable to key eligibility. This measure is also used in another HUD designation scheme, the Community Need Index, which is discussed below.

Relative Distress/Need Indices. All of the Relative Distress/Need Indices employ some housing measure to rank need. By far the most popular measure, which may in fact be the weakest, is *overcrowded housing,* expressed as percent of all housing units with 1.01 persons per room. This measure is directly employed by both Brookings Hardship Indices (Intercity, Intrametropolitan) and indirectly by the Congressional Budget Office Urban Need Designation Scheme which has, as two of its components, the Brookings Hardship Indices. Overcrowding is also used in the presence of other variables in the HUD Community Need Index and the IFTF Evaluation Index.

Other housing variables are also occasionally found in the Need Ranking Systems. HUD (Community Need Index) uses *new private housing units authorized* over a two-year period as a percent of total housing stock in its "Age and Decline Factor" and *percent rental of all housing units* in its "Density" factor. Thus, including the aforementioned overcrowding in its "Poverty" factor, and the age variable (pre-1940, year-round housing) in its "Age of Decline" factor, the HUD Need Index employs four housing-related variables to rank cities. Property value change, a large portion of which is housing value change, is used by the Treasury Department to determine "Urban Fiscal Strain." Since this can be construed much more as a tax effort than a housing variable, it will be discussed under the fiscal measures section of this section.

Resource Allocation Formulae. Of the three resource allocation formulae discussed here only HUD's Community Development Block Grant (CDBG) Program uses housing-related variables as indices to distribute revenues.* CDBG uses both overcrowded housing (number of housing units with more than 1.01 persons per room) and housing age (number of year-round housing units built prior to 1940). The housing variable is one of three factors in each of two formulas (1974 and 1977); in the latter formula housing age is weighted 1.5 to 2.5 as much as the other inclusive variables.

---

*Neither Revenue Sharing nor CETA employ housing variables to allocate revenues.

EXHIBIT 17

Housing and Income Variables Used in Program Eligibility, Distress/Need Indices and Resource Allocation Formulae

DISTRESS/ ALLOCATION CLASSIFICATIONS (VARIABLE GROUPINGS)	Housing-Related Variables				Income-Related Variables		
	Age	Quality	Crowding	Other	Poverty	Low Income	Income or Income Change
PROGRAMMATIC AREA ELIGIBILITY							
UDAG-URBAN DISTRESS	X				X		X
UDAG-POCKETS OF POVERTY						X	
EDA-LONG TERM ECONOMIC DETERIORATION (TITLE IX-LTED)							X
EDA-SPECIAL IMPACT AREA							X
EDA-REDEVELOPMENT AREA (TITLE I)							X
RELATIVE DISTRESS/NEED INDICES							
BROOKINGS INTERCITY HARDSHIP INDEX		X	X		X		X
BROOKINGS INTRA-METROPOLITAN HARDSHIP INDEX		X	X		X		X
CONGRESSIONAL BUDGET OFFICE-SOCIAL, ECONOMIC, FISCAL NEED	X						X
HUD (1979)-COMMUNITY NEED INDEX	X	X	X		X		
INSTITUTE FOR THE FUTURE-EVALUATION INDEX	X	X	X		X		X
TREASURY-URBAN FISCAL STRAIN INDEX							X
RESOURCE ALLOCATION FORMULAE							
COMMUNITY DEVELOPMENT BLOCK GRANT	X		X		X		
REVENUE SHARING							X
COMPREHENSIVE EMPLOYMENT TRAINING ACT						X	X

Source: Rutgers University, Center for Urban Policy Research, Spring 1980.

Housing variables are found most frequently in Relative Distress/ Need type rankings than the other two categories of distribution systems. As one might surmise the agency which has national housing responsibility, i.e., the U.S. Department of Housing and Urban Development, is the one which most frequently employs housing-related variables as city need determinants.

Housing variables are most prone to be used in their static, absolute form. Few dynamic or change constructions or even relative comparisons are made using either one or several of the housing variables.

INCOME-RELATED VARIABLES (EXHIBIT 17)

Programmatic Area Eligibility. All Programmatic Area Eligibility programs, with the exception of the Economic Development Administration's Sudden and Severe Economic Dislocation Program (Title IX—SSED)* use income-related variables to determine eligibility. Most programs use either a *(1) fraction of average national income or (2) percent of families/households below the poverty level or both* to trigger program applicability. The UDAG (Urban Distress) eligibility designation uses *per capita income growth lag* (net increase in per capita income 1969-1974) as well as *poverty rate* (percentage of population at or below the poverty level—1970).

The UDAG Pockets of Poverty Program employs *only* income-related variables to sift for eligibility. The first income criterion is that 70 percent of residents residing in the Pocket of Poverty must have incomes below *80 percent of the jurisdiction's median income.* The second is a poverty measure in which 30 percent of residents must have *incomes below the national poverty level.*

The Economic Development Administration's Long-Term Economic Deterioration (Title IX—LTED) program has income measures in two of three factors leading to eligibility designation. As part of its Chronic Distress Index, *five-year absolute change in per capita income (less than the national average)* is used. In addition, a seperate income-related variable, *75 percent of the current national per capita income average,* is employed to sort competing jurisdictions. The remaining two EDA programs, Special Impact Area and Redevelopment Area (Title I) employ the poverty-derived measure of a majority of persons residing in the jurisdiction whose *incomes fall below 50 percent of national median income.*

---

*Uses two employment-related variables (number of direct jobs lost; change in unemployment rate).

Thus, the bulk of program area eligibility qualification systems depend heavily on income or income-related variables. The major HUD programs and one of the EDA programs have two income criteria (change in per capita income, poverty rate); the remaining EDA programs employ a single, poverty-defined, income variable.

Relative Distress/Need Indices. All of the Relative Distress/Need city ranking systems employ income variables to determine the severity of distress in one city versus another. This classifying system (Distress/Need Index), perhaps more so than any other allocation mechanism, exhibits both the preponderance and diversity of the income variable.

The Brookings Indices employ two income-related variables, *adjusted per capita income* (median–1970 Census) and *adjusted poverty* (percentage of families below 125 percent of low income) to compare intercity and intrametropolitan differences. Both variables are "adjusted" by a budget index compiled by the Bureau of Labor Statistics to create a measure of "effective" income.

The Congressional Budget Office in the development of its equally weighted, three part, need determinant measure (social, economic, and fiscal) uses the income variable multiple times to determine its city ranking. In the social need category it is used once directly *(1973 per capita income)* and twice indirectly *(by employing the Brookings indices as individual variables).* In its economic need criterion it is again used directly *(percent change in per capita income 1960-1973)* whereas in fiscal need it is used indirectly to determine jurisdictional service needs by using two 1976 HUD Needs Indexing systems which employ the income variable in multiple forms. These latter indices of Community Need use *percent of occupied housing containing low income families and children under 18* as its income-related or poverty measure.

The two remaining indices discussed here, i.e., the Institute for the Future's (IFTF) Evaluation Index and U.S. Department of Treasury's Urban Fiscal Strain measure use single income variables to sort cities. In the first case, IFTF uses a poverty measure *(families with income below $7,000 in 1970)* as an index of service requirements as part of its Health Needs determinants. In the second, the Treasury Department uses *relative (jurisdiction to national average) per capita income change (1969-1974)* as the second-highest weighted of five Fiscal Strain criteria.

Resource Allocation Formulae. Of the three Resource Allocation programs discussed in this section, all have a single, static income measure which serves as a guide to revenue distribution. Revenue Sharing uses the *mean of total money income received during 1975* (1970 Census updated to 1975 based on income tax returns and state/county money income estimates); the Community Development Block Grant Program employs a poverty measure consisting of a *ratio (jurisdiction to SMSA) of the persons with income below the poverty level;* CETA also uses a poverty variable to distribute funds, *families with a 1969 CPI-adjusted $7,000 income* which is a ratio of local conditions to a statewide average.

By far, the most widely used indicator of need, regardless of allocation or classification system, is the income variable. It is particularly evident in the Program Area Eligibility and the Hardship/Distress indices where it is often found represented more than once. Dynamic (change over time) income measures seem to characterize Programmatic Area Eligibility systems; these are combined with static measures for Relative Need/Distress gradient designations—in the Resource Allocation schemes, only static measures are found. The most common variable for the dynamic measure is income change either absolute or relative; comparable frequent static measures are percent low income or percent below the poverty level.

SOCIAL-RELATED VARIABLES (EXHIBIT 18)

Programmatic Area Eligibility. None of the jurisdictional, pass-fail eligibility systems examined here contain a direct social variable to trigger program qualification.

Relative Distress/Need Indices. The two Brookings Hardship Indices each contain education and dependency measures to rank cities according to need. The education measure is *percent of persons 25 years and older with less than a twelfth grade education;* the dependency index is *the proportion of the population youthful (less than 18) and aged (over 64).*

The Congressional Budget Office indirectly uses these same two measures by employing the Brookings Index Rankings as separate variables. It also uses the HUD Community Need Social Variables indirectly (see below) by employing the 1976 HUD Indices as variables in its combined index.

By far, the two greatest users of social variables to determine need are the 1979 HUD Community Need Index and the Institute for the Future Evaluation Index. The HUD Index, in its Age/Decline, Density and Poverty Factors uses a measure of social distress, *percent of families with a female head.* In its Density Factor, the variable

EXHIBIT 18

Social and Fiscal Variables Used in Program Eligibility, Distress/Need Indices and Resource Allocation Formulae

DISTRESS/ ALLOCATION CLASSIFICATIONS — VARIABLE GROUPING	Social-Related Variables				Fiscal-Related Variables			
	Minority Population	Education	Female Headed Household	Dependent Population	Tax Effort	Fiscal Capacity	Own Source/ Intergovern- mental Burden	Property Value
PROGRAMMATIC AREA ELIGIBILITY								
UDAG-URBAN DISTRESS								
UDAG-POCKETS OF POVERTY								
EDA-LONG TERM ECONOMIC DETERIORATION (TITLE IX-LTED)								
EDA-SPECIAL IMPACT AREA								
EDA-REDEVELOPMENT AREA (TITLE I)								
RELATIVE DISTRESS/NEED INDICES								
BROOKINGS INTERCITY HARDSHIP INDEX		X						
BROOKINGS INTRA-METROPOLITAN HARDSHIP INDEX		X						
CONGRESSIONAL BUDGET OFFICE-SOCIAL, ECONOMIC, FISCAL NEED INDEX					X	X		
HUD (1979)-COMMUNITY NEED INDEX	X	X	X	X	X	X		
INSTITUTE FOR THE FUTURE-EVALUATION INDEX	X	X	X	X				
TREASURY-URBAN FISCAL STRAIN INDEX							X	
RESOURCE ALLOCATION FORMULAE								
COMMUNITY DEVELOPMENT BLOCK GRANT							X	X
REVENUE SHARING					X		X	
COMPREHENSIVE EMPLOYMENT TRAINING ACT								

Source: Rutgers University, Center for Urban Policy Research, Spring 1980.

female-headed families is repeated and is joined with variables describing both *incidence of crime* (number of violent crimes per 10,000 population—1976) and *minority populations* (change in black population 1960-1970—percent of population non-white 1970). A final Poverty Factor repeats the percent non-white variable and adds to it the Brookings education measure of *percent of the population over 25 with less than high school education.*

The IFTF Evaluation Index, under Service Requirements, has Health, Social Service and Educational Needs each of which contain numerous social-related variables. Under Health alone are found: *suicide rate, infant mortality rate, birth rate, death rate, one person households, aged/youthful population incidence. etc.*

Resource Allocation Formulae. None of the Resource Allocation Formulae discussed here use social variables to distribute funds.

Social index variables are almost nonexistent in either Programmatic Area Eligibility or Resource Allocation Formulae. They are present to a moderate level in the classic (Brookings) Relative Need/ Distress Indices and, in significant fashion, in the more recent hardship-ranking systems represented by the HUD (1979) and IFTF indices. They do not appear, at all, in the Treasury Department's Index of Urban Fiscal Strain.

There appears to be little agreement in the field on what to employ as a measure of social distress. Female-headed households and proportion of minority populations are the few social variables which appear more than once.

FISCAL-RELATED VARIABLES (EXHIBIT 18)

Programmatic Area Eligibility. Fiscal-related variables are not employed as criteria in any of the Programmatic Area Eligibility programs under scrutiny.

Relative Distress/Need Indices. Of the six Relative Distress/ Need Indices discussed in this section, five employ fiscal-related variables for city ranking purposes. The Congressional Budget Office in its fiscal need index uses *tax effort* (taxes as a percent of personal income), *property tax base* (real property valuation per capita), and *indirect measures of service capacity* (HUD 1976 City Need Indices), such as changes in retail sales—a surrogate for dwindling real property tax revenues. The 1979 HUD Community Need Index uses a similar fiscal-related variable as is found in the 1976 HUD Community Need Indices.

The Institute for the Future Evaluation Index employs two fiscal measures to rank cities—*equalized real property valuation per capita* and *tax effort* (total municipal revenues excluding schools compared to the sum of all municipal revenues in a county).

The Treasury Department uses fiscal measures in three of its five Fiscal Strain Indices. The first is *own-source revenue burden change* (percentage change in average local own-source revenue per capita 1969-1976 compared to the percentage change in average local per capita income 1969-1974). In addition, it uses percent change in local, equalized real property value for the period 1971-1976. Each of these fiscal variables is equally weighted at one-third the value of the weighting of the population change variable.

Resource Allocation Formulae. Of the three Resource Allocation Formulae discussed in this chapter only the Revenue Sharing Program uses fiscal variables to distribute revenues. Revenue Sharing uses the *local tax effort* variable discussed above as well as a measure of the *local incidence of intergovernmental transfers.* The latter variable only interacts as a limiting measure, however—Revenue Sharing Allocation cannot exceed 50 percent of the jurisdiction's adjusted taxes and intergovernmental transfers.

The greatest concentration of fiscal variables is found in the Relative Distress/Need Indices. Again, the newer ranking schemes tend to depend more heavily on the inclusion of a wider variety and form of measurement variables. As was the case with the housing measures employed by the U.S. Department of Housing and Urban Development, the agency function, need determinant relationship is obviously apparent. The U.S. Department of the Treasury, whose general concern is the fiscal solvency of local governments, employs distress measures which heavily reflect fiscal condition. The preponderance of variables and their diverse nature reflect this agency's insights to both the causes and relative importance of the fiscal strain indicators.

VARIABLE COMPOSITION OF ALTERNATIVE
DISTRESS MEASURES: SIMILARITIES AND DIFFERENCES

Discussing each distributive program or distress/need designation system by its representation on various classic variables sets enables at least tentative conclusions to be drawn about the sophistication and diversity of the measures found within them.

1. *The Programmatic Area Eligibility and the Resource Allocation groups limit their variable representation to a tighter set of categories than is the case for Relative Distress/Need Indices. Population, employment, housing and income variables are criteria for the former two groups; social and fiscal criteria supplement these four for the latter group.*

2. *Resource Allocation Formulae almost always employ variables which are geographically relative measures (individual jurisdiction to a larger host jurisdiction) as opposed to Programmatic Area Eligibility and Relative Hardship/Need Indices which primarily use non-comparative (to host jurisdiction) criteria. All distribution programs or need/distress designation systems have relative comparisons among inclusive cities as their ultimate objective.*

3. *Functional government agencies' development of need distribution or indexing mechanisms tend to favor variable selection based on mission familiarity. HUD uses more housing variables than most agencies, EDA concentrates heavily on employment indicators, Treasury employs multiple fiscal indicators, etc. Oversight agencies (GAO, CBO) and research institutions (Brookings, IFTF) recommending alternatives to indices, or developing their own, tend to include a broader array of measurement variables.*

4. *Functional government agencies' development of need distribution or indexing mechanisms tend to employ incisive and pointed variables in their own area of expertise and classic (more general and sometimes weaker) variables to measure phenomena with which they are less familiar. Treasury, in its Urban Fiscal Strain Index, uses Own-Source Revenue and Long-Term Debt Burden Change in tandem to measure fiscal strain yet it employs unrefined population change measured at intercensal periods to gauge jurisdictional shrinkage.*

5. *Individual components of the three categories of distributive systems or hardship/need indexing devices span a ten-year development period. The newer indices appear to use more complicated variables introducing relative comparisons and tracing changes over time in most variables. Several of the newer indices, which as a group also have expanded the measurement varible set, may now be more subject to the criticism of double counting than has been the case.*

6. *Income and employment related variables clearly dominate most of the distribution/need-indexing mechanisms. These two variable sets are followed very closely by population variables and less so by housing and social variables. Fiscal variables, to signal hardhip or trigger revenue allocations, are least often represented.*

SECTION FIVE–DEGREE OF CONSISTENCY IN CITY HARDSHIP DESIGNATION

Previous sections have analyzed *what the distress measures consist of* with attention paid to the similarities and differences in objectives, structure, variables and statistical treatment. This section considers the *consistency in the operation or throughput of the distress measures,* namely, what is the level of agreement or disagreement of the measures in ranking the hardship of a common set of cities. This type of investigation deals directly with the question of whether city hardship designation is or is not independent of the mechanism with which it is determined, i.e., that there *is* consistency in city hardship designation regardless of selection scheme or rather, hardship designation is linked to or varies directly with the mechanism of designation.

DISTRESS MEASURES/CITIES SELECTED FOR COMPARISON

To insure an appropriate comparison, only those distress measures with a similar objective were considered. The ranking systems selected were relative distress/need indices and programmatic area eligibility standards whose prime objective was to relatively compare *cities* in terms of *economic* impaction or frailty. Five distress measures were considered including: an Urban Development Action Grant (UDAG) Ranking, the Brookings Institution's Intercity Hardship Index, the Congressional Budget Office's Composite Measure of Economic Need, the Department of Housing and Urban Development's City Need Index and the Treasury Department's Urban Fiscal Strain Index.

The UDAG ranking consists of a two-fold measure. First, cities are ordered according to the number of UDAG criteria they meet from six to zero (1./ age of housing, 2./ per capita income growth lag, 3./ population growth lag, 4./ unemployment, 5./ employment, and 6./ poverty). Second, the group of cities satisfying the different number of the threshold points are rank ordered by the HUD Impaction Rankings* within each threshold point. The four remaining distress measures-Intercity Hardship, Economic Need, City Need and Urban Fiscal Strain have been described already and are summarized in Exhibits 8, 9, 10 and 12 respectively.

The analysis considers 30 cities containing at least 250,000 population as of 1975. For each classification system, original rankings are readjusted slightly to reflect this paired number of cities (30 cities in each). The Treasury Department's city set, ultimately reduced to twenty-five cities for comparability, as explained above, was subsequently augmented to include five additional cities at the moderate-to-low end of the economic need scale not originally considered by this ranking scheme.

Exhibit 19 presents the final rankings under each of the five distress measures for the similar set of thirty cities. Cities are ordered 1-30 in the first column of Exhibit 19 reflecting the UDAG ranking with the rankings of each of the other four designation systems appearing to the right of the UDAG list.

THE RANKING SYSTEMS' ABILITY TO
DESIGNATE CITIES MOST SEVERELY IMPACTED

How consistent are the different hardship rankings? Prior to statistical analysis which will measure both the correlation and concordance of rankings, some visual observations bear mention. If one views each system's ranking of the "top 20" there is reasonable consistency across all hardship rankings systems of those cities heavily and moderately distressed. UDAG versus Brookings, UDAG versus CBO, UDAG versus HUD and UDAG versus Treasury have only two to four discrepancies in their selection of the twenty most impacted cities. While the same level of discrepancy holds for the "bottom ten cities," obviously the proportion or percentage of discrepancy is doubled, i.e., two to four discrepancies out of a possible ten selections.

These visual observations are presented statistically in Exhibit 20. Four 2 x 2 matrices show that out of the top 20 cities, UDAG and HUD have eighteen in common, UDAG and Brookings have seven-

---

*See footnote 24 for description of the Impaction Ranking.

EXHIBIT 19

Distress Criteria Rankings: UDAG, Brookings, CBO, HUD, Treasury
Distress/Need Designation Systems

Distress Ranking (1 = most severe distress)
(30 = least severe distress)

City	UDAG (Rank-Weighted)	BROOKINGS (Intercity)	CBO (Economic)	HUD (Need)	Treasury (Fiscal Strain)
ST. LOUIS	1	2	5	3	11
NEWARK	2	1	1	1	2
CLEVELAND	3	7	3	4	5
PITTSBURGH	4	17	8	16	18
NEW ORLEANS	5	3	22	2	20
CINCINNATI	6	11	14	10	16
BUFFALO	7	9	4	12	4
ROCHESTER	8	18	10	19	21
BOSTON	9	19	6	9	8
PHILADELPHIA	10	15	9	14	17
CHICAGO	11	16	7	11	6
DETROIT	12	8	12	7	7
BALTIMORE	13	6	17	6	27
NEW YORK	14	20	2	13	1
LOUISVILLE	15	10	23	15	15
AKRON	16	21	15	24	23
ATLANTA	17	14	25	8	14
SAN FRANCISCO	18	29	11	20	13
BIRMINGHAM	19	5	26	5	19
MILWAUKEE	20	23	16	22	26
KANSAS CITY	21	24	19	25	12
COLUMBUS	22	26	24	29	24
LOS ANGELES	23	25	20	26	3
MINNEAPOLIS	24	28	18	23	9
SEATTLE	25	30	13	30	10
DENVER	26	27	21	27	29
NORFOLK	27	22	29	18	28
TAMPA	28	12	30	21	25
SACRAMENTO	29	13	27	28	22
MIAMI	30	4	28	17	30

Cities > 250,000 population (1975)

Source: Rutgers University, Center for Urban Policy Research, Spring 1980.

teen in common, and UDAG and CBO/Treasury each have sixteen in common. These results are significant at .001 to .10 levels. Thus, both the tabular and statistical presentations point to relatively high consistency among systems in their designation of those cities most severely impacted.

CLOSENESS OF FIT IN THE
ORDER OF THE RANKINGS

Spearman Correlations. In order to view closeness of fit in the rank orders of pairings of UDAG versus other hardship designation systems, two statistical tests will be employed. The first, Spearman Correlation, measures the simple correlation of the individual city ranks. This measures the amount that the knowledge of Chicago's or any other city's ranking on one scale aids one in predicting that city's exact ranking on another scale. As is indicated by the first row of Exhibit 21, for the *thirty cities,* UDAG exhibits a .50 to .75 correlation with the other four measures. UDAG correlations with Treasury and Brookings are at the .50 level; UDAG correlations with CBO and HUD are at .75 level. These represent a 25 percent (.50 x .50) to 56 percent (.75 x .75) decrease in the average squared error of prediction of the rankings in one system due to the knowledge of the other system's rankings. These results are significant at the 0.0001 and 0.005 levels respectively (two-tailed tests).

Kendall's Tau. Another measure of consistency in ranking may be obtained using the results of a Kendall's Tau analysis. The advantage of this statistical procedure is that it compares the relative position of pairs of cities across ranking systems. It evaluates the frequency with which one versus another designation procedure ranks two cities in the same relative position.

One step in computing Tau is noting if the cities of Chicago and Denver, say, are ranked consistently, i.e., either Chicago is higher than Denver on both scales or lower on both scales. Totally, the procedure is carried out for all pairs of cities, i.e., Chicago and New York, Chicago and Atlanta, Atlanta and New York, etc. This leads to a measure of concordance—the percentage of pairs of cities ranked in the same order—and a measure of discordance—the percentage of cities in reverse order. Kendall's Tau is the difference of the concordant and discordant percentages. The concordance percentage, Pc, appears in the final column of Exhibit 21. When UDAG is compared to (1) Brookings, and respectively to (2) Treasury (3) HUD and

EXHIBIT 20

Consistency of the Most Severely Distressed Cities in UDAG Ranking Versus
the Brookings, CBO, HUD and Treasury Ranking Systems

Brookings (Intercity)

		Top 20	Bottom 10	Statistics
UDAG (Rank-Weighted)	Top 20	17	3	x^2 = 6.77 p < .01*
	Bottom 10	3	7	Z = 2.60 p < .01**

CBO (Economic)

		Top 20	Bottom 10	Statistics
UDAG (Rank-	Top 20	16	4	x^2 = 3.17 p < .01*
	Bottom 10	4	6	Z = 1.78 p < .05**

HUD (Need)

		Top 20	Bottom 10	Statistics
UDAG (Rank-Weighted)	Top 20	18	2	x^2 = 11.72 p < .001*
	Bottom 10	2	8	Z = 3.42 p < .001**

Treasury (Fiscal Strain)

		Top 20	Bottom 10	Statistics
UDAG (Rank-Weighted)	Top 20	16	4	x^2 = 3.17 p < .10*
	Bottom 10	4	6	Z = 1.78 p < .05**

*two-tailed test
**one-tailed test

Source: Rutgers University, Center for Urban Policy Research, Spring 1980.

(4) CBO, rank order similarity of cities, taken two at a time, occurs in 70 to 80 percent of the cases.

EXHIBIT 21

Basic Rank Correlations and Significance Levels of UDAG, Brookings, CBO, HUD and Treasury Ranking Systems

Spearman Correlation

Correlation	UDAG (Rank-Weighted)	Brookings (Intercity)	CBO (Economic)	HUD (Need)	Treasury (Fiscal Strain)
UDAG (Rank-Weighted)	1	.50	.76	.74	.47
BROOKING (Intercity)		1	.09	.80	.04
CBO (Economic)			1	.40	.69
HUD (Need)				1	.32
TREASURY (Fiscal Strain)					1

Kendall's Tau

Correlation	UDAG (Rank-Weighted)	Brookings (Intercity)	CBO (Economic)	HUD (Need)	Treasury (Fiscal Strain)
UDAG (Rank-Weighted)	1	.38	.59	.53	.31
BROOKINGS (Intercity)		1	.07	.65	.05
CBO (Economic)			1	.31	.52
HUD (Need)				1	.20
TREASURY (Fiscal Strain)					1

Spearman Correlation and Kendall's Tau

Significance & Pc	Spearman Correlation	2-tailed Significance	Kendall Tau	2-tailed Significance	Pc
BROOKINGS-HUD	.805	.0001	.651	.0001	.83
UDAG-CBO	.763	.0001	.586	.0001	.79
UDAG-HUD	.741	.0001	.531	.0001	.77
CBO-TREASURY	.685	.0001	.517	.0001	.76
UDAG-BROOKINGS	.502	.0050	.384	.0030	.69
UDAG-TREASURY	.468	.0100	.315	.0200	.66
CBO-HUD	.397	.0300	.310	.0200	.66
HUD-TREASURY	.319	.0900	.205	.1100	.60
BROOKINGS-CBO	.093	—	.071	—	.54
BROOKINGS-TREASURY	.041	—	.048	—	.52

W Statistic = 0.585   Significance @ .001 level

Source: Rutgers University, Center for Urban Policy Research, Spring 1980.

A final measure of the similarity of the designation procedure is a view of the ranking of a single city across all five hardship indices. This is available using the Kendall Coefficient of Concordance (W) which pools the individual Spearman's Correlations (*not* the Kendall Tau's) into a singular measure of association.

The aggregate measure for the UDAG, Brookings, CBO, HUD and Treasury rankings, which may be read similarly to R^2, is $W = 0.585$ (significant at the .001 level). Essentially what is being said here is that if one were to guess a ranking for the City of Chicago on an individual system, the first guess would be 15 ½ or $(\frac{n+1}{2})$. Using the mean rankings for the city as the predictor of this individual rank would, on average, reduce the original squared error of prediction, by 58.5 percent.

Thus, the consistency of the five ranking systems is robust both in terms of its error reduction as well as its statistical significance. Generally, when the W statistic is judged to be as strong as it is here, one can rearrange the individual observations by average rankings. Following this logic and applying it to the distressed cities, we would rank them as indicated in Exhibit 22.

In summary, the empirical analysis described in this section reveals the following close relationship between several of the various hardship rankings.

UDAG VERSUS THE OTHER
FOUR DISTRESS DESIGNATION SYSTEMS

Isolation of Most Distressed or "Top 20" Cities (2 x 2 matrices)	*80-90 % Consistency*
Relationship of Exact City Rankings (Spearman Correlations)	*.50-.75 Correlation*
Similar Ordering of Pairs of Cities (Kendall's Tau)	*70-80% Consistency*
Predicting a Ranking Using a Derived Mean Ranking (Kendall Coefficient of Concordance)	*60 % Error Reduction*

EXHIBIT 22

Mean Rankings of Cities on Combined UDAG, CBO, HUD,
Treasury and Brookings Indices

Ranking	City	Average Rank
1)	NEWARK	1.4
2.3)	ST. LOUIS	4.4
2-3)	CLEVELAND	4.4
4)	BUFFALO	7.2
5)	DETROIT	9.2
6)	NEW YORK	10.0
7-8)	BOSTON	10.2
7-8)	CHICAGO	10.2
9)	NEW ORLEANS	10.4
10)	CINCINNATI	11.4
11)	PITTSBURGH	12.6
12)	PHILADELPHIA	13.0
13)	BALTIMORE	13.8
14)	BIRMINGHAM	14.8
15)	ROCHESTER	15.2
16-17)	LOUISVILLE	15.6
16-17)	ATLANTA	15.6
18)	SAN FRANCISCO	18.2
19)	LOS ANGELES	19.4
20)	AKRON	19.8
21)	KANSAS CITY	20.2
22)	MINNEAPOLIS	20.4
23)	MILWAUKEE	21.4
24)	SEATTLE	21.6
25)	MIAMI	21.8
26)	TAMPA	23.2
27)	SACRAMENTO	23.8
28)	NORFOLK	24.8
29)	COLUMBUS	25.0
30)	DENVER	26.0

Source: Rutgers University, Center for Urban Policy Research, Spring 1980.

These findings show that the urban distress measures have a *high level of consistency* in ranking the hardship of a common set of cities. Despite differences in their variable selction/expression and statistical treatment, the distress measures are *similar in their practical operation or throughput, namely the ordering of urban distress.* City hardship therefore appears to be largely *independent* of the mechanism from which it is determined.

CONCLUSION

This paper has considered the state-of-the-art of measuring urban distress. This topic, having historical antecedents dating from the turn of the twentieth century, has currently moved to front-rank interest as a result of the worsening economic conditions in many central cities and the need to effectively channel dwindling federal and state subsidies to those communities with the greatest need. Following this historical background, the paper presented an organizational framework for considering urban hardship and, using this framework, analyzed fifteen urban distress approaches. This review, while showing individual differences in the measures' variables, linkages, threshold standards and other characteristics, also indicated many broad *similarities* in conceptual approach, data selection and statistical treatment. The distress rankings typically gauge common elements of distress, i.e., physical, social and economic decline; establish easily understood threshold points; i.e., the median value for all cities; utilize similar multiple evaluative stages, i.e. area eligibility followed by project selection; utilize some different statistical treatments, i.e., means, standard scores or factor scores; and as a practical matter, refer to comparable data sets, i.e., U.S. Census housing and population variables, Department of Labor unemployment statistics, etc. This theme of rough similarity in the composition of the urban distress measures is repeated when the operationalization of these measures is considered—all yield similar rankings when applied to a common set of cities.

NOTES

1. United States, The President's Urban and Regional Policy Group, *Cities and People in Distress: National Urban Policy Discussion Draft* (Washington, D.C., U.S. Department of Housing and Urban Development, 1977).
2. Jacob A. Riis, *How the Other Half Lives: Studies Among the Tenements of New York* INew York: Scribner and Sons, 1890).
3. President's Conference on Home Building and Home Ownership, *Slums, Large-Scale Housing and Decentralization,* Vol. III (Washington, D.C.: Government Printing Office, 1932).
4. Mabel L. Walker, *Urban Blight and Slums: Economic and Legal Factors in Their Origin, Reclamation, and Prevention* (Cambridge: Harvard University Press, 1938).
5. Ibid.
6. President's Conference on Home Building and Home Ownersip, *Housing Objectives and Programs,* Vol. XI (Washington, D.C.: Government Printing Office, 1932).
7. Ibid.

8. See U.S. Commission on Urban Problems, *Building the American City* (Washington, D.C.: Government Printing Office, 1968).
9. U.S. Department of Housing and Urban Development, *Housing in the Seventies* (Washington, D.C.: Government Printing Office, 1975).
10. Ibid., See discussion on evolution of federal housing programs.
11. Comprehensive City Demonstration Program, Public Law 89-754 Sec. 103(2).
12. See footnote 1.
13. United States Congress, Joint Economic Committee, Subcommittee on Economic Growth and Stabilization, Subcommittee on Fiscal and Intergovernmental Policy, *The Current Fiscal Condition of Cities: A Survey of 67 of the 75 Largest Cities: A Study. . .95th Congress, 1st Session, July 28, 1977* (Washington D.C.: Government Printing Office, 1977); George E. Peterson, *et al., Monitoring Urban Fiscal Conditions* (Washington, D.C.: Urban Institute (forthcoming); Thomas Muller, *Growing and Declining Urban Areas: A Fiscal Comparison* (Washington, D.C.: Urban Institute, 1975).
14. See T.D. Allman, "The Urban Crisis Leaves Town," *Harper's* (December 1978), U.S. Department of Housing and Urban Development, "Wither or Whether Urban Stress," (1978).
15. United States Congress, House Committee on Banking, Finance and Urban Affairs, Subcommittee on the City, *City Need and the Responsiveness of Federal Grants Programs. . .95th Congress, 2nd Session/August 1978* (Washington, D.C.: Government Printing Office, 1978).
16. Richard P. Nathan, *et al., Block Grants for Community Development* (Washington, D.C.: U.S. Department of Housing and Urban Development 1976); Richard P. Nathan, *et al.,* "Cities in Crisis: The Impact of Federal Aid," League of Women Voters, *Current Focus;* Richard P. Nathan and Charles Adams, Jr., *Revenue Sharing: The Second Round* (Washington, D.C.: Brookings Institution, 1977); Richard P. Nathan and Charles Adams, Jr., "Understanding Central City Hardship," *Political Science Quarterly,* Vol. 91, No. 1(Spring 1976); Richard P. Nathan and Paul R. Dommel, (Federal Aid for Cities: A Multiple Strategy *(Washington, D.C.: Brookings Institution, 1976); Richard P. Nathan and Paul R. Dommel, "Federal-Local Relations Under Block Grants," Political Science Quarterly, Vol. 93,* (Federal Aid for Cities: A Multiple Strategy (Washington, D.C.: Brookings Institution, 1976); Richard P. Nathan and Paul R. Dommel, "Federal-Local Relations Under Block Grants," *Political Science Quarterly,* Vol. 93, No. 3 (Fall 1978), p. 421.
17. United States Congress, Subcommittee on the City of the Committee on Banking, Finance and Urban Affairs, *How Cities Can Grow Old Gracefully* (Washington, D.C.: Government Printing Office, 1977); *New York City's Fiscal Problem: Its Origins, Potential Repercussions, and Some Alternative Policy Responses* (Washington, D.C.: Congressional Budget Office, 1975).
18. David T. Stanley, *Cities in Trouble,* (Columbus: Academy for Contemporary Problems, 1976).
19. George E. Peterson, *et al., Urban Fiscal Monitoring* (Washington, D.C.: Urban Institute, 1978); see also, George E. Peterson, *The Fiscal and Financial Capacity of City Governments,* paper prepared for the Deputy Assistant Secretary of Urban Policy, United States Department of Housing and Urban Development, 1979.

20. See footnote 13.
21. The legislative intent is expressed in Public Law 95-128, 95th Congress:

> The Secretary is authorized to make urban development action grants to severely distressed cities and urban counties to help alleviate *physical* and *economic* deterioration through reclamation of neighborhoods having excessive housing abandonment or deterioration, and through community revitalization in areas with population out-migration or a stagnating or declining tax base. Grants made under this section shall be for the support of severely distressed cities and urban counties that require increased public and private assistance in addition to the assistance otherwise made available under this title and other forms of Federal assistance. . .

22. Ibid.
23. Ibid.
24. UDAG *does* employ an impaction/distress ranking procedure for use in project selection. An *impaction* score is defined as the weighted sum of the standardized scores of the poverty, age of housing and population lag/ decline variables, with weights respectively of 3, 5 and 2. A *distress* score is the sum of the standardized scores of the per capita income, job lag/ decline and unemployment variables. The distress score is computed only for metropolitan cities and urban counties. The impaction score is computed for each of several "peer groups": metropolitan cities and urban counties (50,000 or more population); cities 25,000 to 40,000 in population; cities 2,500 to 25,000 in population; and cities with a population of less than 2,500.
25. The Economic Development Administration has many area designations including:

   a. *Redevelopment Areas* (RA)—counties, labor market areas, and cities over 25,000 where measures of unemployment and/or family income indicate economic distress.

   b. *Economic development districts* (EDD)—multi-county areas containing at least 1 RA and 1 economic development center (EDC) that can support economic development for the district. Unemployment and income levels are the factors considered in this designation.

   c. *Economic development centers* (EDC)—cities under 25,000 that are located in EDDs, that are included in the district's Overall Economic Development Plan and that are capable of developing a diversified economy that can contribue to the EDD's economic growth goals.

   d. *Redevelopment centers*—areas meeting the criteria of EDCs (but with no limit on population size) and that are located in redevelopment areas.

   e. *Special impact areas*—pockets of poverty or unemployment surrounded by relatively well-off areas.

   See U.S. Department of Housing and Urban Development, *Local Economic*

Development Tools and Techniques: A Guidebook for Local Government
(Washington, D.C.: Government Printing Office, 1979). See also, Bureau of
National Affairs, "Economic Development Programs," *Housing and Devel-
opment Reporter*, Vol. 1 (Reference File) Section 15 (Washington, D.C.:
BNA, 1979); Economic Development Administration, *1978 Annual Report*
(Washington D.C.: Government Printing Office, 1979).

26. The description, "Suffering Substantial and Persistent Unemployment," is
found in the Statement of Purpose in PUblic Works and Employment Act
of 1965 (42USC 3121).

27. The objective of Title IX-LTED isdescribed in 43 FR 57919, December
11, 1978 as follows:

> Long-term economic deterioration is the steady decline of the economy
> of an area due to the loss of productive economic activity. It is manifested
> by the loss of jobs and icnome; by the physical deterioration and devalua-
> tion of land, buildings and public infrastructure; and by human suffering
> and social disintegration
>
> The goal of the LTED program is to help states and communities design
> and carry out strategies to arrest and then reverse long-term deterioration.

28. Note: Chronic distress is specifically described as one of the three economic
standards considered by Title IX-LTED. See 43 FR 57919, December 11,
1978. Current Economic Distress, in contrast, is a term formulated by this
study.

29. For a detailed specification, see 43 FR 57918, December 13, 1978.

30. See, for example, 43 FR 52433, November 9, 1978.

31. See HUD, *Local Economic Development Tools and Techniques*, p. 24.
See 45 FR 10740, February 15, 1980 for "Pockets of Poverty" regulations.

32. These two indices are detailed in Richard P. Nathan and Charles Adams,
"Understanding Central City Hardship." The Intrametropolitan Hardship
Index gauges the social and economic hardship of the central city in relationship to its own surrounding suburbs. The Intercity Hardship Index
measures relative hardship between central cities. (See footnote 16 for
other studies.)

33. See Subcommittee on the City of the Committee on Banking, Finance and
Urban Affairs, House of Representatives, *City Need and the Responsiveness
of Federal Programs.* (Written by Peggy L. Cuciti of the Congressional
Budget Office.)

34. Harold L. Bunce and Robert L. Goldberg, *City Need and Community
Development Funding* (Washington, D.C. Government Printing Office,
January 1979), U.S. Department of Housing and Urban Development,
Office of Policy Development and Research, Division of Evaluation. See
also, Harold Bunce, *An Evaluation of the Community Development Block
Grant Program* (Washington, D.C.: U.S. Department of Housing and Urban
Development, 1976); Harold Bunce, "The Community Development Block
Grant Formula: An Evaluation," *Urban Studies Quarterly*, Vol. 14, No. 4
(June 1979), p. 443. For further evaluation of CDBG, see Comptroller
General of the United States, *Why the Formula for Allocating Community
Block Grants Should be Improved* (Washington, D.C.: U.S. General Accoun-
ting Office, 1976); Richard Nathan, *et al.*, *Block Grants for Community*

Development; Robert Goldberg, *et al.,* "CDBG Formula Change" (Washington, D.C.: U.S. Department of Housing and Urban Development, 1977).
35. Gregory Schmid, Hubert Lupinski and Michael Palmer, *An Alternative Approach to General Revenue Sharing: A Needs Based Formula* (Menlo Park, CA: Institute for the Future, 1975).
36. U.S. Department of the Treasury, Office of State and Local Finance, *Report on the Fiscal Impact of the Economic Stimulus Package on 48 Large Urban Governments* (Washington D.C.: Treasury, January 1978).
37. See E. Terrence Jones and Donald Phares, "Formula Feedback and Central Cities: The Case of the Comprehensive Employment and Training Act," *Urban Affairs Quarterly,* Vol. 14, No. 1 (September 1978), p. 31-54, For further discussion of Revenue Sharing see Richard Nathan and Charles Adams, Jr., *Revenue Sharing: The Second Round* (Washington, D.C.: Brookings, 1977); Otto Stolz, *Revenue Sharing: Legal and Policy Analysis* (New York: Praeger, 1974); Burry Molefsky and Dennis Zimmerman, "General Revenue Sharing and Alternatives: Economic Rationales Past and Present," in Fund for Public Policy Research, *Studies in Taxation, Public Finance and Related Subjects—A Compendium,* Vol. 3 (Washington, D.C.: Fund for Public Policy, 1979), p. 33; Robert Inman, *et al., Financing the New Federalism* (Washington, D.C.: Resources for the Future, 1975); Richard Thompson, *Revenue Sharing—A New Era in Federalism?* (Washington, D.C.: Revenue Sharing Advisory Service, 1973).

John E. Petersen - BIG CITY BORROWING COSTS AND CREDIT QUALITY

This paper deals with trends in the financial structure and credit quality of the nation's forty-five largest cities over the past decade.[1] The period covered by the interval from the late 1960s to the late 1970s has been a turbulent one for city government. Commencing during the recession of 1973-74 and spot-lighted by the events surrounding the New York City crises of 1975 and 1976, academics, analysts, and the public at large became increasingly aware of the financial plight of many of the nation's cities. Almost all observers acknowledge that many cities were suffering dramatic demographic and economic declines. But the causes, severity and reverseability of these phenomena are very much in dispute, as are, of course, the appropriate policies which cities, states and the federal government should take to cure this situation.[2]

The first aspect to be examined in this paper will be a brief review of the changing revenue and expenditure patterns of the large cities. After a discussion of the recent performance of the municipal bond market and big-city borrowing costs and difficulties, are the historical record to the largest cities reviewed with respect to their credit quality as represented by the ratings on their general obligation bonds as conferred by Moody's Investor Service. The levels and trends in ratings are then examined in relationship to various socioeconomic and financial indices that are commonly associated with credit quality.

PATTERNS OF BIG CITY FINANCE

As a whole, the state and local sector has undergone considerable change in the magnitude and structure of its financing over the last decade. The largest forty-five cities have shared in these changes and have seen their budgets grow under the impact of inflation and an increasingly rich array of services delivered to the public. On average, however, they have had to contend with declining populations and with residents' personal incomes that have been growing more slowly than those of the nation at large. But, as we shall see, the use of averages in describing even the largest cities is a perilous exercise and that most jurisdictions have found new sources of revenue to finance most—if not all—of their growing expenditure needs.

Exhibit 1 documents, on a per capita basis, what has been the trend in outlays and receipts of the largest forty-five cities, using the unweighted averages and showing annual rates of growth in the individual items. As shown, between 1967 and 1977 (the latest year for which complete information is readily available), city per capita general expenditures and general revenues grew at an average rate of approximately 12 percent, from $184 in per capita expenditures in 1967 to $551 by 1977 in the case of general expenditures.[3]

Skimming over the items listed in Exhibit 1, it may be seen that city current outlays grew much more rapidly than capital outlays and, looking at the revenues, those received in the form of intergovernmental payments grew at more than three times the rate of those revenues collected locally from the city's own sources. Also, the largest 45 cities during the decade under review saw their general government (non-utility) long-term debt rise at a fairly modest annual rate of 7.2 percent.

Several definitional and conceptual caveats need to be borne in mind when reviewing the city averages, and these are discussed in the appendix to this paper. But certain generalizations about city behavior are possible with the assistance of other items shown in Exhibit 1. First, growth in expenditures was driven to a large extent by the inflation in prices that cities had to pay for goods and services. Between 1967 and 1977, the state and local price deflator (as shown in Exhibit 1) rose from 72.5 to 148.5, an annual rate of inflation equal to 7.4 percent. As a result, real per capita expenditures and revenues (adjusted for the rate of price increase) rose at a rate of approximately 4.5 percent per capita.

As Exhibit 1 also indicates, among the items shown, per capita expenditures for the state and local sector were rising more slowly than was the case for the largest cities. Intergovernmental aid, while

EXHIBIT 1

Selected Financial Items for 45 Largest Cities, Per Capita Amounts and
Rates of Growth, With Comparisons to Overall State and Local Sector:
1967-1977

	1967	1977	Annual Rate of Growth
General Expenditures	$184.06	$550.64	11.6%
Current Outlays	$141.99	$449.27	12.2%
Capital Outlays	$ 42.07	$101.40	9.2%
General Revenues	$179.63	$578.97	12.4%
Own-Source Revenues	$133.44	$244.89	6.3%
Intergovernmental Payments	$ 46.19	$334.08	21.9%
Gross City Debt Outstanding	$351.57	$655.49	6.4%
General Government Long-term			
Debt Outstanding	$226.61	$455.95	7.2%
Items:			
State and Local Price Delfator			
(1972=100)	72.5	148.5	7.4%
State and Local Sector			
(per Capita):			
General Expenditures	$472.66	$1268.37	10.4%
Revenues from Own Sources	$383.93	$1029.30	10.4%
Intergovernmental Aid	$ 77.82	$289.30	14.0%
Total Debt Outstanding	$575.49	$1190.62	7.5%

growing rapidly at 14 percent a year, was also growing more slowly
for the sector as a whole than for the largest cities. Outstanding
debt of the 45 largest cities—both the gross debt and that sold for
general government purposes—grew at a relatively leisurely rate and
only slightly more slowly than that of the state and local sector
as a whole.

Despite the relatively faster rates of growth in per capita expenditures and revenues in the 45 largest cities in comparison to the
state and local sector as a whole, the cities actually saw their relative
importance in the aggregate of state and local finances decline. The
percentage of total state and local general revenues represented by
the 45 largest cities was reduced from 10.1 percent in 1967 to 8.4
percent in 1977. The reason for this, of course, can be found in the
decline in city population.[4]

Exhibit 2 illustrates the major underlying trends in total population and per capita income in the 45 cities, contrasting their performance and relative stature in relationship to the rest of the nation.

EXHIBIT 2

Population and Per Capita Personal Income of 45 Largest Cities
Compared to National Figures:
1967-1977

	1967	1977	Annual Rate of Growth
Resident Population (millions)			
45 Cities Total	38.4	37.5	−0.2%
U.S. Total	197.5	216.9	0.9%
Cities as % of U.S.	19.5%	17.2%	—
Per Capita Personal Income			
45 Cities Average	$2790	$5967	7.9%
U.S. Average	$3153	$7051	8.4%
Cities as % of U.S.	88.5%	84.6%	—

As noted, total population in the largest 45 cities declined over the decade 1967-1977 at a rate of 0.2 percent a year (of course, some cities lost population much more rapidly, as will be discussed below). Perhaps of greatest interest is the slower rate of growth in city personal income (7.9 percent versus 8.4 percent nationally). As a result, the average per capita personal income in the 45 largest cities slipped from 88 percent of the national average in 1967 to 85 percent by 1977.

The consequences of increasing expenditures, own revenues, and outstanding debt in the face of declining personal income are reported by the three percentages shown in Exhibit 3. First, for the 45 largest cities, general expenditures as a percentage of personal income rose from 6.6 percent to 9.2 percent between 1967 and 1977, an average annual rate of growth in total state and local expenditures as a percentage of average personal income in the nation, which grew at an annual rate of only 1.8 percent during the decade. However, because cities were enjoying an appreciably higher rate of increase in intergovernmental aid, revenues raised locally as a percentage of personal income actually diminished during the decade for the largest 45 cities, while it increased for the state and local sector as a whole. Last, the burden of debt, as measured by the percentage of gross debt outstanding as a percentage of personal income dropped for the cities at a somewhat faster rate than for the state and local sector in the aggregate.

As indicated above, perhaps the most important development in the finances of the largest 45 cities has not been the rate of

EXHIBIT 3

Selected Financial Items as a Percentage of Per Capita Personal Income,
45 Largest Cities and Overall State and Local Sector:
1967-1977

	1967	1977	Annual Rate of Growth
General Expenditure as % of Personal Income:			
45 Cities	6.6%	9.2%	3.4%
State and Local Sector	15.0%	18.0%	1.8%
Own Revenue as % of Personal Income:			
45 Cities	4.8%	4.1%	−1.6%
State and Local Sector	12.2%	14.6%	1.8%
Debt Outstanding as % of Personal Income:			
45 Cities	12.6%	11.0%	−1.3%
State and Local Sector	18.3%	16.9%	−0.8%

growth in expenditures, but rather the revolution in the way in which cities have been financing them. Exhibit 4 focuses on the changing composition of the sources of revenue, giving the percentage breakdown among the various sources.

The largest 45 cities, from 1967 to 1977, saw their reliance on general revenues raised from their own local sources drop from 74% of total revenues in 1967 to approximately 58 percent by 1977. The largest decline came in the property tax, whose proportionate share fell from 36 percent to 23 percent of total general revenues during the decade. The slack, of course, was picked up by the growth in intergovernmental payments. And within the intergovernmental category, the most impressive growth was found in federal aid. In 1967 federal aid payments represented 4.7 percent of total general revenues; ten years later, its share was more than 21 percent.

Cities have been financing the growth in their expenditures through sources of funds other than those raised locally. Moreover, reflecting on trends of indebtedness, it is clear that cities on average have been using other financing sources, rather than relying more on the capital markets. In fact, own source revenues and debt have both declined as a percentage of personal income, even in cities that lag considerably behind the national average in personal income. The most interesting conclusion, aside from any speculation on the necessity and desirability of such growth in intergovernmental payments, is that the fiscal fortunes of cities have become intertwined progressively with those of the states and, to a great extent, the federal government.

EXHIBIT 4

Percentage Composition[1] of General Revenues:
45 Largest Cities,
1967-1977

	1967	1977
General Revenues	100.0	100.0
Own Sources	74.3	57.7
Property Tax	36.2	22.7
Other Taxes	24.9	23.2
Charges & Fees	13.2	11.8
Intergovernmental	25.7	42.3
State	18.6	19.3
Federal	4.7	21.1
Local	2.4	1.9

[1] Unweighted average of city per capita amounts.

It is important to note, before passing on to other topics, that using 1977 as a terminal year does not catch a large part of the sizable growth in federal assistance that occurred in fiscal 1978. As we discuss later, projections of the 1978 data indicate a dramatic increase in the reliance of cities—even during the relatively good times recently—on federal aid. The implication of this growth for the long-term revenue structure and creditworthiness of cities is discussed below.

COSTS OF CITY BORROWING

In late 1975 and early 1976, several major city borrowers were either excluded from the tax-exempt market or forced to pay very high rates of interest to borrow.[5] A division between stronger and weaker borrowers—a two-tiered market for big-city general obligation bonds—rapidly emerged.[6] Several factors converged to cause these borrowing difficulties. For the greatest part, the difficulties were associated with investor concerns over the credit quality of cities and their ability and willingness to repay loans in the face of deteriorating fiscal and economic circumstances. Doubts about creditworthiness, while bad enough, were compounded by uncertainties regarding legal responsibilities in disclosing fiscal conditions and, in the final analysis, the enforceability of bondholders' rights of repayment against competing claims in the case of default.[7]

A vivid illustration of the tangible costs of such a decay in confidence is found in the large cost differentials that grew among the various grades of municipal bonds, reversing a decade-long trend of declining risk premia among the highest and lowest grades.

An examination of new-issue general obligation bond sales by those cities among the largest 100 in the country during the period 1976-1978 gives a summary of what happened to city borrowing costs in relationship to those in the rest of the municipal bond market. Exhibit 5 presents, by Moody's rating category of the bonds sold, the average reoffering yield on 20-year city general obligation bonds as measured in basis points (hundreths of a percentage point) deviations from the *Bond Buyer* Twenty Bond Index during the week of the bond sale. (This adjustment is made to take account of trends in the general level of interest rates.) The period covered is from the first quarter of 1976, the peak of the crisis in the municipal bond market, through the 1977 and 1978 market recovery. The final column in the exhibit shows the spread between the highest grade, "Aaa," and lowest investment grade "Baa," also in basis points.

As may be seen in Exhibit 5, the difference between the yields on new-issue city bonds of the highest (Aaa) and lowest ratings (Baa) was an astronomical 374 basis points in the first quarter of 1976.[8] By the last half of 1976, the spread between Aaa and Baa new-issue city bonds began to shrink but was still about 200 basis points. The shrinkage was evident at both ends of the credit spectrum: the interest advantage of the highest grades diminished as did the added costs of the lower grades, when compared to the overall market average. By 1977, the market began a relatively smooth glide into smaller, but still significant spreads among the grades.

The experiences of 1975 and 1976 dramatized the costs of suspect credit quality and having a low bond rating. As Exhibit 5 shows, units with the highest quality benefited—at least relatively—from the flight to quality, while the lower grades suffered. Having a low bond rating was highly correlated to paying more money to borrow.[9] But the interest cost was not the only factor; a low rating and the threat of loss of access to credit has manifold political and economic repercussions. Threats of default or bankruptcy demoralize and freighten and conjure up all sorts of vision of stopping city services and civil unrest. It's not only the bondholders that abhor that kind of uncertainity.

EXHIBIT 5

City New Issue Bond Sales:
Spread Between 20-Year Reoffering Yield and Bond Buyer Index:
By Quarterly Averages 1976 I to 1977 IV and 1978 Semi-annual Averages.

Year/Quarter	Moody Rating				
					Baa-Aaa
	Aaa	Aa	A	Baa	Aaa
1976 I	−94	−20	(1)	270	374
1976 II	−72	−31	22	231	303
1976 III	−82	−51	32	130	202
1976 IV	−89	−42	−25	(1)	(1)
1977 I	−52	−34	10	121	173
1977 II	−43	−24	3	128	171
1977 III	−19	−29	−17	(1)	(1)
1977 IV	−46	−29	− 7	95	141
1978 (First one-half)	−56	−32	− 6	27	83
1978 (Second one-half)	−62	−37	−38	56	118

(1) = No observation

Source: Based on 148 general obligation bond sales of cities among largest 100 cities
in the nation.

TRENDS IN CITY BOND RATINGS

The turmoil of the municipal bond market in the mid-1970s and the well-advertised misery of certain cities tends to associate the big city credits generally with the difficulties of certain, mainly Northeastern, cities. However, the fact is that there has generally been an uptrend in the ratings of the major cities over the past decade. Unfortunately, the popular perception of the difficulties among the Northeastern cities is not misplaced. The upgrading in ratings has shown a heavy regional orientation, with the cities in the West and—to a lesser extent—in the South, enjoying the upgradings.

Exhibit 6 presents a description of the distribution of Moody's ratings and changes in ratings of general obligation bonds of the largest 45 cities for the 13-year period, 1965 to 1978. Only the major rating categories are shown; the subcategories A-1, Baa-1 are grouped in the respective major category (i.e., A-1 is assigned to A, etc.) The distribution of ratings in effect in 1965 for the cities can be read across the bottom of the exhibit; that for 1978 may be read in the right-hand stub of the exhibit.

EXHIBIT 6

Ratings and Rating Change of 45 Largest Cities' General Obligation Debt:
1965-1978
(Moody's Ratings)

	Aaa	Aa	A	Baa	Ba-B	Total	
Aaa	3	5	1			9	
Aa		11	11			22	
A		1	4	1		6	1978
Baa			3	2		5	Ratings
Ba-B		2	1		0	3	
	3	19	20	3	0	45	

1965 Ratings

As may be seen in Exhibit 6, the city ratings were evenly clustered in 1965 around the A and Aa categories. However, over the next thirteen years, the number of Aaa and Aa ratings given to city bonds increased, while the number in the lower grades also increased but on a smaller scale. Thus, while the median grade carried by city bonds rose from "A" to "Aa," the number of lower-rated city credits also increased: the distribution of bonds became more dispersed and, to an extent, developed into a two-tiered system of "strong" and "weak" credits.

There was a good deal of movement by the cities among the rating categories. The figures of the boxed diagonal in Exhibit 6 give the number of credits either rising or falling, showing from which rating in 1965 to which rating in 1978 the movement took place. For example, of the 19 borrowers rated "Aa" in 1965, 11 retained that rating in 1978, five moved up to "Aaa," one dropped to "A," and two dropped to below "Baa" (Buffalo and Cleveland).

Looking at the overall totals, only 20 of the 45 city borrowers (44 percent) retained the same rating during the interval 1965 to 1978. Eighteen borrowers were upgraded (40 percent) and seven were downgraded (16 percent) during this period. Not shown in Exhibit 6 but of some interest is the fact that 15 rating changes—10 of the upgradings and five of the downgradings—occurred between 1972 and 1978. Thus, there was a pronounced tendency to upgrade city credits, despite the problems of the mid-1970s.

EXHIBIT 7

Direction of Changes in General Obligation Bond Ratings
Of 45 Largest Cities:
1965-1978

	Upgrade	Unchanged	Downgraded	Total Ratings
Northeast	0	1	5	6
Midwest	4	8	2	14
South	6	8	0	14
West	8	3	0	11
	18	20	7	45

The changes in ratings had a strong regional flavor to them, as is illustrated in Exhibit 7. The heavy concentration of downgradings occurred in the weakening Northeastern quadrant of the nation. Conversely, the prospering South and West have seen their credit ratings improve. Of the 18 upgradings, eight occurred in the West (out of a total of 11 cities), six in the South (out of 14 city credits), and four in the Midwest (out of 14 cities). At the same time, the Northeast saw five of its six big-city credits go down; the only one that remained unchanged (Boston) was already marginal ("Baa") in the sense of its credit quality.

Exhibit 8 gives a listing of the individual cities and their rating changes between December 1965 and December 1978.

CITY ECONOMIC AND FINANCIAL CONDITIONS AND RATINGS

Several recent studies have identified specific cities that are suffering from a host of long-term social, economic and fiscal problems.[10] Numerous factors have been selected as registering these difficulties, but the substance of analysis appears to be that older, formerly heavily industrial areas have suffered reductions in population, loss of jobs, slow growth in per capita income and property values, and a loss of economic activity, wealth and people to the surrounding suburban areas. Municipal credit ratings as conferred by the major rating agencies, of course, are determined by much of the same complex of factors that go into forming an index of city hardship or measuring fiscal performance. Thus, they should generally comport with many of the concerns of the urbanologist or policymaker, translating the many indices of urban economic and fiscal stress into summary ratings to be used in the dollars-and-cents calculations

EXHIBIT 8

Changes in Ratings on General Obligation Bonds
(Moody's Ratings) 1965 and 1978

Rating Upgraded	Rating Unchanged	Rating Downgraded
Phoenix, AR	Long Beach, CA	St. Louis, MO
Los Angeles, CA	Oakland, CA	Newark, NJ
San Diego, CA	Denver, CO	Buffalo, NY
San Francisco, CA	Miami, FL	New York, NY
San Jose, CA	Atlanta, GA	Cleveland, OH
Jacksonville, FL	Louisville, KY	Philadelphia, PA
Honolulu, HI	New Orleans, LA	Pittsburgh, PA
Chicago, IL	Baltimore, MD	
Indianapolis, IN	Boston, MS	
Oklahoma City, OK	Detroit, MI	
Tulsa, OK	Minneapolis, MN	
Portland, OR	Kansas City, MO	
Dallas, TX	Omaha, NB	
Fort Worth, TX	Cincinnati, OH	
Houston, TX	Columbus, OH	
San Antonio, TX	Toledo, OH	
Norfolk, VA	Memphis, TN	
Seattle, WA	Nashville-Davidson, TN	
	El Paso, TX	
	Milwaukee, WI	

of the investor. As has been discussed, the ratings are not of academic interest: the premiums charged borrowers with low credit ratings increased drastically in the mid-1970s, and for many large cities, borrowing was difficult and expensive.

Exhibit 9 displays the largest 45 cities, grouped by rating category, arrayed against 11 indicators that have been widely used to measure city fiscal and economic condition. Shown are the group means for each rating category and their associated standard deviations (shown in parentheses). The first bracket—focusing on income, population change, income disparity, job growth and unemployment—shows a fairly regular association between the jurisdiction's economic condition and the rating: the lower the rating, the poorer its situation as measured by the indicators.

Note, however, that the standard deviations tell us that the group averages are not necessarily tight; there is considerable wiggle room for a city that may not do well in one respect to still "buck the averages" and be classed in a higher rating category. For example, recent population loss, which has been associated with economic

EXHIBIT 9

Relation of Selected Factors to Rating Categories: Average Values for Largest
45 Cities As Classified By Moody's 1978 Rating on City General Obligation Bonds
(Standard Deviation in Parentheses)

Economic and Demographic Items	City G.O. Rating:			
	Aaa	Aa	A	Baa
Per Capita Personal Income[1]	$6563	$6090	$5231	$5260
	(512)	(664)	(511)	(640)
Change in Population (1970-75)	−.5	−.2	−.1	−1.9
(Annual Percentage Change)	(1.5)	(1.6)	(2.1)	(.8)
Per Capita Income Disparity (1973)	106.1	103.1	87.2	88.4
Central City as Percent of Rest of SMSA	(9.5)	(18.2)	(10.6)	(17.5)
Unemployment Rate (January 1977)	7.3	7.5	9.9	11.3
(Percentage Rate)	(2.1)	(1.7)	(2.0)	(3.5)
Employment Growth (1970-1977)	18.3	22.4	10.6	−.8
(Percentage Rate)	(14.2)	(21.8)	(15.1)	(5.7)
Urban Conditions Index[2]	103.7	96.0	182.1	252.3
	(55.8)	(59.0)	(118.4)	(49.3)
Fiscal Items				
City Revenue Effort (1977)	4.4	5.0	5.6	9.3
(Own Revenue/Personal Income)	(2.1)	(2.2)	(2.3)	(4.8)
City General Debt Burden (1977)	5.9	7.4	6.6	11.5
(General Debt/Personal Income)	(2.6)	(4.0)	(2.5)	(5.7)
Local Revenue Effort (1976)	10.0	9.5	9.7	13.4
(Central City Co./Personal Income)	(2.1)	(2.6)	(2.6)	(3.6)
Local General Debt Burdent (1976)	11.8	13.8	14.2	17.3
(Central City Co./Personal Income)	(3.9)	(7.4)	(2.4)	(5.8)
(Number of Cities)	(9)	(22)	(6)	(8)

[1]   Author's estimates based on historical relationship of city personal income to national
personal income.

[2]   Consists of housing stock age, percent poverty population and rate of population
change. See Richard Nathan, Paul Dommel and James Fossett, Testimony Before
the Joint Economic Committee, U.S. Congress, July 28, 1977.

deterioration and fiscal stress, does not show a very strong relationship with rating category.

The next bracket of indicators deals more directly with the burdens of city and city area finance. As may be seen, the relationship between the group means are quite consistent. In the case of city government own revenue effort and debt, the highest grade cities ("Aaa") show only half the effort and burden as exhibited by those cities with the lowest ratings ("Baa" and below).

To take into account that city governments do not provide all the services to citizens, we can also look at the overall revenue and debt burden of local government finance on city residents. This is approximated by the ratio of the general revenues and general debt of all local jurisdictions in the central city area to central city income. The result of using this indicator is largely consisent with just looking at the city government alone: revenue effort and debt burden increasing, although not so steeply as with the city data, the lower the rating.

General measures such as the above show susceptibility to fiscal crisis, but in the end, crisis usually comes down to a shortage of cash. Any government—including a city—is likely to find itself in immediate financial difficulty when expenditures exceed revenues by any great amount for any prolonged period of time. The root causes of these inbalances may be many, but the final result—an accumulated budget deficit—is what signals potential or actual financial emergency.[11] Analysis of the current financial accounts is difficult because of a lack of timely data and differing bookkeeping methods used by state and local governments. To make the data reasonably comparable, detailed adjustments are usually required.

One consistent set of studies of city financial conditions as reflected in their operating results has been performed by Philip Dearborn.[12] Exhibit 10 represents the results of his analysis of city operating budget performance, summarized for cities grouped by major region and by rating classification. The results are usually for the fiscal years 1973 through 1975, the period of the most recent recession. Therefore, they should provide insights into the cities' resilience to adverse economic developments. As may be seen, the major cities in the Northeastern region generally experienced much sharper financial difficulties, experiencing operating deficits as a result. Cities in the other regions, even during this recession, tended to experience small operating surpluses on average.

The sample of cities may also be classified by the rating on their general obligation debt. As may be seen in the second panel of Exhibit 10, those rated "Baa" through "B" showed both accumulated deficits for the period (3.5 percent) and a greater propensity

EXHIBIT 10

City Accumulated Surplus and Years of Operating Deficits

	Accumulated Surplus As % of Three Years Of Expenditures	Number of Years Oper. Deficits Past Three Years[1]
By Region:		
Northeast	−4.8%	2.3%
Midwest	1.3	1.0
South	2.0	0.9
West	2.0	1.0
By Moody's Rating:		
Aaa	2.30	1.00
Aa	2.30	1.00
A	1.40	1.20
Baa-B	−3.50	1.83

[1]   Either interval of 1974-76 or 1973-75.

Source: Philip M. Dearborn, *Elements of Municipal Financial Analysis: Parts I and II.*
First Boston Corporation, 1977.

to have annual deficits (1.83). Operating results are consistently better for the "A" rated cities and are identical for the "Aaa" and "Aa" rated cities, which on average had accumulated surpluses (2.3 percent) and fewer years of deficit (one out of three) on average.

Of course, more sophisticated forms of analysis can be employed to explain what goes into city credit ratings. But the above exercises demonstrate that the ratings—as an ordinal ranking system—do about as well as any in describing where cities stack up in relation to one another in terms of long-term notions of economic future and fiscal capacity.[13] This is not surprising in that a multiplicity of factors enter into such credit estimations because they are intended to rate long-term obligations and, theoretically, give gradations of a credit risk that historically has been quite small.[14]

It is also interesting to observe that the cities' bond ratings—although intended to rank the credit quality of long-term obli-gations—are by no means static. They have responded to changes in the fiscal and economic conditions of cities and regions, typically leading in time the popular and academic perceptions of problems.[15]

SOME NEW FACTORS INFLUENCING CREDIT QUALITY

There are some important new factors that are entering into determining city financial prospects and credit ratings that have not yet received sufficient attention. In part this is because of the slowness of analysts to recognize their importance to city finances and, in part, because of a lack of data. The position of bonded debt, for example, as a liability on a city's balance sheet may be overshadowed by unfunded employer pension liabilities.

Analysts and others are now paying much more attention to this factor. But quantification of impacts is difficult because of data gaps and the great importance of assumptions about future behavior. At a minimum, and even under the best of circumstances, many cities will sooner or later find their level of contributions to retirement funds will have to grow rapidly.

Another source of fiscal uncertainty is the impact of the growing dependency on federal and state assistance payments. These can be of particular importance to city finance because so much of the money flows directly or indirectly (via the state, in the case of some federal money) through the city's financial structure. The problem is what this increasing dependency on outside sources will mean in terms of a city's ability to cope with a withdrawal or slowing down of funds from these sources. Current budgeting pressures at both the federal and state level may soon give us some real-life experience in this regard.

For example, a highly visible reaction to the big cities' fiscal problems has been the three Countercyclical Programs—Anti-recessionary Fiscal Assistance (ARFA), Local Public Works (LPW), and Title VI of the Comprehensive Employment and Training Act, (CETA). Representing a belated federal response to the 1974-75 recession, they combined to pump about $14.5 billion into the state and local sector between late 1976 and early 1978. By in large, the programs were targeted to high employment areas and to cities that would rank high in terms of both socioeconomic and fiscal distress.[16]

The sudden influx of federal assistance clearly brought fiscal relief to many governments, although not necessarily stimulating additional state and local spending—its nominal policy objective.[17] Besides substituting against local-financed expenditure, the assistance to some extent was used to restore run-down cash balances, and this constituted a form of saving, adding to the sector's surpluses. The restoration of city fiscal balances may have been inimical to the aims of the aid programs but, of course, was viewed initially with delight by credit analysts who were becoming increasingly concerned about cash balances and liquidity. Better financial conditions in 1977 contributed to an improvement in bond market reception of city securities and the units' ability to finance themselves.[18] And, although fiscal year 1978 information is not yet available for analysis, it may be supposed the heavy influx of federal assistance that continued during that period—plus generally easy credit conditions—further improved city finances.

The current reliance on federal (and state) assistance may prove to be a mixed blessing for cities. While it obviously eased the near-term burdens, it presents a new worry as dependency on external funds has grown. At present, the prospects for further growth in federal aid are bleak and retrenchment in such assistance—which in many cases accounts for 40 to 60 percent of a city's revenues— may set off new crunches in some cities as they attempt to lower expenditures.[19] The collateral threat of state and locally induced tax and expenditure limitations, depending on the severity and design of the limitation, also can cause problems for local borrowers.

NOTES

1. For purposes of the analysis, the forty-five largest cities are defined in terms of their population as of 1975. The District of Columbia has been excluded because of its unique city-state characteristics.

2. One of the more recent debates surrounding the importance of financial analysis in measuring fiscal stress. A recent study by the First National Bank of Boston and Touche-Ross & Company challenges the notion that socioeconomic indicators are reliable predictors of fiscal stress and carries strong implication that a government that is managed correctly can "buck the trend" of high taxes, debt and expense ratios. One of its conclusions is the statement that "fiscal stability between the demand for public services and financial resources appears to be within the grasp of most cities." The study has been attacked by the Department of Housing and Urban Development on the basis of methodology, sample selection, and generally for taking a myopic view of the long-term trends of economic decline and loss of population, jobs and tax bases. See Touche-Ross and The First National Bank of Boston, *Urban Fiscal Stress: A Comparative Analysis of 66 U.S. Cities* (1977) and "HUD Attacks Bank Study on Cities' Stress," *New York Times* (March 27, 1979), pg. A-6.

3. General expenditures are those expenditures carried out by the city government for purposes that are defined as being of a general governmental nature by the U.S. Bureau of the Census. The principal exclusions are expenditures by what the Census defines as local utility functions, namely water supply, gas, electric and transit utilities. The expenditure figures (nor revenue figures) do not reflect expenditures and revenues made by independent entities such as counties, special districts and school districts

that are local government jurisdictions under separate political control. It is always necessary to remember when dealing with city government revenues and expenditures that only part of the supply of public services and, consequently, revenues are being counted, since many services are rendered and taxes and fees collected by jurisdictions other than the city in a given geographic area.

4. A Fundamental problem in dealing with the aggregates in big-city data involves the impact of New York City, only one but by far the statistically predominant city in the nation. In fact, in the aggregate, New York City's finances tend to swamp those of the largest 45, it being so much the largest. In 1967, New York City expenditures represented 44 percent of the total of the largest 45 city expenditures. In 1977 (despite two years of retrenchment on the part of New York City), the city's total general expenditures still represented 45 percent of the total of the largest 45 cities. Use of unweighted per capita averages corrects for this influence, since New York City's finances then account for only 2 percent (as opposed to 45 percent) of the experience.

5. New York City and Yonkers got most of the headlines, but Buffalo, Detroit, Boston, Newark and Philadelphia had worrisome episodes. Even relatively strong borrowers—such as Richmond, Virginia—suffered scrapes in a confused and jumpy market.

6. See Ronald Forbes and John Petersen, "Costs of Credit Erosion in the Municipal Bond Market," Chicago, Municipal Finance Officers Association (1975).
   Lynne Browne and Richard Syron, "Big City Bonds After New York," *New England Economic Review* (July 1977).

7. For a more extended discussion, see John Petersen "New Developments in the Municipal Bond Market," in *Fiscal Choices of State and Local Government*, George Petersen, Editor, Washington, D.C., Urban Institute (forthcoming).

8. Ratings below Baa are so marginal as to make public sales practically impossible and no sales by cities with such ratings are included.

9. To borrow one million dollars at 9 percent a year instead of 6 percent a year (300 basis points more) with a "level debt service" maturity schedules (like a home mortgage) costs a city $101,000 a year instead of $87,000 in debt service. Such as price effect is hardly enough to drive a city to the poorhouse. The nub of the problem is that it signals the possible, perhaps imminent, cutting off of credit. The latter event can take a city to the poorhouse if it has no other way to raise cash to pay its bills and wages.

10. Useful summaries are found in U.S. Treasury, *Report on the Fiscal Impact of the Economic Stimulus Package on 48 Large Urban Governments*, January 1978, and Subcommittee on the City, U.S. House of Representatives, "City Need and the Responsiveness of Federal Grants Programs," August 1978.

11. For example, a city may not be funding its pensions sufficiently and this means that later on there will be required a higher level of current outlays to meet payments to retirees. The crisis may be delayed, but will ultimately show up as unaffordable claims on current revenues and a drastic increase in taxes or cuts in expenditures.

12. Philip M. Dearborn, *Elements of Municipal Financial Analysis: Parts I and II*, First Boston Corporation, 1977. Dearborn's analysis covers only 29 of the major cities.

13. Municipal note issues (less than one-year original maturity) have a separate rating system developed by Moody's.

14. See Robert W. Doty and John E. Petersen, "The Federal Securities Laws and Transactions in Municipal Securities," *Northwestern University Law Review* (July-August, 1976), pp. 329-333.

15. For a fuller discussion of borrowing costs and rating changes by region, see Ronald Forbes *et al.*, "Public Debt in the Northeast: The Limits of Growth," *Managing a Way Out*, Boston, Council for Northeast Economic Action (1977).

16. See Advisory Commission on Intergovernmental Relations, *Countercyclical Aid and Economic Stabilization*, Washington, D.C. (December, 1978). p. 15-27.

17. Studies of CETA, ARFA and LPWA all show fairly high levels of substitution of federal funds for local funds. See Robert Reishauer, "The Economy, The Federal Budget, and The Prospects for Urban Aid," in *The Fiscal Outlook for Cities* (Syracuse: Syracuse University Press, 1978).

18. According to a recent study of big-city financial conditions: "No *reported* city with the exception of New York, was showing indications of severe financial problems at year end 1977." Philip Dearborn, *The Financial Health of Major U.S. Cities in Fiscal 1977,* First Boston Corporation (1978), p. 1. Dearborn attributes improved financial conditions to strong revenue performance and tight expenditure restraint. Chicago and Cleveland did not have 1977 financial information available and were not included in Dearborn's analysis.

19 See Congressional Budget Office, *Cities' Five Year Projects and Alternative Budget Strategies for Fiscal Years 1980-1984* (January 1979), pp. 48-56.

George E. Peterson - TRANSMITTING THE MUNICIPAL FISCAL SQUEEZE TO A NEW GENERATION OF TAX-PAYERS: PENSION OBLIGATIONS AND CAPITAL INVESTMENT NEEDS

INTRODUCTION

It is difficult to ask the mayor (or taxpayers) of a city operating under budgetary pressure to look beyond the near term future. The temptation is great to cut corners where it is easiest to do so, even if this means postponing the day of reckoning to a future generation of taxpayers.

Perhaps the most obvious mechanism for transmitting budgetary difficulties from one generation to the next is simply to bequeath a tradition of costly service provision and a depleted tax base. These conditions virtually assure that future taxpayers will have to wrestle with the same budgetary problems that troubled their predecessors.

But there are less obvious means of burdening the future. In one form or another, the current generation of service recipients may fail to pay for the services it consumes, or draw down the stock of assets it inherited from the past. The issuance of large amounts of long term debt is one means of borrowing from the next generation of taxpayers. So is the failure to fully fund the retirement benefits that are part of the compensation earned by today's public sector workers. And so, too, is the failure to maintain and replace the public capital stock of a city.

Several cities have reacted to the fiscal pressure of the past several years by cutting back on their capital spending, including the maintenance and preservation of their basic infrastructure. It is commonly thought that cities have skimped on pension funding, too, as a means of easing the pressure on current taxpayers.

If city governments are to remain viable operations, these postponed bills must be paid at some point. The timing, of course, is uncertain. Pay-as-you-go pension financing can defer the moment of fiscal truth for a considerable period, as can a policy of squeezing the last useful service out of an aging capital plant for which no replacement is planned. But the bills may be collected swiftly if the federal or state government intervenes. If Congress were to impose on the state and local sector the same pension funding standards it has legislated for the private sector, this would force an immediate and large jump in many cities' pension fund contributions.

This paper explores pension funding and capital investment needs as part of the "hidden" municipal fiscal squeeze—the part that is not visible in current municipal spending levels. Quite the opposite is true. The seriousness of both pension and capital financing liabilities is best measured by the *gap* between actual spending levels and the spending levels that would be necessary if the present generation were to pay its full way for the public services it consumes. By failing to finance its current consumption, the present generation of public service recipients, like a profligate private consumer, can relieve some of its budgetary pressure at the expense of those yet to come.

Given the charge of this paper, I have directed special attention to comparing the magnitude of pension and capital burdens in declining and growing cities. It is an open question whether these categories help to organize an analysis of deferred spending burdens as they have helped to organize an understanding of other aspects of the municipal fiscal squeeze.

PENSION FUNDING

One of the most important liabilities of state and local governments is their obligation to make future pension payments to retired workers. Anyone who ventures a prognosis of city financial conditions must take into account the impact that discharging these obligations will have on government budgets.

The eventual expense of city retirement benefits has been increasing at a rapid pace as a result of the increase in public employment and wage levels. The average earnings by state and local employees increased by 225 percent over the period 1955-1976, or about one-fourth faster than private sector wage levels. The number of state and local employees increased by 200 percent during the same period. This bulge in public employment and wages has built in the certainty of large future increases in pension payments, as the new workers retire on pensions tied to their higher wage levels. Unlike current wage payments, however, pension obligations are not being fully funded, creating a debt that future generations of taxpayers must redeem.

Employer pension contributions already are among the most rapidly rising components of state and local budgets. They increased from $1.2 billion in 1975 to $10.5 billion in 1976. Gains in the past few years have been at a still faster rate. State and local contributions to retirement systems surged by 21 percent between the first quarter of 1975 and the first quarter of 1976, another 26 percent between the first quarters of 1976 and 1977, and 28 percent more between the first quarters of 1977 and 1978. Although government contributions to pension funds are still relatively modest compared to total government budgets (amounting to 3.4 percent of state-local general expenditures in 1976), they are a much more important share of General Fund spending by most big cities. Exhibit 1 illustrates the share of pension contributions in the General Funds of six of the nation's most fiscally distressed cities. As can be seen, employer pension costs in these cities are of the same general magnitude as debt service requirements, but have been growing much more rapidly. Both elements constitute unavailable costs that greatly limit local budgetary flexibility. Since pension contributions are one of the expenditure burdens not significantly defrayed by federal aid, the importance of rising pension burdens to locally generated revenues has been still greater.[1]

The lag between government hiring and retirement makes pension funding especially critical for cities that are forced to cut back on their expenditure levels in response to budgeting pressure. In the normal course of events, the number of beneficiaries in a retirement system will peak some 15-20 years after the number of current employees reaches its maximum. As a consequence, cities are obliged to finance continually growing retirement costs. If the cities are on a pay-as-you-go pension financing system, or have otherwise under-funded their pension liabilities, they will be forced to make steadily

EXHIBIT 1

Debt and Pension Costs as Percent of Total
General Fund Spending (1976)

City	Debt Service	Pension & Social Sec. Contributions	Total
Detroit	7.3%	17.9	25.2
Newark	12.9%a	9.0	21.9
Philadelphia	10.9%	9.3	20.2
Boston	10.3%	8.4	18.7
Buffalo	12.8%	18.0	30.8
Cleveland	19.7%	11.7	31.4

a Includes 4.9 percent of school debt service delivery supported by state aid; debt is general obligtion of city.

Source: Local Financial Statements

increasing employer contributions even after they have reduced current payrolls and suffered the loss of service capacity that accompanies employment reductions.

Exhibit 2 illustrates the expenditure experience of the City of Pittsburgh over the period 1970-75, when the city made a full-scale effort to reduce public spending levels. During this time, the number of current employees was cut by more than one-fourth from 7,084 to 5,186. General fund expenditures for current services rose by a mere 11 percent in these five years, despite rapid price inflation. However, Pittsburgh's reliance on pay-as-you-go financing of its retirement system made it impossible to cut into the growth of pension costs. The city's contributions for retirement benefits increased by more than 125 percent, greatly limiting its efforts to curtail overall spending growth. Future rapid growth in Pittsburgh's pension contributions is unavoidable, whatever the city should do to restrain current service commitments.

Pension financing in the public sector presently is one of the least standardized of government financial practices. At one extreme of current funding practice is the pay-as-you-go financing method. Under this arrangement only the current costs of making benefit payments are covered, with little or no accumulation of assets. Current pension contributions by employees and employers are used to discharge the benefit entitlements of former generations of employees, rather than to pre-fund retirement for current workers. This is essentially the method the U.S government uses to finance Social Security. As we have discovered at the federal level,

EXHIBIT 2

Expenditure Growth for Current Services and Pensions,
Pittsburgh, 1970-75
(thousands)

Item	Year		Growth
	1970	1975	
Current Service Costs			
Public Safety	$32,641.6	$34,044.8	
Public Works	16,607.9	16,537.7	
Parks and Re-			
creation	5,947.7	6,156.9	
Library	1,976.5	2,443.5	
Land & Buildings	2,315.8	2,404.3	
Supplies	271.8	4,490.0	
Total	$59,781.4	$66,472.2	+ 11.2%
Benefits			
City Contribution to			
Pension Funds	3,151.0	7,144.0	+126.7%
Other Fringe Benefits	2,074.8	7,305.5	
(Workman's Compen-			
sation, Hospitalization,			
Group Insurance &			
Severance Pay)			
Total	5,225.8	14,449.5	+176.5%

Source: Annual Financial Statements for Pittsburgh, Pa., 1970, 1975.

the pay-as-you-go principle can impose stiff and rapidly rising tax burdens once the working population matures and begins to retire, without large numbers of new workers to finance its retirement costs.

At the other extreme of funding practice is full advance funding. There are a number of variations in full funding methods, but they all have the same concept of accumulating the assets necessary to pay retirement benefits prior to actual retirement. Under advance funding, each generation of taxpayers is asked to pay the full costs, including the costs of deferred benefits, of the public services it receives.

In practice, the great majority of public pension plans have some degree of pre-funding but are not fully funded. The unfunded liability of a plan represents the present value of promised pension benefits less the accumulated assets in the system. Some states and cities which now report estimates of the unfunded liability of their pension systems have reported startling numbers, as large as $11 billion according to one estimate for the Commonwealth of Massachusetts, or some $1,900 per capita, and an estimated $20 billion for all state-local governments in the State of California.

In addition to the size of the unfunded liability, which ultimately must be discharged, uncontrollable forces can change the rules governing the timing of payment, placing severe short-term burdens on local budgets. For example, the City of Philadelphia was forced by court order to more than triple its annual pension fund payments in 1968, because beneficiaries contested the adequacy of the city's contributions, fearing that there would not be sufficient asset accumulation to pay contractual benefits. Subsequent court orders in 1973 further stiffened Philadelphia's contribution levels. Court orders forced Detroit in 1972 to make a back payment into its pension funds, raising total employer contributions in that year to 23 percent of city general expenditures and necessitating imposition of a special property tax levy. A minimum pension funding program established by the Minnesota legislature has systematically forced all local governments to increase pension contributions by requiring them to amortize accumulated unfunded liabilities over a specified period. Sudden increases in contributions also may result from periodic updates of actuarial studies indicating that previous levels of funding were inadequate because of outdated actuarial assumptions, increased benefits, or poor investment performance. Finally, federal legislation potentially can affect the level of government contributions. When the Employee Income and Security Act of 1974 (ERISA) was passed, establishing minimum funding standards for private pensions, many employer contributions were raised substantially. Parallel regulations affecting the public sector are not under consideration.

In short, the potential liability of local government pension obligations is large, uncertain in the magnitude of governmental contributions that will be required, and still more uncertain in the timing of its discharge. This inherent risk makes it imperative to understand the true cost of pension obligations and the financing that will be needed to meet them.

A COMPARISON OF CITY PENSION FUNDING POSITIONS

Ideally, in assessing a city's pension funding position, one would want to compare its accumulation of financial assets with its accumulation of future retirement benefit obligations. Unfortunately, at present there is no comprehensive or comparable information available on future pension liabilities.[1] Therefore it is necessary to rely upon comparison of system assets with currently paid retirement benefits. Although such a comparison has little actuarial significance, it provides a simple measure of the magnitude of assets relative to current needs and the trend in this ratio over time. Given the vast disparity in local pension funding practice, there is no doubt that this comparison serves effectively as a preliminary screen of pension funding adequacy.

Use of the asset/benefit ratio to compare pension system positions can be difficult, however, when growing and declining cities are being contrasted. There is a natural life cycle fluctuation to this ratio, even under advanced funding approaches. During periods of strong growth in covered employment, the ratio will tend to be high, since assets are being accumulated on behalf of workers who are not yet entitled to receive benefit payments. As the work force ages and the labor force ceases to grow, the asset/payout ratio will tend to rise, for the simple reason that there are now more retirees in relation to active workers. This fact will tend to make growing cities' pension systems look better funded, on an asset/benefit payout test, than declining cities' systems.

With this caveat in mind, we can make the city comparisons. Exhibit 3 compares asset/benefit ratios for 27 large cities. (The Exhibit omits three cities—Cleveland, Buffalo and Columbus—which participate in state operated systems. Although these cities must still make contributions to their pension systems, the systems in question are statewide in their operation.) The Exhibit shows that in 1976 several big cities—Cincinnati, Milwaukee, Kansas City, Dallas, Nashville and Phoenix—had enough pension fund assets on hand to finance more than 20 years of benefit payments at recent annual rates. At the other extreme, seven cities—Boston, New Orleans, Philadelphia, Pittsburgh, Atlanta, Indianapolis and Jacksonville—had the equivalent of six years current payments or less. Pittsburgh and Indianapolis at that time had essentially no assets at all, as they operated on pure pay-as-you-go plans.[1]

Although the growing cities have, on average, somewhat stronger asset/benefit ratios than the other cities, there is considerably more variation within categories of cities than between category averages. Some fiscally hard pressed cities, such as St. Louis and Milwaukee, have been able to maintain very strong pension funding positions in the face of budgetary pressure. As a class, the declining cities at least held their own in pension funding over the period 1971-1976.

EXHIBIT 3

Asset/Benefit Ratios for Pension Systems of Large Cities

City and Class	Assets Equivalent to Current Payments, in Year 1971	1876	Change 1971-76, in Year
Declining			
Baltimore	17.4	19.7	+ 2.3
Boston	5.9	4.0	− 1.9
Chicago	11.9	11.2	− 0.7
Cincinnati	23.3	23.4	+ 0.1
Detroit	10.8	10.5	− 0.3
Milwaukee	30.7	27.2	− 3.5
Minneapolis	8.1	8.9	+ 0.8
New Orleans	3.1	4.3	+ 1.2
Philadelphia	3.0	5.8	+ 2.8
Pittsburgh	0.2	0.1	− 0.1
St. Louis	16.9	19.0	+ 2.1
San Francisco	13.7	14.0	+ 0.3
Simple Average	12.1	12.3	+ 0.2
Formerly Growing, Now Declining			
Atlanta	3.4	6.1	+ 2.7
Denver	5.3	8.2	+ 2.9
Indianapolis	0	0.1	+ 0.1
Kansas City	20.0	22.0	+ 2.0
Los Angeles	10.3	10.8	+ 0.5
Seattle	10.1	8.1	− 2.0
Simple Average	8.2	9.2	+ 1.0
Growing			
Dallas	21.9	14.2	− 7.7
Houston	17.7	16.4	− 1.3
Jacksonville	3.4	2.7	− 0.7
Memphis	16.3	17.1	+ 0.8
Nashville	23.3	23.4	+ 0.1
Phoenix	37.4	27.3	−10.1
San Antonio	12.1	10.8	− 1.3
San Diego	12.9	15.1	+ 2.2
Simple Average	18.1	15.9	− 2.2
New York	12.8	12.4	− 0.4

Source: Bureau of the Census

EXHIBIT 4

Percentage Amount by Which Retirement System Receipts Exceed Payments

City and Class	1971	1976
Declining		
Baltimore	281	251
Boston	35	7
Chicago	90	123
Cincinnati	185	233
Detroit	108	110
Milwaukee	277	312
Minneapolis	80	90
New Orleans	33	74
Philadelphia	51	71
Pittsburgh	5	(−5)
St. Louis	175	242
San Francisco	145	152
Simple Average	122.1	138.3
Formerly Growing, Now Declining		
Atlanta	68	113
Denver	80	123
Indianapolis	(−2)	(−7)
Kansas City	333	341
Los Angeles	129	126
Seattle	66	46
Simple Average	112.3	123.7
Growing		
Dallas	335	155
Houston	281	251
Jacksonville	18	53
Memphis	161	172
Nashville	50	93
Phoenix	514	410
San Antonio	200	190
San Diego	165	190
Simple Average	215.5	190.0
New York	111	132

Source: Bureau of the Census

Exhibit 4 compares total current receipts of city pension systems (from employer contributions, employee contributions and investment earnings) with total payout for current retirement benefits. The average for all cities in the Exhibit in 1976 was 121 percent, indicating that pension systems in the aggregate took in more than twice as much as they expended on retirement benefits. This average increased from 101 percent over the period 1971-1976.

Once more, growing cities perform somewhat better on this cash flow measure. However, their margin of advantage is not greater than one would expect automatically from the younger age of their employment mix. The gap between city categories also closed substantially over the five-year period. By this measure, too, declining cities as a group strengthened their pension funding position between 1971 and 1976.

The same individual cities stand out from Exhibit 4 as having poorly funded pension systems, with built-in guarantees of future cost escalation. Pittsburgh and Indianapolis both paid out more in retirement benefits in 1976 than they received in funding additions. Boston barely covered its costs on a cash basis.

The costs to cities of maintaining relatively healthy pension funds has been substantial. Over the five years, 1971 to 1976, local government employer contributions for these cities as a whole rose by 89 percent, from approximately $950 million to $1.8 billion. By comparison, total general fund expenditures over the same period increased only 58 percent.

Again, the categorization of cities by declining and growing does not distinguish obvious groupings of pension funding experience. Individual cases of strong deferred costs can be found in all categories. The slow increase in contributions by Boston, Philadelphia, Indianapolis and San Francisco, for example, all signal the probability of the need for future funding jumps. (Baltimore's decline in employer contributions is explained by state takeover of responsibility for some of the city's retirement benefit payments.)

CONCLUSIONS

It is clear that, despite their very rapid growth in contributions, almost all big city pension systems remain less than fully funded. In that sense, tax obligations are being deferred to future generations of taxpayers. It is less clear whether cities as a group are incompletely funding currently incurred pension obligations and thus adding further to their liabilities. This probably is the case.

EXHIBIT 5

Local Government Contribution to Local Retirement Systems

City and Class	Percent Change, 1971-76
Declining	
Baltimore	− 22
Boston	28
Chicago	128
Cincinnati	85
Detroit	96
Milwaukee	203
Minneapolis	104
New Orleans	149
Philadelphia	38
Pittsburgh	94
St. Louis	111
San Francisco (1975)	46
Simple Average	68.3
Formerly Growing, Now Declining	
Atlanta	+ 86
Denver	104
Indianapolis	44
Kansas City	79
Los Angeles	81
Seattle	64
Simple Average	76.3
Growing	
Dallas	81
Houston	141
Jacksonville	297
Memphis	73
Nashville	83
Phoenix	110
San Antonio	108
San Diego	124
Simple Average	127.1
New York	96

Source: Bureau of the Census

Nonetheless, like the rest of the state and local sector, big cities have made a serious effort over the last five years to provide for future retirement benefits. By the standards used in this paper, big cities as a class have not fallen further behind in their pension funding; rather, they were in a modestly stronger financial position in 1976 than in 1971. This trend appears to have continued in 1976-1978, as the need for pension funding attracted more public attention. If cities have large pension burdens laying ahead of them, they have begun to acknowledge these burdens and prepare for them. The greatest financial risk for city budgets now would appear to lie not in paying for eventual retirement costs but in the possibility that the federal government will extend the strict funding standards now applicable to the private sector to state and local pension plans. Should this occur, several cities will face large, immediate jumps in employer contributions which will have to be financed from general tax revenues.

As always, generalizations about big cities as a class can be badly misleading. Our analysis has pinpointed several cities whose pension funding is extremely precarious. These cities face the certainty of escalating public cost in their pension systems, if they are to meet their obligations to retired workers. Boston, Pittsburgh, Philadelphia, Jacksonville and Indianapolis (as well as Washington, D.C.) are cities that find themselves in this position.

Although the pension systems of declining cities on average appear to be modestly less well funded than those of growing cities, the variation within each grouping is more pronounced than the systematic differences between classes of cities. The fiscal pressures on older, declining cities do not seem to have caused them to systematically "borrow" assets from their pension funds. More frequently, they have reacted to budgetary difficulties by cutting back on retirement benefit levels, thus actually strengthening their funding positions.

CAPITAL STOCK DETERIORATION AND CAPITAL INVESTMENT NEEDS

Like underfunding of pension obligations, disinvestment in capital facilities represents a means by which a community may, for a time, borrow against the future. If a city fails to maintain and replace its inherited capital facilities, it in effect liquidates capital assets by converting them to cash. The cash saving takes the form of reduced outlays for maintenance and lower levels of new capital investment.

The terms on which physical capital can be converted into cash, however, become more unfavorable as deferred maintenance and repairs are allowed to accumulate; for each dollar saved in maintenance spending, a much larger burden of capital repair or replacement eventually must be shouldered. However, these costs may be shifted to a different group of taxpayers at a future date that is difficult to pinpoint. This fact has made disinvestment in capital plant an attractive alternative for cities struggling with budgetary difficulties.

Estimation of capital investment "needs" for cities is one of the most elusive tasks in public finance. Usually little help is to be found in the formal capital budgets that city governments prepare. More often than not, these are nothing more than wish lists that have little to do with actual city intentions. The City of Detroit, for example, has not financed more than 25 percent of its annual capital budget in any of the last five years.

The analyst who would compare the magnitude of capital stock problems is thus forced to rely on other methods of examination. Where federal laws prescribe the type and quality of capital stock that a community must have in place, these methods in principle are straightforward. They involve estimating the capital costs that would be required to meet the mandatory federal standards. Unless federal legislation is modified, this capital expenditure will have to be undertaken by a city within the foreseeable future. Most mandatory federal programs now have uniform "needs" assessment procedures which provide a good basis for comparative information.

In the absence of clear federal standards, one can estimate the capital spending that would be necessary to achieve a uniform level of capital stock quality in different cities. Or, alternatively, one can scrutinize the record of capital stock performance, identifying those cities where average service quality is below average and where performance levels are trending downward. Such cities are disinvesting in their real capital. If they are to restore it to former service levels, or to national performance levels, they will be forced to undertake new investment. The severity of the local shortfall in capital stock performance is a good first index of the magnitude of future capital investment that will be necessary.

Finally, it is possible under some conditions to infer deterioration of capital stock quality from a record of steadily declining capital spending, especially when the share of capital outlays devoted to repair, maintenance and replacement of existing facilities can be separated from new undertakings. Since this topic has been treated in another paper prepared for this conference, I have omitted it from the comparisons below.

It should be acknowledged that comparisons of capital stock deterioration or performance quality, like comparisons of the capital spending that would be required to meet uniform standards of performance, carry with them a certain bias. They imply that it is *appropriate* for a community to replace deteriorated capital facilities or upgrade them to the designated standard. For a city suffering severe population loss or economic pressure, this may not be the most viable alternative. It may well be that a city of this type should be shrinking its capital facilities, allowing some pieces of its capital plant to disintegrate into uselessness, rather than bear the costs of maintaining a former standard of service provision. This issue becomes particularly acute for what might be called optional services, such as capital spending on parks and recreation or high standards of school space per pupil.

We have attempted to avoid these difficulties in the comparisons below by concentrating attention on four functional areas that are basic to the core service responsibilities of cities: their sewer and water systems, streets and bridges. Any deterioration in these facilities is likely to be perceived as degradation in basic services. It must be acknowledged, nonetheless, that (except where performance standards are prescribed by federal or state law) there is an inescapable element of arbitrariness in any standard that is used for capital stock evaluation. As a practical matter, however, this fact is of secondary importance. As proved to be true of city pension funding, the range of capital stock conditions is so great—far greater than the variation in any of the current spending or taxing elements of city budgets—that qualifications about the exact interpretation to be given to performance standards is overwhelmed by differences in the order of magnitude of capital condition.

STREETS

In compliance with federal law, the Federal Highway Administration (FHWA) in cooperation with state and local planning officials, is mandated to provide a biennial assessment of future national highway needs as a basis for program funding authorizations. The most recent survey—the 1976 National Highway Inventory and Performance Study (NHIPS)—was organized to collect data, on a sample basis, which would permit identification of changes in the performance and condition of the national highway system since 1970 when a similar effort was undertaken.

Highway condition is measured in terms of the Present Serviceability Rating (PSR)—a 5 point scale used to rate pavement surface condition. In its survey, NHIPS accepted other rating systems as long as they could be converted to PSR equivalents.

The actual data gathering for the 1976 survey was conducted with the cooperation of the highway agencies of 44 states, the District of Columbia and Puerto Rico. They provided inventory, condition and performance data for their functional highway systems, according to the specifications outlined in the "National Highway Inventory and Performance Study Manual," which was then compiled, summarized and analyzed at both the state and national level by the Federal Highway Administration. While efforts were made to involve regional and divisional offices in the development of the Study Manual through workshop sessions, monetary and personnel constraints precluded extensive efforts to insure standardization in reporting.

The data collected on highway conditions for the 1976 NHIPS are subject to several limitations which affect their usefulness as indicators of roadway conditions in urban areas. The data were collected on a sample basis with the following required minimal sampling rates for each functional system:[4]

System	Percent of Functional System Miles
Interstate	100%
Principal Arterials	50%
Minor Arterials	25%
Collectors	10%

No data were collected on local streets. Coupled with the relatively low sampling rates for Minor Arterials and Collectors, the exclusion of local roads resulted in condition assessments for only a small portion of total urban street mileage. Finally, trends and conclusions about highway conditions were based on changes over a six-year period. Additional surveys over a longer time frame should increase the reliability of the results.

With these caveats in mind, the results of NHIPS can be analyzed as they pertain to urban area street conditions. Exhibit 6 provides a comparative summary (1969, 1975) of system condition by functional category for both rural and urban areas. As is to be expected, the Interstate System, due to its relative newness and high construction standards, had the highest percentage of roadway

EXHIBIT 6

Summary Table of Highway Condition and Performance 1970-1975

Measure of Condition or Performance	System Status as of December 31, 1975 Percent		Changes Over 6-Year Period December 31, 1969 or December 31, 1975 Percent		Remarks
	Rural	Urban	Rural	Urban	
Pavement Condition (mileage)					Pavement condition is classified by Present Serviceability Rating (PSR), that ranges from 5 for pavement in very good condition to 0 for completely deteriorated pavement.
Interstate			Interstate	NA	NA
Good	74	68			
Fair	22	29	Arterial (excluding Interstate)		PSR of 5.0 – 3.5 = good
Poor	4	3	Good	–1	–5
			Fair	2	5
Arterials (excluding Interstate)			Poor	–1	–
Good	47	48			
Fair	46	46	Collectors		PSR of 3.5 – 2.5 or 2.0 = fair
Poor	7	6	Good	–3	–7
			Fair	2	7
Collectors			Poor	1	–
Good	30	36			PSR of 2.5 or 2.0 – 0.0 = poor
Fair	60	55			
Poor	10	9			Large changes in pavement condition significantly affect vehicle operating costs.

EXHIBIT 7

Comparison of Street and Highway Conditions
As Classified by Present Serviceability Index (1975)

Urbanized Areas

Category of Urbanized Area	Percent of Highway Mileage on Federal Aid System by Condition Rating		
	Good	Fair	Poor
Large Cities[a]	40%	49%	11%
Declining Cities[b]	36%	50%	14%
Formerly Growing Cities[c]	62%	35%	3%
Growing Cities[d]	64%	27%	9%
Texas Cities[e]	16%	76%	8%

a   Chicago, Los Angeles, Philadelphia, Detroit, New York (not available).

b   Baltimore, Chicago, Cincinnati, Cleveland, Detroit, Louisville, Milwaukee, Minneapolis, New Orleans, Philadelphia, Pittsburgh, St. Louis, San Francisco, Seattle, Washington, D.C.

c   Atlanta, Columbus, Denver, Indianapolis, Kansas City, Los Angeles, Nashville, Norfolk, Oklahoma City, Portland, Toledo, Tulsa.

d   Baton Rouge, Charlotte, Jacksonville, Memphis, Miami, Omaha, Phoenix, San Diego, San Jose, Tucson.

e   Houston, Austin, El Paso, San Antonio, Dallas, Fort Worth.

Source: U.S. DOT, Federal Highway Administration, Computer Print-Out on Urban Mileage and Travel by Pavement Condition and Pavement Type from the 1976 National Highway Inventory and Performance Study.

in good condition followed by Arterials and finally Collectors with the lowest percentage of roadway in good condition. The two functional categories for which comparative data were available— Arterials and Collectors—both showed larger declines in pavement condition in urban than in rural areas over the six-year period.

A more detailed analysis of the highway conditions for a sample of streets, declining cities (i.e., those cities showing a continuous population decline since 1960) had the largest percentage of highway mileage rated in fair and poor condition. (Refer to Exhibit 7.) Growing and formerly growing cities (i.e., those with population declines only since 1970) reported as in good condition almost twice the mileage of declining cities. These data refer to entire urban areas; follow-up studies with individual jurisdictions show the differences in street conditions to be larger at the local level.

Exhibit 8 provides a view of the intermediate term decline in capital spending and maintenance on the street and road systems of large cities.

BRIDGES

The Silver Bridge collapse at Point Pleasant, West Virginia, over ten years ago provided the impetus for enactment of a National Bridge Inspection Program in 1968 and establishment of the Special Bridge Replacement Program in 1970. National Bridge Inspection Standards were in effect by May 1971, requiring a biennial inspection of all bridges on the Federal-Aid System.

State highway departments, in consultation with the Federal Highway Administration (FHWA) are responsible for inventorying all on-system bridges, conducting inspections to determine physical condition of the structures. These condition assessments provide the basis for apportionment of the Special Bridge Replacement Program funds to the states.

Extensive efforts have been made to standardize the bridge inspection process to increase the reliability and comparability of individual state's condition assessments. In practice, however, the inventorying and inspection process has suffered from several limitations. While FHWA has attempted to establish national bridge inspection guidelines, the states are ultimately responsible for the designation and training of inspection teams. Considerable variation exists not only in the size and training of inspection crews, but also in the depth in which surveys are conducted. For example, cost estimates for bringing bridges up to standard are frequently considered, by federal officials, to be unreliable "guesstimates." And finally, in the absence of an independent, outside authority to monitor and evaluate the assessment process, the states have strong incentive to provide a pessimistic picture of need, since actual program funds' apportionments are based in part on the assessments the states provide.

Despite these limitations, the biennial surveys do give an indication of the magnitude and extent of the nation's bridge problem. The most recent analysis (1977) of current inventory data concerning on-system bridges and estimates of off-system bridge condition indicate that there are a total of 105,500 deficient bridges—approximately one out of every five bridges—in the United States. An estimated $25.1 billion, equally divided between on- and off-system bridges, is required to replace these structures. Federal funding has increased from $180 to $900 million per annum for replacement

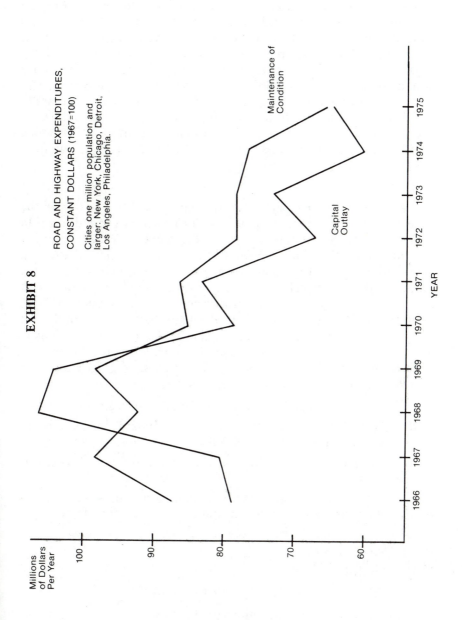

EXHIBIT 8

ROAD AND HIGHWAY EXPENDITURES,
CONSTANT DOLLARS (1967=100)

Cities one million population and
larger: New York, Chicago, Detroit,
Los Angeles, Philadelphia.

purposes. Still, the burden of bridge replacement appears to be well beyond the financial capability of many local governments.

An analysis of the data in DOT's Bridge Inventory File on condition of on-system bridges in a sample of the 50 largest cities indicates that the bridge problem is most severe in the very largest cities (i.e., those with populations over 1 million) and declining urban areas (i.e., those cities which have experienced continuous population declines since 1960). (Refer to Exhibit 9.) In growing and formerly growing urban areas, the number and percent of structurally deficient and functionally obsolete bridges is less than half the large and declining city averages. The special difficulties of declining cities reflect not only the age of their bridge structures, but their greater exposure to cold climates.

SEWERS

Spending for municipal water treatment facilities is by far the fastest growing segment of state and local capital expenditures. In compliance with the provisions of the Federal Water Pollution Control Act, the Environmental Protection Agency (EPA), in cooperation with the states, is mandated to provide a biennial estimate of the capital investment costs required to comply with the water quality standards established by the legislation. This "Capital Needs Survey" provides the basis for the distribution of federal grant allotments among the states. The formulas are largely determined by comparing the estimated construction costs in each state to the total costs of such facilities in all states. Currently, cost estimates are made for six categories of need:

(I)   Achieving secondary treatment for all discharges.

(II)   Achieving more stringent treatment standards than secondary where quality of the receiving water requires.

(III A) Correction of Infiltration/Inflow problems on existing sewer networks.

(III B) Replacement and/or major rehabilitation of sewer systems which are structurally unsound or in danger of collapse.

(IV A)   Need for new collector sewer systems.

(IV B)   Need for new interceptor sewers.

(V)   Control of combined sewer overflow.

(VI)   Treatment and/or control of stormwaters.

The accompanying table (Exhibit 10) provides a summary of investment needs by category from the most recent 1976 Survey. Because

EXHIBIT 9

National Bridge Inventory Survey Information by Type of City

Category of City	Total Bridge Count	Count of Structurally Deficient Bridges[1] (percent of total)	Count of Functionally Obsolete Bridges[2] (percent of total)
Large City Average[a]	375	6 (1.6%)	37 (10.0%)
Declining City Average[b]	170	4 (2.3%)	23 (13.5%)
Formerly Growing City Average[c]	288	2 (0.7%)	12 (4.0%)
Growing City Average[d]	206	1 (0.5%)	13 (6.0%)

a	Chicago, Detroit, Houston, Los Angeles (New York and Philadelphia not available).
b	Baltimore, Chicago, Cincinnati, Cleveland, Detroit, Louisville, Minneapolis, Oakland, St. Louis, San Francisco, Seattle.
c	Atlanta, Columbus, Dallas, Denver, Fort Worth, Indianapolis, Kansas City, Long Beach, Los Angeles, Nashville, Norfolk, Oklahoma City, Portland, Toledo, Tulsa.
d	Austin, Baton Rouge, Charlotte, El Paso, Jacksonville, Memphis, Miami, Omaha, Phoenix, San Antonio, San Diego, San Jose, Tucson.
1	A structurally deficient bridge is one that has been restricted to light vehicles only or closed.
2	A functionally obsolete bridge is one whose deck geometry, load carrying capacity, clearance or approach roadway alignment can no longer safely service the system of which it is an integral part.

Source: U.S. Department of Transportation, Federal Highway Administration, Bridge Inventory File print-out by city, data as of October 4, 1978.

of the large total of projected investment requirements, Categories IV and VI currently are receiving little or no federal funding.

The Needs Survey, the first of which was conducted in 1973, should provide a measure of local sewer facilities' condition and deficiencies which can be monitored over time and compared across localities. In practice, two problems have prevented full achievement of these objectives. First, changes in investment needs as indicated by the surveys frequently reflect changes in the methodology for estimating needs rather than actual changes in condition. Second, while improvements have been made in the standardization of survey procedures and refinement of cost estimating techniques, estimates for certain categories of need such as stormwater control (Category VI) are still tentative, at best.

EXHIBIT 10

Summary of 1976 EPA Needs Survey

Category		Estimated Capital Cost (1976 Dollars, Billions)
	I	13.0
	II	21.2
	III A	3.0
	III B	5.5
	IV A	17.0
	IV B	17.9
	V	18.3
Total	I-V	95.9
	VI	54.1

Source: Officer of War Program Operations, *Cost Estimates for Construction of Publicly-Owned Wastewater Treatment Facilities–1976 Needs Survey*, Environmental Protection Agency, Washington, D.C., February 10, 1977, p. 7.

Drawing on the experience of prior surveys (1973, 1974), EPA decided to conduct the 1976 Needs Survey with the assistance of an independent consultant utilizing a consistent nationwide methodology. As in 1974, cost estimates for needs categories I-IV were to be determined on a facility-by-facility basis. Cost estimates for categories V and VI were derived from a computer model which attempted to incorporate local cost factors. The results in 1976 reflected two major improvements over prior surveys: 1) inclusion of more adequate cost estimates reflecting local and regional construction cost variations and 2) more consistent and reliable reporting resulting from personnel training and precise specification of reporting procedures for conducting the survey. Quality control procedures were coordinated by federal EPA and involved the contractor as well as state EPA offices.

As indicators of system deficiencies and need, Categories I, II and IV B—secondary treatment, more stringent treatement and new interceptor sewers respectively, are considered the most accurate, given years of experience in planning and constructing facilities in these categories. In category III A, cost estimates for infiltration and inflow (I & I) correction have significantly improved with the completion of numerous I & I studies and increased experience in this area. Category III B—sewer replacement and/or major rehabilitation needs—yields a less accurate estimate, given the frequent lack of routine inspection and anticipation of substantial sewer deterioration and/or collapse at the local level.

EXHIBIT 11

Per Capita Sewer Investment Needs by SMSA: 1976 Estimates [1976 Dollars]

Type of SMSA	Category I & II	Category III	Category IV	Total
Large SMSA[a]	$180 (45%)	$70 (17%)	$153 (38%)	$403 (100%)
Declining SMSA[b]	$160 (40%)	$66 (17%)	$169 (43%)	$395 (100%)
Formerly Growing SMSA[c]	$168 (50%)	$35 (10%)	$133 (40%)	$336 (100%)
Growing SMSA[d]	$114 (45%)	$13 (5%)	$129 (50%)	$256 (100%)
SMSA Average	$156 (45%)	$46 (13%)	$146 (42%)	$348 (100%)

a   Chicago, Detroit, Houston, Los Angeles, New York, Philadelphia.
b   Baltimore, Buffalo, Boston, Chicago, Cincinnati, Cleveland, Detroit, Milwaukee, Newark, New Orleans, New York, Philadelphia, Pittsburgh, St. Louis, San Francisco, Seattle, Washington, D.C.
c   Atlanta, Columbus, Dallas, Denver, Indianapolis, Kansas City, Los Angeles, Miami.
d   Austin, Baton Rouge, Charlotte, El Paso, Houston, Jacksonville, Louisville, Memphis, Minneapolis, Nashville, Norfolk, Oklahoma City, Omaha, Phoenix, Portland, San Antonio, San Diego, San Jose, Toledo, Tucson, Tulsa.

Source: EPA 1976 Needs Survey, unpublished computer print-out of needs data by SMSA.

Exhibit 11 provides a summary of the 1976 Needs Survey on a per capita basis by SMSA for those categories that provide the most accurate and reliable estimate of condition and need. Categories I & II indicate the need for additional investment in treatment facilities. Category III—repair and rehabilitation of sewer lines and I & I correction—represents major costs in cities with older infrastructure systems, while Category IV's new collectors and interceptors are major items in growing areas. The federal government has recently taken the position that local jurisdictions should be expected to finance this latter category of needs without extensive federal assistance.

Needs for expanded and upgraded treatment facilities still represent the major cost category for most SMSAs, accounting for between 40-50 percent of total need, or approximately $156 per capita on average. In growing and declining metropolitan areas (i.e., those SMSAs which experienced population increases and population declines respectively since 1960), Category IV needs for new interceptor and collector sewers superseded treatment facility requirements, reflecting system expansion needs in growing areas and upgrading of older systems with inadequate capacity in declining areas. The greatest difference among SMSAs is reflected in Category III estimates. The estimated cost of sewer line rehabilitation and repair and I & I correction in large and/or declining metropolitan areas is twice that of formerly growing areas (i.e., those experiencing population declines since 1970) and more than five times the cost in growing areas. This category is perhaps the best indicator of comparative condition and rehabilitation needs of existing municipal collection systems.

Although certain generalizations can be made about "declining" cities, or their metropolitan areas, as a class, exhibit 12 once again illustrates how highly variable are the capital investment needs of individual regions. Cleveland has more than 300 times the estimated per capita spending need of St. Louis for repair and rehabilitation of existing sewer lines, and almost 10 times the per capita spending need for sewer and water treatment investments of all kinds. Generalization by city category thus is a poor substitute for case-by-case consideration of individual cities' prospects.

WATER

There is, at present, no federal aid for urban water distribution systems and no national measurement of system conditon. Most cities do maintain roughly comparable records on such performance measures as water leaks, pipe flow characteristics in relation to original design standards, and water loss from the distribution system, Exhibit 13 illustrates one such comparative measure, water main breaks per 1,000 miles of pipe system.

The Exhibit illustrates the by now familiar conclusion that there is tremendous variability in individual system conditions, and that this variability is only moderately reduced by classifying cities as growing and declining and looking at average performance within classifications.

CONCLUSION

This section has shown that declining cities do indeed face the need for greater future capital investment than growing cities if they are to maintain existing capital infrastructure. However, the variation in investment requirements within city classifications is so large as to make such a grouping only moderately helpful in understanding the nature of urban capital stock deterioration and future capital investment needs.

Most sobering, perhaps, is the fact that certain cities appear in the greatest "need," whatever measure of capital requirements is used. The City of Cleveland stands at the top of the list in per capita spending requirements for sewer and water treatment facilities, just as it does in per capita spending needs for bridge replacement and in deterioration of its water distribution system. Cleveland, of course, also faces extraordinary difficulties in most other aspects of its budget. Buffalo is another city that faces large across-the-board capital spending needs. In contrast, St. Louis, which has suffered even more severe population decline, has relatively low capital spending requirements to maintain its public infrastructure; it also has been able to maintain a well funded pension system and low tax rates. Cincinnati, too, has been able to perform well on the two scales examined in this paper, despite population and job loss. This suggests that analysts must look to other factors in explaining the observed differences between cities.

Two important questions have remained unanswered by this review. First, has the recent fiscal squeeze on municipal governments contributed importantly to capital stock deterioration in selected areas or to the current differences in capital stock condition between cities? A detailed answer to this question is the subject of another paper, but in abbreviated form the answer, at least in selected cases, is "yes." Maintenance and replacement cycles for basic capital facilities have in several instances been cut back dramatically because of local budgetary pressure, with discernible impacts on the average age and condition of facilities.

Second, how important are future capital investment requirements in the overall fiscal picture for cities? Are they a significant factor in cities' fiscal outlook, or are they of only secondary importance? These questions, too, are best answered on a case-by-case basis. But the case of New York City may offer a representative illustration of the importance of capital spending in big city budgets. The city's ten-year budget plan, which served as the basis for securing renewal of federal loan guarantees for the city, calls for an average of $1.2 billion per year in city funds to be spent over the next decade in "bricks and mortar" capital spending. This total is up from less than $230 million in fiscal 1978, as the city sets about the long-term process of rebuilding its public infrastructure. It also accounts for by far the largest projected growth in spending from the city's own funds. Thus the costs of a full capital recovery are large, both in

EXHIBIT 12

Per Capita Sewer Investment Needs, by SMSA: 1976 EPA Estimates [1976 Dollars]

Classification and City	Repair and Rehabilitation of Sewer Lines, Correction of Infiltration and Inflow	Secondary Treatment Plant Upgrading to Meet Discharge Standards	Total: Includes construction of new sewer lines, further investment in treatment plants to meet ambient water quality standards; excludes investment to eliminate overflow and separate sanitary sewers from stormwater systems
Declining			
Baltimore	$ 13	0	$150
Boston	18	192	575
Buffalo	46	5	262
Chicago	8	0	227
Cincinnati	13	1	455
Cleveland	345	0	723
Detroit	113	0	446
Milwaukee	96	3	533
Newark	29	239	503
New Orleans	60	81	241
New York	257	223	947
Philadelphia	1	4	222
Pittsburgh	1	14	165
St. Louis	1	28	87
San Francisco	16	203	372
Seattle	74	81	539
Washington	44	0	331
AVERAGE	$ 67	63	$399

EXHIBIT 12 (continued)

Per Capita Sewer Investment Needs, by SMSA: 1976 EPA Estimates [1976 Dollars]

Classification and City	Repair and Rehabilitation of Sewer Lines, Correction of Infiltration and Inflow	Secondary Treatment Plant Upgrading to Meet Discharge Standards	Total: Includes construction of new sewer lines, further investment in treatment plants to meet ambient water quality standards, excludes investment to eliminate overflow and separate sanitary sewers from storm-water systems
Formerly Growing			
Atlanta	$ 10	0	$267
Columbus	34	0	485
Dallas	3	0	151
Denver	170	29	332
Indianapolis	31	15	466
Kansas City	53	198	485
Los Angeles	3	74	163
Miami	23	76	337
AVERAGE	$ 35	49	$336
Growing			
Albuquerque	$ 0	67	$ 83
Houston	37	0	408
Jacksonville	1	14	716
Memphis	4	7	55
Phoenix	0	0	154
San Antonio	47	0	322
San Diego	3	157	247
AVERAGE	$ 13	44	$284

Source: Unpublished EPA data compiled for 1976 Need Study.

EXHIBIT 13

Average Annual Municipal Water Main Break Record

City	System Miles	Average Breaks	Period	Breaks per 1000 Miles
Seattle	1675*	19	1969-73	11
Los Angeles	6766*	321	1970-74	47
Boston	1077	54	1973	50
St. Louis	1372*	99	1969-73	72
Chicago	4148**	304	1970-73	73
New York City	6137*	488	1970-74	80
Denver	1794**	188	1970-73	104
Washington, D.C.	1350**	158	1970-74	117
Baltimore	1530*	227	1969-73	148
San Francisco	1168*	181	1969-73	155
Milwaukee	1800**	373	1970-73	207
Kansas City	1924	403	1973-74	209
Philadelphia	3233*	801	1970-74	248
Detroit	3393*	1253	1970-74	369
New Orleans	1426	730	(averages)	512
Houston	3988	5144	1973	1290

*   Average for period
** During last year of period

Source: Sol Galler, "City Plans to Combat Water Main Break Problem," *Public Works*,
109:10 (October 1978), p.89.

budgetary terms and in terms of the impact anticipated on the rest
of the city. Though perhaps to a lesser extent, the commitment
necessary to "catch up" in capital facility performance will be an
important part of the budget burden in other large, old cities, as well.

NOTES

1. No federal programs directly support local pension funding. The rules
   governing the federal Public Service Employment program, for example,
   prohibit the use of federal funds for pension funding on the grounds
   that the workers are meant to be temporary employees who will not be
   eligible for retirement benefits. Of course, the general fundibility of
   much federal aid limits the usefulness of looking at directly authorized
   purposes of aid programs.
2. Such data are now being compiled by The Urban Institute and Howard
   Winklevoss & Associates (actuaries) for 100 representative state and
   local pension plans.
3. As of January 1977, Pittsburgh adopted a normal funding plan whereby
   it pays the currently incurred employer cost of retirement benefits for
   new employees only.

Thomas Muller - CHANGING EXPENDITURES AND SERVICE DEMAND PATTERNS OF STRESSED CITIES

INTRODUCTION

Approximately four years ago, a conference on Post-Industrial America organized by George Sternlieb was the first major forum to discuss the emerging patterns of interregional change and fiscal as well as other effects associated with migration. During the conference, some participants expressed doubt that the early 1970s represented part of a longer term change. Indeed, it was argued that losses in central city population were the result of a particular set of conditions unlikely to be duplicated in future years.

This paper examines demographic, income and related changes during the first seven or eight years of the decade, with emphasis on changes in service demand and municipal outlays in selected large growing and declining cities.

The timing of this conference seems appropriate, since a number of articles, one or two possibly aimed at the science fiction audience, have raised a serious issue: Do we now see a re-emergence of the central city as the hub of economic activity? While this paper does not deal with this broad issue, data presented provide information on current and likely future directions in several areas.

DEMOGRAPHIC AND INCOME CHANGES

CHANGES IN CENTRAL CITY POPULATION

During the 1970s, the decline in large central city populations which lost population in the previous decade exceeded by a factor of two the population decline during the 1960s. However, the rate of decline between 1973-1976 was somewhat lower than during the early 1970s, changing from an annual average decline of 262 thousand to 170 thousand (see Exhibit 1). In the 1973-1976 period, only two large cities, Baltimore and Milwaukee, had an accelerated rate of loss; two others, Buffalo and New Orleans, show no change in the rate of decline; one, Boston, had no decline; while the remaining nine show lower rates of decline.

Among large cities in the growing category, the pattern is mixed. Four cities gaining population during the 1960s reversed this pattern in the early 1970s: Dallas, Indianapolis, Los Angeles and Kansas City. The decline in these cities in the mid 1970s accelerated in all but Dallas, while Denver, which had no loss prior to 1974 now shows substantial decline. Among the other eight cities, three show accelerated growth, five, lower growth rates in mid 1970s. Collectively, the annual gain in population among large cities was reduced from 89 thousand to 34 thousand. With natural increase taken into account, this means that these cities, on the average, had more persons leaving than moving in.

Only five large cities appear to have substantial net migration. Gains in three (Houston, San Antonio, Phoenix) appear to be attributable primarily to annexation during the 1970s. Only San Diego and Honolulu seem to be gaining population by infill into areas incorporated prior to 1970. Differences in population growth among large cities, between the early and mid 1970s, are directly linked to reduced annexation activity (see Exhibit 2).

New York City (shown separately, since its population is equal to one half of all cities in the declining group) had a stable annual loss of population during the 1970s.

NET MIGRATION

Migration from central cities appears to be continuing at the same rate in the mid 1970s as in the early 1970s although there is some indication that it may have accelerated slightly between 1975 and 1978 compared to the previous five years. By adjusting the 1975-1978 data to reflect increased movements from abroad and age of population included in the sample, differences in the rates of net

EXHIBIT 1

Population Change—Large U.S. Cities
1960-1976 (in thousands)

Year	No. Cities	Total Change	Annual Change
Cities With Declining Population Between 1960-1970			
1960-1970	14	−1,048	−105
1970-1973	14	− 787	−262
1973-1976	14	− 527	−176
1970-1976	14	−1,314	−219
Estimated Net Outmigration 1970-1976		−1,813	−302
Cities With Growing Population Between 1960-1970			
1960-1970	13	511	51
1970-1973	13	266	89
1973-1976	13	103	34
1970-1976	13	369	62
Net Migration	13		
New York City			
1960-1970	1	3	—
1970-1973	1	− 250	− 83
1973-1976	1	− 222	− 74
1977	1	− 112	−112
New Migration 1970-1977		− 801	−134
All Large Cities			
1960-1970	28	− 534	− 53
1970-1973	28	− 771	−257
1973-1976	28	− 629	−210
1970-1976	28	−1,400	−233
Net Migration 1970-1976	28	−2,885	−481

migration between the two time periods are basically the same. (See Exhibit 3). Data from the CPS (Current Population Survey) are not published at the individual city level. Therefore, it is necessary to estimate net migration from the two groups of cities indirectly (see Exhibits 4 and 5).

It is self-evident that net migration from cities exceeds population loss, since in all large cities there were more births than deaths. The rate of natural increase depends on location—growing southern cities

EXHIBIT 2

Annexations By Large Cities 1970-1975

City	Square Miles Added 1970-1973	1973-1975	Percent Change in Land Area 1970-1975
Dallas	5	39	17%
Houston	64	10	13
San Antonio	70	10	44
Denver	19	0	16
Columbus	23	15	28
Memphis	44	20	28
Phoenix	21	4	11
San Diego	6	0	2
Total	252	98	–
Per Annum	84	49	–

Source: Bureau of the Census

EXHIBIT 3

Central City Migration 1960-1978

Intra-National[a]	1960-1970	1970-1975[a]	1975-1977	1975-1978[b]
Central Cities[c]	−3,449	−7,018	−3,321	−4,628
Suburbs	8,756	5,423	2,718	3,527
Total Metropolitan Area	5,307	−1,595	− 603	−1,101
Annual Migration Rate from Central Cities	− 345	−1,403	−1,661	−1,543
Movers from Abroad		3,604	2,010	2,697
Central City		n/a	786	1,066
Suburban		n/a	792	1,105
Outside States		n/a	732	526
Annual Movers from Abroad		285	393	355

a. Population 5 years old and over. Central city migration 3 years and older-about−7,215
b. Population 8 years old and over.
c. Data relates to city boundaries as of 1970.

Source: Bureau of the Census. *Geographic Mobility March 1970 to March 1975* and *Geographic Mobility March 1975 to March 1978*.

EXHIBIT 4

Net Migration From Central Cities
Using The Current Population Survey 1970-1976

Year	Category	Estimated Net Migration	Percent of Base Population (Annual)
1970-1975	All Central Cities	−7,018	−2.5%
1976	All Central Cities	−1,665	−3.2%
1970-1976	All Central Cities	−8,683	−2.6%

EXHIBIT 5

Net Migration By City Size 1970-1976

Large Central Cities (From Exhibit)	−2,207	1.2%
All Other Cities	−5,976	3.1%
Total	−8,683	2.3%

have higher rates than northern cities which are losing population. Net migration data are only available for central cities that are counties (such as Denver, New York, New Orleans, Philadelphia) and for urban counties. Applying these relationships to growing and declining cities, the total estimated population migration from large central cities between 1970 and 1976 was 2.2 million. The growing city category, despite population gains, collectively sustained small migration losses (see Exhibit 6). New York City alone had 800 thousand more people leave than move in during this six year period.

Since the Current Population Survey extimated the total 1970-1976 loss in central city population (based on their 1970 boundaries) at 2.9 million, the residual population loss, about 700 thousand, had to take place in smaller central cities. This is consistent with data showing that smaller central cities tend to lose a smaller share of their population than those with half a million or more residents. The level of outmigration between 1970 and 1976 from central cities estimated at 8.6 million based on the population survey is more questionable. If one subtracts the 2.2 million identified in large cities from this total (see Exhibit 6), the residual of almost six million would have to be attributed to smaller cities, an unacceptably high number. How

EXHIBIT 6

Population Change And Estimated Net Migration
1970-1976 (in thousands)

City Category	N	Population[b] Change	Estimated Net Migration 1970	1976
Large Central Cities				
Declining[a]	14	12,412	−1,314	−1,813
Growing[a]	13	11,391	369	− 93
New York City	1	7,423	− 472	− 801
Total Larger Cities	28	31,226	−1,417	−2,207
Smaller Central Cities[b]				
Total	215	29,481	− 762	−5,976
All Central Cities				
Total	243	60,707	−2,179	−8,683c

a. See Exhibit 1 for definition.
b. Data derived from subtracting large central city population change from total central city change from the Current Population Survey. See Bureau of the Census, *Population Profile of the United States in 1977*, April 1978.
c. Derived from Bureau of the Census *Mobility of the Population of the United States, March 1970 to March 1975* and *Mobility of the Population of the United States, March 1975 to March 1977*.

does one explain this discrepancy? Probably the rationale is that central cities have been gaining population, both legal and illegal migrants, from other nations. This immigration is maintaining high central city populations despite substantial outmigration. An example of this pattern can be found in Newark, New Jersey. In 1979, about eight thousand students, or about 13 percent of total school enrollment, are bilingual. This phenomenon is a result of substantial recent immigration from Portugal and other, Hispanic, nations.

CHARACTERISTICS OF MIGRANTS

One of the issues arising in any discussion of the demand for and ability to pay for services by residents of central cities are changes which result from net migration. As noted earlier, most large central cities are continuing to lose population. The significant fiscal question, however, concerns changes in income and household compo-

EXHIBIT 7

Central City Mobility-Median Income Of
Males 25-34, 1975-1978

Population Group	Total Population	Migrants From Central City	Migrants To Central City	Percent Difference
All Males 16 Years and Over	$9,766	$12,031	$9,574	26.4
Married, Wife Present	13,358	14,053	13,328	5.4
Head 25-34 Years of Age	12,978	14,523	13,282	9.4
Other Marital Status	5,643	7,739	6,360	17.8

Source: Bureau of the Census

sition. In particular, it has been argued that central cities are currently attracting many young, above average income households, off-setting outmigration of other families. The most recent data on this subject do not support this argument. As shown in Exhibit 7, the average male moving to the central city has a slightly lower income than the base population, while the average male moving out has an income 23 percent higher than the base. Married immigrating males have about the same income as those moving out, while single or divorced males have low incomes. Unfortunately, from the perspective of the central city, almost three times as many married males move out as move in (see Exhibit 8).

While only 1.4 single males move out for every one moving in, these persons have incomes only one-half of the married male. Between 1975 and 1978, over one million more males with wife present (thus, over two million married adults) moved out as moved in. Those moving out had 1.4 children; those moving in, the same number. However, for married households in the 25 to 44 age group, the number of children is below average, suggesting that those with large families moved out earlier.

What can we conclude from these demographic data?

(1) Cities which had population declines in the 1960s are continuing to decline at a faster rate during the 1970s. There appears to be one exception which requires close monitoring: Boston.

(2) The rate of population decline was reduced somewhat in most cities during the mid 1970s. In some instances, sharp losses

EXHIBIT 8

Central City Mobility For Males By Marital
Status And Age, 1975-1978
(in thousands)

Marital Status	From Central Cities	To Central Cities	Ratio Out/In
All Males 16 Years and Over	2,822	1,467	1.9/1.0
Married, Wife Present	1,799	720	2.5/1.0
As above, Ages 25-44	1,187	429	2.8/1.0
Number of Children under 18	1,623	584	2.8/1.0
Other Marital Status	1,023	747	1.4/1.0

Source: Bureau of the Census, *Geographic Mobility: March 1975 to March 1978*,
November 1978.

during the 1960s and early 1970s would indicate that a new equilibrium is close to being reached. A group of four cities lost a large share of the population between 1960 and 1976 (St. Louis, −31 percent; Cleveland, −29 percent; Pittsburgh, −26 percent; and Detroit, −21 percent). These cities had lower losses between 1973 and 1976 compared to the early 1970s, which suggests their population may be stabilizing.[1]

(3) Growing cities had lower growth rates in the mid 1970s as a result of fewer or no annexations during the 1970s. If annexation rates continue to decline, so will the growth of large cities, although several exceptions can be anticipated, namely San Diego, Honolulu and Miami, due to their favorable geographic location.

(4) Outmigration from central cities is more rapid than population change data indicate. This pattern, presumably due to legal and illegal immigration, is maintaining high central city populations despite substantial relocation movement to suburbs and non-metropolitan areas.

(5) Outmigrants from cities continue to be predominantly married households with above average incomes.

INCOME GROWTH

The ability to pay for services is directly linked to personal income. As one would expect, the rate of income growth in declining cities, on a per capita basis, was below the level of growing jurisdictions. The pattern between 1972-1975 changed only marginally from the

EXHIBIT 9

Changes in Per Capita Money Income
1969-1975

	Percent Change 1969-1972	Percent Change 1969-1975
Growing	22%	61%
Declining	18%	52%
New York City	–	41%

Source: Bureau of the Census

previous three-year period, and the gap between the two categories remained about the same (see Exhibit 9). There were, however, numerous exceptions to the general pattern. Income growth in New Orleans (63 percent) exceeded the level of many growing jurisdictions between 1969 and 1975 (the city had population growth between 1973 and 1976, but not in earlier years), while Indianapolis had below average income growth (50 percent) during the six-year interval. Boston, with no loss in population, had the second lowest nominal gain (45 percent). Apparently, unlike other cities, persons are willing to reside in this city and accept lower income gains. The city also has large " non-profit" sectors such as universities, where wage increases have been below average. Despite these exceptions, there is a correlation, although not particularly a strong one, between growth rates and per capita income gains, if regional location is taken into account.

CHANGES IN COST OF AND DEMAND FOR PUBLIC SERVICES

A recently released report by D.B. Matz of the Joint Economic Committee provided useful data on the importance of public services and city characteristics in the decision process of private firms to remain in or relocate from large central cities. There is little doubt that this is the most extensive survey of its kind in terms of obtaining data on perceptions of city conditions.

Among the 26 city characteristics the following is the ranking of those related to public services:

Characteristics	Rank of Importance	Difference of Means Most/Least Favorable
City Government Attitude	1	0.75
Crime Level	2	0.79
Adequacy of Public Facilities	3	0.42
Adequacy of Public Services	5	0.80
Quality of City Schools	6	1.29[a]
Cultural Attractions	7	0

a. Highest among 26 characteristics.

Source: D.B. Matz, *Central City Business—Plans and Problems*, Joint Economic Committee, January 1979.

As shown in the above tabular display, among the 26 characteristics, 6 of the 7 ranked by importance are related to the provision of public services. The first, attitude of local government, is reflected in the provision of adequate services to businesses and their employees and in local conditions, such as reasonable taxes on business.

In the analysis of results, the study groups ten cities into three categories: those with highly favorable business climates (Dallas, Seattle, Phoenix, Atlanta); cities with least favorable business climates (Detroit, New York City); and those with somewhat favorable climates. The most and least favorable basically correspond to cities with growing and declining economies, although causality has not been established. Among the two characteristics identified by business are crime rate and quality of city schools, specifically, adequacy of facilities and adequacy of services. Respondents from growing cities view their cities as typically positive in these areas, while those with a negative perception of business climate hold a negative view of the provision of services in general, schools and police protection in particular.

Given the importance attached to schools and police, these services will be among the four discussed in this section.

EDUCATION

Education accounts for almost one-half of total outlays at the local level: about 45 percent of all school revenue continues to be raised locally. Thus, education continues to be the most costly single function provided by local government. Since, however, the majority of city school districts are fiscally independent, education data are difficult to assemble from one source.

This section discusses changes in the demand for education for sixteen of the largest school districts nationally. These are grouped into those located in declining northern states and those located in growing cities in the southern and western regions. As shown in Exhibit 10, school enrollment declined by 12.6 percent in the eight declining cities and by 7.4 percent in growing cities.[2] The percentage reduction in school enrollment for declining cities collectively is almost exactly equal to the percentage of outmigration. Sharpest declines were in Memphis (−18.4 percent), Indianapolis (−20.3 percent), Detroit (−18.3 percent), Milwaukee (−17.4 percent), and Baltimore (−16.8 percent). New York City and Newark are among the exceptions, since the annual decline in school enrollment is about the same as their population loss. This suggests that children of migrants from nations with high birth rates are causing enrollment to remain relatively high. In fact, migrants from Portugal and Hispanic nations in Newark now comprise almost fifteen percent of the school enrollment.

With the exception of New York City, the number of teachers has remained stable while average teacher wages increased more rapidly than inflation. It is somewhat surprising that wages for teachers in declining cities increased more rapidly than in the growing cities (see Exhibit 11). In 1972, teacher wages in declining cities exceeded the average of other jurisdictions by 11 percent, while in 1977, their wages were 17 percent higher.

Teacher/pupil ratios improved in all districts except New York City, where fewer teachers brought the city ratio in line with other large jurisdictions. As a result of more teachers per pupil, higher transportation costs and other above average increases, outlays per pupil almost doubled (97 percent increase) in declining cities, and increased by 78 percent in those growing. Three school districts—Boston, St. Louis and Milwaukee—had per pupil outlays increasing by over 22 percent annually between 1972 and 1977 (see Exhibit 11).

RELATION BETWEEN SCHOOL ENROLLMENT AND POPULATION

School enrollment in growing cities is more rapid than the reduction nationally, although the rate of population change is similar. In contrast, the decline of school enrollment in declining cities is less than one would expect based on national patterns. This may be due to two factors: immigration from other nations and above average birth rates among minority populations in older cities. Immigration appears, however, to be the more important cause (see Exhibit 10).

EXHIBIT 10

Changes in Enrollment And Population

City Category		School Enrollment (in thousands)				Population (in thousands)			
		1972	1977	Percent Change	Per Annum	1970	1976	Percent Change	Per Annum
Growing	7	1,550	1,436	− 7.4	−1.5	7,592	7,964	4.9	0.8
Declining	8	1,816	1,587	−12.6	−2.5	7,857	7,085	−9.8	−1.6
New York City	1	1,149	1,097	− 4.5	−0.9	7,894	7,423	−6.0	−1.0
U.S. Total		46,081	44,335	− 3.8	−0.8	203.8	214.7	5.3	0.9

EXHIBIT 11

Teacher/Student Characteristics

City Category	N	No. Teachers (in thousands)			Average Teacher Salary		
		1972	1977	Percent Change	1972	1977	Percent Change
Growing	7	66.4	66.7	0.8	$ 9,901	$14,048	41.9
Declining	8	73.2	72.5	– 1.0	$11,013	$16,513	50.0
New York City	1	59.0	52.0	–11.8	$11,600	$19,000	63.8
U.S. Total		207.0	2,193	2.0	$ 9,690	$13,347	37.8

Student Characteristics

City Category	N	Teacher/Student Ratio			Outlays Per Pupil (ADA)		
		1972	1977	Percent Change	1972	1977	Percent Change
Growing	7	23.3	21.5	– 7.7	$ 798	$1,421	78.1
Declining	8	24.8	21.9	–11.7	$1,116	$2,194	96.6
New York City	1	19.5	21.1	8.2	$1,647	$2,607	58.3
U.S. Total					$1,647	$1,578	68.9

SELECTED COMMON SERVICES

Four services are selected for comparison—two with non-discretionary outlays, police and fire, and two where outlays tend to be at least partially discretionary, recreation and highways.

Outlays for police services in growing cities increased by 74 percent on a per capita basis between fiscal 1972 and 1977, compared to a 54 percent increase in declining cities, reducing the expenditure gap between the two categories, a pattern repeated in fire services. (See Exhibit 12). Among growing cities, outlays for police increased by 126 percent in Houston, 103 percent in Phoenix, in San Antonio by 89 percent and in Memphis by 78 percent during the five-year period. Among declining cities, lowest increases were in Detroit (48 percent) and Buffalo (33 percent); the highest in Cleveland (84 percent). However, police expenditures were above the average of other services in most cities due to higher crime rates and above average wage increases.

Increases for fire protection were most modest, except in Phoenix (123 percent) and San Antonio (110 percent). Among cities declining, Cleveland had the highest increase in outlays (67 percent).

Unlike protective services, growing cities spent slightly more for recreation in both 1972 and 1977 than those declining, although the rate of increase among declining cities was larger, since both Cleveland and St. Louis had increases of over 100 percent, possibly because of the use of CETA employees. Outlays for highways were similar, on a per capita basis, in the two-city categories.

The most notable difference between the two groups of cities was in debt service. Among the declining cities, the average increase was only 18 percent, the increase among the growing cities was a modest gain, 48 percent. By fiscal 1977, per capita debt in the growing cities exceeded the level in those declining! Two cities, San Diego and Baltimore, had absolute debt declines.

New York City shows the effects of its fiscal crisis, with all service outlay increases very small (in effect substantial declines in absolute dollars), reflecting sharp cutbacks in employment.

Combining the four services, one finds the rate of change in outlays in declining cities to be only 15 percent lower than in growing cities. In 1972, declining cities spent 41 percent per capita more than those growing for the four services; in 1977, 33 percent more. At this rate, it would take *another twenty years* or so for outlays to equalize between the two groups of cities. Somewhat surprisingly, by 1977 outlays in New York City dropped to a level below the average of all declining cities and exceeded outlays in growing cities by only 25 percent.

EXHIBIT 12

Per Capita Outlays for Selected
Common Services 1972 And 1977

City Category	N	Police			Fire			Recreation			Highways (Incl. Capital)		
		1972	1977	Percent Change	1972	1977	Percent Change	1972	1977	Percent Change	1972	1977	Percent Change
Growing	8c	$30	52	74%	$19	30	59%	$21	28	33%	$16	28	75%
Declining	8d	58	89	54	27	40	48	18	27	50	18	28	56
New York City	1	79	95	20	35	40	14	15	17	13	20	21	5
All Cities		30	47	57	17	26	53	12	18	50	21	31	48

City Category	Total Debt			Total-Four Services			Consumer Price Index		
	1972	1977	Percent Change	1972	1977	Percent Change	1972	1977	Percent Change
Growing	$425	628	48%	$86	138	60%	124a	182a	47%
Declining	522	615	18	121	184	52	126b	181b	44
New York City	1423	1989	39	149	173	16	131	189	44
All Cities	$400	523	31	80	122	53	129	190	47

a. Northern State Average
b. Southern and Western Average
c. Growing cities are Dallas, San Antonio, Houston, San Diego, Phoenix, San Jose, Jacksonville and Oklahoma City.
d. The declining cities are New York, Buffalo, Detroit, Cleveland, Philadelphia, Pittsburgh, St. Louis and Chicago.

Source: Bureau of the Census, *City Government Finances in 1971-1972 and 1976-1977.*

Per capita outlays for the selected services in declining cities increased at the same rate as all municipalities nationally and at a rate 18 percent above the cost of living increases. Outlays in growing cities were above the total city average and exceeded inflation by 28 percent.

Lower rates of increase for police service outlays in declining cities reflects both fiscal pressures and relatively lower rates of increase in crime. As noted in a recent paper by this author, there has been a convergence in crime rates between large growing and declining cities. This phenomenon is probably linked to lower birth rates and fewer persons in the 14-24 age group residing in declining cities. Persons in this age group committed about 52 percent of all crimes in the nation based on arrest records. Changes in density as a result of population movement is an added factor, since high density tends to correlate with crime activity.

Despite the recent convergence, crime rates in older declining cities remain above the level of newer, lower density growing cities. This should not, however, be considered a new phenomenon.

CHANGES IN ABILITY TO PAY FOR SERVICES

REVENUE BY SOURCE

The rise in per capita operating outlays in declining cities was 58 percent more rapid, in growing cities 69 percent more rapid, and in New York City 62 percent more rapid than gains in money income. This would indicate rising tax burdens in central cities (see Exhibit 13). In reality, this was not the case. Local taxes increased at a substantially lower rate than total revenue from all sources. Local taxes as a share of total revenue declined in both growing and declining cities, but not in New York City (see Exhibit 14). The reduction was twice as rapid in the group of selected cities compared to all cities in the nation. However, the relative share of state aid did *not* increase between 1972 and 1977. The total reduction in the share of local taxes can be attributed to increased federal assistance. Thus, the share of local taxes in declining cities was reduced by 11 percent, while the state and federal aid increased by 12 percent. In growing cities, the local tax share was reduced by 9 percent, while federal funding increased by 11 percent, and state aid dropped by one percent. In New York City, the state share was reduced by three percent; federal funds increased by eight percent. Finally, at the national level, there was a relative decline in state aid and local taxes, totally absorbed by higher federal assistance.

EXHIBIT 13

Per Capita Outlays for Selected
Common Services 1972 and 1977

City Category	N	Police			Fire			Recreation			Highways (Incl. Capital)		
		1972	1977	Percent Change	1972	1977	Percent Change	1972	1977	Percent Change	1972	1977	Percent Change
Growing	8	30	52	74%	19	30	59%	21	28	33%	16	28	75%
Declining	8	58	89	54	27	40	48	18	27	50	18	28	56
New York City	1	79	95	20	35	40	14	15	17	13	20	21	5

	Total Debt			Total-Four Services		
	1972	1977	Percent Change	1972	1977	Percent Change
Growing	425	628	48%	86	138	60%
Declining	522	615	18	121	184	52
New York City	1423	1989	39	149	173	16

EXHIBIT 14

Percent Revenue by Source: 1972 and 1977

City Category	N	1972	1977	1972	1977	1972	1977	1972	1977
Declining	8	19	20	10	22	71	58	53	42
Growing	8	10	9	12	23	78	68	53	44
New York City	1	44	41	3	9	53	50	44	42
All Cities		24	23	7	15	69	62	48	43

Percent Change 1972-1977

	State	Federal	Local Tax
Declining	5	120	-21
Growing	-10	92	-17
New York City	-7	200	-5
All Cities	-4	114	-10

In declining cities, per capita money income increased at about the same rate as local taxes. However, taxes increased more rapidly than income in growing cities, indicating higher tax burdens. Nevertheless, considerable differences in tax burden remain.

CHANGES IN HOUSING DEMAND AND
RESIDENTIAL PROPERTY TAXES

Between 1966 and 1976, the demand for housing in large declining cities was reduced as a result of rapid outmigration from these cities. Among nine large declining cities, the aggregate number of single family units was reduced by six percent. However, Boston, Chicago, Philadelphia and New York City had more such units in 1976 than in 1966, indicating that the number of households increased despite population losses in these cities. On the other hand, several cities had steep losses. St. Louis had 39 percent fewer units and Cleveland 38 percent fewer units in 1976 compared to ten years earlier. The average value of units in these cities increased by 95 percent, while property taxes increased by three percent.

By contrast, if one separates the three largest declining cities and the three cities with the sharpest population losses, a different pattern emerges. The characteristics of the three largest declining cities resembles those of the growing cities (see Exhibit 16). In these cities, the market value of single family property increased by 166 percent, and taxes from these sources by 129 percent despite lower effective tax rates. In the "worst" cities, the total value of single family units declined by two percent in current dollars. Thus, the revenue flow only could be sustained by rate increases of 34 percent, which produced an additional 31 percent in revenues.

In the growing cities, the value of single family property increased by 184 percent and taxes from these sources by 116 percent. The sharpest appreciation in property value occurred in New York City (176 percent), Chicago (147 percent), San Diego (188 percent), Houston (173 percent) and San Jose (163 percent).

During 1976, the average market value of a single family unit in New York City ($60 thousand) was similar to that in Los Angeles and San Diego, while a typical home in Detroit, Baltimore and St. Louis was worth only about $16 thousand. The typical house in the growing city was worth 46 percent more than in a declining city, where property taxes were 60 percent higher. Thus, taxes paid on the units were similar in the two categories of cities.

EXHIBIT 15

Per Capita Local Taxes and Outlays 1972-1977

City Category	N	Local Taxes			Operating Outlays			Capital Outlays		
		1972	1977	Percent Change	1972	1977	Percent Change	1972	1977	Percent Change
Declining	7	$143	$274	42%	$320	$537	68%	$ 52	$ 91	75%
Growing	8	91	145	59	127	236	86	54	89	65
New York City	1	485	806	66	1017	1574	55	134	55	−66

	Change in Local Taxes	Change in Money Income	Difference
Declining	42%	43	2.4
Growing	59%	51	−13.6
New York City	66%	34	−48.5

EXHIBIT 16

Changes in the Number, Value and Tax Rate
On Single Family Units in Selected Cities 1966-1976

City Category	N	Number of Units (in thousands)			Average Value (in thousands)			Effective Tax Rate		
		1966	1976	Percent Change	1966	1976	Percent Change	1966	1976	Percent Change
Declining Cities										
Sharp Population Loss[a]	3	587	419	-29	$12.8	17.6	38	1.79	2.39	34
Slow Losses[b]	3	1030	1070	4	15.9	40.8	156	2.18	1.91	-12
Total	9	1971	1848	-6	14.0	22.4	95	2.41	2.49	3
Growing Cities										
All Except Texas[c]	5	753	925	23	19.3	44.6	131	1.97	1.49	-24
Including Texas[c]	8	n/a	–	–	17.3	40.1	132	2.00	1.56	-22
U.S. Total		40.8	48.7	21	15.2	32.6	114	1.85	1.80	– 3

a. St. Louis, Cleveland, Detroit.
b. New York, Chicago, Philadelphia.
c. San Diego, San Jose, Los Angeles, Phoenix, Memphis, Dallas, Houston and San Antonio.

FINDINGS

DEMOGRAPHIC CHANGES

Central cities are continuing to lose population, although there appears to be a slow reduction in the rate of loss. As a result of reduced annexation activity, many of the cities growing in the 1960s and 1970s are now faced with outmigration. Outmigration from cities is more rapid than can be explained by reduced population, implying that substantial immigration from other nations is masking the outflow. It appears, based on the experience of New York City and Newark, that this migration may have a positive effect on older, poorly maintained neighborhoods.

While older central cities continue to lose population, their per capita nominal income has not been substantially higher than income gains in growing cities. A major exception is New York City, where income gains have been particularly low.

The data suggest a continuation of outmigration from older and many newer large central cities, but at a lower rate of loss than that experienced in the early 1970s. Cities with substantial immigration— New Orleans, New York, Newark, Boston—may have no population loss whatsoever.

CHANGES IN COST OF PROVIDING AND DEMAND FOR MUNICIPAL SERVICES

The importance of municipal services is illustrated by a recent survey that places these services, particularly police protection and quality of schools, as more important than tax incentives or other direct means of encouraging economic development. The demand for schools, as measured by school enrollment, is lower in almost every large city, with Phoenix the one exception. However, aggregate outlays have remained very high. In the group of declining cities, per pupil outlays almost doubled during a five-year period and in all cases exceeded the cost of living. Except for New York City, the number of teachers remained basically the same and teacher wage increases were above average in cities with declining populations.

Unlike school outlays, per capita expenditures for other local public services increased more rapidly in cities defined as growing. However, outlays are converging at a low rate. At the current rate, it would take twenty years to equalize outlays on a per capita basis.

The sharp rise in police outlays in growing cities is due to the steep rise in crime. These cities are experiencing continuing crime growth, while crime in many of the older cities has stabilized.

CHANGES IN ABILITY TO PAY FOR SERVICES

Local government in all city categories increased outlays more rapidly than local revenue collections as a direct result of increased federal aid. State assistance, with the exception of aid to local school districts, remained basically static.

Changes in property tax revenue reflect to a considerable extent changes in residential construction activity and changes in the value of residential property. Among declining cities, several, including the largest three, had increases in the number of single family units and substantial growth in the market value of these units. However, cities with rapid population losses had declines in the number of units and real declines in the market value of their housing stock during the last ten years. In all cities, effective tax rates have been reduced, with steepest declines in rapidly growing communities such as Houston.

NOTES

1. Cities with sharp population losses are northern cities which had rapid population growth between 1900 and 1910. By 1976, Pittsburgh and St. Louis had populations substantially lower than in 1910.

2. In a number of cities, school district boundaries are not coterminous with political boundaries. In Texas, for example, school districts typically reflect boundaries of cities prior to the major annexation of the last two decades.

Roy W. Bahl and Larry Schroeder - FISCAL ADJUSTMENTS IN DECLIN- ING STATES

INTRODUCTION

The relative decline of economic activity in the industrial North-east and Midwest has by now been well documented.[1] Likewise, there has been considerable attention paid to the fiscal problems of state and local governments, many of which are located in this same region.[2] This would appear to be no mere coincidence, and there has been increasing recognition of the linkages between a declining economy and a strained fisc.[3] In fact, public policymakers may have begun to recognize this linkage, although it is difficult to ascertain if their response is based upon the economic environ-ment or is merely political rhetoric in light of the Proposition 13 or Proposition 9 climate throughout the country.

The objective of this paper is to describe and analyze the linkage between variations in economic and demographic changes and state and local government finances. For the declining regions, particularly the mid-Atlantic states, the analysis shows an imbalance between public sector growth and the capacity to finance such growth. While this imbalance may have begun to be altered recently, there still

remains considerable disparity between the relatively declining
Northern Tier of states and the growing South. Yet the discussion
here is not without implications for southern states currently experiencing economic growth but facing a similar set of factors that
led to the increase in government costs in the North: inflation,
in-migration, growing public service demands and increasing strength
of unions.

An initial assumption of this paper is that regional shifts in population and employment are not undesirable *per se* and therefore
should not be the object of remedial public policy. Nor is a trend
toward interregional income equality or a growing homogeneity in
the provision of public services across geographic areas necessarily
detrimental to the public welfare. What is harmful about regional
shifts and what ought to be at the center of concern about public
policy to deal with such shifts are their effects on unemployment,
poverty and the fiscal position of state and local governments. In
a sense, all three of these concerns can be translated into a more
general concern for the distribution of income—more specifically,
to a concern for the share of purchasing power or public services
accruing to low income families.

The problems of decline—those faced by the industrial Northeast
and Midwest—would appear more difficult to resolve than the
problems of growth—those experienced by the Southern Tier states.
Migration barriers tend to hold the jobless in central cities in declining regions and institutional barriers tend to lead to a worsening
fiscal position for jurisdictions in the declining region. But most
importantly, the problems are the result of past decisions which are
not easily reversed, and the solutions to the problems of decline are
beyond purely state and local government actions. Federal subsidies
will be imperative to ease the adjustment of northern states to a
new, lower economic equilibrium. This is not to say that there are
not severe fiscal and poverty problems in the southern region, but
rather, to say that the adjustment problems associated with regional
shifts are likely to be more severe in the Northeast. Moreover, many
of the fiscal problems of northern cities and states need not be
repeated in the South.

Regardless of one's view as to where problems are most serious or
of how they might be resolved, it is clear that an understanding of
the linkages among regional shifts in employment and population,
the unemployment problems particularly of large cities and the fiscal
problems of state and local governments are essential to formulating
a remedial public policy. This paper is a very modest attempt to deal

with one dimension of this linkage, the relationship between regional economic shifts and state and local government finances.

The analysis here is necessarily concerned with regional variations, more specifically, with the variation in finances of jurisdictions—state and local—in growing and declining regions. If any regularities are to be ferreted out, some form of aggregation of these jurisdictions must be used. Since the concern in this paper is with how the fisc has been compromised by regional movements in population, jobs and income, the financing jurisdictions are aggregated by state and region.[4] We follow the general convention of labeling "Northern Tier" the aggregate of the East North Central, Middle Atlantic and New England Census Regions, and "Southern Tier," the South Atlantic,[5] East South Central and West South Central regions.[6]

The danger with such aggregation is that there remain very wide differences in fiscal structure and performance across states in a region and even across local jurisdictions within a state. The reader should remain cognizant of such variations, expecially when this analysis is overenthusiastic in identifying "clear" regional variations.

After reviewing the interregional differences in changes in economic activity over the past one and one half decades in Section I, we turn to a discussion of aspects of public sector differences in the "Snow-" and "Sunbelt" regions. Section III considers more explicitly the linkages between these changes in economic activity and the state of sub-federal fiscs in the regions. Particular attention is paid to the most recent short-term changes in economic activity—the recessionary period of 1974-1975 and the general upturn of 1976-77. The final section discusses implications of these findings.

INTERREGIONAL DIFFERENCES IN ECONOMIC GROWTH

The shift in economic activity from the northern to the southern states has been well documented in the literature. Jusenius and Ledebur have described this shift in terms of population movement,[7] Greenberg and Valente[8] and Garnick[9] have studied the trends in employment, and the Congressional Budget Office has described the pattern of growth in earnings and personal income.[10] For purposes of this paper it is necessary to examine these trends in order to determine their potential effects on the taxable capacity and public servicing requirements of states in each region. Unfortunately, none of these indicators of economic expansion or contraction is an adequate measure of taxable capacity, partly because the tax structures of the fifty states vary so widely. Nevertheless, these measures give some notion of how regional shifts in economic activity enhance or compromise the ability of state and local governments to finance public services. Insofar as possible, four time periods are considered. The 1962-67 period saw the beginnings of a southern movement of population and economic activity, a trend which accelerated between the period 1967 to 1972. The 1972-75 period includes the recession which heightened the "Sunbelt" movement, and the 1975-77 period accounts for the effects of the present recovery period.

INCOME

Per capita income is a composite measure which perhaps more than any other single index, indicates the average level of well-being of citizens in a region. Since per capita income is influenced by changes in population size, it may or may not provide a proxy measure of changes in the capacity to finance. As may be seen in Exhibit 1 below, the per capita income growth in the Southern Tier was greater than in the North for all four time periods considered here. It is interesting to note that the disparity in the rate of growth in per capita personal income narrowed during the recession period, and continued to narrow during the recovery. Between 1967 and 1972, per capita income in the Southern Tier was growing about 27 percent faster than in the North, but the differential growth rate fell to about 14 percent between 1972 and 1975. This narrowing in per capita income growth is due to a combination of relatively heavy loss of population in the Northern Tier states, a continued rapid growth of population in the Southern Tier states and, possibly, the flow of income-compensating transfer payments to the Northern states. In the recovery period, the process of convergence slowed—per capita income grew 4 percent faster in the Southern than in the Northern Tier states.

EMPLOYMENT

In terms of changes in the level of employment, the Southern Tier states have been growing more rapidly for all four time periods considered (see Exhibit 2). Even though the rate of employment growth has slowed in the southern states, it still remains considerably higher than that in the North. Perhaps even more importantly in the context of this analysis is the fact that the relatively low rate of employment growth in the Northern Tier between 1967 and 1972 turned to literally no growth and in some cases declince between 1972 and 1975 and has been very slow during the recovery.

EXHIBIT 1

Percent Increase In Per Capita Personal Income:
By Region For Selected Time Periods

State and Region	Unweighted Regional Means				1977 Level
	1962-1967	1967-1972	1972-1975	1975-1977	
NORTHERN TIER	33.2	38.0	28.5	20.0	7072
East North Central	33.2	37.9	29.4	22.1	7256
Illinois	31.3	36.6	32.9	15.1	7768
Indiana	33.1	36.9	30.0	23.4	6921
Michigan	38.1	39.3	24.6	27.1	7619
Ohio	33.1	38.4	28.3	22.3	7084
Wisconsin	30.7	38.5	31.5	22.7	6890
Mid Atlantic	31.9	38.3	28.3	17.7	7514
New Jersey	29.7	40.9	27.6	17.7	7994
New York	32.2	35.5	25.8	15.6	7537
Pennsylvania	33.8	38.7	31.5	19.7	7011
New England	33.7	37.9	27.9	19.4	6697
Connecticut	31.3	32.7	27.2	18.4	8061
Maine	34.1	41.0	30.8	20.4	5734
Massachusetts	28.6	40.1	26.1	19.3	7258
New Hampshire	31.6	38.7	28.7	20.8	6534
Rhode Island	36.6	34.0	28.7	19.1	6772
Vermont	40.1	41.0	25.7	18.6	5826
SOUTHERN TIER	40.9	48.3	32.6	20.8	6210
South Atlantic	39.2	49.9	30.5	19.3	6547
Delaware	27.1	36.3	28.6	17.4	7692
Maryland	29.8	47.7	30.0	17.9	7571
North Carolina	43.6	51.0	30.2	20.0	5935
Virginia	41.3	52.0	31.8	19.0	6864
South Carolina	48.3	53.8	32.3	20.7	5628
Georgia	46.2	51.4	27.4	19.7	6014
Florida	36.8	58.4	26.5	18.5	6684
West Virginia	40.3	48.9	37.0	20.9	5987

continued on next page

EXHIBIT 1 (cont'd)

	Unweighted Regional Means				
	1962-1967	1967-1972	1972-1975	1975-1977	1977 Level
East South Central	43.3	51.1	32.7	22.0	5596
Alabama	40.2	52.1	35.0	21.2	5622
Kentucky	39.1	47.2	35.5	21.8	5946
Mississippi	52.0	54.0	30.4	24.6	5031
Tennessee	41.7	51.3	29.8	20.6	5785
West South Central	42.0	42.4	36.8	22.5	6151
Arkansas	44.6	48.8	35.9	23.2	5540
Louisiana	43.8	37.2	37.0	23.6	5914
Oklahoma	39.6	41.5	37.1	20.7	6346
Texas	39.7	42.2	36.9	22.6	6803
	Weighted Regional Means				
NORTHERN TIER	32.5	37.6	28.3	19.3	7371
East North Central	33.4	37.8	29.3	21.3	7347
Mid Atlantic	32.2	37.5	27.8	17.2	7460
New England	31.2	37.4	27.0	19.7	7183
SOUTHERN TIER	41.1	49.0	32.4	20.7	6310
South Atlantic	40.3	52.4	29.5	19.1	6485
East South Central	42.3	50.9	32.7	21.7	5651
West South Central	41.0	42.0	36.9	22.7	6458

Source: Bureau of Economic Analysis, U.S. Department of Commerce, *Survey of Current Business,* 56, No. 8 (Washington, D.C.: U.S. Government Printing Office, 1976), and 58, No. 8 (1978).

In the Southern Tier, on the other hand, while the growth rate slowed between 1972 and 1975, only one state (Delaware) showed an absolute job loss. As may be seen from the weighted growth rates in the last column in Exhibit 2, the southern region has participated to a much greater extent than northern states in the recovery.

POPULATION

Yet a third way to measure the change in economic activity in the two regions is to examine the pattern and trend of population growth. On the revenue side, a declining population may mean a diminished capacity to finance public services if the population losses are higher earning families. If out-migration is primarily of low income families, service requirements may be reduced by more

EXHIBIT 2

Growth In Employment: By Region

Region	1962-1967 Percent Change	1967-1972 Percent Change	1972-1975 Percent Change	1975-1977 Percent Change
	Unweighted Means			
NORTHERN TIER	16.7	7.6	1.9	6.4
East North Central	19.8	7.5	2.4	6.4
Middle Atlantic	12.6	6.0	−0.2	2.6
New England	16.3	8.6	2.5	8.2
SOUTHERN TIER	24.0	18.7	7.2	7.5
South Atlantic	24.5	20.4	5.8	6.1
East South Central	23.7	17.5	6.9	9.0
West South Central	23.3	16.4	10.4	8.8
	Weighted Means			
NORTHERN TIER	15.2	5.8	0.8	4.3
East North Central	19.4	6.8	2.2	6.1
Middle Atlantic	11.6	4.7	−0.8	1.8
New England	14.1	6.0	1.5	5.8
SOUTHERN TIER	24.7	20.2	8.4	7.6
South Atlantic	25.7	23.0	6.7	6.4
East South Central	23.6	17.3	6.5	8.8
West South Central	23.6	17.7	12.6	8.8

Source: Bureau of Labor Statistics, U.S. Department of Labor, *Employment and Earnings, States and Areas* 1939-75, Bulletin 1370-12; *Employment and Earnings* 25 No. 5 (May 1978) (Washington, D.C.: U.S. Government Printing Office, 1977).

than taxable capacity thereby enhancing the government's fiscal position. Population growth and changing demographic makeup are likely to influence the level of public expenditures. Weinstein and Pirestine, for example, have carefully studied and analyzed the relations between migration, demographic change and state-local government budgets and find evidence of positive effects of in-migration spending levels.[11]

The North-South differentials in population growth rates are predictable. The growth in the Northern Tier has slowed markedly since 1962 and growth has been negligible since 1972 (see Exhibit 3). Among the southern states the rate of population growth also slowed but remained well above the northern rate. No state in the

Southern Tier showed a population decline since 1972, while five northern states—Ohio, New Jersey, New York, Pennsylvania and Rhode Island—lost population (see Exhibit 3). Though most of the population changes were due to migration, it is interesting to note that because of higher fertility rates, the Southern Tier would have grown faster than the Northern Tier even in the absence of migration between the regions.[12] With respect to the composition of population change, little data are available by way of the income level and employment characteristics (i.e., occupation, industry) of migrants.[13]

The inference one might draw from these trends is that the declining population in the North likely reduced certain servicing needs, but these reductions may have been offset by increasing concentrations of the poor, particularly in central cities.

REGIONAL DIFFERENCES IN FISCAL ACTIVITY

While this section reviews the major regional differences in quantifiable indicators of state and local fiscal activity, it should be recognized that there are also general differences in governmental structures and responsibilities between regions. In general, Southern Tier states are more likely to be state-dominated, whereas local government dominance is more likely to be found among Northern Tier states.[14] Local dominance, with its heavy reliance upon state aids to localities, may create barriers to roll-backs in general expenditure levels within a logrolling political environment where legislators find it difficult to alter historical state-aid formulas.

Additionally, there appears to be greater metropolitan fiscal disparity in the North than in the South. Eleven of the fourteen cities scoring poorest on Nathan and Dommel's "hardship index" are in the Northern Tier while only Atlanta and Richmond are in the South.[15] Likewise, Sacks found greater central city population densities in the North than in the South with city-suburban per capita income ratios less than one in the North but greater than one in the South.[16] While the general newness of these southern cities may help explain these lesser disparities, they also may be due to greater success in annexation and consolidation in the South. For example, Marando argues that consolidation is essentially a southern regional phenomenon, and that annexation has occurred extensively throughout the United States with the exception of the northeastern region.[17] With these structural differences in mind, we now turn to several empirical measures of fiscal activity.

EXHIBIT 3

Population Growth: By Region For Selected Time Periods

Region	Unweighted Means (Percent Increase)				
	1962-1967	1967-1972	1972-1975	1975-1977	1977
NORTHERN TIER	6.5	4.8	0.6	0.7	90,336
East North Central	6.9	3.8	0.6	0.5	41,056
Middle Atlantic	4.7	3.3	−0.6	−0.4	37,038
New England	7.1	6.3	1.2	1.5	12,242
SOUTHERN TIER	5.4	6.2	3.8	2.2	69.158
South Atlantic	8.0	7.7	4.0	2.0	33,616
East South Central	2.1	3.2	2.9	2.2	13,836
West South Central	3.6	6.2	4.4	2.8	21,706
	Weighted Means (Percent Increase)				
NORTHERN TIER	5.6	3.4	−0.1	0.02	
East North Central	6.7	3.6	0.3	0.4	
Middle Atlantic	3.9	2.8	−0.9	−0.5	
New England	7.8	4.6	0.7	0.5	
SOUTHERN TIER	5.9	7.4	4.7	2.6	
South Atlantic	8.7	9.0	5.2	2.1	
East South Central	2.5	3.3	2.9	2.3	
West South Central	4.3	7.6	5.0	3.5	

Source: Bureau of the Census, *Current Population Reports*, Series P-25, various issues.

EXPENDITURE LEVEL AND STRUCTURE

There are important variations between the Northern and Southern Tier states in the level and functional distribution of expenditures. The northern states spend more—about 16 percent more on a per capita basis— than do the Southern Tier states (see Exhibit 4). This pattern holds for most states within the two regions. Only one Northern Tier state (Indiana) spends less than the southern mean, and only three Southern Tier states (Delaware, Maryland and Louisiana) spend above the northern mean. This relatively low expenditure level in the South, even in the midst of an increased flow of resources to that region, is important in understanding the possibilities for fiscal adjustment.

EXHIBIT 4

Expenditure And Employment Characteristics of State And Local Governments By Region In 1977

State and Region	Per Capita Expenditures	Percent of Current Expenditures			State and Local Government Employees	
		Education	Welfare	Health & Hospitals	Per 10,000 Population[a]	Average Wage[b]
Unweighted Regional Means						
NORTHERN TIER	1261	39.5	16.3	7.3	459	1076
East North Central	1208	43.4	15.3	8.5	451	1112
Middle Atlantic	1429	35.6	17.4	7.3	464	1159
New England	1221	38.1	16.5	6.2	463	1004
SOUTHERN TIER	1082	42.2	11.9	10.8	497	901
South Atlantic	1145	42.6	10.4	10.5	514	949
East South Central	1005	41.4	13.4	11.6	473	846
West South Central	1033	42.3	13.3	10.6	486	860
Weighted Regional Means						
NORTHERN TIER	1342	37.8	17.0	7.9	459	1144
East North Central	1218	42.8	15.8	8.2	447	1132
Middle Atlantic	1502	34.0	18.0	8.0	470	1184
New England	1268	35.8	17.3	6.8	464	1065
SOUTHERN TIER	1062	42.4	11.3	11.2	499	912
South Atlantic	1105	42.4	9.9	11.3	514	943
East South Central	1003	41.3	13.4	11.5	472	851
West South Central	1033	43.3	12.2	10.8	491	898

[a] Fulltime equivalent employment
[b] October payroll divided by fulltime equivalent employment

Source: U.S. Bureau of the Census, *Government Finances in 1976-77, Series GF 77, 6* (Washington, D.C.: U.S. Government Printing Office, 1978); *Public Employment in 1977, Series GE77, No. 1* (Washington, D.C.: U.S. Government Printing Office, 1978).

In terms of expenditure distribution, the southern states allocate a slightly greater share of total public resources to education. The same holds true for health and hospitals, though there is much variation among states within the two regions. But perhaps the major regional difference in expenditure structure is that the northern states spend proportionately more for public welfare. Only one northern state allocates as little to public welfare as the southern mean of 11.9 percent.

PUBLIC EMPLOYMENT AND WAGE LEVELS

On the average, there appears to be a greater level of state and local government employment, relative to population, in the South (see Exhibit 4). Nine of the sixteen states in the Southern Tier are at or above the U.S. median of 498 employees per 10,000 population while only one of the fourteen northern states is above this median. Though there are some outliers, there is not a great deal of variation among these two groups of states.

Some evidence has shown an association between the level of local government employment and the rate of population growth. Muller compares twelve growing cities and fourteen declining cities on the basis of common function[18] employment per 1,000 residents. From this relatively small set of observations, he finds declining cities to have 12.1 workers per 1,000 residents as compared to 8.7 in the growing cities.[19] Perhaps even more interesting is his finding that the gap widened between 1967 and 1972. No such relationship between the level of state and local employment and population growth or decline can be found among the Northern or Southern Tier states examined here.

Average public employee wages are higher in the Northern Tier by almost any standard (Exhibit 4). While per capita income is only 14 percent higher in the North, the gap in average public sector wages is over 19 percent. There are a number of possible reasons why public sector workers receive such low wages in the southern states: low productivity, the absence of strong unions, or the possibility that governments in southern states do not perform the same range of public subfunctions and hence, do not require as expensive a mix of labor skills. Another possibility is that these comparisons are not valid because of data and conceptual problems.

There are many problems inherent in a comparison of average wage levels across states. The estimates presented in Exhibit 4 are of average payroll per full-time equivalent employee. These data miss the wide variation in pay levels by class of employees (including full-versus part-time) and mix nine-month employees (teachers) with twelve-month employees. There are also inadequate data to measure interstate variation in the level of pensions and fringe benefits.[20] However, since many benefits are tied to wage levels (e.g., pensions and social security contributions) it is possible that the regional differences in total compensation are greater than those in average wages. Finally, even if the payroll per full-time equivalent employee is a reasonable benchmark for comparison, there remains the problem of cost-of-living differentials which may tend to change this pattern of interstate differences. Generally higher costs-of-living in the North would suggest that real differences in compensation are not as great as indicated in Exhibit 4.

If all of these caveats are disregarded, or if the data problems somehow cancel out, the greater average wage in the Northern Tier suggests that a substantial part of the state and local expenditure difference in the northern and southern states is due to public employee compensation differences. If it is further accepted that differentials in average wages across regions are not the result of public employee productivity differentials, then the higher level of per capita spending in the northern states substantially overstates the difference in the quality of services provided between the two regions. Muller has studied wage variations among local governments using his growth/decline dichotomy, and for his sample, has determined that average wage levels tend to be higher in older and declining cities. His plausible explanation of this difference is the greater ability of municipal employee associations in older cities to press for more favorable contract terms, coupled with cost-of-living differences and perhaps a necessary premium for what is perceived as a lower quality of life in older, more congested cities of the Northeast and industrial Midwest.

SOURCES OF FINANCE

Three aspects of the financing of state and local government expenditures are important in describing regional variations in fiscal systems: reliance on debt, the structure of taxes raised and the level of revenue effort exerted. With respect to borrowing, the level of general obligation debt in the Northern Tier is higher on both a per capita basis and as a percent of personal income than in the South though large variations do exist (see Exhibit 5). The level of debt in the east northcentral states is lower than that in any

EXHIBIT 5

Debt Levels: By Region For 1977

State and Region	Unweighted Means Long Term Debt Outstanding	
	Per Capita	As a Percent of Personal Income
NORTHERN TIER	1053	14.9
East North Central	744	10.2
Middle Atlantic	1500	20.1
New England	1087	16.2
SOUTHERN TIER	867	13.7
South Atlantic	937	13.9
East South Central	821	14.6
West South Central	771	12.5
	Weighted Means	
NORTHERN TIER	1193	16.2
East North Central	767	10.4
Middle Atlantic	1657	22.2
New England	1214	16.9
SOUTHERN TIER	798	12.7
South Atlantic	777	12.0
East South Central	827	14.6
West South Central	814	12.6

Source: U.S. Bureau of the Census, *Government Finances in 1976-77*, Series GF77, 5 (Washington, D.C.: U.S. Government Printing Office, 1977).

southern subregion, attesting again to the problems with inferences from regional averages. The higher level of per capita debt suggests a greater fixed commitment for debt service in the annual budget of the states. In addition debt contracted to build an infrastructure to support a growing economic base may be less burdensome than that contracted primarily in response to fiscal difficulties.

In terms of revenue structure there are distinct and important differences between the regions. Southern states are more heavily reliant on sales taxes and northern states on property taxes (see Exhibit 6). This difference is largely a reflection of the division of financial responsibility for services between the state and local level. Where local government involvement in the delivery of services is strong, there tends to be much heavier use of the property

EXHIBIT 6

Revenue Structure: By Region For 1977

| | Unweighted Means | | | | |
| | Percent of Own Source Revenues Raised From | | | | Federal Aid as a Percent of |
State and Region	Property Taxes	Sales Taxes	Income Taxes	Per Capita Federal Aid	Total General Revenue
NORTHERN TIER	33.1	13.4	17.3	$291	22.2
East North Central	29.2	16.5	19.3	246	19.8
Middle North Atlantic	30.9	13.1	20.9	299	20.3
New England	37.4	11.0	13.9	325	25.1
SOUTHERN TIER	17.2	18.5	14.9	277	25.1
South Atlantic	19.4	15.8	19.1	279	24.1
East South Central	14.3	23.8	12.8	281	27.3
West South Central	17.8	18.8	8.8	271	25.1
	Weighted Means				
NORTHERN TIER	30.9	14.3	20.7	$283	20.3
East North Central	29.5	16.2	19.1	248	20.1
Middle North Atlantic	29.7	13.6	23.2	314	20.0
New England	39.8	10.5	17.2	307	22.4
SOUTHERN TIER	20.4	18.4	11.9	260	23.8
South Atlantic	21.6	16.3	16.6	261	23.2
East South Central	14.4	23.8	12.7	279	27.1
West South Central	21.9	18.8	4.1	246	22.7

Source: U.S. Bureau of the Census, *Government Finances in 1976-77*, Series GF77, 5 (Washington, D.C.: U.S. Government Printing Office, 1977).

tax. But, as noted above, the southern states tend to be more state government dominant, hence, there is heavier reliance on non-property taxation. This difference is of considerable importance to the potential response of the fisc to growth or decline in the economic base. In the South, with its heavy reliance on sales taxes, a combination of real growth and inflation will automatically generate substantial new revenues for expansion of the public sector. In the Northern Tier, where property taxation dominates, even the tax base growth generated by inflationary increase in income is unlikely to be fully or easily captured.[21] In terms of the controversial issue of the regional distribution of federal aid, both regions receive about the same per capita amount, but southern states—because of their lower level of fiscal activity—are more dependent on federal aid as a revenue source.

FISCAL RESPONSES TO DIFFERENTIAL REGIONAL GROWTH

The observed differences in relative economic growth between the North and South and conditions of the fisc in the same regions provide the opportunity for a more detailed examination of their linkages. Here we will consider both expenditure and revenue response to these changes with special interest on the years 1972-77. The period 1972-75 was characterized by nationwide inflation culminating in the general recession of 1974-75. While the recovery of 1975-77 was sustained, it has apparently seen a continuation of the general relative decline of the industrial Northeast and Midwest. Coming in the wake of the well-publicized New York City crisis and the apparent cutback mood of many taxpayers, it is interesting to see whether the general trends in fiscal actions have been reversed.

EXPENDITURE GROWTH

Given the relatively slower growth in financial capacity in the northern states, a slower growth in fiscal activity might have been expected. In fact, expenditure growth in the Northern Tier states was not considerably different from that in the southern states through 1975 (see Exhibit 7). Expenditures grew at a rate roughly 20 to 30 percent faster than personal income in both regions in the three time periods considered, except for the 1967-72 period, when per capita expenditures in the Northern Tier grew 93 percent faster than per capita income (see Exhibit 8). Even in the 1972-75 period, when total employment increased by about 7 percent in the South and less than 1 percent in the North, per capita expenditures grew by about the same percentage in both regions. From this evidence, one might conclude that there was not a strong relationship between the growth in public expenditures in the two regions and the capacity to finance that growth.

Some evidence of greater fiscal restraint in both regions shows up in the recovery period (1975-77) when the growth in expenditures fell below that of the growth in income. One plausible explanation of this lagged and long-overdue response to slow growing economic activity is that the New York City financial collapse and the near disasters in several other cities finally drove home the reality that the public sector, especially in many Northern Tier states, could

EXHIBIT 7

Indicators Of Fiscal Expansion: By Region

Region	Means Percent Increases in Per Capita General Expenditures*			
	1962-1967	1967-1972	1972-1975	1975-1977
NORTHERN TIER	42.8	73.4	34.5	17.2
East North Central	41.0	67.8	34.5	18.9
Middle Atlantic	47.8	91.4	34.6	15.7
New England	41.8	69.1	34.4	16.7
SOUTHERN TIER	51.8	64.5	38.0	18.6
South Atlantic	55.2	71.0	40.9	16.2
East South Central	47.0	64.5	36.5	19.6
West South Central	49.6	51.5	33.8	22.5

* As noted above, we are interested in state level changes so utilize unwieghted means in this and the remaining tables.

Source: U.S. Bureau of the Census, *Governmental Finances in 1976-1977* (1961-62, 1966-67, 1971-72, 1974-75) Series GF77, 5 (Washington, D.C.: U.S. Government Printing Office, 1977).

EXHIBIT 8

Per Capita Income Elasticity[a] Of State and Local Government
Expenditures: By Region

	Northern Tier	Southern Tier
1962-1967	1.29	1.27
1967-1972	1.93	1.34
1972-1975	1.21	1.17
1975-1977	0.86	0.89

[a] Percent increase in per capita expenditure divided by percent increase in per capita income.

Source: Computed from Exhibits 1 and 7.

no longer sustain itself. Reduction, cutbacks and deferrals became the centerpieces of state and local government fiscal policies.

If the growth or decline in taxable capacity does not explain the growth of the state and local government sector through 1975, then attention might be turned to two other possible explanations: (a) on the demand side, growing requirements for services resulted primarily in increased numbers of public employees and an upward pressure on expenditures, (b) on the supply side, increased public employee compensation resulted from union pressures and inflation and forced up expenditure levels. Either explanation would be consistent with the observed absence of a consistent, long-term relationship between economic base and public expenditure growth.

There is a wealth of literature on expenditure determinants which attests to the difficulties of separating demand from supply influences to explain expenditure growth and variations.[22] Those difficulties notwithstanding, we proxy the growth in service demand here with three variables: population growth, increase in AFDC recipients and increase in primary and secondary school enrollments. To the extent these factors increased over the four periods studied, an increase in state and local government employment levels might have been expected. The number of AFDC recipients increased at a greater rate in the North than in the South during 1962-75, while the reverse was true for total increases in population (see Exhibit 9). During the 1975-77 recovery the number of AFDC recipients declined more rapidly in the Southern Tier, hence, the gap in the proportion of low income population has been increasing. This would imply a stronger pressure on public expenditure levels in the northern states.

Primary and secondary school enrollments increased at a more rapid rate in the North over the 1962-72 period and have declined at a more rapid rate since 1972. From these aggregates, one might again infer an increasing concentration of high cost citizens in the North, and a considerably greater demand for increased school personnel—at least during the 1962-72 period. Though these results do not appear to provide strong support for a demand thesis, it is important to emphasize the very great diversity across states which is disguised in such an aggregate analysis. This diversity is particularly great in the case of the rate of increase in AFDC recipients.

During the 1975-77 period, the Northern Tier states have suffered a population stagnation and a reduction in enrollments which implies reduced expenditure demands, but an increase in welfare recipients and in the proportion of poor, suggesting increased expenditure

EXHIBIT 9

Indicators of Growth In Servicing Requirements

	Percent Increases							
	1962-1967		1967-1972		1972-1975		1975-1977	
	North	South	North	South	North	South	North	South
AFDC	44.1	33.4	152.3	115.6	12.8	4.7	−5.7	−8.2
Population	6.5	5.4	4.8	6.2	0.6	3.8	0.7	2.2
Enrollment	15.2	9.4	9.1	3.3	−2.4	−1.7	−1.5	−1.5
Public Employees	25.0	30.9	20.3	24.3	8.8	13.1	3.0	6.7
Per Capita Expenditures	42.8	51.8	73.4	64.5	34.5	38.0	17.2	18.6

Sources: Computed from Exhibits 3, 7 and U.S. Bureau of the Census, *Statistical Abstract of the United States: 1978* (1963, 1968, 1973, 1977), (Washington, D.C.: U.S. Government Printing Office, 1978); Bureau of the Census, *Public Employment in 1977* (1962, 1967, 1972, 1975), Series GE77, 5 (Washington, D.C.: U.S. Government Printing Office, 1978).

requirements. The situation in the South was almost exactly the reverse. As may be seen in Exhibit 9, state and local governments in the South increased their fiscal activity considerably more in terms of employment and only slightly more in terms of expenditures. The 1975-77 expenditure and employment growth rate differences would not appear to be explained by changes in the demand for services.

These results suggest that the explanations for expenditure increases in the two regions are at least partially to be found on the supply side, i.e., in terms of increases in the level of public employee compensation. As may be seen in Exhibit 10, the percentage increase in payroll per employee was higher in the northern than in the southern states over the 1962-72 period—this despite the fact that the capacity to finance such increases in northern states was declining. By the 1972-75 period, the rate of increase in average wages in the North had fallen below that in the South. This pattern continued for the 1975-77 period. The rates of increases in expenditures closely parallel increases in public employee compensation rates.

REVENUE GROWTH

According to the scenario above, the fisc in the northern states has expanded at about the same rate as that in the southern states, despite considerable differences in the growth of their respective economic and demographic bases. As a consequence, revenue effort

EXHIBIT 10

Growth In State And Local Government Employment Per Capita And Public Empoyee Wages: By Region

Region	Employment Per 10,000 Population				Payroll Per Employee			
				Percent Changes				
	1962-1967	1967-1972	1972-1975	1975-1977	1962-1967	1967-1972	1972-1975	1975-1977
NORTHERN TIER	17.6	14.9	8.1	2.2	28.8	38.3	21.8	12.4
East North Central	17.0	13.5	7.1	2.1	24.4	39.2	22.4	12.9
Middle Atlantic	24.1	14.1	7.9	0.6	28.8	40.1	24.0	10.8
New England	14.7	16.4	9.0	3.2	30.1	36.7	20.1	12.8
SOUTHERN TIER	24.2	17.1	8.9	4.3	27.2	34.3	26.9	14.8
South Atlantic	24.1	19.3	9.2	5.1	28.5	36.5	24.2	15.2
East South Central	23.9	17.5	7.7	4.1	27.0	34.1	29.2	14.4
West South Central	24.9	12.4	9.7	3.1	24.8	30.1	29.9	14.5

Source: U.S. Bureau of the Census, *Public Employment in 1977* (1962, 1967, 1972, 1975), Series GE77, 5 (Washington, D.C.: Government Printing Office, 1978).

in the Northern Tier states must have increased more rapidly, or the flow of federal aid to the northern states must have increased. The reality of an increase in revenue effort is borne out by a recent ACIR publication which attempts to classify states with reference to both the level and direction of tax effort.[23] Of the states classified as having high and rising levels of tax efforts, nine are in the Northern Tier and three are in the South.

A comparison of the growth in own source revenues to the growth in personal income shows a greater revenue-income elasticity[24] in the North in the 1967-72 period (see Exhibit 11). In the other three periods, however, these crude elasticities were not substantially different.

The presentation in Exhibit 12 disaggregates increases in state and local government revenue by source of increase. Southern states financed expenditure increases through the use of sales and income taxes while in the North the increments were derived relatively more from property taxes. Also noteworthy within the 1972-75 period was the substantial increase in the reliance on federal grants to finance expenditure increments in the Northern Tier.

This pattern of revenue increase may reflect the greater automatic responsiveness of tax systems in the South which rely more on sales and less on property taxes. While detailed comparisons are not readily available, it would seem reasonable to assume that relatively more of the revenue increase in the North was the result of discretionary changes in the tax system. Data for 1975-76 suggest that the rate and base changes in the income and sales taxes occurred with greater frequency in the North, especially among the harder pressed states.[25]

FISCAL ADJUSTMENTS TO DECLINE

Certain of the data above, e.g., Exhibit 8, suggest that the state and local sector has begun to cut back on their levels of activity. While it would be desirable to carry out an in-depth analysis of recent fiscal retrenchment, time and data constraints have precluded a full analysis of recent fiscal actions in the declining states. Nevertheless, it may be useful to consider briefly recent fiscal changes within New York State as possibly indicative of behavior in other declining states.[26] In the 1975-77 period full-time equivalent state and local employment in New York State declined by 5.2 percent while it grew by 3.8 percent in the rest of the nation.[27] Likewise, average public employee compensation grew by 10.1 percent in New York compared to 12.3 percent in the remainder of the nation during the same

EXHIBIT 11

Overall Responsiveness of Revenue To Economic Activity:

Change	Northern Tier				Southern Tier			
	1962-1967	1967-1972	1972-1975	1975-1977	1962-1967	1967-1972	1972-1975	1975-1977
Percent Increase in Revenues from Own Sources	46.6	84.8	28.9	21.4	56.8	75.5	39.7	22.8
Percent Increase in Personal Income	41.8	44.6	29.3	20.9	48.3	57.6	37.6	23.5
Own Source Revenue-Income Elasticity*	1.11	1.90	0.99	1.02	1.18	1.31	1.06	0.97
Percent Increase in Total Employment	16.7	7.6	1.9	6.4	24.0	18.7	7.2	7.5
Percent Increase in Population	6.5	4.8	0.6	0.7	5.4	6.2	3.8	2.2

*Percent Increase in Revenues from Own Sources divided by Percent Increase in Personal Income.

Source: Computed from sources used in Exhibits 1, 2, 3, and U.S. Bureau of the Census, *Government Finances in 1976-77* (1971-62, 1966-67, 1971-72, 1974-75), Series GF77, 5 (Washington, D.C.: U.S. Government Printing Office, 1977).

EXHIBIT 12

Increases In General Revenues of State and Local Governments

Region	1962-1967 Percent Increase due to			1967-1972 Percent Increase due to		
	Sales & Income Taxes	Property Taxes	Federal Aid	Sales & Income Taxes	Property Taxes	Federal Aid
NORTHERN TIER	21.0	22.6	19.5	22.6	25.5	19.5
East North Central	25.0	21.8	17.6	25.5	23.9	17.8
Middle Atlantic	24.4	22.8	18.6	24.9	24.0	20.4
New England	15.9	23.2	21.4	19.1	27.6	20.5
SOUTHERN TIER	19.3	14.2	26.6	25.4	11.0	23.5
South Atlantic	21.5	15.9	23.1	26.1	12.9	22.2
East South Central	21.0	9.5	31.1	27.1	7.9	26.0
West South Central	13.5	15.3	29.0	22.3	10.5	23.4

	1972-1975 Percent Increase due to			1975-1977 Percent Increase due to		
	Sales & Income Taxes	Property Taxes	Federal Aid	Sales & Income Taxes	Property Taxes	Federal Aid
NORTHERN TIER	33.0	21.3	31.0	31.5	18.2	29.8
East North Central	40.4	13.3	26.0	38.7	15.5	28.6
Middle Atlantic	34.8	20.4	26.9	36.9	19.5	27.0
New England	25.8	28.4	37.2	22.9	19.7	32.1
SOUTHERN TIER	31.1	10.5	28.5	28.7	12.6	29.2
South Atlantic	32.7	11.7	29.0	28.8	14.5	29.2
East South Central	31.2	8.3	28.5	33.3	9.6	30.5
West South Central	27.9	10.2	27.7	23.7	12.1	27.7

Source: U.S. Bureau of the Census, *Government Finances in 1976-1977* (1961-62, 1966-67, 1971-72, 1974-75) Series GF77, 5 (Washington, D.C.: U.S. Government Printing Office, 1977).

1975-77 time period.[28] This slower growth in compensation was accomplished, at least in part, through no scheduled wage increases at the state level during FY1975 and FY1977. This wage freeze followed a period of compensation growth that was greater than the rest of the nation in spite of the obvious long-term relative decline in the economic base of New York State.

The slowdown in the fiscal activity at the state level in New York is indicated by its growth rates in expenditures within state agencies of 7.5 percent (FY1975 to FY1976) and 2.3 percent (FY1976 to FY1977).[29] These growth rates were considerably less than the double-digit rates in the several preceding years.

Since grants to localities within New York constitute approximately 60 percent of its consolidated expenditures, it is also interesting to note that the growth in these grants has slowed considerably. Between FY1976 and FY1977, the growth was only 4.4 percent. This is extremely likely to have constraining effects upon the lower levels of government in the state.

On the revenue side there has been increasing pressure to provide tax relief to both individuals and business. Relatively large tax cuts that show up in the 1978 data are indicative of these efforts. While New York still has a distance to go in bringing these tax levels closer to the median for the rest of the nation (which, itself, has not been immune to such tax cut pressures), it does indicate a response to the overall decline in the economic base.

We did attempt to carry out several correlations between different measures of fiscal activity in the states analyzed here with the three measures of economic base. If there has been a reasonably widespread response to economic decline since 1975, one might expect that for the 1972-75 period correlations between growth in economic base and fiscal activity would be significantly smaller than correlations between the same set of variables for the 1975-77 period. The results did not, however, indicate such a response. While there were some minor alterations in these correlations, there were no strong indications that, indeed, the overall pattern of relationships between economic base and fiscal activity had altered greatly between the two periods. In part this is likely due to the heterogeneity of activities in the several states as well as to the fact that the growing states in the South also have held back their growth in expenditures to a rate less than the rate of increase in personal incomes.

IMPLICATIONS FOR PUBLIC POLICY

The basic dilemma faced by several of the declining states in the Northeast is that their public sector has become overdeveloped relative to financial capacity. As a result, tax burdens are thought to be too high, there is little additional public money to be devoted to what are thought to be serious city fiscal problems, fixed debt and pension committments are high, union compensation demands will likely parallel cost-of-living increments and there seems to be no short-term reversal of existing economic trends. To be sure, this pattern does not fit all state and local governments in the north-eastern and midwestern regions and likely describes some Southern metropolitan area governments. But the pattern tends to hold for many governments in the Northern Tier and tends not to hold for most in the Southern group.

While there may have been some recent responses to these trends, there still are policy issues associated with the retrenchment period. This is especially true for the income distributional implications of the response taken in the declining states. The strategies for dealing with these fiscal problems would seem to be of four types: reversal of the economic decline, both in the central cities and the region; assistance during the transition period; strengthening of the fiscal position of the poorest local jurisdications through a grants program and federal welfare assumption; and fiscal planning in the declining region to bring about a better balance between the size of the public sector and the size of the economic base available to support that public sector.

An alternative strategy would be to take no action to correct the fiscal problems of governments in the declining region. This argument would hold that market forces are already underway which are cor-recting regional disparities in income, employment and population; and that the regional disparities in public service levels also should narrow. Eventually, as the resource base continues to grow slowly, the public sector in the Northeast also will grow slowly. The problem with this line of reasoning is that shrinkage in the public sector in the Northeast will likely mean a cutting of service levels in those areas where expenditures are greatest—health, education and welfare. This may imply that much of the painful burden of the transition to a lower level of public services will be borne by lower income residents in the declining regions.

Given these strategies, there would seem to be five policy directions open: cut services, raise taxes, increase productivity, increase federal assistance, or improve the local economy. The first three are options for state and local government action while the last two require federal action.

STATE AND LOCAL GOVERNMENT OPTIONS

Increased productivity in the public sector is a favorite policy recommendation in that it resolves fiscal problems without requiring governments either to raise taxes or cut services. While there is clearly room for improved management at the local government level, large savings (relative to projected deficits) from increased productivity in the public sector is not a realistic expectation.[30]

Revenues might be increased through further increase in the effective tax rate. The argument against this is the possible retarding effect on economic development given that state and local government revenue effort in many of the northeastern and midwestern regions is already high relative to the South.

Service level reductions are the most likely route. While there will continue to be absolute cutbacks in some areas and reductions in the scope of some services, this will mostly take the form of services not expanding to accommodate increasing needs, and increasing unit cost of provision. This does not mean that expenditures will decline. Increasing wages and benefits can drive up expenditures by a significant amount, without raising service levels.

FEDERAL OPTIONS

The federal government could increase the flow of aid to the state to prop up the public sector during this period of decline. A program of increased aid during a transition period in which the state sought to balance its long-term spending expectations with its likely future economic growth would be a sane program. On the other hand, federal grants to maintain an overdeveloped public sector would only prolong the period of continuing annual fiscal crisis.

There are a number of federal policies that might be undertaken during the fiscal adjustment period—that period when the public sector in the North is moving to a lower level which is commensurate with its capacity to finance. One element of such fiscal reform would be a higher level of federal financing of public welfare. The removal of a substantial share of welfare costs from the declining states in the Northeast would free substantial resources for other uses.

A similar position might be taken with respect to regional development subsidies. Such subsidies would prolong the period of transition to a lower, but stable level of activity. The longer the period of this transition, the greater the uncertainty with respect to business investment and the greater the chance for a snowballing effect of the decline. Yet, if regional subsidies worked, they could have a strong positive effect on the finances of governments in the declining region. There are two caveats, however, even to the potentially favorable governmental finance effects. One is that the fiscal problems in the declining region are very much the fiscal problems of the central cities in those regions. Historically, these cities have not always shared in the economic growth of the region, and therefore it is not clear how much their fiscal positions would improve in the event the regional shifts slowed. A second and related caveat, is that the states in the declining region tend to be more heavily dependent on local property taxation which may make it difficult to fully capture increases in regional income and employment in the public sector. But the most important issue with respect to regional subsidies remains whether or not they induce any *net* improvement in private sector economic activity.

The fiscal problems of many Northern Tier states is that their public sectors are overdeveloped. The states' resource bases will no longer support the high level of public services provided in the state, unless tax rates are continuously increased. While shifts in population and economic activity are tending toward equalizing income across the country, the northern states have retained dominance in their relative national role in state and local fiscal activity. This can no longer be done. A downward transition must be recognized, and policy should center on selecting priorities in the adjustment of public service levels. With appropriate federal aid, this need not mean severe service cutbacks in all areas, but rather a slow growth in services while the rest of the nation catches up.

NOTES

*Larry Deboer and Linda Svetlik, graduate assistants in the Metropolitan Studies Program, compiled much of the data for this analysis. This paper is one result of a larger research project financed by the National Science Foundation (APR77-15730). The current paper extends and updates portions of the analysis contained in Bahl's "The Effects of Regional Shifts in Population and Economic Activity on the Finances of State and Local Governments: Implications for Public Policy," presented at the September, 1977 conference, *National Policy Towards Regional Change,* held at the University of Texas and revised in a paper prepared for the Southern Regional Growth Policies Board as "Regional Shifts in Economic Activity and Government Finances in Growing and Declining States."

1. See, for examples, William H. Miernyk, "The Northeast Isn't What it Used to Be," in *Balanced Growth for the Northeast* (New York State Senate, 1975); Lawrence K. Lynch and E. Evan Brunson, "Comparative Growth and Structures: The South and the Nation," in *The Economics of Southern Growth*, edited by E. Blaine Liner and Lawrence K. Lynch (Durham: The Southern Growth Policies Board, 1977): 11-34; and Roy Bahl and David Puryear, *Economic Problems of a Mature Economy*, Occasional Paper No. 27 (Metropolitan Studies Program, The Maxwell School, Syracuse University, April 1976).

2. See, for example, George E. Peterson, "Finance," in *The Urban Predicament*, ed. William Gorham and Nathan Glazer (The Urban Institute: Washington, D.C., 1976); and Roy Bahl, Bernard Jump, Jr. and Larry Schroeder, "The Outlook for City Fiscal Performance in Declining Regions," in *The Fiscal Outlook for Cities* (Syracuse, New York: Syracuse University Press, 1978).

3. Notable exceptions here are Richard P. Nathan and Paul R. Dommel, who in "Understanding Central City Hardship," (*Political Science Quarterly* Vol. 21, No. 1 (Spring 1976), argue a relationship between regional shifts and urban fiscal problems; Tom Muller, who argues that population decline is a reasonable proxy for fiscal distress in "The Declining and Growing Metropolis—A Fiscal Comparison," in *Post-Industrial America: Metropolitan Decline and Regional Job Shifts*, eds. George Sternlieb and James W. Hughes (New Brunswick, New Jersey: The Center for Urban Policy Research, Rutgers University, 1975): 197-220; and Roy Bahl, Alan Campbell and David Greytak, *Taxes, Expenditures and the Economic Base: Case Study of New York City* (New York, New York: Praeger Publishers, 1974).

4. In comparing the performance of the public and private sectors, between regions, there is the problem of selecting the appropriate "average". Assuming, as we do, that the arithmetic mean is a better measure of central tendency than is the median, there remains the choice of comparing the average value for the entire region and the average state performance. For example, in the case of per capita expenditures, the former would be $\dfrac{\Sigma E_i}{\Sigma E_i}$ and the latter, $\displaystyle\sum_{i=1}^{N} (\dfrac{E_i}{P})/N$ where E_i and P_i represent expenditures and population respectively both for the ith state among N in the region. The latter, the average state performance measure, has the disadvantage of giving the same weight to all states in determining the regional average and may be a misleading indicator if there are wide variations in population size within the same region. Nevertheless, our interest in this chapter is with fiscal jurisdictions, hence in the text we usually discuss the "average state" measure since it is more appropriate for our purposes; however both weighted and unweighted means are provided for the measures of economic base and fiscal activity.

5. Excluding the District of Columbia.

6. The states included in each region are enumerated in the first exhibit. The remaining exhibits report results only for the two tiers and their constituent regions. For the state-by-state breakdowns see Bahl, "Regional Shifts in Economic Activity and Government Finances in Growing and Declining States." Some authors have followed a procedure of excluding certain states in these regions on grounds that they are qualitatively different in terms of economic base. For example, Jusenius and Ledebur exclude Maine, Vermont and New Hampshire because the industrial bases of these states differ in kind and degree from the rest of the region. See C.L. Jusenius and L.C. Ledebur, *A Myth in the Making: The Southern Economic Challenge and the Northern Economic Decline* (Economic

Development Administration, U.S. Department of Commerce: Washington, D.C., November 1976), p. 2.

7. Jusenius and Ledebur, *A Myth in the Making*, pp. 3-5.

8. Michael R. Greenberg and Nicholas J. Valente, "Recent Economic Trends in the Major Northeastern Metropolises" in *Post-Industrial America: Metropolitan Decline and Inter-Regional Job Shifts*, George Sternlieb and James Hughes, eds. (New Brunswick: The Center for Urban Policy Research, Rutgers University, 1975), pp. 77-100.

9. Daniel Garnick, "The Northeast States in the Context of the Nation," in *The Declining Northeast*, pp. 145-159.

10. Congress of the United States, Congressional Budget Office, "Troubled Economies and the Distribution of Federal Dollars," (Washington, D.C.: U.S. Government Printing Office, August, 1977).

11. Bernard Weinstein and Robert Firestine, *Regional Growth and Decline in the United States* (New York: Praeger Publishers, 1978).

12. Jusenius and Ledebur, *A Myth in the Making*, pp. 1-5.

13. For some evidence, see Julie DaVanza, "U.S. Internal Migration: Who Moves and Why," in *Consequences of Changing U.S. Population*, Hearings before the Select Committee on Population, June 6, 1978, pp. 188-201.

14. D. Puryear, R. Bahl and S. Sacks, *Federal Grants: Their Effect on State and Local Expenditures, Employment Levels, Wage Rates* (Washington, D.C.: Advisory Commission on Intergovernmental Relations, February, 1977), Chapter 2.

15. Richard P. Nathan and Paul R. Dommel, "The Strong Sunbelt Cities and the Weak Cold Belt Cities," Hearings before the Subcommittee on the City, of the House Committee on Banking, Finance and Urban Affairs, *Toward A National Urban Policy*, 95th Congress (Washington, D.C.: U.S. Government Printing Office, 1977), pp. 19-26; and "Understanding Central City Hardship," *Political Science Quarterly*, Vol. 21, No. 1 (Spring 1976), pp. 61-62.

16. S. Sacks, *Trends in Metropolitan America*, Tables 4 and 10.

17. Vincent Marando, "The Politics of Metropolitan Reform," in *State and Local Government: The Political Economy of Reform*, Alan Campbell and Roy Bahl, eds. (New York: The Free Press, 1976), pp. 24-49.

18. Common municipal functions exclude education, hospitals and other variable functions as defined by the Census.

19. Muller, "The Declining and Growing Metropolis—A Fiscal Comparison," pp. 203-206.

20. For a good discussion of these measurement problems, see Bernard Jump, Jr., "Public Employment, Collective Bargaining and Employee Wages and Pensions," in *State and Local Government Finance and Financial Management* (Municipal Finance Officers Association, Washington, D.C., 1978), pp. 74-85.

21. David Greytak and Bernard Jump, Jr., "Inflation and Local Government Expenditures and Revenues: Method and Case Studies," *Public Finance Quarterly*,

22. R.G. Ehrenberg, "The Demand for State and Local Government Employees," *American Economic Review* 63, No. 3 (June 1973): 366-79; T.E. Borcherding and R.T. Deacon, "The Demand for Services of Non-Federal Governments," *American Economic Review* 62, No. 5 (December 1972): 891-901.

23. Advisory Commission on Intergovernmental Relations, *Measuring the Fiscal Blood Pressure of the States* (Washington, D.C.: U.S. Government Printing Office, 1977).

24. Revenue-income elasticity is the percent increase in revenue divided by the percent increase in personal income. A more rigorous measure of the revenue-income elasticity would require adjusting the revenue data levels for discretionary changes in both the rates or bases of the tax systems within the several states.

25. Advisory Commission on Intergovernmental Relations, *Significant Features of Fiscal Federalism*, 1976-77 Edition, Vol. II (Washington, D.C.: ACIR): Tables 34-37.

26. More specific analysis of the New York case is found in Roy Bahl, "Fiscal Retrenchment in a Declining State: The New York Case" paper presented to a HUD-sponsored *UCSB Conference on Tax Limitation,* December 14-15, 1978, University of California, Santa Barbara, California.

27. U.S. Bureau of the Census, Public Employment in 1975, 1976, 1977. We recognize that the special problems of New York City may unduly distract these changes; nevertheless, the change is considerable, especially in light of the long-term trends within New York State.

28. U.S. Bureau of the Census, Governmental Finances in 1974-1975, 1975-1976, 1976-1977.

29. All data from Comptroller of the State of New York, *Annual Report, 1977.*

30. A review of the issues surrounding productivity measurement and improvement is present in Jesse Burkhead and John P. Ross, *Productivity in the Local Government Sector,* (Lexington: D.C. Heath and Company, 1974).

SECTION III

Municipal Expenditures - Cause and Control

David Greytak and Donald Shepard - TAX LIMITS AND LOCAL EXPENDITURE LEVELS

INTRODUCTION

The idea and the fact of statewide legislated controls on the spending and taxing of local governments has a fairly long history in this country.[1] Historically the most common limitation imposed on local governments were rate limits which set maximums on the nominal rates at which the assessed value of property could be taxed. Limits of this variety have not been considered to be particularly binding for they could be easily avoided by the specifications of the value of the taxable base. Perhaps it has been the recognition of the ease of circumventing the intent of rate limits which underlies the fact that, of the forty-one states with limitations in effect in 1977, fourteen had adopted new legislation in the 1970s. For the most part, the recent enactments involve the imposition of the more stringent levy limits which establish the maximum revenue that can be raised through the taxation of property.[2]

In addition, four states have adopted full disclosure laws which require that the populus be informed of, and local governing bodies explicitly approve of, any increase in the tax levy. One state has established an "expenditure lid" which places a maximum on the annual growth in appropriations.[3] Whether this new legislation effectively restrains the increase in local government expenditures or the growth in public service levels is an open question for it generally does not preclude the cultivation of alternative sources of local government revenues, higher levels of intergovernmental aid or the transfer of the responsibility for some services to other governments. The range of possibilities give rise to a variety of research questions. A number of these are identified in the following section. Following that, the relation between limits and local government revenues and expenditures will be evaluated. The final section briefly summarizes the implications of this analysis.

LIMITS AND LOCAL GOVERNMENT EXPENDITURES/ TAX BURDENS

For the purposes here, four sets of questions are of interest. The first relates to the most general concern with the effectiveness of limits; that is, do limits reduce the growth in local government expenditures and property tax burdens. Despite the obvious import of this question, the volume of empirical research specifically focused on this issue is limited to two studies, one by Helen Ladd (1978) and the other by Michael Bell and Ronald Fisher of the Advisory Commission on Intergovernmental Relations (1977). Both verify that high levels of property taxation and rapid rates of expenditures increases are likely to lead to the imposition of new limits. However, only the ACIR study evaluated the impact of limits on expenditures and property taxes. Bell and Fisher conclude that local government expenditure levels in states with limits are roughly 6-to-eight percent below what they would be if there had been no limit.

Beyond this, ACIR's general findings indicate that limits are not associated with greater diversification in local revenue systems. The implication is one that coincides with the conclusion of an earlier (1962) ACIR study. That is, that limits cannot generally be associated with the extent to which local governments rely on the property tax as a revenue source. These findings in and of themselves would seem to imply that, while limits may be an effective means of imposing restraints on local government expenditures, their ability to reduce property tax burdens remains an open question.

The second area of concern has to do with the relation between limits on local governments and the role of state governments. Here the issue is whether limit-induced reductions in local government expenditures elict action on the part of state government. In this regard past research is limited to the ACIR study in which the relation between tax limits and combined state and local government expenditures was examined. The findings here, of no significant connection between these two variables, combines with the negative relation between limits and local expenditures to indicate compensatory action on the part of state governments. This, of course, is consistent with at least the initial reaction to Proposition 13 in California.

The third issue is whether the new tax limits more effectively restrain local governments than do old limits. Not surprisingly, this is an issue which has not been directly evaluated. However, the recent ACIR study does consider whether the type of limits which have been recently enacted, levy limits, are more effective than the older rate limits. The analysis indicates, although it does not specifically conclude, that levy limits are associated with somewhat lower levels of local expenditures. In addition, although not subject to specific discussion, ACIR's statistical finding seems to imply that rate but not levy limits lead to less reliance on property tax. Given these findings, it would seem reasonable to anticipate that the effects of new limits will differ from those of old limits.

The fourth and last concern here is to cast the above identified issues within the content of urban growth and decline. The research question at hand is whether limits affect state and local fiscal outcomes in the same fashion in growing and declining areas. This is an issue which does not appear to have been addressed nor empirically evaluated by past empirical studies.

LIMITS VERSUS WHO PAYS FOR LOCAL PUBLIC SERVICES

The issues raised in the previous section can be addressed in a general way by an examination of selected indicators of state and local government activity (Exhibit 1). Over the decade 1967-77, the picture is one of growing importance of state governments as a collector of state and local government revenues, a decline in the relative importance of the property tax as a source of local tax revenues and a growth in locally financed local government expenditures which has been only slightly greater than the growth in personal income.

EXHIBIT 1

Trends in State and Local Government Finances by State, Grouped According to Tax Limit [1]

	State Government Percentage of State and Local Tax Revenue			Property Taxes as a Percent of Local Tax Collections			Local Own Source General Expenditures as Percent of Personal Income [2]		
	1977	1967	Percentage Point Increase	1977	1967	Percentage Point Increase	1977	1967	Percentage Point Increase
All States	62.2	56.8	5.4	83.8	88.6	−4.8	6.48	6.43	.05
Non-Limit States[3]	58.6	54.9	3.7	90.2	94.5	−4.3	6.32	6.04	.28
All-Limit States[4]	63.4	57.8	5.6	82.1	87.2	−5.1	6.49	6.50	−.01
Old-Limit	63.7	58.9	4.8	80.1	86.3	−6.2	6.38	6.39	−.01
New-Limit[5]	62.8	55.4	7.4	86.2	89.0	−2.8	6.74	6.74	.00

1. Unweighted averages of states within each group
2. Total direct general expenditure minus federal and net state aid
3. Non-limit states are Connecticut, Delaware, Maine, Maryland, Massachusetts, New Hampshire, Rhode Island, Tennessee and Vermont
4. Old-limit refers to states whose limits were enacted before 1970 and were unaltered between 1970 and 1976. Those with rate limit states are Alabama, Arkansas, Georgia, Idaho, Illinois, Kentucky, Louisiana, Michigan, Mississippi, Missouri, Nebraska, Nevada, New Mexico, New York, North Carolina, North Dakota, Oklahoma, Pennsylvania, South Carolina, South Dakota, Texas, Utah, West Virginia and Wyoming. Those with levy limit states are Arizona, Colorado, Oregon. For a discussion of these classifications see ACIR, 1977. New-limit states are those which enacted new or altered limits and old-limits during the period 1970-71; those with full disclosure laws are Florida, Hawaii, Montana and Virginia.

Sources: Advisory Commission on Intergovernmental Relations, *Significant Features of Fiscal Federalism, 1978-79 Edition,* M-115 (Washington, D.C.: U.S. Government Printing Office, May 1979), Tables 32 and 39.

Advisory Commission on Intergovernmental Relations, *State Limitations of Local Taxes & Expenditures,* A-64 (Washington, D.C.: U.S. Government Printing Office, February 1977).

U.S. Bureau of the Census, *Governmental Finances in 1976-77, 1966-67,* Series GF 77, 67, No. 5 (Washington, D.C.: U.S. Government Printing Office, 1978, 68).

Underlying these generalities are differences that are consistent with the hypothesis that limits make a difference. In particular, states without limits lagged behind the national trend of decreasing reliance of local governments on property taxes and increasing state participation in the raising of state and local revenues. Perhaps of greater importance is the rather marked difference between limit and non-limit states in the growth of own source expenditures relative to income and in the reliance of local governments on property taxes. The fact that on the average, local expenditures relative to personal income declined slightly in limit states while increasing in non-limit states would seem to constitute a prima facie evidence of the effectiveness of tax limits. The attendant growth in state government role as a revenue raiser, being larger in limit than non-limit states, is consistent with a compensatory response on the part of state government to local tax limit.

Just as there are differences between limit and non-limit states, so too are there differences among states with limits. Most importantly, the old-limit states show a decrease in reliance on the property tax which exceeds that of new-limit states and a slower growth in state revenue share than do new-limit states. However, in terms of the change in the relation between local expenditures and personal income, new and old-limit states do not differ much. While these data would seem to imply that new and old limits have an operative impact on local revenue systems which differ, it is not clear that the difference extends to local expenditures.

Suggestive as these findings may be, they must be considered tentative for they are based on averages of statewide aggregates. Given our concern with urban growth and decline, a more disaggregate approach is desirable. Thus the analysis turns to a consideration of the relation between limits and the structure of local revenues in the nation's larger urban areas.[4] The analysis is based on the growth of property taxes, state aid and other taxes as measured by simple income elasticities (Exhibit 2, Part A). As areas have been classified by type of limit, significant differences (Exhibit 2, Part B) in the elasticities supports the proposition than tax limits affect the composition and growth of local government revenues.

The mean income elasticity of property tax revenues is highest for no-limit areas and the difference between it and that for all limit areas is significant. While this would seem to verify the hypothesis that limits do affect the growth in property taxation, such a conclusion would be premature for there are significant differences among the various limit classifications. Most importantly, property tax elasticity in no-limit and old-limit areas do not appear to be

EXHIBIT 2

Income Elasticities of Selected Local Revenues,
Counties Classified by Limit and Population Growth, 1971-76

A.   Means and Standard Deviations (in parentheses)

		Income Elasticity of:		
Group	Sample Size	Property Tax	State Aid	Other Taxes
No-Limit	31	1.14 (.40)	1.72 (.91)	1.38 (.93)
All-Limit	92	.92 (.43)	1.80 (.97)	1.86 (.37)
New-Limit	39	.79 (.46)	1.97 (1.22)	1.66 (1.03)
Old-Limit	53	1.01 (.39)	1.67 (.72)	2.00 (1.57)
Growing	83	.99 (.39)	1.55 (.69)	1.57 (1.07)
Declining	40	.92 (.51)	2.25 (1.23)	2.09 (1.62)

B.   Two Group Analysis of Variance for Equality of Means

	Income Elasticity of:			
Groupings Compared	Property Tax	State Aid	Other Taxes	Simultaneous Equality [1]
No-Limit and All-Limit	6.37 (.01)	.17 (.68)	3.28* (.07)	3.55* (.025)
No-Limit and New-Limit	11.27* (.001)	.96 (.33)	1.43 (.24)	4.27* (.025)
No-Limit and Old-Limit	2.08 (.15)	.07 (.79)	4.06* (.05)	2.38* (.10)
New-Limit and Old-Limit	6.36* (.01)	2.26 (.14)	1.39 (.24)	2.84* (.05)
Growing and Declining	.73 (.39)	16.33* (.0001)	4.50* (.04)	6.53* (.001)

The figures not in parentheses are the F-statistics under the hypothesis of equality of means. Figures in parentheses are the probability of getting an F-statistic larger than that reported, given that the hypothesis holds.

EXHIBIT 2 (Continued)

1 Simultaneous equality refers to the joint hypothesis that all three means are simultaneously equal between two groups.
* Means are statistically different at a .10 level of significance.

Sources: U.S. Bureau of the Census, *County and City Data Book, 1977, A Statistical Abstract Supplement,* Table 2, (Washington, D.C.: U.S. Government Printing Office, 1979).
U.S. Bureau of the Census, *Local Government Finances in Selected Metropolitan Areas and Large Counties: 1975-76, 1970-71,* Series GF-76, 71, No. 6, (Washington, D.C.: U.S. Government Printing Office), Tables 2 and 5.
Advisory Commission on Intergovernmental Relations, *State Limitations of Local Taxes & Expenditures,* A-64 (Washington, D.C.: U.S. Government Printing Office, February 1977).

significantly different. Alternatively, the property tax elasticity in new-limit areas is lower than that in no-limit and old-limit areas and these differences are significant. The implication is that between 1971 and 1976 new limits appear to have effectively restrained property tax growth while there is no strong indication that property tax growth in no-limit and old-limit areas differs to a significant degree.

The case with the state aid is much different. Although the state aid income elasticities vary in an expected way, these variations are not significantly different in a statistical sense.

Turning to other taxes, the income elasticity is highest for old-limit states, and the difference between it and that in no-limit states is significant. For new-limit states, the elasticity falls between that of no-limit and old-limit areas but is significantly different from neither. These findings, in conjunction with the data in Exhibit 1, are consistent with the hypothesis that limits lead to the cultivation of alternative local government revenue sources.

While the variations in these elasticities provide support for the hypothesis that new limits are more stringent than old limits and a tentative indication that limits may underlie a diversification in local revenue systems, they provide but an indication of the full effect of limits. In this regard, the test for the simultaneous equality of all three measures between pairs of groups provides a more comprehensive test.[5] The fact that this test indicates there is significant difference between all areas supports the conclusion that tax limits affect the composition and growth of local revenues.

Thus, to this point, the analysis lends verification to the contention that limits affect local fiscal performance and that new limits are more stringent than old limits.

Turning to the issue of population growth and decline, comparisons of the property tax, state aid and other tax elasticities yield a similar conclusion: the revenue composition and revenue increases of growing areas differ significantly from that of declining areas. However, the property tax elasticities do not differ significantly. Thus it is the large and significant differences in the state aid and other tax elasticities which produce this finding.

Although showing that the structure and growth of local revenues are affected by tax limitation and by population growth gives some support to the view that tax limits and growth affect local government expenditures, it does so in an extremely tentative way. The purpose of the next section is to design a model for explaining local government expenditure increases and to test for the expenditure effects of tax limits and population change.

LIMITS, POPULATION CHANGE AND LOCAL GOVERNMENT EXPENDITURES

The objective of this section is to investigate the relation between tax limits, population change and local government expenditures. The model developed here is a variant of the "determinants approach" traditionally employed in the analysis of state and local government expenditures.

Although estimation of a determinant relationship is typically done in per capita amounts, the model used here will be estimated in the aggregate, using percent changes. The reason for this break with the traditional approach is two-fold and related to the fact that the use of per capita amounts does not stem directly from the theoretical formulation but from the use of population as a scale factor to correct the heteroscedasticity and to reduce the importance of extreme values. An assumption inherent in the use of population as a scale factor (and one which has received little discussion in the determinants literature) is that per capita expenditures are unrelated (ceteris paribus) to population size.

This has been termed the homogeneity assumption and when applied to a model using percent changes, can be expressed as: if population increases at the same percentage as all other independent variables, then the resulting percent change in per capita expenditures is zero. For example, if income was the only variable explaining per capita expenditures, then an equal percentage change in aggregate income and population (leaving per capita income un-changed) would result in no change in per capita expenditures.

A failure of this assumption may lead to biased estimates of the coefficients of the original theoretical model, the extent of which depends on the variation and covariation of the variables in the model, plus population. As there is a substantial body of literature which has verified the existence of an empirical relation between per capita expenditures and population, interpretations of coef-ficients of a model estimated on per capita values would be dif-ficult. In addition, Kah and Meyer (1955) point out that while this homogeneity assumption may be appropriate when analyzing cross-sectional differences at a point in time, its use in time series analysis is questionable. Given that the study here is concerned with the temporal phenomena of growth and decline, these considerations imply the use of an alternative to the traditional determinants model.

These implications are verified by the following considerations. Using E to denote local government expenditures and for expository purposes assuming there are four independent variables, X_1, X_2, X_3 and X_4 respectively, a general form constant elasticity determin-ants model can be expressed as

$$(I) \quad E = \beta_0 X_1^{\beta_2} X_2^{\beta_3} X_3^{\beta_4} X_4^{\beta_5}$$

For the sake of clarity in the interpretation of the parameter estimates and in the use of population as an explanatory variable, it is useful to compare equation (I) with its formulation in per capita terms.

$$(II) \quad \frac{E}{P} = \beta_0 \left(\frac{X_1}{P}\right)^{\beta_1} \left(\frac{X_2}{P}\right)^{\beta_2} \left(\frac{X_3}{P}\right)^{\beta_3} \left(\frac{X_4}{P}\right)^{\beta_4}$$

Taking natural logarithms of both sides of this expression, it first reduces to

$$(III) \quad \ln\left(\frac{E}{P}\right) = \ln\beta_0 + \beta_1 \ln\left(\frac{X_1}{P}\right) = \beta_2 \ln\left(\frac{X_2}{P}\right) + \beta_3 \ln\left(\frac{X_3}{P}\right) + \beta_4 \ln\left(\frac{X_4}{P}\right)$$

and then further to

$$(IV) \quad \ln E = \ln \beta_0 + \beta_1 \ln X_1 + \beta_2 \ln X_2 + \beta_3 \ln X_3 + \beta_4 \ln X_4 + (1 - (\beta_1 + \beta_2 + \beta_3 + \beta_4)) \ln P$$

Alternatively, population could have been introducted directly into the model, i.e.,

$$(V) \quad E = \beta_0 X_1^{\beta_1'} X_2^{\beta_2'} X_3^{\beta_3'} X_4^{\beta_4'} P^{\beta_5'}$$

Taking natural logarithms of both sides gives

$$(VI) \quad \ln E = \ln \beta_0' + \beta_1' \ln X_1 + \beta_2' \ln X_2 + \beta_3' \ln X_3 + \beta_4' \ln X_4 + \beta_5' \ln P$$

At this point, it is desirable to discuss two issues. The first relates to the problem of spurious correlation and the second concerns the interpretation of the coefficient of the population term. Equation III is expressed in (percent changes of) per capita amounts and could possibly be adopted to handle population change by the addition of $\beta_5 \ln P$ to the right hand side.[6] As was stated earlier, the estimates $(\beta_1', \ldots \beta_4')$ from the estimation of this formation may not be the same as those $(\beta_1', \ldots \beta_4')$ from VI if the homogeneity assumption does not hold. Comparing equation (IV) and (VI), the homogeneity assumption holds if

$$(VII) \quad \beta_5' = 1 - (\beta_1' + \beta_2' + \beta_3' + \beta_4'),$$

or, alternatively,

$$(VIII) \quad \beta_1' + \beta_2' + \beta_3' + \beta_4' + \beta_5' = 1$$

Stated in words, a one percent increase in all independent variables leads to a one percent increase in expenditures, or, if per capita amounts of all four explanatory variables remain unchanged, then so does per capita expenditures.

If the homogeneity assumption is rejected then the sign of the independent effect of population on per capita expenditures is given by the sign of

$$(IX) \quad \beta_5' - (1 - (\beta_1' + \beta_2' + \beta_3' + \beta_4')).$$

If the value of (IX) is positive, then an increase in population, holding per capita amounts of the other explanatory variables constant, would increase per capita expenditures. A negative sign would imply an inverse relationship between population and per capita expenditures.

The foregoing clearly indicates that in the analysis of the determinants of local government expenditure increases, an estimation model of the form of equation VI is preferable to the more common form, i.e., equation III.

In the empirical analysis which is to follow, the relation between local government own source expenditures and their determinants is specified as log-linear (equation IV). As the variables are defined in terms of percent changes between two points in time, the coefficients (i.e., the β's) are the partial elasticities of own expenditures and with respect to the independent variables. The observations on which the regressions are estimated are 123 counties with populations greater than 300,000 in 1975. The analysis is of the growth of own source expenditures in the period 1971 to 1976.

The problem of functional responsibilities arises in all cross-sectional analyses of local governments. That is, the responsibility for providing municipal services within an area may be met by one or more local governments and the extent of state responsibility varies between states. The two methods most commonly used for handling this problem of fiscal responsibility are 1) the analysis of common functions, and 2) the use of counties as a unit of analysis. It is the second of these methods which is used here, the implicit assumption being that the local governments within a county act as a unit. This permits combining expenditures on all functions, allowing for differences in state responsibility by the use of an appropriate independent variable. The analysis is restricted therefore, by the additional assumptions that expenditures (and aid) can be meaningfully aggregated between functions, while separate relations for each function may well exist.

The variables in the analysis are

E = Total local direct expenditure net of state aid and federal aid

X_1 = Net state aid to local governments

X_2 = Net federal aid to local governments

X_3 = Personal Income

X_4 = State expenditures

P = Population

Observations are in terms of percent changes in the selected variables between the fiscal years 1971 and 1976. Using ln to denote percentage change, the basic estimating equation is:[7]

$$\ln E = \ln \beta_0 + \beta_1 \ln X_1 + \beta_2 \ln X_2 + \beta_3 \ln X_3 + \beta_4 \ln X_4 + \beta_5 \ln P.$$

The expected signs of the coefficients, are as follows. The coefficients of the aid variables may be positive or negative, depending on whether aid is stimulative or substitutive. The coefficient of the income term is expected to be positive; greater than, or less than one depending upon whether local services are a superior or a normal good. The coefficient for state expenditures will be negative if state expenditures are, on the net, a substitute for local expenditures. It may be positive if state expenditure is complementary to local expenditures, or, if states exhibit control over local expenditures to keep their growth in line with the growth of state expenditures.

With respect to the adjusted population coefficient ($\beta_5 - (1 - (\beta_1 + \beta_2 + \beta_3 + \beta_4))$), if the sign of this term is positive, then an increase in population, holding per capita amounts of other explanatory variables constant, would increase per capita expenditures, while a decrease in population would decrease per capita expenditures. A negative sign would imply the opposite. It may be reasonable to expect that this expression is not significantly different from zero with respect to growing communities and less than zero with respect to declining communities.[8]

The effects of growth and decline as well as the impacts of new and old limits are evaluated by separate estimation of the model described above for subsets of the observations differentiated by their limit and population change characteristics.

The findings of the regression analyses are presented in Exhibits 3 and 4. Of particular importance are the mean square errors (MSE) listed for each grouping (Exhibit 3) along with the F-test for the significance of the regression equation. Immediately apparent is the fact that expenditure growth in non-limit areas appears to be independent of the determinants (F-test not significant at any reasonable level of significance). This finding would seem to lend support to those who argue that in the absence of explicit constraints, local government expenditures will grow independent of constituent demands. Moreover, the fact that local government expenditures are significantly related to the identified determinants in areas with limits lends evidence to those who would argue that tax limits are necessary if expenditure growth is to be tied to voter preferences.

EXHIBIT 3

Summary Statistics for Regression Analysis, By Group According to Limit, Population Change

	Sample Size	Means Square Error	F	Pr>F	R²
No-Limit Counties	31	456.6	1.36	.27	.21
Growing	21	387.3	.69	.64	.19
Declining	10	803.8	.56	.73	.41
Limit Counties (All)	92	643.4	10.10	.0001	.37
Growing	62	743.9	4.88	.001	.30
Declining	30	328.1	5.41	.002	.53
Old-Limit Counties	53	663.7	7.16	.0001	.43
Growing (I)[1]	36	716.3	4.84	.002	.45
Declining (II)[1]	17	312.8	5.25	.01	.70
New-Limit Counties	39	598.7	4.29	.0004	.39
Growing	26	758.3	1.52	.23	.27
Declining (III)[1]	13	108.1	6.29	.02	.82

MSE is the estimate of the variance of the disturbance term.
F-test here is for significance of regression equation.
1. Further results for these groups given in Exhibit 4.

Source: See Exhibit 4.

The analysis also suggests a difference between growing and declining areas. For all areas with limits, the variance in error terms is greater (higher MSE) for growing than declining areas, and in new-limit areas the regressions are insignificant for growing areas.[9] This, coupled with the fact that the proportion of variation explained is generally lower for growing areas, indicates that growing and declining areas, whether classified by limit or no-limit, should be considered separately.[10] That is to say, the relation between expenditure growth and its determinants depends on the nature of population change, the existence of a limit and whether the limit is new or old.

Exhibit 4 contains the additional regression results for old-limit/growing, old-limit/declining, and new-limit/declining counties. For areas in old-limit states which experienced a decrease in population, the only estimated elasticity significantly different from zero is that of state expenditures, indicating by its negative sign a substitution of state for local expenditures. For declining areas, there are large differences in the coefficients for new-limit and old-limit areas. For

EXHIBIT 4

Regression Results[1] for Selected Groups of Counties, Percent Change in Own Source Expenditures, (1971-76)

A. Estimated Coefficients[1] and Pr > T (in parentheses)

	Intercept	State Aid	Federal Aid	Personal Income	State Expenditure	Population
			Percent Change In:			
I. Old-Limit, Growing	105.28	.02	−.00	.35	−1.02*	2.02
	(.05)	(.88)	(.68)	(.69)	(.02)	(.22)
II. Old-Limit, Declining	−33.97	−.25	−.02	2.08*	.47	.88
	(.51)	(.33)	(.33)	(.01)	(.40)	(.59)
III. New-Limit, Declining	65.08	−.97	−.01	−1.94	1.00*	5.90*
	(.19)	(.36)	(.68)	(.11)	(.00)	(.02)

B. Test of Homogeneity Assumption

	Group (As Noted Above)		
	I	II	III
Point Estimate for the independent effect of population	.36	2.15	3.87*
F-statistic for null hypothesis: $\beta_1 + \beta_2 + \beta_3 + \beta_4 + \beta_5 = 1$	.17	1.83	6.10
Pr > F	.68	.20	.04

1. Other statistics reported in Exhibit 3.
* Coefficient different from zero at .05 level of significance.

Sources: U.S. Bureau of the Census, *Governmental Finances in 1975-76, 1970-71*, Series GF 76, 71, No. 5 (Washington, D.C.: U.S. Government Printing Office, 1977, 72).

U.S. Bureau of the Census, *County and City Data Book, 1977 A Statistical Abstract Supplement* Table 2. (Washington, D.C.: U.S. Government Printing Office, 1978).

U.S. Bureau of the Census, *Local Government Finances in Selected Metropolitan Areas and Large Counties: 1975-76, 1970-71, Series GF-76, 71, No. 6, Tables 2 and 5.* (Washington, D.C.: U.S. Government Printing Office).

Advisory Commission on Intergovernmental Relations, *State Limitations of Local Taxes & Expenditures A-64* (Washington, D.C.: U.S. Government Printing Office, February 1977).

old-limit areas the estimated income elasticity is significantly positive, while others are not significantly different from zero at the .90 level. For new-limit areas, the state expenditure elasticity is positive and equal to its expected value equal to 1.00. Part B of Exhibit 4 shows statistics relevant to the test of the homogeneity assumption. They show that this assumption can only be rejected (at .90 level) for new-limit areas with declining populations. For this group, the adjusted coefficient is significantly positive.

CONCLUSION

The principal findings of this analysis, tentative as they may be, are that limits tend to restrain local government revenue and expenditure growth. The indication is that new-limits which, for the most part, have been levy rather than rate limits, have had a more stringent effect on local governments. As would be expected, this effect of new limits is most apparent in the relatively slow growth of property tax revenues. These findings confirm those of past studies (ACIR, 1977). Beyond this, the analysis here indicates that limits are associated with local government cultivation of nonproperty tax revenue sources, i.e., revenue diversification, but provides no confirmation for the hypothesized limit induced increase in state aid to local government. These findings are contrary to the implications of the earlier study which addressed this issue (ACIR, 1977).

In addition, the findings of this analysis lend at least some support to the following propositions. First, during the years 1971-to-1976, local own source expenditures in counties without limits increased at a rate not associated with the demand factors commonly used in studies of local government expenditure determinates. This supports the basic tenets of the tax-payer revolt, casting additional doubt on the efficacy of the process by which consumer-voter preferences are translated into local service levels.

Second, for localities with tax limits, the effect of such limits on linking own source expenditures with demand factors and/or affecting the response of expenditures to these factors depends on the age of the limit and on whether the county has had a population increase or decrease. For counties with increasing population, old-limits have the effect of strengthening the relationship between expenditures and demand factors, while new-limits in growing areas are shown to have been ineffective at doing the same. This may imply that new-limits in growing areas restrain expenditures to a growth lower than, and independent of, what the demand factors indicate. For declining areas with old-limits, the relationship between expenditures and income appears to be strongly positive. An interesting implication of this is that, once they are adjusted to, old-limits in declining areas help maintain a level of expenditure more in line with demand.[11]

For the group of counties with new-limits and decreases in population, it appears that tax limits may have had the effect of establishing a closer link between decreases in population (decreases in tax base) and decrease in own source expenditures. This result may be regarded as a mixed blessing as a decrease in expenditures may reflect either a decrease in service levels or a decrease in costs.

In sum, the analysis here provides tentative indications of the effectiveness of tax limits. However, it also indicates that this effectiveness is conditioned by the type of limit and may differ depending on whether population has been growing or declining. What these findings indicate most clearly are the distinct possibilities that limits of whatever variety will have affects which are conditioned by the structure and performance of the local economy.

An earlier version of the paper was presented at the Twenty-Sixth North American Meetings of the Regional Science Association, Los Angeles, California, November 9-11, 1979.

NOTES

1. Generally the academic as well as popular discussion of tax limits has focused on limits related to the raising of revenues for the funding of general purpose expenditures. In addition there exist limits related to the raising of revenues for the purpose of debt service. The variety and chronology of tax and expenditure limitations has received extensive consideration in the publications of the Advisory Commission on Intergovernmental Relations. See ACIR (1977) and their previous publications cited therein.

2. States adopting levy limit type legislation are Alaska, California, Indiana, Iowa, Kansas, Minnesota, Ohio, Washington and Wisconsin.

3. The four states which have adopted full disclosure laws are Florida, Hawaii, Montana and Virginia, and New Jersey has imposed expenditure limitation. For a discussion of the specifics of these new limits, see ACIR (1977).

4. The data discussed in this section pertain to all local governments in counties with a 1975 population greater than 300,000 with the exception of those counties which compose New York City and Honolulu. Interarea differences in the assignment of revenue and expenditure functions and the overlapping nature of local governments preclude the use of cities as the units of analysis.

5. This test for simultaneous equality is identical to the F-test for a regression using all three measures as independent variables to discriminate between

two groups (i.e., linear probability model with dummy independent variable).

6. Compared with the results given later in Exhibits 3 and 4, the estimations of this alternative specification yield lower R^2's and regression F statistics, while the coefficients for the independent variables (excluding the population term) were only slightly different. These differences in coefficients were greatest in the case where the hypothesis of homogeneity (described later) was rejected.

7. Implicit in the use of this model is the assumption that previous to the population change, expenditures per capita were at an "equilibrium" level given per capita amounts of the independent variables and no lags are involved in the response of expenditures. Since percent changes in aggregate values are used (instead of actual changes), there is no a priori reason to believe that the estimation formulated here will be prone to the problem of heteroscedasticity or extreme values. There is in fact more reason to believe, based on previous studies, that the use of percent changes in per capita amounts would lead to heteroscedastic or non-normal disturbances.

8. These expectations are based on the assumptions that there are no significant economies of scale and that the supply of public services is relatively elastic as service levels are increasing and inelastic, due to the demands of existing capital and labor unions, as service levels decrease. For a discussion of the factors which lead to this expectation, see Peterson (1976).

9. The variances of the error terms are significantly different between the groupings: old-limit growing and old-limit declining; new-limit declining and old-limit declining. Also, as noted above, the model does not explain a significant proportion of the variation in expenditure growth for new-limit, growing areas.

10. The results of the usual statistical tests (e.g., Chow test) for the equality of the functional relationship between two groups (in this case, growing and declining counties) are not appropriate in the presence of the significant difference between variances of the error terms in the regression in the two groups (heteroscedasticity) or a high degress of multicollinearity within them (see Maddala [9, 1977], p. 199). This being the case, apparently large and significant differences in the sizes of coefficients will be used to further justify the separation into subgroups prior to further interpretation of coefficients, etc.

11. This follows from an income elasticity close to what would be expected and the goodness of fit of the regression model for old-limit declining areas.

REFERENCES

Advisory Commission on Intergovernmental Relations. *State Limitations on Local Taxes and Expenditures,* Report A-64. Washington, D.C.: U.S. Government Printing Office, February 1977.

Advisory Commission on Intergovernmental Relations. *State Constituional and Statutory Restrictions on Local Taxing Powers,* A-14. Washington, D.C.: U.S. Government Printing Office, October 1962.

Bahl, Roy. "Studies on Determinants of Public Expenditures: A Review," in Selma J. Mushkin and John F. Cotton, *Functional Federalism: Grants-in-Aid and PPB Systems.* Washington, D.C.: State-Local Finances Project of the George Washington University, 1968, pp. 184-207.

Beck, Samuel H. "A Political Scientist's View of Fiscal Federalism," in *The Political Economy of Fiscal Federalism,* Willace E. Oates, Ed. Lexington, Mass.: D.C. Heath and Company, 1977, pp. 21-46.

Bell, Michael and Ronald C. Fisher. "State Limitations on Local Taxing and Spending Powers: Comment and Re-evaluation," *National Tax Journal,* XXXI, No. 4.

Fox, William F., J.M. Stam, W.M. Godsey, and S.D. Brown. "Economics of Size in Local Government: An Annotated Bibliography," Rural Development Research Report No. 9. Washington, D.C.: U.S. Department of Agriculture, Economics Statistics and Cooperative Service.

Friedman, Milton J. "The Limitations of Tax Limitations," *Policy Review* (Summer 1978), reprinted in Sheldon D. Englemayer and Robert J. Wagman, *The Taxpayer's Guide to Effective Tax Revolt.* New York: Dale Books, 1978, pp. 264-269.

Kah, Edwin and John R. Meyer. "Correlation and Regression Estimates When Data are Ratios," *Econometrics* (October 1955), pp. 400-416.

Ladd, Helen F. "An Economic Evaluation of State Limitations on Local Taxing and Spending Powers," *National Tax Journal,* XXXI (March 1978), pp. 1-18.

————. "State Limitations on Local Taxing and Spending Powers: A Response." *National Tax Journal,* XXXI, 4 (December 1978), pp. 397-398.

Maddala, G.S., *Econometrics.* New York: McGraw-Hill, Inc. 1977.

Peterson, George E. "Finance," in *The Urban Predicament,* William Gorham and Nathan Glazer, eds. Washington, D.C.: The Urban Institute, 1976, pp. 35-118.

Helen F. Ladd - MUNICIPAL EXPENDI-TURES AND THE RATE OF POPU-LATION CHANGE

INTRODUCTION

The decline of many old industrial cities in the Northeast and the rapid growth of cities in the Southwest have forcefully drawn attention to the fiscal implications of population change.[1] Although the major urban areas receive most of the attention, other smaller cities confront many of the same issues. This paper focuses on these smaller cities with the specific purpose of determining the impact of population change on per capita local public expenditures. Since the analysis is limited to communities in metropolitan areas within a single state, population change measures can be embedded in a fully specified local public expenditure model; we can therefore isolate the expenditure effects of population shifts from the effects of other factors influencing demand for local public services.[2]

In the following section, we hypothesize that per capita local public expenditures are a U-shaped function of the rate of population change. That is, expenditures per capita will be highest for the most rapidly declining cities and towns; will fall as the rate of population decline slows, reaching a minimum at a positive rate of population growth; and will rise again in rapidly growing cities. To test this hypothesis, we performed a multivariate cross-section regression analysis, based on 1975-1976 non-school expenditures in Massachusetts cities and towns. The major findings are reported in the final section of this paper.

THE BASIC HYPOTHESIS

We expect communities experiencing absolute population decline to spend more per capita for public services than otherwise similar but stable communities. The public good character of many city services means that the benefits received by current users vary more with the size of the facility than with the number of users. Consequently, an expenditure reduction commensurate with the fall in city population would lower the benefits received by remaining residents. As a city's population decreases, therefore, elected officials find it difficult to reduce expenditures proportionately. These political problems of cutting services are exacerbated to the extent that the population outmigration is associated with a high level of private sector unemployment, thereby leaving to the public sector the responsibility of providing jobs.

In addition, certain expenses such as debt service and maintenance for roads, sewers and city buildings do not decrease as the population decreases; these costs are simply spread over a smaller population. This particular problem is aggravated in older declining cities where antiquated capital stocks require larger maintenance expenditures. A second type of fixed expense, pension payments to retired municipal workers, also may have a serious impact on expenditures in a declining community. To the extent that pension liabilities incurred in previous years were not fully funded, current residents must pay part of the costs of the public services enjoyed by city residents in the past. The burden of these uncontrollable costs can be substantial in declining cities.

Moreover, as people migrate out of the city, the vacant and abandoned buildings they leave behind increase the probability of fire and vandalism. To provide a constant level of protection to remaining residents, cities may thus need to increase expenditures on police and fire fighting services. If the city's decline also results in a shift toward a more dependent population, increased per capita expenditures may again be necessary just to maintain service levels. In both cases, higher per capita expenditures reflect the changed relationship between the public sector inputs—city expenditures on public services—and public sector outputs—the things of primary interest to citizen consumers.

A community experiencing positive, though limited, population growth may confront some of these same problems, particularly if some neighborhoods of the city are losing population while others are gaining; if the city has an antiquated capital stock; or if the population mix is changing toward the poor and the elderly. Unlike declining areas, however, these cities can spread fixed expenses over a slowly increasing rather than decreasing population. Hence, we expect slowly growing cities to have lower per capita expenditures than declining cities.

Communities with moderate growth rates are likely to have the lowest per capita expenditures. For some of the same reasons that per capita expenditures are high in declining cities, they may be low in growing areas: population growth may not require proportionate increases in expenditures to maintain service levels; fixed expenses can be spread over a larger population; and the relation between public sector inputs and outputs may be more favorable than in other types of communities. Rapidly growing communities, in contrast, may have relatively high expenditures per capita, reflecting the adjustment problems associated with increasing the capital stock and raising service levels in anticipation of continued growth.

These considerations lead to the hypothesis that the effect of population change on per capita public expenditures is U-shaped, with the minimum expenditure occurring at a moderate rate of population growth. Since the appropriate statistical test requires that we control for other factors affecting per capita expenditures (especially those that might be correlated with population change), the following section specifies a full model of local public expenditures.

LOCAL PUBLIC EXPENDITURE MODEL

Our local public expenditure model is based on individual utility maximization behavior.[3] This model implies that, within a particular community, the public service levels residents desire vary with their income or wealth, their tax prices and their preferences for public services. To translate residents' conflicting demands for services into a single community demand function, we assume majority rule; in general, the effective demand is thus the level demanded by the voter desiring the median quantity of the public service.[4]

We estimate a model of this type for 1975-76 non-school expenditures across 103 Massachusetts cities and towns having more than 10,000 residents in 1975.[5] Because local municipalities in Massachusetts have responsibility for most public functions, cities and towns are the appropriate units for observing fiscal decisions. Moreover, the use of the local town meeting, in either its pure or representative form, makes the model's individualistic utility maximizing assumption appropriate. It should also be noted that the property tax is the only tax source available to local governments in Massachusetts.

The model to be estimated has the form:

$$EXP = AY^{\alpha_1}\ R^{\alpha_2}\ P^{\alpha_3}\ \overline{B}^{\overline{\alpha}_4}\ \overline{T}^{\overline{\alpha}_5}\ Z^{\alpha_6}\ \overline{G}^{\overline{\alpha}_7}\ e^{\beta_1 X + \beta_2 X^2}\ u$$

where:

EXP = per capita non-school expenditures,

Y   = median household income,

P   = a proxy for the cost of public services,

$\overline{B}$ = a vector of business-related variables that reflect production function and direct demand effects of business property.

$\overline{T}$ = a vector of community characteristics affecting the demand for public services through either preference or production relationships,

Z   = 1975 population,

R   = residential fraction of the assessed tax base,

$\overline{G}$ = a vector of intergovernmental aid variables,

X   = 1975 population divided by 1970 population,

u   = a random error,

A is a constant,

$a_1, \alpha_2, \alpha_3, \alpha_6, \beta_1, \beta_2$ are parameters, and

$\overline{\alpha}_4, \overline{\alpha}_5, \overline{\alpha}_7$ are vectors of parameters.

In the reported regressions, the dependent variable (expenditures per capita) takes two different forms: municipal operating expenditures per capita (MUN), and non-school tax levy per capita (NSLEVY). The variable MUN includes all 1975-76 expenditures on general government, public safety, health, sanitation, hospitals, recreation, highways and libraries other than those for capital outlays, regardless of whether they were financed from the local property tax or intergovernmental aid. Although NSLEVY is broader than MUN because it includes fixed costs such as debt service, pension costs and assessments on cities and towns by the state and county, it represents the portion of expenditures financed only by the property tax.

Although not strictly correct, we follow the convention of representing the income of the median voter as median household income (Y).[6] We updated 1970 census data on the 1969 median income of families and individuals with estimates of 1969-75 change in per capita income, as calculated for the purposes of general revenue sharing.

The tax price to the median, or decisive, voter is represented by the residential fraction of the tax base (R) and a proxy for the cost of providing public services (P). Assuming that the property tax is the only local revenue source, that residents perceive they bear only the portion of the tax that they pay directly as consumers or owners of residential property, and that the community receives no matching aid, the tax price to the median voter per unit of public services per family is:[7]

$$TP = P \cdot R \cdot H_M/H_A$$

where:

TP = the tax price to the median voter,

P = the resource cost per unit of public services,

R = the residential fraction of the taxable assessed base and

H_M/H_A = the ratio of the assessed value of the median voter's house to the average assessed value of residential property in the community.

The lower any of the three components is, the lower the price of public services resident voters perceive, and thus the larger the demand for public services. The constructed variable representing the distribution of residential property (H_M/H_A) has been omitted in the estimated equations because it is unlikely to vary across communities enough to have any statistical impact.[8]

Since no data are available on the price per unit of public services across communities, price (P) is proxied crudely in the equations by the total population of the metropolitan area. The argument is that land prices, and consequently wages and the cost of living, will be higher the larger the metropolitan area. Use of this proxy implies that within each metropolitan area factor inputs to the production of public services are bought and sold in a single market.

The coefficient of P is expected to be positive since the negative effect on quantity demanded of a higher price most likely would be offset by the positive impact of a higher price on expenditures, i.e., on price times quantity.

The residential fraction of the tax base (R) accurately reflects the tax base component of the tax price only under the simplest assumptions about property tax incidence. Realistically, resident voters probably perceive that they bear part of the property tax levied on local firms. If resident voters believe, for example, that firms are mobile in response to intercommunity fiscal differentials, higher resident-related public expenditures—and therefore higher tax liabilities for firms—in the current period will adversely affect the local commercial and industrial tax base in the future. In this case, residents might recognize that they would assume part of the property tax levied on firms in the form of a potentially reduced future tax base. Alternatively, residents may fear that they will bear the burden of higher business taxes by having to pay more for locally consumed goods and services. This requires that the firms have sufficient market power—or at least that residents believe that they have such power—to increase prices. In both cases, R underestimates the tax base component of the tax price as perceived by local residents.[9] Unfortunately, a more theoretically correct specification cannot be estimated here because of the inclusion of the $\overline{B}$ vector in the equation.

In all the reported regressions, commercial workers (CWOR) and manufacturing workers (IWOR), both expressed as a fraction of the resident population, are included as the business-related variables in the vector $\overline{B}$.[10] By increasing the non-resident population in a community, business property may lower the effective level of public service outputs (such as protection from crime) produced from any given quantity of public sector inputs (such as police patrols and cruisers), thereby increasing local demand for public sector inputs. Business property also may affect the total demand for public services by exerting direct demands for business-related services, demands that must be made effective through threat of exit, price increases, or wage decreases.

The taste vector $\overline{T}$ includes the fraction of the population living in households with income below the poverty level (POV), the fraction of total housing units occupied by renters (REN), and the number of manufacturing workers *residing* in each community expressed as a fraction of the resident population (BLUE). A positive coefficient on POV can have a variety of interpretations: (1) non-poor voters, including the median voter, received consumption externalities from providing services to the poor; (2) the presence of poor people alters the production relation between, say, police service inputs and protection from crime outputs, thereby affecting the median voter's derived demand for police services; or (3) poor people in any one community have relatively strong demands for public services and are able to make their demands effective through the political process.

The coefficient of REN also can be interpreted in several ways. A common argument is that renters have strong demands for public services because of their perception that they do not pay the property tax (implying a perceived tax price close to 0). For this to have a positive impact on expenditures, renters would either have to be numerous enough to affect the demand of the median voter or to have sufficient political power to impose their will on the majority. Another explanation for a positive coefficient of REN is its positive correlation with other community characteristics, such as density, that might affect expenditures positively.

The number of manufacturing workers residing in a community (BLUE) is included to control for the taste differences of resident voters that may be correlated with the amount of nonresidential property, particularly industrial property, within a city. The variable is expected to have a negative effect on the demand for expenditures.

The expected sign of the population variable (Z) is ambiguous. On the one hand, as a proxy for density, it may cause an increased demand for public services. On the other, economies of scale in either the production or provision of public services may reduce per capita expenditures in larger cities, controlling for other factors. This variable has been included in the equation so that the effects of population change can be separated from those of population size.

Three intergovernmental aid variables ($\overline{G}$) are included in some of the reported regressions to control for the effects of federal revenue sharing grants (RS), state lump-sum grants (SLS), and state categorical aid (CAT). No attempt has been made to separate the multitude of state categorical grants into matching and non-matching grants. All three types of aid are likely to increase local operating expenditures (MUN) by increasing the community's resources and to decrease the non-school tax levy (NSLEVY) by substituting intergovernmental funds for local tax revenues.

The final term of the expenditure model ($e^{\beta_1 X + \beta_2 X^2}$) reflects the basic hypothesis that population change has a U-shaped effect on per capita expenditures. It should be noted here that, since the expenditure model is estimated in logarithmic form, this specification requires that the ratio of 1975 population to 1970 population

EXHIBIT 1

Municipal Expenditures
(Absolute values of t-statistics in parentheses)

Equation I-1. No aid variables

LMUN	=	.3764 LY	−	.2399 LR	+	.0502 LP
		(1.799)		(1.891)		(2.062)
	+	.1121 LCWOR	−	.0088 LIWOR	+	.2820 LPOV
		(1.910)		(.2841)		(2.718)
	+	.0440 LREN	−	.3760 LBLUE	+	.0537 LPOP
		(.6951)		(4.057)		(1.232)
	−	7.662 X	+	3.216 X^2	+	5.155
		(2.496)		(2.261)		(2.128)

R^2 = .65   S.E.E. = .2020
$\bar{R}^2$ = .61   D.O.F. = 91

Equation I-2. Aid variables included

LMUN	=	.3552 LY	−	.2667 LR	+	.0518 LP
		(1.632)		(1.894)		(2.042)
	+	.1063 LCWOR	−	.0136 LIWOR	+	.2422 LPOV
		(1.784)		(.4322)		(2.195)
	+	.0472 LREN	−	.3576 LBLUE	+	.0548 LPOP
		(.7274)		(.2008)		(1.228)
	+	.0370 LCAT	+	.0199 LRS	+	.0424 LSLS
		(.9301)		(.2008)		(.7854)
	−	7.423 X	+	3.156 X^2	+	4.862
		(2.390)		(2.198)		(1.904)

R^2 = .65   S.E.E. = .2038
$\bar{R}^2$ = .60   D.O.F = 88

The variables are defined as follows:*

MUN   =   Municipal non-school operating expenditures per capita (including general government, public safety, health sanitation, hospitals, recreation, highways, and libraries).
MUN = $163

(X) and the square of that ratio (X^2) be included in the equation. A U-shaped relationship implies a negative β and a positive β^2.

The estimated equations for municipal expenditures (MUN) are reported in Exhibit I and for non-school tax levies (NSLEVY) in Exhibit II. Since all variables (except X and X^2) are expressed in logarithmic form, the coefficients for the independent variables can be interpreted as expenditure elasticities.

EXHIBIT 1 (cont'd)

NSLEVY	=	Non-school property tax levy per capita. NSLEVY = $197
Y	=	Median income of families and individuals. Y = $15,330
R	=	Residential fraction of the assessed value of property subject to local property taxation. R = .70
P	=	Metropolitan area population as proxy for the price of public services across metropolitan areas. P = 1,702,000
CWOR	=	Commercial workers per capita. CWOR = .145
IWOR	=	Industrial workers per capita. IWOR = .109
POV	=	Fraction of population living in households with income below the poverty level (1970). POV = .06
REN	=	Fraction of housing units occupied by renters (1970). REN = .30
BLUE	=	Manufacturing workers residing in the community divided by the population of the community (1970). BLUE = .119
POP	=	Total 1975 population (State Census). POP = 37,659
CAT	=	State categorical and to local governments per capita. CAT = $4.20
RS	=	Federal revenue sharing grants per capita. RS = $19.74
SLS	=	State lump aid to local governments per capita. SLS = 7.56
X	=	1975 population (estimates) divided by 1970 population. X = 1.027

* Prefix L refers to the natural logarithm; see appendix for sources.

The signs and magnitudes of the coefficients are resonable across all equations, although in several cases multicollinearity prevents precise estimates. The statistically insignificant variables have been retained in the equations for control; since there is a possible correlation between REN and the variables of primary interest, for example, we retain REN in the MUN equations even though its

EXHIBIT 2

Non-school Tax Levy
(Absolute values of t-statistics in parentheses)

Equation II-1. No aid variables.

LNSLEVY	=	.7837 LY	−	.5812 LR	+	.0702 LP
		(4.085)		(4.994)		(3.145)
	+	.1055 LCWOR	−	.0474 LIWOR	+	.2750 LPOV
		(1.961)		(1.673)		(2.890)
	+	.0739 LREN	−	.4711 LBLUE	+	.1150 LPOP
		(1.273)		(5.541)		(2.874)
	−	10.51 X	+	4.521 X^2	+	1.760
		(3.732)		(3.465)		(.7922)

R^2 = .79   S.E.E. = .1853
R^2 = .77   D.O.F. = 91

Equation II-2. Aid variables included.

LNSLEVY	=	.8061 LY	−	.5802 LR	+	.0642 LP
		(4.194)		(4.665)		(2.862)
	+	.1133 LCWOR	−	.0473 LIWOR	+	.2953 LPOV
		(2.151)		(2.151)		(3.030)
	+	.0965 LREN	−	.4283 LBLUE	+	.0983 LPOP
		(1.686)		(5.014)		(2.457)
	+	.0629 LCAT	+	.0097 LRS	−	.1098 LSLS
		(1.738)		(.0111)		(2.304)
	−	10.26 X	+	4.454 X^2	+	1.916
		(3.740)		(3.511)		(.8491)

R^2 = .81   S.E.E. = .1800
R^2 = .78   D.O.F. = 88

See Exhibit 1 for variable definitions and means.

coefficient is statistically insignificant. Unfortunately, we are unable to control fully for 1970 community characteristics because of data limitations. In particular, POV, REN and BLUE come from the 1970 census, while the median individual and family income variable (Y) is the 1970 census figure adjusted to the 1975 level by the estimated change in per capita income from 1969-75. We are therefore unable to separate completely the expenditure effects of changes in population size from the effects of changes in the population mix.

By comparing equations I-1 and I-2, it is clear that adding the three intergovernmental aid variables does not change the results. Indeed, all three variables are statistically insignificant and have virtually no impact on the magnitudes of the other coefficients. On the basis of the $\bar{R}^2$ and the standard error of estimate, equation I-1 is preferable to equation I-2. In contrast, the aid variables play a more important role in the NSLEVY equations shown in Table II. Here, state lump-sum aid (SLS) permits communities to decrease their non-school tax levies as predicted; revenue sharing apparently has little impact; and state categorical aid results in higher local tax levies. This last finding reflects the matching requirements of many state categorical programs.

As the equations are specified, increases in both commercial and industrial property decrease the tax price term (R) equivalently, thereby increasing expenditures by comparable amounts. Commercial property, however, has an additional impact through the commercial worker variable (CWOR) which reflects the adverse production function and direct demand effects of such property. The preferred equations (I-1 and II-2) imply that a community with a ratio of commercial workers to the total population two standard deviations above the simple mean has per capita operating expenditures 16 percent and a non-school tax levy 21 percent above those in otherwise similar communities.[11] In contrast, the industrial worker variable (IWOR) appears to exert a negligible or negative impact on expenditures and tax levies, even after controlling for the taste differences of resident voters.[12]

EFFECTS OF POPULATION CHANGE

The statistically significant positive coefficient of X^2 in all equations confirms the U-shaped effect of population change on per capita expenditures.[13] Exhibit III summarizes the expenditure implications of the parameter estimates. The fractions in the exhibit compare the expected level of per capita expenditures in a community experiencing the given rate of population change with the expected level in an otherwise similar community with no population change. For example, on the basis of equation I-1, a community with 1975 population equal to 90 percent of its 1970 population is predicted to have municipal expenditures 17 percent higher than a comparable community with no population change during 1970-75. Again according to equation I-1, a growing community with 20 percent more people in 1975 than in 1970 would have per capita expenditures approximately 11 percent below those of a comparable community

EXHIBIT 3

Effects of Population Change of Per Capita Expenditures*

Equation Number	1975 Population/1970 Population						
	.80	.90	1.00	1.10	1.20	1.30	1.40
I-1	1.45	1.17	1.00	.91	.89	.92	1.026
I-2	1.42	1.15	1.00	.92	.91	.95	1.062
II-1	1.61	1.21	1.00	.90	.89	.97	1.15
II-2	1.57	1.20	1.00	.91	.91	.99	1.19

*The entries in the exhibit represent the estimated per capita expenditures for a community with the given ratio of 1975-1970 population expressed as a fraction of the estimated per capita expenditures for a comparable community with no 1970-1975 population growth.

with no population change. Because of the way the equations are specified, these ratios are independent of actual expenditure levels. The population change values cover the entire range of the sample, i.e., a 20 percent decrease to a 40 percent increase during the five-year period. The mean population change in the sample is a 2.7 percent increase and the standard deviation is 8.6 percentage points.

Because non-school tax levies include more of the difficult-to-reduce costs such as debt service and pension payments, we hypothesize that per capita differentials associated with population change should be greater for this category than for municipal operating expenditures. Moreover, non-school tax levies include the tax burden effects of the debt service necessary to finance new capital in growing communities. As Exhibit 4 demonstrates for the preferred equations (I-1 and II-2), the NSLEVY parameter estimates do, in fact, imply a steeper U-shape than the estimates for operating expenditures.

We also hypothesized that communities with a moderate rate of population growth would have the minimum per capita expenditure level, all other factors held constant. For municipal operating expenditures the minimum level occurs at a 17 to 19 percent population growth rate; for non-school tax levies at a 15 to 16 percent growth rate. Although per capita expenditures are higher in communities with more than moderate growth rates, it should be noted that expenditures in rapidly growing communities do not exceed those in stable, urban areas until the population growth rate is higher than 30 percent. Only the most rapidly growing communities, therefore, have a per capita spending disadvantage: those experiencing a 40 percent population increase (the largest in the sample) are

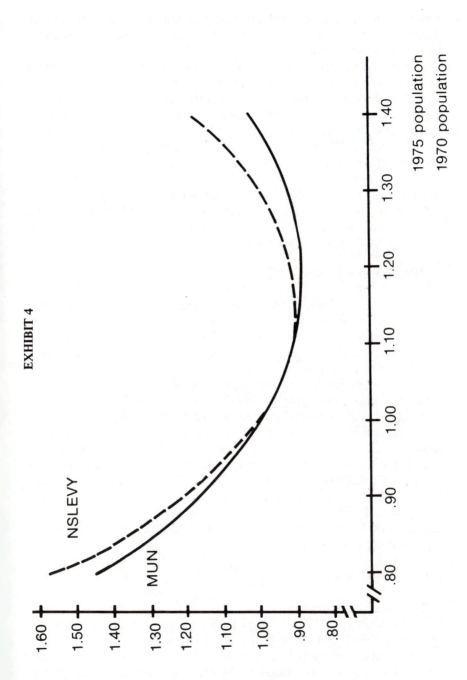

EXHIBIT 4

predicted to have municipal operating expenditures 3 to 6 percent higher than those in stable communities, with non-school tax levies 15 to 20 percent higher.

The per capita spending and tax burden differentials for declining communities are particularly striking. In the most rapidly declining areas (1975 population/1970 population = .80), per capita operating expenditures are 45 percent higher and nonschool tax levies 60 percent higher than in stable communities. Residents in communities experiencing a 10 percent decline face municipal expenditures 16 percent higher and non-school tax levies 21 percent higher than in comparable, but stable communities. Since these differentials are too large to be explained fully by the spreading of a fixed level of expenditures over a smaller population, it is likely that antiquated capital stock, adverse production function effects and rising private sector unemployment also play important roles.[14]

SUMMARY AND CONCLUSIONS

In making fiscal comparisons across communities, the convention is to base them on per capita expenditures or tax levies. Such comparisons must be interpreted carefully, however, especially to the extent that expenditures are out of equilibrium because of changing population levels. This study contributes to our understanding of spending differentials by focusing on the per capita spending implications of population growth and decline. Specifically, we find that population change has a U-shaped impact on per capita expenditures, with minimum spending levels occurring in communities with moderate growth rates. In the case of rapidly declining communities, and differential per capita spending effects are sufficiently large to suggest that the political and economic problems of reducing expenditures need further investigation. A better understanding of these issues would allow policymakers to design more effective intergovernmental and other programs for communities experiencing rapid population change.

DATA SOURCES

The operating expenditure data were derived from Schdule A forms sent to the Massachusetts Department of Revenue (formerly the Department of Corporations and Taxation) by towns and cities for the fiscal year 1975-76. Although nominally required by law, completed forms were available for only 103 out of a total of 118 metropolitan area communities with population over 10,000.

The percent breakdown of the assessed tax base among property types comes from LA-EQV-19 forms used by the Massachusetts Revenue Department of Revenue in its biennial property tax equalization study. The non-school tax levy is calculated from the school tax rate, the total tax rate, and the total tax levy by community available from the Massachusetts Taxpayers Foundation.

Employment data by place of work are from the Massachusetts Division of Employment Security, *Massachusetts Cities and Towns: Employment and Wages in Establishments Subject to the Massachusetts Employment Security Law by Major Industry Divisions, 1967-75.*

The state intergovernmental aid variables are derived from fiscal 1976 cherry sheets, Massachusetts Department of Revenue. Revenue sharing payments are reported in U.S. Department of the Treasury, Office of Revenue Sharing, *Sixth Period Entitlements.*

The 1975 population used in calculating per capita figures is from the Massachusetts State Census; the 1975 population estimate used for the 1975-1970 population change variable is from the U.S. Department of the Treasury, Office of Revenue Sharing, General Revenue Sharing, *State and Local Data Elements,* Entitlement Period 9. Other socio-economic data are from either the 1970 Census of Population or the 1970 Census of Housing. Per capita income estimates, available by community for 1975 from the U.S Department Office of Revenue Sharing, *State and Local Data Elements,* were used to update the 1970 Census median income to 1975 levels.

NOTES

1. For a thorough discussion of the fiscal dilemma of the declining city, see Peterson (1976).

2. The more common approach is simply to compare per capita expenditures on common functions in declining cities with those in growing cities. See, for example, Peterson (1976).

3. The model is developed most fully in Ladd (1974); parts of the model are summarized in Ladd (1975) and Ladd (1976).

4. It can be shown that as long as preferences are single peaked, the budget preferred by the median voter is the only budget that will win a majority of the votes when paired against any other budget. See Duncan Black (1948).

5. The sample is restricted to those communities for which complete 1975 expenditure data were available from the Massachusetts Department of Revenue.

6. Recent theoretical work has shown that even without the monotonicity assumption, use of median household income is still appropriate provided that income distributions across communities meet certain regularity assumptions. See Bergstrom and Goodman (1973).

7. This tax price expression is derived in Ladd (1975). Note that the R used here is equivalent to the RB used in my earlier paper.

8. This conclusion is based on previous work. In my earlier study of municipal expenditures, the constructed variable H_M/H_A had insufficient variation across communities to have any explanatory impact. See Ladd (1974).

9. This complication is addressed in Ladd (1974) and Ladd (1975). Briefly, the tax base component can be generalized to R^* as follows:

$$R^* = 1 - \alpha \cdot C - \beta \cdot I$$

where C and I are the commercial and industrial fractions of the tax base. As the parameters α and β approach 0, R^* approaches 1 in spite of the presence of business property. Previous empirical work on the demand for education expenditures suggests that α is greater than β for communities in the Boston metropolitan area. See Ladd (1975). This finding implies that industrial property, in not being tied to the local market, is perceived to be more responsive to fiscal factors than commercial property.

10. In Ladd (1976), the vector $\overline{B}$ includes tax base variables in some equations as well as employment variables. As reported in that paper, however, the results are essentially invariant to the particular business property variables used.

11. This estimate includes both the effect through the variable CWOR and the indirect effect through the variable R. The estimated expenditure effects of commercial property, it should be noted, are sufficiently large to imply that differences in nonschool tax rates across communities are positively associated with differences in commercial property, *ceteris paribus*. In other words, the presence of commercial property increases the demand for public services by an amount sufficient to offset the tax rate benefits of the larger tax base. The tax rate implications of similar results are discussed more fully in Ladd (1976).

12. To the extent that the location decisions of industrial property are responsive to fiscal factors, the negative coefficient of IWOR may reflect simultaneous equations bias.

13. Since the 1975 Massachusetts State Census uses a definition of resident population that differs slightly from the federal definition, the 1975 population used in the population change variable is the figure estimated by the Federal Government for the purpose of distributing general revenue sharing grants. The equations also were estimated using a 1969-1975 population change variable based completely on Massachusetts State Census data. Those equations are very similar in their implications to the equations reported in the text.

14. Ideally, the equations would control for the changing population mix leaving for the variable X only the change in size, but as noted above, the absence of data on 1975 socioeconomic characteristics means that some mix effects may be included in the population change variable. Even if the population mix remained constant, however, a decrease in the population would change the environment by increasing the number of abandoned buildings.

REFERENCES

Bergstrom, T.C. and R.P. Goodman, "Private Demands for Public Goods," *American Economic Review* 63, 3 (June 1973), pp. 280-97.

Black, Duncan. "On the Rationale of Group Decision Making," *Journal of Political Economy,* Vol. 56 (February 1945), pp. 23-34.

Booth, Douglas P., "The Differential Impact of Manufacturing and Mercantile Activity on Local Government Expenditures and Revenues," *National Tax Journal* XXXI, 1 (March 1978), pp. 33-44.

Deacon, Robert T., "Private Choice and Collective Outcomes: Evidence from Public Sector Demand Analysis," *National Tax Journal* XXX, 4 (December 1977), pp. 371-86.

Ladd, Helen F., "Local Education Expenditures, Fiscal Capacity, and the Composition of the Property Tax Base," *National Tax Journal* XXVIII, 2 (June 1975), pp. 145-158.

Ladd, Helen F., "Local Public Expenditures and the Composition of the Property Tax Base," Unpublished Ph. D. Dissertation, Harvard University, 1974.

Ladd, Helen, F., "Municipal Expenditures and the Composition of the Local Property Tax Base," in Arthur D. Lynn, Jr., *Property Taxation, Land Use and Public Policy* (TRED 8) (Madison: The University of Wisconsin Press, 1976), pp. 73-98.

Peterson, George, E., "Finance," in Gorham and Glazer, eds., *The Urban Predicament* (Washington, D.C.: The Urban Institute, 1976).

Seymour Sacks, George Palumbo and Robert Ross - THE DETERMINANTS OF EXPENDITURES: A NEW APPROACH TO THE ROLE OF INTERGOVERNMENTAL GRANTS

INTRODUCTION—THE EMERGENCE OF FEDERAL-TO-LOCAL INTERGOVERNMENTAL AID

The fiscal relationships of the various levels of government have increased in scope and complexity since the early literature on expenditure determinants: Fabricant (1952); Sacks and Harris (1964); Brazer (1959) and Fisher (1964).[1] There is indeed an entire literature surveying the determinants literature: Miner (1963); Bahl (1968), Gramlich (1970), Barro (1974) and Gramlich (1976).[2] Our concern in this work is with the integration of the intergovernmental dimension into the traditional determinants literature and the new "theoretical" following the work of Borcherding and Deacon (1972), Perkins (1977), Inman (1979) and Barro (1972).[3] Emphasis is placed upon the impact on state and local expenditures of the rapidly expanding grants system. While there is an immense literature which is at least peripherally concerned with this issue, virtually no studies have been done reflecting the massive shift of federal involvement on an aggregate basis in the mid-1970s. The analyses have been focused on individual programs or have had to

369

rely on earlier, non-comparable, circumstances. The emergence of direct federal aid to local government as an important instrument of intergovernmental policy along with increasing information about the two major components of federal aid, the direct and pass-through elements, as well as the state aid from own sources (ACIR, 1980), forces a new focus in the interpretation of grants-in-aid as a determinant of expenditures.[4]

BACKGROUND–THE NATURE OF EARLY INTERGOVERNMENTAL TRANSFERS

The early literature on the determinants ignored the role of grants-in-aid for two major reasons. The first was the limited amount of aid. State grants for education and federal grants for welfare dominated the patterns. Once these patterns were in place they tended to remain unchanged. In a determinants context the importance was placed on own circumstances rather than on the intergovernmental context which has since emerged. The early determinants literature moreover could not resolve the difficult problem of pass-through federal aid when dealing with local governments. State aid as reported by the Census Bureau is the only uniform data set available. It includes federal aid distributed by state governments. On the other hand federal aid encompassed only direct federal to local flow of funds. In the period for which most of the early literature is relevant, the pass-through component was far more important than its direct counterpart, but estimates of its size were not available. The result was a great deal of confusion of the role of aid at the local level.

Pass-through aid originates at the federal level and is mainly designed to aid local governments, but it must first pass through a state government. In some cases it merely acts as a neutral conduit, as in most educational aid. A second kind of pass-through aid emerges at the volition of the state government. The main example of this form of pass-through aid is the case of the local provision of categorical public welfare programs. In this case, state aid contains the federal welfare aids less the amount retained at the state level. The pass-through exists as a consequence of state rather than federal policy. Finally, there is the possibility that a state government might pass-through, of its own volition, the federal aid which it receives. The most important example of this case exists in the state share of General Revenue Sharing. This pass-through is purely at the discretion of the state government. Some of these issues have been discussed recently by Stephens and Olson (1979).[5] Pass-through aid, direct federal aid and state aid from its own sources are three different aid streams for local goverments. The early determinants literature often could not identify the pass-through component and direct federal aid did not begin to emerge as important until the middle of the last decade. This study analyzes the impact of each of these aids on local expenditures. For purposes of comparison, federal aid to state governments and to the combined state-local totals also will be considered.

By the Census year 1977, local expenditures had experienced the impact of a massive amount of noneducational direct federal aid. It is this event that has altered the basic financing structure of local expenditures in the United States. Earlier analyses were unable to deal with the manner in which most federal aid entered into local finances, namely, via the pass-through, because it was embedded in the state aid figure. As a result, interstate analyses using Census data commingled these three streams of aid to local governments. At the local level the limited amount of direct federal aid in the earlier years was incorrectly viewed as indicative of the federal component, when in fact the pass-through was more important. The emergence of massive federal to local aid, while associated with General Revenue Sharing, was far more extensive. The combined effect of direct and indirect federal aid on local noneducational fiscal behavior has not been dealt with, although there have been analyses of individual programs.

THE STRUCTURE OF THE ANALYSIS:
EXAMINING THE EFFECTS OF INTERGOVERNMENTAL TRANSFERS ON LOCAL FISCAL BEHAVIOR

The question to be dealt with here is what has been the effect of these new developments on local fiscal behavior. The answer will be presented in terms of an econometric model in which the grants will be disaggregated into the two major expenditures sectors, local educational and noneducational. In addition to the three exogenous grants variables, two endogenous variables, income and tax base, also will be incorporated into the analysis. Finally, a variable indicating the extent of the local assignment of expenditure responsibility will be included to permit interstate comparisons. For purposes of comparison, analyses of state and state-local expenditure totals also are presented with only federal aid as an exogenous variable.

EXPENDITURE DETERMINANTS ANALYSIS:
CRITICISMS—THE QUESTION OF SIMULTANEITY

A number of criticisms are generally made about the early determinants literature. They can be placed in three categories: 1) the lack of a theoretical structure which may lead to specification error in the estimating equations; 2) the aggregation of state and local government activity; and 3) simultaneous equation bias, which might result from the inclusion of intergovernmental aid and expenditure in the same equation. While the early determinants literature is too broad to be attacked en masse, many early studies were subject to one or more of these problems.

The aggregation problem is one that is generally valid and is addressed in this work specifically. The estimating equation presented in this work is in terms of local, state, and state and local patterns; the lack of immediate relevance of the state and local combination in evaluating the nature of aid is evident from the equations.

The more serious criticisms pertain to the structure and the relationship of the variables. Inman (1979) has argued that the lack of a theoretical structure may lead to a misspecification of the model, due to omitted variables.[6] Fiscal base, a variable generally missing from the "theoretic" as well as the "atheoretic" models, may be correlated with income, which is generally included in both sets of models. The resulting specification error may lead to biased and inconsistent estimators. It is our contention that while the fiscal base is definitely related to income in a systematic way, it is not a unique relationship. It is necessary for a tax base variable to separate out the demand and supply aspects of income. The systematic relationship between income and the fiscal base worked in conjunction with the presence of "nonresidential" tax base and "nonresidential" demands. While the problem is greatest at the local jurisdictional level, it also exists in the case of nationwide aggregates. If there is a shortcoming of the existing literature concerning the intergovernmental fiscal relationships of different governments, it lies in their failure to accurately mix the demand and supply effects of the nonresidential tax components with the income-determined residential side. It is uncertain why the demand models that have followed Borcherding and Deacon (1972) fail to include a nonresidential component, but in effect, the median voter model also fails to ascribe any demands from the industrial and commercial section.[7] What is even more surprising, the more difficult questions of tax shifting, tax exporting, the intermediate nature of public goods, and the real tax price of public goods also are ignored. In the analyses the inclusion of tax base as well as income variables in part allows for a nonresidential demand and supply impact. The variables included in our model generally reflect the reality of, or serve as proxies for, unavailable data on intergovernmental relationships.

A more realistic criticism is that of the simultaneous nature of several of the variables which often appear in empirical models, Bahl (1969) has suggested that aid and expenditures are jointly determined through tax effort in a variety of aid formulas, a problem that would be most serious in the determination of flat or lump sum grants like General Revenue Sharing.[8] This type of aid is of minor importance even in terms of total direct federal-local intergovernmental transfers, and tax effort is only one of several factors in determining this aid. A broader indictment of including intergovernmental aid in an estimating equation is levied by Pogue and Sgnotz (1968) who claim that state and local expenditures and federal expenditures can be explained by a third set of explanatory variables; and that their inclusion in the same equation would result in unreliable estimates of the impact of grants on local expenditures.[9] Though later studies fail to support this claim, it should be noted that, in general, grants-in-aid may be correlated to expenditures when allocations are at issue, but present allocations may be determined by past tax effort, income, expenditures, grants or other circumstances and not future or present values of these variables.

In essence, it has been argued that the presumed simultaneous equation bias is caused by including the dollar amounts of the grants as an independent variable. This issue is far more complex when one uses grants as *received,* rather than the allocations process, where certain things are true by definition. In some cases, grants are reimbursements for prior expenditure; in other cases, the timing of grants may be inconsistent with the expenditure process, especially in periods of rapid change. Third, and perhaps most important, is the fact that there is a multitude of grant programs, rather than a single program, in operation.

SIFTING THE VARIOUS INTERGOVERNMENTAL FLOWS

The recent micro-based literature has emphasized the character of the grant as a variable as well as the necessity for having a price variable. The price variable is usually stated as essential, but except for special circumstances, cannot be dealt with in a direct fashion, as a matching ratio, a tax-price, or a "product" price. In dealing with the character of the grant variable, the major complexity emerges again because of the multiplicity of grant programs involved which themselves may interact with each other.

This work builds a cross-sectional model which attempts to assess the reaction of state and local governments as separate statewide entities to various levels of grants, as well as to "own" circumstances. In an attempt to get to the real tax price of expenditures, we attempt to dissaggregate the aid into direct federal, pass-through, and own state aid for education and noneducation sectors as well as in total.

While the question of fungibility and various matching formulas cloud the issue, the following models are presented and estimated in the hope that they can serve to identify the effects on local and governments of intergovernmental aid relative to other factors which determine the ability of these governments to provide goods and services.

The model used to analyze the impact of intergovernmental aid takes the general form:

Per Capita General Local Expenditure = f

(Per Capita Direct Federal Aid, Per Capita Pass-Through Federal Aid, Per Capita Aid from Own Sources, Per Capita Income, Per Capita Tax Base, State Proportion of State and Local General Expenditures).

This model is estimated for education and non-education expenditures using OLS estimators linearly, to measure impacts, and log linearly to obtain elasticities. The model is estimated for statewide totals of local governments in the United States in 1977, excluding the District of Columbia. This model is reestimated for 50 state governments using federal aid received and used by states, and finally, state and local expenditure activity is analyzed using total federal as the exogenous variable.

The three streams of aid vary in importance by function. In order to postulate our expectations of the impact of aid one must go back through the development of this aid.

As already noted, one of the outstanding developments in recent years has been the emergence of a direct federal-local set of intergovenmental grants. This is shown in Exhibit 1 and Appendix Exhibit 1 where the overall patterns of aid are divided into the three conventionally reported categories plus estimates of the pass-through of federal aid and the state aid from own sources. As reported in the successive volumes of *Historical Statistics on Governmental*

Finances and Employment as late as 1957, federal aid to states was mainly concentrated on state own purposes with the exception of the pass-through of public welfare where the responsibility was assigned to local governments.[10] There was little direct federal aid to local governments, and of that, almost 46 percent of the total went to the District of Columbia. State aid to local governments was considerably larger than federal aid to states. The amount of pass-through of federal aid was restricted mainly to public welfare. The period after 1957 witnessed considerable change in the amount of federal aid to states. New programs were introduced aimed primarily at state-type functions, but had the consequence of showing up on the local level when the fucntion was assigned to local governments. While the increase in federal aid to local governments was large in relative terms, it remained small in absolute terms. The big shift occurred after 1972, as shown in Exhibit 1, when direct federal aid to local governments changed in its absolute importance. As already noted, the system of aid to local governments had become fundamentally more complicated with three different aid streams; federal to local, pass-through of federal funds, and state aid out of its own funds. If one also divides these streams into their education and non-education components, one finds the analytical framework becomes more reasonable for reasons that will become obvious.

The aid streams as has been noted have been dominated by two categories, federal public welfare aid to states and state education aid to local governments. (This categorization has recently been recognized in *Governmental Finances in 1977-78.*)[11] The analysis will focus on these two problem areas. But one should recognize the changes which had important consequences on earlier analyses. One category in particular is of importance on the state level, namely highways. In the early 1960s, highway aid temporarily exceeded public welfare assistance in the aggregate and, based on the per capita amounts, also dominated the pattern of federal aid to states. Even in the year 1977, on an unweighted per capita basis, federal aid to states for highways still has an inordinate importance. In the middle 1960s the passage of the Elementary and Secondary Education Act involved the federal government in the provision of education aid on a more massive scale than in the limited directly provided "Impact" Area aid. While the ESEA and related aids went nominally to the state governments, they were distributed to the local governments providing education, with the notable exceptions where "local schooling" was provided on the state level. Later in the decade the introduction of Medicaid altered the relative importance of public welfare once again.

EXHIBIT 1

Per Capita Intergovernmental Aid and the Federal Component of State Aid to Local Government:
National Totals, 1977
(millions of dollars)

Intergovernmental Aid Flows	Total Expenditure	Expenditure Function				
		Education	Highways	Public Welfare	Health and Hospitals	All Other
Nominal Federal Aid to States	$215	$42	$30	$88	$7	$48
Nominal Federal-Local Aid	78	6	*	1	1	69
Nominal State-Local Aid	283	171	2	43	7	46
Pass-through	58	24	1	23	2	7
Net Federal Aid to States	158	18	29	65	5	41
Net Federal-Local Aid	135	30	2	24	3	76
Net State-Local Aid	225	147	15	20	5	39
Percent difference in federal-local aid due to pass-through	74.1%	393.6%	236.7%	3,068.5%	200.5%	10.0%
Pass-through as a percent of total federal aid.	19.6	49.9	3.6	26.3	23.8	5.9

Source: ACIR, *Recent Trends in Federal and State Aid to Local Government*

The major shifts occurred in the 1970s when a host of new programs were introduced (Exhibits 1, 2 and 3). Some of these programs were aimed at local governments, but for special circumstances funds channeled through states where local governments were not viewed as large enough or where there were other compelling reasons. The state share of Federal Revenue Sharing also was included in this total. Nevertheless, given all these circumstances, the major shift in the 1970s was in the case of direct federal-to-local grants. There was a major difference however in this period, illustrated, but not completely covered by, General Revenue Sharing, namely the emergence of lump sum aid to certain classes of governments which had previously been kept out of the intergovernmental stream, such as municipalities and other local general purpose governments. Counties, insofar as public welfare was a local function, had received aid for that purpose. School districts and any other governments assigned the educational responsibility received aid for that purpose. Except where municipalities also were counties and/or school districts they usually did not receive direct federal-to-local aid. In a few states there was some general purpose aid, often a consequence of some earlier tax sharing scheme.

The early literature reflected these underlying institutional arrangements, but in the case of federal aid there was increasing complexity caused by the pass-through phenomenon. This made it very difficult to analyze state or federal aid and the sum of the two was not completely identified as to its nature.

The use of aggregates tends to obscure the fundamental dichotomy between local government aid received for educational and noneducational pruposes. Direct federal aid for education in 1971-72 was equal to 2.1 percent of direct educational expenditures. Nominal state aid to education was equivalent to 42.5 percent of expenditures. If one allocates the pass-through of federal aid, then federal aid was equivalent to 8.2 percent of all educational expenditures and state aid to 36.3 percent. The period from 1971-72 to 1976-77 witnessed a rough stability in the federal proportion of educational expenditure, 8.5 percent in the aggregate as opposed to the earlier 8.2 percent. On the other hand, the net state proportion of educational expenditure rose from 36.6 percent to 41.5 percent of the total. There was thus an almost 50-50 division between local sources and exogenous aid in the case of education.

The roles of the state and federal governments were reversed in the case of noneducational aid. Clearly the outstanding development of the period was in the direct federal to local aid. From a level of

EXHIBIT 2

Percent Change in Intergovernmental Aid and the Federal Component of State Aid to Local Government:
National Totals, 1972-77

Intergovernmental Aid Flows	Total Expenditure	Expenditure Function				
		Education	Highways	Public Welfare	Health and Hospitals	All Other
Nominal Federal Aid to States	71.3%	51.0%	30.6%	52.4%	154.9%	236.1%
Nominal Federal-Local Aid	263.7	27.3	108.5	128.2	150.4	352.4
Nominal State-Local Aid	71.5	76.2	38.2	35.5	113.5	117.5
Pass-through	73.4	69.4	415.6	36.7	624.6	418.2
Net Federal Aid to States	70.5	31.8	27.0	58.9	105.7	217.2
Net Federal-Local Aid	147.9	58.8	258.7	38.4	219.1	357.7
Net State-Local Aid	71.1	77.3	31.2	34.1	65.2	97.0

Source: ACIR *Recent Trends in Federal and State Aid to Local Government.*

EXHIBIT 3

Average Expenditure Values for Education and Non-Education,
and Total Expenditures for Local, State and State and Local Governments

Per Capita Expenditure Category	Unweighted (A) Mean	(B) St. Div.	(B÷A)	(C) Mean	Weighted (D) St. Div.	(D÷C)
Local						
Education	$332.84	$ 89.51	26.9%	$349.55	$ 70.17	20.1%
Non-Education	371.43	134.47	36.2	436.23	178.04	40.8
Total	704.27	198.77	28.2	785.77	235.78	30.1
State	565.66	262.62	46.4	472.51	121.16	25.6
State & Local	1272.58	360.46	28.3	1264.71	255.34	20.2
Aid Category Local						
Federal Direct Education						
Aid	7.12	5.82	87.1	5.84	3.74	64.0
Federal Pass-Through						
Education Aid	22.32	8.37	37.5	23.95	7.33	30.6
State Own-Source						
Education	140.58	58.43	41.6	144.95	36.64	25.3
Federal Direct						
Non-Education	61.84	19.86	32.2	65.49	15.75	24.0
Federal Pass-Through						
Non-Education	20.30	24.85	122.4	32.85	42.51	129.40
State Own Source						
Non Education	55.25	46.03	83.3	77.76	63.12	81.2
Federal Direct	68.96	19.91	28.9	71.32	15.53	21.8
Federal Pass-Through	42.63	26.35	61.8	56.79	43.10	75.9
State Own-Source	195.83	85.20	43.5	222.70	88.34	39.7
Federal-to-State "Lodging"	197.77	91.88	46.5	156.02	48.81	31.2
Federal-to-all Levels	309.36	93.38	30.2	284.14	57.02	20.1
State Expenditures						
Assignment	.44	.094	21.4	.382	.085	22.3
Per Capita Income	6153	952	15.5	6367	736	11.6
Tax Base Index	98.9	16.4	16.6	99.9	10.91	10.9

6.2 percent of noneducational general expenditures in 1971-72, it rose to 16.0 percent in 1976-77 (Exhibit 2). Given the increase in the pass-through, the aggregates roles of the state and federal governments were reversed by 1976-77. Federal aid was equivalent to 23.5 percent of local expenditures as compared to 16.3 percent in the case of state aid. In fact, the overall increase of aid as a proportion of local noneducation expenditure was from 31.2 percent in 1971-72 to 39.8 percent in 1976-77.

There is a fundamental difference between the pass-through of education and public welfare federal aid. In the case of education, most of the pass-through is a reflection of statewide characteristics, but not of state policy. Federal aid is channeled through states with very little consequence, no mandating, and no necessary local matching except in certain types of minor aid. While most of the programs in the noneducational side are of a similar nature, the quantitatively dominant program, public welfare, is very different. There is no requirement that public welfare aid to states be channeled through to local governments. Only a small number of states actually pass-through public welfare aid, and of these only one, New York, channels through both public assistance and medical assistance. As already noted, unlike other types of pass-through aid, there is an additional set of mandates established by the state which generally are in excess of the federal guidelines. This will have consequences on the hypothesized values for pass-through noneducational aid.

Information on expenditures are drawn from *1977 Census of Governments* (Exhibit 3).[12] The information on the assignment of expenditure responsibilities is also drawn from the Census of Governments. Only the tax base data is drawn from outside this network. It is the 1975 counterpart of the "Representative" tax base as developed by Selma Mushkin for the Advisory Commission on Intergovernmental Relations and updated by Karl Halstead (1978).

The question as to what is specifically included in intergovernmental revenues is answered in part by the *Classification Manual for Government Finances* issued by the Governments Division of the Census Bureau.[13] It classifies intergovernmental revenue as including the following: ". . . grants, shared taxes, and contingent loans and advances for support of particular functions or for general financial support, any significant and identifiable amounts received from other governments as reimbursement for performance of governmental functions, and any other form of revenue representing the sharing by other governments in the financing of activities administered by the receiving government. Intergovernmental revenue excludes

EXHIBIT 4

Parameter Values for Education and Non-Education, and
Total Expenditures for Local, State and State and Local Governments

Local Government	Direct Federal	Pass-Through	Net State	Income	Tax Base	Assignment Variable
Impact						
Education	>1	0	>0;<1	>0	0	0
Non-Education	>1	>1	>0;<1	0	>0	<0
Total	>1	>1	>0;<1	>0	>0	<0
Elasticity						
Education	>0	0	>0	1	0	0
Non-Education	>0	>0	>0	0	1	−1
Total	>0	>0	>0	>0;<1	>0;<1	<0
State Government						
Impact	>1			>0	>0	>0
Elasticity	>0			1	1	>0
State and Local Total						
Impact	>1			>0	>0	0
Elasticity	>0			1	1	0

amounts received from the sale of property, commodities and utility services to other governments. All intergovernmental revenue is classified as general revenue."[14]

THE IMPACT OF FEDERAL-TO-LOCAL INTERGOVERNMENTAL AID

The complex nature of grants makes our expectations of the impacts of aid difficult to summarize as a single unit. We expect different impacts from aid which is basically tax sharing than from aid which mandates local expenditures. These are reflected in the expected parameter values which appear in Exhibit 4. They may even have important interactive properties. The analysis also recognizes that the inclusion of additional variables has an effect on the other variables included in the estimating equation. Given the division into three separate aid variables by function on the local levels it appears that the expected results may differ from earlier results based on other models.

EXHIBIT 5

Estimates of Impacts and Elasticities of Education and Non-Education, and
Total Expenditures for Local, State and State and Local Governments
(weighted model)

Impact	Federal Direct	Pass-Through	Net State Aid	Per Capita Income	Per Capita Tax Base	Expenditure Assignment	R^2
Local : Education	2.111 (1.412)	−.695 (.759)	.523 (.162)	.047 (.012)	−.910 (.755)	−365 (78)	.749
: Non-Education	1.596 (.447)	1.740 (.249)	.962 (.180)	.009 (.015)	2.220 (.898)	−321 (103)	.957
: Total	2.111 (.561)	1.582 (.281)	.988 (.140)	.057 (.019)	1.720 (1.116)	−575 (133)	.960
State Total	1.575 (.215)			.082 (.017)	−1.909 (1.087)	546 (140)	.817
State and Local	3.083 (.205)			.098 (.027)	1.257 (1.620)	−948 (145)	.913
Elasticity							
Local : Education	.031 (.023)	−.093 (.053)	.182 (.059)	.891 (.220)	−.188 (.222)	−.406 (.100)	.750
: Non-Education	.283 (.095)	.064 (.019)	.091 (.024)	−.138 (.315)	.731 (.302)	−.876 (.131)	.908
: Total	.221 (.067)	.076 (.028)	.248 (.045)	.435 (.198)	.269 (.195)	−.458 (.095)	.928
State Total	.397 (.063)			.909 (.183)	−.352 (.184)	.454 (.102)	.804
State and Local	.662 (.050)			.443 (.142)	.205 (.138)	−.291 (.052)	.898

Values in parentheses are the standard errors.
Significance values are not shown because of different hypotheses as shown in Exhibit 3.

Some of the hypotheses are held with stronger conviction than others. Of these, the strongest held hypothesis is that educational expenditures are unit elastic with respect to income using statewide totals. In a similar fashion it is felt that the tax base rather than income is the principal determinant of noneducational expenditures when combined with the assignment of expenditure responsibilities. As is shown in Exhibit 5, both of these hypotheses are confirmed. Also confirmed are the significantly low, but positive elasticities for the separate aid variables. These values are consistent with the new "theoretical" literature on the response of expenditures to grants. While the general feeling of this analysis is that cross-sectional models are not appropriate in dealing with responses to changes in aid, the results are consistent with the models as currently interpreted.

In terms of the more conventional approach in which the "impacts" of grants on expenditures have been analyzed in conjunction with other factors, the results are generally consistent with different types of grants. What has to be recognized is that interstate differences, rather than the more conventional inter-local or intrastate models, are under consideration.

CONCLUSIONS

The determinants approach to the explanation of inter-state differences in expenditures yields answers that are roughly in accord with underlying hypotheses. This approach, which disaggregated information on grants-in-aid for educational and noneducational purposes, indicated some of the limitations in using improperly specified data. The introduction of tax base information also indicated a major difference between the effects of income on educational as opposed to noneducational expenditures.

The determinants approach, while criticized, has been incorporated into the new theoretical literature on the response of expenditures to grants. There is no evidence that a cross-sectional approach yields the same hypotheses, let alone the same observed patterns as a time series analysis. Grants-in-aid should be distinguished as to their nature, but a cross-sectional approach which explains differences in levels of fiscal activity requires the inclusion of differences in the levels of aid. The effects of changes in the levels of aid has to be incorporated into a more complex intertemporal model.

NOTES

1. Solomon Fabricant, *The Trend of Government Activity in the United States Since 1900* (New York: National Bureau of Economic Research, 1952) Ch. 6; S. Sacks and R. Harris, "The Determinants of State and Local Government Expenditures and Intergovernmental Flow of Funds," *National Tax Journal,* March 1964, 17 (1), pp. 75-85; Harvey E. Brazer. *City Expenditure in the United States.* Occasional Paper 66 (New York: National Bureau of Economic Research, 1959).

2. Jerry Miner, *Social and Economic Factors in Spending for Public Education* (Syracuse, N.Y., Syracuse University Press, 1963); R. Bahl, "Studies on Determinants of Public Expenditures: A Review," *Sharing Federal Funds for State and Local Needs: Grants-in-Aid and the PPBS System,* edited by Selma J. Mushkin and John F. Cotton (New York: Praeger, 1969); R. Inman. "Dissecting the Urban Crisis, Facts and Counter-Facts," *National Tax Journal,* XXXII, no. 2; S. M. Barro, *Theoretical Models of School District Expenditure Determination and the Impact of Grants-in-Aid,* (Santa Monica: Rand Corporation, 1972) Report R-867-FF; E.M. Gramlich, "Intergovernmental Grants: A Review of Empirical Literature," Paper presented at the International Seminar on Public Economics Conference, Berlin, Germany, January 1976; E.M.Gramlich and H.Galper. "State and Local Fiscal Behavior and Federal Grant Policy," *Brookings Papers Economic Activity,* 1973 (1), pp. 15-58; E.M.Gramlich. "Alternative Federal Policies for Stimulating State and Local Expenditures," *National Tax Journal,* June 1968, 21 (2), pp. 119-129.

3. T.E.Borcherding and R.T.Deacon. "The Demand for the Services of Non-Federal Governments," *American Economic Review,* December 1972, 62 (5) pp. 891-902; George M. Perkins. "The Demand for Local Public Goods: Elasticities of Demand for Own Price, Gross Prices and Income," *National Tax Journal,* XXX, no. 4; S.M.Barro, *Theoretical Models of School District Expenditure.*

4. Advisory Commission on Intergovernmental Relations, *The Role of Intergovernmental AIDS in the Financing of Local Governments,* (forthcoming).

5. Ross Stephens and Gerald W. Olson. *Pass through Federal Aid and Interlevel Finance in the American Federal System, 1957 to 1977,* University of Missouri–Kansas City, August 1, 1979.

6. Inman, "Dissecting the Urban Crisis."

7. Borcherding and Deacon, "The Demand for the Services of Non-Federal Governments."

8. Bahl, "Studies on Determinants of Public Expenditures."

9. T.F.Pogue and L.G.Sgontz. "The Effects of Grants-in-Aid on State and Local Spending," *National Tax Journal,* June 1968, 21 (2), pp. 190-199;

10. U.S. Department of Census, *Historical Statistics of the U.S.: Colonial Times to 1970. Part II,* 1975.

11. U.S. Bureau of the Census, Governments Division, *Government Finances Classification Manual,* 1977.

12. U.S. Bureau of the Census, Governments Division, *Government Finances,* 1977.

13. See footnote 11.

14. Ibid.

REFERENCES

Advisory Commission on Intergovernmental Relations, *The Role of Intergovernmental AIDS in the Financing of Local Governments*, (Forthcoming).

Bahl, R. "Studies on Determinants of Public Expenditures: A Review", *Sharing Federal Funds for State and Local Needs: Grants-in-Aid and the PPBS System*, edited by Selma J. Mushkin and John F. Cotton (New York: Praeger) 1969.

Barro, S.M. *Theoretical Models of School District Expenditures Determination and the Impact of Grants-in-Aid* (Santa Monica: Rand Corporation) Report R-867-FF, 1972.

Borcherding, T.E. and Deacon, R.T. "The Demand for the Services of Non-Federal Governments," *American Economic Review,* December 1972, 62 (5) pp. 891-902.

Brazer, Harvey E. *City Expenditure in the United States.* Occasional Paper 66 (New York: National Bureau of Economic Research) 1959.

Fabricant, Solomon. *The Trend of Government Activity in the United States Since 1900* (New York: National Bureau of Economic Research) 1952. Ch. 6.

Gramlich, E.M. "Alternative Federal Policies for Stimulating State and Local Expenditures," *National Tax Journal*, June 1968, 21 (2), pp. 119-129.

_____. "Intergovernmental Grants: A Review of Empirical Literature," Paper presented at the International Seminar on Public Economics Conference, Berlin, Germany, January 1976.

Gramlich, E.M. and Galper, H. "State and Local Fiscal Behavior and Federal Grant Policy," *Brookings Papers-Economic Activity,* 1973 (1), pp. 15-58.

Inman, Robert. "Dissecting the Urban Crisis, Facts and Counter-Facts," *National Tax Journal,* XXXLL, No. 2.

Miner, Jerry. *Social and Economic Factors in Spending for Public Education* (Syracuse, N.Y., Syracuse University Press) 1963.

Perkins, George M., "The Demand for Local Public Goods: Elasticities of Demand for Own Price, Gross Prices and Income," *National Tax Journal,* XXX, No. 4.

Pogue, T.F. and Sgontz, L.G. "The Effects of Grants-in-Aid on State and Local Spending," *National Tax Journal,* June 1968, 21 (2), pp. 190-199.

Sacks, S. and Harris, R. "The Determinants of State and Local Government Expenditures and Intergovernmental Flow of Funds," *National Tax Journal,* March 1964, 17 (1), pp. 75-85.

Stephens, Ross and Olson, Gerald W. *Pass through Federal Aid and Interlevel Finance in the American Federal System, 1957 to 1977.* University of Missouri-Kansas City, August 1, 1979.

U.S. Bureau of the Census, Governments Division, *Government Finances, 1977.*

U.S. Bureau of the Census, Governments Division, *Government Finances Classification Manual, 1977.*

U.S. Department of Health, Education and Welfare, The National Institute of Education, *Tax Wealth in the Fifty States,* 1977.

Margaret A. Corwin and Judith Getzels - CAPITAL EXPENDITURES: CAUSES AND CONTROLS

INTRODUCTION

We are by now well acquainted with municipal fiscal problems. The part played by capital expenditures in adding to these problems is a matter of substantial concern to many communitiees. Although the fiscal situation is some cities appears to be such that even the most necessary capital expenditures will be put off in the face of what seem to be even more pressing needs, expenditures for capital improvements cannot be delayed indefinitely. Even in communities in relatively good fiscal condition, capital improvements are scrutinized in an attempt to evaluate their consequences for the future development of the city. Capital improvements are too costly to construct and reconstruct, and too lasting in their effects to be undertaken with careful consideration.

Professionals interested in efficient and well-managed government have tried to see that capital improvements are made logically and wisely. Planners, who are concerned with the physical development of cities, have a particular interest in capital improvements. For over 50 years planners have prepared master plans to guide this development, and more recently they also have worked with elected officials and citizens to prepare goals, objectives and policies to govern the physical character of cities.

But as we all know, the real world makes it difficult to carry out good intentions expressed in plans and policies. Local governments operate in a constantly changing environment, where problems and opportunities are unpredictable; where social and economic forces—such as escalating interest rates, population shifts, and the requirements to finance pension liabilities—are beyond local control; and where political factors—such as Proposition 13 fever and vested interests—influence decisions of elected officials. Because of this constant change and because plans and policies have symbolic as well as literal meanings, it is difficult to build or not build capital improvements to further local objectives.

In 1976, HUD and the National Science Foundation funded the American Planning Association and several subcontractors[1] to examine the attempts of communities to make capital expenditures in accordance with their stated development plans and policies. The capital improvements program was initially the focus of this research because it was believed to be an important and underused tool that planners might employ to advance development objectives. Eventually, the scope of the project was broadened to include the political aspects of policy setting and budget making in addition to technical questions about the compilation and monitoring of the capital improvements program.

The first phase of the project, an extensive literature review, resulted in an interim report, *Local Capital Improvements and Development Management*. The second phase involved field work in eight communities. Hypothesizing that problems, policies and procedures would differ systematically in rapidly growing and mature cities, we selected four of each type to visit: Atlanta, Baltimore, Dayton, and St. Paul were the mature cities, Aurora, Colorado; Salem, Oregon; San Jose, California and Montgomery County, Maryland were the rapidly growing ones. (Montgomery County, which has many of the powers of a municipality, was included because of its countywide planning and budgeting process.)

While it is an oversimplification to categorize each of the eight cities as growing or mature, for purposes of this research we focused on their dominant characteristic. Further, since the eight communities selected were believed to have unusally good methods of using capital expenditures to carry out their policies, these eight may not be typical of growing or mature cities generally. What I will present today is a summary of observations from the field work phase of our research.

CAPITAL NEEDS OF GROWING CITIES

I will first describe the problems that rapidly growing cities faced with capital expansion, the policies and procedures that were devised for solving them, and the difficulties in using such policies and procedures to meet the problems of rapid growth. Then, I will describe the major capital problems in mature cities, the policy statements that indicated efforts to solve them, and the ways that policy objectives achieved political legitimacy, so that capital expenditure decisions could be said to further them.

To begin, I will consider the communities undergoing rapid development. A major problem in these communities was that rapid expansion created greater demands for urban services than the cities could afford. Thus, the services provided to existing residents deteriorated and the tax base was strained. As a result, existing residents in the four growing cities were generally supportive of measures to control the expansion of capital facilities so that already developed areas of the city would not be adversely affected.

To do this, the rapidly growing cities formulated explicit policies which related capital expansion to their development objectives and sometimes designed regulations to prevent development when public facilities did not meet certain standards or were otherwise inadequate. Capital expenditures are affected in two ways. First, these growing communities are increasingly trying to shift the cost of capital expansion to new development through fees and taxes. Thus, new residents, who were believed to benefit most from the provision of new facilities and services, would bear the costs.

The second trend is to use the inadequacy of off-site capital facilities as the basis for denying permission for new development. This policy has one of two meanings: there will be no development unless certain capital facilites (and thus a certain level of municipal services) are present or promised by some level of government, or provided (in some cases) by the developer. And further, capital facilities will not be automatically provided by the local government—the right time and place will be determined by the local government.

Certain difficulties arise both with attempts to make development contingent on the existence or promise of adequate services and capital facilities, and with the attempt to shift costs. The effort to limit new development when municipal services and facilities were inadequate was primarily because local government was unable to exert control over the crucial off-site facilities.

The basic problem here was the lack of control of necessary revenues. Although growing cities obviously had more sources of revenue for capital improvements than mature cities, the source of some of their revenue uniquely constrains local governments' ability to meet their development objectives. Often revenues for major growth-inducing facilities came from and thus were controlled by other levels of government (the state), publicly-owned utilities (special districts or utility departments) and private utility suppliers (private water companies).

Growing cities rely on intergovernmental transfers to fund highways and major sewage treatment plants. As a result, these local governments did not have complete—or sometimes any—control over the timing and location of major capital improvements, control that their policies sometimes implied they did have. For example, Montgomery County has devised sophisticated standards to determine the adequacy of roads adjacent to proposed developments and intends to deny individual projects next to overburdened roads, even when improvements must be made by the state. In such cases, developers talked about suing the county for a "taking" of their property.

Even when the major facilities could be financed within a given area, the local government often lacked jurisdictional control over these facilities. The goals and policies of general purpose local governments pertaining to capital expansion often implied a desire to limit services delivery as a way of meeting their problems. These goals and objectives, however, sometimes conflicted with the mandates of the special districts and the legal obligations of publicly-owned utilities that actually provided the service. Their primary obligation was to offer service when economically feasible, more or less in response to consumer demand. In Aurora, for example, the water department's plans resulted in commitments to an oversized water facility that has largely determined the extent of development. Conflicts between the Sanitary District's service extensions and development plans of Montgomery County caused the county to get state legislation amended in 1975 to give them responsibility for preparing facility plans. Statutes that require sanitary districts to make capital expansion based on a jurisdiction's development plans, however, are rare. Even when utilities are municipally owned, if they are monopolies and act in a proprietary capacity, in most states they cannot decline legally to provide service on the basis of municipal development policies, rather than on their capacity to provide services.

There are, however, circumstances when development policies may apparently justify refusal to provide service. It appears that courts *may* support a withholding of extensions on non-utility related grounds when service extensions are made in concert with other land use regulations. Within municipal boundaries, there may be grounds for a publicly operated utility department to withhold extensions that conflict with the city's development policies, when there are other land use regulations in effect to serve the same objective. However, because service extensions often make urban densities possible, they typically precede a local government's control over land use. Thus, control over extensions outside of municipal boundaries is lacking where local governments have no extraterritorial planning powers. Thus, where most needed, this control in unavailable.

These problems may be addressed in other ways. For example, state-mandated controls over the provision of public services outside municipal boundaries existed in two of the four rapidly growing cities studied. Both California and Oregon have empowered countywide agencies—such as the Santa Clara County Local Agency Formation Commission in California and the Marion-Polk County Local Government Boundary Commission in Oregon—to plan for and enforce development policies. These agencies have powers to review annexations, control special district formations, and regulate the private suppliers of municipal services.

As a result of these special agency controls, developers building at urban densities outside of Salem, Oregon did not have alternatives to municipal services provided by cities and existing special districts. In Aurora, Colorado, on the other hand, there were no such controls on dense county development or special districts, and city residents probably bore some of the costs of urban services benefiting county developments. Despite the fact that Santa Clara County Local Agency Formation Commission provides control over development outside San Jose, the county still approves development at certain densities in unincorporated areas that San Jose does not favor.

While local interviewees frequently said that agencies set up to review county development and service providers did little to force cities to make cost/efficient service extensions within the city's boundaries or sphere of influence, county controls did seem to restrict the private provision of municipal services and to prevent some non-urban development not annexed to cities.

Problems of another kind arise when attempts are made to grant permission for new development on the basis of the adequacy of off-site facilities. There are technical problems involved in formulating standards of adequacy, particularly for certain services such as streets and highways. Off-site road improvements were a serious problem in each of the four growing cities visited, and standards have been the subject of dispute in two of them. For example, Aurora was unable to deny development where major roads were inadequate. San Jose did use road standards to enact a moratorium that permitted the city to deny development on the basis of inadequate street capacity. As a result, residential development was restricted temporarily in certain areas of the city until facility problems were solved. Montgomery County has adopted the most technically sophisticated methods of setting standards, but they are essentially untested because the amount of development has been limited by a shortage of sewage treatment capacity; it is the Sanitary District's allocations of sewer taps rather than the service standards that now control the location and timing of new development.

The attempt to shift costs of new development which had previously been borne by the public to the private sector (developers and thus, new residents) is a second way by which the growing communities we visited tried to cope with the demand for capital expansion. This attempt ran into problems of a legal, technical and political nature.

Local governments in some states faced legal problems with shifting costs. State and federal constitutional provisions mandate equal protection and prohibit treating similar classes of residents differently. As a result, developers can only be charged (through dedication requirements or special taxes) for capital facilities that primarily benefit their developments. Nevertheless, new development can seldom literally be made to "pay its own way." Some off-site improvements and service expansions clearly would not be undertaken by a community in the absence of new development. Yet it is difficult to assign all the costs and benefits of the new facilities to the new development alone. The "lumpiness" of some capital facilities, such as additional fire stations or a new treatment plant, makes it likely that their costs will be borne, in part, by existing residents.

Where capital costs were clearly attributable to new development and thus legally could be shifted to the developer, the staff of local governments sometimes faced technical problems in assessing those costs. When major facilities, such as storm drainage improvement, benefited an area where new development was occurring, it was often hard to determine legally defensible ways of dividing the costs between developers. And for a community's network facilities, such as roads and sewers, it was even more difficult to decide how costs should be allocated. For example, because a road had ramifications through the transportation network, an improvement in one area changed traffic patterns on major and minor arteries throughout the city.

Given resources, a technically sophisticated staff and a good lawyer, it is probably possible to surmount such technical difficulties; clearly if the costs of determining precise standards outweigh the financial revenue to the city, then cruder measures seem preferable. But there are political as well as technical difficulties in an explicit shifting of the costs of capital expansion to new development.

For example, although the Rand Corporation prepared a series of reports discussing service pricing schemes as a solution for San Jose's problems with urban sprawl, only one person we spoke to in San Jose had even heard of the reports. He dismissed them as completely infeasible in the prevailing political situation.

Political considerations are often prior to technical ones when local governments try to determine the costs and benefits of development. Occasionally, what looked at first like a technical problem turns out to be a political one. For example, in San Jose, the staff is trying to set standards to determine the net fiscal, economic, social and environmental benefit of development to the city. One of their planners observed that the meaning of the term "net benefit" had changed 180 degrees since the assessment was first proposed. He explained that the council decided to do such analyses at the height of the environmental movement, when public sentiment favored limiting development to preserve natural amenities, and environmental benefits were weighed heavily. Now the process allows the council to give more emphasis to other benefits, particularly fiscal ones.

The overall political context in which these capital expenditure decisions were made cannot be overlooked. Decisions about capital improvements inevitably have political consequences and create equity problems. In rapidly growing cities, these problems become obvious. As in mature cities, the benefits of capital improvements must be distributed among existing residents, but in rapidly growing areas, further tradeoffs are necessary between existing residents and developers who represent future residents.

In the growing cities we studied, elected officials were heavily involved in development concerns, and often favored growth over the objections of the administrative staff, who had to worry about service delivery. The city manager was often caught in the middle, and in two of the four growing cities, the manager lost his job in the last year over growth control issues.

Election by ward seemed to make elected officials more responsive to existing residents, rather than to the interests of future residents. On the other hand, at-large elections in combination with development pressures might very well mean that elected officials, who need to conduct expensive, citywide campaigns, are supported by those with money and a desire to see the city grow—developers, labor unions and businessmen. Thus, the recent change in San Jose from at-large elections to a ward system is likely to have a dramatic effect on the council's attitude towards new development and its support for development controls.

In sum, making capital expansion respond to development policies is extremely difficult for some very real political, financial, technical and legal reasons. To simplify or ignore these in determining plans, goals and objectives, or to fail to realize the symbolic political functions they serve, means that capital improvements will not be made as planned.

CAPITAL NEEDS OF MATURE CITIES

In the case of mature cities, the problems met in trying to link development policy and capital allocation are primarily financial and political. Mature cities lack funds to address even the most serious capital needs. They are seeking to finance capital renovation and maintenance at the same time they are beset by demands for increased delivery of social services. While citizens expect service levels to increase or at least to be maintained, the exodus of tax-paying residents and businesses makes this increasingly difficult, creating an ever-widening gap between needs and revenues.

As many reports have indicated, mature cities now face major problems with renovation of their capital plants. In the case of Dayton, for example, all major improvements such as bridges were built in the 1920's and all are wearing out at once, forcing the city to anticipate refinancing of major facilities in addition to normal capital replacement. One person said that the cost of needed capital maintenance was so great in his city that improved levels of service and capital replacement were impossible for anyone to consider seriously.

Mature cities are already exploiting available revenue sources to the fullest that state laws permit and their taxpayers will tolerate. They now are heavily dependent on the federal government not only for capital funds, but also for operating revenues. Nevertheless, each of the four mature cities has devised a means of securing some local funds to be used for capital improvements. In Baltimore, a "loan package" is prepared for voter and state approval, and then bonds are issued for specific improvements. Atlanta and St. Paul secured state legislation that allowed them to issue a fixed amount of annual general obligation bonds for capital improvements exempt from voter approval, and these provided a small but regular infusion of revenues for systematic capital maintenance and renovation. Ohio municipalities can levy income taxes that voters approve every five years, and thus, Dayton was able to make capital improvements "income tax promises" to voters, enabling the city to raise some capital funds.

Prerequisite to any process of setting policies and undertaking capital improvements to meet those objectives are some resources to allocate. Because the capital funds that cities do have are often earmarked and because they depend on other levels of government for additional "bequests," mature cities are forced to be responsive and reactive, making the formulation of long-range plans to solve problems enormously difficult. Even so, Atlanta, Baltimore, Dayton and St. Paul are attempting to draft written goals and objectives, to develop processes for identifying capital improvements that will meet them, and to use revenues—although constrained in different ways—to make whatever capital improvements can be funded to further these objectives to the extent possible.

Everyone in mature cities is only too painfully aware of his city's needs. Plans that provided additional documentation of needed capital improvements often were frustrating to those who knew that most recommendations would be unaffordable. If these plans or surveys stirred up unrealistic hopes of neighborhood residents, they were politically unpalatable for elected officials, and where plans made the fight with operating departments more difficult, they were dreaded by budgeters. One local finance director said that he viewed the city's plans as something the city could turn to if it ever had any money. When resources were extremely limited, plans that ignored the city's fiscal limits were viewed by many as pointless and even wasteful of staff time, money and energy.

Because there was little money for new large or small improvements, traditional functional plans of planners were not needed, and plans for capital maintenance and rennovation were often prepared by operating departments. Policy formulation in planning documents often tended to be closely related to the budgeting process. Thus in mature cities development policy is often budget policy.

The policy departments of mature cities looked different from those in growing communities. For example, the capital improvements programs of Baltimore and Dayton are printed in the same document as the city's policy objectives. In St. Paul, a separate document called the *Capital Allocation Policies* is prepared *solely* to guide capital budgeting and programming.

The time frame of policy documents in mature cities is also shorter than in growing municipalities, to relate policies more closely to revenue cycles and political terms. For example, St. Paul's *Capital Allocation Policies* covers three years to relate to CDBG[2] funding cycles. Dayton and Atlanta prepare annual as well as multi-year objectives for use in the yearly budgeting process, and these objectives either are incorporated in the budget itself or in a document prepared in the budget's format. This short-range policy focus means that the policy and budget decisions of elected officials must be made within their political time horizons.

The policies in these short-range documents tended to be more specific to budgetary concerns, both operating and capital, than the objectives and policies in growing cities. While the general goals of local governments of both types are similar, the policy documents of mature cities often included more specific statements incorporating decision rules for budget requests and project evaluations. For example, St. Paul's *Capital Allocation Policies* includes such directives as "there will be no expenditures for swimming pools in 1979-81," and "any conflict in project requests between citizens and operating departments automatically disqualifies both project requests." Such policies were used to circumscribe budget requests and to prevent unrealistic proposals. As a result, capital improvement requests were more realistically related to the city's political and fiscal limitations.

Sometimes policies were prepared relating development objectives to budgetary concerns because the city was adapting experimental budgeting and personnel processes—such as PPBS and MBO[3]—to meet local needs. Dayton and Atlanta have organized policy statements into a program framework, provided background on specific areas to inform or explain decisions, and related funded or proposed projects to specific local objectives. Using an MBO type process, Dayton related policies set by their commission to departmental goals spelled out in annual contracts with the staff. Thus the use of new budget and personnel systems forced attention to the city's objectives into the budgeting process.

It is difficult to generalize about the effects of political forms on these policy setting and budgeting processes, although each city's particular political environment contributed significantly both to the nature of its policies and its processes. Political support for development policies and for capital expenditures to further those objectives seemed to arise in a number of ways. First, support was sometimes achieved by involving citizens in policy development and budget making. Second, when development policies were part of the agenda of a popularly-elected mayor, they acquired ligitimacy. Third, when elected officials focused consciously on policy setting, some measure of political commitment to policy was obtained. Finally, the socio-économic homogeneity and local traditions of a community itself meant in some cases that support for some policies and actions was a foregone conclusion. Since the last conditions are a given, I will discuss the first three in the communities we studied.

Each of the four mature cities allowed citizens to participate in policy and budgeting through semi-official neighborhood networks to comply with CDBG regulations and to develop mechanisms for regular citizen feedback. Having formal procedures for input did seem to change the character of budget decisions. For example, council members were less influenced by operating departments and more responsive to neighborhood interests as a result of the process. Although many mentioned that it was difficult and time-consuming to involve citizens, there was public support for this process of arriving at decisions, if not always for the individual projects.

Political legitimacy was also accorded to policy and budget decisions when they were part of the agenda of a popularly-elected mayor. In Baltimore, for example, development policy *was* the mayor's agenda. His staff prepared the policy and budget document—the *Development Program*—which was clearly an executive document. His appointments on the Board of Estimate ensured approval of the budget, and his physical development coordinator monitored the city's operations to make sure that decisions were carried out. Perhaps because his policies were written down in only the broadest terms, the mayor was able to respond quickly to expressions of neighborhood needs or development opportunities presented by the private sector.

In both Atlanta and St. Paul, a charter amendment instituting a strong mayor form of government also required the use of policies to guide budget decisions. In Atlanta, an annual process of planning and budgeting was mandated in the new charter, giving a department reporting to the mayor more budgetary control, because the finance director reports directly to the council.

In St. Paul, the shift from a commission to a strong mayor form of government also resulted in centralization of authority in the executive branch. St. Paul has, in addition, involved citizens extensively in setting policy *and* has shifted responsibility for determining capital priorities to them. It is required both by state law and charter that a citizens' committee use a priority rating sheet to determine priorities for expenditure of capital improvement bond funds. This citizens' budget committee, with the assistance of the mayor's budget staff, makes multi-million dollar decisions on the capital budget that for the most part were ratified by the mayor and council.

In mature cities with a council/manager form of government—where in theory the council sets policy—elected officials struggled with policy-oriented processes. Dayton's elected officials underwent policy leadership training to assume a more conscious policy role, allowing the staff to administer policy and monitor the city's progress. Commissioners have prepared a *Policy Guidebook* to record policy decisions and they use policy discussion forms to consider agenda items. Budget discussions, we were told, did not include mention of dollars and cents, rather of problems and alternative solutions.

But where there was local disagreement about the meaning of policies, the written words in the *Guidebook* were of little help. For example, approval of an emergency bypass resulted in a dispute about whether Dayton's "role in the regional leadership" meant that Dayton should act first to strengthen its economic base or the region's, when the latter might be to the disadvantage of the city in the short run. Thus, the *Guidebook's* written policies could only be an imperfect guide.

Regardless of the form of government, the way in which council members are elected appears to determine whose interests are represented and thus has implications for the city's policy and budgeting processes. At-large elections make it easier for elected officials to support capital improvements for the good of the whole city, while ward systems mean that capital funds must be spread, sometimes making sorely needed improvements in particular areas impossible. And in mature, as in growing communities, election by ward seems to make a city more responsive to neighborhood rather than business interests.

Thus, faced with financial and political problems in using policies, some mature cities did appear to have achieved a measure of success in using policies in the capital budgeting process. Having now discussed the policies and problems in rapidly growing and mature cities, I would like to conclude with more general comments.

Perhaps when capital improvements were financed primarily by issuing general obligation bonds to systematically replace and expand capital facilities, it made sense to think that local governments could list capital expansion or renovation needs and take regular steps to meet them. But now, because many capital improvements are no longer locally financed, it makes little sense to conceptualize the process in this way. Thus, the capital improvements programs cannot literally implement plans as they once might have done.

Futher, when we talk about implementation of policies through better control over capital budgeting, this primarily means political, not technical improvements. When a local government sets out to more closely relate policy to capital expenditures, it is important that it recognize that this is not a politically neutral effort.

While there were some systematic differences between growing and mature cities, we were struck with the unique historical traditions and local pecularities that made policy-oriented budgeting processes function on various levels. Informal relationships, the character of the business community, the income level of citizens, the availability of certain revenue sources, and the character of political leadership, among other reasons, seemed to account for local variations. As a result, it is difficult to recommend successful aspects of these processes for other communities, regardless of the seeming similarity of their situation.

CONCLUSION

In examining the policies of these eight cities and in trying to assess how their capital expenditure decisions were made, we observed that fiscal concerns are the central and perhaps the controlling ones. The basic objectives of mature cities are economic development and neighborhood revitalization, both of which augment tax base and minimize taxes to existing residents. Although citizens in growing communities also share these concerns, they did not want to assume the costs of capital expansion and to have their services diluted as a result. Thus their development objectives also were at base fiscal— to shift costs and to set service standards that preserved existing service/cost ratios. While local development policies often included non-financial objectives, such as environmental protection and minimization of energy consumption (and some people believed in them), the main reason that there is political support for compact and efficient development is because this reduces the capital and operating costs to the city, and thus to its taxpayers.

In the case of rapidly growing cities, it is important to note that planning and budgeting processes designed to manage capital expansion were the product of local governments in states with strong judicial and legislative support for planning. California, Oregon and

Maryland in particular give statutory support to certain planning policies, and the courts in these states are sympathetic to planning efforts by local governments. Such factors, again make practical recommendations for growing communities in different states inappropriate.

In the end, we are skeptical about the overall usefulness of written policies to influence budgeting decisions, although symbolic and legal benefits of policies cannot be ignored. While in several municipalities these policies were recognized as useful in the budgeting process, this seems to be as much the result of unique local factors and social homogeneity as it is the particular character of policy statements. Since cause and effect relationships were impossible to establish, it was hard for anyone to prove that written policies had made a difference in budget outcomes, although some felt that they had.

If capital improvement decisions are to be made in the "public interest," we sense that better policies will go farther to achieve this than elaborate policies. If a clearly understood process is developed, in which participation by departments, neighborhoods, elected officials, administrative staff and business interests is carefully managed and controlled, decisions will be, by definition, less insular. Planners might spend their time more usefully in determining the probable consequences of capital improvements and making this information available to the public, elected officials and department heads, than in trying to exert their influence on local governments to make capital improvements that follow long-run plans and policies. Whether or not the individual capital improvement decisions are in accordance with long-run concerns is a political decision that citizens should recognize and elected officials must make. For professionals in local government, this will not be a comforting thought, because as a result, expediency and parochial interests will sometimes win out. But after all, local governments have two not-always-compatible functions—the delivery of services and the adjudication of political conflicts.

NOTES

1. Peat, Marwick, Mitchell & Co; Ross, Hardies, O'Keefe, Babcock and Parsons; Municipal Finance Officers Association; and Dr. Carl Patton.
2. Community Development Block Grant.
3. Planning programming and budgeting system and managment by objectives.

Astrid E. Merget - ACHIEVING EQUITY IN AN ERA OF FISCAL CONSTRAINT

INTRODUCTION

The urban malaise of the sixties, followed by a period of sustained urban decline, has raised unsettling questions: Is the condition of American cities fair? Is it just? Is it equitable? Or, what is the acceptable course for public policy in dealing with the decline of urban America?

In searching for answers, the philosopher, the policy analyst and the social reformer are all vexed by the proverbial riddle: What is equity? The riddle is further conplicated by the dilemma of how equity meshes with other enduring values of the American civic culture such as stability, liberty and equality. Most social scientists have evaded these normative issues; they prefer to chart the course of urban change by documenting the disparate conditions within and among metropolitan areas. However, if the equity consequences of urban change are to be understood, we must deal with more than the obvious symptoms of inequity such as the fiscal disparities which popularly characterize the urban crisis. We must begin to deal with the underlying structure and dynamics of local government, and we must contemplate the moral underpinnings of the American federal system.

EQUITY in a TIME of FISCAL STRAIN

In 1978, as analysts sort out the process of urban change,[1] they uncover a racial pattern perhaps more extreme than the one presented by the Kerner Commission ten years ago. As the redistribution of people and jobs progressed, the older, more industrialized and densely-settled cities of the Northeast and Midwest have suffered population losses, economic decline and fiscal strain. Suburbanization coupled with regional movements has been selective in its effects. Cities in general, but particularly the declining ones, have come to contain larger fractions of the poor, principally concentrated among minority groups. The fiscal strain, squeezing municipal budgets, is all the more attenuated by the pressing needs of these dependent people for municipal services.

Since the "politics of bankruptcy" has gripped cities like New York and Cleveland, policymakers and policy analysts have riveted their attention on the economic and financial plight of municipalities.[2] For municipal officials, the nub of the problem is balancing the budget— finding added revenues (sometimes through budget gimmickry) and controlling expenditure increases by cutting back services and resisting claims for higher wages and salaries on the part of municipal workers. The revenue-expenditure crunch is a mere sympton of a more funda- mental problem arising from the dynamics of urban change. Raising revenues and spending them results from a municipality's function as a service provider. Fiscal strain thus portends a decline in the quantity and quality of urban services.

The evidence on fiscal emergencies suggests that the effects are felt disproportionately by the disadvantaged: minority-member civil servants are usually the first to be unemployed; social-welfare pro- grams are witnessing if not absolute cutbacks, then slower increments relative to the cost of living; and basic municipal services such as police, fire and sanitation also are being curtailed. Another indication of strain is the disinvestment in the infrastructure and capital facilities of many municipalities. Further limiting the fiscal capacity of muni- cipal governments to respond to service demands and needs are Proposition 13 and the prospect of similar kinds of expenditure- revenue controls in other states and localities.

Declining services may further accelerate the urban exodus for those with the ability to exit. For some who opt to stay, their incomes permit seeking private-sector alternatives to complement or substitute for municipal services; the most obvious indication is the choice of many urban residents to enroll their children in private schools. For those without these options, owing to poverty and the persistence of racial discrimination, service declines signify an absolute loss in welfare.

The racial and poverty dimensions of urban change are more profound now than they were a decade ago. Even the hopeful, although isolated and modest signs of urban redevelopment, captured in "gentrification," augur further problems: the displacement of the poor and minority families from their neighborhoods. The initiatives proposed under the new urban policy of the Carter Administration last March (1978) recognize the economic and fiscal consequences of urban change, but beg the moral dilemma: are the heightened disparities—across neighborhoods, cities, suburbs and regions—fair? Are they just? Are they equitable? Are most of the residents in declining cities who are compelled to stay, destined to suffer the material consequences of fiscal strain and deteriorating services?

The legacy of recent judical decisions implies a "no" to these questions. The landmark case of *Hawkins v. Town of Shaw* (461 F.2d 1171 [1972]) in Mississippi proscribed discrimination on the basis of race in the provision of basic municipal services. Expanding that precedent beyond the small, rural towns of the South has met resistance. Yet, public-interest lawyers, civil rights groups and other municipal reformers, often assisted by foundation support,[3] continue to press the issue of equity in service provision. While inspired by the successes of the school-finance reforms, the urban fiscal crisis itself seems to frustrate the cause. Redistribution to offset inequities is simply more painful, when many municipal infusions of state and federal aid are bleak and when the overall economy is hamstrung by inflation and a sluggish growth rate.

IN PURSUIT of EQUITY

Like most public values—accountability, efficiency, effectiveness, responsiveness and representativeness—the norm of equity is elusive. Perplexing the translation of equity into reasonable rule for the distribution of municipal services are the unanswered riddles:

(1) What is to be equalized? inputs? activities? output? outcomes?

(2) What is the basis for equalizing? needs? preferences? effort? willingness to pay?

(3) What is the appropriate unit? individuals? jurisdictions?

(4) What is the level of equalization? a minimum standard? uniformity?

There is no consensus on answers to these questions. Nor is there a coherent theory of the political economy from which answers can be deduced logically for policy purposes. Yet, the fact of the matter is that policymakers, including the providers of services, do answer these questions every day, whether consciously or not. The police chief, the fire marshall, the civil engineer, the librarian, the school superintendent and a host of other service providers—all make decisions on equity.

The overall objective of this paper is to clarify how the norm of equity does and can operate in the provision of municipal services even in an era of fiscal strain. Three aspects of equity are explored: first, equity as a moral issue; second, equity as a legal principle, third, equity as a decision rule in public policy. Finally, a political economy framework for grappling with the equity issue as both an intellectual and practical matter is offered in an effort to resolve many of the distortions which have crippled our thinking about this critical public value.

EQUITY AS A MORAL ISSUE

The last decade is rich in examples of political events and policy disputes which have revived interest in the public value of equity. The politics of confrontation convulsed many cities in the mid-sixties and underlies sustained tensions between city hall and minority neighborhoods; the politics of fiscal bankruptcy seized New York and Cleveland and threatens the capacity of many other municipalities to provide public services; and the politics of tax revolt extends beyond California's borders to other states and municipalities and promises to limit the scope and discretion of local officials. These events signal a crisis in the basic institutions of local government. They also communicate a concern for the outcomes of public policy; that is, for the impact public action has on the conditions of different sets of individuals and jurisdictions.

Over the decade, national policy responses to urban problems have come to reflect changing conceptions of what policy can and should do. Recent debates over the Carter Administration's proposals for urban policy no longer manifest the sharp distinctions between liberals and conservatives. Many "liberals" are now uncertain about the appropriate scope of governmental intervention in the market economy and in the affairs of state and local government; there is also uncertainty about the preferred set of policy instruments for dealing with urban problems. Many policy initiatives recommended to assist local governments in coping with urban change encompass options once regarded as "conservative": local institutional capacity-building, vouchers, unrestricted aid and block grants plus a host of public incentives to leverage private action Merely rechannelling federal funds to distressed areas is no longer the preferred, let alone feasible, course of policy action.

NORMATIVE THEORY REAWAKENED

Intellectuals also have responded to these disturbing events with a renewed concern for public values. Normative discourse in the social sciences has resurged, as analysts question the significance of their "objective" findings. In search of meaning, conventional theories of politics, administration and public finance have come under attack. Political scientists are reassessing their conceptions of American pluralism.[4] Scholars of public administration are challenging the hierarchical model of bureaucracy and questioning the field's historic commitment to such values as efficiency and neutral competence.[5] Even for economists, the statistical, descriptive term of fiscal disparities provokes a moral concern: Campbell and Bahl discerned that metropolitan fiscal disparities posed "the central moral dilemma for reformers of the late sixties" and that recast in the context of an equity framework, the goal of relating services to needs "is closely allied with current economics usage of efficiency, as related to demand."[6]

As social scientists wrestle with problems as complex as those in our cities, barriers between disciplines have weakened and the fact-value dichotomies have dissipated. Contemporary policy analysts are vitally concerned with the impact public policy has on the social well-being of various groups within society. Their new preoccupation with policy outcomes lends the riddle of equity a substantive reference point in ongoing policy research.

Equity has been a recurrent theme in political philosophy dating back to Aristotle[7] and reaching up to the current, provocative work of John Rawls.[8] Philosophers locate equity within the larger concepts of justice. Their many theories of justice evolve from complex, sometimes torturous and arcane, modes of reasoning. Rawls, for example, defines such a procedure for deriving a morally just society. The logic envisions an original position, an intellectual state rather than a state of nature, which is essential for assuring the conditions whereby moral discourse, not political bargaining, will promote consensus on the rules of justice. In the original position, men focus on themselves as men. Put another way: they operate under a veil of ignorance such that they are unaware of their place in society and of the differences in their socio-economic, genetic and intellectual endowments. From the discourse ensue the rules of justice, of fairness, of equity. In short, what results is the difference principle which permits the redistribution of resources across society's members in order to improve the relative condition of those worse off. Redistribution may occur even if some members are made worse off, providing they were among the better off.

Rawls, like other philosophers, offers both a procedure and a set of principles which facilitate appraising the actions of government and their consequences for the relative condition of individuals within society. In the realworld of political bargaining, where the resources of power are not uniformly distributed, his theory seems unworkable, and for many it is plainly undesirable. However, judging by the commentary and debate his theory has inspired, the topic has animated many in the academic, legal and political communities.[9]

PRAGMATIC MORALITY

Until recently, many policy analysts and policymakers have constricted their view of equity to the process of political choice. The practical message of Rawls is the profound importance of both process and outcome and their interrelationship.[10] Certainly calling for a constitutional convention to simulate the original position seems somewhat far-fetched. But even in the absence of a coherent and acceptable theory of equity confining policy efforts to equal opportunity, equal representation and other procedural reforms seems unduly shortsighted and even vaguely immoral; it neglects the results of the decisionmaking process. Who gets what? Who benefits? Who pays?—these questions are the essence of practical politics. In pointing to the outcomes of public action, these questions speak to equity as a public value. Equity pertains to the relative condition of individuals in society. In searching out the meaning of equity in public policy, the test is a simple one to frame: What difference does public policy make in the relative condition of people? Are they worse off, better off or just the same as a result of public action (or inaction)?

With those questions providing the test, the old conceptions of incremental, pluralistic politics are most unsatisfying. Consensus may be a practical, even necessary, condition for policy in a heterogeneous, conflict-oriented society, but it is not a sufficient one.

Economists have also backed away from the issue of equity. Although concerned with the substantive conditions that warrant governmental intrusions into a free-market economy, public-goods theorists define the allocation function in a subordinate way: public provision of goods and services is legitimate to promote economic efficiency, when the market-place fails. This line of argument deprives government of any distinctive, purposeful mission beyond law and order and national defense. Only in delineating the distribution function is there any faint attention to what Madison envisioned as the premier purpose of government: "Justice is the end of government. It is the end of civil society." (Federalist No. 52.)

In effect, practical policymakers are left to decide what equity is, with few philosophic principles to judge the consequences of their decisions. Political philosophy seems too abstract and often contradictory to apply to the daily choices that confront officials. Political scientists furnish some procedural guides, while economists confine the distribution function to some equity principles for taxation.

The reaction in the sixties to policy decisions still haunts our cities. Then, as now, a substantial fraction of Americans did not accept the outcomes of the political process as fair. In fact, so outraged were the poor and the minorities that they violated the rules of pluralistic politics and exchanged compromise for confrontation. To be sure, an alternative—a coherent, acceptable theory of equity—is probably unrealistic in a heterogenous society. But, in ignoring that possibility, officials have abdicated some of the hard choices about equity to the judiciary. Judges have become the "philosopher-kings" on the fairness of municipal service provision.

EQUITY AS A LEGAL PRINCIPLE

Several decisions reached by the courts have come to endow the norm of equity with substantive meaning. When claims alleging discrimination in service provision have been litigated, the courts have had to judge the policies and practices of local governments as fair, just or legal. On a case-by-case basis, the body of law begins to furnish partial answers to what equity is. Three streams of litigation help clarify what fact situations warrant being labelled inequitable and what tests of equity the courts invoke to make such judgments. A review of the salient cases offers some practical guidelines for policymakers charged with allocating scarce resources in an equitable way.

FACT SITUATIONS

The most pertinent legal tradition began with the decision in *Hawkins* v. *Town of Shaw*, when, in 1971, the U.S. Court of Appeals for the Fifth Circuit ruled on the claims of black residents in Shaw, Mississippi. The opinion of Judge Elbert Tuttle in speaking for the court appeared to many social reformers and policy analysts as prophetic of a new era in municipal reform:

> Referring to a portion of a town or segment of society as being 'on the other side of the tracks' has for too long been a familiar expression to most Americans. Such a phase immediately conjures up an area characterized by poor housing, overcrowded conditions and, in short, overall deterioration. While there may be many reasons why such areas exist in nearly all of our cities, one reason that cannot be accepted is the discriminatory provision of municipal services based on race.[11]

The *Shaw* decision rendered a narrow standard for equity in the provision of municipal services. The current legal meaning is very simply: minority citizens in a community should receive roughly the same quality and quantity of services as are received by its white residents. With race as a suspect classification commanding the strict scrutiny of the court, the judges found that discriminatory service provision served no useful state purpose.[12] Rather, discriminatory treatment conferred some kind of stigma, harm or abuse.

The conditions in the town of Shaw were indeed extreme. The case for litigation rested on the fact of near absolute deprivation. The disparity in services between whites and blacks was of gross proportions. The pattern of "with" vs. "without" services was all too vividly reinforced by rigid residential segregation. Shaw was a relatively small community in population, thus permitting the plaintiffs to compile an exhaustive inventory of services. The services in dispute were quite tractable—roads, lights, sewers, water drainage; their conditions were readily described in simple statistical terms (*e.g.*, the proportion of houses fronting on unpaved roads).[13] Interpreting the evidence before the court merely required a common-sense, logical deduction: the severe disparities, as they correspond to racially-defined neighborhoods within the town, constituted a *prima facie* case of service discrimination. This pattern of inequity is a simple one to discover. The obvious problem in expanding the precedent is that few metropolitan urban centers display such blatant patterns of service discrimination. The prototypical rural town of the South finds few counterparts in the large central cities of other regions.

Following the decision, the precedent was strengthened by a series of similar cases: the progeny of *Shaw*.[14] Most mirrored the same fact situations and successfully reached settlements either in or outside of court. However, efforts to stretch the precedent to cover service conditions in large urban centers failed. Two such cases are illustrative: *Beal* v. *Lindsay* (468 F.2d. 287 [2nd Cir. 1972]) and *Burner* v. *Washington* (C.A. No. 242-71 [D.D.C. 1972]). While neither undermined the *Shaw* principle, both introduced confusion into the documentation of facts and into the legal meaning of equitable service conditions.

Beal v. *Lindsay* attacked the conditions of selected parks in the City of New York.[15] It was alleged that a park in the Bronx serving a predominantly black and Puerto Rican population was poorly maintained and was not staffed as well as the three other parks in other sections of the borough. The park was not only unsightly; the gounds and facilities were also in disrepair and disarray. Users could suffer harm. The City in its defense established that is was spending proportionately more on the park in question; it also pointed to higher rates of vandalism in the adjacent community. The court rules in the City's favor. In a sense, the court appeared to be adopting an input standard to judge fairness rather than the resulting condition or outcome implied in *Shaw*.

Unlike the New York case, an action filed against the District of Columbia encompassed a wide range of services including fire and police protection, recreational facilities, refuse collection, the provision of sidewalks and mass transit. In *Burner* v. *Washington* the court was presented with more complex dimensions of service delivery as well as more sophisticated evaluations of service conditions.[16] The facts on police protection, for example, looked to workload statistics, crime rates and clearance rates. There was an at least implicit attempt to discern the demand, need and efficiency dimensions of the service. In assessing the facts the court looked for "substantial differences" across a few black and white communities selected for comparison within the City. The court did not find that the disparities were "substantial" enough to warrant a finding of racial discrimination. However, while the case was in litigation, the City took steps to redress some of the disparities alleged in the case.

A second, impressive category of lawsuits surrounds the financing of public education at the state-local level. The best known of these numerous actions are: *Serrano* v. *Priest* (483 P.2d. 1241, 1244 [Cal. 1971]), *San Antonio Independent School District* v. *Rodriguez* (411 U.S. 1, 58 [1973]), and *Robinson* v. *Cahill* (62 N.J. 473, 303 A 2d. 273 [1973]).[17] Initially, some of these cases shared with *Shaw* a reliance on the equity principles to be derived from the Equal Protection Clause, but most have come to depend on comparable provisions in state constitutions. In *Serrano*, the original case looked to both the U.S. Constitution and the California state constitution. In reviewing the variable tax bases supporting the state's numerous school districts, the state court scrutinized tax-base inequalities and considered their implications for the quality of education a student would receive. The range of the fiscal disparities was so extreme that the court concluded it was unfair to make the quality of education a child could receive dependent upon the average wealth of a school district. The court amplified the notion of suspect classification beyond race to include wealth. The standard of fiscal neutrality[18] was invoked and the remedy envisioned a new financing system, predicated on district power equalization.[19] Furthermore, the court acknowledged that education commanded special importance among the array of municipal services offered by the state and local governments; education verged on becoming a fundamental interest[20] requiring special constitutional protection.

While in the wake of *Serrano* many states became targets for litigation or initiated school-finance reforms under pressure, the Constitutional footing behind these reforms was eroded by the Supreme Court ruling in *Rodriguez*. The Court, confronted with a similar pattern of tax-base inequities in Texas, refused to elevate wealth to the status of a suspect classification. It also refused to dignify education as a fundamental interest, and it proceeded to legitimate the authority of the state and local governments with a federal system to design the financing systems for local services. In effect, the pursuit of equity in the courts now must be sought in the states. Upon opening the case again, *Serrano* was upheld in the California state court in 1976. Other actions in an assortment of states have also resulted in favorable rulings.[21]

In the past, these challenges concentrated on the financing arrangements for local elementary and secondary education. The facts focused on disparities in the tax bases available to school districts and on the impacts of state aid for education. Over time the facts have come to comprehend more refined dimensions of local education, going beyond financial inputs to look at education activities and to contemplate the outcomes and the entire process of "producing" educated children. Evidence presented in court now includes student-teacher ratios, measures of teacher quality, attendance ratios, as well as data on achievement levels, reading and other test scores. The case which is probably most distinctive is *Robinson* in that it bypasses the equity issue as such to tackle the meaning and achievement of a "thorough and efficient" education.

In more recent school finance cases, two other features of the education function have gained recognition both as evidence in the court and as part of the remedy. Under the classical test of fiscal neutrality, many urban areas did not stand to benefit from district power equalization because they rank relatively high in assessed valuation per pupil.[22] Sensitive to the fiscal strain besetting many municipalities, reforms now address the high costs of municipal over-burden[23] as well as the special educational needs of urban children.[24]

A third category of legal challenges indirectly pertains to municipal services. These cases differ from the *Shaw-* or *Serrano*-type actions because inequity in service delivery was not the single, central fact or legal issue in dispute. Instead equal protection and due process issues associated with local policy practices under General Revenue Sharing,[25] municipal annexation,[26] voting rights,[27] as well as zoning and land use,[28] furnished the basis for filing complaints in federal and state courts. In a number of these cases, data on disparities in service provision were cited as evidence of the discriminatory effects of the policies in question. Where claims are targeted to federal courts, a clear finding of racial discrimination remains imperative. However, in a few state courts, judges have been willing to expand the meaning of equity. Perhaps, most notable was the New Jersey Supreme Court decision in *Southern Burlington County NAACP* v. *Township of Mount Laurel* (67 N.J. 151, 336 A2d 713 [1975]) which invalidated exclusionary zoning practices. Not only did the court reject local policies, which intentionally or not, had the impact of excluding low-income, and primarily minority, residents; it also mandated local governments to act affirmatively in absorbing a "fair share" of that component within the regional population. Other state actions have repudiated an often-heard defense of local exclusionary zoning: the claim local officials make that the admission of lower-income families will impose fiscal and economic burdens is not defensible is some states. Not unlike the reasoning in school-finance cases, the federal courts have largely upheld the constitutional basis of local zoning practices and thus indirectly have permitted residential segregation to institutionalize services disparities within metropolitan areas. As in the financing of education, selected states are advancing equity claims of the poor and the minorities.

STANDARDS: LEGAL GUIDELINES

In reviewing the fact situations presented in these diverse cases, the courts have begun to design some standards for assessing service conditions. Generally there are three kinds of standards or tests of equity to be found in the legal proceedings.

First, there are those essentially technical in nature. These guidelines pertain to the qualitative and quantitative characteristics of a service itself. Most often, these standards are framed by the professionals responsible for actually producing and delivering a service. For instance, civil engineers go a long way to determine how a road, or bridge, or other capital facility should be constructed; what it will cost; where it is to be built; who are the users; and how effective or safe or convenient it is. Similarly, the librarian will influence the allocation of resources to branch libraries within a city and will determine what constitutes an appropriate collection of materials and services for a branch system as well as the central library. In the courts, these standards are typically introduced through the testimony of technical experts who are frequently called upon to evaluate the service in dispute and to elucidate the practices underlying an alleged inequity. Such testimony helps establish the reasonableness (or unreasonableness) of a particular pattern of service provision.

Second, policy and general administrative guidelines also are invoked. Sometimes a pattern of municipal services is defended as a consequence of the local decisionmaking process; thus, it represents an expression of distinctive and legitimate local preferences for public goods and services. Such broad standards as local discretion, accountability to constituents and responsiveness are cited, despite the ambiguity of these terms. Additionally such canons of public administration as efficiency and economy are included. These standards usually enter legal deliberations when municipal officials are summoned to explain the package of municipal services. Their arguments attempt to defend service conditions on procedure; that is, the pattern of service provision results from the policies and practices of a duly-constituted democratic political body within the federal system.

Third, and obviously key to the development of equity politics, are the emergent constitutional and legal norms applying to municipal services. Most legal challenges invoking the Equal Protection Clause have extended only to those blatant instances of service discrimination on the basis of race. Under the Berger Court, equity claims have been further constrained by the tightening up of legal procedures.[29] The Supreme Court's decision in *Washington* v. *Davis* (426 U.S. 229 [1976]) imposed severer requirements on evidence. Although the case dealt with alleged racial discrimination in the entrance tests for police officers, the Court addressed the larger question of the kind and extent of proof necessary to support claims of discrimination. It concluded that evidence showing a racially-biased impact was not sufficient. Thus ruling opened up the slippery question of whether it is essential to prove the intent to discriminate; in a footnote the opinion specifically referred to *Shaw*-type cases. In fact, the court will accept evidence documenting service disparities, whereby an inference of intent to discriminate can be confidently made. Even more compelling facts—extreme disparities and longstanding historical patterns of difference—are now needed to invoke the *Shaw* principle, but the intent dimension has not been construed as requiring evidence on motivation. Similarly, the Court's ruling in *Alaska Pipeline* limited attorneys fees to only those claims specified by Congress in statute, thus making the relief from many unfair conditions sought by the poor and minorities through litigation prohibitively expensive. Curiously, equity claims brought under statute have generally secured more favorable rulings from the Berger Court, as occurred in the Chicago case of *Hills* v. *Gautreaux* (U.S. Sup. Ct. 74-1047 [1976]). Further reinforcing the *Shaw* precedent has been the expansion of the legal basis to include statutory requirements on non-discrimination in the use of federal funds like General Revenue Sharing.[30]

The pursuit of equity in state courts has, by contrast, expanded the scope of legal protection against unfair service practices. The expansion has proceeded incrementally on a service-by-service basis—in education, in zoning and land use and so forth. Furthermore, wealth as well as race figures into the tests of discrimination. Frequently, judgments contain more than findings in equity and exhoration for remedial action; they often prescribe guidelines for affirmative action to undo past patterns of discrimination.

THE PRACTICAL MEANINGS of EQUITY

In deliberating the cases alleging service inequity—that is, where service disparities are treated as inequities—that courts have grappled with a number of questions that ultimately go to the heart of the municipal service sector:

First, what is the mix of services to be undertaken by a municipality?

Second, what services, if provided insufficiently or not at all, are of such public significance that the disparity implies some kind of stigma, deprivation or harm?

Third, how are the quality and quantity of services to be described and measured?

Fourth, how are various groupings of citizens who benefit from as well as pay for services to be classified and treated?

Fifth what is the permissible rate of variation of such dimensions of services as inputs, outputs and outcomes, particularly among the relevant groupings of the municipality?

Sixth, what is the magnitude of resources required to offset those variations which may be deemed unfair? And how are such resources to be secured?

Although often ambiguous or even conflicting, the courts have offered partial answers to these queries. Federal courts regard decisions on the mix of services to be provided within a municipality to be within the province of local policymaking, as constrained by the various state assignments of service responsibility. But the federal courts are unequivocal on at least one dimension of municipal service delivery: once a municipality undertakes to provide a service, that service must be made available to all residents. There are several refinements on this point of law. *Shaw* proscribes discrimination on the basis of race alone, not wealth. Consequently, a city may use special assessments which are tied to wealth or ability-to-pay in order to finance services.[31] The practice most likely will be declared illegal, if a city moves to invoke special assessments when services are to be provided to a black neighborhood after comparable services have already been made available to white residents through the general budget.

In addition, municipal governments will be held in violation of the Equal Protection Clause, if over time the redefinition of city boundaries through annexation demonstrates the exclusion of black communities on the periphery of a city. The effect has been to deprive them of city services. Similarly, in the design of electoral schemes, a city will be considered as undercutting the law, if the voting power of black residents in effectively diluted, thus denying them meaningful political participation. Indirectly these voting rights issues reach to service delivery. An essential component of the proof is typically a demonstration that discriminatory electoral systems are linked to inferior, inadequate or simply disparate service levels. The service inequity manifests a substantive indication of the material harm conferred by unfairly-constituted decisionmaking bodies.

However, the federal courts have not extended this logic to local zoning and land use practices. Exclusionary zoning creates barriers to mobility and has the effect of denying some citizens access to better municipal services in jurisdictions with richer fiscal endowments. Nonetheless, the federal courts accord local jurisdictions the right to determine the character of their communities.[32]

Unlike education, which commands constitutional primacy in many states, other municipal services do not warrant such special privilege. In other words, the courts have not moved to sort out the essentialness of certain services over others. Indirectly, the litigation strategy entailed in municipal service cases is predicated on differences across services. The point is often made by establishing a connection between a service disparity and the social consequences which ensue. For example, a compelling argument in the courtroom will demonstrate the harm associated with failure to supply a service adequately or at all: a faulty water system in a town takes on special significance when linked to an outbreak of hepatitis. Direct bodily harm with overtones of mortality weighs heavily as evidence of the substantive impact of a service inequity. Clearly not all services have such import. Where amenities like parks, recreation facilities or libraries are in question, the connotation of a stigma or implication of inferiority takes on a more persuasive meaning than harm.

In *Shaw* and its companion cases, the disparities were so severe that the evidence did not have to depend as much on establishing such a causal link with analytic precision or rigor. The *Beal* case signalled the court's hesitancy to advance the proposition that service disparities in inputs could ultimately lead to material harm or stigma. The fact that the City spent an equal or greater amount on the park redeemed the municipality. The intervening variable of vandalism, which influenced the eventual condition of the park, was discounted as a feature of service provision for which the City could have been held responsible. In short, the courts appear quite confused over the essential differences across services, over the appropriate dimension on which to measure inequity—inputs, outputs, outcomes—and over the interrelationship of these factors through some underlying production function.[33]

Education offers a distinct contrast. Although the *Serrano* tradition accentuates input disparities, the proof has extended to demonstrate the likely social consequences of tax-base inequalities. More and more evidence delineating the various elements of service production and delivery is presented to the court. The input standard, implied by fiscal neutrality, has been modified in states, which acknowledge the special educational needs of children, especially those in central cities, as well as the higher service costs of the municipal service sector. The "thorough and efficient" standards in New Jersey potentially enlarges the analysis of service provision beyond inputs.

The courts also have had to decide at what point a disparity becomes an inequity and in turn what magnitude of resources is required to remedy the situation. In *Shaw*, the answer was simple. The pattern of service disparities presented a "with" vs. "without" set of conditions. The solution was to level up the services in the black community to those of the white community. In *Burner*, the court phrased the test as one of "substantial differences." Although the meaning was never clarifed, the term implied a disparity not nearly so extreme as in *Shaw* and it was affixed to the workload and conditions of services. However, in *Beal*, equal or proportionate inputs were accepted as proof of nondiscrimination, while in *Shaw* the remedy implied that varying inputs would be needed to compensate for past practices of discrimination in achieving equality in service conditions. The court seemed to be focusing on what might be called service outputs or measures of an intermediate rather than final good: fire hydrants, paved roads, street lights and so forth.

In education, the remedy of district power equalization presumes levelling up poorer districts and levelling down wealthier ones to some statewide average. In fact, grandfather or hold harmless provisions precluded the latter. The result usually meant a jump in state aid to pull up poor local districts. Increasingly, the input standard and state-wide average have given way under special remedies for urban areas. The courts appear to be moving toward a concept of equal outputs or even outcomes, whereby variable inputs are permitted to accomodate the different needs of service consumers.

The pursuit of equity through the courts is most auspicious for education but significantly less so for other municipal services. Advancing the *Shaw* tradition to urban areas will mean that the Equal Protection Clause must embrace not just race but also wealth. Even if that unlikely possibility materialized, the proof would probably necessitate establishing a connection between a disparity and some harmful, undesirable social consequence. Analysts of service delivery have long fretted over the definition of service production functions, which precisely relate inputs, activities, outputs and eventual outcomes. Also, there lurks the question as to whether the scope of comparing disparities should be confined to selected, perhaps "sampled", neighborhoods or should extend to all neighborhoods within a city and even to city-suburban differences within a metropolitan area.

Merely replicating *Shaw* will bring relief to some municipalities where egregious practices of racial discrimination persist. But for residents in larger urban centers, a litigation strategy will not be simple. In growing and expanding cities, the tradition of law on annexation and voting rights may afford some indirect assurance of fairness in service provision. In declining, land-locked cities, however, such recourse may not be appropriate. Claims filed under statute in federal court may fare better. That will probably mean attacking service disparities on a more limited service-by-service basis. It will also critically depend on the wording of the non-discrimination provisions in a statute, rather than on a simple clearcut principle of equity. State courts appear a more promising route certainly for education and in a few states for zoning and land use, which again indirectly may promise a more equitable service sector in metropolitan areas. Despite these diverse avenues, there remains another unsettling question as to whether or not the courts are institutions capable of and appropriate for judging the shades and nuances of complex fact situations and for offering up policy remedies.

EQUITY AS A DECISION RULE IN PUBLIC POLICY

The pattern of public services within any municipality does not just happen. It results from a complex set of policy and administrative decisions which public officials make in allocating scarce resources. Daily, they make choices about who gets what, who benefits, who pays. Since some people are made better or worse off as a consequence, these decisions manifest equity rules. Local decisions on resource allocation are made differently from jurisdiction to jurisdiction and from service to service; they are also in varying ways altered by intergovernmental policies. In practice, there is no single answer to what is equity. Instead, there are many.

In an effort to discover these numerous answers, a starting point is the accumulated body of policy analysis which has struggled to explain variations in the levels and mixes of municipal services. From the diverse and sometimes contradictory findings, three broad sets of influences can be delineated for their significance in elucidating how equity rules translate into patterns of local services. The first influence pertains to the structure of local government, particularly the scale or the boundaries of a jurisdiction. The second set of influences encompasses local finances, specifically the revenue-raising capacity of a municipality and its reliance on intergovernmental funds. The third, perhaps most neglected in policy analysis until lately, concerns the administration of local budgets; that is, the conversion of resources into services that are made available to local citizens. On each dimension choices are made, whether consciously or not, that affect the eventual distribution of municipal services. Further, the emphasis on one influence over another in research has given rise to at least three popularly-held prescriptions for promoting greater equity in municipal service

provision: some structuralists call for the redesign of local governments; the fiscalists recommend rechanneling funds, leaving the
basic structure of government intact; and the students of administration contemplate alternate modes other than bureaucracy for
delivering services and interacting with clients. The validity of their
prescriptions crucially depends on their conceptions of how equity
fits in the complex scheme of service provision and on the methods
of research they develop to generate findings.

Presented here is a brief summary of several research perspectives
on the structure, finances and administration of local governments,
as they affect service provision and in turn determine who benefits.
A more critical and intensive review of relevant research, yet to be
done, will go a long way to clarify what equity means: how the norm
actually works as a decision rule in public policy; what the consequences of different equity rules are on service provision and on
the relative conditions of service consumers; and what the opportunity
costs may be of preferring one equity rule over another. Further,
a critical review of these disparate research traditions will indicate
how equity had been conceptualized and measured in policy analysis
and how understanding what equity is and should be might benefit
from a new framework of analysis.

STRUCTURING LOCAL GOVERNMENT

The structure of local government establishes not only the formal
institutions of policymaking but also the scale or territorial area
captured within its jurisdiction. Scale has profound impact on local
service sectors because it delineates who and what are included or
excluded. Hence, scale influences what the resulting demand for
public services will be and the locality's capacity to support a public
sector on its own. The size of a jurisdiction, measured both by
geography and by population size, helps determine the proximity
or accessibility of government to its citizens. Boundaries also define
the degree of homogeneity a community exhibits in its socio-economic and cultural character.

In addition, structure also affects the process of decisionmaking
in that it specifies the electoral schemes as well as the authoritative
institutions for policymaking. To the extent that outcomes result
from political processes, the nature of official institutions helps
determine the allocation of scarce resources.

Thus, in describing and explaining variations in the quality and
quantity of services available within and across governments, structure is of crucial import. Whether a jurisdiction expands its boundaries

through annexation or city-county consolidation, or whether it adopts a ward- rather than an at-large electoral scheme, or whether it moves to centralize authority in a strong mayor or not—these choices may alter the eventual distribution of public services.

The structural issue, particularly as it pertains to the scale of local government, resurrects the historical debate over centralization vs. decentralization[34] in the American federal system. Although a topic of long-standing controversy, modern analysts have moved beyond the normative issues to inform the debate with empirical evidence on the service consequences of varying scale and altering boundaries.[35]

On the issue, two current schools of thought clash. The public choice approach, for example, rests its argument for small-scale units on an analogy between public-sector allocation and the private marketplace. As formulated by Tiebout, Bish, Ostrom and others,[36] the analogy works as a rationale for a multiplicity of local governments, each offering a distinct package of services and taxes from which mobile consumers/voters may choose. Carried to its extreme, this line of reasoning justifies disparities in service provision as a legitimate expression of different preferences on the part of consumers for services and their willingness to pay for them. There is resistance to the centralizing tendencies, threatened by metropolitan forms of organization which are often recommended for promoting some form of fiscal redistribution from wealthier to poorer jurisdictions. Instead, forms of inter-local cooperation, improvisation and co-production[37] are encouraged. Despite the compelling criticism targeted at this approach by those who assail the marketplace construct and construe local service disparities as reflections of the mismatch between needs and resources, the public choice theorists provoke a central question of equity: the preferred structure of the intergovernmental system for realizing genuine and legitimate preferences for public services and taxes. A critical perspective they offer on equity is their concern for consumer preference—that is the demand side of the local public sector; smaller-scale jurisdictions more readily admit of revealing preference, and to the degree that they are more homogeneous, consensus is more easily struck internally on what services should be provided.

There is a healthy empirical tradition rooted in the public choice approach. Its primary focus is the effect of alternative organizational scales and related bureaucratic arrangements for public-service provision. In the analysis of municipal budgets, there has been an ambitious effort to move beyond simple revenue-expenditure indicators and look at service performance and productivity.[38] Considerable attention has been focused on the outcomes of service provision, as they are comprehended in the satisfaction derived by citizens/ consumers from the various services they receive. In general, the findings are in the direction of favoring small-scale units for production and delivery. These studies have generated voluminous data on the varieties and disparities in services. In so doing they go a long way to isolate the convoluted dimensions of service provision spanning inputs to outcomes, plus they bring together objective measures with the perceptions citizens hold.

Rejecting the public choice argument are the traditional municipal reformers who favor increased centralization. They stress the resource base of local government, as it relates to the service needs of constituents as well as the larger economic region. Further, they forsee increased efficiencies by containing externalities and realizing economies of scale. Their emphasis is on the supply side of the local public sector. By expanding municipal boundaries to capture the wealthier tax bases in the suburbs and by assigning redistributive powers to an area-wide government, they envision offsetting fiscal disparities and achieving greater equity in services.[39]

Unfortunately, the few experiences with area-wide governments makes the record of empirical evidence somewhat limited to defend the claims of the metropolitanists.[40] To be sure, where boundary expansion has occurred, the effect has been to enrich the tax base and relieve tax pressures, thereby allaying fiscal strain. However, whether these fiscal effects have been translated into service improvements shared by the poorest segments of the population is somewhat difficult to ascertain.

Part of the problem in reconciling these two approaches to policy analysis is that they conceptualize and measure equity quite differently. The public choice approach stresses the demand side of the service sector, whereas the centralists emphasize the supply side. The former links equity to the quality and quantity of services provided, especially as the consumer evaluates them; the latter limits the view to an input consideration with more assumption than fact that an improved financial situation will translate into better services, especially for the least well off.

FINANCING MUNICIPAL GOVERNMENTS

Although the sharing of service or allocational responsibilities within a federal structure permits, even encourages, disparities to occur, adjustments are rationalized when externalities give rise to suboptimal production and when inequities arise reflecting the mismatch of fiscal resources and service needs. Some form of fiscal redistribution is typically recommended wereby the basic structure of local government remains intact. In theory and in practice, these policy instruments, most notably the grant-in-aid, contain equity rules. A long tradition of normative inquiry and empirical research into fiscal federalism helps locate a series of such rules and their impact on local budgets as well as the capacity of local governments to provide services.

A common adjustment takes the form of a grant-in-aid from the national government to the state-local sector and from states to their localities. Equity in the sense of offsetting the imbalances between service needs and revenue capacity frequently constitutes the basis for intergovernmental fiscal relations. There are a number of suggested equity rules incorporated into grant policies which determine the distribution of assistance. For example, the U.S. Advisory Commission on Intergovernmental Relations some years back identified several such alternative rules for equalization; specifically, they included: (1) a uniform amount to each state or community; (2) an equal sum per unit of program need; (3) an amount varied directly with need and capacity to foster equal program levels; and (4) an amount designed to raise program levels especially in poor states to some minimum level.[41] In the normative literature on grants, there are varied prescriptions such as Buchanan's rule of a "fiscal residum"[42] which specifies redistribution to assure that the net differences between tax burdens and expenditure benefits are equalized for individuals across jurisdictions. Concealed in the increasingly complex structure of intergovernmental grants is a set of answers to the esstential question of equity; simply put: grants-in-aid specify equity rules, which answer what is to be equalized.

A central target for empirical research has been the local budgetary effects of federal and state intergovernmental arrangements, concentrating largely on the grant-in-aid and its equalizing effects. Typically these empirical studies have classified the fiscal effects of grants as to whether they are substitutive, additive or stimulative within municipal budgets.[43] Few analyses go beyond the identification of these fiscal consequences, defined exclusively in financial or input terms, to trace the effects on service levels and their distributional impact within a city. The normative concepts ingrained in this type of research do take account of the equity features in fiscal federalism, but where this occurs redistribution pertains to inter- rather than intrajurisdictional disparities.

A related approach has been moderately successful in isolating the variables which account for disparities in local public spending. The determinants studies, originating with the seminal work of Fabricant and accumulating a long tradition of findings and methodological improvements,[44] have been able to pinpoint the relative contributions of such factors as local socio-economic characteristics, land-use features, governmental structure and intergovernmental fiscal flows on the observed variations in local public spending. The findings of these studies have invited many empirically-founded hypotheses on why some local governments spend as they do. However, these studies are highly aggregative and look to interjurisdictional disparities in spending rather than eventual service levels.[45] Further, in the absence of an underlying theory of spending determination, many of these findings are considered to be the results of statistical artifacts; that is, correlation and multiple regression.[46] This approach has been somewhat explored to explain variation in services within a city; the search is for a statistically-significant correspondence between service disparities and such factors as race, ethnicity and class.[47]

The focus on local finances also has included studies on the probable consequences of reassigning financing responsibilities from local to state governments[48] as well as of devising tax-base sharing plans.[49] More often than not the research concentrates on shifting tax burdens. Equity, as it pertains to taxation, has been at a great advantage in empirical research because policymakers and analysts have more readily reached consensus on equity rules such as ability-to-pay and on their translation into operational, measurable indicators.[50] The expenditure side of the budget, as it pertains to service benefits, lags notably behind.

ADMINISTERING MUNICIPAL SERVICE SECTORS

Equity rules also crystalize in the way resources get converted into actual services which are made available to citizens. In the past, looking at how services get produced and delivered borrowed heavily from studies into production functions. But, the simple input-output model does not furnish an accurately refined concept for analyzing local public sectors.

Depending on the elusiveness of the service in question—that is, its resistance to quantitative measurement—the studies of production functions can present very technical analyses which rely on the methods of operations research.[51] This research strain goes a long way to specify in quantitative terms the connection between service inputs and outputs and their conversion processes. Also, it has ably enlarged the range of indicators to describe service provision beyond simple expenditures. Its shortcoming is that it seldom addresses the distributional outcomes of service delivery. Many production-function studies are more technically defined than policy oriented; in exploring capital-labor relationships and the effects of new technology, they often examine only selected sub-services rather than take a comprehensive view. The inherent normative bias is efficiency rather than equity.

Yet, for many public services, understanding the production and delivery process necessitates a very different approach to analysis. The conversion of inputs into services occurs within the bureaucracies of municipal service agencies, wherein policy practices and procedures are often mysterious to citizens and policymakers and where for the analyst, they are elusive and seldom amenable to quantification. Yet, it is in the process of administration or implementation where the eventual services get produced and delivered.

The field of public administratiom finds its historical, intellectual preoccupation with the implementation side of service provision. In the late sixties, Frederickson, as an advocate of the new public administration, extolled the norm of social equity as an ethical precept for public servants; thus he challenged the traditional values of efficiency and neutral competency.[52] A complementary strain of the new public administration has scrutinized the bureaucratic structures of government dominated by hierarchical decisionmaking processes in an effort to draw out their implications for fair, responsive service delivery.[53] Their analytic focus has narrowed down to the day-to-day interactions between the service provider and service consumer.[54] At this micro-level of investigation, equity rules materialize in the transactions between service providers and service consumers.

Reinforcing this perspective on bureaucracy was the study of service provision as present in *Urban Outcomes* by Levy, Meltsner and Wildavsky.[55] They explored resource allocation for three municipal services—schools, libraries and streets. They were able to identify disparate patterns of service distribution against three standards of equity—market equity, equal opportunity and equal results. The objective data on inputs, service activities and outputs were endowed with added meaning as the analysts searched out the bureaucratic practices behind them. While all the other analytic approaches help to highlight one or another dimension of service equity such as structure or finances, it is the approach initiated in the Oakland study which is most promising to pursue, both for analytic and reform purposes. It has practical import when restructuring local government seems politically unpalatable and when radical redistribution of financial resources appears unlikely in a time of fiscal restraint.

The multiple measures approach is rich in generating empirical data on service outcomes. Although somewhat eclectic in method— some have even depicted it as a nonmethodology—it combines the production-function approach with an analysis of administrative decisionmaking. It calls for a host of indicators and data which yield evidence on the inputs, conversion process and outputs to describe roughly what goes into the ultimate delivery of services. Unlike the conventional production-function analyses, this approach is not preeminently concerned with systematizing relationships between inputs and outputs into mathematical formulas. In entertaining numerous indicators, not just expenditures, it becomes possible to differentiate among services. Also, within individual services, the effect of regulations associated with intergovernmental policies become more clearcut. But the most critical contribution of the study was the insight gained. The researchers probed for the professional judgments service providers make in allocating various inputs and distributing services. What the analysts uncovered was the impact of the professional mores held by librarians, educators and civil engineers; each possessed a distinctive conception of how to produce and deliver a service "properly," within broad policy and financial constraints, and of how to treat various categories of citizens/consumers within a jurisdiction. Since such practices vary from service to service, the analytic approach dictates a case study method. This approach begins to illuminate the "how to" or the technology of converting inputs to services.

Building on this tradition is a promising study recently completed by Lucy and Mlandenka which confirms the profound importance of the decision rules service providers invoke in allocating scarce municipal resources.[56] The researchers begin to untangle a number of the riddles behind equity in their search for the real world, practical answers service providers offer when prompted to explain a particular pattern of service disparities. The framework for analysis, their exploratory study suggests, is more rigorous than that presented in *Urban Outcomes* in a number of respects. First, they stretch the service-by-service analysis to span a fuller range of municipal services. Thus, it becomes possible to grasp the distinctive nature of various services and to expose the different standards of "good" across them. Second, their study classifies several types of equity rules which operate in service provision. These include not only the equality rule which means sameness or uniformity but also various equity standards sensitive to demand, or to need, or to preference, or to willingness-to-pay. Third, they locate how these rules come into play at discrete stages of the service production function: inputs, activities, outputs and outcomes.

The study advances a framework which can be applied across numerous municipal jurisdictions in order to clarify what equity rules are actually in operation. Based on the limited set of interviews with actual service providers, the study suggests that rules vary somewhat predictably by service and that more than one equity rule may be invoked in producing and delivering a service. For example, in libraries, additional budgetary resources are usually allocated among branches according to home-use circulation patterns, thus revealing equity with respect to demand. At the same time, the initial contents of branch libraries often are standardized, which implies an equality rule. In the allocation of police manpower across precincts, several equity rules were spotlighted: where response time was key, equity with respect to demand operates to achieve equalized activities; where crime or victimization rates provide the standard, then equity in relation to need to achieve some equal outcomes can be inferred; and where the number of calls received by precincts dominates, then again a demand or preference dimension is characteristic. In a number of services, the allocation rules which contain choices affecting equity are set forth by national professional organizations, which is often the case in parks and recreation.

To be sure, the framework requires careful application across a range of municipalities if any generalizations are to be comfortably made with appropriate conceptual refinements. Empirical analysis by and across municipalities as well as services promises to demonstrate how equity operates as a rule in resource allocation. Potentially, the findings permit calculating the opportunity costs associated with one equity rule versus another. But even without such conclusions, the value of the study is to point out the obvious fact, far too often obscured by the pursuit of abstract theories of equity, misunderstood in the legal proceedings and neglected in policy analysis: decisions about equity are made every day by the service providers themselves. The pursuit of equity is far less elusive than it seems.

A POLITICAL ECONOMY FRAMEWORK
FOR UNDERSTANDING EQUITY

CONCLUSION

For social reformers the pursuit of equity in the late seventies is a frustrating cause. During times of economic prosperity, when revenues swell municipal tax coffers, redistribution in favor of the disadvantaged can take place without necessarily making anyone worse off. This is not the case when the politics of bankruptcy plagues city halls. Funds simply may not be available to sustain even the current package of services, inequitably distributed as it may be. When municipal budgets are squeezed, a reform strategy seems unrealistic, if it entails freeing up some funds to redirect them to services for that fraction of the community deprived of its "fair share" in the past. More ambitious strategies for reform, including proposals for restructuring local government, are also too costly to entertain seriously. Just the start-up or transitional costs seem extravagant,[57] when the annual increments to the budget are shrinking, at the same time seemingly fixed costs coupled with inflation are pushing service expenditures upward. Appeals to higher-level governments for fiscal assistance are also challenged by competing claims on the state and federal treasuries; by conditions of widespread inflation and symptoms of slowdown and scarcity in the national economy; by the renewed concerns over managing unwieldy public bureaucracies; and by the recurrent tensions within the federal system between local autonomy and intergovernmental intrusion.

If the pursuit of equity in service provision is to have any political reality within the late seventies, reformers must begin to envision solutions within the resource constraints of the times. Rather than whole-scale reform, tinkering with the existing system of allocating public funds may be an interim, pragmatic strategy. A critical look at the administrative practices for producing and delivering services may hold a promising clue for redistribution.

Whatever avenue to reform is pursued for practical purposes, the achievement of equity will remain an elusive objective so long as we continue to fracture our thinking about it. As the earlier discussion implies, analysts have compartmentalized their thinking about equity. The tendency to explore one facet of the problem at the expense of another not only promotes academic rivalries but also leads to sometimes competing and contradictory prescriptions for reform. While we may never agree on a single answer to what is equity, we can improve our understanding of equity from a more comprehensive inquiry, building on the philosophic, legal and analytic foundations of the subject.

A more enlightened treatment of the subject can result by casting equity within a political economy framework. Such an approach dignifies the interplay of normative and empirical inquiry; it encourages a lively tension between principles and facts. The essential premise of a political economy approach is not highblown; it is a simple, practical one: because the scarcity of resources means that not all wants, needs and preferences can be fulfilled, conflict–politics–necessarily ensues. The functions of government–to resolve conflict and to provide services–are inextricably bound up. Such a simple view will go a long way to resolve the "dualisms" which have crippled our thinking about equity and which have perpetuated some fallacies in the recent traditions of policy analysis and policy reform. Some perspectives on these distorting dualisms are offered below:

(1) Government vs. the marketplace in service provision. Public goods theory defines the allocation function of government in a subordinate way: government interventions are legitimate to promote efficiency when the private market fails. Such logic omits a positive purpose except in its casual reference to a social welfare function which most concede is impossible to specify. What equity is all about is the relative position and condition of individuals in society. Equity is a social concept, not a market concept. It is the premier function of government.

(2) Equity vs. efficiency. Despite the broad logic of public goods theory, the popular view of efficiency is a narrow one, accentuating productivity. Where efficiency comprehends demand as well as supply in the allocation of scarce resources, equity can emerge as a complementary rather than competing goal for public policy.

(3) Process vs. substance in policymaking. Understanding equity requires a political economy perspective which looks at both the procedural and substantive features of urban policy. In this framework, municipal government is seen to affect the material well-being of its citizens as it manages conflict over the allocation of scarce resources to produce and deliver public services.

(4) Stability vs. change. Although forging consensus by limiting controversy to marginal policy changes assures stability, the incrementalist view of American politics stresses procedure and begs the issue of the substantive content of government's role in society. Framing policy to effect change in the social conditions of citizens, as they coexist and interact in a community, is the mission of government.

(5) Centralization vs. decentralization. Redistribution of fiscal resources–the traditional policy prescription for achieving greater equity–usually implies increased centralization. However, if equity is understood as more than a fiscal problem, the vitality of local government becomes essential. The capacity of local institutions to respond to the various needs and demands of citizens is salient in pursuing equity.

NOTES

1. Current studies of the urban condition have focused on growing and declining cities across regions of the nation. See, Harvey A. Garn, Thomas Muller, *et al.,* "A Framework for National Urban Policy: Urban Distress, Decline and Growth," Urban Institute Working Paper No. 0259-2. (Washington, D.C.: The Urban Institute, December 1977); Committee for Economic Development, *An Approach to Federal Urban Policy* (Washington, D.C.: CED, December 1977); and Richard P. Nathan, Charles F. Adams and Associates, "Understanding Central City Hardship," *Political Science Quarterly.* Volume 91 (Spring 1976).

2. George Peterson, "Finance," in William Gorham and Nathan Glazer, eds., *The Urban Predicament* (Washington, D.C.: The Urban Institute, 1976.) Two recent studies have attempted to sort out the impacts of federal policy on the economic and fiscal plight of central cities; see, George Peterson, *Federal Tax Policy and Urban Development* (Washington, D.C.: The Urban Institute, 1978)–summarized in "Shaping and Misshaping the Metropolis" *Search* Volume 7 (Spring 1977), pp. 4-8. Also, see the Rand Corporation, *The Urban Impact of Federal Policies* (–in four volumes). (Washington, D.C.: Rand Corporation, 1978)–summarized in Mark J. Kasoff, "The Urban Impact of Federal Policies," *Nation's Cities,* Volume 15, (November 1977), pp. 25-32.

3. A locus of reform energies is to be found at the Government Services Equalization Center (GSEC) at the Lawyers' Committee for Civil Rights Under Law, Washington, D.C. GSEC was financed by grants from the Ford Foundation, the Trinity Parish Church, the Veatch Foundation as well as the Lawyers' Committee itself. The impetus to establish the Center was felt at the Trinity Parish Conference on Public Service Equalization, New York City, May 16, 1974; the Conference produced a report entitled, *The Next Step?* (New York: Trinity Parish, 1974.) Some time prior to the setting up of GSEC, the NAACP issued a manual for lawyers and citizens seeking to press claims of racial discrimination in the provision of municipal services; see, Jonathan Shapiro, *A Manual for Lawyers on Litigation for Equalization of Municipal Services* (Washington D.C.: U.S. Civil Rights Commission, Clearinghouse Publication No. 49, September 1974). An interesting contrast with the accomplishments of the school finance reforms can be derived from Rochelle L. Stanfield, "Why Johnny Can't–the Problem of State School Financing," *National Journal,* (April 24, 1976).

4. Kenneth Newton, "American Urban Politics: Social Class, Political Structure and Public Goods," *Urban Affairs Quarterly,* Volume 11, (December 1975); Robert L. Lineberry, "Equality, Public Policy and Public Services: The Underclass Hypothesis and the Limits to Equality" *Politics and Policy* Volume 4 (December 1975); and Jewel Bellush and Stephen M. David, eds., *Race and Politics in New York City* (New York: Praeger Publishers, 1971.)

5. Frank Marini, ed., *Toward a New Public Administration* (Scranton, Pennsylvania: Chandler 1971). Also Dwight Waldo, ed., *Public Administration in a Time of Turbulence* (Scranton, Pennsylvania: Chandler, 1972.)

6. Alan K. Campbell and Roy W. Bahl, eds., *State and Local Government: The Political Economy of Reform* (New York: The Free Press, 1976), pp. 2, 13. Also see David M. Gordon, "Introduction," in David M. Gordon, ed., *Problems in Political Economy: An Urban Perspective* (Lexington, Massachusetts: D.C. Heath, 1971), pp. 2-9. A more complete selection of essays on economic justice is available in: Edmund S. Phelps, ed., *Economic Justice* (Middlesex, England: Penguin Books, 1973); see, especially, "Introduction," pp. 26-27. Also Edmund S. Phelps, ed., *Altruism, Morality and Economic Theory* (New York: Russel Sage, 1975.)

7. Dalba Winthrop, "Aristotle and Theories of Justice." *American Political Science Review.* Volume 72 December 1978.

8. In recent years perhaps no other book has revitalized interest and critical inquiry into the moral dilemma of justice as John Rawl's *The Theory of Justice* (Cambridge, Massachusetts: Harvard University Press, 1971), The book has provoked commentary in such diverse fields as philosophy, the law, economics, political science and public administration.

9. The commentary is voluminous. See, for example, John W. Chapman, *et al.* "Justice: A Spectrum of Responses to John Rawls' Theory. . . ," *American Political Science Review,* Volume 69 (June 1975). Also, see David K. Hart, "Social Equity, Justice and the Equitable Administrator" *Public Administration Review* Volume 34 (January/February 1974).

10. At a normative, philosophic level this line of argument is being developed by Professor Michael Harmon of the Department of Public Administration, The George Washington University, in a manuscript on theory of public administration.

11. *Hawkins* v. *Town of Shaw.* (437 F. 2d 1268 [5th Cir. 1971]), p. 1287.

12. A fundamental interest or right like voting or freedom of speech commands special constitutional protection. Consequently, differential treatment or classification of individuals when a fundamental interest is at stake can occur only if the government has extraordinary reasons. The burden of proof falls to the government and the strict scrutiny of the court is invoked. Similarly, a suspect classification triggers the test of strict scrutiny compelling the government to present more than reasonable grounds for the differential treatment of individuals.

13. A table describing the detailed condition of services appears in Astrid D. Merget, "Equalizing Municipal Services: Issues for Policy Analysis," *Policy Studies Journal* (Spring 1976) and in "Equity in the Distribution of Municipal Services," (a paper prepared for the Academy for Contemporary Problems, April 1978; forthcoming in Herrington Bryce, ed. *The Future of Our Cities: Places to Live and Work,* exp. 1979).

14. The Lawyers Committee filed complaints in October 1975 against six Mississippi towns: *Richardson* v. *Ikolona, Ely* v. *Byhalia, Adams* v. *West Point, Yarborough* v. *Ackerman* and *Johnson* v. *Greenwood.* Also, immediately after *Shaw*, several other cases were successfully litigated or settled out of court; they included: *Harris* v. *Town of Itta Bena* in Mississippi; *Dupee* v. *City of Chattanooga* in Tennessee; and *Fairfax County-Wide Citizens Association* v. *County of Fairfax* in Virginia.

15. For a more detailed discussion, see Astrid E. Merget and William M. Wolff, Jr., "The Law and Municipal Services: Implementing Equity," *Public Management* (August 1976).

16. Merget and Wolff, *op. cit.* Also, see Peter B. Bloch, *Equality of Distribution of Police Services: A Case Study of Washington D.C.* (Washington, D.C.: The Urban Institute, February 1974), and Donald Fisk and Cynthia A. Lancer, *Equality of Distribution of Recreation Services: A Case Study of Washington, D.C.* (Washington, D.C.: The Urban Institute, July 1974.)

17. A detailed account of these major cases is presented in: Joel S. Berke. *Answers to Inequity: An Analysis of the New School Finance.* (Berkeley, California: McCutchan Publishing Corporation, 1974.)

18. The test of fiscal neutrality finds its origin in the constitutional doctrines formulated in: John E. Coons, William H. Clune and Stephen D. Sugarman, *Private Wealth and Public Education.* (Cambridge, Massachusetts: Harvard University Press, 1970.) Against this test, the constitutionality of a state school financing system turns on whether the money available for a child's education is constrained by the wealth of the local school district. Under fiscal neutrality, the relevant standard is the state's overall wealth not that of the individual district. Put another way: the quality of education a child receives should be neutral with respect to the wealth of the particular district in which he or she resides.

19. Flowing from the test of fiscal neutrality is the logical remedy of district power equalization, which calls for equalizing across a state the per-pupil property tax base. In theory, the system works, as Peterson cogently describes: "In its purest form, the power equalization principle allows local school districts to continue to set their own school tax rates. For the purpose of computing individual tax bills, the locally selected tax rate is applied to the assessed valuation of property, just as before. However, the revenue per pupil that the school district receives from its school tax levy is determined by applying the tax rate it had chosen to the average property valuation per pupil for the state as a whole. If the tax payments made on local property fall short of the amount a community is entitled to receive by law, the difference is made up by state assistance. Should local tax payments per pupil exceed the statewide average that can be raised from the same tax rate, in theory the excess revenue collected would be turned over to the state to assist below-average districts. In practice, several states have dispensed with the requirement that excess tax collections be delivered to the state. Such programs in effect guarantee all school districts access to the statewide average property tax base, but permit some districts (usually for a limited number of years) to continue to benefit from their above average property wealth. This leveling up explains why power equalization plans generally have required higher overall levels of state assistance." See, Peterson, "Finance," *op. cit.* p. 98.

20. In asserting that education was a fundamental interest, and that wealth constituted a suspect classification, the *Serrano* case placed an extreme burden of proof on the state, for which it could not demonstrate a compeling interest or reason to defend its financial practices. See, Berke, *op. cit.*, pp. 15-17. The constitutional foundation for casting education in this fashion was originally envisioned in: Arthus Wise, *Rich Schools, Poor Schools* (Chicago: University of Chicago Press, 1968).

21. Of late, favorable rulings were rendered by the state courts in Connecticut *Horton* v. *Meskill* (172 Conn. 615 [1977]), New York—*Levittown* v. *Nyquist* (Index No. 8208/74 [1978]) and Ohio—*Board of Education of the City School District of the City of Cincinnati* v. *Walter* (Declaratory Judgment Order and Judgment Entry No. A 7602725). Projects on school finance reform closely monitor the legal and legislative activities in the various states; among the most active research and reformist groups are the Education Commission of the States, the National Conference of State Legislatures, the Education Policy Research Institute and the Lawyers' Committee for Civil Rights Under Law.

22. Early ones to flag this eventuality were Joen S. Berke and John J. Callahan in their essay, "*Serrano* v. *Priest*: Milestone or Millstone for School Finance?," *Journal of Public Law,* Volume 21, (1972). Some years later, Robert L. Bish argued that power equalization schemes can have an adverse impact on poor children residing in districts with a predominantly industrial tax base. Central to his argument is that different levels of taxes services get capitalized into the value of the land. The relevant yardstick for equalization then is not the disparity in local wealth per se under the test of fiscal neutrality; rather it is the difference between tax costs and benefits derived. See Robert L. Bish, "Fiscal Equalization Through Court Decisions: Policy Making Without Evidence," in Elinor Ostrom, ed., *The Delivery of Urban Services: Outcomes of Change* (Beverly Hills, California: Sage, 1976), pp. 75-102.

23. The concept of municipal overburden has been hotly debated among public finance economists. The "overburden" is presumed to beset central cities because they devote a smaller fraction of their budgets to education in order to sustain a broader spectrum of urban services. The overburden is attenuated by the larger shares of dependent people residing in central cities, the higher costs of living in cities and related cost pressures on the public budget plus the benefits of services spilling out to suburbanites which go uncompensated. Some argue that the burden or overburden is offset through tax exportation. The existence of a presumed overburden prompted several major cities to join as intervenors in the case challenging New York State's school financing system (*Levittown* v. *Nyquist*). In a favorable ruling rendered in June, 1978, the New York State Supreme Court declared the State's system of financing unconsititional; the opinion accepted the facts of the alleged municipal overburden. The remedy will undoubtedly call for special treatment of the cities. A similar, successful argument was asserted in the Cincinnati case.

24. Cities contain larger fractions of children who have language problems, learning disabilities and other problems impeding their education within a traditional school curriculum. Many states take the higher costs of educating these children into account in their financing systems. For

example, Florida assigns weights in its computation of property valuation per pupil according to the relative costs of providing services for children in need of special education. A critical case in protecting the educational rights of non-English-speaking children was *Lau* v. *Nichols* (414 U.S. 563 [1974]).

25. The Lawyers' Committee participated in a case in Louisiana, *Cain* v. *Simon*, which alleged the discriminatory use of General Revenue Sharing (GRS) funds as racially-biased and as reinforcing past patterns of discrimination in service provison. The case was brought under the statute of the State and Local Assistance Act of 1972 containing nondiscrimination provisions and regulations. The willingness of the federal courts to entertain such a case was suggested by the decision in *U.S.* v. *City of Chicago* (405 F. Supp. 48 [1975]); the City was spending a large chunk of GRS funds on its police department which had demonstrable discriminatory practices in hiring.

26. Boundary practices can be highly discriminatory in their racial impact and their consequences for equitable service provision. A superb volume devoted to this subject was prepared under the guidance of Professor Donald G. Hagman of the School of Law, University of California, Los Angeles: see, "Symposium—The White Curtain: Racially Disadvantaging Local Government Boundary Practices," *University of Detroit Journal of Urban Law,* Volume 54 (1977).

27. The annexation of adjacent territory by the City of Richmond, Virginia, was originally challenged in federal courts under the Voting Rights Act of 1965, wherein the dilution of black voting strength concentrated within the central city was alleged to be a discriminatory feature of the boundary change. See Peter H. Weiner. "Boundary Changes and the Power of the Vote," in *University of Detroit Journal of Urban Law, op. cit.,* pp. 981-990. The case in question went to the U.S. Supreme Court, *City of Richmond* v. *U.S.* (422 U.S. 385, 372 [1975]). The Urban Institute prepared a report and one of its authors appeared before federal court as a technical expert to explain the fiscal and economic effects of annexation for the City of Richmond. See Thomas Muller and Grace Dawson, *The Impact of Annexation on City Finances: A Case Study in Richmond, Virginia* (Washington, D.C.: The Urban Institute, May 1973) and *An Evaluation of the Subsequent Fiscal Impact of Annexation in Richmond, Virginia* (Washington, D.C.: The Urban Institute, 1975.)

28. *Southern Burlington County NAACP* v. *Township of Mount Laurel* (67 N.J. 151, 336 A 2d 713 [1975]); for a useful summary of critical decisions in federal and state courts, see Michael N. Danielson, *The Politics of Exclusion* (New York: Columbia University Press, 1976), Chp. 7.

29. Professor A.C. Dick Howard of the University of Virginia School of Law advanced this interpretation in a seminar at the Woodrow Wilson International Center for Scholars, Washington, D.C., December 7, 1978.

30. A far-reaching dimension in the *Shaw*-type cases brought by the Lawyers' Committee was the allegation that General Revenue Sharing (GRS) funds were being spent by the communities in question to reinforce existing patterns of discrimination. At the prodding of the committee, the federal court in the Fifth Circuit escrowed the FRS funds pending a decision on the merits of each case or until a municipality sought an out-of-court

settlement. The funds were to be reserved for the remedy, whereby services in the black side of a town were to be levelled up to those enjoyed by its white residents. The GRS feature not only furnished the cases with statutory foundation, since the receipt of such funds is contingent upon a compliance with non-discrimination regulations; it also undercut a common defense offered by the towns that in upgrading services for black residents the municipal budget would go broke.

31. Although the courts, on balance, have conferred substantial discretion on local governments in their performance as service providers, the limits of *Shaw* apply only to racially discriminatory service provision. Beyond that, the courts also examine the evenhandedness of the administrative practices behind service provision. Even in *Hadnott* v. *Prattville, op. cit.*, which permitted wealth disparities to obtain with special assessment financing, the court scrutinized the municipality's administrative practices in search of their fairness in application. Of course, were a service or set of services declared a fundamental interest, then wealth would come to take on the character of a suspect classification. Further, the courts look to whether current practices of service provision, which may be on their face fairly administered, have the effect of freezing in past practices of discrimination; if that is the case, the municipality will be held in violation of the law; see, *Hawkins* v. *Town of Shaw, op. cit.*, *Selmon Improvement Association* v. *Dallas County Commission* (399 F. Supp. 477 [1972]).

32. *Village of Belle Terre* v. *Borass*, (416 U.S.___[1976]). The court noted that zoning did not involve a fundamental interest or right. Also, the court presumed the validity of local zoning and land use practices; see, *Village of Euclid* v. *Ambler Realty Co.* (272 U.S. 365 [1926]).

33. For further elaboration on the confusion in the courts, see William M. Wolff, Jr., "School Financing and Municipal Service," in Mark Rosentraub, ed., *Financing State and Local Governments: New Approaches to Old Problems* (Ann Arbor, Michigan: Social Science Journal/Xerox Publishing Company, February 1977).

34. Herbert Kaufman, "Administrative Decentralization and Political Power," in Waldo, ed. *Public Administration in A Time of Turbulence, op. cit.*

35. Robert L. Bish, *The Public Economy of Metropolitan Areas* (Chicago: Markham, 1977).

36. A succinct statement of the public choice theory as it applies to local government and service delivery is presented in: Robert L. Bish and Vincent Ostrom, *Understanding Urban Government: Metropolitan Reform Reconsidered* (Washington, D.C.: American Enterprise Institute for Public Policy Research, 1973). Also, see Robert L. Bish, *The Public Economy of Metropolitan Areas* (Chicago: Markham Publishing, 1971); Vincent Ostrom, Charles Tiebout and Robert Warren, "The Organization of Government in Metropolitan Areas," *American Political Science Review* Volume 55 (December 1961); Charles M. Tiebout, "A Pure Theory of Local Expenditures," *Journal of Political Economy*, Volume 64 (October 1956).

37. Producing and delivering services, let alone assuring that their outcomes are effective, often entail the direct efforts of citizens/consumers themselves, as individuals or as organized into community groups. Beyond their efforts at supplementing public services by direct production, neighbor-

hood associations can augment the effectivness of available services by acting as "co-producers." The quality of services, therefore, often depends on residents' actions as much as those of public servants. See Richard C. Rich, "Neglected Issues in the Study of Urban Service Distribution," (a paper prepared for presentation at the Annual Meeting of the Midwest Political Science Association in Chicago, Illinois, April 20-22, 1978.) Also, see Richard C. Rich, "Equity and Institutional Design in Urban Service Delivery," *Urban Affairs Quarterly,* Volume 12 (March 1977).

38. Several years ago the RANN Division of the National Science Foundation sponsored a competition under the heading of "Division Related Research on the Organization of Service Delivery in Metropolitan Areas." One of the projects awarded funds entailed the study of police services and their alternative organizational arrangements; the research endeavor was conceived of and directed by Professor Elinor Ostrom of the Political Science Department at Indiana University. Serving as Co-Principal Investigator along with Professor Gordon P. Witaker of the University of North Carolina, Dr. Ostrom has explored a range of indicators and measures on the effectiveness, efficiency, equity and responsiveness of local police services. The inquiry, before and after the RANN award, has generated numerous publications. Selected articles include: Elinor Ostrom, "Institutional Arrangements and the Measurement of Policy Consequences," *Urban Affairs Quarterly* (June 1971); Elinor Ostrom and Roger B. Parks, "Suburban Police Department: Too Many and Too Small?," in Louis Massoti and John Hadden, eds., *The Urbanization of the Suburbs* (Beverly Hills, California: Sage, 1973); Elinor Ostrom, Robert B. Parks and Gordon P. Whitaker, "Do We Really Want to Consolidate Urban Police Forces? A Reappraisal of Some Old Assertions," *Public Administration Review,* Volume 33 (1973); Elinor Ostrom, "The Need for Multiple Indicators in Measuring the Output of Public Agencies," *Policy Studies Journal,* Volume 2 (1973).

Also, see Roger B. Parks, "Police Patrol in Metropolitan Areas—Implications for Restructuring Police" in Elinor Ostrom, ed., *The Delivery of Urban Services: Outcomes of Change, op. cit.,* Contained in that same volume is a set of essays summarizing the initial results of the other research projects sponsored by RANN on service delivery in solid-waste management, fire protection and health care.

Other publications and materials on measuring services and assessing the effects of alternative organizational arrangements are available through the Workshop in Political Theory and Policy Analysis, Department of Political Science, Indiana University.

39. Alan K. Campbell, "Approaches to Defining, Measuring and Achieving Equity in the Public Sector," *Public Administration Review,* Volume 36 (September/October 1976). The classic statement recommending a metropolitan form of organization for local government appears in: Committee for Economic Development, *Reshaping Government in Metropolitan Areas* (New York: CED, 1970). Also, see Alan K. Campbell and Roy W. Bahl, eds., *State and Local Government: The Political Economy of Reform* (New York: The Free Press, 1976).

40. Thomas Murphy and Charles R. Warren, eds., *Organizing Services in Metropolitan Areas* (Lexington, Massachusetts: D.C. Heath, 1974).

41. U.S. Advisory Commission on Intergovernmental Relations, *The Role of Equalization in Federal Grants* (Washington, D.C.: U.S. Government Printing Office, 1964), p. 46.

42. James Buchanan. "Federalism and Fiscal Equity" *American Economic Review*. Volume 40. September 1950. Also, see Jesse Burkhead and Jerry Miner, *Public Expenditures* (Chicago: Aldine/Atherton, 1971). pp. 252-294.

43. George F. Break, *Intergovernmental Fiscal Relations in the United States* (Washington, D.C.: The Brookings Institution, 1967), pp. 99-100. Also, Richard P. Nathan and Charles F. Adams, *et al., Revenue Sharing: The Second Round* (Washington, D.C.: The Brookings Institution, 1977).

44. A superb summary of this research tradition—its hypotheses, findings and methodology—is contained in Roy W. Bahl, "Studies on Determinants of Public Expenditures: A Review," in Selma J. Mushkin and John F. Cotton, eds., *Functional Federalism: Grants-in-Aid and PPB Systems* (Washington D.C.: State-Local Finances Project of the George Washington University, 1968.) A landmark study in this tradition was: Alan K. Campbell and Seymour Sacks, *Metropolitan America* (New York: Free Press, 1967).

45. A critique of this approach on this very point is offered in: Frank S. Levy, Arnold J. Meltsner and Aaron Wildavsky, *Urban Outcomes* (Berkeley, California: University of California Press, 1974), pp. 10-12.

46. Bahl, *op. cit.*, points to the inherent tautological problems in the statistical models.

47. Robert L. Lineberry, *Equality and Urban Policy* (Beverly Hills, California: 1977). Also, see Kenneth Mladenka, "The Distribution of Urban Public Services," (a dissertation prepared at Rice University, Houston, Texas, May 1975).

48. Roy Bahl, Alan K. Campbell and David Greytak. *Taxes, Expenditures and the Economic Base.* (New York: Praeger, 1977).

49. Katharine Lyall, *op. cit.*

50. George F. Break, "The Incidence and Economic Effects of Taxation," in Alan S. Blinder, *et al., The Economics of Public Finance* (Washington, D.C.: The Brookings Institution, 1974). Also, see for an example of the incidence of local property tax, Henry J. Aaron, *Who Pays the Property Tax? A New View* (Washington, D.C.: The Brookings Institution, 1975).

51. Much of the work developed at the Rand Institute in Santa Monica and formerly in New York City is of a highly quantitative nature often relying on operations research techniques. See, for example, the following reports available through The Rand Institute, Santa Monica, California: Jan M. Chaiken and Richard C. Larson, *Methods for Allocating Urban Emergency Units: A Review* (1971); Arthur J. Swersey, *Reducing Fire Engine Dispatching Delays* (1973); Warren Walker *et al., An Analysis of the Deployment of Fire Fighting Resources in Wilmington, Delaware* (1975); Jack Housner *et al., An Analysis of the Deployment of Fire Fighting Resources in Yonkers, New York* (1974); Edward H. Blum, *Deployment Research of the New York City Fire Project* (1972); and Richard C. Larson, *Measuring the Response Patterns of New York City Police Patrol Cars.* (1971).

52. H. George Frederickson, "Toward a New Public Administration," in Frank Marini, ed., *Toward a New Public Administration* (Scranton, Pennsylvania: Chandler, 1971). Also, see "Symposium: Social Equity and Public Administration," *Public Administration Review* Volume 34 (January/February 1974).

53. Larry Kirkhart, "Toward a Theory of Public Administration," in Marini, *op. cit.*

54. Michael M. Harmon. "Toward An 'Active-Social' Theory of Administrative Action: Some Empirical and Normative Implications," (a paper in draft available through the Department of Public Administration, The George Washington University, Washington, D.C.). Also, see Robert P. Biller. "Toward Public Administrations Rather Than An Administration of Publics: Strategies of Accountable Dissaggregation to Achieve Human Scale and Efficiency and Live Within the Natural Limits of Intelligence and Other Scarce Resources," (a paper prepared for presentation at the Annual Meeting of the American Society of Public Administration, Washington, D.C., April 21, 1976.)

55. Levy, *et al. Urban Outcomes, op. cit.*

56. The author wishes to thank Lucy and Mladenka for sharing the draft manuscripts on their research which describe the study, its framework and methodology. William H. Lucy and Kenneth R. Mladenka. *Equity and Urban Service Distribution.* (A Study conducted at the University of Virginia, Charlottesville, under contract to The Urban Management Curriculum Development Project, The National Training and Development Service, Washington, D.C.: financed by the U.S. Department of Housing and Urban Development, 1978.) Also, see William H. Lucy, Dennis Gilbert and Guthrie S. Birkhead "Analysis of Equity in Local Service Distribution," *Public Administration Review,* Volume 37 (1977).

57. Donna E. Shalala and Astrid E. Merget, "Transition Problems and Models," in Thomas Murphy and Charles R. Warren, eds., *Organizing Services in Metropolitan Areas, op. cit.*

SECTION IV

Traditional Municipal Revenues - Reworked and Retooled

Glenn W. Fisher — WHAT IS THE IDEAL REVENUE BALANCE? — A POLITICAL VIEW

Economists have had a major impact upon state and local tax structure in the last few decades. In that period of time, they have participated as staff members in hundreds of tax studies. But the greatest impact has come not because policy makers immediately have accepted the recommendations made in carefully reasoned staff papers. Rather, the teachings of economists have become part of the intellectual equipment of those who make tax decisions and have been disseminated by publication in tax studies, journal articles, in the news media and through classroom teaching. Long-run impacts of this type are difficult to measure, but the widespread use of economic terms and concepts by those who make tax policy would appear to be a very good *prima facie* evidence that economic thinking about tax matters is influential.

Examples are easy to find. Thirty years ago the term "regressive tax" scarcely was heard outside the classroom, and those who attempted to explain the term or to invoke it as a sanction against the sales tax risked being considered slightly subversive. Today the term is widely used and approved. As this is written a Republican controlled legislature in Kansas is considering strongly the removal of food from the sales tax base in order to reduce the regressivity of the tax. The importance of this lies not in the fact that it will create a fiscal problem for a newly elected Democratic governor, though this is not unimportant, but rather it lies in the fact that the Republican Party in a rather conservative state would choose the regressivity of the tax as the stated reason for the attempt.

Many legislators are familiar with the "tax elasticity" concept, and "coefficients of dispersion" are often cited as measures of the horizontal equity of the property tax. Even though such terms and concepts are often used in political rhetoric to justify positions already taken for other reasons, I believe that the frequency with which these terms and concepts are used suggests that economists are held in considerable respect and that the widespread use of economic arguments by legislators, administrators, lobbyists and ordinary citizens has a substantial long-term effect on policy decisions.

The problem with this state of affairs is that non-economic aspects of tax policy may be overlooked or that the results of economic analysis undertaken in one setting or at one particular time may be misapplied in another setting or at a later time. The principal argument of this paper is that more emphasis should be placed upon the political aspects of taxation.

PUBLIC POLICY ANALYSIS AND TAX POLICY

The analysis of public policy involves several steps. Among the most important are:

1. Choosing goals and objectives,
2. Measuring or appraising various alternatives in light of the goals and objectives adopted,
3. Determining priorities or weights to be accorded the various goals in order to arrive at a recommendation.

The second phase of these is largely a technical, value-free task properly performed by the analyst in his or her role as a scientist or technician. Steps 1 and 3, on the other hand, are value-laden processes, and the analyst should act with care to avoid attributing scientific validity to his or her own value judgments.

One common "model" of rational decisionmaking calls for "society" or some agency within the political system to define goals and objectives. It then becomes the job of the analyst or technician to determine the most effective or efficient way of achieving these goals and objectives.[1] Although examples of decisionmaking which conform essentially to this model can be cited, rational decisionmaking is not the usual way of making the hard decisions.[2] A colleague of mine once told a state legislature that he could design a tax system if he were provided a clear statement of what the tax system was to accomplish. Predictably, he never received the statement of objectives. Any close student of legislative behavior knows that it would be far more difficult for a legislative body to draft such a statement than to make specific changes in the tax system without drafting such a statement.

ECONOMIC CRITERIA FOR A REVENUE SYSTEM

The failure to receive a statement of goals, objectives and priorities has not kept the economists from doing applied work in the field of revenue policy. Lacking an authoritative directive, economists have utilized their own knowledge and experience to formulate criteria for revenue systems and have then analyzed the various revenue sources in light of these criteria. The long history of this activity is emphasized when we recall that among the most quoted portions of the *Wealth of Nations* are the four maxims of taxation which Adam Smith formulated. In fact, these maxims—equality, certainty, convenience of payment and economy of collection—bear striking resemblances to the criteria utilized in recent revenue policy analyses.

Typical of the present-day criteria are the six utilized by George Break in analyzing local property taxation in California.[3] These criteria, as listed by Break are:

1. Horizontal Equity

   Equal burdens should be placed on people who enjoy equal amounts of local government services and own equal amounts of property.

2. Vertical Equity

   In a broad sense, vertical equity requires that people who are in different economic circumstances pay tax burdens that are different from each other in some systematic and rational sense. . . . Opinions differ widely concerning the choice among taxes with varying degrees of progressiveness and the choice between progressive and proportional levels.

3. Fiscal Efficiency

The third test of a good tax system deals both with the administrative costs that the government must incur in order to obtain revenue from different kinds of taxes and with the time and effort and money . . . required on the part of the taxpayer in order to determine the amount of his tax liability.

4. Fiscal Flexibility

If local governments are to maintain their fiscal autonomy, they need at least one major source of revenue that can easily be varied from year to year in response to changing demands for local government services.

5. Economic Efficiency

This fifth test concerns the impact of different taxes on the effectiveness with which economic decisions to consume, to save, to work and to invest are made.

6. Growth Sensitivity

Local governments have found themselves in financial difficulties in recent years largely because the demand for their services appears to be highly sensitive to economic growth, whereas their traditional revenue sources are not.

Though differing somewhat in organization and emphasis, a similar list of criteria was utilized in a recent study of the Washington, D. C. tax system.[4] This list is as follows:

1. Revenue Productivity

The primary job of a tax system is to produce revenues. Thus, the system as well as each particular tax must be judged on the basis of its revenue generating potential. For those who want the jurisdiction's revenue to expand at least as rapidly as its population and economic activity, there is an advantage in selecting taxes whose revenues are automatically responsive to changes in employment, volume of business, price level, or as a general proxy, the dollar value of personal income received in the jurisdiction.

2. Neutrality

Neutrality in taxation requires that taxes accomplish certain *intended* objectives, but beyond this they should minimize interference with private economic decisions. Special emphasis here must be placed on the word "intended." Sometimes a government deliberately chooses to raise some prices through taxation and thus discourage consumption.

3. Equity

Few questions of public finance are more obviously judgmental—and therefore political—than the question of "who should pay." Nevertheless, tax equity is a proper concern in economic analysis and must be addressed as objectively as possible. For our purposes here, there are two types of equity concepts which can be distinguished: "horizontal" and "vertical."

4. Tax Exporting

Most state/local governments rely—sometimes quite heavily—on taxes which are designated to be paid by non-residents. This design to "export" taxes should not be based on a political preference to "beggar our neighbors," but from the realization that non-residents may generate substantial costs to a jurisdiction in traffic policing, health problems, congestion and environmental degradation.

5. Investment and Economic Growth

It is frequently alleged that state or local taxes will frighten away prospective investors and producers, but there is a large literature which testifies that neither tax increases nor tax exemptions have had significant effects on the location of industry within the U.S. At some point, of course, extremely high, discriminatory or uncertain taxes could have adverse effects on the jurisdiction's economic growth.

6. Administrative Feasibility

Another basis commonly advanced for choosing among tax alternatives is the ease or difficulty, costliness or cheapness of collecting any levy in a reasonably uniform way. Surely, other things being equal, it is preferable to choose taxes which are easy to collect . . . .

Indeed, there are few taxes proposed to city councils or state
legislatures which, assuming that they are constitutional and
otherwise lawful, cannot be administered if government has
the will, the facilities and staff to do so.

7. Taxpayer Compliance Costs

There is a wide range of compliance costs—the costs borne by
the individual or business taxpayer in keeping records, computing and filing tax returns, undergoing audits, etc. . . .
Failure to consider the taxpayers' views in the mechanics of
tax preparation can result in widespread tax evasion and con-
tempt for the government legislative body.

The authors of the D.C. study conclude the discussion of criteria
for evaluating a revenue system by pointing out that there must be
tradeoffs among the criteria and that there is no perfect tax. This
leads them to the widely held conclusion that a good tax system
must be a balanced system utilizing several different taxes.

Both lists of criteria cited above are strongly oriented toward
economic factors. In this regard, the two studies probably are typical.
An underlying assumption appears to be that the private sector is
working well generally and that the tax system should alter the
operation of that system only in limited, consciously arrived at
instances. Discussion of administration of the revenue system is
confined almost entirely to the costs of administration. The authors
of the D.C. study go out of their way to downplay the importance
of administration by suggesting that all common types of taxes can
be administered satisfactorily if the political will and resources are
present. Concern about revenue adequacy is expressed, but this
seems to be only a concern that existing units of government maintain
existing levels of services without undue political conflict. Nowhere
in the lists of criteria do the authors indicate concern that revenue
systems have a major impact upon the structure of government.
Concern about public attitudes is minimal, and there is no explicit
recognition that taxes might be related to the alarming decline in
the capacity of our political insitutions to govern.

This state of affairs has come about because economists predominate among the groups of persons thinking and writing systematically
about government revenue. Political scientists, with a few exceptions,
have been uninterested and uninformed about the technical aspects
of revenue, and those who have become interested often have been
so impressed by the metholdology of economics that they sometimes

fail to emphasize sufficiently their own expertise in government structure and in the processes of authoritative decision making.

THE CASE FOR POLITICAL CRITERIA

The major theme of this paper is that it is time to add explicit political criteria to the list of tax criteria used in tax policy analysis and that these should be given rather high priority—especially when urban fiscal problems are under consideration. In formulating revenue criteria economists generally have taken the political and administrative structures of government as given. Adam Smith, living much closer in time to major struggles over the constitutional rights of the sovereign in matters of taxation and also living before the development of the modern administrative state, appears to have been more sensitive to these matters than are many modern writers. His words on the "certainty" maxim are worth recalling:

> The uncertainty of taxation encourages the insolence and favors the corruption of an order of men who are naturally unpopular, even where they are neither insolent nor corrupt. The certainty of what each individual ought to pay is, in taxation, a matter of so great importance, that a very considerable degree of inequality, it appears, I believe, from the experience of all nations, is not near so great an evil as a very small degree of uncertainity.[5]

Economists writing in more recent times have been concerned about administrative feasibility or fiscal efficiency. They have emphasized the economic costs of administration and compliance or sometimes, as illustrated by the quotation from Break's study, the effects of administration upon equity. These are basically economic, not political concerns. In almost every case, economists who make tax studies have assumed the basic political system, including the administrative and governmental structure, as given. The question has been how to adjust the tax system to the existing political system which is taken as a constant. *This procedure ignores the fact that taxes are major determinants of the structure and operation of the political system.* It may be simplifying history to say that this nation exists because of the tax policies of King George III, but surely those policies were a major factor in bringing about the American Revolution. Closer to the present it is surely true that the rapid fiscal centralization of government occurring in this country has been greatly facilitated—it may not be too strong to say caused—by the discrepancy between the elasticity coefficients of Federal taxes, on the one hand, and the income elasticity coefficients of state and local taxes, on the other hand. The tax rate is the politically sensitive variable in the basic tax equation, Tax = Base × Rate.[6] Because the rate is *very* sensitive, a tremendous political advantage accrues to any governmental unit that obtains a major portion of its revenue from a base that increases automatically in years of rapid growth in money incomes. The fiscal centralization occurring in recent years has been an almost inevitable result of elasticity of the federal tax system. The fiscal centralization, in turn, is transforming the political system in this country in ways which we do not fully understand but which may represent very far reaching and fundamental changes.

Tax structure is also an important determinant of the horizontal structure of local governments. I have argued elsewhere that there is a symbiotic relationship between fragmented local government and the property tax. The highly fragmented, overlapping units of government which exist in the United States could not exist and maintain any real semblance of independence if the real property tax were not available as a revenue source. Conversely, it is likely that the decline in the importance of the property tax would have been much more rapid if satisfactory alternative revenue sources had been available to local units of government—especially to the smaller ones. This symbiotic relationship makes it highly unrealistic to judge the property tax apart from its effect on government structure.

Authors of tax studies not only commonly assume that the broad political structure is given, but they also neglect to make any real analysis of administrative capabilities as they exist in a political context, although attention may be given to administrative capabilities in a narrow or technical context. The appraisal profession has the skills to do a good job of assessing most kinds of real property. Computer assisted methods are being improved rapidly, and the statistical techniques for measuring the quality of assessment and pinpointing trouble spots are available.[8] Within the technical context it is correct to say that good administration of the property tax is feasible. In a broader political context, however, this conclusion is much more doubtful. To bring about this result in many states it would be necessary to appropriate rather large sums of money to employ highly skilled appraisers at salaries very near the top range of state and local government salary scales. These individuals would be allowed to make decisions which would bring about drastic changes in the size of property tax bills. All this must occur at a time when distrust of government is high, when populist-like distrust of experts seems closer to the surface than usual and when property tax is the major focus of tax revolts in several states.

It is common to respond to such a recital of problems by suggesting the need to educate citizens as to the nature of the property tax and to the separation between technical administrative matters and policymaking. This approach implies that the citizen's attitude is the operational policy variable. It may be, however, more useful to recognize that in many states to propose the achievement of high-quality assessment by employing highly qualified professional appraisers is to propose a major change in the decisionmaking process. The authority to make decisions determining individual shares of the property tax levy would be placed in the hands of persons who are new to the political process. These persons would obtain their positions by an entirely different route than that followed by those presently holding power and would use an entirely different procedure to make decisions. This is a political change of considerable magnitude—not a minor administrative change.

Aaron Wildavsky, an early and persistent critic of PPBS, pointed out repeatedly that some of the changes proposed by budget reformers represented major changes in the political system.[9] In one memorable passage he chided Arthur Smithies for not realizing that he had reinvented the parliamentary system of government. Property tax reformers should be alert to avoid similar oversights, and students of taxation might well devote some time to a systematic study of the political capacity of governments to raise revenue.

The political aspects of public revenue are especially important in a conference devoted to the Municipal Fiscal Squeeze. The fiscal crisis which have plagued American cities in recent years are far more political than economic. New York City, Newark, Cleveland and the other cities with well publicized fiscal problems are located at or near the heart of some of the greatest concentrations of wealth and income in the history of the world. If there are any little men in flying saucers who have been observing this planet for the past few hundred years, they must be amazed that one of the worst fiscal crises of that period occurred in New York City in the 1970s. It must be perfectly clear to them that the problem is not lack of economic resources but failure in the public decisionmaking mechanism. This of course, is not news to students of public finance. Unfortunately, however, those who give advice on municipal financial problems often have limited their responses to suggestions that taxes be adapted to the political structures. In some cases they have called for reform in the political structures. Rarely have they paid adequate attention to the effect that taxes themselves have upon political structures.

Tax matters also play an important role in citizen attitudes toward government and in the growth of alienation shown by opinion polls in recent years.[10] Taxpayers in many states are aware of the gross inequities in property tax assessments which exist in their communities. The report of the 1976 assessment/sales price ratio study recently released by the U.S. Bureau of the Census shows that only 42 percent of 1,569 jurisdictions had a coefficient of intra-area dispersion of less than 20 percent.[11] This is for single family (non-farm) houses, which are probably the best assessed class of property. In those assessment areas with a population of more than 50,000 the record is even worse— only 36.5 percent had a coefficient of less than 20 percent. Although the average taxpayer is probably not aware of such studies or of their significance, many are very much aware of individual instances of poor assessment. Many taxpayers can point out similar properties which are assessed at widely different levels of value. This undoubtedly is one of the reasons that the property tax is consistently selected as the "most unfair" tax.[12]

Other instances of the effect of taxation upon public opinion are easy to cite. The dramatic drop in public confidence in the federal income tax which followed revelations of the Nixon Administration's attempt to use the tax to punish those on its list of enemies, and the publication of information about the number of wealthy individuals who paid no taxes, has been well reported. It is difficult to prove how much effect these revelations have had upon general attitudes toward government, but it is clear that public dissatisfaction with government has been rising and that much political activity has focused on attempts to reduce taxes. It seems reasonable to assume that dissatisfaction with the tax system is an important factor in dissatisfaction with government.

TWO PROPOSED POLITICAL CRITERIA

The relationship between finance and the political system is recognized widely, and references to various aspects of the relationship are common in the literature. But little systematic consideration has been given to the importance of these relationships. The inclusion of specifically political criteria in the list of those utilized in tax policy analysis would spotlight the importance of these factors and encourage policymakers to give more weight to them. Explicit consideration of political factors in policy analysis also might encourage systematic research of these questions.

Political criteria could be formulated in many ways, but perhaps it would be appropriate to begin by focusing upon the effects of taxation upon government structure and the public acceptability of various tax measures:

1. *Effects on Government Structure.* The analysis of the effect of taxation upon government structure, like the analysis of tax equity, can conveniently be divided into vertical and horizontal components. Vertical structure refers to the relationships among governments at different levels—federal, state and local. There is little doubt that the revenue structure has had a powerful influence upon these relationships in the past few decades. In a period of rapidly growing money income, the highly elastic federal income tax produced abundant revenues without any need for Congress to initiate the highly unpopular act of raising tax rates. Local officials, on the other hand, have found it impossible even to maintain the existing level of services without periodically taking concrete, visible steps to raise tax rates or, in some jurisdictions, to take the equally visible step of raising assessed valuation. The centralizing force represented by this simple fact about tax structure probably has been far more powerful than have all the economic analyses of efficiency or externalities and all the academic debates about the proper structure of federalism.

The horizontal structure of government—especially at the local level—also has been powerfully affected by tax structure. The real property tax is ideally suited to finance small and overlapping local governments. Jurisdiction is simple to establish and because the tax is an automatic lien on the property, its collection is certain except in those cases where the tax makes up an unusually high proportion of the value of the property. This means that small units of government are able to survive even though they lack the administrative capacity to administer other kinds of taxes and lack the support to obtain funds from higher levels of government. Some of these units are relics of a rural past, but others have been created largely or partly to take advantage of concentrations of taxable wealth. The existence of such tax enclaves fragments the tax base available to local units of government and reduces their ability, as a group, to provide local services. This gives further impetus to the trend toward fiscal centralization.

The latest chapter in the story is provided by Proposition 13 and its consequences. Not only did Proposition 13 in California reduce the ability of local governments to raise revenue, but it imposed an overall limit upon property tax rates that required the intervention of the state government to "ration" the available property tax revenues among the various local governments having jurisdiction over a parcel of property. The state legislature responded to the problem by enacting temporary measures which allocated state aid and property taxes according to a variety of formulas and imposed a variety of limitations upon the fiscal independence of local governments. Special districts fared the worst, as the legislature allocated an arbitrary sum and assigned counties the task of allocating it. Since that time the Post Commission has issued a report recommending that the state assume the full costs of welfare, health costs and, to the extent feasible, major costs of the court system. The commission also recommended that the major share of school funding be assumed by the state. The commission underscored the growing pressure for reorganization and restructuring of local government, which may turn out to be among the most important consequences of Proposition 13.

Proposition 13 has been the inspiration for a large number of tax limit proposals in other states. Although it is far too early to appraise the impact and direction of this movement, it is clear that many of the proposals, if adopted, will have major effects upon the structure of state and local governments. These include not only changes in the powers and functions of local governments but also structural changes within state governments. The establishment of joint legislative budget committees or the employment of ceilings related to price indexes, personal income, state product or projected revenues will all result in changes in the decisionmaking process and shifts in the balance of political power.

It is widely admitted that many local governments are too small to deal with many of the problems of a modern economy. Externalities in both the public and private sectors make it impossible or inequitable for local governments to attempt to solve many kinds of problems or to provide certain kinds of services. Suggested approaches to solving these problems include consolidation of government and various kinds of cooperative measures, such as consolidation of specific departments, councils of government, contracting for services and mutual aid pacts. Other approaches usually initiated by state or federal government include transfer of functions to higher levels of government, grant-in-aid programs and the mandating of services or standards.

Often, arguments for or against modifications in government structure revolve around questions of cost, efficiency and equity in the provision of services. These arguments often seem to favor major horizontal consolidation or vertical concentrations of the decisionmaking power. Countering this are arguments involving questions of local democracy and citizen participation. At one time these arguments were advanced largely by those opposed to change, who wanted to preserve existing units of government and existing functions and privileges. More recently, similar arguments have been advanced in support of new citizen participation structures within existing governmental units. Often these demands come from the poor or disadvantaged who are seeking a role in the system.

The analyst cannot settle all of these questions, but in view of their importance and the impact that tax structure has upon governmental structure, it appears that for the analyst to ignore these questions is to do a disservice.

2. *Public Acceptability.* A government exists only so long as its legitimacy is widely accepted. Recent events in Iran illustrate once again that even an established government with an abundance of modern arms and the support of powerful allies cannot continue to exist once it becomes obvious that public support is lacking. Because taxation is one of the most unpopular functions performed by governments, it would seem to follow that one of the first questions to be asked about a revenue source should be, "How acceptable is it to the taxpayers?" Although knowledge of what makes a tax more or less acceptable is limited, it appears that most people favor taxes which seem to be fair and which can be uniformly administered. If so, it would seem that tax policymakers should pay more attention to polls which measure people's attitudes toward taxes. In addition, concern about administrative feasibility should emphasize uniformity and fairness of administration rather than the cost of administration. The historical record shows that certain taxes rarely are enforced fairly or accurately. The erosion of the personal property tax base over time and the almost universal failure to assess real property accurately are prime examples. To state that the tax could be enforced if the unit of government had the will, facilities and staff is not a sufficient answer to the problem when more than one hundred years of history shows that it rarely has been done.

APPLYING THE CRITERIA

To agree that political criteria should be considered when appraising a tax system would be an important and desirable step toward solving problems of fiscal squeeze, but that alone provides limited guidance to the revenue analyst. It is necessary to develop methods of appraising various revenue sources on the basis of these criteria and to determine the weights or priorities to be accorded the various economic and political criteria.

Unfortunately, the literature relating revenue systems to the structure of government is not a rich one. There are many scattered references to the connections between finance and government structure. For example, it is often pointed out that constitutional debt or tax limits have encouraged overlapping special districts or school districts. There are many references in the literature of urban finance to the desire to minimize tax burdens as one of the factors promoting urban sprawl as well as many references to the multiplicity of governments in urban areas. For the most part, however, these have been incidental references, and generally the emphasis has been upon designing revenue systems for existing governmental structures. Of course, there are some exceptions. The tax-base sharing arrangement in the twin city area of Minnesota was adopted with structural considerations in mind, and governmental structure has been considered in grant-in-aid programs. Probably the outstanding example of the latter was the use of fiscal powers to encourage the consolidation of school districts. At the federal level, structural questions are often debated when grant programs are under consideration, but there is not much evidence that the results have been positive. On balance, the results of federal grant programs probably have been to fragment governmental structure and further to confuse the taxpayer who wants to understand state and local finance. Structural questioms often have been cited as a reason for the adoption of revenue sharing. It is unfortunate that this act was passed only after a political alliance was put together in such a way as to insure that the formula would help to perpetuate rather than reduce fragmentation of government.

There are at least two reasons for the failure to give more attention to government structure as a dependent variable. One is that the scholarly literature is not well developed, and the other is that the frame of reference of most revenue studies has not been one in which it appeared appropriate to consider government structure.

Because the scholarly literature has not been developed, we lack the intellectual frame of reference to analyze the relationships. The very words "government structure," for example, are vague and poorly defined. In writing this paper I have found myself using the term to refer to such diverse concepts as the internal decisionmaking and administrative mechanism within a unit of government or branch of government and also to the intergovernmental structure represented by the existence of hundreds of local governments in a metropolitan area. There is a great need for a Musgrave-like *Political Theory of Public Finance* that would provide the concepts and framework for discussion and research.

In the realm of applied tax studies, the frame of reference often does not permit the analyst to consider questions of government structure. If one is appointed or employed by the legislative branch of a municipal government to study financial problems of the municipality, there is little scope for considering innovations in the organization of the municipal government and even less opportunity seriously to consider measures which would lead to consolidation or elimination of the municipality itself. Studies of minicipal finance by state governments would seem to be a more appropriate occasion for such considerations. However, the attention span of state officials when the problems of local governments are concerned often is not very long. Local problems are considered when bankruptcy threatens a city or a Proposition 13 creates a crisis, but concern rapidly shifts back to the state's fiscal problems.

The information needed to apply the "citizens attitude" criteria to tax policy questions is more readily available than is information about the connection between revenue and government structure. Established survey research groups have included questions about taxation in many national and local surveys. The periodic studies undertaken by the Advisory Commission on Intergovernmental Relations are the most widely quoted. Oddly, however, these appear to have been given little attention by tax analysts. Perhaps economists see themselves as educators, who should influence public opinion rather than tailor their recommendations to fit existing public opinion.

One of the crucial steps in appraising a revenue system is the assigning of priorities or weights to the various criteria utilized. In the present and foreseeable future this remains a judgmental rather than a technical process. This means that not only will final conclusions be affected by the values of the person or persons making the judgment but that the priorities will depend upon the situation in the place and at the time that the judgment is made. It is, therefore, not possible to specify just how much weight should be given to political criteria or to rank the various political and economic criteria. In my own opinion, however, political criteria often deserve a high priority. There is ample evidence that public confidence in government is eroding and that the fiscal squeeze in many areas is more political than economic. In these circumstances it would seem to be folly to recommend an unpopular tax because of a minor point of equity when a less unpopular tax is readily available. Similarly, it is unwise to ignore the effects that a revenue system has upon the structure of government. A reappraisal of priorities would, in my opinion, often have a major impact upon how we view particular taxes. For example:

1. *The Property Tax.* The reader is undoubtedly aware of the debate over the degree of regressivity, if any, of the property tax.

Concern with the vertical equity of the tax in many situations may be less appropriate than concern with the horizontal equity and the closely related question of public attitudes toward the tax. When assessment/sales ratio studies show that coefficients of dispersion in many jurisdictions are 30 percent or higher and apparently rising, there is much cause for concern on both economic and political grounds. Such inequities cannot be corrected or offset by other taxes or low-income credits. To say that the tax can be administered well if resources and political will are present is to hide the important question. If we rule out totalitarian methods, political will somehow must involve the feelings and desires of the governed. I suggested a few years ago that perhaps the property tax survives only because it is poorly and corruptly administered. One of the economists present when I read the paper suggested that such a statement was immoral. Immoral or not, it is a regrettable but tenable hypothesis. The passage of Proposition 13 in a state generally considered to have good property tax administration unfortunately lends support to the hypothesis.

In appraising the property tax one also must consider that it has been consistently voted the least popular tax in opinion polls. We have little knowledge of the extent to which that unpopularity is related to poor administration and to taxpayer misunderstanding of the tax, but research into these questions would be more useful, from a policy viewpoint, than further analysis of the burden of a hypothetical, perfectly administered property tax. Pending further findings in the area I would suggest that the principal "advantage" of the property tax is that it permits fragmented, overlapping units of local government to raise a great deal of money and to retain a considerable degree of fiscal independence. To the extent that we want to continue such a local government structure, the property tax plays a useful role. Otherwise, we should be giving attention to taxes that will support reorganized urban or regional governments and to methods of delivery of intergovernmental grants which will facilitate and encourage the kinds of intergovernmental structures and relationships we desire to see develop. Revenue matters should not be considered isolated from these questions.

2. *The Sales Tax.* The sales tax usually fares poorly in tax studies. It has been cited as the prime example of a regressive tax, and that reputation has spread widely. In my contacts with legislators I am often startled at the frequency with which persons of all political persuasion and of all degrees of economic literacy condemn the tax as regressive. Perhaps it is time for a reappraisal of the importance

of that fact. Concern about the regressivity of the tax originated in the 1930s when the tax was widely adopted by states. At that time the country was in the midst of a major depression. Redistributive transfer payments were small, and the imposition of a tax upon the absolute necessities of life (which make up the bulk of the taxable retail sales) was a serious matter. It was entirely appropriate to be very concerned about the burden the tax imposed on the very poorest. Today the situation is different. There are many well financed programs which redistribute income, and federal taxes now dwarf state and local taxes as instruments of social policy. Much public unrest centers around doubts about government's ability to administer the laws which have been passed—including the tax laws. It seems strange that we so often dismiss as unworthy the tax that is consistently voted the least unpopular in public opinion polls, that is cheap to administer and raises the fewest doubts that everybody is paying his share. Several years ago Professor Kenneth Galbraith defended the sales tax as a lucrative source of revenue that could provide revenue for social programs which would benefit the poor. Today one could add that the sales tax can be a useful tool to maintain the strength and integrity of state and local government, which may, in the long run, benefit rich and poor alike.

The principal disadvantage of the sales tax, as a locally imposed, state administered source of revenue, is that the existence of large shopping centers in small suburban muncipalities creates inequities in the distribution of the tax. It would require only a little ingenuity, however, to overcome this disadvantage. One possibility would be to develop a regional tax-base sharing scheme similar to the property tax-base sharing scheme utilized in Minnesota. Another possibility would be to make the tax available only to large metropolitan or regional governments and to use the tax as an instrument that would encourage governmental reorganization according to a well thought out plan balancing equity, efficiency and participation.

3. *Grants-in-Aid.* The application of political criteria to intergovernmental fiscal programs may be the most promising approach of all. This is because the framework in which policy is made may be more favorable for consideration of political issues. Because the "superior" government normally takes the initiative, it is in a position to consider structural effects of the program. The school consolidation programs are prime examples. However, unless the issues are well articulated and carefully researched, the results many be mindless overcentralization or equally mindless protection of the status quo. Because this is a very complex issue and one that receives attention

in other chapters in this volume, no attempt is made to develop it further here.

CONCLUSIONS

Economists have been influential in the formation of revenue policy not only because of the analytical methods they have developed, but also because of the role they have played in formulating the criteria for judging a revenue system.

At the present time the major reasons for the fiscal squeeze facing municipalities are political rather than economic. Resources are heavily concentrated in the metropolitan areas of America, but fragmented government structure and political alienation place resources beyond the reach of the municipal governments which have the greatest need. Political mechanisms do balance the expenditure = revenue equation but only after a great deal of conflict and confusion.

It has been suggested in this paper that a proper revenue balance can be achieved only if greater attention is given to political criteria for appraising revenue sources. Specifically, it was suggested that much more weight should be given to the effect of a revenue source upon the structure of government and to the acceptability of the revenue source to the taxpayers. Instead of considering the political system as an independent variable to which the tax system must conform, it was suggested that the political system be considered a dependent variable that is greatly affected by the revenue sources used. For example, the property tax helps perpetuate fragmented local government, and intergovernmemtal grants can transform both the structure and function of governmental systems.

NOTES

1. Edward Banfield, *Political Influence, A New Theory of Urban Politics* (New York: The Free Press, 1965), p. 357.
2. A study of decision-making in the Illinois Constitutional Convention concluded that it is reasonable to describe the decisionmaking process involved in writing the finance article as rational. There was a general consensus concerning the objectives, and the process of arriving at the outcome was systematic and relatively efficient. Decisions about the much more controversial revenue article were made in an entirely different manner. Compromise and ambiguity, rather than systematic thought and clarity, made it possible to make a social choice. Joyce D. Fishbane and Glenn W. Fisher, *Politics of the Purse: Revenue and Finance in the Sixth Illinois Constitutional Convention* (Urbana: University of Illinois Press, 1974), p. 199.

3. George F. Break, *Agenda for Local Tax Reform* (Berkeley: Institute of Governmental Studies, University of California, 1970), pp. 7-35.

4. District of Columbia Tax Revision Commission, *Financing an Urban Government* (Washington, D.C., 1978), pp. 11-14.

5. Adam Smith, *An Inquiry into the Nature and Causes of the Wealth of Nations,* (Modern Library Edition), p. 778.

6. This statement requires some modification as regards the property tax. Because the assessed value of a piece of property is legally established by a highly visible administrative act, reappraisal may focus attention upon the base rather than the rate. This, however, only reinforces the main point, since the result is often the postponement of reappraisal which reduces the "effective" elasticity of the property tax.

7. Glenn W. Fisher, "Property Taxation and the Political System," in *Property Taxation, Land Use and Public Policy*, ed. by Arthur D. Lynn, Jr. (Madison: The University of Wisconsin Press, 1976), pp. 5-22.

8. The International Association of Assessing Officers have recently published a handbook for assessors based on information collected as part of a major study of assessment. This handbook summarizes much current knowledge regarding the practices and appraisal of the assessment process. International Association of Assessing Officers, *Improving Real Property Assessment: A Reference Manual* (Chicago: International Association of Assessing Officers, 1978), p. 444.

9. Aaron Wildavsky, "Political Implications of Budgeting Reform," *Public Administration Review*, Vol. 21 (Autumn, 1961), pp. 183-90.

10. For a concise summary, see Jacob Citrin, "The Alienated Voter," *Taxes and Spending* (Oct./Nov. 1978).

11. U.S. Bureau of the Census, 1977 Census of Governments, *Taxable Property Values and Assessment/Sales Price Ratios* (Washington, D.C.: U.S. Government Printing Office, 1979), p. 21.

12. Advisory Commission on Intergovernmental Relations, *Changing Public Attitudes on Government and Taxes*, 1977 (Washington, D.C.: U.S. Government Printing Office, 1977), p. 11.

Dick Netzer - THE PROPERTY TAX IN THE NEW ENVIRONMENT

The "new environment" in the title refers to a set of characteristics that are not brand-new, but sharply different from those that obtained and were expected to persist during the decade or so—from roughly 1960 to, say, 1973—during which the now conventional wisdom about the property tax and its proper role in the financing of large-city governments was formed.[1] The "new" characteristics relevant to discussion of the property tax include the following:

1. The probability that whatever the rate of measured aggregate economic growth, the rate of growth in variables important for the property tax base—the *physical* aspects of taxable property in general and the price aspects closely tied to population growth (e.g., land values in rapidly growing places)—will be considerably slower than has been the case in this country historically.

2. The dispersion of geographically-specific growth rates around the national averages will be large, not small.

3. The rejection of the notion that state-local government financial aggregates must continue to grow more rapidly than GNP; conceivably, there may be further increases in the state-local share (and in the overall public sector share), but that will be heavily contested, not least by property tax ceilings of one kind or another.

4. The end of the long era in which individual property tax
   burdens were adjusted informally and extra-legally by administrators and elected officials, with departures from uniform
   treatment from here on requiring explicit legislation and
   class actions.

This paper addresses, without providing conclusive answers,
several questions implied by these and other changes. The first
question is whether the topic itself is not essentially trivial: do
recent institutional changes in state-local finance suggest that the
demise of the property tax as an important revenue source is
approaching, willy-nilly? Assuming that the property tax has *not*
fallen into such disfavor and that there will be public acceptance
of the notion that the property tax *should* continue to play a
significant role, what is likely to be happening to the property tax
base over time, in the aggregate and for declining cities in particular?
Given the answer to this question and the institutional change cited
in (4), above, what should be happening to the structure of the
urban property tax? What is likely to happen?

THE DECLINING ROLE OF THE PROPERTY TAX

It is reasonably well understood that the role of the property tax
in state-local finance declined marginally during the 1950s and early
1960s, principally as a result of some expansion in the utilization
of local non-property taxes and relatively modest increases in state
aid to local governments. But beginning in the middle and late 1960s,
the property tax role declined much more rapidly, mainly because
of an expanded federal role, some shift of functional responsibilities
to state governments (e.g., public assistance) and school finance
reforms resulting in greater state government shares. It is not
generally understood just how rapid that decline has been.

For this purpose, I used Census data to attempt to depict the
change in the role of the property tax in financing those local government outlays it is generally expected to finance. Local governments
generally do not finance capital outlays from current revenues
(other than intergovernmental grants for capital purposes), so the
property tax has little or no role in financing capital outlays when
they are made; however, it does, or can, have a role in financing
debt service. In general, American local governments that operate
water supply and electric power utilities segregate the utility
finances and do not expect them to generate deficits financed from
current general revenues, such as the property tax; in most cases, they

do not expect to produce current surpluses to be used to finance general government operations. But, by now, most American local governments that operate transit systems expect those systems to realize deficits that *are* charges against current general revenue. So, the property tax is ordinarily relied upon to play a role in financing the following Census local government expenditure items:

(a) general expenditure excluding capital outlay;

(b) current deficits of transit systems;

(c) retirement of long-term debt, excluding debt issued for utility systems (transit aside);[2] and

(d) local government contributions to employee-retirement systems operated by local governments.[3]

Exhibit 1 shows the change in these expenditure items and in property tax revenue, for all local governments combined, over a twenty-year period. In the first half of the period, the property tax share declined by 6 percentage points, in the second by 10 percentage points; in relative terms, the decline was about twice as great in the more recent decade. Moreover, although this is not shown by the exhibit, the decline in the property tax share accelerated over the decade, even before the massive effects of the federal anti-recession package showed up, in local government fiscal years beginning after July 1, 1977.

These data apply to all local governments. It might have been expected that the municipal governments serving large central cities would have been less affected by the structural changes, because (a) few of them operate school systems directly (and so would not be affected by school finance reforms) and (b) even in 1957 and still more in 1967, they were relatively heavy utilizers of non-property taxes and user charges as revenue sources. The reality, as Exhibit 2 shows, is that the decline proceeded even more rapidly for the municipal governments of the 46 cities with a 1975 population in excess of 300,000, from 1966-67 to 1976-77.[4] The property tax share declined by one-third, to 24 percent of the relevant expenditure total. In fiscal 1978, the percentage may have fallen below 20 (although there should be some rebound as the anti-recession package expires).

Analogous calculations were done for whole metropolitan areas, this time for 1975-76 versus 1965-66, undertaken to ascertain how ubiquitous the shift has been, while avoiding the influence of such

EXHIBIT 1

The Property Tax in U.S. Local Government Finance,
1957, 1966-67 and 1976-77.[a]
(dollar amounts in billions)

Expenditure or revenue item	1957	1966-67	1976-77
1. General expenditure other than capital outlay	20.9	49.0	149.7
2. Current deficits of transit systems[b]	*	0.1	1.6
3. Retirement of long-term general debt[c]	1.6	3.4	6.9
4. Contributions to local-government-administered employee-retirement systems	0.5	1.0	3.4
5. Total, 1 through 4	23.5	53.4	161.7
6. Property tax revenue	12.4	25.4	60.3
7. 6 as % of 5	53.8%	47.6%	37.3%

Note: Totals and division from unrounded data

*   Less than $50 million (actually, $9 million current surplus)

a   Adapted from U.S. Bureau of the Census, Governments Division publications, notably the 1957, 1967 and 1972 Census of Government and the annual series for 1976-77.

b   Current operating expenditure plus interest on transit debt less transit revenue.

c   Partly estimated on the basis of outstanding debt. Properly speaking, this should include retirement of transit debt as well.

differences in local government structure as whether the city government or another unit runs the schools or transit system. The property tax share declined by more than one-third in 16 of the 37 SMSAs for which this comparison was possible and by between one-fourth and one-third in another 9. In no SMSA did it decline by less than one-tenth. By now, there is no major SMSA outside New England in which the property tax finances more than one-half of the relevant local government expenditures. In the Sunbelt and in the Frostbelt, in growing areas and in declining areas, the property tax role has declined and sharply.

If this decline means that the property tax in another decade will "have become an all-but-forgotten relic of an earlier fiscal age" (a forecast made in 1956 for 1976),[5] then this paper should end at this point. However, the guess here is that the institutional changes that caused the rapid structural shift of the past dozen or so years will not be repeated with anything like the same effect over the next dozen years. This guess rests on two suppositions. The first is that the federal role in state-local finance will not increase as rapidly

EXHIBIT 2

The Property Tax in the Finance of the Municipal Governments
of Cities with a 1975 Population over 300,000, 1966-67-1976-77[a]
(dollar amounts in millions)

Expenditure or revenue item	1966-67	1976-77
1. General expenditure other than capital outlay	8,148	25,204
2. Current deficits of transit systems[b]	81	355
3. Retirement of long-term general debt[c]	825	1,828
4. Contributions to city-government-administered employee-retirement systems	680	2,184
5. Total, 1 through 4	9,734	29,571
6. Property tax revenue	3,563	7,111
7. 6 as % of 5	36.6%	24.0%

a   Adapted from U.S. Bureau of the Census, *City Government Finances in 1966-67* and *City Government Finances in 1976-77*. Cover 46 cities with a 1975 population in excess of 300,000.

b   Current operating expenditure plus interest on transit debt less transit revenue.

c   Partly estimated. Properly speaking, this should include retirement of transit debt as well.

as in the recent past and to the extent that it does increase, it will affect the finances of the state governments rather than the local governments, e.g., by absorbing state/government-borne public assistance and Medicaid costs. The second is that the pace of school finance reform will slacken, at least in aggregative dollar terms: school finance reform already has occurred (and will go only marginally further) in a fair number of states and those in which there is much scope for reform are either small or hard cases without neat solutions (such as New York State), upon which the imperial judiciary may well founder.

The *deus ex machina* relieving the need for property-tax-generated revenues may be less likely, but this does not make the property tax any more popular, nor does it make the property tax base grow. The revenues will be needed, but can they be generated and, if so, how?

THE AGGREGATE TAX BASE

Twenty years ago, those of us who were early fanciers of the now-popular indoor sport of long-range economic projections for public-sector finances had some disputation about whether or not the proper tax base to consider for these purposes, in connection with the property tax, was the assessed value or the market value of taxable property. In small part because of the persuasive powers of the purists (we held that long-term economic projections ought to project economic variables, not the behavior of assessors), but largely because of reforms in assessment procedures that gave a great deal of cognizance to market values, no one today would pay attention to anything other than trends in the market values of property subject to tax.

The property tax base early in this century was composed of privately-owned land, buildings and tangible personal property not specifically exempted because, for example, it was owned by churches or other worthy non-governmental entities. Today, because of state enactments removing whole classes of nonreal property from the tax base and other actions providing for more tailored abatements and exemptions, the tax base nationally may be described as follows:

(a) virtually all nonfarm business structures, and the land on which such structures are built;

(b) about one-half of the book value of nonfarm business and farm equipment;

(c) perhaps 35-40 percent of the book value of nonfarm inventories on the assessment dates in the various states;

(d) nearly all farm land and structures, mostly valued on the basis of current use (not market) and with farm structures contributing little, if anything, incrementally to taxable values;

(e) a small fraction of the average annual value of farm inventories;

(f) perhaps 95 percent of the value of privately-owned nonfarm residential structures and land;

(g) 25 percent or less of the market value of nonbusiness-owned motor vehicles; and

(h) privately-owned vacant urban land.[6]

What should be striking about this list is the extent to which the tax base is made up of reproducible *physical things.* The property tax base, being comprised of the value of physical assets, differs sharply in character from a tax base—like that of taxes on gross receipts, income, profits or value added—comprised of the value of transactions in that changes in the base of the property tax are peculiarly dependent on physical changes, notably construction of buildings and other structures. That is, the property tax base is sensitive to the nation's product mix and input mix.

It seems inevitable that, over time, real GNP should become less structure-intensive, with slow rates of population growth (which have obvious impacts on the need for residential structures) and a continued shift in the product mix from physical goods to intangible services. The corollary may be that there will be (relatively) more equipment in (relatively) fewer buildings, but much equipment is not subject to tax and it is reasonable to expect recent trends toward removal of tangible nonreal property from the tax base to continue. Slow population growth should imply slow growth in land value in the aggregate; changes in population distribution, e.g., among regions, should wash out in their effects on overall land values.

Obviously, this is a vastly oversimplified model of the relationship of taxable property values to GNP, even for the country as a whole for periods of a decade or more. Nonetheless, I am persuaded that we should expect the GNP elasticity of the property tax base to be lower in future than it has been over the past generation. Most of the 1960's studies of the elasticity of the property tax base with respect to some measure of income or overall economic activity came up with values clustered close to unity. It seems reasonable to forecast somewhat lower values, as a general tendency, in looking ahead.

But there is little evidence of this general tendency as yet. A goodly portion of the property tax base is covered by Department of Commerce estimates of business "fixed capital" and residential structures; the principal exclusion, of course, is the value of land. Exhibit 3 utilizes those estimates to calculate an indicated GNP elasticity of this part of the property tax base. For the twenty years from 1949 to 1969, the elasticity figure is just over 1.0. *A priori,* one might have expected to begin to observe a decline in the years since 1969, given the almost uninterrupted series of national or worldwide economic difficulties since that year (U.S. recession in 1970-71; worldwide hyperinflation in 1972-73; the oil embargo and price rises in 1973-74; worldwide recession in 1974-75; etc., etc.).

However, as Exhibit 3 also shows, the GNP elasticity of the property tax base components included here was marginally higher, at 1.1 or 1.2, not lower, than it had been in the previous twenty years. To be sure, in the earlier period, 60 percent of the growth in property values was real, rather than price, while in the 1969-77 period only 27 percent of the growth was real. But this paralleled GNP movements. The relative price of fixed capital rose only slightly (about 8 percent), according to these data.

My conclusion from all this is that it makes no sense to forecast property tax base inadequacy over the next decade or two, in aggregate terms, whatever the general tendencies. Nonetheless, the general tendencies provide a constraining backdrop against which to consider regional differences.

DECLINING AND GROWING CITIES

A starting point: there are *no* reliable and nationally-applicable data on recent changes in the market value of taxable property in all major cities or in a list that includes most of them. The Census of Governments data have serious omissions (e.g., for the cities of Chicago and Cleveland in the 1977 Census), problems of comparability over time and major conceptual difficulties. Thus, the empirical discussion in the literature of the relation between property values (in market terms) and city economic fortunes is anecdotal, either explicitly or implicitly (because it relies on noncomparable local data).[7] Here, too, the empircal evidence is anecdotal.

However, it is clear that the property tax base of a city *should* be powerfully affected by longer-term economic changes specific to that city. Indeed, the property tax base should reflect relative long-term economic trends in magnified form, that is, the elasticity of the rate of change in a city's property tax base relative to the national average with respect to its rate of change in city gross product relative to GNP should be well above 1.0. If the city's population is declining fast enough to yield a decline in the number of households, the value of the housing stock and of land potentially available for residential use must be declining in relative terms at a fast clip. If real economic activity in the city is declining, the same will be true of its stock of nonresidential buildings and, very likely, even more true of the value of land in or available for nonresidential uses. Indeed, a notable characteristic of declining cities is the existence of large amounts of land with zero or negative values in private ownership just beyond the possibly-thriving central business district.

EXHIBIT 3

The GNP Elasticity of the "Fixed Capital" Components of the Property Tax Base," U.S., 1949-1977[a]

	1949	1969	1977
Current dollar data:			
Privately-owned fixed capital assumed to be in the property tax base, 1977 ($ billion)[b]	325.5	1,209.5	2,760.1
Average annual percent increase	---	6.79%	10.87%
GNP ($billion)	258.0	935.5	1,887.2
Average annual percent increase	---	6.65%	9.16%
Indicated elasticity	---	1.02	1.19
Constant (1972) dollar data:			
Privately-owned fixed capital assumed to be in the property tax base, 1977 ($72 billion)[b]	591.1	1,323.8	1,670.4
Average annual percent increase	---	4.12%	2.95%
GNP ($72 billion)	490.7	1,078.8	1,332.7
Average annual percent increase	---	4.01%	2.68%
Indicated elasticity	---	1.03	1.10

a   Derived from data in *Survey of Current Business*, April 1976 and September 1978, and *The National Income and Product Accounts of the United States, 1929-74.*

b   It is assumed that the nationwide property tax base in the U.S. as of 1977-78 includes (in addition to land, some inventories and a limited amount of consumer durables, notably autos):

  100% of nonfarm business structures;
  50% of nonfarm business and farm equipment; and
  95% of privately-owned nonfarm residential structures,

measured by value. The exclusions reflect the statutory coverage of the property tax in the various states and a variety of partial execptions, principally for nonfarm housing. It is also assumed that farm structures, residential or nonresidential, form a non-independent element of farm land values, for property tax purposes, reflecting conventional assessment practices. For the coverage of the property tax, see the introductory narrative discussion in U.S. Bureau of the Census, *1977 Census of Governments*, Vol. 2, *Taxable Property Values and Assessment/Sales Price Ratios* (1978).

The limited Census of Governments evidence on changes in property values is utilized, for selected cities, in Exhibit 4.[8] The first six are old, declining cities in the Midwest or Northeast; the last two, San Diego and Washington, are growing cities included for comparative purposes. If a city grew at the national GNP rate and if the 1969-77 elasticity figure of 1.1 is an appropriate one for these purposes, then the "expected" rate of increase for such an "average" city would have been roughly 67 percent between 1971 and 1976. San Diego far exceeded this as one would expect, but Baltimore also matched this target and prosperous Washington fell below. Residential property values in Washington, however, conformed to the gentrification scenario; that is, they increased extraordinarily rapidly in a central city without population growth.

Nonresidential property value changes in the declining cities other than Baltimore are consistent with what any observer would have predicted—large absolute declines (12 percent in just five years) in Detroit and Milwaukee, stability in Pittsburgh and increases in New York and Philadelphia far below any plausible national average expectations (and those increases probably are exaggerated by the estimating methods). Moreover, because the price level increased by nearly 50 percent during the five years from 1972 to 1977, stability of property tax revenue in real terms would have required increases in effective property tax rates in five of the six declining cities.

It is possible to devise scenarios in which the decline in the population of most of the large old cities is a good deal slower than, say, New York in the post-1970 period or Detroit and St. Louis since the early 1950s, and in which the real level of economic activity remains roughly stable in most such cities; it is difficult to devise plausible scenarios in which these cities do much better. But the moderating-population-loss/stable-real-economy model probably implies continued declines in the real value of taxable property, albeit modest declines, through net disinvestment and land value decreases for taxable residential property and nonresidential property outside the CBD that are only partly offset by net investment and land value increases within the CBD. And this model is probably overly optimistic if the slowly declining real tax base leads to steady increases in effective property tax rates. Thus, the conclusion here is that property tax yields in real terms can be expected to decline in the large older cities in the Northeast and Midwest. How that decline will be distributed, or should be distributed, among the various types of property is a separate question, dealt with below.

EXHIBIT 4

Estimated Percentage Changes in Market Value of Real Property,
1971 to 1976, in Selected Cities[a]

| City | Percent change in market value of— | | | Exhibit: Single-family as % of total 1976 market value |
	All real property	Single family houses	Other types	
Baltimore	+ 70	+ 73	+ 66	49.3
Detroit	− 4	+ 6	− 12	49.2
Milwaukee	+ 12	+ 35	− 12	60.7
New York	+ 38	+ 46	+ 37	12.5
Philadelphia	+ 45	+ 65	+ 25	57.9
Pittsburgh	+ 30	+ 82	+ 3	47.1
San Diego	+130	+108	+169	57.7
Washington	+ 49	+138	+ 12	47.0

a Derived from data in 1972 and 1977 Census of Governments (Volume 2 in each case). Market value estimates are based on "measurable sales." To the extent that there are important classes of property underrepresented in "measurable sales" and that have ratios of assessed to market values wholly different from the rations for those classes adequately represented in the sales data, the estimates in columns (1) and (3) are distortions. It is probable that the distortions lie in the direction of overstating the increase in nonresidential property values in Baltimore, New York and Philadelphia, especially in the latter two.

What about the San Diegos? The limited Census of Governments data suggest that, in the 1970s through 1977, effective property tax rates typically *did* decline somewhat in rapidly growing Sunbelt cities and SMSAs. That is, the market value of taxable property rose more rapidly than property tax revenues, although the latter in fact also rose rapidly. Proposition 13 followed a period of declining, not increasing, effective property tax rates in most California cities. This is not the place to review the endless exegesis of the causes and effects of Proposition 13; clearly there *were* factors specific to California, including highly visible uniform and up-to-date reassessments.

But a more general factor is the almost universal hostility to the taxation of unrealized capital gains, which was occurring in property taxation in California, despite modest declines in the ratio of property tax liability to the market value of taxable property. That hostility is especially intense when it is perceived, accurately or not, that the unrealized capital gains are largely or wholly a result of inflation in general. In other words, there seems to be a demand for some form of implicit indexation in the property tax. If that demand is as effective politically as it appears to be, then property tax yields will increase relatively slowly in growing cities, as effective rate reduction becomes the dominant response to rapid growth in property values.

THE FORM OF THE URBAN PROPERTY TAX

The story thus far is a forecast of declining property tax yields with stable effective rates in declining cities and slowly growing yields with decreasing effective rates in growing cities. What form should/will these reductions/ceilings take?

At this point, note should be made of the "new view" or "revisionist" conception of the property tax, as one that falls efficiently and progressively in incidence on the owners of capital, when the property tax is examined on a national basis: *efficiently* in the sense that the tax does not have major macro consequences for resource allocation and *progressively* when compared to the distribution of incomes. The geographic and sectoral non-uniformities yield both inefficiencies (effects on location decisions and micro intersectoral effects) and, under some circumstances, regressivity. Thus, the fairly obvious policy conclusion is that the more uniform the property tax is, the better.

The alternative and more "traditional" view, now espoused by some "new view" theorists, among others, is that the property tax for most policy purposes can be analyzed usefully only as a geographically-specific revenue instrument: how does it work in a given city, SMSA or state? From this standpoint, there is no special virtue to uniformity as such. If some features of the tax have undesirable efficiency or equity results, then those features should be addressed directly and specifically, even at the cost of making the property tax as a whole less uniform, within or among jurisdictions.

Even in the heyday of the "general property tax" in the mid-nineteenth century, when nearly all forms of property, real and personal, tangible and intangible, were theoretically subject to taxation at a uniform rate within a given jurisdiction, the tax in practice was far from uniform. And reformers roundly denounced the departures from uniformity as a sign of bad government. Bad government there was, but it is more reasonable to ascribe systematic and long-continued differentials in the property tax treatment of different kinds of property (initially via assessment discrimination but over the years also via statutory exemption, abatement and classification) to efforts to respond to social and economic realities.

These realities include reluctance to tax heavily that "necessity," housing (and to tax it regressively); recognition that—at least in the short-run—taxation of business property might be partly exportable; reaction to repeated bouts of sustained hard times in agriculture in earlier generations; differential difficulties in discovering and valuing different types of property; and worry about the consequences for local economies of tax burdens that are thought to discourage new investment.

These realities are no less pressing today. But, increasingly, local governments are constrained from responding by the time-honored method of informal and extra-legal assessment discrimination, by court decisions and legislative enactments. There is, thus, far more pressure for uniformity than in the past. As noted earlier, a high order of uniformity is surely one factor in the circumstances leading to Proposition 13. Proposition 13 is one form that the reductions/ ceilings might take: more or less across-the-board reductions or ceilings applying to all types of taxable property.

Another form also exists, in practice: increasingly widespread use of non-uniform property tax reduction adjustment mechanisms, like the circuit-breaker, other residential abatements and partial exemptions, new-industry abatements and outright classification and differential taxation of the various property-use classes. All such devices are designed to shelter specified types of taxpayers from the rigors of uniformity and/or to encourage investment that might not be undertaken unless so sheltered. Inevitably, such devices yield some degree of both inequity and inefficiency. For example, they inequitably shelter some rich homeowners and farmers along with poorer homeowners and farmers. They inefficiently reduce taxes on some investments that would be undertaken even at higher effective tax rates, along with making other, previously submarginal investments, attractive. The real question, of course, is the magnitude of the inequities and inefficiencies relative to, say, across-the-board reductions in property tax yields.

The "new view" is an inappropriate theoretical framework for answering this question for a given city. There is, however, another set of theories applicable here. This theorizing concludes that the optimal local-source revenue system for a large central city is one that consists entirely of user charges and taxation of land values. Such a system meets the canons of equity fully and, simultaneously, eliminates any local-tax deterrent to economic development.

If the theory is valid, then the policy implication is fairly obvious: the property tax in large cities should be stripped down to one on land values; buildings should be taxed only to the very limited extent that the taxation of improvements is, and is perceived by taxpayers to be, the equivalent of appropriately-designed user charges. Selective abatements and exemptions within classes thus are a poor idea if they are highly selective. If, however, they are freely available and so widespread that they might become universal in time, such as the untaxing of all new investment in housing and business structures (including both new construction and rehabilitation), they are consistent with the theory. The old investment-denied tax reduction will disappear in time, and there is no special point in affording windfall gains to the holders of such assets.

This approach has the significant advantage of minimizing immediate revenue losses. The revenue losses, such as they are, accrue over the years: that is, the reductions/ceilings that seem likely in any case take this particular form. Clearly, this kind of change in property taxation requires significantly higher effective rates on land values. This will produce capital losses whether done instantaneously or over time, a non-trivial political consequence. Moreover, there should be no illusions that land values in declining cities—even after the initial capital losses have been assimilated—will increase rapidly, and probably not at all in real terms. There is no change in the local tax system that will transform Milwaukee into San Diego: old declining cities will tend to have weak tax bases. The choice is between weak and weaker.

Only the credulous would accept this prescription as the most likely course of action. After all, advocates of land value taxation have been offering their remedy for a long time—1979 is the 100th anniversary of the publication of *Progress and Poverty*. But perhaps municipal poverty will concentrate minds more than municipal progress has done heretofore.

NOTES

1. I accept my share of the blame for the conventional wisdom. We all should recognize that the shelf life of most conclusions about urban public policy is short, surely less than ten years.

2. The Census defines long-term debt as debt with a maturity of one year or more. Generally, short-term debt is seasonal borrowing, retired within the fiscal year in which issued. Thus, year-to-year comparisons can ignore short-term debt changes as a general matter, New York City to the contrary notwithstanding.

3. The Census does not include such payments in current general expenditure, treating them as intra-governmental fund transfers. However, contributions to pension funds run by other governments, notably state governments, *are* part of general expenditure. In 1976-77, about 55 percent of local government pension fund contributions went to state-administered pension funds.

4. 1957 has been dropped from this comparison, because some cities in the Sunbelt that were over 300,000 by 1975 were small places in the 1950s, possibly with very different fiscal structures.

5. George W. Mitchell, "Is This Where We Came In?" *Proceedings of the Forty-Ninth Annual Conference on Taxation,* National Tax Association (1956), p. 494.

6. This catalog excludes a variety of specialized property types like forest land, mineral properties and mineral rights, subject to highly varied property tax treatments among the states.

7. Disgracefully, a fair number of writers slide over, deny or are ignorant of the serious weaknesses of the property value data they employ to prove their points and have not been appropriately rebuked by referees, reviewers or rejoiner-writers.

8. Limitations in either 1972 or 1977 Census of Governments data prevent extending a comparable analysis to any additional central cities other than Honolulu, Minneapolis, St. Paul, Oklahoma City, Memphis and California SMSA central cities.

Lennox L. Moak - THE REVENUE SOURCE WITH VITALITY - A NEW LOOK AT SOME ANCIENT CONCEPTS - NON-TAX REVENUES

THE (LARGELY) OVERLOOKED RESOURCE

Without bespeaking or criticizing my good friends who have planned this symposium, the relegation of non-tax resources of our city governments to such an insignificant position in the program can be appropriately interpreted as typifying the tendency of our thinkers to fail to give appropriate emphasis to non-tax revenues of our city governments.

Local finance officers are not guilty of this sin.

They have long recognized the non-tax sources as one of the most viable and flexible sources of income. They have been busy tilling this sector and exploiting its use with increasing vigor.

THE THIRD-THIRD

How many of you realize that the non-tax revenues of city governments in 1977 stood substantially upon a par with local taxes in the support of these governments?

How many of you realize that these non-tax revenues stood only just shortly below intergovernmental revenues in support of municipal governments? And, if one eliminates the educational subsidies in those city governments that operated public school systems,

475

that non-tax revenues of city governments exceeded the amount of intergovernmental revenue receipts in 1977?

The time is not only at hand but well past in which serious students of public finance should devote a suitable amount of their energies to this sector of revenues!

Of the $73.8 billion of city government revenue reported by the Bureau of the Census for 1977[1], there were three thirds:

First Third: Local taxation $26.1 billion   35.3 percent
Second Third: Inter-governmental   24.2 billion   32.8 percent
Third Third: Non-Tax Revenues   23.5 billion   31.9 percent

Yet, except for Selma Mushkin[2] and regrettably few others, where are the students who seriously studied this segment in recent years?

In this era of weariness and rebellion against high tax levels; in this era of disenchantment with the view that our social problems can be solved by yet another appropriation financed from yet another tax; in this period of disillusionment with the capacity of the governmental bureaucracy to manage our money better collectively than we can manage it individually, the realization is coming home that:

> The typical American prefers the right of
> *individual* choice in the allocation of the
> fruits of his labor.

Within the governmental sphere, this right of choice is best epitomized through the rendition of services on a basis where there are price tags affixed and where the individual has substantial latitude in determining just how much he wants to purchase of the services rendered.

It is to this subject that this paper is largely, although not exclusively, devoted.

THE STATISTICS

This is not a paper devoted to statistics, yet, some hard data concerning trends is useful in conceptualizing the relative importance of the different sectors of municipal revenues, especially of the non-tax revenues.

To that end, Exhibit 1 sets forth data from the Bureau of the Census for the four years selected for comparison purposes—1977, 1976, 1967 and 1957.

EXHIBIT 1

Tax Revenues and Selected Non-Tax Revenues
Municipal Governments
1957, 1967, 1976 and 1977
(dollar amounts in billions)

	1977 (1)	1976 (2)	1967 (3)	1957 (4)
	Amounts			
Taxes	$26.07	$23.34	$10.45	$ 5.86
Selected Non-Tax Revenues	21.27	18.87	7.36	3.88
Current Charges	6.87	6.16	2.20	0.92
Other Selected Non-Tax Revenues	14.40	12.71	5.16	2.97
Interest	1.33	1.44	.38	.11
Special Assessments	0.53	0.53	.31	.223
Utility Charges	10.68	9.05	4.17	2.32
Water	3.83	3.45	1.81	1.08
Electric Power	5,29	4.60	1.57	.76
Transit	0.94	0.93	.56	.38
Gas Supply	0.63	0.52	.23	.10
Employee Retirement Systems	1.89	1.69	.66	.32
	Amounts as Percentages of Tax Revenues			
Selected Non-Tax Revenues	81.6	80.8	70.4	66.2
Current Charges	26.4	26.4	21.1	15.7
Other Selected Non-Tax Revenues	55.2	54.5	49.4	50.7
Interest	5.1	6.2	3.6	1.9
Special Assessments	2.0	2.3	2.9	3.8
Utility Charges	41.0	38.8	39.6	39.6
Employee Retirement Systems	7.2	7.2	6.4	5.5

Sources: U.S. Bureau of the Census, *City Government Finances in 1957*, p. 7; *in 1966-67*, p. 5; *in 1976-77*, p. 5.

Obviously, the tremendous deflation in currency values during this period robs raw dollar data of much of its significance. Only when trends in different series are compared do useful indications appear.

From Exhibit 1 it is noted that in 1957 these selected non-tax revenues of municipal governments accounted for funds equal to about two-thirds of municipal tax revenues. By 1977, this ratio had risen to 82 percent.

For the entire period, the consumer price index rose at an average compound annual rate of about 4 percent; taxes at about 8 percent; and non-tax revenues at above 9 percent.

If 1977 data are deflated to 1957 values by use of the consumer price index, the comparisons become:

	1957	1977	Average Compound Annual Rate of Increase
Taxes	$5.86	$12.14	3.8
Selected non-tax revenues	3.88	9.91	4.9

Therefore, the rate of increase in the non-tax category in terms of constant dollars was about one-fourth greater than that of the taxes. In the decade 1967-1977, the difference was even greater with taxes increasing at a rate of about 3.2 percent in constant dollars compared to 4.8 percent for the selected non-tax items.

Exhibit 2 distributes per capita tax and current charge data by size of cities.

It is not surprising that on a per capita basis the very large cities tend to develop greater income per resident than do the middle range and smaller cities. Thus, in 1977 the average income from current charges amounted to $50.28 per capita for all cities; cities with populations of more than 300,000 being well above that average. Yet, it was only in the smaller cities (populations of less than 50,000) that the yield dropped to low dollar levels.

When per capita income from current charges is related to per capita city tax income, it is noted that with the exception of the 300,000-500,000 population cities, the relative dependence upon current charges vis-a-vis city taxes tends to be inverse to the population size of the city. Thus, the cities of over 17 percent of per capita tax revenues compared with 31 percent for those under 50,000 population.

Exhibit 3 presents information generally parallel to that presented in Exhibit 1; however, it is restricted to the larger cities—those with a population of 250,000 or more in 1957 and 300,000 or more in the other years. This data again emphasizes the fact that the degree of dependence of these larger cities upon the non-tax revenues being considered is considerably less than overall dependence by all cities as has been shown in Exhibit 1.

EXHIBIT 2

Per Capita Taxes and Current Charges
Municipal Governments, According to Population-Size Groups
Selected Years, 1957-1977

Year	Total (1)	Over 1,000,000 (2)	500,000 999,999 (3)	300,000 499,999 (4)	200,000 299,999 (5)	100,000 199,999 (6)	50,000 99,999 (7)	Under 50,000 (8)
Taxes								
1977	$190.70	$475.49	$273.55	$200.23	$196.56	$189.28	$158.90	$102.90
1976	170.72	432.63	236.16	180.97	181.22	169.51	142.50	91.14
1967	89.76	194.58	126.00	82.83	87.43	90.10	90.47	48.12
1957	60.99	110.91	86.06	56.68*	n.a.	63.11**	48.40	34.62
Current Charges								
1977	$ 50.28	$ 80.30	$ 60.06	$ 75.64	$ 47.54	$ 52.65	$ 46.78	$ 32.22
1976	45.07	74.30	54.49	68.57	43.11	48.37	41.34	32.50
1967	18.92	27.91	22.13	23.91	19.13	22.50	17.98	14.04
1957	9.60	14.09	10.33	10.60*	n.a.	10.54**	11.47	6.60
Current Charges as a Percent of Taxes								
1977	26.4	16.9	22.0	37.8	24.2	27.8	29.4	31.3
1976	26.4	17.2	23.1	37.9	24.0	28.5	29.0	35.7
1967	21.0	14.3	17.6	28.9	21.9	25.0	19.9	29.2
1957	15.7	12.7	12.0	17.8*	n.a.	16.7**	23.7	19.1

* In 1957, 250,000-499,999

** In 1957, 100,000-249,999

Sources: U.S. Bureau of the Census, *City Government Finances in 1957*, p. 8; *in 1966-67*, p. 8; *in 1975-76*, p. 8; *in 1976-77*, p. 8.

EXHIBIT 3

Tax Revenue and Selected Non-Tax Revenues
Largest U.S. Cities[a]
Selected Years, 1957-1977

(dollar amounts in billions)

Item	1977 46-cities (1)	1976 46-cities (2)	1967 43-cities (3)	1957 47-cities (4)
	Amounts			
Tax Revenues	$13.42	$12.08	$ 5.55	$ 3.21
Selected Non-Tax Revenues	8.94	8.15	3.28	1.78
Current Charges	2.89	2.58	0.94	0.43
Other Selected Non-Tax Revenues	6.05	5.61	2.34	1.35
Interest [b]	0.68	0.71	0.20	0.08
Special Assessments	0.12	0.11	0.08	0.09
Utility Charges	3.73	3.34	1.49	0.93
Employee Retirement Systems	1.52	1.46	0.57	0.28
	Percentage Distribution			
	Non-Tax Revenues as a Percent of Tax Revenues			
Selected Non-Tax Revenues	66.6	67.5	59.1	55.5
Current Charges	21.6	21.0	28.7	13.4
Other Selected Non-Tax Revenues	45.1	47.3	42.1	41.9
Interest [b]	5.1	7.4	3.6	2.5
Selected Assessments	0.9	1.0	1.5	1.9
Utility Charges	27.8	26.8	26.9	28.9
Employee Retirement Systems	11.4	12.1	10.2	8.7

a   In 1977, 46 cities with estimated population of 300,000 or more; in 1976, same 46 cities; in 1967, 43 cities with 300,000 population or more; 1957, 47 cities with population of 250,000 or more.

b   Interest reported here excludes interest earnings of employees' retirement systems, which interest is reported as a revenue of such systems.

Sources: U.S. Bureau of the Census, *City Government Finances in 1957*, pp. 37-38; *in 1966-67*, p. 56; *in 1975-76*, p. 98; *in 1976-77*, p. 97.

On the other hand, even among these larger cities, there has been a decidedly greater growth in these non-tax revenues during the two decades under consideration than in local tax revenues. Thus, these non-tax revenues represented about 56 percent of tax revenues in 1957 but has risen to 67 percent by 1977.

The annual average compound rate of increase for taxes during this period for these larger cities amounted to 8.0 percent; for the non-tax revenues being considered, the rate of increase was 8.6 percent.

From Exhibit 4, a limited insight into the components of the *current charge* group is afforded.

In terms of relative importance within the current charge group, revenues from hospitals, sewage and airports all showed growing importance within this group vis-a-vis the other elements of the group. More about this later in the paper.

The remainder of this paper is devoted to a commentary upon several aspects of the subject. The order of presentation is without significance.

WATER SUPPLY, WASTE WATER, AND STORM WATER

Public policy has a way of developing in curious and uneven steps.

WATER SUPPLY

The history of urban conurbations is replete with the wide swings of the pendulum insofar as charges for the public water supply are concerned.

Generally as municipal water supply systems developed in the United States, there was a tendency to apply some type of charge for use. In the absence of meters, the household, number of residents and fixture charges were among the favorite methods of apportioning a part or all of the cost.

Most of the cities developed during the 20th century installed water meters early in their history. The older cities tended to depend upon other types of proration of costs well into the present century and, in some instances, universal metering has yet to be attained.

Systems of charge, even with metering, varied from flat-rate charges to inverse graduation. The largest customers were sometimes able to secure water at rates below the costs of providing the service.

Some cities used the water charge in peculiar ways. Thus, New Orleans, for example, followed a policy from the turn of the century

EXHIBIT 4

Current Charges, by Functional Groupings
Selected Years 1957-1977
Largest U.S. Cities

(dollar amounts in millions)

	1977 46-cities (1)	1976 48-cities (2)	1967 43-cities (3)	1957 47-cities (4)
	\multicolumn{4}{c|}{Amounts}			
Total	$2,895	$2,575	$943.1	$427.461
Education	247	176	97	39.6
School Lunch Sales	38	44	24	19.6
Other Local Schools	4	5	8	20.0
Higher Education	204	127	65	
Highways	222	195	85	58.4
Hospitals	489	476	79	35.3
Sewage	509	448	129	54.3
Sanitation, Excl. Sewage	87	79	28	11.4
Parks and Recreation	155	144	63	28.0
Housing and Urban Renewal	293	270	155	44.5
Airports	403	365	111	27.5
Water Transport & Terminals	120	109	45	29.5
Parking Facilities	112	97	49	19.2
Misc. Commercial Activities	32	28	20	n.a.
Other	225	186	82	48.5
	\multicolumn{4}{c|}{Percentage Distribution}			
Total	100.0	100.0	100.0	100.0
Education	8.5	6.8	10.3	9.3
School Lunch Sales	1.3	1.7	2.5	4.6
Other Local Schools	0.1	0.2	0.8	4.6
Higher Education	7.0	4.9	6.9	
Highways	7.7	7.6	9.0	13.7
Hospitals	16.9	18.5	8.4	8.3
Sewage	17.6	17.4	13.7	12.7
Sanitation, Excl. Sewage	3.0	3.1	3.0	2.7
Parks and Recreation	5.4	5.6	6.7	6.6
Housing and Urban Renewal	10.1	10.5	16.4	10.4
Airports	13.9	14.2	11.8	6.4
Water Transport	4.1	4.2	4.8	6.9
Parking Facilities	3.9	3.8	5.2	4.5
Misc. Commercial Activities	1.1	1.1	2.1	–
Other	7.8	7.2	8.7	11.3

Sources: U.S. Bureau of the Census, *City Government Finances in 1957*, pp. 37-38;
in 1966-67, p. 56; *in 1975-76*, p. 98; *in 1976-77*, p. 97.

of providing specified amounts of free water on a per capita basis for the population of each household both as an economic adjustment to the poorer families but more especially to encourage personal cleanliness and the use of public sewage facilities.

Currently most cities impose water charges in patterns sufficient to finance the costs of supplying water to all who use it. Rate systems vary widely, both in theoretical basis and in application. Ineffectual practices of meter maintenance frequently have the effect of nullifying segments of scientific rate structures.

WASTE WATER CHARGES

Public policy for the handling of waste water has been changing rapidly during recent years. It seems destined to change much more rapidly in many communities under the policies being pursued by the state and federal environmental officials.

Of course, many cities did not institute any treatment of waste water until after World War II. The prevailing practice was to dump the waste water into the nearest available stream, lake, or ocean.

This policy worked rather well when the urban population was low and when levels of ignorance/indifference were great. But as urban population increased rapidly and the characteristics of waste water also changed dramatically, treatment of effluent became more and more imperative. This moved gradually from primitive treatment to sophisticated levels of removal of offending matter before return of the waste water to the watercourses, lakes and oceans. Nor have we begun to reach the full level of treatment required to restore a better balance in this important element of our environment. The questions are:

Who shall pay?
How?

The sewer service charge has been with us now for more than a half century. During the past two decades, it has increased at a rate substantially higher than the rate of growth of most other city revenue sources. Although strictly comparable data are not available, it has been found, for example, to have grown from 13 to 18 percent of the aggregate service charge revenues of the larger cities. (See Exhibit 4.)

For the 46 cities with a population of 300,000 or more in 1975, it is noted that aggregate reported sewer service charges in 1977 amounted to only about 13 percent of aggregate water charges for the same cities. However, this is destined to change rapidly as more and more cities are obliged to bring their sewage treatment procedures up to standard and as they find the waste water charges the most acceptable manner in which to finance local elements of this expensive operation.

In some cities where the sewage treatment process has developed to a much higher degree than others, it is found that the sewer service charge already produces annual income that is greater than that produced by water supply systems.

STORM WATER CHARGES

Generally the costs of handling storm water is, to the extent it is a current expense, still charged to the tax budget. Yet, a number of cities regularly handle relatively low storm flows and miscellaneous seepage through their sanitary sewage treatment systems. This is especially true where the combined sewer serves for both sanitary and storm purposes.

The environmentalists now frequently press for treatment of the full storm flow because study has revealed that much of the pollution in our streams, lakes and oceans arises from street debris carried away through the storm water system.

Some cities are already shifting parts of the storm water budget to the water supply/waste-water budget, with financing being at least partially picked up through the system of waste water charges.

This has proved a useful way in which to help conserve tax funds for other priority purposes.

INDICATION

On the basis of trends during recent decades, it seems appropriate to assume that within a relatively short period of years, not only will all water supply costs be almost universally borne from service charges but that this will have been extended to costs of handling waste water.

It is too early to offer conclusions as to the extent to which storm water handling costs will be first greatly increased through requirements for treatment and secondly shifted from the tax to the service charge basis.

Problems of finding a suitable basis for charge are significant. If, as some contend, the automobile is once again the major source of pollution, consideration to shifting this cost to some kind of automobile user charge must inevitably be most carefully weighed.

ELECTRICITY AND GAS

Although eastern cities are not greatly involved in municipal (or other governmental) ownership and operation of electric generating and distribution systems, it will come as a surprise to some who study Exhibit 1 to find that the aggregate revenues of municipal electric power systems in 1977 greatly exceeded the aggregates for municipal water systems—$5.3 billion vs. $3.8 billion.

The number of cities with water supply systems outnumber those with electric supply systems; however, where the electric systems exist, electric system revenues may be several times water revenues; e.g., Los Angeles, with a 6 to 1 ratio.

In almost all cases, where electric generating and/or distribution systems are present, these are operated on a basis that is at least self-supporting.

Municipal gas supply systems are few in number. These tend to be self-supporting and, with rare exceptions, to be restricted to gas distribution systems, although a few cities have gas manufacturing capabilities.

TRANSIT

Municipal interests in transit date from the 19th century when they were ordinarily the grantors of private transit franchises for the use of their streets for transportation of persons. Gradually some developed elements of rapid transit. But, until after World War II, public transit systems were very largely privately owned and privately operated. A variety of developments following World War II brought cities once again into the transit operations as a means of saving the public transit systems that could no longer be operated profitably on a private basis.

The past two decades have been a period of great transition for the industry. It has not been feasible to make these public utilities support themselves. Revenues have grown at a snail's pace and, in terms of constant dollars, actually have decreased.

As long as energy is relatively plentiful, it appears that price alone will have to increase very dramatically before there is any significant transfer from personal automobiles to mass transit. Some of the newer systems are securing new riders but the process is not one that promises realization of revenue at a rate sufficient to reduce dependence upon the tax budget.

On the other hand, if this author is correct in his view that we are now at the end of the Indian Summer of availability of energy in the United States at economic and political prices we can afford to pay, there must be a resurgence of the use of mass transit. I believe that within a decade, the demand will exceed the supply of good mass transportation services.

Should this occur, the opportunity for repricing of this public service will be present. Perhaps one can move once again in a pattern that will initially stabilize and subsequently reduce the dependence of the public transit system upon tax subsidies.

That is the hope.

CHARGES FOR USE OF MONEY

We have travelled through a number of cycles in respect to the concept of charges for the use of money. In the 1950s and 1960s concept, demand deposits of municipal governments were deemed to be *non-interest bearing*. In other words, the deposits were placed with commercial banks and the interest derived from the use of such deposits "belonged" to the bank.

The law still forbids payments of interest by commercial banks upon demand deposits; however, through the use of savings accounts associated with demand deposits and other devices, vast revenue is now produced.

As the interest rates rose gradually for more than a decade after 1957 and then precipitously in another decade, it became increasingly important that municipal governments take a careful look at the interest to be derived from funds temporarily in their hands.

From this has come a wide interest among municipal finance officials in the whole range of considerations involved under the term *cash management*. These officials have come to realize that the dollars earned from idle balances are very real dollars. Many of them have become surprisingly sophisticated concerning the potentials for arbitrage.

The result has been that this new awakening—still only very partially perceived by many finance officers—has led to the search for new and better methods of holding down the uninvested municipal funds. The results to date are still far from the potential implicit in the situation; however, lack of sufficient data forestalls a realistic assessment of the situation. Thus, the 1976-77 data of the Bureau of the Census[3] show that local governments had *cash and deposits* of $44.9 billion (excluding trust fund moneys) at the close of the fiscal years falling within this period. (The report does not show how much of the deposits was in the form of interest-bearing deposits; e.g., certificates of deposit.)

However, the word is now abroad that *thar's gold in them thar hills.*

Obviously, the potential for revenues from this source is limited.

Equally, obvious, the full potential has not been fully exploited.

With $67.7 billion in cash and securities, in other than insurance trust funds, interest earnings might be well above the reported $3.3 billion.

REVENUES OF PUBLIC EMPLOYMENT RETIREMENT SYSTEMS

The financing of public employee retirement systems is one of the significant challenges of the age. Generally, all of our governments have developed public employee retirement systems that are proving very difficult to finance.

The revenues attributed to public employee retirement systems as set forth in Exhibits 1 and 3 are restricted to (1) the contributions of employees and (2) earnings upon the moneys in these funds. These revenues do *not* include the sums that are contributed by the municipalities to their own retirement systems.

In approaching this subject, it is essential that the reader understand that huge numbers of municipalities do not maintain their own employee retirement systems. In many states these are maintained by the state governments, and the financial data concerning their operations are not reported in the financial data of the cities themselves—except that the contributions of the cities are included as a regular expense in appropriate categories. Therefore, the financial data reported in Exhibits 1 and 3 in respect to public employee retirement systems are not fully comparable to the data on other matters of concern in this paper.

Even so, it is important to understand that the cities as a group still realized revenues from these funds equal to about 7 percent of tax revenues for all cities. (Comparable data would produce a much higher percentage; however, it is not available. For example, employee retirement system revenues in Atlanta amounted to 20 percent of tax revenue; in Chicago, 21 percent; Detroit, 21 percent; Houston, 13 percent; Philadelphia, 9 percent; New York, 11 percent.)

It is not easy to evaluate these revenues of retirement systems vis-a-vis overall financing. Yet, inasmuch as we have chosen to provide large amounts of compensation for our public employees in the form of deferred compensation, it is highly important that the cities be encouraged to maximize the earnings and other revenues of such systems beyond the contributions of the governments themselves from tax and non-tax sources.

The huge assets that are piling up at growing rates in these funds offer great potential for effective management of these assets. Until recently, relatively little attention has been devoted to the matter of the most appropriate investment policies for these funds.

Upon the decisions for such investment rests great opportunities for relieving tax funds of demands for contributions that will have to be made in the absence of such earnings.

SPECIAL ASSESSMENTS

Prior to World War II, the special (benefit) assessment was widely used to facilitate the financing of capital improvements deemed to be of direct benefit to adjacent property. The literature of the 1920s abounds with extended discussions of the use and potential use of special assessments.

Not only was the special assessment used and to be used for the public improvements *directly* associated with public facility developments but also the concept of *adjacent benefit assessment* was widely discussed in the literature and in municipal forums. The potentials for financing numerous public improvements, e.g., transit facilities, at least partially from special assessments, was a lively topic in the literature of the period and found its way to statutory and, occasionally, into constitutional provisions.

The Great Depression of the 1930s brought developments that changed the views of officials, investors, developers and the general public toward special assessments.

Defaults were rampant as the assessments derived from speculative real estate development in Florida and elsewhere failed to materialize. Assessments in developed areas for public improvements proved hard to collect. Genuine hardships were visited upon property owners on whom a substantial assessment had been laid in the good times of the 1920s as these notes became due from reduced or nonexistent cash assets in the 1930s.

City after city found it necessary to take actions which, in effect, substituted general revenue for the proceeds of special assessments. Many refused to pursue this course, and the investors were obliged to write off the paper values represented by the funds advanced in good faith.

With the oncoming of the FHA mortgages and developments associated therewith, the financing of improvements incident to development of raw land came in for a new approach. Namely, the new developments (to a mild extent prior to World War II but to a very large extent thereafter) were obliged to furnish a wide range of public improvements as an incident to being able to secure permission to develop new land. Streets, sewers, street lighting, drainage, water mains and others were included in this list.

Although these facilities were developed from non-governmental financing, any proper comparison between the decade of the 1920s and the 1950s must take this development into account.

The 1950s and later periods also were characterized by a significant lessening of the degree of reliance upon special assessments as a means of financing improvements within developed portions of our cities and other municipalities.

The pattern developed was one of substantially greater dependence upon the general revenue sources of the municipality, especially local taxation, to provide the funds that were no longer provided through the widespread use of special assessments.

POTENTIAL FOR RETURN

Although the special assessment has fallen from favor during the halcyon years of the past three decades, there are good reasons once again to examine the potential implicit in this ancient device.

1. Effectively and efficiently administered, the special assessment still provides one of the few *automatic* devices for reconciling demands for public expenditures with the willingness of the citizens to pay.

2. Despite the difficulties and occasional gross inequities created by the system, it does afford a means of equitable financing for a number of types of benefits. Moreover, it also acts to forestall some of the unjust windfall in advantage derived by some property holders from public expenditures being broadly financed by the moneys provided by all.

The contemporary political picture is such that a broadscale early return is not likely. On the other hand, when the pressures derived from limitations upon taxation are broadly felt, this alternative is likely to become more attractive than previously believed to be the case.

While not couched in these terms, the recent resurgence of *respectable studies* concerning the cost of development and the appropriate assessment of such costs among the various economic and social sectors of the community have either explicitly or implicitly reopened the question.

Any return to broad use of special assessments should be accompanied—indeed be preceded by—a significant study of the economic, financial, social and political ramifications of this as a financing device.

But with local revenue systems producing well beyond $100 billion annually from their own sources, this is an important potential that has been too long overlooked.

A resurgent application should search out not only streets, water and sewer facilities but a fairly broad range of other optional facilities, e.g., elements of the recreational, park and cultural activities of the community.

FEES IN COURTS

Fifty dollars and costs!
A traffic violation avenged.

We think nothing of providing a system of fines and fees in the administration of our traffic operations.

Time was that the justice of the peace not only helped to maintain the peace but also helped to finance both his own services and those of various attendants through a system of *costs.* The fines went to the general treasury; however, the costs went to pay the justice, the constable and other functionaries.

But by some quirk, we do not regularly impose costs upon litigants who tie up the courts at great expense to many of our cities in the settling of their civil differences.

If two great corporations are willing to spend millions of their dollars in order to litigate a point, what is the obligation of the taxpayer to provide court facilities to accommodate them?

Maintenance of the king's peace requires that there be a court for adjudication. However, maintenance of king's peace does not require that the king's other subjects pay the bill.

Any fair analysis of the aggregate costs of courts in the United States will show that by far the largest amount of court time and facilities is required to handle civil litigation. And, it is likely that most of this time and facilities are required by cases where one or more of the litigants can well afford to pay for use of personnel and facilities in obtaining justice.

Although most of the court expenses are at the county level, the city-county governments find this as a part of the municipal budget.

The potential for significant relief to the tax budget is present through a well-designed system of charges which will, on the one hand, not inhibit social and economic justice for those of limited means but, on the other hand, discourage misuse of the courts and misdirection of economic responsibility for the costs involved in the other cases.

Perhaps some charges in criminal cases would not be altogether out of order in some cases.

THE MOTOR VEHICLE

The motor vehicle has at once been one of the greatest gains and losses in our society.

To an extent rarely understood, the motor vehicle pays no taxes in the sense that it contributes to the general financing of governmental services beyond those imposed in providing facilities and services essential to the operation of the motor vehicle.

From the outset, the property owners through direct payments, special assessments and general taxes provided the street system upon which the motor vehicle operated. Little was known initially about the degree and types of pollution associated with this form of transportation. The subsidies have continued and become greater with the years.

If we are to clean up the storm water, we are told that undetermined billions of added capacity for treatment of storm water will be required for both plant and operations.

The huge recent increases in both the capital cost of the motor vehicle and in its operating and insurance costs indicate that here is an element of our system that can stand much broader charges to help defray the costs that are generated as a result of its place in our economy and its operation in our environment.

The so-called motor fuel taxes and motor vehicle taxes are in fact service charges that have been misnamed. A redesignation of them as service charges is long overdue; the expansion in the same manner as waste water charges is also slow in arriving.

The strength of the lobbies is as yet untested by effective public interest groups.

IN CONCLUSION

The wide range of other potentials for application of the service charge can be detected easily upon a bit of reflection.

The growth of these charges, as discussed earlier in this paper, at rates in excess of the growth in local taxes offers real potential for a shifting of considerable amounts of costs from the local taxpayer to the service charge mechanism.

Of course there will be yells from those whose ox is being gored. But, so be it.

Perhaps the so-called *demands* for public service will be much abated when price tags are affixed to these services.

This is not to suggest the denial of needed services to those who cannot afford to pay; it is not to suggest that the services be made fully self-supporting in all instances. It is to assert that evidence of public willingness to pay should be considered a significant element of determination to make the services available.

Few who demand services are in a position that they can make no contribution to the rendition.

More importantly, the willingness of those served to make at least some contribution to the support of the service is a superb market mechanism for testing the legitimacy and the size of demand.

This is a subject that warrants application of our best brain power.

The significance far outstrips the mere subject of making additional moneys available. It goes to the bedrock of our system of values.

The time is at hand!

NOTES

1. Bureau of the Census data for 1977 is for fiscal years ending in the 12 months July 1, 1976 to June 30, 1977. This format has been the same commencing with 1962-63. Prior to that date, data for a year was for the fiscal years ending within the calendar year.

2. See *Public Prices for Public Products,* Selma J. Mushkin, ed., The Urban Institute, 1972, and Selma J. Mushkin and Charles L. Vehorn, "User Fees and Charges," *Governmental Finance,* Vol. 6, No. 4, (November 1977), pp. 42-48.

3. U. S. Bureau of Census, *Government Finances in 1976-77,* p. 39.

Katharine C. Lyall - REGIONAL TAX BASE SHARING - NATURE AND POTENTIAL FOR SUCCESS

INTRODUCTION

The Twin Cities experiment with tax base sharing is now nearly a decade old with roughly five years of actual experience to examine.[1] Originally, tax base sharing was a product of dissatisfaction with the property tax, the way it entered into local competition for industrial development and the desire to modify some its more inequitable distributive effects following the Serrano principle. Today, in the wake of Proposition 13 fever, the political and policy climate is rather different. Tax limitation referenda aim to cap state and local expenditures and, as a consequence, are shifting the composition of local revenues from the property tax towards user fees, sales taxes and local income taxes.

Tax base sharing schemes take many forms. All plans proposed to date share a portion (40-60%) of the growth in commercial and/or industrial assessable base measured from some base date. None has proposed sharing existing tax base. The plans differ, however, in precisely how this "growth pool" is reallocated among participating jurisdictions. Some distribution formulas allocate shares based on relative population or per capita residential assessments (a measure of tax capacity), others include some measure of local tax effort as

The views presented in this paper are solely those of the author and do not represent official policies or positions of the U.S. Department of Housing and Urban Development.

well. The Minneapolis plan redistributes tax base to be taxed by each jurisdiction at its prevailing local rate; the Maryland plan proposes to tax the growth pool at a weighted average tax rate for the region and reallocate the resulting revenues back to participating jurisdictions. (For a more complete discussion of distribution formulas see Simms, 1977.)

Since the Twin Cities took the first plunge in 1974, there has been a steadily growing interest in tax base sharing for a surprisingly wide variety of purposes.

- To compensate local jurisdictions for land designated as environmental wetlands and therefore off limits to development—tax base sharing was incorporated in the Hackensack Meadowlands Act in New Jersey.[2]
- To share the proceeds of primary mineral extraction—tax base sharing has been proposed both by the Province of Alberta, Canada and by the State of Maine as part of its management plan for exploiting off-shore oil.[3]
- As a guide in statewide land use planning in the States of Maryland, Washington, and California.[4]
- As an explicit growth control tool in California and Allentown, Pennsylvania where it has been considered as quid pro quo for extending water and sewer system outside the city limits, and in Virginia where it has been considered as a quid pro quo for not exercising powers of annexation over their suburbs.

Some of these initiatives are proposals incorporated in specific planning and development documents, others, like the Maryland proposal, are bills that have been debated by state legislatures and put aside as premature until evidence from the Minnesota experiment was available.

The objectives sought from tax base sharing are multiple: reduction of fiscal disparities among jurisdictions within a single metropolitan region so that corresponding public services can be more equitably provided throughout the metro area, provision of incentives for more rational land use planning and industrial development by focusing development in jurisdictions where its net public service costs are minimized and rewarding jurisdictions for maintaining valuable open space for environmental and recreational use, general fiscal relief for distressed local jurisdictions, provision of a favorable environment for business development through carefully planned and financed infrastructure investment, and stabilization of the community life cycle of central cities and suburbs.

Critics of the tax base sharing idea, on the other hand, have raised fears that it will discourage new economic development in participating jurisdictions, that fiscal disparities may not be closed fast enough to make a difference, and that the distribution formula may actually produce a less equitable allocation of net revenues and tax burdens among individuals.[5]

THE EVIDENCE TO DATE

Evidence from the Minneapolis experiment to date and from recent public finance literature provide some insights into the extent to which these expectations are likely to be realized.

1. Tax base sharing does reduce fiscal disparities among participating jurisdictions within a metropolitan area, although this narrowing starts rather slowly in the early years of the plan and depends ultimately on the relative rates of growth in the property tax base over time. Evidence from the Minneapolis case indicates that fiscal disparities within that metropolitan area in 1974 and 1975 were reduced approximately 7 percent per year as measured by:

- assessed valuation—disparities in assessed valuation were reduced 4.25 percent in 1974 and 7.2 percent in 1975.[6]
- coefficient of variation of per capita commercial and industrial tax base—average disparities were reduced by 9.77 percent between 1974 and 1975.
- average per capita fiscal capacity of the net gainers ($9,100) compared to that of the net contributors ($11,800)—disparities were reduced by redistributions away from higher capacity jurisdictions to lower capacity areas.[7]

These patterns were found to be largely consistent among individual jurisdictions, as well as for groups of jurisdictions. It should be noted that while average reductions of 4 percent over the first year or two appear quite modest, the cumulative effect of such rates can be substantial. If the underlying growth in the metro area driving these distributions were to persist at the same rates, fiscal disparities within the region could be effectively eliminated within twelve to fifteen years.[8]

2. Tax base sharing appears to do little to reduce the average tax burden of low- and moderate-income residents in the metro area or to reduce horizontal inequities in tax liabilities among individual taxpayers in the region. The reason for this is that there is relatively little correlation between personal income levels of individuals and the fiscal capacity of the jurisdictions in which they live as measured by assessed property values so that jurisdictions with relatively high assessable base may also have a high proportion of poor, elderly, or other low-income residents. Conversely, jurisdictions with relatively low average assessable bases may contain a significant number of high income residents. In the Minneapolis case, Reschovsky finds that despite a low (.38) correlation between personal income and fiscal capacity, there is a rough redistribution in the "right" direction; that is, the average personal income in jurisdictions that were net contributors to the pool was $900 higher than that of residents of of the gainer jurisdictions.[9]

It should be noted that this effect could be heightened by adjusting the distribution formula to focus on concentrations of high cost resident populations such as the poor and elderly and/or by incorporating some measure of tax effort relative to income in the formula as described in the final section.

3. Tax base sharing is not likely to be an effective central city fiscal relief program. A number of critics of tax base sharing have opposed it politically on the grounds that it was thought to be a thinly disguised central city fiscal relief program designed to shift revenues from suburbs to their central cities. In the Minneapolis case, Reschovsky found that the tax base of the Twin Cities increased two and a half percent between 1974 and 1975 as a result of tax base sharing; however, this stemmed almost entirely from the relative growth lag in their commercial and industrial base during that period.[10] Such gains for central cities may be rather ephemeral since a number of distressed older cities are beginning to show modest gains in their CBD values resulting from renewal efforts of the past decade that are finally beginning to take root, statewide uniform reassessment laws that catch up drastically under-assessed central city properties in some areas, and the like. At the same time, a number of older suburban areas are experiencing signs of commercial stagnation similar to their core cities in the 1950's and 1960's.

It has been argued that one benefit of tax base sharing might be the stabilization of long-term community growth and decline cycles by reallocating taxable base to those jurisdictions relatively in most fiscal need, thus moderating the cycles of blight that pass from one neighborhood to another and one locality to another with maturing of the economic base. In such a long-term scheme, central cities should not expect to find themselves perpetual net recipients of tax base.

More importantly, however, it must be remembered that tax base sharing by its nature is primarily a redistributive mechanism and not a method for increasing the total tax revenues for the region. For this reason as well, it should not be looked to as a source of major short term fiscal relief for distressed cities.

4. Tax base sharing does not appear to be a measurable deterrent to new industrial and commercial development within the metro region. To establish definitively the incentive/disincentive effects of tax base sharing on long term economic development would require a rather precise model of industrial location decisionmaking—a methodology far beyond the current state of the art—in order to predict what pattern of development would have occurred in the absence of tax base sharing. Without such precise tools, only very approximate and partial evidence is available. Reschovsky indicates that there appears to have been no noticeable reduction in the overall pace of new economic development in the Twin Cities region over the past five years. Empirical studies of the location determinants of businesses reinforce the notion that local taxes have a negligible effect on gross location decisions although they may influence the micro-decision to locate in one jurisdiction or another *within* a metro area. One reason for this relative insensitivity to local tax differences is that firms often are able to shift part or all of the tax forward to consumers or backwards to suppliers in a national market. In general, then, there is little reason to expect tax base sharing to have a chilling effect on general economic development patterns and indeed it may, in some instances, have a reinforcing effect as a symbol to businesses that a metropolitan area has a mechanism for planning, financing and maintaining its infrastructure investments over time.

OUTSTANDING ISSUES AND POLITICAL PROSPECTS

While evidence from the Minneapolis experience to date can provide some answers to questions about the workings of tax base sharing, several issues remain unsolved. First, considerable work remains to be done in devising more sensitive and sensible distribution formulas that have been used to date. The most obvious candidates are the incorporation of per capita income or per capita assessed valuation and/or some measure of tax effort for each jurisdiction so that distributions from the growth pool would be inversely proportional to fiscal capacity and directly proportional to tax effort. Another suggestion has been to reflect variations in public service costs traceable to specifically identified dependent (high cost) populations such as the elderly and the poor.

These attempts are complicated by both data and measurement problems. Estimates of local public service production functions are not precise enough to permit the separation of high service costs attributable to high cost population characteristics from those attributable to local government inefficiencies. Lack of consistency in local fiscal reporting makes difficult the separation of capital from operating costs; the disentanglement of overlapping school and special service districts; and the netting out of services to non-residents. Such difficulties are more severe in some metropolitan areas than in others and considerable empirical work is necessary to make the distribution formula a more sensitive and equitable instrument.[11]

Second, any unanticipated long-term effects of tax base sharing on the pattern of economic development can be detected only by close observation over much longer periods of time than we have yet had available. Changes in the corporate tax structure, general macroeconomic trends and conditions, or the relative position of the Frostbelt region of the country compared to the Sunbelt might produce greater sensitivity of location decisions to tax base sharing parameters.

Third, the shifting political atmosphere in which local property tax concerns are raised may have a dramatic impact on the prospects for adoption of tax base sharing in other areas. The shifting emphasis over the past two years from a focus on intrametropolitan disparities to a focus on the decline of whole metropolitan regions, including declining suburbs, may make tax base sharing a much less promising tool for addressing fiscal distress, especially in the Northeast and North Central regions of the country.

As pointed out above, tax base sharing is primarily a redistributive not a net tax raising tool. As Proposition 13 and other tax limitation referenda limit the total revenues that can be raised from property taxation, local governments can be expected to turn increasingly to sales taxes, income taxation and user charges. As Bahl and Puryear have pointed out, because sales taxes and user charges are generally more regressive than the property tax, the final mix of revenue sources may very well be more regressive than when the property tax bore a larger share of local tax burden.[12] In this instance, greater inter-jurisdictional equity may be achieved at the expense of greater inter-personal inequity.

Considerable prominence was given in President Carter's Urban Policy Statement a year ago to a "new federal-state-local partnership" in which state initiatives to devise and implement new methods for aiding their urban areas are to be considered. Various forms of fiscal sharing, coupled with more deliberate economic and land use planning, are enticing candidates of this partnership. The evidence to date suggests that tax base sharing, while it should not be looked to as a fiscal bailout for distressed urban areas, may well be a modest tool for the longer term stabilization and revitalization of metropolitan areas.

NOTES

1. The Minnesota Metropolitan Fiscal Disparities Act was passed in 1971 but several years of litigation delayed its implementation until 1974.
2. Hackensack Meadowlands Reclamation and Development Act, 1972; challenged and found constitutional by N.J. Supreme Court, 1973.
3. Provincial-Municipal Finance Council, *Tax Base Growth-Sharing Program for Alberta*, July 1976.
4. See Maryland State Legislature, House Bill 866 and House Bill 1091.
5. For discussion of anticipated benefits and problems see K. Lyall, "Tax Base Sharing: A Fiscal Aid Towards More Rational Land Use Planning," *Journal of American Institute of Planners* (March 1975), pp. 90-100.
6. A. Reschovsky, *Tax Base Sharing: An Assessment of the Minnesota Experience*—Final Report (March 1978), p. 38.
7. A. Reschovsky, *op. cit.*, p. 30.
8. It should be noted that the formulas for contributions to and redistributions from the shared growth pool are asymmetrical. That is, an area with a decline in its commercial and industrial tax base will contribute nothing to the shared pool although it will still be eligible to receive distributions from the pool depending on its relative population, need and tax effort. Thus, the rate at which disparities are narrowed depends on the rate of growth in the commercial and industrial base throughout the region. A region in which no growth occurred would have no contributions to the growth pool and no narrowing of the disparities by any measure of fiscal capacity.
9. A. Reschovsky, *op. cit.*, p. 42.
10. A. Reschovsky, *op. cit.*, p. 47.
11. For a full discussion of several modifications to the distribution formua, See A. Reschovsky, *op. cit.*, pp. 24, 55-56.
12. R. Bahl and D. Puryear, "Regional Tax Base Sharing: Possibilities and Implications" *National Tax Journal*, September 1976, pp. 328-335.

REFERENCES

Bahl, Roy and David Puryear "Regional Tax Base Sharing: Possibilities and Implications" *National Tax Journal* (September 1976), pp. 328-335.

Fischel, William, "An Evaluation of Proposals for Metropolitan Sharing of Commercial and Industrial Property Tax Base," *Journal of Urban Economics*, Vol. 3 (1976). pp. 253-263.

Gilze, Paul, "Recent Developments in Metropolitan Tax Base Sharing," (memo to Citizens League Board of Directors, October 19, 1977).

Haskell, Mark, "Toward Equality of Educational Opportunity," *Urban Education*, Vol. XXI, No. 3 (October 1977), pp. 313-326.

Lyall, Katherine, "Tax Base Sharing: A Fiscal Aid Towards More Rational Land Use Planning," *JAIP*, (March 1975), pp. 90-100.

Rahm, Karen, "Tax Base Sharing: A Fiscal Tool for Land Use Planning in Washington State?" *Washington Public Policy Notes* (University of Washington, Institute of Governmental Research, Vol. 5, No. 3, Summer 1977).

Reschovsky, Andrew, *Tax Base Sharing: An Assessment of the Minnesota Experience*—Final Report (March 1978).

Reschovsky, Andrew and Eugene Knaff "Tax Base Sharing: An Assessment of Minnesota Experience" *JAIP* (October 1977), pp. 361-370.

Simms, Margaret, " Metropolitan Tax Base Sharing: Is It The Solution To Municipal Fiscal Problems?" (Working Paper 9-237-7, Urban Institute, August 20, 1977).

Special Subcommittee on Community Development, *A Draft Proposal for a Tax Base Growth Sharing Plan for California* (July 11, 1977).

W. Patrick Beaton - REGIONAL TAX BASE SHARING: PROBLEMS IN THE DISTRIBUTION FUNCTION

It has long been recognized that large differences in the fiscal conditions of cities within our metropolitan areas exist. The old declining central cities and many older suburban communities have been found poorly endowed for the production of adequate levels of public services as well as the revitalization of their capital infrastructure vis-à-vis the newer developing cities of their region (ACIR, 1967). The local real property tax has been given the responsibility for many of these problems (Netzer, 1968). In addition, it has been observed that the property tax system creates a set of land development incentives within suburbanizing cities that can frustrate the goals of long-run land use planning (Lyall, 1975). Within the past decade, regional tax base sharing (TBS) has been advanced as a policy to address these problems (Weaver, 1972). In addition, its use has been encouraged by the President's Urban Policy Task Force.

The commendable nature of these goals makes it difficult to criticize such policies; however, in a policy which of necessity involves gainers and losers it is essential to ask ourselves if the losers are truly those municipal corporations intended and capable of being losers vis-a-vis the other cities in the affected region. In theory, TBS is a policy by which jurisdictions within a legally defined region share for tax purposes the growth in business valuation occurring within any one jurisdiction. In its operational aspects, however, little consideration has been given to three problem areas:

1. municipal life cycles,
2. municipal costs incurred through business development, and
3. the components and determinants of change in the municipal business tax base.

Given these omissions, it is the goal of this paper to examine the ability of several current TBS formulations to restore the sagging fiscal structure of the older declining cities. Clearly, this is but one of several issues for policy analysis. The following analysis is a partial equilibrium approach which confronts only those policy elements that attempt to reduce intermunicipal fiscal disparities.[1]

The following analysis will be performed in three steps. The initial section will center upon a description of TBS, its pooling formula and its redistribution formula. Second, several unanticipated consequences flowing out of the current TBS formulations will be examined. Lastly, two forms of TBS, the Minnesota and Maryland plans, will be imposed for research purposes upon the New Jersey system of cities and the long-term fiscal consequences from the simulated intervention of these policies on the local fisc examined.

TBS: AN INTRODUCTION

Regional tax-base sharing programs are now operating in two areas, one in New Jersey (Hackensack Meadowlands Development Commission, 1972), and the other in Minnesota (Reschovsky & Knaff, 1977). Of the several proposed programs currently under consideration in state legislatures, Maryland's TBS proposal has been reported in the professional literature (Lyall, 1975). All of these programs are organized around two formulas: a pooling formula and a redistribution formula.

The pooling formula places within a regional resource pool a fraction of the growth in assessed valuation (Minnesota) or equalized assessed valuation (Maryland and New Jersey) of each jurisdiction's business tax base (Minnesota) or property tax revenue (Maryland and New Jersey). The redistribution formula divides the pool among the jurisdictions within the region. In short, the pooling formula places a tax on the municipality for providing a site for business development independent of its current fiscal and economic development condition. The redistribution formula provides an unconditional grant to the municipality the size of which is usually determined by the city's relative size and wealth.

IMPACTS OF THE POOLING FORMULA

The pooling formula appears to be at the heart of the effort to stimulate long-term regional planning (Lyall, 1975). (See appendix 1 for the pooling and redistribution formulas for Minnesota and Maryland.) For all jurisdictions within a region, a fraction of the growth in the business tax base is placed in the regional pool. The pooling fraction is 40% in the Minnesota program and 60% in the Maryland proposal. It is anticipated by TBS proponents that the removal of a significant fraction of the growth in business ratables will reduce windfall fiscal dividends to their municipal and school district treasuries. Such a policy will, it is claimed, promote effective long-run rational land use planning.[2] Similarly, it is asserted that procedure assures municipalities that the integrity of their existing tax base will be maintained (Lyall, 1975). It is to this latter issue that we shall now proceed.

TAX BASE INTEGRITY

The rationale behind pooling the growth in the business tax base is the intention to share only the real as opposed to the monetary increments to the value of the business tax base (Peterson, 1976, pp. 80-1). Current TBS policies and proposals are based on changes in assessed valuation (Minnesota), or equalized assessed valuation of business property (Maryland and New Jersey). Here, however, it must be recognized that the aggregate business tax base will grow over time because of both real increases in the value in business property and increases due to inflation in excess of depreciation.

Recent experience has shown that property values and, as a consequence, the municipal property tax base have risen during inflationary periods (Greytak & Jump, 1977). Where and why the aggregate value of the business tax base has risen is a topic that has received scant attention.[3] Given the current formulations of TBS, however, a municipal corporation can become a net loser only if its business tax base grows in value. Who suffers is, it would seem, a legitimate question that must be examined. To assume that all declining cities or fiscally needy cities have either an absolute loss or sufficiently low rates of tax base growth to insure them against loss from TBS is an empirically testable hypothesis that may not be born out by the facts. Given our ignorance of municipal life cycles either from the point of view of descriptive characteristics of change or determinants of change, some forms of TBS may lead to a situation where a redeveloping old declining city will be penalized for its redevelopment. The penalty may be of such a magnitude as to trigger a new round of Tiebout type outmigration of business and population (Mills & Oates, 1975).

Separating the influences of real growth from the inflationary growth factor in the value of real property has seldom been done; however, a recent study out of the Maxwell School suggests that on a nationwide basis, the average property tax base grew due to inflation by 42.6% between the years 1967 and 1972 (Metropolitan Studies Program, 1975).

In the specific case of inflationary growth of the local business property tax base, there is placed within the control of the TBS pooling formula, an existing tax base and this in a broad sense, violates the claim that current formulations of TBS do not deal with the existing tax base. This may be considered only a technical matter involving the wording of a statute; however, one also must consider the use to which the lost tax base was put. In the case of new development and its tax base, the tax base must only support the short-run marginal cost of the new facility; in the case of the existing property and its associated tax base, the tax base must yield the average cost for supplying services. If it is accurate to assume that the short-run marginal cost is less than the average cost, then every dollar of existing tax base taken over by inflation will be more costly to the municipality than the dollar of tax base added to the tax rolls through real growth.

While we currently cannot separate real from inflationary growth increments to assessed valuation, it may be informative to examine the growth of total business valuation (equalized) across different types of municipalities. In New Jersey, for example, the average municipality experienced a 20% annual rate of growth in industrial ratables between the years 1970 and 1974. Of even more crucial importance to the implementation of TBS, it has been found that within New Jersey's larger declining cities there has been on the average a 10% annual rate of growth in the equalized valuation of the aggregate business tax base in spite of an average annual loss of 3% in the number of firms located within these cities (Exhibit 1).

Similarly, it may be useful at this point to examine the rates of change in property values in each of the declining cities mentioned above. Exhibit 2 displays the relevant data for 18 of New Jersey's

EXHIBIT 1

Average Annual Rates of Change in Business Related Characteristics
1970-74 for New Jersey Municipalities

	New Jersey	Suburbanizing Cities	Declining Cities
Commercial Ratables (equalized assessed valuation	19.8%	24.3	9.2
Industrial Ratables (equalized assessed valuation)	24.6%	14.9	10.8
Commercial Firms	0.3%	3.8	−3.1
Industrial Firms	−3.8%	5.5	−2.4
n of Cities	567	112	33

Source: Thirty-Seventh Annual Report of the Division of Local Government Services: 1974, State of New Jersey Division of Local Government Services; Trenton, NJ 1974.

cities that have been estimated by the New Jersey Department of Community Affairs to have declined consistently in population for the years 1960 to 1975. Annual growth rates range from a - 2% for Asbury Park's commercial property to a high of 32.3% for industrial property within the city of Summit. In only two cities is there found in fact an absolute drop in either component of the municipal business property tax base: Asbury Park and East Orange. To the extent that these figures reflect price level increases, tax base integrity is lost. If, for the sake of argument, the average inflation rate for business property were 7.4%, then by compounding this rate annually, the monetary value of the base would double in size over a 10-year period, while 31% of the real value of the old tax base would be now within the control of the pooling formula. That is, if tax rates are held constant, 31% of the existing tax base could not be counted upon to generate its pre-pooling revenues to the city.

The removal of the existing tax base from municipal control through the inflation of business property values independent of the redistribution formula cuts into the ability of the municipality to generate revenues needed to meet the costs of current business activity. In summary, when considering real economic growth in the context of TBS, the tax base controlled by the municipality must be capable of meeting the marginal costs of servicing the new

EXHIBIT 2

Equalized Assessed Valuation of Commercial and Industrial Property
And Rates of Change from 1969 to 1974 for 18 Declining
New Jersey Municipalities

City	1974 Market Value (X1000)		Change in Estimated Value 1969-74 (X1000)		Annual Percentage Change of Market Value 1969-74	
	Commercial	Industrial	Commercial	Industrial	Commercial	Industrial
Atlantic City	$218,301	$ 1,100	$29,080	$ 282	3.0%	6.8%
Dumont	10,943	926	4,455	362	13.8	12.8
Englewood	53,100	51,687	15,800	15,735	8.4	8.8
Camden	88,308	55,868	13,212	12,022	3.6	5.4
Bridgeton	18,312	18,896	2,507	5,759	3.2	8.8
Belleville	40,603	41,652	15,911	12,550	12.8	8.6
East Orange	115,155	9,162	32,584	−558	7.8	−1.2
Newark	589,295	283,542	28,555	2,890	1.0	0.2
Orange	34,138	10,747	6,448	1,577	4.6	3.4
Bayonne	77,476	189,739	23,637	53,671	8.8	7.8
Hoboken	51,857	62,778	10,237	22,572	5.0	11.2
Jersey City	214,916	239,236	30,714	62,469	3.4	7.0
Trenton	128,377	38,877	23,845	1,873	4.6	1.0
Asbury Park	27,307	623	−3,378	378	−2.2	30.4
Morristown	75,975	6,937	34,175	2,646	16.4	12.4
Hillside	22,435	66,730	6,389	17,918	8.0	7.4
Summit	55,121	49,086	16,637	24,408	8.6	32.2
Phillipsburg	16,632	28,268	7,146	13,339	15.0	17.8

Source: Thirty-Seventh Annual Report of the Division of Local Government Services: 1974, State of New Jersey. Division of Local Government Services, Trenton, NJ 1974.

business activity; however, under the conditions imposed by inflating property values, the tax base remaining under local control must also be capable of meeting long-run average costs for the business development currently in place within the municipality.

THE REDISTRIBUTION FORMULA

As stated earlier, the pooling formula appears to be aimed at minimizing competition for new business tax ratables among cities in a region. On the other hand, the goal of the various redistribution formulas appears to be the reduction of intermunicipal fiscal disparities that so adversely affect our older and declining cities. The construction of such formula is intended to promote purely fiscal ends such as reducing taxes or increasing fiscal capacity in order to meet social needs. As with other formula allocation systems, in TBS redistribution formulas one or more surrogates of social need, fiscal capacity or fiscal effort are placed within a formula along with floor, ceiling and time phasing factors, etc., that lessen the full impact of the formula on those who might be made worse off through its implementation (Isserman and Majors, 1978).

The two TBS formulas examined here utilize several need and fiscal capacity indices to redistribute their respective resource pools. The Maryland proposal redistributes a revenue pool. In this case, redistribution is affected by population size as well as relative per capita residential wealth. In the case of Minnesota, the resource to be redistributed is a pooled tax base. The individual municipalities then tax this base in the same manner as they do their existing tax base. In this case, redistributed shares are proportional to population size and inversely proportional to per capita property tax base for all classes of property with a limiting provision protecting the higher wealth municipalities.

If inflation is not a significant factor in the growth of municipal business property valuation and if the removal of a constant 40 to 60 percent of the growth in valuation truly removes only windfall benefits to municipalities, then the redistribution formulas are purely political in nature and correctly reflect the values governing the decisions to use surrogates of social need as the instruments to redistribute public wealth. If, on the other hand, either of these conditions do not hold, the redistribution formula should, from the perspective of equity, redress the economic biases created by the other parts of the specific TBS policy. From a purely pragmatic viewpoint it has been intimated by proponents of TBS that the arguments of the redistribution formula guarantee a sufficient flow of revenue to declining cities that even if there are problems vis-a-vis tax base integrity or business related service costs, these cities will still be net beneficiaries of the policy. We shall shortly test this assumption using a net benefit test on tax base and population projections for the 10th year following implementation of TBS.

Given the strong emphasis in the redistribution formulae on wealth, the extreme cases—poor, older declining cities, undoubtedly will gain financially from TBS. However, TBS is a regional policy; its impact along the full line of metropolitan cities: large, small; rich, poor; growing, stable and declining should be examined. It is a simple matter to draw a line through the break-even point of a rank order (in terms of taxable wealth) distribution of cities and determine that poorer cities are net beneficiaries of TBS. However, since poor is a relative term, how poor *is* poor becomes a relevant issue for those not benefiting from the program, and it follows that the consequences of TBS for their own fiscal and economic stability as well as that of their region become, I would think, relevant issues. It is to the empirical examination of these problems that we now proceed.

PROJECTING THE FISCAL IMPACT OF TBS

1. THE NET BENEFIT TEST

There are at least two tests that can be used to judge the direct fiscal consequences following the implementation of the TBS: the net benefit test and the inflation-municipal cost test. The former is used by Lyall in her Maryland study (1975). Here, net benefits are defined as the community's share of the revenue pool minus the foregone property tax revenues contributed to the regional pool.

The previous use of this test has been under relatively static conditions in that the values for the terms in the formulas are limited to the time period 1971-72. However, since our metropolitan areas are constantly in the process of change, the stability of the long-term fiscal consequences must be examined before a particular TBS system is advocated for regional use.

In the analysis to follow, the net benefit approach is used to judge the impact of TBS on cities that may be loosely termed to be in the different stages of the urban life cycle. As an example of this type of analysis, we have taken as the region the full set of New Jersey cities and calculated estimates of the net benefit accruing to each city after 10 years in the operation of TBS. For purposes of comparison across cities, the set of 567 cities is partitioned into 16 sets according to population size, relative size of the property tax base, and the long-term rise or fall in population (Beaton, 1975).

Each of the variables used to define the pooling and redistribution formulae are projected (linearly) from the base year (t_0 = 1970) to the test year (t_{10} = 1980) at rates based upon the observed rates of change of each variable from 1970 to 1974. The results, therefore, reflect each city's historic growth or decline in population, total valuation (equalized) as well as commercial and industrial valuation change (equalized).

Exhibit 3 displays the per capita average net benefit for each class of city. Not surprisingly, cities with above-average property tax bases are net losers in the two types of TBS program; in each set of cities, the Maryland formulation has a larger negative net

EXHIBIT 3

Average Net Benefit in Per Capita Dollars by Class of City
After 10 Years of TBS
(Maryland/Minnesota)

City Population Size	Growing Cities		Declining Cities	
	Below Average Wealth (1)	Above Average Wealth (2)	Below Average Wealth (3)	Above Average Wealth (4)
Below 1000	27.96/3.19	−79.35/− 5.04	4.89/−3.16	−4678.37/−552.76
1000-7000	15.74/4.58	−64.63/−18.18	7.93/ 18.93	− 59.56/− 17.41
7000-25000	6.04/1.82	−40.57/−12.79	−.58/−1.09	− 57.77/− 27.15
Over 25000	5.52/3.16		4.89/ 9.65	− 57.41/− 18.92

benefit value than that for Minnesota. In an unanticipated finding, one class of below-average wealth cities is also shown to be a net loser from both TBS policies. There also is shown to be a gradual lessening of the value of the average net benefit or net loss as one moves down the column of figures to larger size classes of cities. Lastly we see that TBS as currently formulated is relatively neutral to the growth or decline of cities as indexed by long-term population change. In fact, in three of the above-average wealth categories, declining cities are on the average larger net losers than are growing cities. This is not really surprising in that both TBS fromulations are weighed by population size.

While class averages are useful as summary numbers they necessarily hide intraclass variation and thus the scope of the unanticipated consequences of the TBS formulation. Exhibit 4 displays the percentages of cities within each class that are net losers due to the two TBS policies after 10 years of the operation. Again, not unsurprisingly, the classes of cities with above-average wealth are almost universally net losers as a result of these policies; perhaps of greater interest is the size of the fraction of below average wealth cities that turn out to be net losers. For example, of the 43 large (over 15,000) New Jersey cities losing population, over 30% are found to be donors in the program.

2. THE INFLATION-MUNICIPAL COST TEST

The second technique for evaluating the effectiveness of a specific TBS formulation is the inflation-municipal cost test. It has been stated earlier that, if uncorrected through the use of index numbers, inflation places progressively more of the base year tax base within

510   TRADITIONAL REVENUES

EXHIBIT 4

Percentage of Cities Within Each Class With a Negative Net Benefit From TBS
(Maryland/Minnesota) After 10 Years of Operation

City Population Size	Growing Cities Below Average Wealth	Above Average Wealth	Declining Cities Below Average Wealth	Above Average Wealth
Below 1000	9.0%/ 9.0% (11)*	100.0%/50% (6)	33.3%/77.8% (9)	100.0%/100.0% (5)
1000-7000	12.8%/22.2% (158)	100.0%/96.2% (25)	35.1%/42.2% (57)	92.8%/ 85.7% (14)
7000-25000	26.9%/33.1% (97)	100.0%/100.0% (9)	40.0%/50.6% (105)	100.0%/100.0% (4)
Over 25000	23.8%/42.8% (21)	NC (0)	34.9%/37.2% (43)	100.0%/100.0% (2)

* Value in parenthesis represents the number of cities within the particular cell.

control of the pooling formula. If the business activity that exists within the municipality at the time of the base year generates municipal service needs (municipal expenditures), it should be of no small interest to determine the city's post-TBS ability to generate revenues from the business tax base from which to service these needs.

In order to assess the importance of these issues, the contributions to total municipal costs made by various sectors of the local business community must be estimated and the inflationary growth in the business tax base extracted from the growth in its total aggregate assessed value. Municipal expenditure determinants analysis can provide estimates of the former entity (Ladd, 1975). However, the lack in the availability of data from which to partition real and inflationary growth in business assessed valuation requires a less direct approach than the above.

For the purpose of demonstration, then, let us assume that the test region has had no real growth in business activity during the time interval since implementation of TBS. All change in assessed value occurs through inflation. If sufficient time is allowed to pass, almost the entire base year's tax base will be subject to the pooling formula.

Under such a restricted circumstance, the net benefits received by the city can be compared with the costs it incurs in servicing the existing business activity. Such an example is of course not a realistic appraisal of real world economic processes; however, given the limitations of data and resources, it serves to demonstrate hitherto unrecognized problems for current versions of TBS.

COST ESTIMATION

Cost estimation techniques are broken down logically into marginal and average costs. In this example, an estimate of the long-run average costs born by the municipal corporation is appropriate for our purposes. Cross-sectional multiple regression techniques such as those used by Ladd (1975) can be used to produce long-run municipal operating expenditure coefficients reflecting the service needs generated by business activity. Appendix 2 describes these methods and their application to the problem at hand. The estimates of the business related costs for several types of cities found within metropolitan areas are shown in Exhibit 5.

THE FISCAL CONSEQUENCES OF
REGIONAL TAX BASE SHARING

In the empirical analysis that follows, the impact of the Maryland and Minnesota TBS formulations upon the fiscal status of 18 large New Jersey cities declining in population between 1960 and 1976 will be assessed. The estimates are based on the assumption that the total business tax base has come under the control of the pooling formula as a result of inflation.

Two types of measurements will be taken in order to assess the municipal fiscal condition before and after the imposition of the tax-base sharing plans. The "before" condition will be assessed by comparing the revenues derived from the city's business sector through the property tax with the expenditures needed to meet its service needs. These results are obtained by finding the estimated expenditure requirements due to commercial and industrial activity, (shown in Exhibit 5), subtracting total expenditures from total revenues derived from each business component, and, lastly, for comparative purposes, scaling all values by population size.

The second index to be calculated is a measure of a city's ability to meet the service needs of business through either of the proposed programs. In this case, total business-related municipal service costs are subtracted from total business-related property tax revenues (withheld fraction plus regional pooled fraction). The service needs gap index is then expressed in terms of per capita dollars.

Exhibit 6 displays the calculated values for each index for the 18 declining New Jersey cities. Column 2 shows that in 16 of the 18 cities the business sector prior to the implementation of TBS did not pay its way with respect to municipal services. A comparison of columns 3 and 4 with column 2 reveals the extent to which the various

TRADITIONAL REVENUES

EXHIBIT 5

Municipal Service Expenditures Assigned to the Needs Brought About by the
Operation of Commercial and Industrial Activity Located Within the City
(Values Scaled in Terms of Dollars of Operating Expenditures
Per Business Employee)

	TYPE OF CITY			
Type of Cost	Small Growing Cities	Intermediate-Sized Growing Cities	Large Growing Cities	Large Declining Cities
Commercial Costs	99.9	56.4	108.1	348.4
Industrial Costs	23.2	31.6	69.6	***

Source: See Appendix 2. Exhibit A1.
*** extremely high standard error makes this value questionable

cities have benefited from the two types of tax-base sharing programs
when viewed from the perspective of the need to cover the costs of
business activity. In the Minnesota plan, 8 of the 18 cities are made
worse off by the implementation of the plan; in the Maryland plan,
12 of the 18 are made worse off with the implementation of that
proposal.

Why, under conditions of inflationary growth, are many declining
cities poorly treated by these programs? In the Minnesota plan,
cities are penalized for having above-average per capita business
property values; while, in the Maryland plan, the tax base increment
from the regional pool is taxed at the regional average, a value that
in some cases will be significantly less than the local rate such that
the gain in tax base will not be translated into a gain in tax revenues.

When viewed in terms of helping declining cities meet the basic
service needs of their business sector, neither program explicitly
recognizes the fact that the business sector places costs upon the
municipality. It is more a matter of serendipity than purposefulness
that certain municipalities have been able to improve their basic
business-related expenditure revenue balance.

POLICY CONSEQUENCES

While we cannot say for certain, it is assumed that these results
were not anticipated by the design of the two tax base sharing plans
now under investigation. What can be done to reverse these results?

Tax Base Sharing—Cons   513

EXHIBIT 6

Per Capita Business Sector Municipal Revenue-Expenditure Gaps
For 18 Declining New Jersey Cities*

City	Business Sector's Municipal Revenue Minus Expenditure Gap *Before* Tax Base Sharing	Business Related Revenue Minus Expenditure Gap *After* Tax Base Share	
(1)	(2)	(3) Minnesota	(4) Maryland
Atlantic City	−23.8	−54.16	−71.34
Dumont	−13.2	−11.68	− 7.12
Englewood	−56.5	−70.29	−77.78
Camden	− 3.1	15.83	− 7.15
Bridgeton	−31.5	−27.56	−21.85
Belleville	−31.9	−34.34	−30.97
East Orange	− 0.4	17.58	13.76
Newark	−10.8	− 9.02	−26.86
Orange	−12.1	− 5.19	−11.61
Bayonne	−50.3	−57.84	−54.85
Hoboken	8.3	23.72	−12.50
Jersey City	4.8	19.30	− 6.05
Trenton	− 3.9	14.19	− 9.63
Asbury Park	−31.9	−32.86	−34.44
Morristown	−79.7	−88.26	−85.14
Hillside	−50.7	−60.38	−62.12
Summit	−77.4	−82.66	−85.92
Phillipsburg	−25.9	−21.92	−18.87

* For the raw data used to calculate these values see Appendix Exhibit A2.

From a technical point of view, two problem areas must be reexamined by policy makers. First the formulae must be modified for purposes of equity across cities to include the costs borne by the city in supporting its business sector. Only that fraction of the tax base net of that which is used to support the needed local services should be placed in the regional pool. If total costs are considered, the objection based upon inflation may go by the board.

Second, the various arguments within the pooling and redistribution formulae must be examined for their effectiveness within the context of the system of cities being placed in the plan. In regional or statewide plans in which all municipalities are treated as equal participants, the existence of several industrial enclaves with per capita property tax bases anywhere from a hundred to a thousand times larger than the median will reduce the effectiveness of the 40% or 60% pooling factor and render ineffective the use of the per capita tax base value relative to the regional average as a mechanism to redistribute taxable wealth to poorer cities.

Third, the distribution of commercial and industrial ratables across the regional system must also be examined. In the New Jersey system, those cities classified by this writer as declining are precisely the cities with the greatest concentration of business assessed valuation as well as employment and, therefore, service needs exist.

The final problem faced by these programs is theoretical. The formulae are indifferent as to all consequences of the plans other than the fact that a tax base redistribution has taken place. Which municipalities lose and which ones ultimately gain are not related to any model showing how cities evolve over time as well as how the evolutionary paths may be altered beneficially.

APPENDIX 1: TAX BASE SHARING FORMULAE

CONTRIBUTIONS FORMULAE

$$C_i = 40\% \ (V_{i,\,c} - V_{i,\,b})$$ Minnesota

$$C_i = 60\% \ (V_{i,\,c} - V_{i,\,b}) \, \overline{t}$$ Maryland

$$\overline{t} = \frac{t_i \, (V_{i,\,c-1})}{\Sigma \, V_{i,\,c-1}}$$

REDISTRIBUTION FORMULAE

$$D_i = \frac{I_i}{\Sigma \, I_i} \ (C)$$ Minnesota

$$I_i = 2N_i \ (\overline{Y}/Y_i) \ \ \text{or}$$

$$I_i = N_i, \ \text{whichever is greater}$$

$$D_i = aN_i \ (2 - r_i)$$ Maryland

$$a = \frac{\Sigma C_i}{\Sigma N_i}$$

$$r_i = \frac{R_i \,/\, N_i}{\Sigma R_i \,/\, \Sigma N_i}$$

C_i : contributed tax base or tax revenue to regional pool

t_i : property tax rate

V_i : assessed or equalized assessed valuation of real property within municipality

c : current year

b : base year

i : municipality

I_i : redistribution index value

N_i : population

Y_i : total per capita equalized valuation of real property in i

R_i : total assessed valuation of residential property in i

APPENDIX 2

The Measurement Of Business Related Municipal Costs

Within the last several years, efforts have been mounted to measure the impact of business upon the municipal budget. Efforts have ranged from intensive case studies requiring researchers to interview many local officials to econometric methods requiring an extensive data base for use in either time series or cross-sectional expenditure determinants analyses (Burchell, Listokin, *et. al.,* 1978). Given the nature of the techniques used in these various methods, case study analyses are favored when estimates of the direct costs of business development are required; for the total expenditure impact, however, econometric methods are preferred. Several econometric based studies focusing upon the role of business activity have been reported recently. A common thread runs through each of these works. Each assumes that the expenditures attributed to the presence of business activity within a municipality can be validly measured by using cross-sectional per capita expenditure determinants analyses techniques. The basic problems faced by each of these analyses are the same: the categorization of business activity into areas with common service needs, the specification of surrogates, as well as the equation or equations capable of measuring that set of characteristics of business activity that necessitate the provision of services by municipal government, and lastly, the separation of the business sector's service needs and revenue effects vis-a-vis municipal expenditure levels. Each of these problem areas will now be examined.

Business activity has been classified by the U.S. Office of Management and Budget into a system of 10 divisions as well as a set of 2, 3 and 4 digit categories. Each category is defined in terms of the principal activity performed by the firm at its geographic location. Each fundamental category of firm can be hypothesized to vary in its need and demand for local services. All firms require local government to deliver basic housekeeping services such as assessments, tax collections, local planning, budget management and legislative decisionmaking; however, firms may differ significantly in the level of direct and indirect services required of local government (Hirsch, 1959).

Direct services relate to the services delivered at the site of the business activity; while, indirect services refer to the class of economic externalities requiring the provision of services at locations other than at the site of the business activity (Ladd, 1976, p. 79).

This distinction is significant for it clearly recognizes the municipality's need to maintain the total public infrastructure and not merely the interface between public and private property. The cost of dealing with the total requirements of business activity is necessarily related to the types and quantities of inputs and outputs from firms. Factors such as the number of person-to-person contacts generated, the types of equipment used to store and transport goods, domestic and industrial waste and other forms of pollution should be considered in the municipality's production function.

Both in the empirical work that follows as well as the previously cited research, local business activity has been partitioned into those firms engaged in commercial or service-related activities and those involved in the manufacture or handling of processed materials.

The second problem deals with the specification of surrogates of commercial and industrial activity. As with many a fledgling science, municipal cost analysis has yet to develop the knowledge with which to test the various published characteristics of business activity with a truth set. Indices are put forward and assumed to measure the relevant characteristics found in the municipal production function. Indices such as the number of employees, value of real property and acreage of land utilized for a particular purpose have in the past been used as surrogates of business activity; continuing that pattern, this work uses per capita employment and property value as the most useful surrogates of business-related municipal service need.

The third problem deals with the distinction between a service needs effect and the revenue effect. The revenue or tax price effect of business activity within a municipality stems from the perception by local citizens *qua* voters that only that fraction of the local tax burden that falls directly upon them as homeowners is the tax price for municipal goods and services (Ladd, 1976, p. 76). Economic theory suggests in this case that the smaller the resident voters' share of these costs, the larger will be the quantity demanded. The surrogate used to identify the tax price effect follows directly from this logic. This is the percentage of the property tax base that is residential. The higher this fraction, the more completely the residential tax base must support the municipal budget. As a consequence, the higher the residential percentage of the property tax base, the lower will be the level of expenditures for goods and services not directly required to meet basic residential needs.

ECONOMETRIC MODELS

The estimation procedures used in this work are derived directly from two recently published works in this field. These are Helen Ladd's determinants analysis using 50 cities within the Boston SMSA (1976) and Douglas Booth's work with 47 Wisconsin municipalities (1978, p. 37). Both of these efforts utilize multiple regression techniques on a cross-sectional sample of metropolitan cities. In light of the applied nature of this research, only a brief description of each model will be made herein with the readers referred to the published texts for a more complete justification of the models.

The cost estimation technique used by Booth expresses per capita municipal police and fire expenditures as a function of family income, the per capita employment levels of commercial and industrial activity, the percent of the tax base that is residential, population size and population density. The coefficients for the employment terms are interpreted to measure the full cost to the municipality for providing a level of services adequate to satisfy direct and indirect service demands. Because of the use of the percent residential tax base term, the coefficients of the per capita employment terms are assumed to be free from any revenue effects derived by the municipality from the presence of the business tax base. Ladd's basic formulation of the determinants equation is somewhat the same as Booth's with the exception that a larger set of independent variables are used and the revenue effect attributable to the business tax base is treated differently. The procedure used in this work combines the set of variables used in the Ladd study with the linear ordinary least squares model specified by Booth.

The other break from the two models comes in the selection of the sets of cities used in the cross-sectional determinants analyses. It has been hypothesized earlier that the costs incurred in servicing the direct and indirect needs of business activity varies by type of city. For purpose of demonstration, four types of cities have been selected in order to test this hypothesis. The typology contains 1) small growing cities referred to as suburbanizing cities, 2) intermediate-sized growing, 3) large growing cities, and 4) large old cities which have lost population over the past 16 years; these cities are referred to as declining cities.

While this classification procedure is of immediate value from the point of view of the principal hypothesis, it is also necessary from the statistical point of view. Cross-sectional determinants analyses often have been plagued by problems of heteroscedasticity (Gramlich, 1969). When a statewide system of cities is partitioned by direction of population change and size of city, this problem has been found to be significantly reduced (Beaton, 1974).

REGRESSION RESULTS

Exhibit A1 displays the 4 regression equations through which the costs of servicing business activity can be estimated. Seven of the eight commercial and industrial service costs coefficients representing business are significantly different from zero at the 0.05 level and all these coefficients have a positive sign. In the case of the set of cities identified as small and growing over the past decade, it is found that each additional employee classified as commercial requires an additional $99.9 in total municipal operating expenditures. Moving across the four types of municipalities, commercial expenditures ultimately rise in a "U" shaped fashion to $348 per employee while industrially-related needs, where measurable, rise from $23.2 to $69.6 per employee in the class of large growing cities.

EXHIBIT A1

The Determinants of the 1974 Per Capita Municipal Operating Expenditures
For New Jersey Municipalities

TYPE OF MUNICIPALITY

	Small Growing	Intermediate Sized-Growing	Large Growing +	Large Declining
Commercial				
Service	99.9*	56.4*	108.1*	348.4*
Needs	(27.2)	(38.4)	(54.2)	(143.7)*
Industrial				
Service	23.2*	31.6*	69.6*	−111.2
Needs	(15.0)	(21.9)	(27.5)	(108.9)
R Base	.00092*	.012*		.0105
	(.00053)*	(.001)		(.01)
Y	.018*	.0092	.00066	
	(.003)	(.0048)*	(.002)	
POV	.20	2.8*	2.5*	3.73
	.94	(1.5)	(1.4)	(3.33)
REN	−.44*	−.71*	−.57*	2.04*
	(.20)	(.20)	(.18)	(1.33)
RESTOT	−13.4	−74.3*	4.3	−350.1
	(19.1)	(28.4)	(25.5)	(231.0)
CRAFTS	.62		−5.8*	
	(.77)		(2.9)	
R^2 (adj.)	.33	.43	.507	.46
F	12.5	17.6	13.9	3.7
n	213	133	102	20

* Significant at 0.05 level
+ Intercorrelation between the commercial and industrial service needs indices

GLOSSARY:

The regression equations displayed throughout this work made extensive use of symbolic abbreviations in place of definitions for the dependent and independent variable sets. The glossary contains the symbols used in the equations, their operational definitions and the source for the data.

SYMBOL OF VARIABLE AS USED IN THE EXHIBITS	OPERATIONAL DEFINITION	SOURCE
Commercial Service Needs	The ratio of persons employed in the trade, commercial, financial industries and covered by state unemployment insurance in 1970 to municipal population, 1970.	III
Industrial Service Needs	The ratio of persons employed in the construction, transportation, utility and manufacturing industries and covered by state unemployment insurance in 1970 to municipal population, 1970.	III
REN	Percentage of housing units occupied by renters	II
POV	Percentage of the population below poverty guidelines	II
R	Non-linear tax price term devised by Ladd (1976) $(1 - .4 \, (\% \, \text{Residential}))$.	
Restot	Fraction of the property tax base classified as residential	I
Crafts	Percentage of resident population employed as craftsmen	II

R Base   Per capita equalized assessed valua-   I
                          tion of residential property within the
                          municipality.

Y   Median family income of municipality   II
                          1970.

Types of
Municipalities

Small
Growing   Municipalities ranging between 1,000
                          and 7,000 in population and growing
                          in population between 1960 and 1970

Intermediate-   Municipalities ranging between 7,000
sized Growing   and 15,000 and growing between 1960
                          and 1970.

Large Growing   Municipalities with a population in excess
                          of 15,000 and growing in population
                          between 1960 and 1970.

Large Declining   Municipalities with a population over
                          15,000 and declining in population
                          between 1960 and 1970

SOURCES

I *Thirty-third Annual Report of the Division of Local Finance: 1970.* State of New Jersey, Department of Community Affairs; Division of Local Finance: Trenton, New Jersey.

II *1970 Census of Population,* Fourth Count: Population Summary Tape, File B.

III *1970 New Jersey Covered Employment Trends by Geographical Areas of the State,* 27th Annual Edition, State of New Jersey, Department of Labor and Industry, Division of Employment Security, Trenton, New Jersey.

EXHIBIT A2

Raw Data Used in the Calculations Reported in EXHIBIT 6

City	I_i	Pop. 1970 N_i	% of Pool $I/\Sigma I_i$	D_i Minn $ Redistribution (X1000)	ppc Per Capita Property Tax Base Y_i
Atlantic City	148,327	47,859	.47%	25,284	6,519
Dumont	40,390	17,534	.13	6,885	8,771
Englewood	42,144	24,985	.13	7,184	11,978
Camden	668,368	102,551	2.14	113,933	3,100
Bridgeton	115,230	20,435	.37	19,643	3,583
Belleville	99,676	34,643	.32	16,991	7,022
East Orange	313,684	75,471	1.00	53,472	4,861
Newark	2,037,540	382,417	6.51	347,327	3,792
Orange	143,817	32,566	.46	24,516	4,575
Bayonne	254,714	72,743	.81	43,420	5,770
Hoboken	324,896	45,380	1.04	55,383	2,822
Jersey City	1,527,140	260,545	4.88	260,322	3,447
Trenton	671,145	104,638	2.14	114,406	3,150
Asbury Park	64,748	16,533	.21	11,037	5,159
Morristown	41,007	17,662	.13	6,990	8,702
Hillside	50,841	21,636	.16	8,667	8,598
Summit	37,149	23,620	.12	6,333	12,846
Phillipsburg	93,838	17,849	.30	15,996	3,843

$\overline{Y}_{Minn}$ = $10,102

$\overset{n}{\Sigma} I$ = 31,295,272

n = 561 cities

ΣC_{iMinn} = $5,334,719,800

$\overline{t}_{md}$ = $1.03 tax per 100 dollars of equalized assessed valuation

Per Capita
Regional = a = 11.44
Growth Pool
(revenue)

Regional
Average
Per Capita = r_i = $4,850
Residential
Wealth

EXHIBIT A2 (cont'd)

	Muni Tax Rate[*]	Comppc[*]	Indppc[*]	Resppc[*]
Atlantic City	2.70	4,111	19	1,498
Dumont	.72	358	31	6,740
Englewood	1.40	1,614	1,554	7,401
Camden	3.08	783	458	1,707
Bridgeton	1.01	775	643	1,968
Belleville	1.26	722	851	4,306
East Orange	2.93	107	126	1,947
Newark	2.86	1,410	705	1,119
Orange	2.45	886	292	2,168
Bayonne	1.24	853	2,156	2,133
Hoboken	3.60	1,005	972	400
Jersey City	3.51	747	716	1,229
Trenton	3.16	961	339	1,683
Asbury Park	1.97	1,768	15	1,819
Morristown	1.04	2,753	287	3,961
Hillside	1.19	748	2,278	5,364
Summit	.60	1,745	1,116	8,942
Phillipsburg	1.23	557	876	2,240

[*] Muni Tax Rate: Equalized municipal property tax rate
[*] Comppc: Equalized municipal per capita commercial property tax base
[*] Indppc: Equalized municipal per capita industrial property tax base
[*] Resppc: Equalized municipal per capita residential property tax base

NOTES

1. In a general equilibrium approach such as taken by William Fischel (1976) the effects of a TBS formulation that does not explicitly include a shadow price for the maintenance of the residential ambiance is shown to affect the rate and pattern of development in those areas capable of controlling their land use through zoning policies.

2. Whether TBS in any of its several operational forms contains the necessary or sufficient conditions to meet this goal is a matter still open to empirical testing.

3. Changes in the assessed valuation of a jurisdiction's business property depends upon the addition and deletion of real property from the tax rolls, depreciation on existing improvements and any across-the-board inflation adjustments the local tax assessor is authorized to apply to all property within his jurisdiction. The equalized assessed valuation adjusts the value of the assessed valuation by the average sales/assessment ratio for qualified sales within each class of property. Given the preponderance of residential sales within most jurisdictions relative to sales of other classes of property, inference from the sample sales/assessment ratio to jurisdiction-wide aggregate market values can be expected to have a

relatively low standard error given that sales can be assumed to be randomly distributed throughout the full range of available parcels. However, the relatively low level of business property sales (occasionally 0) and our relative ignorance of the degree of congruence between the distribution of assessed value and potential market values of business property leaves the inference of the aggregate market value of business property open to a higher level of error than in the former case. In the absence of valid business sales, the equalized valuation of this class of property is imputed from the sales/assessment studies from the residential class of property.

Since TBS formulas that rely upon changes in assessed valuation of business property may significantly lag the market value of business property (as valuated by a professional appraiser), the decision to reappraise or update assessments to account for inflation may now have a new political hurdle to cross given the perception of a regional tax on a jurisdiction's tax base growth. On the other hand, TBS formulas that rely on change in equalized business valuation can be strongly dependent upon an extremely small number of sales or upon the growing values of the residential property market and thus not to factors that have been necessarily intrinsic to the changes in value of the jurisdiction's industrial or commercial sector.

REFERENCES

Advisory Commission on Intergovernmental Relations, (1967), *Fiscal Balance in the American Federal System.* Vol. 2, Metropolitan Fiscal Disparities Washington, D.C.: USGPO.

Bahl Ray and David Puryear, (1976), "Regional Tax Base Sharing: Possibilities and Implications," *National Tax Journal.* Vol. 29, pp. 328-35.

Beaton, W. Patrick, (1974), "The Determinants of Police Protection Expenditures" *National Tax Journal* No. 2.

Beaton, W. Patrick, (1975), "Environmental Structure and Municipal Costs." *Municipal Needs Services and Financing,* edited by W. P. Beaton (New Brunswick: Center for Urban Policy Research), pp. 249-80.

Booth, Douglas E., (1978), "The Differential Impact of Manufacturing and Mercantile Activity on Local Government Expenditures and Revenues," *National Tax Journal,* Vol. 30, No. 1, pp. 33-43.

Burchell, Robert W. and David Listokin, *et. al.,* (1978), *The Fiscal Impact Handbook.* (New Brunswick, N.J.: Center for Urban Policy Research, Rutgers University).

Fischel, William A., (1976), "An Evaluation of Proposals for Metropolitan Sharing of Commercial and Industrial Property Tax Base." *Journal of Urban Economics* (July), pp. 253-63.

Gramlich, Edward M., (1969), "The Effect of Federal Grants on State-Local Expenditures: A Review of the Economic Literature," National Tax Association, *Proceedings of the Sixty-Second Annual Conference on Taxation,* pp. 569-93.

Greytak, David and Bernard Jump, (1977), "Inflation and Local Government Expenditures and Revenues: Method and Case Study." *Public Finance Quarterly,* Vol. 5, No. 3 (July), pp. 275-301.

Hackensack Meadowlands Development Commission, *Intermunicipal Tax Sharing Theory and Operation.* State of New Jersey. (October, 1972).

Hersch, Werner Z., (1959), "Expenditure Implications of Metropolitan Growth and Consolidation" *Review of Economics and Statistics,* Vol. 39 (August), pp. 232-41.

Isseman, Andrew M. and Karen L. Majors, (1978), "General Revenue Sharing: Federal Incentives to Change Local Government," *Journal of the American Institute of Planners,* Vol. 44 (July), pp. 317-27.

Ladd, Helen F., (1976), "Municipal Expenditures and the Composition of the Local Property Tax Base," In *Property Taxation Land Use and Public Policy.* Edited by Arthur D. Lynn, Jr. (Madison: University of Wisconsin Press). pp. 73-98.

Lyall, Katharine, C., (1975), "Tax Base Sharing: A Fiscal Aid Towards More Rational Land Use Planning," *Journal of the American Institute of Planners.* 41, (March), 2.

Mills, Edwin S. and Wallace E. Oates, (1975), "The Theory of Local Public Services and Finance: Its Relevance to Urban Fiscal and Zoning Behavior," *Fiscal Zoning and Land Use Controls* edited by Edwin S. Mills and Wallace E. Oates, Lexington Books: Lexington Mass.

Netzer, Dick, (1968), "Impact of Property Tax: Effect on Housing," *Urban Land Use, Local Government Finance.* Washington, D.C.:USGPO.

Peterson, George, (1976), "Finance," *The Urban Predicament,* edited by William Gorham and Nathan Glazer (Washington, D.C.: Urban Institute).

Reschovsky, Andrew and Eugene Knaff, (1977), "Tax Base Sharing: An Assessment of the Minnesota Experience," *Journal of the American Institute of Planners,* 43 (October) 4.

The Metropolitan Studies Program of the Maxwell School. (1975) *The Fiscal Implications of Inflation: A Study of Six Local Governments.*

Weaver, Charles R., (1972), "The Minnesota Approach to Solving Urban Fiscal Disparity," *State Government* XLV (Spring), pp. 100-105.

SECTION V

*The New Dominance of
Intergovernmental Transfers*

Richard P. Nathan - FEDERAL GRANTS - HOW ARE THEY WORK-ING?

INTRODUCTION

The 1980 Federal Budget is a watershed budget for federal grants-in-aid. Actually the last two budgets taken together mark the turning point in federal grants policy. Focusing on non-welfare grants and looking at the 1979 and 1980 budgets together, there has been a substantial decline in *real* terms in the value of non-welfare federal grants, that is, subtracting out from total federal grants those for the AFDC, Medicaid and Section 8 programs. (The programs eliminated are transfers to individuals administerd through states and localities, as opposed to transfers to jurisdictions for their own services and activities.)

Using the Administration's conservative estimates for the GNP price deflator, non-welfare grants from the federal government to states and localities are projected to *decline* in *real* terms by 3.3 percent in 1979 and by 6.8 percent in 1980. These declines are unprecedented in recent experience. Ironically, the biggest reductions come in the programs expanded in 1977 to fight the last recession just as the current recession is about to be felt on the economic horizon. The effect of these reductions is going to hit very

The author is a senior fellow at the Brookings Institute and heads the Institute's Monitoring Studies Group. The views and interpretations in this paper are those of the author and not necessarily those of the trustees, officers and other staff members of the Brookings Institute.

hard as a result of enaction of the 1980 budget. Assuming there is a recession late this year or early next, with rising unemployment, lowered tax receipts (viz. for sales and payroll taxes) and simultaneously higher prices, these cuts in federal grants are bound to cause especially severe problems for the nation's most distressed cities. This is so because the federal grant-in-aid programs most affected by the cutbacks in 1979 and 1980 are also the programs best targeted on community distress—CETA public service jobs (PSE), local public works (LPW) and the anti-recessional fiscal assistance program (ARFA).

Federal grants are estimated in the new budget at $82.9 billion[1] for 1980, of which $28.1 billion is for grants for payments to individuals and $54.8 billion is for other—i.e., non-welfare—grants to states and localities. Total grants are projected to account for 23.6 percent of total state and local expenditures in 1980 compared to 26.7 percent in 1978, which was the highest such percentage in history.

Cities, the subject of this paper, are now major recipients of federal grants. Federal grants to local governments account for approximately half of all non-welfare federal grants to states and localities. The growth in direct federal-local grants over the past fifteen years is one of the most fundamental changes in our intergovernmental finances in the recent period. The heightened flow of federal grants directly into city coffers (revenue sharing, CETA, CDBG, ARFA, UMTA, wastewater treatment) is of such consequence as to challenge the basic characterization of the American governmental system as federal.

There are by most counts five major federal governments in the world. They are Australia, Canada, Switzerland, West Germany and, according to most observers, the U.S. However, aside from the U.S., the central government's predominant fiscal and regulatory relationships are with the regional or middle level—states in Australia, provinces in Canada, cantons in Switzerland and the laender in West Germany. It is essentially correct to say that *no* central government grant-in-aid funds are provided directly to local governments in the other four political systems.

Federal grants to local governments in the U.S. are the main focus of this paper. Several projects of the Monitoring Studies Group at Brookings shed light on federal grants-in-aid to cities and help us to deal with the question: How are they working? We are conducting monitoring studies of the general revenue sharing, community development block grant (CDBG) and CETA-public service employment programs. In addition, a number of the individual field-research associates are presently writing case study chapters for a forthcoming book on the overall and cumulative impact of federal grants in fiscal year 1978 in twelve selected large cities included in the monitoring networks.[2]

A word is needed here about the way in which the discussion in this paper is organized. It is currently fashionable among social scientists to "de-mythologize." This paper identified and discusses seven myths about federal grants and how they work, bringing our research findings and those of others to bear on what, to me at least, appear to be some popular ideas—sometimes mistatements and often overstatements—about federal grants-in-aid.

MYTH # 1: FEDERAL GRANTS HAVE PROLIFERATED LIKE RABBITS

There is in the literature still the recurrent theme that, despite the general revenue sharing program, there has continued to be a steady and unremitting growth in the specificity and narrowness of federal grants-in-aid. "We've let a thousand programs bloom," it is said; "there may even be more than a thousand, but we've lost count."

I would urge a word of caution about this view of the rabbit-like proliferation of federal grants. The fact of the matter is that proliferation rate seems not to be increasing, but rather to be tailing off. True, the Carter administration has introduced some new categorical programs, particularly in the youth employment field, where we now have (if I recall the names correctly), YIEP, YETPA, SPEDY and YAC. But in spite of these developments, the fact of the matter is that more than one third of all non-welfare federal grants to states and localities currently is in the form of what the OMB classified as "general-purpose" grants and "broad-based" grants. If one adds to that federal aid for public service employment (PSE), which is administered through the CETA block grant system, general and broad-based grants, plus CETA-PSE funding, account for 52 percent of all non-welfare grants estimated for 1978. The "New Federalism" is very much with us. The domestic program of the Nixon years was one of expenditure growth and quite fundamental changes in policy with the adoption of broader and less conditional—decentralizing—grant program initiatives. These changes have made their mark on our political and governmental system.

Totalling up the number of federal grant-in-aid programs is often done in the literature on a basis that counts peanuts and watermelons the same way. A $7 billion revenue sharing program, $8 billion for CETA-PSE and $3.5 million per year for CDBG are not equal to one project grant. There may be a few more peanuts, but the increasing importance of watermelon-sized, broad-based grants cannot be overlooked. In short, while it may be politically useful for some observers to highlight what they perceive as a problem of grant proliferation, the tendency in doing to often is to mythologize what is really happening to federal grants.

MYTH # 2: THE THROUGH-THE-ROOF THEORY OF GRANTS

Myth number 2 does not need much comment since it already has been considered in the introductory section. It is the commonly held belief that federal grants are growing not only in number, but in size, and that, in technical terms, they have "gone through the roof." Not so anymore. The last big spurt in grantmaking came in 1977 with President Carter's $13 billion Economic Stimulus Program (funds for job creation, local public works and countercyclical revenue sharing). Although President Carter proposed to annualize this supposedly countercyclical package in 1979, the Congress would not go along. The Administration's proposals to keep the stimulus package alive—converting some of it to urban policy initiatives—were overtaken by Proposition 13 fever in the waning days of the 95th Congress. The text of the 1980 Federal Budget has a somewhat unreal tinge to it where the Administration talks about cuts in the stimulus programs in 1979 in terms that appear to take credit for taming the spending machine of federal grants.

Prior to Carter's now conveniently semi-forgotten stimulus package, big spurts in federal grantmaking came in the Republican years with the advent of revenue sharing (which produced a 37 percent jump in non-welfare grants in 1973) and the introduction of the block grant programs of the "New Federalism." These increases demonstrate what in the old days—pre-Proposition 13—was a basic law of federal grants: *New concepts cost money*. No matter who you are or were, if you were a President of the United States pre-Jarvis-Gann, in order to "reform" a federal grant program you had to keep the old money and add some more to it, a "sweetener" as it is known in the trade. The net result was to *ratchet up* the total. Those days are gone forever, or so it would seem. In any event, those who think that federal grants are still growing through the roof have missed the turning point; it was last year.

MYTH # 3: IT ALL GOES DOWN A SEWER
IN BIG CITY SLUMS

Myth number 3, perhaps less common than the others, is nevertheless one we often hear—namely, that federal grants are pouring into the big old tired and declining cities (with all of their political muscle) and that the rest of us—lucky enough to live in wealthy growing cities or well-off suburbs—are paying the freight. Not so. We have in a number of studies written about the "spreading" versus the "targetting" effect of federal grants. The fact of the matter is that the spreading effect has predominated in recent years and that targeting is a very recent and modest development that already seems to be losing ground. The advent of the computer (and "the politics of the print-out") plus the "New Federalism" of the Nixon-Ford period produced a marked spreading effect in the distribution of federal grants. Jurisdictions which had never seen a U.S. Treasury check before began getting them regularly. In many cases, they get just as hooked on the new money as anybody else. Revenue sharing payments are made to over 38,000 local governments. All of us have heard stories of local officials receiving checks under new federal programs (GRS, ARFA, even LPW and CDBG) and not knowing what they were for. They found out in a hurry!

As mentioned above, the Monitoring Studies Group is presently conducting a set of case studies on the cumulative and overall impact of federal grants in a dozen large cities. Rather fortuitously, we took as our observation period, fiscal year, 1978; the research has been under way for over two years. The methodology is a simple one. A group of social scientists (about evenly divided between economists and political scientists) is writing individual chapters on the cities in which they are located. The authors are using a uniform analytical framework; all are obtaining the same types of basic data. This research is being sponsored by the U.S. Departments of Labor and Commerce, with the Office of Program Evaluation of the Labor Department having the lead and primary responsibility.

It is too early to present general findings from these case studies. They are to be submitted to the Labor Department's Office of Program Evaluation in blocks as they are completed.

However, with such a big group of scholars and such an interesting subject, some of the findings have been discussed publicly and in these cases it is possible to indicate at least some of the preliminary results. Two of the case studies, which are furthest along and which have been the subject of some public discussion, concern healthy Sunbelt cities—Tulsa, Oklahoma and Houston, Texas.

The authors of the federal aid case study of Tulsa, Professors Steve B. Steib and R. Lynn Rittenoure of the University of Tulsa, have completed a draft of their paper and have discussed their findings with community leaders and interested experts. They found that Tulsa in 1978 received $48 million in federal grants and that these funds accounted for over one-quarter (actually 27 percent) of the city's spending for the traditional or primary city services. This was a five-fold increase from 1972.

In Houston, Texas, the author of the federal aid case study, Professor Susan A. MacManus of the University of Houston, developed data on federal aid in 1978 which was recently discussed at a conference at the University of Houston.[3] Professor MacManus found that Houston received $210 million in federal aid allocations in 1978, of which $140 million was for capital purposes and $70 million for operating purposes. Total available federal aid in 1978, including funds in the pipeline, was over $450 million. (These funds can be expected to spend out over a period of years; included are large grants for mass transit and wastewater treatment projects.) From 1973 to 1978, federal aid to Houston increased by more than seven-fold.

The picture that many of us carry in our minds of massive federal aid bailing out the nation's most distressed cities, but with healthier cities resisting Washington's blandishments, simply isn't true. Whatever ultimately happens in 1980 to the rate of spending for the three programs in the Carter Administration's 1977 Economic Stimulus Package, the fact of the matter is that federal grants are now—and will continue to be—big ticket items for all cities in the U.S.

MYTH # 4: THE POINTY-HEADED BUREAUCRAT MYTH

One of my favorite myths about federal grants, because I have lived in Washington for twenty years, is the impression one often gets from commentaries on the subject that federal grants are controlled by federal bureaucrats who observe every move of every recipient local government and as a result are taking over the country. Watch out for that one. I suggest that the best therapy for persons afflicted with this myth about federal grants is to try to get information about what is happening under any one of your favorite federal grant-in-aid programs. The Feds—in many cases—simply do not know. Not only do they lack sophisticated control mechanisms with which to implement grandiose grant plans, they simply do not know what is being done. Even if they have information about the allocations to major functional areas by recipient jurisdictions under a particular grant program, they are likely to have relatively little information about specific programmatic uses of these funds and even less information about the effects and effectiveness of the dollars spent.

I do not mean to disparage either federal bureaucrats or state and local officials. I don't believe that federal bureaucrats can or should know how every federal grant dollar is spent. Under many programs the cost of finding out would be four or five times the amount spent on the program. This reflects the essential character of our federalism. It is a highly pluralistic, open and competitive system. Personally, I like it that way, and have only sympathy for federal officials called on the carpet by a Congressional committee because of the limitations of their knowledge of what happens under a particular federal grant program.

Local democracy in the United States is really quite healthy; the trend of the past decade towards broader and less conditional federal grants has aided and abetted localism as a basic value of our political system. This may not always be the case. A new centralism yet to come may make these selfsame grants instruments of national control, but I doubt it will happen soon and I would—if it makes any difference—be against such a development.

The odd man out in all of this lately has been the states, the all-important middle-man of the federal system. However, the states have basically good prospects down the road. John Shannon makes this point effectively. Proposition 13 (cutting local property taxes) pushes responsibilities up to the state level. Likewise, the slowing down in the growth of federal grants is likely to cause a reduction in the importance of federal-local fiscal and regulatory relationships. The elasticity of state income taxes in inflationary periods (and inflation seems always to be with us) is another point in favor for the states over the long run.

While states have been losing ground, there is a tendency to ignore their prospects for the future. In any event, I think one of the biggest gaps in our knowledge about contemporary American federalism has to do with the role of the states. I would like to see a national monitoring study undertaken in this important and fast-changing subject area.

MYTH # 5:THE URBAN CRISIS IS OVER;
YOU CAN TURN OFF THE WATER NOW

Thanks to that new household word on urbanology—T.D. Allman—there is a growing impression that the urban crisis is over. We can bring the troops home. I refer, of course, to Mr. Allman's provocative and skillful—but *wrong*—article in the December 1978 issue of *Harper's* magazine. The world is more complex than suggested in a few judiciously selected quotes. Yes, urban conditions (thanks in part to increased federal grants) are improving in some older cities with natural locational and institutional advantages, for example, Boston, Chicago, Baltimore. At least this is *"suggested"* (I emphasize the word) by some recent analyses. But the data to look at such trends are limited for the current period.

On the other hand, an analysis we did recently shows that in older and declining cities without locational and institutional advantages, facing deep and more serious structural problems, the urban crisis is getting worse.[5] Data for Detroit, Newark, St. Louis, Cleveland and Buffalo indicate that the case for targeting lives on. One may want to cut federal grants to these distressed (as well as non-distressed) local governments for other reasons. All I am saying is that it cannot be shown that there has been a quantum change in the conditions of the nation's older and declining cities such that there is now a basis for arguing that their water should be turned off.

MYTH # 6: STATES AND CITIES HAVE HUGE SURPLUSES
AND ALL BY THEMSELVES COULD BALANCE
THE FEDERAL BUDGET

Another item making the rounds, especially in relation to the proposal for a Constitutional Amendment to balance the federal budget, is the idea that the federal budget could be balanced by simply devoting the huge surpluses that state and local governments are holding to this purpose. Proponents of this position cite the $29.6 billion surplus shown in the national income accounts for state and local governments in 1977 and wistfully compare it with the projected deficit in Carter's proposed budget for 1980.

The issue is indeed a complex one. The state-local surplus is *less* than meets the eye. It has already declined by an estimated $6 billion from $29.6 billion in 1977 to $23.4 billion in the third quarter of 1978. But even more important is the fact that most of this surplus is in the form of social insurance funds, primarily retirement funds for state and local government employees. Out of the third quarter 1978 surplus of $23.4 billion, $21.6 billion is in the form of insurance funds. Public finance experts for years have advocated that state and local employee-retirement insurance funds be made actuarially sound by having reserves which reflect what is needed to pay the retirement benefits of the state and local government employees who will eventually draw upon these funds. In essence, fiscal responsibility accounts for most of the surplus on hand. *The surplus is not easily and automatically transferable to purposes that could offset federal budget cuts.*

Moreover, the state-local fiscal picture is a fast-changing one. The Congressional Budget Office projects a net deficit in 1979 and 1980 for the state and local government sector, exclusive of social insurance funds. This is said to be due to Proposition 13 in California and the tapping of accumulated surpluses to maintain service levels. The CBO projects a $3.3 billion deficit in 1973 in "other funds" and a $3.7 billion deficit in 1980. This follows three years of NIPA surpluses for "other funds" in the state-local sector.

One more point. Even with what look like surpluses in some places, good fortune in the state-local sector reflects what is in reality a very mixed picture. The continuing great fiscal strain faced by many distressed cities (local governments cannot officially run a deficit) is unaffected by growing fund balances in wealthy jurisdictions.

MYTH # 7: NOTHING WORKS

The final item on this myth parade is the idea that nothing works. Everything is broken. The governmental system is in chaos. Federal grants only make it worse. I exaggerate, of course, even in paraphrasing the views one hears on this subject, but there is indeed a strong negativism afoot about federal spending, including and often featuring, federal grants-in-aid. I would like to deal with this subject on a more philosophical basis that pertains to governmental goods and the elements and ideas of our federalism.

You can't have or do everything at once. Too many programs in Washington have as their goals fixing up everything, solving every problem, spending a minimal amount of money in the process, and doing it on a basis that gives broad discretion to state and local governments with maximum citizen participation and an environmental review of every major project undertaken.

In short, the more goals you have, the less likely you are to fulfill them. The federal grants system deserves a patent for perfecting the art of multiple and conflicting goals. Again, the problem is not that we do this; it is that we don't understand what it means.

The Brookings Monitoring Studies Group is studying three programs with classic symptoms of multiple and conflicting goals—CETA—PSE, CDBG and general revenue sharing. In all three cases, if you like the idea of local self-government (and I do), there is much good than can be said about the flexibility and inventiveness of state and local governments in the use of federal grant funds. The *Reader's Digest* can find ten examples of anything, and its favorite subject for such surveys is often fraud and abuses under federal grant programs. So be it. Its provocative article on CETA has made this program a new four-letter term of disparagement in the popular lexicon.[6] But our monitoring study of the CETA-PSE program (the second report on PSE will soon be out) shows that the rate of job creation under this program is quite high, that local governments undertake many projects that are related to the major activities or services they provide, and that the program is quite well targeted on disadvantaged persons, though some would disagree on this later point.

We conclude our second report on the PSE program with a discussion of the two-dimensional policy bargain of CETA-PSE.[7] The program involves a constantly shifting policy bargain at the national level among three basic objectives or sets of objectives—job creation, providing useful services at the state-local level, and aiding the disadvantaged in the process. It is also a vertical policy bargain in terms of working out a treaty, if you will, between the national government and states and localities in order to get the later to do its business for it—in this case the business of job creation and economic stimulation. The recipient jurisdictions want and expect to get something out of the bargain. In some cases it is the job displacement which does occur under PSE. But in more cases it is the fact that the recipient state and local governmental jurisdictions receive free labor to provide certain previously marginal services. This is a big subject and I have only touched upon it here. The point is that—yes, CETA-PSE has its problems—but from the vantage point of our monitoring research, there are a number of ways in which one can say the program works. I venture to add that if one can show that CETA works, he has gone a long way in at least raising questions about the popular conception that *nothing* works.

* * * * * *

This is my myth parade. While I grant you (pardon me) that this paper is not quite conventional, I believe these are serious points about our grant system and how it works which do not receive as much attention as they should in policy and popular discussions of the role and efficacy of federal grants-in-aid.

NOTES

1. This total ($82.9 billion) for grants-in-aid in the 1980 federal budget includes some programs that are not actually grants to state and local governments. For example, it includes the Corporation for Public Broadcasting, the National Foundation on the Arts and Humanities, the Community Services Administration and TVA shared revenue. However, there are some highway funds not included which probably should be. In any event the net change that would result from adjusting these items would be small.

2. The cities are: Boston, Chicago, Cleveland, Houston, Los Angeles, New Orleans, New York, Phoenix, Rochester, St. Louis, San Francisco, and Tulsa. See *Case Studies of the Impact of Federal Grants in Large Cities in 1978*, transcript of working conference proceedings prepared for Office of Program Evaluation, Employment and Training Administration, U.S. Department of Labor, The Brookings Institution, Washington, D.C., Feb. 2, 1978.

3. The Outlook for Sunbelt Cities, University of Houston, February 12, 1979.

4. Richard P. Nathan and James W. Fossett, "Urban Conditions—The Future of the Federal Role," Paper prepared for presentation to the National Tax Association, Philadelphia, Pa., Nov. 13, 1978.

5. Ralph Kinney Bennet, "CETA: $11-Billion Boondoggle," *Reader's Digest* (August 1978), p. 72.

6. Richard P. Nathan, Robert F. Cook, V. Lane Rawlins, Janet M. Galchick and Associates, Monitoring the Public Service Employment Program: The Second Round, U.S. National Commission for Employment Policy, March, 1979, Chapter 6.

John Shannon and Bruce Wallin - FISCAL IMBALANCE WITHIN THE FEDERAL SYSTEM: THE PROBLEM OF RENEWING REVENUE SHARING

The General Revenue Sharing renewal debate is highlighting recent and fairly dramatic changes in the fiscal positions of the federal and state governments. While local governments are still the low men on the intergovernmental fiscal totem pole, the fiscal position of the states has improved markedly while that of the federal government has deteriorated. These trends have made continued inclusion of the states the central issue of General Revenue Sharing renewal. This development, in turn, now threatens the state-local coalition that successfully pressured a reluctant Congress into program enactment and later into initial renewal.

The views presented are those of the authors and do not necessarily reflect the views of the Commission on Intergovernmental Relations.

BACKGROUND AND RATIONALE

The General Revenue Sharing program provides on a formula basis nearly seven billion dollars a year in relatively unrestricted support, one-third to states and two-thirds to local governments. The program was enacted in 1972 and renewed in 1976. It will expire on October 1, 1980, if not reenacted by Congress.

The leading rationale for the program's passage was that of imbalance—both fiscal and political. Fiscal imbalances were of two types:

Vertical imbalance. The federal government had a revenue system which responded readily to the growth in the economy and which was progressive. In contrast, state and local governments carried the major share of domestic expenditure responsibilities and were financed by less elastic and more regressive revenue systems.

Horizontal imbalance. There was also a widespread recognition that some states and local governments were more needy than others. The major central cities of the Northeast and Midwest were considered especially deserving of fiscal support.

The decisionmaking imbalance in the federal system was caused by the growth in federal categorical programs and a concentration of power in Washington—a "hardening of the categories" with power entangled with rigid rules sometimes having duplicatory and contradictory effects. The categorical buildup forced local governmental officials to make "grantsmanship" a pressing priority in an attempt to manipulate the red tape which characterized these grants. Moreover, grantsmanship ability varied widely, with small governments having the greatest difficulty playing the game. State and local government officials, it was decided, needed more flexibility in order to respond to their diverse needs.

In sum, the intent of the General Revenue Sharing program was to accomplish a decentralization of decisionmaking power through general fiscal support with no hamstrings attached.

THE CHANGED INTERGOVERNMENTAL
FISCAL ENVIRONMENT

While the need for decentralized decisionmaking in the federal system remains relatively unchallenged, opponents of the General Revenue Sharing Program argue that the rationale of fiscal imbalance is no longer valid in the 1979 intergovernmental fiscal environment. This increasingly voiced objection to renewal relies on recent changes in the federal fiscal system, most notably the "deterioration" of the federal fiscal position, coupled with the substantial improvement in the fiscal position of the states.

FEDERAL GOVERNMENT: DETERIORATION

The federal government has recently found itself in the middle of a four-way squeeze between continuing pressure for new programs, soaring costs of ongoing programs, a hobbled income tax and a taxpaying public demanding more tax relief.

Perhaps the single most telling evidence of growing fiscal tensions at the federal level was the Carter Administration's recommendation that certain social security benefits be cut back—hard on the heels of the January 1979 social security tax hike.

The federal government's income tax is badly hobbled. In recent years, Congress has considered it necessary to cut federal income tax rates repeatedly for purposes of economic stabilization. Now federal income tax cuts also are justified to offset social security tax hikes and to prevent inflation from creating income tax "windfalls." Moreover, public agitation about "loopholes" has not resulted in tax reform legislation.

There is widespread public resistance to continued rapid growth in government spending in general and to federal spending in particular. Proposition 13 has not only produced clones in other states, but has created a national mood of public sector retrenchment. Underlying reasons include:

(a) the recent strong growth in total tax burden for individuals (Exhibit 1);

(b) the dramatic loss of confidence in government in general and in the ability of elected representatives to contain growth in particular (Exhibit 2);

(c) A significant post-Proposition 13 drop in public regard for the effectiveness of federal government. Prior to Proposition 13, the federal government came out first, local governments second, and state governments third, when respondents were asked to select the most efficient level of government. (Exhibit 3). After Proposition 13, when asked to single out the most wasteful level of government, 62% of the respondents cited the federal government, 12% state government and 5% local government. (CBS-New York Times Poll, June 19-23, 1978) (Exhibit 4).

EXHIBIT 1

A Comparison of Direct Tax Burdens Borne by Average and
Upper Income Families, Calendar Years 1953, 1966, and 1977.

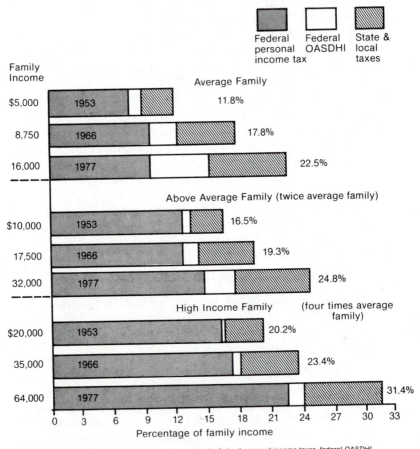

*These estimates assume a family of four and include only: federal personal income taxes, federal OASDHI,
state and local personal income and general sales taxes, and local residential property taxes.

Source: ACIR staff.

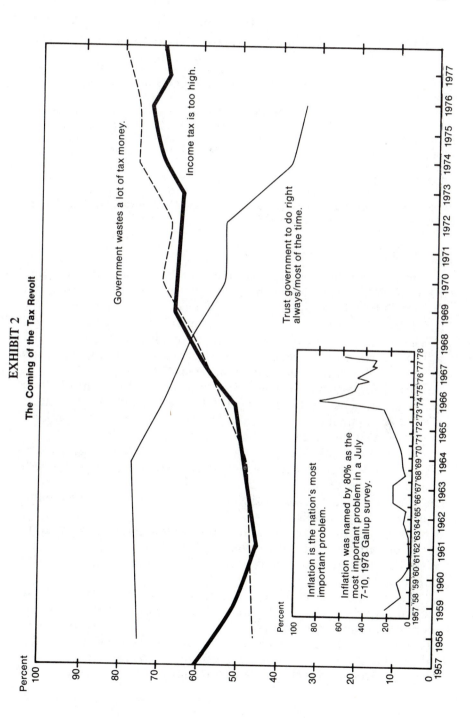

EXHIBIT 2

The Coming of the Tax Revolt

Government wastes a lot of tax money.

Income tax is too high.

Trust government to do right always/most of the time.

Inflation is the nation's most important problem.

Inflation was named by 80% as the most important problem in a July 7–10, 1978 Gallup survey.

EXHIBIT 3

From Which Level of Government Do You Feel You Get the Most for Your Money—
Federal, State, or Local?

Percent of U.S. Public

	May 1978*	May 1977	March 1976	May 1975	April 1974	May 1973	March 1972
Federal	35%	36%	36%	38%	29%	35%	39%
Local	26	26	25	25	28	25	26
State	20	20	20	20	24	18	18
Don't Know	19	18	19	17	19	22	17

* Opinion Research Corporation—2,110 adults, personal interviews, May 11-30, 1978. ORC also conducted the earlier polls for ACIR.

There is growing public resistance to federal deficit financing. Fear of double-digit inflation has placed powerful constraints on federal deficit financing and has produced a strong movement for a federal constitutional convention to mandate a balanced budget.

The trends on the expenditure side are explosive. There has been a massive increase in federal domestic expenditure commitments in the social security and federal aid areas. In 1954, federal expenditures in these two areas amounted to less than 2 percent of Gross National Product. In 1978, they total an estimated 8.1 percent of GNP. The dramatic increase in direct federal aid to the nation's largest cities is one manifestation of this trend (Exhibit 5).

On the social welfare side, the federal government has assumed responsibility for financing an increasing share of the programs with the fastest growth—income maintenance for the elderly and the poor and the health care costs for the elderly, the poor and the near poor. For example, population over 65 has grown 17.6 percent since 1970 and now constitutes 10.9 percent of the population; average monthly social security benefits rose from $123 in 1970 to $300 last year, with the federal cost jumping from 33.8 billion dollars to 93.8 billion dollars.

Meanwhile, there has been a "bottoming out" of national defense reductions. Between 1954 and 1978, defense outlays including interest payments on the defense-related share of the national debt dropped from about 13 percent to 6.7 percent of GNP. In effect, a substantial part of the resources generated by the creation of a powerful federal revenue system was shifted from defense to the

EXHIBIT 4

Selected Opinion Polls

The Gallup Poll for Newsweek
June 7-8, 1978
Telephone Interviews—750 Adults

Which level of government gives you the most value for your tax dollars?

Local Government	State Government	Federal Government	Can't Say
35%	23%	22%	20%

NBC-AP Poll
June 12-13, 1978
Telephone Interviews—1,600 Adults

Do you feel that you get your money's worth from the tax dollars you pay to the federal government [state government, local government, local schools], or don't you think you get your money's worth?

	Yes. Get Money's Worth	No. Don't Get Money's Worth	Not Sure	Total
Federal	21%	73%	6%	100%
State	30	63	7	100
Local Government	39	53	8	100
Local Schools	45	44	11	100

CBS News-New York Times Poll
June 19-23, 1978
Telephone Interviews—1,527 Adults

Which level of government do you think wastes the biggest part of its budget—the federal government, the state government or local governments?

Federal	62%	None/All Equal	13%
State	12	No Opinion	8
Local	5		

EXHIBIT 5

Direct Federal and State Aid to the Nation's 47 Largest Cities,[1]
Selected Years 1957-1978

Source of Funds		Fiscal Year			
		1957	1967	1976	1978 est.
Total Federal and State Aid (in millions)					
Federal		$ 65.3	$ 406.0	$3,182.6	$5,400.0
State[2]		444.3	890.4	2,759.9	3,040.0
	Total	$509.6	$1,302.4	$5,977.6	$9,240.0
Per Capita Federal and State Aid[3]					
Federal		$ 2.33	$ 13.14	$ 101.56	$ 172.16
State[2]		15.84	29.00	89.19	122.44
	Total	$ 18.17	$ 42.14	$ 190.75	$ 294.60
Federal and State Aid Per $1.00 of Own Source General Revenue					
Federal		$ 0.03	$ 0.09	$ 0.34	$ 0.50
State[2]		0.18	0.21	0.30	0.35
	Total	$ 0.21	$ 0.30	$ 0.64	$ 0.85

[1]　Excluding New York City.

[2]　Includes an unsegregable amount of federal aid passed through the states.

[3]　Based on the following population estimates:
1957, 1950 population; 1967, 1960 population; 1976 and 1978, 1975 population.

Source:　ACIR staff computations based on U.S. Bureau of the Census, *City Government Finances in 1957, 1967, and 1976.* Estimated own source general revenue and state aid for 1978 based on annual average increases between 1971 and 1976. Federal aid estimates for 1978 based on Department of the Treasury, *Fiscal Impact of Economic Stimulus Package on 48 Urban Governments*, A Memorandum for the Urban and Regional Policy Group, November 8, 1977; and ACIR staff estimates.

domestic sector. In view of the present international situation and strong pressure by NATO allies, it no longer appears possible to continue this redeployment of federal funds from defense to non-defense programs.

In sum, federal expenditure responsibilities are fast growing while both its revenue raising and deficit financing ability are becoming increasingly constrained. This fiscal fact of life has prompted Senator Long and Chairman Ullman to mention the unmentionable—the need for a major new federal tax—a value added levy.

STATE GOVERNMENTS: MARKED IMPROVEMENT

The fiscal position of the states has improved considerably over the past two decades. States have more balanced revenue systems— today 37 states make use of both the personal income tax and the general sales tax as compared to only 19 states in 1960. State-local tax systems are less regressive—29 states now partially shield home owners from property tax overload situations through state financed circuit-breakers. More than half of the sales tax states now remove much of the regressive sting from the sales tax with food and drug exemptions or with income tax credits.

As a group, the states now have dramatically forged ahead of local governments on the revenue front. In 1964, the 50 states were collecting about one dollar for each dollar raised locally. Now the states are raising almost $15 for each $11 collected at the local level (Exhibit 6).

This striking state revenue advance is due in no small measure to the remarkable performance of the state personal income tax—the fastest growing revenue instrument in our intergovernmental revenue system; it is also making it increasingly difficult for state policy-makers to argue that the federal government has "preempted" the income tax field (Exhibit 7). For example, in 1953, the four person family earning $10,000 turned over to the "median" income tax state about 10 cents for each dollar paid to the federal income tax collector; in 1977, the $10,000 family of four turned over 33 cents for each one dollar paid to the IRS (Exhibit 8).

Two primary factors account for the fact that the state income tax turtle is slowly but steadily closing the long lead held by the federal individual income tax rabbit. The federal government has cut its effective rates repeatedly over the last two decades, in order to both spur the economy and offset the built-in tax increases due to inflation. In sharp contrast, the states have held their rates fairly

EXHIBIT 6

State Government Percentage of State and Local Tax Revenue,
By State, Selected Years, 1959-1977

State	1977	1975	1971	1967	1963	1959	Percentage point increase or decrease (−)[1] 1975 to 1977	1969 to 1975
United States	57.5	56.7	54.2	52.1	49.9	48.9	0.8	7.8
Alabama	75.0	74.1	74.0	71.0	69.2	69.4	0.9	4.7
Alaska	82.8	68.4	69.9	68.5	69.8	71.0	14.4	− 2.6
Arizona	61.1	64.1	61.1	57.3	55.7	56.3	− 3.0	7.8
Arkansas	75.8	76.1	72.6	72.5	68.8	70.2	− 0.3	5.9
California	52.8	52.0	46.5	43.8	45.7	46.8	0.8	5.2
Colorado	49.9	54.2	50.2	49.0	46.6	49.0	− 4.3	5.2
Connecticut	53.0	49.1	48.4	48.1	47.0	44.9	3.9	4.2
Delaware	81.0	79.9	79.7	78.8	79.8	80.1	1.1	− 0.2
Dist. of Columbia	−	−	−	−	−	−	−	−
Florida	61.7	64.1	60.1	53.2	52.8	56.3	− 2.4	7.8
Georgia	62.0	61.9	63.9	65.8	64.8	65.9	0.1	− 4.0
Hawaii	78.6	78.1	76.4	73.2	74.8	81.7	0.5	− 3.6
Idaho	67.1	68.8	64.0	62.5	53.1	50.3	− 1.7	18.5
Illinois	55.0	54.2	54.6	44.6	42.2	41.3	0.8	12.9
Indiana	62.2	60.2	49.7	50.0	44.0	48.6	2.0	11.6
Iowa	60.0	58.0	49.8	50.1	43.1	47.4	2.0	10.6
Kansas	57.3	56.7	49.2	49.6	43.2	44.0	0.6	12.7
Kentucky	75.0	76.1	73.2	68.5	68.4	61.8	− 1.1	14.3
Louisana	68.9	71.2	70.7	72.3	73.8	74.4	− 2.3	− 3.2
Maine	65.6	61.0	55.5	51.4	48.5	50.0	4.6	11.0
Maryland	57.6	58.0	56.8	53.6	56.0	55.7	− 0.4	2.3
Massachusetts	50.7	46.8	47.4	47.7	40.6	41.6	3.9	5.2
Michigan	60.4	55.8	57.5	55.2	54.4	51.5	4.6	4.3
Minnesota	69.0	68.3	56.8	51.6	47.2	45.7	0.7	22.6
Mississippi	76.9	76.2	73.7	66.6	65.6	68.5	0.7	7.7

[1] The state percentage increased in 29 states by an average of 2.4 percentage points between 1975 and 1977, and in 42 states by an average of 8.4 percentage points between 1959 and 1975.

[2] Fiscal year 1960. Not included in United States total since Hawaii did not become a state until August 1959.

Source: U.S. Bureau of the Census, *Governmental Finances*, various years.

EXHIBIT 6 (cont'd)

State Government Percentage of State and Local Tax Revenue, By State, Selected Years, 1959-1977

State	1977	1975	1971	1967	1963	1959	Percentage point increase or decrease (−)[1] 1975 to 1977	1969 to 1975
Missouri	54.7	52.3	49.9	51.3	48.7	47.4	2.4	4.9
Montana	53.6	50.8	54.3	44.1	43.7	42.1	2.8	8.7
Nebraska	50.7	47.6	45.1	34.9	34.0	37.2	3.1	10.4
Nevada	58.3	58.5	58.7	51.5	59.1	56.5	− 0.2	2.0
New Hampshire	38.1	40.1	41.4	37.5	36.5	38.1	− 2.0	2.0
New Jersey	45.5	39.6	41.2	37.7	29.5	28.4	5.9	11.2
New Mexico	80.4	82.7	78.9	74.5	72.9	74.2	− 2.3	8.5
New York	47.9	48.1	49.3	48.3	43.3	38.0	− 0.2	10.1
North Carolina	72.8	71.8	74.9	74.6	74.1	72.0	1.0	− 0.2
North Dakota	66.6	67.7	54.2	50.8	49.2	50.3	− 1.1	17.4
Ohio	52.1	52.9	45.1	44.4	44.7	46.2	− 0.8	6.7
Oklahoma	67.7	67.6	64.1	62.2	67.1	66.8	0.1	0.8
Oregon	51.6	54.6	49.4	51.4	50.2	48.9	− 3.0	5.7
Pennsylvania	61.6	62.9	58.6	54.3	53.2	50.3	− 1.3	12.6
Rhode Island	59.2	58.5	60.8	53.7	51.4	50.7	0.7	7.8
South Carolina	75.2	76.2	76.6	77.2	75.0	73.8	− 1.0	2.4
South Dakota	46.1	46.2	41.7	43.1	40.9	40.2	− 0.1	6.0
Tennessee	63.1	61.0	61.0	62.4	62.3	64.2	2.1	− 3.2
Texas	58.1	57.7	55.9	53.6	53.9	60.2	0.4	7.5
Utah	64.2	65.4	63.1	59.5	56.7	54.6	− 1.2	10.8
Vermont	58.7	56.8	62.2	61.3	55.0	49.6	1.9	7.2
Virginia	59.2	59.5	59.2	58.5	58.8	54.9	− 0.3	4.6
Washington	69.9	64.9	67.0	70.6	68.4	69.1	5.0	− 4.2
West Virginia	78.1	77.3	74.5	70.0	69.9	67.6	0.8	9.7
Wisconsin	67.5	64.6	59.4	62.0	51.3	48.5	2.9	16.1
Wyoming	58.1	59.2	56.7	47.9	52.3	52.7	− 1.1	6.5

[1] The state percentage increased in 29 states by an average of 2.4 percentage points between 1975 and 1977, and in 42 state by an average of 8.4 percentage points between 1959 and 1975.

[2] Fiscal year 1960. Not included in United States total since Hawaii did not became a state until August 1959.

Source: U.S. Bureau of the Census, *Governmental Finances*, various years.

EXHIBIT 7

State Personal Income Tax Receipts in Relation to Selected Federal, State, and Local Revenue Items
Fiscal Years 1953-1977

Fiscal Years	State Personal Income Tax Receipts ($000,000)	State Personal Income Tax Receipts as a Percent of—				
		Federal Personal Income Tax Receipts	State Tax Collections		Corporation Income Tax Receipts	Local Property Tax Receipts
			Total State Collection	General Sales and Gross Receipts		
1953	969[1]	3.2	9.2	39.8	119.6	10.8
1963	2,956	6.2	13.4	53.4	196.4	15.4
1968	6,231	9.1	17.1	59.7	247.5	23.2
1971	10,153	11.8	19.7	65.6	296.5	27.6
1974	17,078	14.4	23.0	75.5	283.9	36.8
1975	18,819	15.4	23.5	75.9	283.3	37.6
1976	21,448	16.3	24.0	78.5	294.9	39.1
1977 Prel.	25,453	16.2[2]	25.2	82.5	277.1	42.2
1978 Est.	29,500	16.6	25.9	84.3	281.0	45.7

[1] Includes corporation income taxes for three states—Alabama, Louisiana, and Missouri

[2] Decrease in percentage from previous year due to change in federal fiscal year.

Source: ACIR staff computations based on U.S. Census Bureau of the Census, Governments Division, various publications, and staff estimates.

EXHIBIT 8

State Personal Income Tax Effective Rates As A Percent of Federal Rates,
Selected Years 1953-1977[1]
[Married Couple With Two Dependents]

Calendar Year	Adjusted Gross Income Class			
	$5,000	$7,500	$10,000	$25,000
1953	5.3	7.4	9.8	12.3
1963	8.3	11.5	12.5	14.3
1968	9.6	15.0	16.3	20.0
1971	13.9	17.1	17.6	20.9
1974	not computed[2]	26.2	21.7	22.6
1977	not computed[2]	not computed[2]	33.3	21.6

[1]   Based on median state rates.
[2]   Negative or minimal federal tax.
Source: ACIR staff computations.

constant thereby permitting inflation and economic growth to push taxpayers into higher effective tax rate brackets—a silent and unlegislated tax rate increase (Exhibit 9).

In "good times", most states no longer have to rely on politically painful tax rate increases now that their revenue systems are much more responsive to economic growth, both real and inflationary. As indicated by the ACIR's latest survey, the net 1978 increase in state revenues came wholly from inflation and real economic growth (Exhibits 10 and 11).

The whole issue of the state surplus is slippery at best. The National Governors' Association does note that states began FY 1979 with a larger balance than they had in FY 1978, 9.2 billion dollars vs. 6.6 billion dollars. Half of this balance is attributable to three states, however—California, Alaska and Texas.

On the expenditure side, demographics are working for the states and their localities. The decline in student enrollment at the elementary, secondary and now even the university level is stabilizing—if not reducing—this important expenditure pressure. Between 1950 and 1970, the number of elementary and high school age children (5-17) increased 70%, while the estimated school age population for 1979 is 10% below 1970, with another 10% decline forecasted for the next decade. For the nation as a whole, the state and local outlays for local schools dropped from 5.3 percent of personal income in 1974 to 4.6 percent in 1978.

EXHIBIT 9

A Comparison of Federal and Median State Personal Income Tax Effective Rates
For Selected Adjusted Gross Income Levels,
Married Couple With Two Dependents, 1953-1977

Calendar Year and Level of Government		Adjusted Gross Income Class			
		$5,000	$7,500	$10,000	$25,000
		Effective Rates[1]			
1953	Federal	7.6%	10.8%	13.3%	20.4%
	State	0.4	0.8	1.3	2.5
1963	Federal	7.2	10.4	12.8	19.6
	State	0.6	1.2	1.6	2.8
1968	Federal	5.2	8.0	10.4	16.0
	State	0.5	1.2	1.7	3.2
1971	Federal	3.6	7.0	9.1	15.3
	State	0.5	1.2	1.6	3.2
1974	Federal[2]	*	4.2	6.9	13.3
	State	0.3	1.1	1.5	3.0
1977	Federal	−6.0	− 0.1	4.5	12.5
	State	−	0.8	1.5	2.7

* Less than .05 percent.
[1] "Effective Rates" are computed as the percentage that tax liability is of adjusted gross income.
[2] After rebates provided for by the "Tax Reduction Act of 1975."

Source: ACIR staff computations.

In sum, the improvement of state revenue system, coupled with a moderate decline in educational expenditure pressure, has greatly strengthened the fiscal position of the states. Pointing to this and to the fiscal deterioration at the federal level, some argue for termination of the federal General Revenue Sharing Program to the states.

LOCAL REVENUE IMPAIRMENT

The fiscal position of local government remains precarious. Vertical imbalance for local governments has its foundation in the fact that local governments are legal creatures of their respective states and thus are dependent upon them for the power to impose taxes. This situation has led to heavy local reliance on the property tax, the poorest administered and most unpopular source of revenue.

But even with unlimited power to tax, local governments are constrained by the limited nature of their jurisdiction, which makes

EXHIBIT 10

Sources of Increased State Tax Collections

1966-1978[1]

		Amount due to Economic Factors in billions				Proportion of Total Increase PRELIMINARY	Economic Factors		
Fiscal Year	Total Increase	Total Economic	Real Growth[2]	Inflation	Political Actions[3]	Total Economic	Real Growth	Inflation	Political Actions[3]
1966	$ 2.7	$ 1.8	$1.3	$ 0.5	$ 0.9	$ 67%	48%	19%	33%
1967	2.3	1.5	0.8	0.7	0.8	65	35	30	35
1968	4.1	1.7	0.8	0.9	2.4	41	20	21	59
1969	4.4	2.6	1.2	1.4	1.8	59	27	32	41
1970	4.9	2.2	0.2	2.0	2.7	45	4	41	55
1971	2.9	2.3	0.4	1.9	0.6	79	14	65	21
1972	5.7	3.4	1.6	1.8	2.3	60	28	32	40
1973	7.0	5.1	3.0	2.1	1.9	73	43	30	27
1974	5.0	5.2	1.0	4.2	− 0.2	104	20	84	− 4
1975	5.1	4.6	− 2.0	6.6	0.5	90	−39	139	10
1976	6.8	5.2	1.9	3.3	1.6	76	28	48	24
1977	10.2	8.7	3.9	4.8	1.5[4]	85	38	47	15
1978	10.5	10.5	4.3	6.2	0[5]	100	41	59	0
13 Year Total	71.6	54.8	18.4	36.4	16.8	77	26	51	23

[1] Taxes included are: general sales tax, individual income tax, corporate income tax and selective sales taxes.

[2] Total economic factors was allocated between inflation and real growth by calculating the proportion that the rate of change in constant GNP represents to the growth of amount of GNP and applying this proportion to the total economic component (as reported by state tax administrators).

[3] Political Action—Discretionary in character such as the adoption or repeal of a tax, the raising or lowering of a tax rate, the legislative expansion or contraction of a tax base, and changes in language enforcement.

[4] Includes Michigan Single Business Tax as a new adoption.

[5] Political actions reduced state tax collections by less than 50 million.

Source: ACIR Annual Survey of state Revenue Growth in cooperation with State Revenue Departments.

EXHIBIT 11

State Government
Revenue Growth, 1970-1978

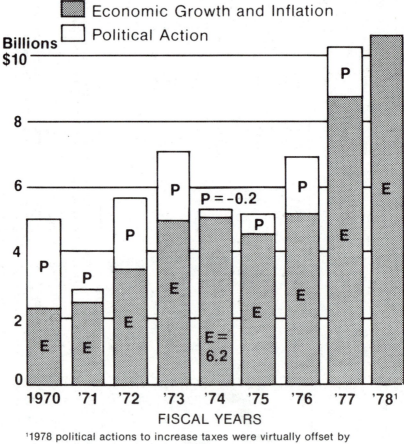

FISCAL YEARS

[1]1978 political actions to increase taxes were virtually offset by the political actions to decrease taxes.

Source: *ACIR staff compilations based on questionnaire returns.*

them more vulnerable than any other level of government to inter-local tax competition, the threat of people, capital and jobs moving to lower tax communities.

The local landscape continues to be characterized by jurisdictions of unequal tax capacity and varying needs (Exhibit 12). This is most evident in comparisons between many of the nation's central cities and surrounding suburbs (Exhibit 13). Most central cities in the Northeast and Midwest display signs of chronic fiscal distress, generated in part by the deep interjurisdictional disparities within their respective metropolitan areas.

If there is one development which has particularly worsened the position of local governments since the passage of General Revenue Sharing it is persistent high inflation, especially in the housing sector. Tolerable at best in ordinary times, the property tax is pushed toward its maximum irritant content in inflationary times, drastically driving up assessed values, especially of single family homes, imposing a stiff tax on an unrealized capital gain.

The easy solution to the problem of rising assessments—rolling back taxation rates—has not proved completely effective. Inflation has pushed residential property values up at a much faster clip than commercial and industrial property values. This, in turn, has brought about a shift in the local property tax burden from income producing property to the homeowners. This trend was one of the clear reasons for the success of Proposition 13 in California and has created a nation-wide atmosphere of active resistance to residential property tax increases in particular.

Inflation hits the spending side of local government, too, driving up program costs. As the most labor intensive of the governmental levels, local jurisdictions confront particularly strong pressures for greater outlays in periods of soaring inflation.

In sum, local governments still reflect the vertical and horizontal fiscal imbalances which General Revenue Sharing sought to moderate. Persistent high inflation has only added to their woes. The argument for continued financial support to units of local government remains strong.

SURGE IN FEDERAL AID

One final trend in fiscal federalism is worth highlighting. Federal aid to states and localities, which had increased greatly during the 1960s virtually exploded in the decade of the 1970s. Over the

INTERGOVERNMENTAL TRANSFERS

EXHIBIT 12

Local Disparities Challenge Indices

State	County Income Disparity[1]	School Equalization Needs[2]	Urban Equalization Needs[3]	Combined Challenge Index[4]
AVERAGE STATE[5]	100	100	98	99
Very Severe Urban Disparity:[3] [6]				
New Jersey	93	153	635	294
New York	103	148	467	239
Missouri	131	91	423	215
Massachusetts	66	328	375	256
Ohio	80	99	367	182
Illinois	80	123	311	171
Severe Urban Disparity:[3]				
Michigan	100	123	290	171
Maryland	116	189	273	193
Connecticut	81	169	268	173
Pennsylvania	94	60	245	133
Georgia	133	32	187	117
Florida	103	7	170	93
Wisconsin	100	46	154	100
Moderate Urban Disparity:[3]				
Minnesota	122	107	100	110
Oregon	92	43	99	78
Alabama	116	32	98	82
California	75	197	77	116
Rhode Island	45	66	76	62
Kentucky	137	109	65	104
Minor Urban Disparity:[3]				
Virginia	150	141	46	112
Indiana	71	37	44	51
Louisiana	98	16	41	52
Texas	127	91	31	83
Arizona	79	116	27	74

EXHIBIT 12 (cont'd)

State	County Income Disparity[1]	School Equalization Needs[2]	Urban Equalization Needs[3]	Combined Challenge Index[4]
No Urban Disparity:[7]				
Wyoming	108	287	–	198
Mississippi	121	191	–	156
Montana	151	183	–	167
Vermont	59	173	–	116
Colorado	111	148	–	130
Washington	80	148	4[a]	114
Arkansas	116	141	–	129
Tennessee[a]	121	136	6[a]	129
Delaware	90	127	–	109
New Hampshire	50	123	–	87
Kansas	127	94	–	111
Maine	64	93	–	79
South Carolina	82	92	–	87
Nebraska	88	79	–	84
North Carolina	100	76	–	88
South Dakota	108	67	–	88
Idaho	104	64	–	84
North Dakota	140	55	–	98
West Virginia	112	45	–	79
Oklahoma	139	43	–	91
Alaska[b]	165[b]	40	–	103
No Urban Disparity and few School Equalization Needs:[8]				
New Mexico[c]	118	25[c]	–	118
Iowa[c]	68	16[c]	7[a]	68
Utah[c]	96	11[c]	–	96
Nevada[c]	58	6[c]	–	58
Hawaii[d]	63	d	–	63

[1] The County Income Disparity Index is based on the coefficient of variations in county income for each state for 1974 weighted by county population size. This is an attempt to compare the interlocal distribution of financial resources as measured by income for each of the fifty states. Data were obtained from the Congressional Budget Office.

EXHIBIT 12(cont'd)

[2]   The School Equalization Needs Index was derived from data published by the Department of Health, Education and Welfare (Lawrence L. Brown III, et. al., *School Finance Reform in the Seventies*, Technical Analysis Paper, Sept. 30, 1977, pp. 62). Essentially the Index is the cost of achieving a 1.2 disparity ratio among the school districts and/or dependent school systems in each state in 1975 (p. 27) divided by total state personal income for 1975. The Index is constructed using the average state, not the national total or median.

[3]   The Urban Equalization Needs Index is a proxy for the amount of revenue base lost to large central cities (150,000 or more 1970) in 1973 as a result of the fragmenation of the metropolitan tax base. It is the total personal income difference re population between the central cities and their suburbs, i.e., the per capita difference multiplied by the suburban population divided by total state personal income for each state, 1973. The range is from .04 to 12.066 percent of state income for the 26 states having such disparities with a median (disparity state) of 1.9 percent. The median is 100 with an average state (total of the indices divided by 50) rating of 98.

[4]   The Combined Challenge Index is simply the total scores of the other three indices divided by three.

[5]   The average state is the unweighted average of the indices for the fifty states. It is very close to the median usually, but often quite different from national totals.

[6]   The states are ranked according to the city-suburban disparity index (see footnote 3):

    (1) very severe   300-700 (311-635)
    (2) severe   150-300 (154-290)
    (3) moderate   50-190 (65-100)
    (4) minor   25-50 (27-46)
    (5) nor urban disparity under 25 (0-7)

[7]   States without an urban disparity problem are ranked on the severity of school equalization needs and the urban disparity index is deleted from the combined challenge index.

[8]   States without urban dispaities and few school equalization needs are ranked according to county income disparities and this is used as the challenge index.

[a]   The amount involved in equalizing urban resources is so small that it can be discounted.

[b]   Much of Alaska is without county governments so the calculation is based on local areas rather than counties, 1969.

[c]   With an index of 25 or less the school equalizing needs are virtually non-existent.

[d]   Hawaii has a school system where all public education is state administered.

Source: ACIR staff compilation.

period 1972 to 1978, total federal aid to state and local government rose from 34.4 billion dollars to 77.9 billion dollars (Exhibit 14). Not only was General Revenue Sharing enacted, but broad-based grants in community development, employment and training, and economic stabilization came on stream.

The new federal grants had two characteristics which distinguished them from most earlier federal financial assistance—they were designed to send more money to jurisdictions in greater "need," particularly hard pressed cities, and further allowed states and localities more discretion than did the usual categorical federal aid. When General Revenue Sharing was enacted in 1972, flexible federal grant funds constituted about 10 percent of all federal aid. By 1978, these flexible funds represented 27 percent of all federal aid.

WHERE DO THESE CHANGED CIRCUMSTANCES LEAVE THE GENERAL REVENUE SHARING PROGRAM?

STATE GOVERNMENTS

An improved fiscal position produces three General Revenue Sharing scenarios for state governments.

1. *Terminate state participation in General Revenue Sharing.* The argument here is that there is no justification for a federal government in deficit to share revenue with state governments now that they are in a relatively robust fiscal condition.

2. *Status quo—keep the states in with no change in responsibility.* * There are several arguments for retention of the states in revenue sharing. First, from a fiscal standpoint, states and localities are inexorably tied together. Much of what Hawaii does at the state level, New Hampshire does at the local level, which accounts for the fact that state revenues finance about 80 percent of state-local expenditures in Hawaii and only 51 percent in New Hampshire.

The exclusion of the states from the General Revenue Sharing program would serve as one more sign that Washington has little interest in strengthening their pivotal role in the federal system. State aid to local governments has risen sharply over the past

---

* At its March 23, 1979 meeting, the Advisory Commission on Intergovernmental Relations recommended that the General Revenue Sharing program be renewed as is, including, then, both state and local governments. In light of persistent inflation, the Commission further recommended that program payouts be adjusted to maintain full purchasing power. Finally, the Commission suggested that further effort toward reform of the categorical grant system might produce desired savings.

EXHIBIT 13

Index of Central-City Hardship Relative to Balance of SMSA and
Selected Population Data for Fifty-five of the Sixty-six Largest SMSAs

Primary Central City of SMSA	Central City Hardship Index (A)	Number of County Areas in SMSA (B)	Total (000) (C)	SMSA Population 1970 Percent Central City (D)	Percent Central County (E)	Region (F)
Newark	422	3	1,857	20.6	50.1	NE
Cleveland	311	4	2,064	36.4	83.4	NC
Hartford	317		664	23.8	e	NE
Baltimore	256	6	2,071	43.7	43.7	NE
Chicago	245	6	6,975	48.2	78.7	NC
St. Louis	231	7	2,363	26.3	26.3	NC
Atlanta	226	5	1,390	35.8	43.7	S
Rochester	215	4	883	33.6	80.7	NE
Gary	213	2	633	27.7	86.2	NC
Dayton	211	4	850	28.6	71.3	NC
New York	211	5	11,572	68.2	68.2[d]	NE
Detroit	210	3	4,200	36.0	63.5	NC
Richmond	209	4	518	48.2	48.2	S
Philadelphia	205	8	4,818	40.4	40.4	NE
Boston	198		2,754	23.3	26.7	NE
Milwaukee	195	4	1,404	51.1	75.1	NC
Buffalo	189	2	1,349	34.2	82.5	NE
San Jose	181	1	1,065	41.9	100.0	W
Youngstown	180	2	536	26.1	56.6	NC
Columbus	173	3	916	58.9	90.9	NC
Miami	172	1	1,268	26.4	100.0	S
New Orleans	168	4	1,046	56.7	56.7	S
Louisville	165	3	827	43.7	84.1	S
Akron	152	2	679	40.5	81.5	NC
Kansas City, Mo.	152	6	1,254	40.5	52.2	NC
Springfield, Mass.	152		530	30.9	86.6	NE
Fort Worth	149	2	762	51.6	94.0	S
Cincinnati	148	7	1,385	32.7	66.7	NC
Pittsburgh	146.	4	2,401	21.7	66.8	NE
Denver	143	5	1,228	41.9	41.9	W
Sacramento	135	3	801	31.8	78.9	W
Minneapolis	131	5	1,814	24.0	52.9	NC
Birmingham	131	3	739	40.7	87.2	S

EXHIBIT 13 (cont'd)

Primary Central City of SMSA	Central City Hardship Index (A)	Number of County Areas in SMSA (B)	Total (000) (C)	SMSA Population 1970 Percent Central City (D)	Percent Central County (E)	Region (F)
Jersey City	129	1	609	42.8	100.0	NE
Oklahoma City	128	3	641	57.2	82.2	S
Indianapolis	124	8	1,110	67.1	71.8	NC
Providence	121		913	19.6	63.6	NE
Grand Rapids	119	2	539	36.6	76.2	NC
Toledo	116	3	693	55.4	69.6	NC
Tampa	107	2	1,013	27.4	48.4	S
Los Angeles	105	1	7,036	40.0	100.0	W
San Francisco	105	5	3,110	23.0	23.0	W
Syracuse	103	3	637	31.0	74.3	NE
Allentown	100	3	544	20.1	47.0	NE
Portland, Oreg.	100	4	1,009	37.8	55.2	W
Omaha	98	3	540	64.3	72.1	NC
Dallas	97	6	1,556	54.3	85.3	S
Houston	93	5	1,985	62.1	87.8	S
Phoenix	85	1	968	60.1	100.0	W
Norfolk	82	4	681	45.2	54.2	S
Salt Lake City	80	2	558	31.5	82.2	W
San Diego	77	1	1,358	51.3	100.0	W
Seattle	67	2	1,422	37.3	81.3	W
Ft. Lauderdale	64	1	620	22.5	100.0	S
Greensboro, N.C.	43	4	604	23.9	47.8	S

Source: Richard P. Nathan and Charles Adams, "Understanding Central City Hardship," *Political Science Quarterly*, Vol. 91, No. 1 (Spring 1976), pp. 47-62.

The hardship index expresses the city-suburban relationship for six measures available from the 1970 census: unemployment, dependency, education, income level, crowded housing and poverty.

EXHIBIT 14

Outlays for General-Purpose, Broad-Based, and Other Grants
(Dollar amounts in millions)

	1972	1975	Actual 1976	1977	1978
General-purpose grants:					
General revenue sharing	–	$ 6,130	$ 6,243	$ 6,758	$ 6,823
Other general purpose fiscal assistance and TVA[1]	516	878	907	2,748	2,780
Subtotal, general purpose grants	516	7,008	7,150	9,506	9,603
Broad-based grants:					
Community development block grants	–	38	983	2,089	2,464
Comprehensive health grants	90	82	128	65	88
Employment and training[2]	–	1,333	1,698	1,756	1,992
Social Services	1,930	2,047	2,251	2,534	2,809
Criminal justice assistance	281	577	519	580	346
School aid in federally affected areas	602	577	558	719	706
Local public works	–	–	–	577	3,057
Subtotal, broad based grants	2,903	4,654	6,137	8,359	11,462
Other grants	30,953	38,170	45,807	50,550	56,824
Total	34,372	49,832	59,094	68,415	77,889
ADDENDUM PERCENT OF TOTAL					
General purpose grants	1.5%	14.1%	12.1%	13.9%	12.3%
Broad based grants	8.4%	9.3%	10.4%	12.2%	14.7%
Other grants	90.1%	76.6%	77.5%	73.9%	73.0%
Total	100.0%	100.0%	100.0%	100.0%	100.0%

[1] For detail see grants in the general purpose fiscal assistance function Table H-11. Amounts in Table H-7 above include shared revenues from the Tennessee Valley Authority shown in the energy function.

[2] Comprehensive Employment and Training Act (CETA). Titles I and II A, B and C. An additional $6,934 billion of CETA grant-in-aid outlays are estimated for 1980, but there are some restrictions on client eligibility for these programs (e.g., income level and employment status) and therefore they are included in other and not broad-based aid.

Source: *Special Analyses Budget Of The United States Government, Fiscal Year 1980.*

decade—from $14 billion in 1965 to $61 billion by 1976. A move to disconnect the states from revenue sharing conceivably could result in a reduction in aid to local governments—the jurisdictions least able to bear the burden.

Some states—such as New York and Massachusetts—are under particularly strong fiscal pressure due to extraordinary tax, public welfare and urban burdens (Exhibits 15 and 16).

An examination of the perennial state surplus issue reveals less than meets the eye. The surplus, after excluding social insurance funds (which are not available for general program purposes), is not all that large. More importantly, the surplus is heavily concentrated in less than a handful of states—Texas, California and Alaska—and thus offers little consolation to New York and Massachusetts (Exhibit 17).

Further, what now looks like a rosy picture for the state government sector could change quickly: as their revenue systems have become more elastic, states have become more vulnerable to the clear and present danger of recessionary forces.

The expected slowdown in the federal aid flow to states will place more pressure on the expenditure side of the state fiscal equation; and the growing movement toward statutory and constitutional limits on state taxation and/or spending, along with expected pressure for indexation of state income taxes, will sap the fiscal strength of some states.

Finally, from a political perspective, a move toward excluding the states would shatter the state-local political coalition which was essential to the passage and original renewal of the program.

3. *Retain States with major "quid pro quo" conditions.* Given their fiscal gains, states might be asked to pay a price for continued General Revenue Sharing support. Two alternatives come to mind.

Keep states in provided they pick up other functions for local governments. Provisions for state assumption of a progressively larger share of the local school bill and/or state assumption of public welfare and medicaid costs might be offered as the price for receiving continued General Revenue Sharing funding. Alternatively, the federal government might make the states inclusion in revenue sharing contingent upon their picking up responsibility for some of the huge number of federal categorical aid programs currently channeled directly to local governments.

Keep states in with the requirement that they undertake or increase efforts to relieve interlocal fiscal disparity. Many local governments still face extraordinary tax burdens in relation to their fiscal capacities. As a condition for receiving revenue sharing funds,

EXHIBIT 15

Rating the States on the Basis of Their Tax, Welfare and Urban Burdens

State and Region	Tax Burden Index[1]	Welfare Burden Index[2]	Metro Disparities Burden Index[3]
New England			
Connecticut	94	103	268
Maine	111	167	0
***Massachusetts	125	328	375
New Hampshire	93	149	0
*Rhode Island	104	225	75
Vermont	182	182	0
Mideast			
Delaware	101	124	0
District of Columbia	—	—	—
**Maryland	105	117	273
**New Jersey	101	149	635
***New York	146	221	467
**Pennsylvania	100	184	245
Great Lakes			
**Illinois	101	142	311
Indiana	95	89	44
**Michigan	103	224	290
Ohio	86	134	357
***Wisconsin	119	180	154
Plains			
Iowa	99	125	7
Kansas	93	96	0
**Minnesota	121	166	100
Missouri	89	100	433
Nebraska	91	99	0
North Dakota	96	49	0
South Dakota	100	92	0
Southeast			
Alabama	84	72	92
Arkansas	82	63	0
Florida	86	59	170
Georgia	93	87	187
Kentucky	95	118	65
Louisiana	109	83	41
Mississippi	102	84	0
North Carolina	92	66	0
South Carolina	90	47	0
Tennessee	86	75	6
Virginia	91	99	46
West Virginia	103	68	0

EXHIBIT 15 (cont'd)

State and Region	Tax Burden Index[1]	Welfare Burden Index[2]	Metro Disparities Burdent Index[3]
Southwest			
Arizona	114	66	27
New Mexico	110	61	0
Oklahoma	85	89	0
Texas	87	51	31
Rocky Mountain			
Colorado	99	101	0
Idaho	94	65	0
Montana	105	61	0
Utah	97	65	0
Wyoming	108	59	0
Far West			
*California	124	257	77
Nevada	110	91	0
*Oregon	103	134	99
Washington	103	117	0[4]
Alaska	94	103	0
Hawaii	123	195	N.A.

***States that stand out on all three burden tests.
**States that score average or above on all three burden tests
 *States that score above average on the tax and welfare burden tests and have a metro disparity burden.
ACIR staff Compilation.

[1] State and local tax collections as a percent of resident personal income. States were indexed by the median state tax burden = 11.1 percent of state personal income in 1975.

[2] State-local welfare expenditures from own source funds as percent of state personal income. States were indexed by the median state welfare burden = 0.76 percent of state personal income in 1975.

[3] The Metropolitan Disparities Burden Index is the total income difference between the central city and its suburbs divided by statewide (total) personal income. This is only for states having central cities of 150,000 population or more, 1970. The range for such states is from .066 to 12.066 percent of state personal income with the median at 1.9 percent, 1973. Twenty-four states either have no such disparity or no central cities of 150,000 plus.

[4] Washington's disparity was only .04 percent, which was rounded to zero.

Sources: Measuring the Fiscal "Blood Pressure" of the States—1964-1975, ACIR Publication M-111, Table 1, and Appendix C.

Trends in Metropolitan America, ACIR Publication M-108, Table 1 and 10.

EXHIBIT 16

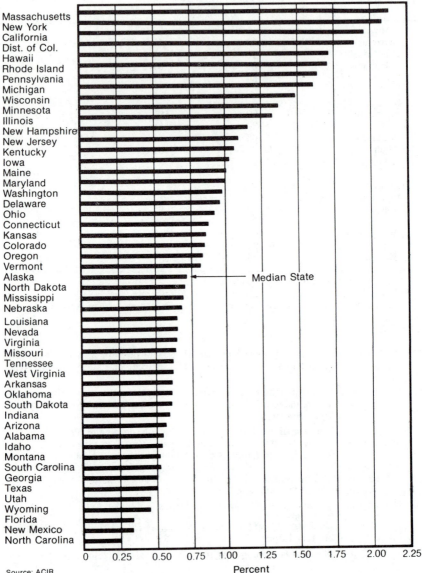

Source: ACIR

EXHIBIT 17

Projected State General Operating Fund Resources, Expenditures, and Balances,
Fiscal Year 1979
(dollars in millions)

State	1979 Projected Resources (including 1978 balance forward)	1979 Projected Expenditures	1979 Projected Balance[a]	1979 Projected Operating Balance as Percentage of 1979 Expenditures
Alabama	$ 1,495.5	$ 1,495.2	$ .3	0.02
Alaska	1,976.1	1,375.0	601.1	47.3
Arizona	1,053.6	1,023.6	30.0	2.9
Arkansas	772.5	772.3	0.0	0.0
California	18,357.7	17,578.4	779.3	4.4
Colorado	1,254.0	1,208.0	46.0	3.8
Connecticut	2,149.6	2,142.2	7.4	0.4
Delaware	556.7	539.7	17.0	3.2
Florida	3,050.7	3,021.4	29.3	1.0
Georgia	2,487.4	2,379.6	107.8	4.5
Hawaii	915.4	907.9	7.5	0.8
Idaho	319.0	319.0	0.0	0.0
Illinois	6,944.0	6,848.0	96.0	1.4
Indiana	1,913.6	1,789.9	123.7	6.9
Iowa	1,594.3	1,491.9	102.4	6.9
Kansas	1,100.1	988.2	111.9	11.3
Kentucky	1,734.2	1,715.9	18.3	1.1
Louisana	3,857.1	3,819.6	37.5	1.0
Maine	471.7	459.0	12.7	2.8
Maryland	2,500.2	2,298.0	202.2	8.8
Massachusetts	3,656.4	3,601.0	55.4	1.5
Michigan	4,260.7	4,256.4	4.3	0.1
Minnesota	3,174.0	3,142.0	32.0	1.0
Mississippi	944.7	892.2	52.5	5.9
Missouri	1,716.2	1,578.4	137.8	8.7
Montana	250.3	240.1	10.2	4.3
Nebraska	574.1	550.8	23.3	4.2
Nevada[b]	–	–	–	–
New Hampshire	235.0	219.0	16.0	7.3
New Jersey	4,421.6	4,394.4	27.2	0.6

EXHIBIT 17 (cont'd)

State	1979 Projected Resources (including 1978 balance forward)	1979 Projected Expenditures	1979 Projected Balance[a]	1979 Projected Operating Balance as Percentage of 1979 Expenditures
New Mexico	760.7	683.5	77.2	11.3
New York	12,041.2	12,022.9	18.3	0.2
North Carolina	2,578.0	2,577.9	0.1	0.004
North Dakota[b]	–	–	–	–
Ohio	4,895.9	4,719.7	176.2	3.8
Oklahoma	779.7	779.7	0.0	0.0
Oregon	1,287.9	1,035.8	252.1	24.3
Pennsylvania	5,786.0	5,786.0	0.0	0.0
Rhode Island	613.5	603.3	10.2	1.7
South Carolina	1,400.1	1,400.0	0.1	0.01
South Dakota	195.2	185.7	9.5	5.1
Tennessee	2,457.0	2,456.5	0.5	0.02
Texas	4,085.1	3,383.0	702.1	20.8
Utah	665.5	656.9	8.6	1.4
Vermont	207.4	207.4	0.0	0.0
Virginia	2,289.0	2,276.5	12.5	0.6
Washington	3,011.9	2,839.6	172.3	6.1
West Virginia	999.7	965.1	34.6	3.6
Wisconsin	4,960.8	4,866.7	94.1	1.9
Wyoming	217.0	182.0	35.0	19.2
TOTAL	$122,968.0	$118,675.5	$4,292.5	3.6

a	Balance does not equal resources minus expenditures in some states in view of statutory provisions to transfer part or all of the year-end balance to a separate fund for uses including debt service, capital outlay, tax refunds or rebates, and future-year expenditures.
b	The reports from these states were incomplete and therefore not included in this report.
Source:	National Governor's Association, *Fiscal Survey of the States, 1978-1979* (Jan. 1979), p. 10.

Congress might mandate efforts aimed at reducing these imbalances (Exhibit 12). This "trade-off," along with the previous one, becomes increasingly important because of the fiscal retrenchment at the federal level.

A third type of quid pro quo would not threaten state revenue sharing entitlements, but would use revenue sharing renewal as an opportunity for working out the respective responsibilities of the federal government and the states for helping the localities deal with problems of inflation, stagflation and recession. For example, if a

EXHIBIT 18

Distribution of General Revenue Sharing Relative to Social,
Economic, and Fiscal Need:
Dollars Per Capita

Category of Need	Number of Cities	General Revenue Sharing to City Government	General Revenue Sharing to City and Overlying County Government
Social Need			
All Cities	39	21.60	27.83
High	10	24.71	30.85
Medium	19	21.25 a	28.23
Low	10	19.18	24.06
Economic Need			
All Cities	45	21.10	27.51
High	10	25.75	30.53
Medium	25	21.10	28.69
Low	10	16.44	21.52
Fiscal Need			
All Cities	38	21.25	27.72
High	10	28.29	31.55
Medium	18	21.74	28.62
Low	10	14.33	22.27

Source: Congressional Budget Office, "City Need and the Responsiveness of Federal Grant Programs" (August 1978), p. 58.

state would agree to compensate its localities for "losses" due to inflationary erosion of their federal revenue sharing entitlements during "good times," the federal government would agree to provide this supplementary assistance during periods of stagflation. Another possibility—if a state would agree to supplement targeted federal aid to hard pressed central cities during "good times," the federal government would assume this supplementary burden during periods of stagflation or recession.

LOCAL GOVERNMENTS

Local governments, still victims of vertical and, in some cases, horizontal imbalance, nonetheless face two General Revenue Sharing scenarios.

The optimistic view. Local governments should emerge from the renewal debate unscathed. Enough vertical and horizontal imbalance remains in the system to justify continued unrestricted aid to the local sector. The General Revenue Sharing program correlates well with local need in general (Exhibits 18 and 19), and is the best equalizer in the current federal aid system (Exhibit 20).

The pessimistic view. Local governments may not be home free in the General Revenue Sharing renewal debate. One pessimistic forecast warns that if the states are cut off from the revenue sharing spigot, local governments are likely to see aid from state governments reduced. The more dramatic result of state expulsion, however, and perhaps even from imposition of strong conditions on the states, could be the destruction of the state-local coalition which was effective in enacting and initially renewing the program. A Congress with mixed feelings at best about the program might then find it much easier to scuttle revenue sharing entirely.

CONCLUSION

Over the past two decades, localities have increasingly bypassed the states in their lively pursuit of outside fiscal support. As a result, the Congress has assumed many of the responsibilities of state and local legislative bodies.

Any scenario for the future of local governments must, however, recognize two "new" realities:

(a) we are entering a period of definite federal regrouping on the domestic front—including a pronounced slowdown in the flow of federal aid funds to states and localities;

(b) states now dominate the fiscal as well as the legal heights of the state-local sector.

Given the weakening of the federal fiscal position and the hypothesis that governments closest to problems are most efficient at solving them, there is a strong need for a sorting out of responsibility for local governments between the states and the federal government, as well as a need for a revitalized state-local partnership. General Revenue Sharing may prove to be onew vehicle aimed at both these purposes.

EXHIBIT 19

Central City and Suburban Cities	Per Capita Entitlement	Per Capita Income
Los Angeles	$12.56	$3,951
Beverly Hills	4.33a	11,159
Cities other than Los Angeles	6.14	3,808
Chicago	19.89	3,402
Winnetka	3.68a	9,904
Cities other than Chicago	6.55	4,356
Detroit	27.79b	3,200
Grosse Point Farms	3.83a	9.011
Cities other than Detroit	16.24	3,858
Minneapolis	14.50	3,483
Edina	4.11a	6,511
Cities other than Minneapolis	4.39	4,137
Cleveland	18.13	2,281
Shaker Heights	2.97a	8,101
Cities other than Cleveland	6.49	4,366
Milwaukee	19.38	3,184
Fox Point	4.55a	7,632
Cities other than Milwaukee	6.47	4,070

a Larger than formula would have provided in the absence of the requirement that no local government receive less than 20% of the statewide average per capita local entitlement.

b Smaller than formula would have provided in the absence of the requirement that no local government receive more than 145% of the statewide average per capita local entitlement.

Source: ACIR staff computations.

EXHIBIT 20

Correlation Between Grants Distribution and
Social, Economic and Fiscal Need

Program	Social Need	Economic Need	Fiscal Need
General Revenue Sharing			
To city governments only	.378	.401	.769
To city and overlying governments	.528	.354	.516
Community Development Block Grant			
1977 actual distribution	.328	.361	.609
1974 formula only	.698	.222[a]	.586
New dual formula	.548	.786	.517
Antirecession Financial Assistance			
To city governments only	.714	.620	.656
To city and overlying governments	.731	.524	.481
Local Public Works	.546	.608	.546
Comprehensive Employment and Training			
Title I	.616	.428	.417
Title II	.509	.399	.028[a]
Title VI	.446	.372	.168[a]

Note: The summary measure used is a Pearson correlation coefficient; if a program receives a score of 1.000 it means that in every instance cities with higher need received a larger per capita grant than cities with lesser need. A perfect correlation also implies that the relationship is consistent and linear, that the size of a city's grant could be predicted precisely based on its need score. A low score indicates that the grant distribution bears little or no relation to differences among cities in the severity of their problems.

a   These correlation coefficients are insignificant at .05 level. It is possible in these instances that there is no relationship between grant size and level of city need.

Source: Congressional Budget Office, "City Need and the Responsiveness of Federal Grant Programs" (August 1978), p. 76.

NOTES

1. The County Income Disparity Index is based on the coefficient of variations in county income for each state for 1974 weighted by county population size. This is an attempt to compare the interlocal distribution of financial resources as measured by income for each of the fifty states. Data were obtained from the Congressional Budget Office.

2. The School Equalization Needs Index was derived from data published by the Department of Health, Education and Welfare (Lawrence L. Brown III, et. al., *School Finance Reform in the Seventies,* Technical Analysis Paper, Sept. 30, 1977, 62 pp.). Essentially the Index is the cost of achieving a 1.2 disparity ratio among the school districts and/or dependent school systems in each state in 1975 (p. 27) divided by total state personal income for 1975. The Index is constructed using the average state, not the national total or median.

3. The Urban Equalization Needs Index is a proxy for the amount of revenue base lost to large central cities (150,000 or more 1970) in 1973 as a result of the fragmentation of the metropolitan tax base. It is the total personal income difference repopulation between the central cities and their suburbs, i.e., the per capita difference multiplied by the suburban population divided by total state personal income for each state, 1973. The range is from .04 to 12.066 percent of state income from the 26 states having such disparities with a median (disparity state) of 1.9 percent. The median is 100 with an average state (total of the indices divided by 50) rating of 98.

4. The Combined Challenge Index is simply the total scores of the other three indices divided by three.

5. The average state is the unweighted average of the indices for the fifty states. It is very close to the median usually, but often quite different from national totals.

6. The states are ranked according to the city-suburban disparity index (see footnote 3):

(1) very severe   300-700 (311-635)
(2) severe   150-300 (154-290)
(3) moderate   50-190 (65-100)
(4) minor   25- 50 (27- 46)
(5) no urban disparity under 25   (0-7)

7 States without an urban disparity problem are ranked on the severity of school equalization needs and the urban disparity index is deleted from the combined challenge index.

8. States without urban disparities and few school equalization needs are ranked according to county income disparities and this is used as the challenge index.

a. The amount involved in equalizing urban resources is so small that it can be discounted.

b. Much of Alaska is without county governments so the calculation is based on local areas rather than counties, 1969.

c. With an index of 25 or less the school equalizing needs are virtually non-existent.

d. Hawaii has a school system where all public education is state administered.

Thomas J. Anton, Jerry P. Cawley, Kevin L. Kramer - FEDERAL SPENDING IN STATES AND REGIONS: PATTERNS OF STABILITY AND CHANGE

INTRODUCTION

Few issues of domestic political concern have generated as much sustained interest in the past half decade as the distribution of federal government expenditures among state and local jurisdictions. The causes of increased interest seem obvious enough. Barely a trickle in the 1950s, and only $7 billion in 1960, federal grants have now reached a level at which they clearly dominate state-local revenue systems, surpassing property, sales and income taxes in significance. Moreover, as Exhibit 1 makes clear, grant expenditures have increased far more rapidly than either GNP or total federal budget outlays.

Extraordinarily rapid growth in federal grants has raised the stakes of participation in the federal grant system and led officials from states, counties and cities to invest more and more effort in generating revenue from the federal treasury. That effort, in turn,

EXHIBIT 1

Growth In Federal Grants-In-Aid and Non-Defense Domestic Outlays
Compared To GNP and Budget Outlays, FY 1960-1978
(In Billions of Dollars)

Fiscal Year	GNP	Budget Outlays		Grants-in-Aid	Grants As % of Budget Outlays	
		Total	Non-Defense		Total Outlays	Domestic Outlays
1960	497.3	92.2	47.1	7.0	7.6	14.9
1965	657.1	118.4	71.0	10.9	9.2	15.4
1970	959.0	196.6	118.0	24.0	12.2	20.3
1975	1457.3	334.2	248.7	49.8	14.9	20.0
1978	2060.4	461.2	356.0	77.9	16.9	21.9
Increase 1960-78	314%	400%	656%	1013%		

Sources: Office of Management and Budget, Budget Review Division, Fiscal Analysis Branch, "Federal Government Finances, January 1980 Edition" (Washington, D.C.: Office of Management and Budget, 1980), and "Federal Grants-In-Aid to State and Local Governments, January 1980 Edition" (Washington, D.C.: Office of Management and Budget, 1980). GNP figures are for fiscal year period. Budget figures are for total budget outlays.

has focused political attention on the criteria for federal fund distribution, particularly since a number of well-publicized reports have argued that federal monies are being delivered to the wrong places, for the wrong reasons. Officials from northern states, many of which are experiencing economic decline, repeatedly complain that their tax dollars are being used to funnel disproportionate amounts of federal funds into southern and western states, many of which are experiencing economic and population growth.[1] A growing "regional" consciousness seems on the verge of replacing more traditional (i.e., partisan) bases of political division in national politics, leading some observers to anticipate a "new war between the states."[2]

Our purpose in this discussion is to lay a foundation for evaluating both the quality and the significance of these arguments. We use the phrase "lay a foundation for" quite deliberately, since answers to the question "who gets what" turn out to be quite difficult to answer in an unambiguous way. Federal data sources provide no definitive information, hence assertions about where federal funds go are heavily influenced by what data are used, how the data are combined, and how they are analyzed. Following a brief review of the more obvious problems in commonly-used federal data systems, we show the advantages of using an alternative data system, based on federal outlays reports, to structure images of federal fund distribution. As will be seen, use of outlays data leads to rather different but more plausible conclusions than any now available. Those conclusions, in turn, provide a foundation for consideration of the political and analytic significance of "region" in explaining federal spending patterns.

FEDERAL DATA AMBIGUITY

Analysts typically assume that authoritative data on federal aid to states are available either from official Census publications, from the Treasury Department publication, *Federal Aid to States,* or from OMB's "Federal Aid to State and Local Governments," published annually as a special analysis appended to the federal budget.[3] These publications do not report all federal spending in states, focusing only on grants-in-aid to state and local governments, but they do purport to report the same flow of funds. Yet, when numbers from these souces are arrayed for comparison, rather large differences appear. Federal grants to states as reported by Treasury for the period 1970 through 1977 differ from Census reports by as much as $3.96 billion (1972), and average nearly $3 billion annually for that 8-year

EXHIBIT 2

Comparison of Grants-In-Aid Totals for the 50 States and D.C.
Reported by Treasury and Census FY 1970-77
(Millions of Dollars)

| Fiscal Year | Grants-In-Aid Total Reported By | | Difference |
	Treasury	Census	
1977	66,084	62,610	3,474
1976	57,719	55,587	2,131
1975	48,570	46,994	1,576
1974	45,092	41,831	3,261
1973	43,057	39,256	3,801
1972	35,217	31,253	3,964
1971	29,272	26,146	3,126
1970	23,717	21,858	1,859

Sources: Data calculated from The Department of the Treasury, *Federal Aid to States*
(Washington, D.C.: U.S. Government Printing Office, 1971-1979); and Bureau of
the Census, Department of Commerce, *Government Finances* (Washington, D.C.:
U.S. Government Printing Office, 1971-1978).

period alone (Exhibit 2). Worse, these total differences are derived
from individual state differences of impressive magnitude. For fiscal
1977, Treasury reports $7.45 billion in federal grants to New York;
Census reports $6.52 billion. For fiscal 1976, Treasury reports
$5.80 billion to California; Census reports $6.23 billion. For fiscal
1974, Treasury reports $2.13 billion to Texas; Census reports $1.90
billion, and so on. Although small from the perspective of national
totals, differences that can exceed $1 billion for a single state in a
single year (New York, 1972) clearly raise questions about how to
interpret such data.

Questions of interpretations become even more pointed when we
consider OMB figures (Exhibit 3). Annual OMB analyses provide
national totals for programs and functions, without disaggregating
these total figures into state or lower-level figures. Disaggreation by
state is done by Treasury, whose officials work closely with OMB
staff to produce a *Federal Aid to States* document that is specifically
designed to provide the financial detail absent from OMB totals.[4]
Despite these high levels of cooperation and coordination, OMB
national totals consistently differ from Treasury totals, by as much
as $2.686 billion in FY 1974. Differences between these figures and
Census data, of course, are equally different.[5]

Some of the differences between OMB and other numbers are
almost certainly due to differences in accounting procedures. OMB

EXHIBIT 3

Comparison of National Totals for Grants-In-Aid to State and Local Governments
Reported by OMB and Treasury FY 1970-78
(Millions of Dollars)

| Fiscal Year | Grants-In-Aid Totals Reported By | | Difference |
	OMB	Treasury	
1978	77,889	77,901	12
1977	68,415	68,437	22
T.Q.	15,909	16,444	535
1976	59,094	59,112	18
1975	48,832	49,723	891
1974	43,354	46,040	2,686
1973	41,832	43,964	2,132
1972	34,372	35,941	1,569
1971	28,109	29,845	1,736
1970	24,018	24,194	176

Sources: "Federal Aid to States and Local Governments," in Office of Management and Budget, *Special Analyses, Budget of the United States Government* (Washington, D.C.: U.S. Government Printing Office, 1978, 1979), Historical Trend of Federal Grant-In-Aid Outlay tables from 1980 budget report and 1979 budget report from T.Q. data; and The Department of the Treasury, *Federal Aid to States,* (Washington, D.C.: U.S. Government Printing Office, 1971-1979).

figures are based on reports of "expenditures" submitted by agency budget officers while Treasury figures are based on reports submitted by agency accounting division officers. Census figures are derived from OMB, Treasury, federal agency and state and local sources. All three "authoritative" sources, however, utilize a definition of "grants," consistent with OMB Circular A-11. Differences amounting to billions of dollars in national totals and hundreds of millions in state-by-state totals are thus both difficult to understand and hazardous to interpret, particularly since there is no consistency in the *magnitude* of year-to-year reporting discrepancies. All three sources show vast increases in federal aid to states, but beyond that, it is extraordinarily difficult to know how to draw reliable conclusions from these data.[6]

DEVELOPING AN ALTERNATIVE DATA SYSTEM

Sorting out the causes of these data discrepancies may be possible, but it has not yet been attempted. For the moment, therefore, we believe it preferable to rely on a fourth data source, known earlier as "Federal Outlays" and now published annually by the Community Services Administration as *Geographic Distribution of Federal Funds*.[7] The outlays data series is driven by OMB Circular A-84, effective 1967, which requires all executive departments and establishments to submit annual reports of obligations incurred from federal funds in state and local areas.[8] Agency reports are summarized and published annually by CSA in 53 volumes: one for each state, one for the territories, and one reporting national totals. Outlays data have several important advantages over other federal data systems. First, outlays reports are *comprehensive,* including payments to individuals, salaries, loans and loan guarantees and procurements as well as grants. This creates the possibility of estimating the total impact of the federal government in a given area, no less than the impact of one kind of obligation, such as grants-in-aid. Second, outlays data have more *depth* than other data systems, which disaggregate only to the state level. Outlays are reported for all states, but they are also reported for all counties, and all cities of 25,000 or more population, creating major opportunities for substate analyses of various kinds.[9] Third, outlays reports have been published since 1968, opening up possibilities for observing changes in federal spending patterns.

These advantages are real enough but, like other federal data sources, outlays data are afflicted with several problems that dictate caution in their use. Because improvements in reporting procedures have been made more or less annually, there are difficulties in comparability from one year to the next and data quality seems significantly "harder" in the period since 1974. Outlays data also credit state and local jurisdictions with some funds that are never used *in* those jurisdictions. Outlays for foreign assistance payments or State Department foreign operations, for example, are credited to states such as New York because funds are channeled through banks located there. Or, outlays reports credit jurisdictions with receipts that are known to be expended elsewhere, in whole or in part. Defense Department procurements, for example, are obtained from prime contractors who are known to issue sub-contracts to suppliers often located elsewhere. Yet outlays are reported only to the location of the prime contractor. Similarly, interest payments on the national debt are credited primarily (52 percent in 1977) to New York, although an important fraction of these obligations are distributed across the country by large New York financial institutions. Or, some agencies simply do not report certain program expenditures to CSA (e.g., selected UMTA programs). Clearly, outlays data require adjustment if they are to be used with confidence.

Solutions to many of these problems are being developed, but are not yet available. In this preliminary discussion, therefore, we have simply adjusted the outlays data to permit analyses that avoid the more perverse consequences of using unadjusted figures. Defense Department procurements, interest payments on the national debt, and other "non-influence" outlays (primarily foreign payments) are all reported separately. Because these obligations are either known to be inaccurate or known to be expended abroad, they are excluded from the calculation of "net domestic outlays," made up of all other federal obligations.[10] For state-regional analysis, we also have excluded the District of Columbia which, because of its heavy concentration of government employees and federal spending, causes outlays totals for the South Atlantic (division) or the South (region) to be artificially inflated.[11] Net Domestic Outlays are now available in total and per capita form for 1975, 1977 and 1978. In this analysis, however, we rely primarily on 1975 and 1978 calculations.

Use of this new "net domestic outlay" data will permit a more plausible state-level analysis than any yet attempted. We propose to move beyond that, however, to three more specific levels of analysis. First, because there has been so much interest in the form in which federal money is distributed, we discuss distributions of formula grants, project grants, direct payments, and other types of federal spending. Second, because federal agencies are crucial political and administrative actors in fund distributions, we analyze spending obligations incurred by the largest 15 agencies in states and regions. Finally, because the politics of federal expenditure is largely a politics of programs, we review several important aspects of program outlays. This review leads to a reexamination of the significance of "region" and a consideration of appropriate conceptual tools for explaining the changing patterns of federal outlays.

PATTERNS OF SPENDING

Total federal outlays grew from $346.5 billion in fiscal 1975 to $502.7 billion in fiscal 1978.[12] When Defense procurements, interest and foreign outlays are removed, these totals are reduced to $280 billion and $416 billion, respectively. These are very substantial reductions from the data base, amounting to more than $395 per person in 1978. As might be expected, removing these sums from total outlay figures has a noticeably different impact on regional totals. The strongest impact is experienced in the East where significant interest and foreign assistance payments are channeled through large banks in New York, New Jersey and Connecticut (Exhibit 4).

EXHIBIT 4

Differences Between Total and Net Domestic Per Capita Outlays,
By Region: 1975, 1978

Region	1975	1978
Northeast	$550.18	$582.70
North Central	175.24	278.78
South	204.44	333.27
West	369.18	526.98

Removing these data from the total removes a substantial portion of reported spending in the Northeast. But the West region, too, loses large sums due to the unusual significance of defense procurements in that region. Per capita defense procurements to the West region in 1975, 1977 and 1978 are the highest of any region. The North Central region, which appears to receive relatively little in either defense or interest outlays, shows the smallest impact from removal of these data. The South also shows a somewhat less impressive reduction than might have been expected, in view of repeated claims that defense spending is unusually concentrated in the South. Excluding these reported outlays from the calculation of a "Net Domestic" total obviously reduces the significance of these data somewhat, but in return we are able to provide a far more accurate estimate of where the bulk of federal outlays go. Let us begin by observing the structure of federal outlays.

Given the rapid recent increases in federal grant outlays and the frequently-asserted proliferation of different types of grant programs, it is easy enough to believe that some fundamental change in the structure of intergovernmental fiscal realtionships has taken, or is taking, place. At first glance, however, these data appear to contradict the "fundamental change" hypothesis. Whether measured in total dollars received or per capita dollars received, there are very powerful correlations between state outlays in 1975 and state-level outlays in 1978: $r = .9987$ for total dollars and $r = .9068$ for per capita dollars, using the adjusted "net domestic" data base. Both scatter plots and rank order correlations (Tau-B $= .76$) make clear, futhermore, that relative state position is also fairly stable from 1975 to 1978. Exhibit 5 displays one aspect of this stability by showing state "winners and losers" in per capita rank order. Among the top fifteen "winners" in 1978, only Nebraska and Georgia were not included at the top in 1975. Among the bottom fifteen "losers" in 1978, only Delaware, Indiana, and Connecticut are not (quite) as badly off in 1975. There are some dramatic changes in ranks across years, to be sure: Nebraska jumps from 27 to 11, or West Virginia drops from 22 to 41. Most of the moves are moderate, however, reflecting a basic stability in these fiscal interactions during the 1975-78 period.

Stability also characterizes the distribution of outlays by Census Division or region. Exhibit 6 compares per capita outlays by division and region with the national per capita amount for both years. At the regional level rank orders are the same for both years, with the West and South not only above the national mean, but moving further away from it. Similarly the North Central and Northeast regions are not only below the national mean in both years, but also moving further below the mean from 1975 to 1978. Divisional rankings are not precisely the same in both years. The Mountain and South Atlantic Divisions increase their lead over other areas through time, while the East North Central, New England, West South Central, and Middle Atlantic Divisions continue to lag behind the national average, by increasing per capita amounts. The only striking shift is the West North Central Division, which moves from a position below the national mean in 1975 to a position far above the mean in 1978. These data, with defense procurements *excluded,* thus confirm the widely discussed conclusion that western states, and to a lesser extent southern states, continue to maintain a commanding lead over other areas in receipt of federal disbursements.[13]

Although these numbers appear to suggest an impressive system stability and, within stability, a continuing domination of western and southern states, we are not inclined to attach a great deal of significance to them. For one thing, regional and divisional aggregations are both arbitrary and highly artificial, masking the considerable state-by-state variation that exists *within* regions or divisions. Demographically, Vermont has more in common with Wyoming than with Massachusetts or Rhode Island, with whom Vermont shares a common regional and divisional assignment. Connecticut and New Jersey, alike in so many ways, nevertheless are assigned to different divisions. Within the same region (west) differences in per capita income by state can exceed $2,200, and differences in per capita outlays can exceed $2,200. Disparities of this magnitude are masked when data are aggregated by region or division, confounding efforts to find regionally based "patterns" in, for example, relationships between personal income and outlays.

EXHIBIT 5

"Winners and Losers"
The Distribution of Federal Expenditures in FY 1975 and 1978

State	Per Capita Outlays		Differences of State Per-Capita Outlays From National Per-Capita Total		Ranking	
	1975	1978	1975	1978	1975	1978
TOP FIFTEEN STATES						
ALASKA	3405	4107	2085	2194	1	1
NORTH DAKOTA	1638	3285	318	1372	9	2
NEVADA	1700	2852	380	939	6	3
NEW MEXICO	1968	2817	648	904	3	4
SOUTH DAKOTA	1620	2714	300	801	10	5
HAWAII	2016	2664	696	751	2	6
MONTANA	1603	2552	283	639	11	7
COLORADO	1749	2480	429	566	5	8
WYOMING	1662	2446	342	532	7	9
IDAHO	1545	2435	225	521	14	10
NEBRASKA	1307	2394	-13	480	27	11
MARYLAND	1785	2392	465	478	4	12
VIRGINIA	1654	2344	334	431	8	13
ARIZONA	1555	2340	235	427	13	14
GEORGIA	1473	2313	153	400	16	15

EXHIBIT 5 (Continued)

State	Per Capita Outlays		Differences of State Per-Capita Outlays From National Per-Capita Total		Ranking	
	1975	1978	1975	1978	1975	1978
	BOTTOM FIFTEEN STATES					
DELAWARE	1229	1769	−91	−145	38	36
TEXAS	1250	1757	−70	−156	35	37
ILLINOIS	1241	1756	−79	−158	36	38
NEW HAMPSHIRE	1255	1712	−65	−201	32	39
VERMONT	1203	1681	−117	−232	39	40
WEST VIRGINIA	1344	1663	24	−251	22	41
LOUISIANA	1150	1643	−170	−271	41	42
NORTH CAROLINA	1136	1609	−184	−304	43	43
PENNSYLVANIA	1142	1589	−178	−325	42	44
NEW JERSEY	1072	1535	−248	−378	44	45
INDIANA	945	1472	−375	−441	50	46
WISCONSIN	1007	1425	−313	−488	46	47
CONNECTICUT	961	1424	−359	−490	49	48
OHIO	962	1403	−358	−358	48	49
MICHIGAN	976	1365	−344	−549	47	50

EXHIBIT 6

Dollar Difference From National Per Capita Domestic Outlays,
By Census Divisions and Regions
1975 and 1978

Region/Division	1975 Per Capita	Rank	1978 Per Capita	Rank
New England	−164.86	8	−227.14	8
Middle Atlantic	−137.22	7	−206.89	7
East North Central	−275.83	9	−411.26	9
West North Central	− 57.91	5	127.54	4
South Atlantic	369.36	1	507.18	2
East South Central	22.42	4	66.70	5
West South Central	− 58.63	6	−129.87	6
Mountain	341.73	2	559.56	1
Pacific	169.87	3	136.80	3
Northeast	−144.03	3	−211.95	3
North Central	−212.73	4	−253.72	4
South	167.06	2	218.68	2
West	213.56	1	245.70	1
Total U.S.	1,320.02		1,913.42	

More fundamentally, it is not at all clear that dividing total outlays by total state population produces a very meaningful number. Per capita calculations are obviously convenient to use and they do provide an easily understood estimate of federal spending activities across state boundaries. The practical and theoretical significance of such rough estimates, however, is not easily discerned. In fiscal 1978, for example, South Carolina ($1,853.26) and Missouri ($1,862.4) both recorded per capita outlay amounts within about $10 of the New York per capita outlay of $1,855.53. The New York per capita figure was based on total outlays of some $32.9 billion, while total outlays in South Carolina were $9 billion, and Missouri outlays reached $5.4 billion. One might use these numbers to argue that South Carolina received "less" and Missouri "more" than New York in per capita terms. Although technically accurate, the assertion would also be misleading, given the outlays actually distributed. Unless more information was available regarding the kinds of outlays made in each state, it would be impossible to know what other conclusions to draw. Payments to individuals are known to have very different impacts from payments to governments, for example, just as capital (or "hard") outlays are known to have different impacts from outlays for government administration, or social services activities. Statements about more or less, in short, are necessarily ambiguous when based on calculations of per capita totals.

The problem of course, is that per capita calculations have no clear relationship to either allocation processes or programmatic purposes for which federal outlays are made. Although state population is commonly used in the design of federal outlays programs, very few programs rely on total population alone. Instead, programs are typically designated for some portion of the total state population: the number or proportion of persons over 65, or under 18, or below a designated income level, or some combination of these proportions with other data elements. Federal outlays, moreover, are not made "as a whole," but through the separate and largely uncoordinated actions of program managers, within agencies, that are related to other agencies in departments, which typically expect and receive annual increments in authorized spending levels, through a complex but highly routinized budget process. Total per capita calculations do not reflect allocation processes or political purposes because they cannot. Before accepting images of stability or change based on such calculations, therefore, it is clearly essential to observe outlay patterns in finer detail.

TYPES OF FEDERAL OUTLAYS

Outlays data permit the analysis of eleven different types of federal obligation. Although distinctions between these types are not always as clear as they might be, the "type" designations come much closer to conceptions of purpose and process than overall per capita figures, and thus offer a useful opportunity for more detailed examination. For this report we have selected five of the most important types and collapsed the remainder into a single category as follows:

1. FORMULA GRANTS.

This category includes all grant funds distributed according to some specific formula. As noted earlier, formula elements often include population, the proportion of a jurisdiction's population

that falls within some specified class, physical or economic characteristics of the jurisdiction, or combinations of various formula
elements. Distribution of formula grant funds is relatively automatic,
once the formula algorithm has been determined. Understandably,
then, recent dramatic increases in dollars allocated for such grants
have been accompanied by considerable conflict over the terms to be
included in various formulas. Dramatic as these increases have been,
formula grants *as a proportion* of net domestic outlays declined from
17.5 percent in 1975 to 15.2 percent in fiscal 1978.[14]

2. PROJECT GRANTS.

Project grants are made available for specified purposes or projects,
defined by legislation and interpreted by federal regulations. Since
nationally defined purposes are the criteria for awarding such grants,
state and local jurisdictions typically are required to submit applications for evaluation by federal program managers. Jurisdictions
selected as recipients of project grants typically are required to submit a variety of interim and final reports to the granting agency,
showing what was accomplished with federal funds and how those
accomplishments contribute to the achievement of national purpose.
Compared to formula grants, project grants assign considerably more
discretion to federal program managers in deciding which units
should receive grant funds. The distribution of project grant funds
thus can be taken to reflect both national political priorities and the
discretionary judgment of national administrators as well as local
"grantsmanship." Project grants increased from 5.3 percent of net
domestic outlays in 1975 to 6.2 percent in 1978.[15]

3. DIRECT PAYMENTS.

Although somewhat ambiguous in concept, this category includes
payments that are primarily made to individuals or nongovernmental
organizations. Various social security, welfare and unemployment
insurance programs are included here, as is Medicare, which transfers
federal funds to vendors of medical services. Medicaid, however, is
not included as a direct payment, since federal funds are distributed
to state governments for distribution to suppliers of medical services
to needy populations. (Medicaid is treated as a formula grant.) Not
surprisingly, direct payments represent the bulk of domestic outlays,
rising from 33.6 percent in 1975 to 38 percent in 1978.[16]

4. DIRECT LOANS.

Various programs loan federal funds directly to individuals or organizations for purposes such as the creation of business enterprises, support of agricultural activities, or disaster relief. While not large relative to total federal obligations, direct loan outlays increased by just over 475 percent between 1975 and 1978, from $1.67 to $9.66 billion. As a proportion of total domestic outlays, direct loans increased from .6 percent in 1975 to 2.3 percent in 1978. Increases of this magnitude in a single type of federal obligation clearly seem both interesting and potentially significant.

5. GUARANTEED LOANS.

For nearly a half century the federal government has guaranteed banks and other financial institutions against losses on loans made to individuals for a variety of purposes. Agencies such as HUD, VA or the Department of Agriculture administer large mortgage programs to encourage home purchase, Commerce and Agriculture Department programs offer loan guarantees for business or agricultural enterprise, and HEW guarantees loans for purposes such as financing the costs of higher education. These programs, too, have increased dramatically, nearly doubling between 1975 and 1978. Guaranteed loans represented some 11.1 percent of total outlays in 1978, up from 8.3 percent in 1975.[17]

6. OTHER DOMESTIC OUTLAYS.

This category, which groups together the remaining classes of federal outlays, is dominated by salaries and expenses paid to federal employees. Other obligations, such as non-defense procurements or commodity distribution, are less significant in total dollars but included in order to provide a comprehensive report of remaining types of federal financial activity. Outlays included in this category fell from 24.2 percent of total outlays in 1975 to 17.6 percent in 1978.

A more comprehensive view of the forms in which federal obligations are incurred permits a more accurate assessment of what is, and what is not, changing. Exhibit 7, which displays per capita allocations for the various types of assistance in 1975 and 1978, makes clear that, while total outlays are increasing over all, some

EXHIBIT 7

Per Capita Types of Federal Outlay,
1975 and 1978

Year	Formula Grants	Project Grants	Direct Payments	Direct Loans	Guaranteed Loans	Other
1975	230.74	69.50	443.34	7.87	109.99	458.59
1978	290.40	118.79	728.37	44.42	212.87	518.57
% Change	+25.86	+70.93	+64.29	+464.67	+93.53	+13.08

types of outlay have far greater rates of increase than others. The quite dramatic increase in direct loans (+465%), coupled with the very substantial increment in guaranteed loans (+94%), seems interesting because neither type of assistance represents an "expenditure" but rather a commitment that, if made, will ultimately be recovered by the federal treasury. Should this pattern persist, it would suggest a change in federal outlay policy of some significance. Formula grants, said by many to represent the cornerstone of a shift to a "new federalism," are increasing far less rapidly (+26%) than many have supposed and in fact constituted a smaller fraction of total outlays in 1978 than they did in 1975. Project grants, whose reduction was a major goal of advocates of the "new federalism," actually increased in significance in 1978 (+71%) totaling $25.8 billion, $11 billion higher than the 1975 spending level. Far and away the largest dollar increases, if not percentage increase, have occurred in direct payments, spurred on by medical, welfare and social security increases. Rankings of states by total federal receipts may not have changed very much, but these figures suggest that *what* the states are receiving may indeed have changed.

When these outlay types are broken down by region, interesting patterns emerge. In Exhibit 8 we show these patterns by comparing differences between national and regional per capita types of outlay. The West, we can now see, achieves its relatively favored position by exceeding the national per capita allocation in formula grants and guaranteed loans. The South achieves its advantage primarily through project grants and guaranteed loans. Although considerably below the national mean in net outlays, the Northeast is further above the mean than any other region in formula grants, project grants and direct payments. Apart from the very dramatic shift in the direct

EXHIBIT 8

Dollar Differences from National Per Capita, By Type of Assistance
Expenditures by Divisions and Regions, FY 1975 and 1978

AREA	Net Domestic Total FY 75	FY 78	Formula Grants FY 75	FY 78	Project Grants FY 75	FY 78	Direct Payments FY 75	FY 78	Direct Loans FY 75	FY 78	Guaranteed Loans FY 75	FY 78	Other Types of Assistance Fy 75	FY 78
REGION														
N.E.	-144.03	-211.95	10.96	43.58	10.98	15.41	17.86	66.15	-4.37	-31.51	-54.48	-110.49	-124.99	-195.08
N.CT.	-212.73	-253.72	-27.17	-38.16	-9.75	-11.81	-20.15	-28.05	-2.60	32.78	-12.87	18.11	-140.19	-190.38
SOUTH	167.06	218.68	1.84	-14.07	.52	4.09	9.67	-8.30	4.70	2.67	27.14	41.42	124.21	192.87
WEST	213.56	245.70	23.54	26.55	1.36	-8.80	-10.19	-25.67	1.28	-13.63	42.36	89.02	155.20	178.24
DIVISION														
N.ENG	-164.86	-227.14	6.56	31.60	16.61	46.93	-9.94	27.75	-2.46	-26.96	-48.04	-112.11	-127.60	-194.35
M.A.	-137.22	-206.89	12.40	47.58	9.13	4.91	26.95	78.94	-5.00	-33.03	-56.58	-109.96	-124.14	-195.33
E.N.C.	-275.83	-411.26	-27.98	-35.46	-8.85	-7.10	-42.48	-68.36	-4.45	-23.04	-34.14	-68.63	-157.94	-208.67
W.N.C.	-57.91	127.54	-25.17	-44.67	-11.97	-23.18	34.63	69.54	1.93	167.85	39.31	104.12	-96.65	-146.11
S.A.	369.36	507.18	3.77	-7.24	21.65	37.95	33.71	43.55	3.91	5.82	31.41	37.79	274.89	400.95
E.S.C.	22.42	66.70	14.45	5.82	-15.79	-17.23	4.45	-28.20	2.80	3.37	20.39	29.51	-3.88	73.43
W.S.C.	-58.63	-129.87	-9.38	-37.20	-25.63	-34.59	-24.89	-75.65	7.19	15.31	24.76	54.54	-30.71	-52.27
MTN	341.73	559.56	38.13	16.55	6.16	-6.90	-27.52	-51.70	4.45	10.11	106.73	289.97	213.76	301.52
PAC	169.87	136.80	18.57	30.02	.28	-9.46	-4.28	-16.64	.21	-21.88	20.41	19.30	135.23	135.47

loans category, the North Central region continues to lag behind other regions in both years.

These patterns become more sharply defined when divisions, rather than regions, are observed. The very large increase in direct loans between 1975 and 1978 clearly benefited the West North Central states of North and South Dakota, Minnesota, Iowa, Kansas, Nebraska and Missouri more than other states, although states in the West South Central and Mountain areas were also considerably above the national mean. Legislation enacted in 1976, which expanded both eligibility criteria and funding for rural electrification and development loans, rural housing loans and emergency disaster loans, appears to be the source of much of this outlay expansion, and for the equally noticeable expansion in guaranteed loans as well. In the Northeast, New England states moved from a position below the national per capita mean for direct payments in 1975 to a position considerably above the mean for direct payments in 1978. Although the per capita increment was similar for the heavily populated Middle Atlantic states of New York, New Jersey and Pennsylvania, the per capita difference from the national mean was much greater in these states than in New England. New England states, however, increased their lead over other divisions in the receipt of project grants.

Analyzing types of outlays rather than total outlays shifts our perspective from what states get to what federal programs give. From the latter perspective, federal outlays assume a more dynamic quality through time. Programs and funding levels change, sometimes in response to economic and demographic change, sometimes in response to new program initiatives on the part of Congress or the Executive Branch. The result, within states and regions, appears as a constant shifting in types of outlay receipts. Under conditions of economic decline, direct payments for welfare assistance, medical costs or unemployment insurance increase more or less automatically in industrial states, as do formula grants tied to economic indicators. Population movements from one state to another have a similar effect on federal transfer payments or formula grants tied in some way to population. As new programmatic concerns make their way onto the national political agenda—environmental protection, energy or mass transportation are prominent recent examples—outlays addressing such issues begin to be made, often in the form of project grants or the recent explosion of direct and guaranteed loan programs. Observing outlay types moves us closer to understanding these patterns than analysis of per capita totals by exposing variety in the type and quantity of federal response to social and political change. We can move still closer by observing patterns of outlay by agency.

AGENCY OUTLAY PATTERNS

Federal departments are far more than administrative agencies. Like all organizations, individual departments represent a particular "mobilization of bias," in favor of some purposes or activities, opposed to others. Departmental biases, however, are supported by constituencies that are represented in Congress and protected by strong alliances between constituency groups, Congress and agency bureaucrats. These alliances create a powerful political claim on a share of each year's national budget that is extremely difficult to adjust in the short run. Because agency biases are shaped by constituencies that are spread unevenly across the country, it is to be expected that federal departments will have closer fiscal relationships to some states than to others.

In general, Departmental outlays are highly correlated with state population, particularly for agencies such HEW, whose programs are dominated (76 percent in 1978) by direct payments, or Labor, whose programs are dominated (74 percent in 1978) by formula grants. The correlations shown in Exhibit 9, however, reveal that the population-outlay relationship is not universally strong, and hardly exists at all for the Department of Interior, whose programs seem directed toward more sparsely populated areas. Among the less robust correlations, Agriculture might appear surprisingly high, in view of that agency's presumptive bias toward less populated farm areas. It must be remembered, however, that Agriculture in fact operates several programs with a decidedly urban focus, among them the very large school lunch and food stamp programs. The rather high 1975 correlation for Agriculture is thus understandable, as is the moderate decline in 1978, when the large new direct and guaranteed loan programs concentrated in agricultural states came into place. A weaker population-outlay relationship for the Small Business Administration in 1978 suggests a "spreading effect" in SBA outlays, away from the more populous states. NASA and Commerce outlays, too, appear to be less concentrated in highly populated states than are outlays for other large agencies.

EXHIBIT 9

Correlations Between State Population and Agency Spending
1975 and 1978

AGENCY	1975	1978
AGRICULTURE	.772	.676
COMMERCE	.668	.581
DEFENSE	.697	.721
EPA	.909	.700
GSA	.878	.855
HEW	.979	.985
HUD	.921	.912
INTERIOR	.188	.271
JUSTICE	.968	.955
LABOR	.957	.950
NASA	.636	.650
SBA	.854	.597
DOT	.883	.889
TREASURY	.954	.782
VA	.924	.900

State concentration of agency outlays can be measured by the proportion of each agency's annual outlay total that is allocated to a given state. These calculations (see Appendix Exhibit 1) make clear that agency outlays are indeed highly concentrated: in no case are more than six states required to accumulate a third of agency outlay totals; only three are required to reach that level for EPA disbursements. For NASA, California alone accounts for nearly 40 percent of agency outlays and nearly 67 percent of the total is achieved by adding Texas, Maryland and Florida. It is also clear that agencies often concentrate their outlays in different states. Michigan, low in Agriculture, heads the list for EPA obligations. Georgia, low in HEW payments, stands first in outlays from the Small Business Administration.

Concentration of agency outlays therefore seems as much a characteristic of recent intergovernmental fiscal relations as is agency specialization in the type of outlay distributed. Outlays are more concentrated for some agencies than others, to be sure, and some agencies—Agriculture, or HEW, for example—distribute several types of outlay rather than one or two. But specialization in outlay form and geographic focus seems a common characteristic among the deliverers of federal funds to states and regions. Depending on the interaction between state characteristics and the mix of programs administered within Departments, different states, at different times, will benefit more or less from agency disbursements.

This conclusion may seem rather too bland. We offer it primarily to call attention to the variability in both federal government activities and the enormously varied characteristics referred to by the words "state" or "region." Variability at the receiving end of the outlays pipeline is captured poorly, if at all, by aggregating data at the state or regional level. Thus, while richer and more populous states seem to do better than their opposites in the receipt of federal funds, there is enough within and between-state variability to undermine the significance of this observation, particularly when outlays are broken down by form or agency. Similarly, aggregating federal outlays by form or agency may have more political and programmatic meaning than total sums, but the increment in our understanding is hardly satisfying. Understanding *what is being delivered* clearly requires a deeper appreciation of federal funding purposes.

PROGRAM OUTLAYS

In creating an improved outlays data system, we have included separate reports for 48 of the largest federal programs, selected according to *Catalog of Federal Domestic Assistance* codes. Apart from capturing as large a proportion of total assistance as possible (70% of net domestic outlays in 1978), programs were selected to represent a broad mix of agencies and a mix of established and new program activities. Thus well-established programs such as Aid to Families with Dependent Children (HEW) or Highway Trust Fund disbursements (Transportation) are included, as are more recently initiated programs such as General Revenue Sharing (Treasury), CETA (Labor), or the Emergency Public Works program (Commerce). Since a number of these programs by-pass the states or are targeted on lower-level jurisdictions, county or city analysis seems a more appropriate vehicle for detailed examination of program distributions. Our focus here on state-level analysis nevertheless permits a brief commentary on three aspects of program outlays that seem both interesting and important.

The first represents a modification of our earlier conclusion that agency outlays are highly concentrated because, we suggested, agency "bias" is directed toward differentially concentrated constituency groups. This formulation overlooks the multiple constituencies serviced by many large agencies; hence the probability that a single agency may have or develop a number of distinctively different funding biases. A clear, if simple, example is the Department of Transportation, which for years has distributed highway planning and construction grants to states with extensive hard-surfaced highway systems. Observing the distribution of such grants in 1975, states such as Texas, California, Michigan or Pennsylvania emerge as the largest beneficiaries. Creation of an Urban Mass Transportation Authority within the Department of Transportation, however, established a different bias, with a different geographic focus. Observing UMTA distributions for 1975 reveals a heavy concentration in New York, New Jersey and Georgia, while states such as Michigan, Texas or Pennsylvania drop to positions closer to the bottom of the funding list. Multiple biases are of course even more noticeable in larger and more complex agencies whose constituencies sometimes do, and sometimes do not, overlap. Thus outlay distributions for two Department of Agriculture programs, Waste and Water Disposal and Low and Moderate-Income Housing, look very different indeed.

Multiple objectives in large agencies, coupled with the obvious but easily overlooked fact that many different agencies often pursue the same (or very similar) objectives, create conditions for competition or cooperation that have scarcely been explored. Agriculture and HUD, for example, both operate large housing assistance programs for low-to-moderate income families, with largest outlay amounts concentrated in the same groups of states. Similarly, Agriculture and EPA both operate water and waste disposal programs that show overlapping patterns in the Midwest, South and West. Agency interest in constituency expansion, in order to broaden support for program appropriations, would suggest patterns of competition in the delivery of these program outlays. Within Michigan, however, Agriculture's waste and water program is concentrated in largely rural counties, while the EPA wastewater treatment program distributes larger amounts to urban counties. In this state, a "high" beneficiary from both programs, there may well be some form of cooperation between agencies in deciding where to allocate funds.

A second aspect of state-level program outlays that is worth a brief comment is the relative proportion of "hard" and "soft" outlays within states. Relying primarily on *Catalog of Federal Domestic Assistance* descriptions, we made an effort to code each of the 46 reported programs as "hard" or "soft," depending on whether they appeared to be designed primarily to deliver services or funds to individuals, or to support capital investment activity. These judgments were not always easy to make: many programs mix "hard" and "soft" purposes, many program descriptions are quite difficult to interpret, and unrestricted programs such as General Revenue Sharing provide no basis at all for discrimination (using the best available information of GRS uses, we coded it "soft"). The results are therefore no more than judgmental, but the effort seemed worthwhile largely because "hard" and "soft" monies are thought to be distributed quite differently, and to have quite different impacts on state and local economies.

Nationwide, some three-quarters of these program dollars turn out to be "soft" and, in contrast to widely held expectations, to be distributed about the same way as "hard" outlays are distributed. As our scatterplot reveals (Exhibit 10), states that do well in the receipt of soft dollars also tend to do well in the receipt of hard dollars (1975: r = .88; 1978 r = .87), probably for similar reasons: they are large states, with large populations and thus likely to attract more of whatever program dollars are available in Washington at a given time. States whose hard-money receipts are unusually high—Mountain states such as Idaho or Wyoming, for example—are states whose total receipts tend to be rather low. At the other extreme, states such as Pennsylvania or Massachusetts receive a greater proportion of soft dollars than other states. Whether hard or soft, federal program dollars tend to flow more to people than places, although some divisional biases are evident. While soft dollars increased by 39 percent from 1975 to 1978 and at relatively equal rates of increase across divisions, hard dollars increased by 85 percent with pronounced differences in rates of increase by division. West North Central (+131%) and Mountain states (+113%) received the largest increase in hard dollars while New England (+59%) and South Atlantic (+66%) states experience much smaller rates of increase. Divisional biases also appear in per capita comparisons: In 1978, West North Central ($602.63) and Mountain states ($620.98) receive almost twice the national average amounts of hard dollars. By contrast, the Middle Atlantic ($201.08) and New England states ($219.67) rank lowest in per capita hard dollars.

Finally, it is extremely important to note the lack of stability in the flow of program dollars through time. We began this discussion by noting an apparent stability in the intergovernmental fiscal system when national totals or per capita totals were used as measures. From 1975 to 1978 total outlays increased dramatically, with some variation in rate of increase from state to state, but with little change in relative position among the states. States that were high

EXHIBIT 10

SCATTERPLOT OF DISTRIBUTION OF HARD AND SOFT DOLLAR OUTLAYS BY STATE

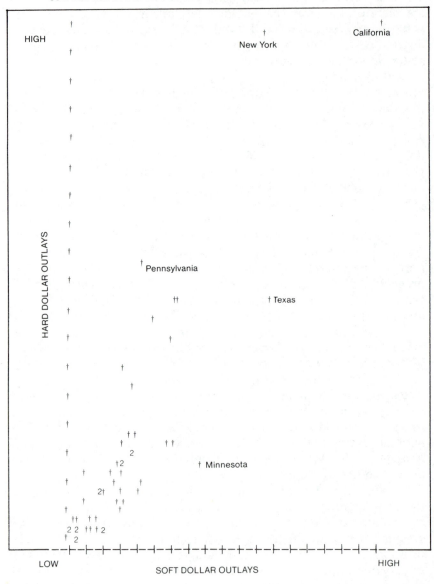

beneficiaries in 1975 remained high in 1978; states that were low in 1975 remained low in 1978. The appearance of stability began to disintegrate, however, when we observed outlay flows by type of financial assistance or by agency. States whose relative position remained low or high in total outlays often were states that experienced shifts from one dominant type of outlay to another. Thus while position remained relatively stable, the components of stability often changed. Similarly, stable position was often maintained despite shifts of dominant support from one agency to another.

At the program level, the appearance of stability virtually disappears, except for large direct payment programs or formula grants tied to population or population characteristics. A clear example of instability is the SBA's Physical Disaster Loan program, which presumably *should* change rapidly. Comparing outlay patterns in 1977 and 1978 for this program reveals that from one year to the next, California and Iowa move from low to high in program outlays, Kentucky moves from high to low, Georgia moves from medium to high, and New York moves from high to medium. Although a program designed to respond to unpredictable physical disasters may seem an extreme case, the pattern is quite similar for a range of more typical programs that deliver either hard or soft money. In Michigan, for example, programs such as CETA move dramatically up, then down, from one year to the next, EPA water treatment moves down, then up, from one year to another, or Vocational Education moves up slightly, then down, then up sharply, from one year to the next (Exhibits 11-13).

These examples typify the classic "good news-bad news" quality of federal disbursement. Because national program priorities change from year to year, and because many programs permit administrators to exercise considerable discretion in their allocation of program dollars, federal outlays can and do respond rather quickly to new needs or new political commitments. That is the good news. The bad news is that such variable responses are often unpredictable, particularly in discretionary programs, thus undermining the ability of state officials to either plan or manage federal receipts very well. Assuming continued growth in federal outlays, the dilemma posed by useful but unpredictable funding flows seems certain to require continued attention.

EXHIBIT 11

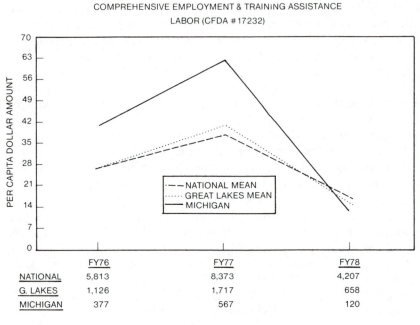

COMPREHENSIVE EMPLOYMENT & TRAINING ASSISTANCE
LABOR (CFDA #17232)

	FY76	FY77	FY78
NATIONAL	5,813	8,373	4,207
G. LAKES	1,126	1,717	658
MICHIGAN	377	567	120

(IN MILLIONS OF DOLLARS)

Comprehensive Employment and Training Assistance is intended to provide job training and employment opportunities for the economically disadvantaged. Given the high levels of unemployment which characterized the Michigan labor force during the 1973-1976 recessionary period, it is not surprising to find Michigan ranked 6th in per-capita C.E.T.A. outlays in 1976 and as high as 3rd in 1977. This position changed radically in 1978, however, as per-capita outlays went from $62.25 in 1977 to $13.17 in 1978 for a reduction in national ranking to 26th.

EXHIBIT 12

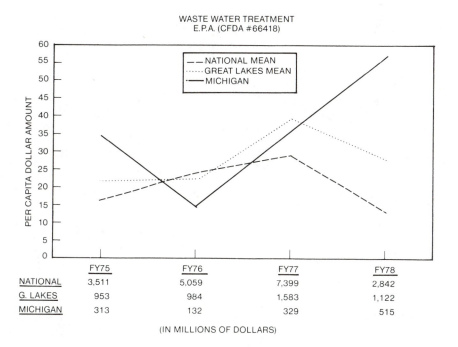

WASTE WATER TREATMENT
E.P.A. (CFDA #66418)

	FY75	FY76	FY77	FY78
NATIONAL	3,511	5,059	7,399	2,842
G. LAKES	953	984	1,583	1,122
MICHIGAN	313	132	329	515

(IN MILLIONS OF DOLLARS)

The Construction (Project) Grants for Wastewater Treatment Works are intended to assist and serve as an incentive in the construction of adequate municipal sewage treatment works and are administered by the Environmental Protection Agency. In contrast to Michigan's rank of 29th (1978) nationally per-capita agriculture waste disposal grants, Michigan ranks 1st in 1978 per-capita E.P.A. construction grant spending ($56 per-capita), at a time when national spending for this program has decreased markedly (−19%) as well as within the Great Lakes states. E.P.A. construction grants to Michigan have increased by 64.5% with all but twenty counties receiving grant assistance.

The following chart compares per-capita Agriculture and E.P.A. Waste Water program outlays, with E.P.A. activities clearly more dominant.

EXHIBIT 13

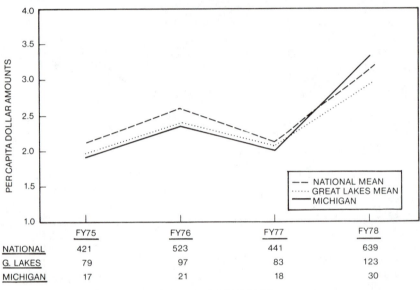

VOCATIONAL EDUCATION
H.E.W. (CFDA #13493)

	FY75	FY76	FY77	FY78
NATIONAL	421	523	441	639
G. LAKES	79	97	83	123
MICHIGAN	17	21	18	30

(IN MILLIONS OF DOLLARS)

Whereas federal Vocational Education program spending has increased by almost 52% since 1975, Vocational Education spending in Michigan has increased by almost 73% from $17 million in 1975 to $30 million in 1978. This dramatic increase in spending has shifted Michigan's national per-capita position from 38th in 1975 to 29th in 1978, although still below Ohio (26th in 1978) and Wisconsin (20th in 1978).

CONCLUSIONS

Several conclusions emerge from the preceding analysis:

1. Although federal outlays continue to grow, there appears to be no major shift in the state or regional distribution of total outlays. Indeed, there appears to be considerable stability in state and regional distributions, when measured by per capita totals. The West and South continue to lead the rest of the nation in total per capita receipts, the Northeast benefits more than the rest of the country from project grants, the West benefits most from formula grants, and the North Central region benefits most from the recent expansion of direct and indirect loans.

2. Project grants are more significant in 1978 than they were in 1975; formula grants, however, decline as a proportion of total outlays.

3. Major federal departments tend to concentrate most of their expenditures in a very few states but, because many departments serve multiple constituencies, the concentration of agency spending among states varies from year to year.

4. Disaggregated by program, federal outlays are often quite unstable through time, both because new programs are created and because existing allocations are made according to changing patterns of administrative discretion. At the program level, therefore, outlays by state tend to be difficult to predict.

5. There is a strong relationship between federal outlays and state population and this relationship remains strong for agency and program outlays. Patterns of distribution for "hard" and "soft" monies are quite similar.

6. Although it is convenient to summarize outlay distribution by region, there is little support in these data for a distinctively "regional" bias in program, agency or functional outlays. When state-level figures are used, per capita income has only a moderate relationship to federal outlays.

7. Agency, functional and program spending all appear to change dramatically from year to year in their respective patterns of state distribution. We take this to indicate an impressive degree of federal responsiveness to changing conditions and political demands.

EPILOGUE–MAKING OUTLAYS SENSE

What theory or theories might be used to account for these patterns of distribution? The patterns themselves seem sufficiently complex to prohibit early development of a single theoretical explanation, particularly if empirical support is desired for theoretical formulations. We believe the data reported here to be far more accurate and useful than other available data, for example, but we nevertheless remain acutely aware of the distance between these data and "good" data. The problem, of course, is not simply that data may be "inaccurate" for various reasons, but more fundamentally that data systems are themselves infused with theoretical assumptions that may be incompatible with alternative theoretical interpretations.

Consider the recent uses of outlays data. These data are collected annually, by program within federal agency, and reported for all states, counties and large cities. Attention is thus focused on federal purposes, as measured by program obligations, and administrative accountability, as measured by the record of state and local jurisdictions into which purposive funds are allocated. Extended over time, these data encourage evaluation of the extent to which purposes are reflected in outlays and the extent to which program administrators are sensitive to purposive goals. The "theory" implicit in outlays data is very much a theory of federal policy and program management.

Most published analyses based on outlays data, however, translate the data into outlay "totals," aggregated by state or region, divided by state or regional population, to arrive at an easily manipulated per capita sum. Attention is thus focused on what states or regions *receive,* rather than on what federal agencies distribute, and on per person allocation rather than *purposive* allocations. Such translations are then used to structure arguments about which regions get more or less from the federal government as a whole or which states show a positive or negative "balance" between federal taxes paid and outlays distributed.

There are two problems inherent in such data transformations. The first, already noted above, is that per capita sums obscure both program differences and the allocation processes that distribute federal dollars. It is therefore difficult to either interpret per capita sums or to use them unambiguously in further analysis. The second, more important, problem is that the theory implicit in such calculations has little, if any, empirical support. Although all federal expenditure programs have distributional consequences, there is little evidence that funding decisions are designed to increase or decrease total outlays to one region or another, little evidence of any federal interest in taking total per capita distributions into account, and no evidence at all of a federal concern for "balancing" taxes paid and outlays distributed. Individual programs may have any or all of these consequences, and it is often useful to understand those distributional results. A vast literature on national budgeting makes clear, however, that program and agency are the building blocks of federal budgets, that decisionmaking is fragmented rather than holistic, and that distributional impact, when it comes into play, is of distinctively less significance than national program purpose.

Of the two theoretical themes woven through our analysis, then, we believe that "who gets" is likely to be far less interesting for state-level analysis than "what is given," at least in the near future. This is not to say that state receipts are unimportant, particularly as a political issue. Within region and within state demographic variations are so pronounced, however, that neither a geographic nor an ecological-theoretical framework is likely to reveal clear-cut patterns of state-federal fiscal interaction. A political framework is clearly essential, given the complexity and changeability of federal outlays from one year to another. Although any political framework is bound to be significantly intergovernmental in content, it seems similarly clear that the place to begin its development is at its federal source.

Apart from program variability, federal outlay patterns are quite complex because they appear on close examination to be in constant flux, despite some elements of a fairly stable structure. We take it, then, that a conceptual scheme to generate theories that might explain this dynamic but structured complexity should be (a) substantively clear, (b) capable of summarizing changes in relationships through time, (c) linked to plausible and available data, and (d) capable of raising questions for further investigation. Since our interest is in the political aspects of outlay distributions, the imagery we seek must also be political in content. Some years ago Phillip Monypenny worked out an analysis of certain federal aid programs that was as useful conceptually as it was empirically interesting.[18] Although our views and purposes are somewhat different from Monypenny's, we borrow freely from his argument in suggesting the following conceptual scheme.

Government activities are organized by *program,* staffed by officials responsible for providing services or goods or both to citizens. Large individual programs or collections of smaller programs taken together can be viewed as policies, generated through *processes of choice.* Depending on the quality of those choice processes, particularly the strength and longevity of *coalitions* that support programs or policies, program activities are maintained or they are changed. Strong coalitions that continue through time can produce programs that also continue through time as institutionalized commitments. Programs supported by weak or brief coalitions can be radically changed or, in some cases, done away with entirely. Because program activity and coalition support can change independently, it can be expected that some programs will continue to operate even as coalition support weakens, or that strong coalitions will exist for some time before a program is enacted.

While simple, these ideas reflect essential political characteristics of outlay programs without imposing artificial summary judgments on the relationships that may exist between those characteristics. A focus on "program" defines activities that can be observed, including funds expended, to which some purpose or purposes have been assigned through official actions. At any given time, a governmental system can be described in terms of an existing mix of programs and, over time, system change can be described in terms of changes in the type and size of programs. Describing governmental systems in terms of programs is plausible, since programs necessarily reflect what governments do, and data for such descriptions are, in principle, readily available in documents of various kinds, as well as through observation. Built as it is on program-level data, the outlays data series provides an unusually comprehensive and detailed "system" description.

Linking programs to coalitions of actors through choice processes is also plausible. Conceived as purposive activity, programs necessarily represent values, which must be defined and advocated. Value definition and advocacy are pursued by individuals but, to become established as government activities, support for values must be obtained from many individuals, hence the necessity for coalition behavior. Depending on the interaction between types of coalitions and types of values pursued, choice processes associated with government programs will exhibit considerable variety, ranging from "crisis" patterns in which widely shared basic values are reaffirmed or redefined by broad-based coalitions, to the largely hidden processes often associated with incremental adjustments to highly specialized programs designed to serve limited constituencies. Processes associated with program initiation are likely to differ from processes associated with program maintenance or change. As with differences in the size, longevity and resources of coalitions, however, these process differences are in principle observable, thus measurable in one sense or another.

Program, choice and coalition are no more than conceptual boxes that, when elaborated and infused with data, can generate statements that may help to clarify changing federal outlay patterns. Relationships between these concepts are assumed to exist and to be significant, but the quality of those relationships can only be defined by empirical investigation. In that sense the scheme is theoretically open ended. Answering the questions "how do government programs come into existence, how are they maintained, and how do they change" can produce insights into both the structural and dynamic properties of government action that presumably will vary from time to time as well as from place to place. Indeed, the scheme demands that attention be given to system dynamics, even as it clarifies system structure.

To illustrate, let us suggest that the current "structure" of the federal outlay system is made up of a number of long-lasting programs, supported by stable coalitions, that represent agreed-upon political commitments. *Core programs* of this kind are relatively few in number, but they represent a large fraction of distributed funds (Exhibit 14).[19] Because they reflect a stable political agreement, core programs are likely to be extremely resistant to anything but incremental change. Fund levels will increase as the national budget increases, but major program changes will occur seldom, usually as a result of some crisis, or perhaps a political realignment that undermines the existing coalition. When such changes occur in core programs, the terms of coalition support are renegotiated in order to ensure future stability for the revised program. Core programs, in short, represent institutionalized political settlements that are durable as well as purposive. Programs such as highway grants, vocational education grants, AFDC or mortgage guarantees are good examples.

In addition to core programs, federal outlays support a wide variety of purposes that reflect current political concerns not yet fully institutionalized. These concerns change from one year to another, and coalition formation is pursued with differing levels of skill. When successful, coalitions organized around new political issues produce new programs to service newly recognized constituencies. At any given time, therefore, the full range of programs can be viewed as a political barometer of sorts, measuring the developing concerns of the political system as well as its lasting political settlements. Success in initiating a new program, however, is no guarantee

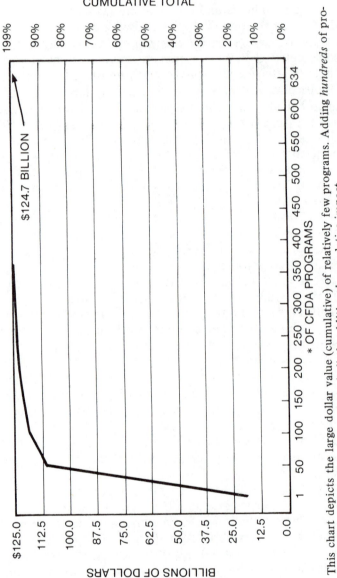

EXHIBIT 14

BULK OF FEDERAL ASSISTANCE CONCENTRATED IN FEW PROGRAMS
STATE & LOCAL ELIGIBILITY FOR 1979 CFDA PROGRAM DOLLARS

This chart depicts the large dollar value (cumulative) of relatively few programs. Adding *hundreds* of programs after the first 10% has relatively little additional cumulative impact.

that the program will become institutionalized; concern over the issue may weaken or coalition members may be unable to sustain cooperative action, or new concerns may arise with stronger claims on national resources. Thus, around the core programs we can observe a fluctuating variety of *barometer programs*, only some of which will achieve stability of support: the Emergency Public Works Program, General Revenue Sharing, or LEAA appear to be good examples. Seen as a whole, the outlays system is both "structured" around core commitments and coalitions, yet constantly changing to accommodate the interests of new or developing coalitions. Viewed this way, structure and change are equally amenable to observation, measurement and analysis.

APPENDIX EXHIBIT 1

AREA	NET Domestic	AG	COM	DOD	EPA	GSA	HEW	HUD	INT	JUST	LAB	NASA	SBA	DOT	TREA	VA	OTHER AGENCIES
ALA	1.72	1.71	1.27	2.31	1.61	1.07	1.66	1.68	.36	.88	1.17	5.03	2.76	1.18	1.16	2.01	1.59
ALK	.41	.38	1.04	.86	.11	.30	.12	.08	6.77	.28	.44	.02	.33	1.60	.27	.27	.18
ARZ	1.33	.94	.27	1.71	.70	.50	1.02	3.39	8.64	1.49	1.78	.33	.64	.93	.88	1.93	.84
ARK	.96	1.85	.34	.80	.51	.57	1.04	.69	.53	.56	.76	.00	.70	.79	.68	1.11	.58
CAL	10.61	4.92	8.29	14.48	9.52	8.04	10.39	14.21	12.63	11.01	12.41	39.97	8.20	6.14	9.87	13.01	8.85
COL	1.61	1.66	2.51	2.26	.91	1.99	1.00	2.19	8.19	1.47	1.15	1.39	1.43	1.36	.91	3.14	1.43
CONN	1.07	.79	1.03	.48	.33	.51	1.43	.91	.18	1.17	1.80	1.64	.88	.95	.99	.87	.87
DEL	.25	.16	2.73	.30	.14	.51	.24	.17	.08	.28	.26	.01	.09	.18	.51	.27	.15
D.C.	3.03	1.00	11.13	1.50	7.54	21.43	1.28	1.57	8.23	17.43	5.69	1.63	1.33	13.01	5.73	1.94	5.00
FLA	4.17	2.31	1.37	5.40	2.81	.90	4.87	4.45	1.54	3.28	3.19	8.65	2.58	3.05	2.66	5.19	3.20
GA	2.82	2.89	.77	3.93	2.67	3.79	1.95	3.11	.95	2.29	1.93	.09	9.68	2.46	12.77	2.98	1.80
HA	.58	.36	.39	2.14	.84	.10	.34	.26	.22	.40	.62	.05	.24	.80	.44	.67	.38
IDA	.52	1.17	.35	.34	.22	.13	.32	.47	2.47	.22	.34	.00	1.05	.55	.26	.57	.74
ILL	4.74	3.36	1.51	2.34	8.98	5.84	5.00	2.66	.71	4.30	4.52	.34	1.72	6.68	3.93	3.64	9.27
IND	1.90	4.13	.95	1.03	2.99	1.16	2.09	1.58	.65	1.42	2.18	.41	1.07	1.31	1.40	1.59	1.32
IOWA	1.26	3.56	.11	.23	.92	.23	1.24	.69	.25	.52	.87	.09	7.74	.91	.76	1.02	.81
KAN	1.17	3.16	.31	1.38	.48	.29	.99	.73	.40	1.05	.67	.10	2.46	.88	.59	1.05	.81
KY	1.55	1.55	.61	2.04	1.42	.86	1.52	1.53	.46	1.46	1.64	.01	.80	1.18	1.42	1.19	2.12
LA	1.57	2.05	9.58	1.53	.75	.42	1.54	1.45	.43	1.10	1.28	2.46	2.50	1.23	1.73	1.62	1.07
MAINE	.48	.56	.43	.48	.30	.49	.52	.25	.18	.44	.68	.01	.93	.38	.50	.54	.35
MD	2.38	.96	11.03	3.43	1.40	2.42	2.18	1.99	.85	1.68	1.61	8.90	.78	3.00	1.56	2.09	3.21
MASS	2.47	.86	1.58	1.24	1.20	2.68	3.18	2.24	1.18	2.49	3.48	1.14	3.05	4.17	2.90	2.08	2.18
MI	3.01	2.02	.93	1.12	14.41	3.83	4.18	3.36	1.15	2.62	3.33	.39	2.06	2.30	3.43	2.10	1.86
MINN	1.88	4.95	.32	.45	1.28	.48	1.74	3.60	1.36	1.29	1.16	.36	1.08	1.38	1.35	2.08	1.24
MISS	1.16	2.65	.89	1.23	.78	.25	1.08	.87	.84	.52	.95	.62	2.79	.70	1.00	1.16	.56
MO	2.17	2.50	2.67	1.75	1.45	4.75	2.29	2.00	1.23	2.27	2.22	.15	3.19	1.61	1.82	1.77	2.48

APPENDIX EXHIBIT 1 (Continued)

AREA	NET Domestic	AG	COM	DOD	EPA	GSA	HEW	HUD	INT	JUST	LAB	NASA	SBA	DOT	TREA	VA	OTHER AGENCIES
MONT	.48	1.38	.38	.29	.21	.19	.32	.50	2.21	.31	.44	.00	.83	.55	.27	.42	.38
NEB	.90	3.37	.16	.71	.47	.16	.65	.49	.62	.29	.40	.00	1.56	.51	.43	.80	.72
NEV	.46	.15	.17	.53	.90	.13	.24	1.88	1.35	.30	.52	.03	.24	.49	.23	.66	.63
N.H.	.36	.35	.15	.62	.81	.08	.36	.14	1.3	.27	.39	.06	.79	.36	.22	.36	.27
N.J.	2.70	1.25	3.07	2.04	1.51	5.13	3.43	2.95	.54	2.23	4.67	1.25	1.37	1.87	2.82	2.16	2.51
N.M.	.82	.79	.35	1.10	.44	.31	.46	.80	5.43	.52	.55	.45	.89	.76	.52	.60	1.81
N.Y.	7.91	6.26	17.38	2.06	2.74	7.76	10.13	8.56	1.41	8.25	11.18	1.34	5.63	9.05	10.87	5.04	7.96
N.C.	2.15	2.98	1.08	3.54	4.72	1.37	2.18	1.50	1.00	1.32	1.54	.08	1.69	1.45	1.62	2.39	1.17
N.D.	.52	2.54	.15	.44	.31	.19	.28	.39	1.14	.24	.23	.00	.41	.35	.18	.30	.21
OHIO	3.62	2.03	.66	2.35	4.44	3.00	4.46	3.61	1.03	2.23	4.00	3.79	1.21	3.03	3.07	4.19	3.84
OKLA	1.40	1.86	.80	2.25	.85	.20	1.27	1.50	1.66	.88	1.11	.01	.68	1.52	.80	1.51	1.19
ORE	1.12	2.12	.69	.46	1.19	1.10	1.13	.69	4.67	.60	.99	.04	.71	1.69	.87	.83	.95
PA	4.49	2.01	2.08	3.03	2.51	2.71	6.09	3.57	1.80	4.03	4.68	1.80	2.27	4.12	4.88	3.71	4.63
R.I.	.40	.11	.40	.50	.35	.13	.50	.36	.12	.25	.64	.02	.88	.26	.37	.39	.31
S.C.	1.29	1.40	.57	2.59	.54	.45	1.09	1.16	.61	.59	.87	.00	2.86	.67	.91	1.48	1.31
S.D.	.45	1.83	.22	.30	.34	.09	.29	.38	1.73	.21	.24	.01	.64	.25	.20	.37	.20
TENN	2.20	2.09	.45	1.10	1.55	.66	1.84	2.55	.44	1.12	1.31	.11	2.84	1.43	1.56	2.01	5.74
TEX	5.51	7.25	2.17	8.71	4.35	4.18	4.72	5.94	1.54	6.92	3.84	9.59	7.24	4.03	4.43	7.53	3.74
UTAH	.69	.79	.26	1.16	.19	.50	.43	1.13	2.52	.35	.66	1.49	1.15	.54	.76	.85	.59
VER	.20	.29	.14	.08	.20	.08	.24	.06	.08	.52	.21	.01	.32	.21	.24	.15	.16
VA	2.92	1.81	2.43	7.68	1.56	3.91	1.83	2.22	2.46	2.28	1.36	5.15	1.07	2.50	1.50	3.85	4.02
WASH	2.00	1.53	2.28	2.88	1.71	2.07	1.62	1.87	3.18	2.08	1.79	.86	2.28	2.89	1.25	1.98	2.82
W.VA.	.74	.74	.65	.21	.76	.36	.95	.43	.63	.85	.72	.00	.74	1.08	.85	.72	.61
WIS	1.60	2.17	.83	.38	2.93	1.60	2.18	1.08	.60	1.32	1.37	.09	.98	1.29	1.49	1.45	1.05
WY	.25	.47	.07	.20	.11	.08	.13	.13	2.62	.11	.14	.01	.62	.35	.12	.35	.29

NOTES

1. For instance, Daniel P. Moynihan, "The Politics and Economics of Regional Growth," *The Public Interest* No. 51 (Spring 1978): 3-21; and The Academy for Contemporary Problems, *Revitalizing the Northeastern Economy— An Action Survey, General Report and Recommendations* (Columbus, Ohio: The Academy for Contemporary Problems, 1978, Second Printing).

2. See, among many others, Joel Havemann, Rochelle I. Stanfield, Neal R. Pierce, *et. al.*, "Federal Spending: The North's Loss is the Sunbelt's Gain," *National Journal* 8,26 (June 1976): 878-891; Joel Havemann, Rochelle I. Stanfield, "A Year Later, The Frostbelt Strikes Back," *National Journal* 9,27 (July 1977): 1028-1037; "The Second War Between the States," *Business Week* (May 17, 1976): 92-114; C.I. Jusenius and L.C. Iedebur, *A Myth in the Making: The Southern Economic Challenge and Northern Economic Decline* (Springfield, Virginia: U.S. Department of Commerce, Economic Development Administration, Economic Development Research Paper, PB 263 631, National Technical Information Service, 1976); and Robert W. Rafuse, Jr.'s review of the literature on this debate (as of early 1977) *The New Regional Debate: A National Overview* (Washington, D.C.: National Governors' Conference, Center for Policy Research and Analysis, Agenda Setting Series, April 1977).

3. Since 1969 Treasury has published *Federal Aid to States* annually as a separate volume; earlier it was part of the *Statistical Appendix to Annual Report of the Secretary of the Treasury on the State of the Finances.* Since the early 1960s "Federal Aid to State and Local Governments" has been included in OMB's *Special Analyses, Budget of the United States Government* volume. The Census data referred to here is from the *Government Finance* series.

4. Pursuant to OMB Circular No. A-11, Treasury Circular No. 1014 and Part 2, Chapter 7000, *Treasury Fiscal Requirements Manual*, the grants-in-aid outlay data reported by Treasury and OMB are supposed to be consistent with each other. Indeed, the OMB report employs the Treasury data in constructing a regional/divisional table on the distribution of grants. For discussion of the OMB and Treasury data collection processes see Jerry P. Cawley and Kevin L. Kramer, *Reconciling Treasury's "Federal Aid to States" Report with Community Services Administration's "Geographic Distribution of Federal Funds" Report* (Ann Arbor, Michigan: Ph.D. Program in Urban and Regional Planning, The University of Michigan, The Intergovernmental Fiscal Analysis Project, Analysis Series Paper No. 10, April 1979), and Mark T. Lilla, "Where Has All the Money Gone? The Distribution of Federal Grants-In-Aid," Unpublished B.A.–Senior Honors Thesis, Department of Political Science, The University of Michigan, 1978; Comparison of OMB and Treasury numbers is complicated by the practice followed by both Departments of revising in latter years the grants totals previously reported. The 1980 "Federal Aid to State and Local Governments" lists, for example, total grant outlays at $43.4 billion for FY 1974, $2.7 billion less than OMB previously reported in its 1976 budget analysis. For further details see the assessment of federal data sources in Thomas J. Anton, Jerry P. Cawley and Kevin L. Kramer, "Who Knows Where the Money Goes: A Comparison of Data Sources for Monitoring Federal Expenditures," in Thomas J. Anton, Principal Investigator, *Report to the Department of Housing and Urban Development.* (Ann Arbor, Michigan: Ph.D. Program in Urban and Regional Planning, The University of Michigan, The Intergovernmental Fiscal Analysis Project, 1979).

5. For a review of the Census data see Thomas J. Anton, "Data Systems for Urban Fiscal Policy: Toward Reconstruction," paper presented for the NSF Conference on Comparative Urban Research, Chicago, Illinois, April 26-27, 1979.

6. For a selection of rather different conclusions regarding the regional distribution of federal monies, based on different data bases, compare Mark T. Lilla, *op. cit.;* the Havemann, *et. al., National Journal* articles, *op. cit.;* the General Accounting Office, *Changing Patterns of Federal Aid to State and Local Governments, 1969-1975* (Washington, D.C.: U.S. Government Printing Office, 1977); Ann R. Markusen and Jerry Fastrup, "The Regional War for Federal Aid," *The Public Interest* No. 53 (Fall 1978): 87-89; and Ann R. Markusen, Annalee Saxenian, and Marc A. Weiss, *Who Benefits from Intergovernmental Transfers?,* paper presented at the Conference on Municipal Fiscal Squeeze, Miami, Florida, March 8-9, 1979 (Berkeley, California: Department of City and Regional Planning, The University of California, Berkeley, Working Paper No. 306, June 1979).

7. For more detailed assessments of CSA's F.I.X.S. information system, see Thomas J. Anton, "Outlays Data and the Analysis of Federal Policy Impact," paper prepared for The Urban Impacts of Federal Policies Conference, Washington, D.C., February 8-9, 1979, to be published in Norman Glickman, ed., *The Urban Impacts of Federal Policies* (Baltimore, Maryland: Johns Hopkins University Press, 1980); Thomas J. Anton, "Creating a Data Base for Intergovernmental Fiscal Analysis" (Ann Arbor, Michigan: Ph.D. Program in Urban and Regional Planning, The University of Michigan, The Intergovernmental Fiscal Analysis Project, Analysis Series Paper No. 1, 1978); the OMB established, *Interagency Task Team Report on Improvements to the Federal Outlays Report by Geographic Region, OMB Circular A-84 Policy and Associated Process* (Washington, D.C.: Office of Management and Budget, July 1974); Congressional Budget Office (Peggy L. Cuciti, main author), *Troubled Local Economies and the Distribution of Federal Dollars* (Washington, D.C.: U.S. Government Printing Office, 1977); Richard P. Nathan, Jacob M. Jaffee, Paul R. Dommel, and James W. Fossett, *Feasibility of Measuring the Geographic Impact of Federal Economic and Community Development Programs* (Washington, D.C.: The Brookings Institution, Report to the Office of Management and Budget, August 8, 1977); Fred K. Hines and J. Norman Reid, *Using Federal Outlays Data to Measure Program Equity – Opportunities and Limitations* (Washington, D.C.: U.S. Department of Agriculture, Economic Development Division, Economics, Statistics and Cooperative Service, Working Paper No. 7711, 1977); and J. Norman Reid, "Understanding Federal Programs; The Need for a Coordinated Data System," *State and Local Government Review* 11,2 (May 1979): 42-47.

8. The F.I.X.S. information system does not cover judicial, Congressional and certain classified expenditures.

9. Only Census data possess comparable geographic depth. Census intergovernmental transfer data, however, systematically under-report federal aid to cities, while systematically overstating the magnitude of state aid to cities. This is due to the way Census treats federal grants-in-aid to lower level governmental jurisdictions that are passed through state governments. Census counts all such assistance as "state" aid while restricting "federal" aid only to direct federal-local payments. For details, see Thomas J. Anton, "Data Systems for Urban Fiscal Policy: Toward Reconstruction," *op. cit.*

10. The net domestic outlay figure encompasses 81, 82 and 83 percent of

the total federal outlays reported in CSA for fiscal years 1975, 1977 and 1978; Defense procurements, interest on the public debt and "non-influence" activities respectively constituted 12, 11, 12, 6.5, 4.5, and 6.5, .4, .5 percent of the total federal outlays.

11. Readers interested in seeing what difference the inclusion of D.C. in regional and division analyses makes are referred to the data presented in Thomas J. Anton, Jerry P. Cawley, Kevin L. Kramer, *I.F.A.P. National Summary Data Tables* (Ann Arbor, Michigan: Ph.D. Program in Urban and Regional Planning, The University of Michigan, Intergovernmental Fiscal Analysis Project, 1980).

12. All subsequent outlay figures cited are calculated from the CSA data.

13. The first and second place rankings of the West and South are maintained when defense civilian and military payrolls are removed from the calculation.

14. Expressed in dollar amounts, formula grants increased from $$8.9 billion to $63.2 billion from FY 1975 to FY 1978.

15. Project grants were $14.8 billion in FY 1975 and $25.8 billion in FY 1978.

16. Direct payments were $94.1 billion in FY 1975 and $158.5 billion in FY 1978.

17. Guaranteed loans were $23.4 billion in FY 1975 and $46.3 billion in FY 1978.

18. Phillip Monypenny, "Federal Grants-In-Aid to State Governments: A Political Analysis," *National Tax Journal,* 13,1 (March 1960): 1-16.

19. Figure 5 is calculated from program data in OMB's *1979 Catalog of Federal Domestic Assistance.*

Ann R. Markusen, Annalee Saxenian, Marc A. Weiss - WHO BENEFITS FROM INTERGOVERNMENTAL TRANS- FERS?

I. INTRODUCTION

In this paper, we address the conceptual and empirical issues underlying the debate on the spatial distribution of intergovernmental transfers. The debate has been embodied in the ongoing and vigorous political battles over formula construction at the federal level and the accompanying rhetoric indicting federal "favoritism" toward certain regions and places. Such political ferment begs a careful accounting of what the distribution currently looks like, to the extent that empirical data exist to reveal it.

Therefore, in Section II, we attempt to answer the question "What is being distributed to whom?" We begin by laying out three dimensions from which to describe the distribution: spatial, functional and

We would like to thank the Center for Urban Policy Research at Rutgers University, the Office of Policy Development and Research of the U.S. Department of Housing and Urban Development, and the Institute of Urban and Regional Development at the University of California, Berkeley, for material support for the research. We are particularly grateful to David Wilmoth, Dan Feshbach, Michael Luger, Michael Teitz, Roger Montgomery, John Mollenkopf, Dennis Keating, and the National Urban Policy Collective for critical comments.

temporal. We discuss briefly the spatial untis that seem to be of interest (regions, states, cities by city size, and central city vs. suburbs vs. rural counties). We talk about two different approaches to the tabulation of intergovernmental transfers: narrowly, by grant data and broadly, by outlay data. And within these two definitions, we consider various functional categories such as welfare, highways and education, which indicate the most significant factors in accounting for spatial differences. Finally, we focus on changes in distribution over a period of time, roughly the last ten years (1967-78). Drawing on work by various authors and directly interpreting some elements from Census and Outlays sources, we construct brief tallies of the evidence on spatial distributions of expenditures from federal and state levels, for both the most recent year available and over the past decade. Where possible, we address distribution by function. The evidence suggests that intergovernmental transfers, while demonstrating wide variation across spatial units, generally do "favor" the northeastern region, large cities and central cities. However, the dispersion within most of these distributions has diminished over the last decade, despite the fact that this period has witnessed great concern over urban fiscal crisis and economic decline in the Northeast.

In interpreting the data, we raise a number of questions about its adequacy. But even more importantly, we caution against the subtle normative connotations which generally accompany discussions of such distributions. We note that, unlike the distribution of income to individuals, which constituted a clear unidimensional criterion for debating the success of welfare programs, no societally agreed upon criterion exists for prescribing what the distribution of governmental transfers to areal units ought to be. Furthermore, the popular claims of "unfairness" suggest some correlation between needy people and particular places. But, in fact, no simple geographical correspondence exists. And even if it did, there is no guarantee that expenditures in particular places will result in concomitant income gains for needy groups, due to the discretionary behavior of local governments and the complexity of the multiplier process by which the various types of transfers filter through a local economy. Finally, it bears reminding that intergovernmental relations are not reducible to intergovernmental transfers: many nonbudgetary policies affect spatial units differentially, and the incidence of the tax burden may also vary spatially.

In Section III, we go on to discuss some more fundamental methodological problems with public finance approaches to the question of intergovernmental transfers. We reflect on the state of positive theories of public finance and on the empirical evidence for them. We caution against the proliferation of expenditure determination studies to explain spatial distributions, by demonstrating that such distributions are not stochastic processes and by suggesting that most such studies will end up merely reducing aggregates to components— a task inappropriate for econometric analysis. Secondly, we note that public finance has increasingly ventured into behavioral theories of expenditure determination, but has oddly restricted its realm of study to the behavior of voters and taxpayers and to the response of state and local governments on receipt of transfers. No behavioral work that we know of fully addresses the complex behavior of federal and state govenments (Congress, legislatures, executives, agencies and their constituents) in determining the supply of inter-governmental transfers. Surely this is a ripe research frontier, one we try to probe in our final section.

In Section III we also reflect on the normative exercises in public finance which attempt to convert formula construction and the determination of appropriate intergovernmental responsibilities into scientific exercises. We suggest that there has been a tendency for such efforts to obscure their normative content and underlying assumptions, with the result that debates over distributions have masqueraded as matters of a technical nature, when in essence they are political and involve conflictual visions. In reality, whether the authors are aware of it or not, different formula prescriptions serve the interests of various parties to the conflict. In our view, this era of scientific pretension to technical answers appears to be coming to an end, as formula construction becomes increasingly politicized. Without advocating any normative criterion for spatial distribution we suggest that public finance needs a good dose of political theory— especially a behavioral theory of the use of political power and resources and a richer specification of the actors in the intergovern-mental process, both those within the public sector and their constituents without.

In Section IV, we offer a political interpretation of intergovern-mental transfers and their spatial distribution. We contend that the distributions over time have been determined by the outcome of particular political coalitions and forces, which can be much more richly described by political analyses. Furthermore, we suggest that the distributional battles have determined not only expenditure receipts but also have reshaped political power among various juris-dictions and actors.

In a brief exercise, with quite imperfect federal outlay data, we suggest that congressional committees and agencies within the federal government have spatial affinities and ties to constituents which shape the distribution of their expenditures. In a further exercise, we look at three waves of federal grants-in-aid from the mid-1960s on: the New Frontier/Great Society, the New Federalism, and the era of Countercyclical Assistance and "targeting." The battles over distribution have increasingly induced the growth of regional lobbies and research efforts. This conflict over formula construction is spilling over into regional debates about the reliability of the data on which formulas are based.

We argue that economists concerned with the distribution of public expenditures must incorporate in their research studies the power relationships within government agencies, between levels of government and between government and the private sector. Further, we also point out that a real understanding of distributional questions requires micro-level documentation of actual receipt of benefits by individuals, groups and classes.

II. THE EMPIRICAL EVIDENCE

A comprehensive attempt to identify the "beneficiaries" of intergovernmental transfers should examine the distribution of government spending in three dimensions. It should show how transfers are distributed spatially, it should examine how this distribution has changed over time, and it should weigh the relative importance of different categories and types of expenditures. This combination of spatial, temporal and functional evidence should provide a clear overview of what is being distributed to whom, how this distribution is changing and which components are the most significant in explaining the distribution.

Particular care must be taken when examining the distribution of federal expenditures to regions or states to first identify exactly what is being distributed. The federal government spent $60 billion in grants-in-aid to state and local governments during 1976. However, during the same year, total federal outlays exceeded $358 billion. This latter includes all federal government expenditures, of which the direct aid to states and localities comprised only 17%. Purchase of goods and services—defense and non-defense—payments to individuals, and interest payments on debt accounted for the remaining $298 billion. Expenditures of this magnitude have substantial distributional effects. In fact, they provide a very different picture of the overall "impact" of federal spending on regions and on states from grant data. It is important, therefore, to examine the distribution not only of federal aid but also of total federal outlays.

(This distinction in terminology between the more narrow category, "aid" and the all-inclusive "outlays," will be maintained throughout.)

In specifying to whom these expenditures are distributed, certain arbitrary choices must be made. Conceptually, many recipient units and categories can be identified, ranging from individuals to classes to regions of varying definition. However, the only available data has been collected on spatial units and has been aggregated according to political boundaries. Therefore, while other distributional foci could prove enlightening, necessity limits consideration to politically defined spatial units such as regions, states, cities and counties.

Currently, there are three principal sources of data from which to examine these elements of governmental spending. The Department of Commerce *Census of Governments* and *Government Finances* itemize federal, state and local intergovernmental transfers of aid by function (e.g., education, highways, public welfare). The Treasury Department's *Federal Aid to States* provides a detailed listing of federal grants paid directly to state and local governments by agency and by specific type of allocation. Both of these sources deal only with aid; grants which pass directly from one local government to another. Finally, the Community Services Administration report of *Federal Outlays* provides a listing of federal outlays—all federal expenditures, both direct and indirect. This source lists dollar outlays according to federal agency, and itemizes them by specific program and function. Thus, *Federal Outlays* provides a comprehensive description of the overall pattern of federal government spending. It is a rich and extensive body of data which has yet barely been tapped. Unfortunately, severe accounting problems render it currently only about 7% accurate (Anton, 1979) so that it must be used with caution.

In what follows, we integrate the existing evidence to provide an overview of the spatial, temporal and functional distribution of government transfers. We have chosen to focus on those distributions which have been most hotly debated of late. In particular, we will examine the distribution of federal expenditures (both aid and outlays) to regions and to states and the distribution of federal and state aid to cities (according to size) and within SMSAs (contrasting central cities with suburbs and non-metropolitan counties). As much as data allows, we will focus on the 1967-1977 time period. Our regional definitions will follow those of the U.S. Census.[1] It is important to remember that variations in spending within regions and within states often exceed the variations reported between them (Vehorn, 1977). Finally, while we will be quoting dollar figures for expenditures, straight comparison of these figures can be misleading due to considerable differences in economic conditions and cost of living across the United States. Unfortunately, we do not have adequate indexes with which to make these adjustments, nor is there a consensus as to how such regional differences ought to temper evaluation of the data.

FEDERAL TRANSFERS TO REGIONS

The Northeast currently receives the greatest amount of federal aid per capita, followed closely by the West, while the Midwest lags decidedly behind the rest of the country. In 1975, the northeastern region received $260 per capita in federal grants, while the midwestern states received only $198. The West and South received $246 and $220 respectively in per capita aid (Vehorn, 1977).

Public welfare grants account for the most significant proportion of this regional variation, with the Northeast receiving 35% more than the South in per capita aid ($116 per capita goes to the Northeast for public welfare, $75 to the South). The Northeast also receives the highest per capita grants for health and hospitals, regional development and general revenue sharing, while the West leads in the receipt of aid for manpower and employment security, highways and transportation, and natural resources. The Midwest remains at the bottom of the distribution per capita grants for education, highways and transportation, general revenue sharing, manpower and employment security, and health and hospitals (Vehorn, 1977).

Despite these disparities, federal aid is now distributed more evenly across regions than it was ten years ago. The relative differences in per capita aid have decreased, suggesting movement towards parity in the regional distribution of federal aid. Per capita grants to the Northeast increased significantly more rapidly than to other regions over the period, thus moving it ahead of the West and South which it had previously followed. The West experienced the greatest decline in federal aid relative to the national average, the relative position of the South also declined somewhat, and the Midwest remained in its former position below the national average (GAO, 1977).

Turning to the more comprehensive category of federal outlays, the West is clearly ahead of the rest of the nation, and the Midwest again remains at the bottom of the distribution. Total federal expenditure in the West during 1976 was $1,852 per capita, while it was only $1,228 in the Midwest. Federal spending in the South and Northeast were fairly close to each other, but well behind the West, with per capita outlays of $1,511 and $1,453 respectively (Havemann and Stanfield, 1977). To underscore the variation between regions, Anton (1979), using slightly different regional aggregations, notes a gap of more than $1,000 per capita between the lowest and highest region in 1977.

Enormous regional variations in defense expenditures account for more than half of these inequalities in federal outlays. Total spending in the West during 1976 exceeded that in the Midwest by $624 per capita, of which 58% ($359) was due to defense spending. Disparities in outlays for welfare programs account for most of the remaining regional variations (as noted in the discussion of federal aid) with the Northeast receiving the most and the Midwest the least. And according to the National Journal (1977) compilations, total spending on highways and sewers and on retirement programs is relatively evenly distributed across regions (Havemann and Stanfield, 1977).

The trend in per capita federal outlays over the past decade does not support the current image of continuing "bias" in federal spending in favor of the "Sunbelt" and at the expense of the "Frostbelt." While federal outlays have more than doubled since 1970, and the rank order of the regions has remained much the same, disbursements to the South and West have actually fallen behind those to the Northeast in their *rate* of increase. If judged by the rate of increase in spending, a slight bias towards the Northeast can be detected, indicating that the higher per capita amounts now going to the West and South are reflection of a past bias, rather than current trends (Anton, 1979).

However, we suggest much caution in viewing distributional outcomes on such an aggregate level. Anton clearly demonstrates that the "Sunbelt-Frostbelt" imagery is too simple in its depiction of regional differences, since part of the Sunbelt and part of the Frostbelt are in very similar relative positions. He calculates per capita outlays and rank orders for all nine subregions and observes the following trends in the 1970's: low disbursements to the North and Northeast getting higher, high disbursements to the South Atlantic, Mountain and Western regions getting higher, and low disbursements to the South and Central regions, increasing less rapidly than other regions (See Exhibit 1). He calculates regional differences from the national mean in 1971 and 1977 and notes that the Midwest and the South Central regions are the only ones which were not only below the national mean in both years, but moving further from it. He thus suggests that we might refer to a bias in favor of a "Ski and Sunbelt" and against the "Middlebelt" (Anton, 1979).

EXHIBIT 1

Sub-Regional Per Capita Federal Outlays
1971 and 1977

1. Mountain	Mountain	95
2. Pacific	Pacific	89
3. South Atlantic	South Atlantic	86
4. Mid-Atlantic	Mid Atlantic	108
5. West South Central	Great Plains	97
6. Great Plains	New England	111
7. East South Central	East South Central	101
8. New England	West South Central	66
9. Great Lakes	Great Lakes	107

Source: Anton, 1979

FEDERAL TRANSFERS TO STATES

The disparities in per capita federal aid to the states are substantially greater than the variation among regions. While in 1975
the Northeast received 31% more in per capita grants than the
Midwest, Wyoming received a full 133% more than Indiana. Clearly,
the regional debate should be approached with skepticism. In 1975,
per capita federal aid to states ranged from $152 (Indiana) to $354
(Wyoming), with $244 for the nation as a whole.

While comparisons of distribution to regions is a relatively simple
(though potentially misleading) task, it is much more difficult to
generalize about patterns of distribution across fifty states. We have
no criteria for judging how much aid different states should receive,
and it is clear that the amount of aid is not directly related to population. Since per capita income is a logical indicator of relative need,
we have chosen to use it as a yardstick with which to measure the
distribution of aid. It has been noted by some that high-income
states frequently receive more aid than low-income states. According
to a GAO study (1977), of the five states that received the most per
capita aid in 1975, three had above average income levels; while all
of the five states receiving the least per capita aid were below average
in income. Though these observations are accurate, enough exceptions
exist (low-income states among the top aid recipients and vice versa)
that evidence does not support consistent, across the board correlations between a state's per capita income levels and the federal aid
it receives (see Vehorn 1977 data).

While the sources of variation in the flow of federal aid to states
are complex, public welfare, highways and transportation, and

education grants account for about half of the total aid allocated and also for much of the variation between states.[2] General revenue sharing and health and hospital grants are fairly evenly distributed, and while development grants, manpower and employment security, and natural resources grants show greater unevenness in distribution, their absolute amounts are not enough to make very much of a difference (GAO, 1977).

During the past decade, there has been a marked trend towards convergence in per capita distribution of federal aid across states. This trend, however, has merely begun to mitigate even greater previous disparities among the states. For example, Maryland, the state which shoed the smallest percentage change in per capita aid from 1970-1975—33.9%, still receives more aid than Michigan, which gained the most during the period—166.5% (Vehorn, 1977).

Turning to the distribution of federal outlays, still greater inter-state disparities exist. In 1976, Alaska received 247% more in per capita federal disbursements than Wisconsin. Again, these differences are largely due to differences in defense expenditures. While Alaska received $3,620 per capita in federal outlays, Wisconsin received only $1,044; and over 50% of this gap is accounted for by defense contracts and salaries (Havemann and Stanfield, 1977).

Perhaps most strikingly, the distribution of per capita outlays varies somewhat consistently with per capita state incomes. The highest income states clearly receive among the highest per capita outlays—eight of the richest ten states (ranked by per capita income) are within the top 22% of the distribution of per capita outlays; likewise, while the correlation is not as great, the poorest states seem to receive lower per capita federal outlays (see Exhibit 2).

Due to the inconsistencies in the CSA federal outlays data over time, it is difficult to trace whether or not convergence in the distribution of federal outlays has been occurring in the way that we noted with federal aid. We look forward to the data-cleaning efforts suggested by Anton (1979) for further enlightment on this issue, as well as further exploration of distributional patterns of federal expenditures.

FEDERAL AID TO CITIES BY CITY SIZE

The smallest cities receive the smallest per capita federal aid, but the largest cities do not receive the greatest. Census data tabulated in Exhibit 3 show that for 1975-76, the six cities with population over 1 million received more than a third smaller per capita allocations than did the eighteen cities whose sizes fall between 500,000 and a million. Nevertheless, the distribution generally favors larger cities,

EXHIBIT 2

Federal Outlays To Selected States,
By Income Rankings, 1976

State	Per capita income 1975 rank	Per capita outlays Rank	Per capita outlays $	Total outlays Rank	Total outlays Millions of $	Outlays as % of total federal outlays
Alaska	1	1	3,887	41	1,368	.4
Connecticut	2	10	1,874	19	5,801	1.6
Delaware	3	45	1,247	49	722	.2
Illinois	4	39	1,372	5	15,290	4.3
New Jersey	5	11	1,815	6	13,281	3.7
New York	6	3	2,243	2	40,641	11.3
Maryland	7	7	2,067	13	8,471	2.4
California	8	8	1,951	1	41,330	11.5
Missouri	9	9	1,902	12	9,058	2.5
Hawaii	10	2	2,500	36	2,162	.6
North Carolina	41	43	1,288	16	7,019	2.0
Maine	42	20	1,641	39	1,738	.5
Tennessee	43	23	1,591	17	6,662	1.9
Louisiana	44	42	1,301	24	4,932	1.4
Kentucky	45	27	1,537	22	5,220	1.5
Alabama	46	30	1,525	20	5,511	1.5
South Carolina	47	29	1,437	28	4,048	1.1
New Mexico	48	4	2,165	34	2,483	.7
Arkansas	49	37	1,382	33	2,925	.8
Mississippi	50	10	1,730	27	4,059	1.1

Source: CSA, *Federal Outlays in Summary, Fiscal Year, 1976.*

Notes: The District of Columbia has been excluded here as it is clearly an exceptional case. Figures include Indirect Federal Support—interest payments on the national debt and outlays for use in other countries—which tend to greatly inflate the amounts received by New York and New Jersey in particular (See Anton, 1979).

EXHIBIT 3

Per Capita Amounts of Intergovernmental Aid Received By Cities
By Population Size Group (In Dollars)

Period	Level of Government	Average	1,000,000 +	500,000 to 999,999	300,000 to 499,999	200,000 to 299,999	100,000 to 199,999	50,000 to 99,999	less than 50,000
'68-69	State	49.56	174.27	53.83	38.12	26.47	33.17	31.44	18.59
	Federal	9.76	16.82	31.18	10.60	11.79	9.24	7.27	3.14
'71-72	State	63.46	222.51	71.31	56.07	56.96	48.71	35.14	23.49
	Federal	18.96	31.06	61.76	28.96	32.78	19.73	11.96	4.75
'72-73	State	79.99	254.66	82.91	68.72	61.62	56.07	38.45	43.01
	Federal	33.11	56.30	82.79	42.13	48.61	33.72	23.58	14.55
	Federal$_{rs}$	12.17	23.39	15.96	12.18	11.34	12.25	9.30	8.55
'75-76	State	100.76	364.65	119.31	88.99	94.02	83.09	58.79	40.43
	Federal	54.45	99.08	137.72	80.78	70.90	56.53	36.91	25.80
	Federal$_{rs}$	15.99	23.18	21.34	20.52	20.22	17.80	14.07	12.18

rs: the general revenue sharing component ot total federal aid

Source: Census, *City Government Finance*, Selected Years

with the smallest cities receiving $25.80 per capita, or less than one-half of the national per capita average of $54.45, and the eighteen in the second largest size group receiving $137.72, two and a half times the average.

Over the period from 1968 to 1976, the federal government has increased its aid expenditures to local governments dramatically. However, the relative positions of different size city groups have not changed in a systematic way. The second largest group, still the biggest recipients of federal aid, gained the least proportionately, suggesting that federal actions are tempering the disparities in the aid distribution. This group, however, includes some of the worst-off cities in the country. On the other hand, the six largest cities (which include Los Angeles and Houston) received the largest per capita increase over the period. The two other size categories which received larger than average increases were the 300,000 to 499,000 group and the less than 50,000 group. The largest and smallest cities gained most. No functional breakdown is currently available to document which types of aid are responsible for these trends.

The role of general revenue sharing (GRS), while less than one-third of total federal aid, is striking. In 1972, the first year of general revenue sharing, the largest per capita shares went to the biggest size cities. But from the beginning the program was less generous to larger cities proportionately than all other forms of federal aid combined. Furthermore, over the period from its adoption through 1976, formula changes favored intermediate size cities even more, so that disparities in the allocations of GRS by city size were substantially diminished. GRS has clearly been a "spreader" program.

No functional distributions are currently available by city size, nor are the federal outlay data compiled by city size. Thus, a conclusion that federal aid favors big cities can be drawn only tentatively on the basis of narrowly defined federal aid allocations.[3] And, the evidence suggests that the disparities within the distribution have diminished, rather than increased, over the decade of urban fiscal crisis.

FEDERAL AID TO CENTRAL CITIES, SUBURBS AND NONMETROPOLITAN CENTERS

Central cities receive higher per capita allocations of federal aid than either their suburbs or nonmetropolitan counties in the same state with the remarkable exception of the Western region (Vehorn, 1977). Using computations from the 1970 and 1975 Census sample, Vehorn suggests that Northeastern central cities receive the greatest per capita aid and Midwest central cities the least, though variations within regions are great. Oddly, the Vehorn study shows (without hypothesizing why) that suburban receipts in the Western region exceeded not only those of their own central cities, but of central cities in the South and Midwest as well.[4]

Over the time period from 1970 to 1975, central cities' receipts grew faster than the other two types of jurisdictions. At the same time, nonmetropolitan counties' receipts grew faster than suburban receipts, so that by 1975, these counties' per capita allocations exceeded suburban allocations in all regions but the West.

While cautioning that inter-group variation exists, Vehorn concludes that "the federal government has attempted to channel more local aid to central cities than to suburbs" over the period.

No central city/suburban comparisons of federal outlay data have been compiled, and it would be unreasonable to attempt it before the Anton (1979) data-cleaning effort has been completed. The inability to compare federal outlays with the narrower federal aid allocations prevents us from concluding that federal expenditures clearly have been redistributed toward greater shares for central cities in the recent period. However, the conclusion can be drawn tentatively that central cities have generally been favored in grants distribution except that a Western regional bias, favoring suburbs and rural areas, dating from an earlier period, still exists.

STATE AID TO CITIES BY SIZE

The record on state aid to cities by size is fairly straightforward: the bigger the city, the larger the per capita allocation. The distribution, from Census sample data, is tabulated for selected years in Exhibit 3.[5] In the most recent period, state allocations (which include federal aid that is passed on through state governments) were almost twice as large as direct federal to local allocations and generally favor larger size cities. The six cities in the biggest size category receive almost three times as much as the next set of cities and more than nine times as much as the smallest size cities.

The historical record for state aid distribution by city size from 1967 to the present is quite revealing. States increased their transfers during this era only a bit more than 100%, compared to the federal increase of more than 500%, though state allocations still remain larger. Intermediate size cities (from 100,000 to 500,000) gained the most percentage-wise, just the opposite of changes in federal aid distributions. Thus it can be concluded tentatively that statehouses, and federal programs run through the states, increasingly have been more generous to intermediate size cities than to those considered most in need of aid infusions in the urban-conscious seventies.

The combined changes in state and federal aid by city size suggest that the cities of over 1 million receive the greatest per capita a- mounts of intergovernmental transfers, whereas in 1962, the 500,000 to 1 million group did. The percent of aid relative to own source revenue, calculated by the ACIR (1977A, p. 49) for 1962-75, shows that cities of all sizes increased their dependency dramatically, but cities in the largest, smallest and 100,000 to 500,000 groups increased their dependency most.

STATE AID TO CENTRAL CITIES, SUBURBS AND
NONMETROPOLITAN COUNTIES

No multi-state studies of the central/suburban/rural distribution of state aid have been undertaken. Harold Hovey (1978, p. 107) cites two studies which are anecdotal rather than quantitative. He notes that while many states have one or more geographical units which claim that their state government discriminates against them in ex- penditure patterns, state level studies have been confined to noting facility locations and financial flows. The Carter administration, in formulating its urban policy, tried to determine whether or not states discriminated against their central cities, but multi-state data were not available to illuminate policy formulation (Hovey, 1978, p. 108).

Interpreting state aid flows is particulary tricky because a large part of the state-to-local distribution consists of pass-throughs from the federal government (ACIR, 1977B, p. 14). A forthcoming GAO study attempts to separate the federal component from the state- originating component, tracing the allocation of each to county jurisdictions for the state of New York. Using three types of counties (nonmetropolitan, metropolitan without a central city and metro- politan including a central city—roughly rural, suburban and central city), they are concluding that per capita state aid favors rural counties most, non-central city metropolitan counties next and central city SMSA counties least; furthermore, this pattern has not changed over the period from 1969 to 1975. Federal aid per capita pass-throughs in 1969 in New York favored rural counties, central city SMSA counties second and suburban metropolitan counties least; by 1975, changes in federal formulas and programs resulted in higher pr capita distributions to central city counties than to rural counties. Thus, to the extent that central city counties are faring better currently from state aid flows, such improvement is due to the federal pass-through component. The state-originated flows, even in a state like New York with a strong urban lobby, favor non-central city counties. A second interesting finding in the GAO study is that state aid favors counties with low fiscal capacity (GAO, 1979).

The ACIR (1977A) has compiled census data on receipt of state aid over time by type of jurisdiction (county, township, municipalities, school districts) over the period from 1952 to 1974. We could assume that townships represent rural jurisdictions and municipalities traditionally have been more dependent on state aid than townships and, furthermore, that such dependency has increased more rapidly for municipalities (ACIR, 1977, Table 8, p. 13). However, counties are even more dependent on state aid, although their dependency has remained the same over the period. Since many rural residents rely more heavily on the county for public services, it is not easy to conclude from this data that the states necessarily favor urban areas. The data, of course, provide no insight into central city vs. suburban jurisdictions.

In general, we might expect wide variation in state treatment of local areas. Most states share revenues with local governments, but some rely primarily on source-of-revenue or per capita criteria for sharing, while others, like Michigan and New York, have criteria that attempt to build in need indicators such as per capita local property values or tax effort. Furthermore, outlays by the state to local areas might be much different in distribution than aid, depending on diverse factors such as the scale of some services which require central city locations (e.g., much special education and some public health) as well as the political clout of various areas. Much interesting work remains to be done on documentation and interpretation of state to local expenditures.

INTERPRETATIONS OF THE DISTRIBUTIONAL DATA

In the above section, we have tried to present the basic cross-sectional and longitudinal evidence on spatial patterns of intergovernmental transfers. We have registered a number of complaints about the data, both in the form it is currently collected and compiled and in its adequacy. We have drawn some tentative conclusions about areal gainers and losers and changes in the distribution across time. From here, we could go on to construct elaborate variants on Gini coefficients that might show in even greater detail how the distributions have changed. However, we have succumbed to the delight of making sense out of numbers without explicitly placing the exercise in its normative framework. There are several points which must be addressed before we can interpret the significance of the trends we have displayed.

First of all, aside from our introductory comments, we have not justified why the distributions and changes over time might be cause for alarm or elation. We have posed no critieron to measure the distributions against so that we could evaluate the appropriateness of certain outcomes. This point has been explored by one of the authors at greater length elsewhere (Markusen and Fastrup, 1978). To summarize, it is impossible to discover any general consensus about what the aggregate expenditure distribution *should* be: should big cities receive more than their suburbs, should Frostbelt states receive more than their southern neighbors? The level of aggregation, both spatially and functionally, lumps qualitatively different recipients and programs together.

In probing for normative criteria, one inevitably concludes that a process of disaggregation must be undertaken. Ultimately, we think of justice as a matter of human, not spatial, consequences. The substitution of spatial units for individual recipients, the logical outcome of the fact that political units (state and local governments) are the major actors in the intergovernmental battle, obscures the patterns of real change in the human condition for various socioeconomic groups and individuals. Individuals are the only ones for whom we have had a societal consensus on the appropriate indicator: the distribution of income. A single criterion emerges for judging the success or failure of various programs in improving the distribution: changes over time in per capita income of individuals in the various income intervals. No spatial characteristic equivalent to income in the individual case has ever been proposed, much less agreed upon. Thus, in the descriptions above, we noted when the distribution, over various sets of spatial groupings, appears to be less skewed or to register greater dispersion over time on either a per capita or an income per capita basis. But we really cannot say whether these outcomes are good or bad.

Unless we could generate one agreed upon index of spatial worthiness (e.g., current efforts to rank cities as more or less "distressed"). our only option is to try to map the incidence of many deserving individuals onto spatial units, a presumption which lurks behind many of the arguments in formula construction for intergovernmental transfers. To champion a particular spatial distribution is to assume this correspondence. Yet there are many difficulties in doing so. The debate about people prosperity vs. place prosperity is not new

(Winnick, 1966; Alonso, 1971); in the 1960s it was employed as a critique of many Kennedy/Johnson programs. Recently it has been rearticulated cogently on the left by Matt Edel (1979) as a criticism of the current drift of national urban policy.

In fact, we know that spatial units do not correspond to needy populations well. Central cities have widely disparate income distributions and many inner ring suburbs have large numbers of poor, unemployed residents. Thus it is impossible to argue single-mindedly that central cities should receive greater intergovernmental transfers or that states with high unemployment rates should receive more. We could only argue reasonably for such aggregate distributions if we knew that the unemployed and poorer groups within each jurisdiction really received the flows. In order to know the latter, we would have to have studies of economic and service flows that are simply not now available. First, we would have to know how each state and local government spends its receipts and how each locally based recipient of federal outlays (including private corporations) spends its dollars. Then we would have to be able to document the multiplier effects, to show us for instance whether or not public employee salaries remain in the neighborhood or city and generate jobs for other residents. With present techniques, the demonstration that intergovernmental transfers by place do reach worthy people is impossible to make. Many of the technical difficulties encumbering even the documentation of flows by place (e.g., which regions do federal military dollars ultimately reach) are addressed in the various papers assembled in Glickman, ed. (1979).

A final caveat for interpreting spatial disparities in expenditure is that intergovernmental relations are not equivalent to intergovernmental transfers. Tax flows are also important, as well as the distribution of tax breaks. The ultimate origin of taxes is quite difficult to trace (Markusen and Fastrup, 1978, p. 89). Nonbudgetary policies such as regulation, licensing, trade and foreign policies also may have severe distributional consequences, but are not available in a spatial accounting of intergovernmental transfers. A great deal of additional work would have to be done before we could say with much certainty that we knew what the distributional consequences of such policies might be. In part, this arises from the fact that such policies frequently affect the supply side of regional growth rather than the demand side. Supply-induced growth is particularly difficult to model and measure quantitatively (Chinitz, 1961).

In addition to the receipt of places and people of expenditures, an entirely different and fascinating question is posed by the political consequences of changes in the pattern of intergovernmental transfers. Research on the effects that changes in levels and requirements of particular transfers have had on political power relationships at the state and local level is almost nonexistent. One notable exception is Yin (1979), who tries to show how local political bureaucracies restructure themselves in response to changes in particular grant programs. Since gains in political power in the long run may be as significant as economic gains, the documentation of such political consequences should be pursued under the question "Who benefits from intergovernmental transfers?"

III. THE INADEQUACY OF CURRENT INTERGOVERNMENTAL FISCAL STUDIES

In a recent review of intergovernmental finance, George Break states, "If fiscal research is stimulated by rapid growth in the programs to be studied, intergovernmental grants should soon be basking in the warm glow of expert attention" (Break, 1978). With the burgeoning debate on the spatial distribution of these grants, we might add that such research will undoubtedly address these spatial patterns. In order to speculate on the direction and value of future public finance research, in this section we reflect on methodology. Fiscal research can be divided into descriptive and prescriptive studies.

Descriptive research efforts use empirical testing to substantiate hypotheses about "explanations" for the variation in fiscal variables (expenditures, tax rates, tax base) cross-sectionally or over time. There are two types of such studies: those which avoid behavioral postulates, focusing on characteristics of jurisdictions as determinants of tax spending patterns and those which employ explicit theories of government behavior. The first type of study generally consists of multiple regression techniques where a dependent variable such as expenditure is regressed on several explanatory variables, such as local per capita tax base, percent of tax base that is commercial and industrial, and intergovernmental transfers. While the exogenous variables in reduced form may be considered proxies for fiscal capacity (ability to pay) and tax price of public servies, they imperfectly represent decision variables in public choice models. Elliott Morss definitively criticized both the empirical and theoretical weaknesses of expenditure determination studies years ago (Morss, 1966).

While such studies have become less fashionable of late, the new interest in spatial distribution of expenditure may revive them. An example is the effort to gauge the state and local fiscal response to demographic changes across a sample of fifty states by Weinstein and Firestine (1978), in which they use 57 different demographic indicators in turn to try to explain the variation in expenditure patterns over time. Undoubtedly, efforts will soon be made to explain the variation in federal and state-to-local expenditures to areas by determination studies, in which the exogenous variables will be characteristics of areas (per capita income, local tax effort, percent proverty population) and functional components of expenditure (defense, health and education). What such studies will tell us is uncertain; the characteristics of places which may be correlated with expenditure levels may not reveal anything about the complex public sector behavior that ultimately determines such distributions, especially in ways that would enable forecasting. And the regression of aggregate levels of expenditure on components of that expenditure (categories such as education, health, etc.) has been shown by Morss to be incorrect use of econometric techniques, which are supposed to be employed on stochastic processes, not on a relationship which by definition is determinate. Similarly, a regression which "explains" expenditure levels by several indicators will not be analyzing a stochatic process if those very indicators are used in the allocation formulas.

The second type of empirical study which has gained popularity in recent years tries more explicitly to describe the behavior of the public sector with methods that have emerged from rational behavior models in microeconomics. The new field of public choice theory focuses directly on such behavior. Unfortunately, to date, public choice studies rely almost totally on individual utility maximization models in which the median voter is assumed to be the active agent in deciding public sector tax and expenditure levels, by pursuing utility maximization (Break, 1978). The empirical work testing voter choice models similarly employs regression techniques that attempt to explain expenditure outcomes on the basis of the greater sector price and income equivalents of consumer choice in the private sector.

The trouble with both these variants of expenditure determination studies is that their modeling of the public sector institutions and behavior requires rather restrictive simplifying assumptions. This is particularly true if we anticipate their application to the determination of intergovernmental transfers. Even the second type of study limits its scrutiny of the relevant actors to voter/consumers, which assumes that the political process is demand-dominated and that government legislative bodies, bureaus and elected officials automatically respond to the median voter's wishes. But in fact, the array of petitioners and decisionmakers includes many whose powers and interests are quite different from the median voter. We map out an alternative approach below.

Intergovernmental prescriptive studies include the original Heller/ Pechman work on revenue sharing, which argued that replacing categoricals by revenue sharing from the federal to state and local levels would solve the fiscal imbalance problem, increase flexibility in decisionmaking and improve efficiency in the public sector by permitting the use of revenue sharing funds to be more responsive to constituents' needs. Since then, Richard Nathan at Brookings and other social scientists have designed specific criteria on which to base revenue sharing, at both the federal and state levels, as well as certain categorical programs such as CDBG. (One of the authors, Markusen, recently designed an indicator for the anti-recessionary program based on changes in employment as a proxy for long run economic health. (GAO, 1977, pp. 103-123.)

In general, such studies identify problems with current formulas (anomalous distributions, for instance) and suggest new indicators for formula construction. The new indicators are generally proxies for "needs" of geographical places and are thus clearly prescriptive and advocatory. This commitment on the part of social scientists and policy analysts to produce prescriptive recommendations is laudable. However, the exercise itself frequently results in scientific claims for the appropriateness of a particular indicator, claims which may originate in the political rather than research sphere but nevertheless accompany the public debate. Whether a particular formula inventor is aware of it or not, any individual indicator will favor certain jurisdictions over others and will embody a normative decision about need. When such formulas are debated, they are frequently shorn of their normative logic and simply championed as better criteria of "need." An example is the age of the housing stock variable in recent federal formulas. And, of course, the particular formulas have frequently been chosen because their indicators correlate with certain impressions of deservedness of their populations, without any guarantee that the expenditures will reach those within the jurisdiction who are, in fact, worthy.

On the basis of the above reflections, we might offer a structural critique of the role of fiscal experts in the formula creation process. With the advent of general revenue sharing in 1972, prescriptive work on formulas reached a new state of development. No longer merely accounting for expenditure and revenue patterns of state and local government post facto, fiscal specialists now played a central role in creating the formulas that allocated revenue to state and local governments. The formulas for general and special revenue sharing were to be based, as President Nixon put it, "on objective criteria" (Feshbach, 1975, p. 15). Fiscal experts came to be relied upon to develop these criteria, a job which has expanded to encompass revisions of the original formulas and the creation of new federal grant programs based on formula distributions.

Social science construction of allocation criteria did not begin with revenue sharing. Economists, sociologists, political scientists, psychologists and other professionals devised the criteria for the New Frontier and Great Society categorical project grant programs in the 1960s. Here, too, "objective criteria" were necessary. Piven and Cloward argue that the criteria functioned to obscure the political purpose of the programs:

> There were other reasons why the political interests at stake were not widely recognized, at least in the beginning. One was the large role played by various professionals, especially social workers and social scientists, who provided the rationales for the Great Society. Each measure was presented at the outset as a politically neutral "scientific cure" for a disturbing social malady. Each concrete program that evolved was couched in the murky, esoteric terminology customarily used by professionals, a terminology that obscured the class and racial interests at stake, so that few groups could be certain who would gain from the new programs or who would lose, or what they would gain or loss. (Piven and Cloward, 1917, p. 277.)

In other words, the apparent scientific character of indicators proposed by public finance experts may have served certain powerful state and local groups who wished to smokescreen their attempts to garner a larger share of the federal budget.

IV. THE POLITICAL DETERMINATION OF INTERGOVERNMENTAL TRANSFERS

Above we have suggested that fiscal analysts have unduly ignored the political and social conflict which ultimately shapes fiscal federalism. In place of an "expenditure determinants" approach to the study of the spatial distribution of transfers, we propose a political study. In what follows, we lay out the elements of such a study, documented by an historical interpretation of the last two decades of federal aid allocations. We do not claim to pose a satisfactory theory of political resources and political power that would explain all of the interrelationships determining the distribution of transfers. This task we commend to fiscal researchers in the future.

ELEMENTS OF A POLITICAL THEORY

Our basic contention is that the spatial distribution of intergovernmental transfers can be explained most easily by studying the politics of the process under which they were produced. To borrow from economics, we can think of the process as having demand and supply sides. Constituents, particularly state and local governments and special interest groups, form the demand for intergovernmental transfers at the federal level. On the private sector side, certain interest groups are better organized and more "well-heeled" and therefore much stronger and persuasive than the median voter. The pattern of federal outlays and grants may be an amalgam of many special interest-oriented porkbarrel programs, whose shape can only be modelled properly by explicit inclusion of those groups in the model. For instance, state shares of federal farm price support payments could be hypothesized to be related to the absolute and relative size of the farm constituency, the seniority of their representatives in Congress, the profitability of their farms, the level of organization among farmers and the campaign contribution "price" they are willing to pay for political power. Similarly, organizations of state and local public officials and employees, who form the major lobby groups for federal aid, will win larger allocations if their lobbying effort is well-articulated and well-financed. Several interesting hypotheses could be posed regarding the strength of such efforts and the expenditure outcomes.

Demanders may be as interested in the functional form in which the money is distributed as in the actual level of government. The relative power between levels of government and among agencies is strongly affected by the form of transfers chosen. For instance, the switch from categorical grants to block grants tends to diminish the power of agencies receiving categoricals and to strengthen the power of general local government. The constituency groups with power within certain local agencies also stand to gain or lose from changes in the grant structure (Friedland, Piven and Alford, 1977).

On the supply side are the federal Congress and state legislatures who actually appropriate the funds and the bureaucracies who propose programs and administer them. Certain congressional committees at the federal level, and their bureaucratic counterparts, may have long histories of relationships with certain constituencies (McConnell, 1966; Wildavsky, 1974). Such links may provide a tremendous momentum to the distributional pattern. But bureaus may also have significant power to shape programs in their own interests. Work on the supply behavior in the public sector is relatively nonexistent in public finance.[6] Adequate models would have to take into account the complexity and diversity of behavior in the public sector itself.

The political interactions among the forces battling over the distribution of federal expenditures are suggested by federal outlays data on an agency by agency basis (rather than by function, as is normally done). In Exhibit 4, we have aggregated the total per capita outlays of selected federal agencies by subregions. Certain agencies seem to have spatial affinities, as evidenced by the uneven distribution of their expenditures across the country. We can hypothesize that these distributions are the outcomes of the interactions among agencies, the interests of their constituents and the congressional committees concerned. For example, the seeds of an explanation of the regional unevenness of spending by the Department of the Interior are found in a history of the mountain West:

> Without the federal factor, the mountain states' economy might not be viable at all . . . The decision to promote the growth of the West, even at the cost of the taxpayers of the other regions, may well have been a wise one in the interests of long term development of the U.S.A. But the decision was not primarily economic, but rather political—the result of adroit maneuvering by Western Senators and Representatives on Capitol Hill.
>
> The House Interior Committee, for instance, is headed by Wayne Aspinall of Colorado's Western Slope. Aspinall has obtained authorization for so many federal dam and reservoir projects in Colorado that even his home-state boosters admit some of them are uneconomic and should never be built. Yet it is interesting to note that no federal water projects deliver subsidized water to cities east of the Mississippi . . . Interior, or course, is the great patron department of the West. (Pierce, 1972; p. 26).

This type of historical and political analysis tells much about the distribution of certain federal expenditures that we could never learn from econometric expenditure determination studies or microeconomic behavior models.

We suggest that further examination of such factors in the supply behavior of the public sector would help explain distributional patterns of outlays. Likewise, demand side forces such as the relative levels of organization and influence of the constituency of an agency

EXHIBIT 4

Per Capita Federal Outlays to Regions, by Agency, 1976

AGENCY	Per Capita Outlays[1] (in thousands of dollars)									
Region	Agriculture	Defense	HEW	HUD	Interior	Transportation	ERDA	EPA	Commerce	Labor
Northeast										
New England	41.5	476.7	635.5	15.7	4.7	53.5	3.5	17.4	5.4	48.4
Mid-Atlantic	51.7	239.2	647.3	9.7	3.5	44.2	13.8	3.8	2.8	46.0
Midwest										
Great Lakes	42.6	162.8	544.6	8.1	2.4	30.8	13.2	19.7	2.4	36.1
Great Plains	82.7	437.6	557.5	11.5	16.1	41.7	8.1	22.2	4.5	33.9
South										
South Atlantic	75.9	462.1	564.6	9.1	8.0	40.4	12.6	24.6	16.5	30.5
E.S. Central	102.8	339.0	552.2	10.1	5.1	36.6	69.3	13.5	4.9	37.8
W.S. Central	86.8	400.8	499.2	10.5	6.7	43.8	2.2	14.6	6.9	34.5
West										
Mountain	87.4	448.8	469.2	10.2	118.1	63.1	87.8	15.0	11.9	44.7
Pacific	62.6	656.2	567.0	10.4	33.9	39.5	30.7	43.8	8.3	50.6

Note: District of Columbia has not been included.
     [1] includes both direct grants and all other indirect oulays.

Source: Community Services Administration, *Federal Outlays in Summmary, Fiscal Year 1976* (Washington, D.C.: U.S. Government Printing Office, 1976).

may be instrumental in the spatial distribution of federal spending. For instance, we might hypothesize that the bias of the Agriculture Department in favor of the West is in part a reflection of the influence of large scale, organized agribusiness.

Demand and supply side actors meet before the legislative bodies at the state and federal levels. Here, the details of outlays and transfers are sketched out, followed, in some cases, by discretionary regulations and implementation at the bureaucratic or state and local levels, also affected by political power and conflict. In what follows, we document how important political coalitions and conflicts are in the determination of certain federal intergovernmental flows.

THE POLITICS OF TWO DECADES: THE SEESAW BATTLE OVER FEDERAL GRANTS

In the previous section we have posited the theory that broad social, economic and political conflict between groups, classes and individuals organized on spatial, functional and ideological lines, accounts for the distribution of federal expenditures. This is true for all federal government activity including tax and regulatory policies, but we have chosen to focus exclusively on spending patterns.

While many interests are brought to bear on the allocation process, including executive and judicial agencies, decisions on the appropriation of funds available for expenditures are worked out in the legislative arena. In this section we take a closer look at the legislative and executive branch politics of one small part of the total federal budget, federal grants to cities. We describe the political conflict that has been responsible both for the changes in the dollar amounts going to different types of cities in different parts of the country and for changes in the structure of the grant programs themselves. In this case, a key impetus for change has been the relationship of the Democratic and Republican parties to various ethnic, economic and political constitutency groups, including state and local government officials.

We have found three distinctive swings in the distribution of federal grants to cities in the 1960s and 70s that correlate highly with Democratic and Republic electoral strategy. As Exhibit 5 demonstrates, federal grants to cities grew by a tremendous amount during this total period, with the northeastern and midwestern cities benefitting most from 1965-72, the southern and western cities benefitting most from 1972-75, and a slight swing back in favor of the first group from 1975-78. The first swing is a function of the large Democratic majorities in Congress in the 1960s, coupled with eight years of a Democratic Presidency. Particularly during the key Great Society years (1965-66), many grant programs were initiated or expanded that were aimed at the traditional New Deal constituency of big city ethnic machines and organized labor in the industrial belt, as well as at the recently expanded and explosive population of minorities in the large northern cities.

However, the focus by the Great Society on blacks and Hispanics in large cities produced a political backlash in the once solidly Democratic south and also among blue-collar white ethnics who were abandoning the central cities for suburbia. Richard Nixon based his "silent majority" election campaign of 1968 on an appeal to these disaffected Democrats and once in office, embarked on what was to be an eight-year strategy of restructuring the post-New Deal two-party alignment and traditional national voting patterns. This strategy, outlined by Kevin Phillips in *The Emerging Republican Majority* (1970), tried to merge the 1968 Nixon and Wallace votes by building a coalition that combined voters from the old Republican suburbia and midwest farm belt with voters in the rapidly growing southern and western regions and the new suburbia of the Democratic ethnics. The redistribution effects of the formulas for President Nixon's general revenue sharing and grant consolidation proposals were a deliberate part of this Republican strategy. The adoption by Congress in modified form of some elements of Nixon's "New Federalism" accounts for the second swing.

The third swing grew out of the Watergate scandal and recession of the mid-1970s. Together they led to a defeat of the Nixon strategy, strong Democratic congressional gains in all regions and metropolitan areas, as well as the election of a southern Democratic President. Congressional Democrats were able to effect mild redistribution toward areas of their greatest voting strength, while not rescinding the increased funding levels that had been awarded to the Sunbelt, small cities and suburbia during the heyday of the New Federalism.

The Politics of Distribution. The politics of distribution involves two elements: who the money goes to and who controls the allocation process at each level through which the funds flow. These two elements are highly interrelated. For example, the recent debate over whether HUD, EDA, the Department of the Treasury or some newly-created agency should control a National Development Bank largely revolved around perceptions by various potential recipients about which agency and distribution structure would most favor their interests. Similarly, the decision between establishing the Bank at one central location or a series of regional offices would influence who ultimately gets what and who would decide who gets what. Even if a grant program employs an automatic formula, the formula itself had distributive consequences. In addition, the recipient state and/or local governments will also shape the distribution, depending on which level of government and which agency within that level controls the program. Political battles also occur over the administrative regulations imposed by both Congress and the federal agencies responsible for grant oversight and the extent to which these regulations are actually enforced (Elazar, 1976).

Federal grants directly to city government agencies began in the New Deal period. President Roosevelt, through relief and public works programs, wanted to get large amounts of money into the hands of millions of unemployed workers, among other things because they were a major force in his electoral coalition. Republican-dominated state governments had proven to be unsympathetic to massive relief and public works efforts. In addition, he channeled the money through city government agencies because big-city Democratic machines were a crucial part of his electoral base, and the various New Deal programs gave Democratic mayors a huge source of money to dispense and thus garner continued voter support, not to mention campaign contributions and outright graft, in some cases. (Schlesinger, 1958, 1960. Piven, 1971).

Republicans during the 1930s and 40s often denounced what they saw as the New Deal's intrusion on state sovereignty. Their preferred method was to funnel grants-in-aid to state governments. Conflict over this issue came to a head in the Federal Airport Act of 1946, when, despite GOP insistence that all aid go to the states, the Democrats included a provision that allowed federal grants to go directly to certain types of cities. In the 1950s the pattern was somewhat reversed, with Republican President Eisenhower's Interstate Highway Act putting billions of dollars nationwide into the hands of state government officials, many (though by no means all) of whom were Republicans, with which they could dispense jobs, contracts and other business to preferred constituents in exchange for political support (Dommel, 1974).

The Three Swings. With the Democrats back in power under Kennedy and Johnson, grants to cities proliferated. Demetrios Caraley, in an analysis of key votes in the House and Senate between 1945 and 1975, argues that party affiliation is the crucial variable in explaining Congressional votes on urban aid. Grant programs to cities were most likely to be passed or appropriations expanded when there was a preponderance of norther Democrats in Congress and when a Democrat was President. Southern Democrats were more likely to oppose urban aid programs than their northern counterparts, but even so Caraley points out that their voting record in general was more pro-urban than Congressional Republicans. Thus, the Johnson years in particular were ideally suited to a major expansion of urban programs (Caraley, 1976).

Piven and Cloward point out that during the 1960s the Democratic practice of targeting grants-in-aid to city rather than state governments was supplemented by a new strategy of targeting aid to particular ethnic and neighborhood groups. Because black and Hispanic people were generally excluded from urban services by local Democratic machines, the Kennedy and Johnson administrations created programs which bypassed local government and put money directly into the hands of minority-controlled community agencies (Piven, 1971).

The increasing use of categorical grants led to the emergence of interest group coalitions that cut across intergovernmental and geographic lines. The more powerful of these, such as the highway and education lobbies, transcended party affiliation as well. But some were more vulnerable to the vagaries of political partisanship. As Nixon ascended to the Presidency in 1968, he prepared to do battle with the Great Society's legacy. The result was a curious admixture known as the New Federalism, which rather than launching a frontal attack on grant programs for out-of-favor constituencies, chose instead a flanking movement by reorganizing the grant system itself (Nathan, 1975 A).

One element of the Nixon strategy was to create a broad grant program that would give aid to all state governments and nearly all general purpose local governments, including very small ones. The money, within certain vague guidelines, could be spent in whatever fashion the recipient desired. Republican sentiment was that certain bureaucratic and constituency groups were better organized at the Congressional committee and federal agency level than at state or local levels, and that placing more decisionmaking power over federal grants at the state and local level would result in a diminution of influence by Democratic party-favored groups and bureaus (Feshbach, 1975; Beer, 1976).

In order to drum up support in Congress for General Revenue Sharing (GRS), President Nixon and the Treasury Department mobilized state and local government executive and legislative officials to lobby for the measure. They did this by promising a large number of these governmental units that they would receive more money under this new program than they were getting under the previous categorical grant programs. The outcome—more for everybody—has been dubbed "spreading" by Richard Nathan. Under the first formula for the GRS program, which began operating in December, 1972, $5.3 billion in aid was divided up between 50 states and nearly 38,000 counties, townships and municipalities (Nathan, 1975 B).

The political payoff for the Republican party was that suburbs and small cities and towns, plus the western and southern regions in general, were the biggest gainers under the formula for the new program (Nathan, 1975 B; 1977). Still since the Nixon administration promised that GRS would be an "add-on" to all existing grants, mayors in hard-pressed northern central cities were supportive. Two key legislators originally opposing the program, Democrats Muskie of Maine and Mills of Arkansas, were both running for the Democratic Presidential nomination in 1971-72 and the mayors in particular prevailed upon them to acquiesce to a modified version of the Nixon proposal (Dommel, 1974). This support turned out to be crucial in breaking the Congressional logjam.

The State and Local Fiscal Assistance Act finally passed in October, 1972, and one month later President Nixon was overwhelmingly reelected. He then began a renewed push for the second element of his "New Federalism" strategy: the elimination of many Great Society categorical grant programs and their replacement by broadly defined block grants with power of administration more firmly vested in state and local general government bodies (Banfield, 1971). His first step was to announce drastic cutbacks in many grant programs, including "impoundment" of funds already appropriated by Congress, claiming that General Revenue Sharing could be used by cities to make up for the lost grant revenues. Thus, despite repeated promise of "add-on" by the Nixon administration over the previous four years, this, as Paul Dommel puts it, "was clearly the language of a policy of substitution." Big-city mayors who had previously supported GRS now turned around and denounced it as a "cruel hoax" and a "gigantic double-cross" (Dommel, 1974, pp. 173-4).

The battle over block grants (also called "special revenue sharing") got bogged down by the Watergate scandal, giving the constituency groups and politicians who opposed the grant regulation added leverage. In the end only two modified versions of Nixon's original special revenue sharing proposals passed Congress, the Comprehensive

Employment and Training Act (CETA) in 1973 and the Community Development Block Grant (CDBG) program in 1974. The latter, as we argue below, involved substantial redistribution of money and power benefitting constituencies to which Republicans at all levels of government pitch their electoral appeals. A smaller grant consolidation, Title XX grants to state governments for social services, also passed Congress in late 1974.

Since the early 1970s, the politics of federal grants have increasingly involved bargaining and conflict between governmental units rather than among private constituencies. In addition, the debates have focused more on regional or other spatial disparities rather than on functional categories of assistance (Wilmoth, 1978). An indication of the first trend is the growth since the late 1960s of the power and organization of the "intergovernmental lobby"[7] represented by groups like the National Governors' Association. The latter trend is characterized by the recent appearance of *regional* lobbies, such as the Coalition of Northeastern Governors (CONEG), (Pierce, 1976).

The formula era brought on by the Nixon administration, despite some serious setbacks, achieved its desired result. The net effect on cities, as noted by one of the architects of General Revenue Sharing, Richard Nathan, was "increased support for smaller city governments in general and also for larger cities in the South and West that were not active participants in the older categorical programs" (Nathan, 1978, p. 80). Our Exhibit 3 (above) shows this clearly for city-size categories. But it only took a couple of years for the Democratic Congress to adapt the Nixon-initiated formulas to better advantage. In July of 1976, with the national elections less than four months away, the Democratic Congress overrode President Ford's veto and passed the Public Works Employment Act of 1976. Title I of this Act, the Local Public Works Program, and Title II, the Anti-Recession Fiscal Assistance Program, combined with Title II and IV of CETA to form the "countercyclical package." These programs also used formulas, but with very different distributional results.

Since the strategy of the Democratic Party in the coming elections was to blame the Republicans for the unhealthy state of the economy and particularly for the high unemployment rate, the countercyclical package, with its economic stimulus and job-creation focus, demonstrated the Democratic commitment to a political alternative (Singer, 1975). And since the programs were all targeted to areas of high unemployment, central cities, particularly in the northeast and north central regions, benefitted substantially (GAO, 1977; Treasury, 1978; ACIR, 1978A). President Carter, upon taking office, expanded the budget for these programs, and further expansions were made with the passage of the Intergovernmental Anti-Recession Act in May of 1977. Also in 1977, Congress passed the new "dual" formula for Community Development Block Grants, which was highly beneficial to the older central cities in the Northeast and Midwest. The net effect of these and other programs was a swing-back of federal dollars to the traditional Democratic constituencies, after the Nixon redistribution of the early 70s.

Exhibit 5, taken from a recent paper by Richard Nathan and extended by us back to 1965-66, illustrates clearly the three cyclical swings of the politics of federal grants to local government. The northeastern and midwestern cities did well in the 1960s, were eclipsed by the Sunbelt cities' gains under the New Federalism, but enjoyed a significant comeback in the Democratic surge of 1975-78.

One element of this comeback is the resurrection of a discretionary project grant program by HUD to take the place (on a much more modest scale) of urban renewal, which was one of the seven programs "folded-into" CDBG. Exhibit 6 shows the distribution of Urban Development Action Grants in 1978:

Printout Politics. The use of automatic formulas for the distribution of grants-in-aid to state and local governments seems to be a steadily rising trend. Even cost-of-living increases in social security benefits, a transfer program to individuals, was tied to an automatic formula during the Republican highpoint in 1972 (Derthick, 1979). The concern with creation of automatic distribution formulas has generated a whole new industry for fiscal analysts, one that we might call "needs measurement." In the last few years a bevy of studies have appeared each trying to develop statistical indices measuring "need" according to various criteria which would, in turn, be inserted into formulas to target the distribution of federal grants (Nathan, 1976, 1977c, 1977d; Stanley, 1976; HUD, 1976; Treasury Department, 1978; Kordalewski, 1978; Barro, 1978; House Banking Committee, 1978). Who should receive the money, by what criteria, through what medium, for what purpose, and at what level of spatial or demographic aggregation, are all questions that are hotly debated.

How can "distress" or "need" be defined? The Congressional Budget Office conducted a study in 1977 of the possibilities of targeting federal spending to relieve "troubled local economies," but ran up against several definitional problems. If one is concerned with the problem of low growth, then the New England, Middle Atlantic and Great Lakes states need the most help. On the other

EXHIBIT 5

Comparative Growth in Total Federal Grants,
Selected Northeastern and Midwestern and Sunbelt Cities, 1965-78
(thousands of dollars)

Eight Northeastern and Midwestern Cities	Total Grants 1965-66	Total Grants 1971-72	Total Grants 1974-75	Est. Grants FY 1978	% Inc. 66-72	% Inc. 72-75	% Inc. 75-78
St. Louis	380	14,145	31,483	109,500	3622	123	248
Buffalo	2,589	15,345	31,844	80,947	493	108	154
Cleveland	6,468	16,782	47,733	110,381	159	184	131
Boston	32,842	61,249	66,782	120,885	179	9	81
Philadelphia	15,836	82,694	130,820	328,134	422	58	151
Detroit	20,770	132,071	166,183	311,142	536	26	87
Chicago	29,804	95,147	166,129	407,726	219	75	145
Baltimore	5,308	43,835	108,015	181,394	726	146	68
Mean value for the eight Northeastern and Midwestern cities:					795	91	133
Nine Sunbelt Cities							
Atlanta	2,341	10,345	38,458	58,994	346	269	53
Dallas	—	4,807	42,165	64,147	—	777	74
Houston	5,496	12,507	45,869	86,395	128	267	88
Phoenix	3,067	8,990	36,556	70,911	193	307	94
Birmingham	1,357	3,240	14,458	31,643	139	346	119
Louisville	8,220	21,588	36,364	67,686	163	68	86
Jacksonville	—	6,247	30,619	40,886	—	390	34
New Orleans	398	14,770	45,670	86,895	3611	209	90
Oklahoma City	4,168	5,540	18,691	38,748	33	237	107
Mean value for the nine Sunbelt cities:					659	318	83

Source: U.S. Bureau of the Census, City Government Finances; (Nathan, 1978, p. 81).

EXHIBIT 6

UDAGs By Cities, and Dollars According to Region

	# of cities	# of dollars (millions)
Northeast	45	137
North Central	27	116
South	17	53
West	2	60

Source: (Lyall, 1979).

hand, if low income is the primary issue, then the South and South-west, "despite relatively high growth rates of past years," deserve the most urgent attention (CBO, 1977).

A recent report by the House Committee on Banking, Finance and Urban Affairs (1978) lists three different ways of discerning need: 1) social needs, such as poverty, crime, or poor health; 2) economic decline, including relative or absolute loss in population, income, manufacturing activity, or retail sales volume; and 3) fiscal problems, ranging from low tax bases and high tax rates, to short-term cash flow problems, severe budget deficits and near bankruptcy.

What size and type of spatial unit should be chosen for distribution, Katharine Lyall, in a forthcoming article on targeting aid to "cities and people in distress," lists four different recipient units for targeting strategies: by city, by people, by neighborhood, and by region (Lyall, 1979). Each one of the measurements of need used in the House Banking Study targets aid on different sets and types of cities in different parts of the United States. As we noted above, individual need may not correlate well with spatial characteristics.

The House Banking Committee Report and the GAO Report (1977) both advocate better understanding of urban economic evolution as a basis for fashioning formulas. The former concludes that:

Better knowledge of urban dynamics—of cause-effect relationships within cities—would facilitate the development of consensus on those aspects of urban need that should be considered.

(House Banking Committee, 1978, p. 77)

We question this optimism. When federal budgetary resources are rapidly expanding, congressional leaders could strike a series of compromises on dual or multiple formulas whereby each unit of government chooses the automatic formula most favorable for its purposes. Such an approach would be the ultimate in "spreading", with the entire range of regional and intra-metropolitan interests in the intergovernmental aid lobby satisfactorily subsidized. But in this age of fiscal restraint, where "targeting" is the watchword, continued, continued bitter controversy is more likely. Groups such as the Northeast-Midwest Congressional Coalition and Southern Growth Policies Board are both launching extensive formula research projects and writing critical reports on "bias" in federal programs.

Some have bemoaned this domination of formula grant construction by "printout politics," but regardless of sophisticated social science input, politics has been and will continue to be the determining factor in the grant process (Stanfield, 1978b). In this sense, there is no such thing as a truly non-discretionary grant program; it's just that some programs have more predictable payout schedules than others.

The Brookings Monitoring Study, in its summary of the history of revenue sharing, points out that printout politics was an integral part of the process from the beginning. In July of 1970, for example, Assistant Secretary of the Treasury Weidenbaum held a press conference releasing a "comprehensive statistical report on how much each individual recipient might expect to receive under the administration's revenue-sharing plan" (Nathan, 1975, p. 357; Friedman, 1971). This direct appeal to state and local pocketbooks received more extensive media coverage than previous announcements about the philosophy of the New Federalism. Similarly, when the bill was in the House Ways and Means Committee, Deputy Treasury Secretary Charles Walker made available a technical staff and computer facilities so that each new modification of the formula could be immediately tested for its political consequences (Nathan, 1975, p. 364).

One of the authors of this paper had her own experience with the politics of formula grant writing. In 1971, the city of Detroit faced impending fiscal crisis. The mayor appealed to the state legislature to find a means of channeling more state revenue to the city. The unearmarked portion of existing state shared revenues was allocated on the basis of population. Markusen, then Staff Economist for the Speaker of the House, wrote a new formula incorporating indicators of per capita tax base and tax effort. The formula would have allocated significantly more to Detroit, the city with the highest local tax rates. Suburban jurisdictions and some rural areas would have lost in comparison since no additional revenues were proposed. The Michigan Municipal League, representing the entire array of city governments, countered by proposing that $50 million more be added to the fund, not to advance Detroit's interests but to ensure that no city government would lose. As the battle shaped up, the staff was required to produce city-by-city tallies, for all 110 legislative districts, for a myriad of variations on the formula. Ultimately, through a process of bargaining and incremental fund increases, the Speaker's right-hand man produced a set of acceptable dollar amounts by city and district which would win the necessary 57 votes in the House. The staff was handed this final tally sheet and asked to produce a new formula which would result in these allocations. This proved literally impossible, unless each district were to be represented by a dummy variable in the formula. The bill which finally passed contained a tax effort formula with a series of ingeniously constructed grandfathering provisions and an extra $23 million.

Data Disputes. The political fight over the determination of the various formulas now has begun to spill over into considerable controversy about the gathering and interpretation of the data on which the formulas are based. Whereas in 1970, $16 billion in federal aid to state and local governments was based on U.S. Census Bureau data, in 1980 roughly $50 billion is at stake. Similarly, the amount of federal aid dependent on unemployment statistics has risen from about $700 million a year in the early 1970s to $17 billion in 1977. A recent change by the Bureau of Labor Statistics in the way it calculates local unemployment rates resulted in the loss of millions of dollars in federal anti-recessionary assistance by 10 large cities last year (Stanfield, 1978A). The specter of large gains and losses by state and local governments has hung heavily over the work of the National Commission on Employment and Unemployment Statistics. Precisely because the stakes are so high, the Commission has thus far been very cautious about proposing any major reforms (Singer, 1979; Lehner, 1979).

Similarly, the Census Bureau has been surrounded by controversy of late, including the resignation of its director and the retirement or resignation of other key officials (Business Week, 2/26/79; Wall Street Journal, 2/8/79). One example of the Bureau's political problems concerns the case of Paterson, New Jersey. The city of Paterson recently pioneered a new technique of conducting its own head count. Its census resulted in substantially greater population figures than the Census Bureau's because it included illegal aliens and people living in illegally converted dwellings and because it canvassed minority neighborhoods quite carefully. The city then convinced the Bureau to accept its methods, resulting in a 13% increase in population count for Paterson and an extra $1.2 million in federal grants. This approach appeals to both Sunbelt and Frostbelt cities; New York, Dallas, Newark and Denver have all requested copies of Paterson's survey techniques. The Census Bureau has tried to adjust the political heat by announcing that its 400 district offices will have staff authorized to consider instant appeals from local public officials should they be unduly displeased with their 1980 census count (Klapper, 1978).

Given that so many federal grant programs now depend on census population data, with a modest flight of fantasy we can well imagine the President and OMB one day declining how much aid each state and local government should receive and then directing the Census Bureau to adjust the population figures to produce the correct amount of aid under the various Congressional formulas. Geographically-based Congressional coalitions might then counterattack by passing laws mandating new survey techniques. Social scientists, of course will throw up their hands in despair and long for the days of the categorical grant programs.

COMMUNITY DEVELOPMENT BLOCK GRANTS: AN EXAMPLE OF POLITICAL DETERMINATION

The Housing and Community Development Act of 1974 grew out of President Nixon's "New Federalism" political strategy. The President's primary goal was to wrest control of several categorical programs from the HUD bureaucracy in order to spread the funds to a much larger group of local government recipients. He proposed combining seven categorical programs into one single block grant to be distributed to eligible local government jurisdictions by an automatic formula. Urban counties were included in the program due to the increasing power of the suburban lobby (Nathan, 1977B pp. 46-49). The formula redistributed community development funds away from the New England and Middle Atlantic states and toward the southern and western regions (see Exhibit 7). In addition, many more local jurisdictions (4,800) were included in the formula than had previously benefitted from the seven categorical programs. Smaller jurisdictions gained at the expense of central cities under the Nixon formula.

The New Federalism also made a direct appeal to big-city Democratic mayors. The Nixon administration promised to reverse the growth of federal legal requirements and administrative oversight procedures in the urban renewal and Model Cities programs that had been mandated by Congress and HUD in direct response to the black ghetto riots of 1964-69. President Johnson and the Democratic majority in Congress had moved to correct past abuses in urban renewal programs by requiring project area committees and adequate

EXHIBIT 7

Total CDBG Funds, 1975 and 1980
Under the 1974 Formula

Region	Entitlement CDBG 1975 ($000s)	Entitlement CDBG 1980 ($000s)	Per cent Change 1975-1980
Northeastern	$712,626	$ 622,935	−13%
North Central	$572,067	$ 675,909	+18%
South	$725,165	$1,029,594	+42%
West	$353,578	$ 486,619	+38%

Source: DeLeon and LeGates, 1977, p. 392.

housing and small business relocation assistance. Model Cities went even further by requiring the local agency to use the federal money to directly benefit residents of low and moderate income neighborhoods (National Commission, 1969, pp. 152-198; Hartman, 1974; Frieden, 1975). Such restrictions were unpopular with the mayors and city managers. Nixon's proposal to redistribute federal block grants by automatic formula that could be spent by local governments in a relatively unrestricted fashion, with no requirements for local matching funds, and virtually no federal oversight, greatly appealed to groups like the National League of Cities and U.S. Conference of Mayors. The CDBG program redistributed power from the local redevelopment and Model Cities agencies to the local chief executives. As A result, the funds tended to be spread around to a greater number of neighborhoods within each city. (Nathan, 1977B; Keating, 1978).

Despite the sweetener of grant reorganization, the Democratic Congress resisted President Nixon's proposal when first introduced in 1971 due to the redistributive consequences of the formula. Senate Democrats from states with large black populations also were concerned about the lack of administrative oversight and about the adverse distribution of benefits within each community, but House Democrats in general were more willing to follow the lead of local executives in pursuing maximum flexibility.

After his landslide reelection in 1972, President Nixon took a hard line with Congress in fighting for the Community Development formula, by imposing a draconian cutback and impoundment of funds for major housing subsidy programs and for the categorical grant programs that were to be "folded-into" CDBG. This forced the

Democrats to compromise, since their constituents were most affected by the impoundment of funds. In early 1974, a deal was struck in the House which provided for a modest amount of HUD oversight of CDBG and Republican support for new housing subsidy programs (Nathan, 1977B, pp. 43-46).

Another element of the compromise was that northern urban Democrats insisted on a "hold-harmless" provision in the distribution formula, ensuring that no jurisdiction would receive less than it was getting under the previous categoricals. By 1974, President Nixon's power base was rapidly eroding due to the Watergate scandal, and he was in no position to oppose this provision. "Hold-harmless" was to be gradually phased out over a six-year period, but big-city and northeastern Democrats hoped that the 1974 and 1976 elections would revive their political fortunes so that they could change the formula.

Ironically, by the time CDBG actually passed Congress in August of 1974, President Nixon had already resigned under threat of impeachment. But by then all the deals and commitments already had been made. The pressures from the various lobbying groups of local government officials to start the money flowing were too great for any major last-minute changes to be considered. As a result, all eyes turned to the anticipated battle over Congressional renewal of CDBG in 1977.

The redistributive effects of the CDBG formula are well documented in the Brookings Study (Nathan, 1977B). DeLeon and LeGates, in a study of California cities, discovered an interesting political pattern that accompanied the geographic shift. Not only did the CDBG redistribute funds toward economically better-off communities, but those communities who had the greatest net relative gains from the new program also tended to have the most politically conservative electorates and the least favorable attitudes towards construction of low-income housing or racial integration of housing. In the politics of automatic formula-writing, conservatives definitely won the first round (DeLeon, 1976).

DeLeon and LeGates also noted shifts in the area of decision-making "dramatically away from the federal-local government-sublocal government authority-neighborhood organization models" to local chief executives and general government bodies (DeLeon, 1976, p. 31). In other words, both community groups and local bureaucrats in some categorical agencies lost part of their power base in the changeover from a federal to a local allocation process. It has taken several years for these groups to recover their strength after the initial setback.

While the full implications of the changes brought about by the CDBG formula were softened by "hold-harmless," social scientists responsive to the concerns of the losers immediately set about developing normative criteria and statistical measurements of "need" so that arguments could be made for a reallocation of funds. Again, both the Brookings Study and the DeLeon and LeGates Report are examples of these efforts, as was work that was conducted in HUD's Office of Policy Development and Research (HUD, 1976). The old formula, based on equal weights for population and overcrowded housing and a double weight for poverty, was seen to be deficient because it rewarded growing rather than declining areas, and because the overcrowded housing and poverty criteria primarily benefitted the South. Since many people in policy and research positions felt that the greatest areas of need were precisely those central cities, particularly in the Northeast, that had been receiving the most under the categorical programs, it was necessary to construct a new formula that would redirect the funds their way (Stanfield, 1977).

Once this normative decision was made, all that remained was to find a variable or set of variables that correlated most highly with the localities most in "need." The new formula finally arrived at by Congress, based on the Brookings and HUD models, is weighted 20% population growth lag, 30% poverty and 50% age of housing (defined as the number of housing units built before 1939). The results appear in Exhibit 8. As Katharine Lyall recently stated, "Age of housing was chosen as a proxy for older infrastructure and because we knew exactly where the old housing was, not because it related to health problems, crime problems, poverty, or other social measures of distress. It's a very pragmatic formula" (Lyall, 1979). In fact, age of housing does correlate highly with various measures of fiscal distress and physical decay, which are most prevalent in the northeastern cities.

This, of course, is precisely why it was chosen over hundreds of other computer-tested variables. The formula, as always, is fitted to the desired results. What's sauce for the goose is sauce for the gander.

The new CDBG allocation formula was passed as a "dual" formula, meaning that communities could choose whichever of the two gave them more money. Of course, should the overall level of funding be reduced, such political compromises eventually mean less for everyone, so that the benficiaries of the old formula still can be relatively worse off as a result of the "add-on."

Political coalitions organized on explicit regional lines (Markusen, 1979) have emerged as another significant feature of this particular

EXHIBIT 8

Aggregate Percentage and Per Capita Changes in 1980 Funding in the Shift from the Original to the Dual Formula Compared with Funding Changes From the Original Formula to Formula B Alone

Region	1 % aggregate increase in entitlements from from old formula to dual formula	2 $ per capita aggregate increase old to dual formula	3 % aggregate increase in entitlements from old formula to Formula B alone	4 $ per capita aggregated increase from old formula to Formula B alone
New England	+86%	+$15	+86%	+$15
Mid-Atlantic	+71%	+$16	+71%	+$16
East North Central	+68%	+$14	+64%	+$13
West North Central	+65%	+$12	+61%	+$11
South Atlantic	+16%	+$ 3	− 5%	−$ 2
East South Central	+14%	+$ 4	−13%	−$ 3
West South Central	+ 3%	0	−33%	−$ 8
Mountain	+ 9%	+$ 2	−28%	−$ 4
Pacific	+20%	+$ 3	− 7%	−$ 2

Source: DeLeon and LeGates, 1978, p. 31.

formula fight. While federal programs always have had skewed spatial distributions, the political constituencies advocating or opposing them have more often tended to be organized around functional or programmatic issues. The CDBG fight cut across many traditional levels of interest group identity. The battle was billed primarily as "Frostbelt" v. "Sunbelt." The Northeast-Midwest Congressional Coalition in the House acted as the mobilizer of forces defending the new formula against an amendment to retain the existing formula. The two California Democratic Congressmen who introduced the amendment both represented districts which were net gainers under the 1974 formula (Havemann, 1977, p. 1031; DeLeon, 1976). Northeast-Midwest solidarity plus a fair amount of legislative horse-trading carried the day, and the "dual" formula passed. However, the price of this victory has been a virtual declaration of war by the Southern Growth Policies Board on any future formula debates.[8] In particular, it is attacking the age-of-housing indicator and the push for incorporation of regional cost of living differentials.

The effects of the formula change are substantial for particular cities. St. Louis, for example, would have received $17.1 million in FY 1980 under the old formula. Under the new CDBG formula, it will receive $36.8 million. But the real question is not how much money any particular jurisdiction is receiving, but how that money is being spent. Here the record is mixed. Among the most publicized abuses have been Community Development funds used to build swimming pools, golf courses and tennis courts. More importantly, municipalities and urban counties have, in many cases, instituted their own local versions of "spreading," whereby the funds are redistributed to more favored and powerful constituencies than the poor (Keating, 1978).

Such a pattern has led HUD to impose new regulations beginning last May which require CDBG recipients to spend 75% of their Community Development funds for the benefit of low and moderate income people. How "benefit" is precisely measured is a difficult question. Thus far, HUD's solution is to focus on the income level of the residents of the census tract in which the money is spent. This criterion still does not adequately identify the income level of the ultimate beneficiaries, (Keating, 1978). But it is a step in the right direction, for at least it is a recognition of the real problems. Just because New Orleans, Louisiana has a large number of poor people does not mean that those people benefit from the formula which sends federal funds to their city, any more than the fact that Philadelphia, Pennsylvania has a lot of old housing means that the housing stock will improve as a result of block grant allocations, or that people currently living in bad housing will benefit. Local governments are becoming so dependent on federal funds that efforts to obtain a larger share have overshadowed concern for the purposes for which the funds should be utilized. More social science research and political activity should be directly addressed to this aspect of fiscal behavior.

THE FUTURE OF INTERGOVERNMENTAL POLITICS AND RESEARCH

Continuing intrametropolitan and interregional demographic changes have combined with the new anti-inflationary mood of public fiscal austerity to produce a situation in which the Democratic upswing of the countercyclical era has now come to a close. The CDBG formula fight may have been a last hurrah for the central cities of the Northeast. Last year in Congress attempts to renew the countercyclical programs were defeated, partly due to opposition from southern congressmen who felt that the emphasis on the rate of unemployment in the distribution formulas discriminated against their region. And despite his announcement of a "national urban policy," President Carter's budget for 1981 indicates a major shift from previous priorities of urban aid. It would appear that we are now on the crest of a fourth swing, a Frostbelt/Sunbelt free-for-all the outcome of which is hard to predict. Caraley has pointed out the extent to which increasing suburbanization of the population weakens the commitment of Democratic Congressmen, Senators and Presidents to aiding central cities, "hardship indexes" notwithstanding (Caraley, 1976). One of the issues in the controversy over the 1980 Census is the fact that reapportionment in the early 1980s will bring political changes that could cost state and local governments millions of dollars, depending on the formulas.

"Targeting" transfers to spatial units, regardless of how much the data improve (and nearly all researchers agree there are massive data problems) or the formulas are refined, is not necessarily any better than "spreading" in addressing needs of people rather than places. Determining which jurisdiction or place receives the money does not really address the question of *who* benefits from intergovernmental transfers. To answer this question we need to know much more about how the money is actually spent, the direct and indirect impacts of the expenditures, interaction with other tax, spending and regulatory efforts and with private sector decisions; and physical, demographic and income effects. One planner recently stated that "redevelopment, after all, was often targeted at poor people, like a gun pointed at their head" (Montgomery, 1979). Knowing which region, SMSA, city, town, or even neighborhood the funds flow to does not tell which people gain from the use of that money, which people lose, and how.

The current Chairman of the Council of Economic Advisers, Charles Schultze, wrote several years ago that federal grants programs would be "significantly improved" if "federal control over *who* got the benefits were maintained or even intensified in selected cases" (Schultze, 1976, p. 369). Schultze adds that an important reason for pursuing this course of action is to assist local public interest groups in their battle for more equitable distribution of expenditures. Whether or not the efforts are federal or locally-based, the politics of federal grant formula redistribution must be supplanted by the politics of genuine economic redistribution. Putting their "needs measurement" skills to use in assisting this latter task is something that fiscal experts have not done often enough.

NOTES

1. The U.S. Census divides the country into four regions and nine sub-regions as follows:

   1. *Northeast*

      A. New England: Maine, New Hampshire, Vermont, Massachusetts, Rhode Island, Connecticut

      B. Mid Atlantic: New York, New Jersey, Pennsylvania

   2. *Midwest*

      A. Great Lakes: Ohio, Indiana, Illinois, Michigan, Wisconsin

      B. Great Plains: Minnesota, Iowa, Missouri, North Dakota, South Dakota, Nebraska, Kansas

   3. *South*

      A. South Atlantic: Delaware, Maryland, Virginia, West Virginia, North Carolina, South Carolina, Georgia, Florida, District of Columbia

      B. East South Central: Kentucky, Tennessee, Alabama, Mississippi

      C. West South Central: Oklahoma, Texas, Arkansas, Louisiana

   4. *West*

      A. Mountain: Montana, Idaho, Wyoming, Colorado, New Mexico, Arizona, Utah, Nevada

      B. Pacific: Washington, Oregon, California, Alaska, Hawaii

2. This evidence suggests caution in interpreting functional causality. Above, we noted that federal *outlays* on highways and sewers were evenly distributed across regions; here, *aid* distributions show disparities among states. These differences may result from the different procedures for aggregating across funtional categories and/or regions.

3. These, moreover, do not include federal transfers to states that are passed through to cities; these the Census tabulates in the state-to-local figures, discussed in the next section. An attempt to compute these pass-throughs and adjust the data for them is contained in Vehorn (1977); since his data suggest that the federal government has increasingly favored central cities, the pass-through amounts may be significantly different in their distribution. However, an alternative interpretation might be that Vehorn's conclusion that central cities are favored may result from his aggregation over various sized cities, in which the *largest* central cities are not the most favored recipients. A full discussion and alternative treatment of the pass-through problem is contained in ACIR, 1977 B.

4. In order of their 1975 per capita allocations, the aggregates for selected jurisdictions are ranked as follows (Vehorn, 1977, p. 13):

Northeast Central Cities	$ 243.76
Western Suburbs	136.54
South Central Cities	103.54
Western Counties	103.06
Western Central Cities	100.12
Midwestern Central Cities	97.30
Northeastern Counties	95.05
Northeastern Suburbs	91.33

Southern Counties	84.16
Midwestern Counties	75.34
Midwestern Suburbs	72.95
Southern Suburbs	66.04

5. The interpretation of these figures as definitive of state-to-local relations must be cautioned by underscoring the narrowness of the categories. See ACIR, 1977 B, pp. 1-2, for a discussion of the various substitutes for aid (state assumption of responsibility and state authorization of revenue-raising powers).

6. Some threads are discernible. In sociology and political science, power structure research attempts to show the links between certain public sector suppliers and private sector powers (Domhoff, 1978, 1979; Carnoy and Weiss, 1973). In public choice theory, work on supply behavior within bureaucracies is only just beginning (Niskanen, 1971; Wamsley and Zald, 1973). A recent paper by Markusen (1979) speculates on the supply behavior of the Carter administration in producing the urban impact analysis. An outline of endogenous and exogenous supply behavior is presented in Capitol Kapitalistate (1977).

7. The seven main organizations of the "intergovernmental lobby" are the Council of State Governments, the National Governors' Association, the National Legislative Conference, the National Association of Counties, the National League of Cities, the United States Conference of Mayors and the International City Management Association.

8. An example of the ferocity of the regional formula fights is the speech given by Governor George Busbee of Georgia to the White House Conference of Balanced National Growth and Economic Development (January 31, 1978). Referring to the 1977 "dual" formula for CDBG, Governor Busbee stated "When this formula was passed into law, the South had no coalition to counter the efforts of the six action coalitions of the North. A Washington newspaper rubbed salt into the wound by telling us what we belatedly discovered—that the South had been caught with its eyes closed and its britches down." (Wilmoth, 1978, p. 18.)

REFERENCES

Advisory Commission on Intergovernmental Relations. 1976. *Significant Features of Fiscal Federalism 1976. Volume 1, Trends* (Washington, D.C.: Government Printing Office).

_____ . 1977A. *Significant Features of Fiscal Federalism, 1976-77, Volume 3, Expenditures* (Washington, D.C.: Government Printing Office).

_____ . 1977B. *The States and Intergovernmental Aids* (Washington, D.C.: Government Printing Office).

_____ . 1976-7-8. *The Intergovernmental Grant System: An Assessment and Proposed Policies*. 14 volumes (Washington, D.C.: U.S. Government Printing Office).

Alonso, William. 1971. "Equity and Its Relation to Efficiency in Urbanization," in John Kain and John Meyer, *Essays in Regional Economics* (Cambridge: Harvard University Press, 1971).

Anton, Thomas J. 1979. "Outlays Data and the Analysis of Federal Policy Impact," in Norman Glickman, ed. *The Urban Impact of Federal Policies* (Baltimore: Johns Hopkins University Press, 1979).

Banfield, Edward. 1971. "Revenue Sharing in Theory and Practice," *The Public Interest*, Number 23.

Barro, Stephen. 1978. *The Urban Impacts of Federal Policies: Volume 3, Fiscal Conditions* (Santa Monica: The RAND Corporation).

Beer, Samuel. 1976. "The Adoption of General Revenue Sharing: A Case Study in Public Sector Politics" *Public Policy*, Volume 24, No. 2.

Break, George, 1978. "Intergovernmental Finance," in John Peterson, Catherine Spain, and Martharose Laffey, *State and Local Government Finance and Financial Management: A Compendium of Current Research* (Washington, D.C.: Government Finance Center).

Bureau of the Census. Selected years. *City Government Finances.*

Business Week. (February 26, 1979) "Troubles Multiply for the 1980 Census."

Capitol Kapitalistate. 1977. "The Study of Studies: A Marxist View of Research Conducted by the State" *Kapitalistate,* Volume 6, pp. 163-190.

Caraley, Demetrios. 1976. "Congressional Politics and Urban Aid" *Political Science Quarterly,* Volume 91, No. 1.

Carnoy, Judith and Marc Weiss. 1973. *A House Divided* (Boston: Little, Brown and Company).

Chinitz, Benjamin. 1961. "Contrasts in Agglomeration: New York and Pittsburgh" *American Economic Association, Papers and Proceedings* (May 1961), pp. 279-89.

Community Services Administration. 1976. *Federal Outlays in Summary, Fiscal Year 1976* (Washington, D.C.: Community Services Administration, compiled for the Executive Office of the President).

Congressional Budget Office. 1977. *Troubled Local Economies and The Distribution of Federal Dollars* (Washington, D.C.: U.S. Government Printing Office).

DeLeon, Richard and Richard LeGates. 1976. *Redistribution of Effects of Special Revenue Sharing for Community Development.* (Berkeley: Institute of Governmental Studies, University of California).

──────. 1977. "Community Development Block Grants: Redistribution Effects and Equity Issues," *The Urban Lawyer* Volume 9, No. 2.

──────. 1978. "Beyond Cybernetic Federalism in Community Development," *Urban Law Annual,* Volume 15.

Derthick, Martha. 1979. "How Easy Votes on Social Security Came to an End," *The Public Interest,* Number 54.

Domhoff, G. William. 1978. *Who Really Rules?* (New Brunswick: Transaction Books).

──────. 1979. *The Powers That Be* (New York: Random House).

Dommel, Paul. 1974. *The Politics of Revenue Sharing* (Bloomington: Indiana University Press).

Elazar, Daniel. 1976. "Restructuring Federal Housing Programs—Who Stands to Gain?" *Publius,* Volume 6, No. 2.

Edel, Matthew. 1979. "People vs. Places in Urban Impact Analysis," in Norman Glickman, ed., *The Urban Impact of Federal Policies* (Baltimore: Johns Hopkins University Press.

Feshbach, Dan. 1975. "History of Revenue Sharing," unpublished manuscript.

Frieden, Bernard, and Marshall Kaplan. 1975. *The Politics of Neglect* (Cambridge: MIT Press).

Friedland, Roger, Frances Fox Piven, and Robert Alford. 1977. "Political Conflict, Urban Structure and the Fiscal Crisis," in Douglas Ashford, ed., *Comparing Public Policy: New Approaches and Methods* (Beverly Hills: Sage Publications).

Friedman, Saul. March 2, 1971. "Cities Would Get Least Under Nixon Plan," *Detroit Free Press*.

General Accounting Office. 1977. *Antirecession Assistance—An Evaluation* (Washington, D.C.: Government Printing Office).

_____. December 1977. *Changing Patterns of Federal Aid to State and Local Governments 1969-75* (Washington, D.C.: Government Printing Office, PAD-78-15).

_____. 1979. *The Interaction of Federal and State Aid: A Case Study of New York State*. Forthcoming, summer.

Glickman, Norman, ed. 1979. *The Urban Impacts of Federal Policies*. (Baltimore: John Hopkins University Press).

Hartman, Chester. 1974. *Yerba Buena* (San Francisco: New Glide Publications).

Havemann, Joel, Stanfield Rochelle L., and Pierce, Neal R. 1976. "Federal Spending: The North's Loss is the Sunbelt's Gain," *National Journal*, Volume 8, No. 26 (June).

_____. 1977. "A Year Later, the Frostbelt Strikes Back," *National Journal*, Volume, 9, No. 27, (July).

Hovey, Harold. 1978. "State-Local Intergovernmental Finance," in John Peterson, Catherine Sapin, and Martharose Laffey, *State and Local Government Finance and Financial Management: A Compendium of Current Research* (Washington, D.C.: Governmental Finance Research Center).

House Committee on Banking, Finance, and Urban Affairs, Subcommittee on the City. 1978. *City Need and the Responsiveness of Federal Grant Programs* (Washington, D.C.: U.S. Government Printing Office).

Keating, Dennis and Richard LeGates. 1978. "Who Should Benefit from the Community Development Block Grant Program?" *The Urban Lawyer*, Volume 10, Number 4.

Klapper, Byron. "Finding the Bodies: Cities Challenge Population Count," *Wall Street Journal* December 27, 1978, p. 10.

Kordalewski, John. 1978. *Ways of Identifying Cities in Distress* (Washington, D.C.: The Urban Institute).

Labovitz, I.M. 1978. "Federal Expenditures and Revenues in Regions and States," *Intergovernmental Perspectives*, Volume 4, No. 4, pp. 16-23.

Lehner, Urban. February 5, 1979. "Method of Computing Jobless Rate Faces Relatively Few Shifts After 2-Year Study," *Wall Street Journal*.

Lyall, Katherine. 1979. "Targeting: Progress on the National Urban Policy," forthcoming in *Commentary*, a journal of the Council on Urban Economic Affairs.

Markusen, Ann. The Urban Impact Analysis: A Critical Forecast. In Norman Glickman, ed., *The Urban Impact of Federal Policies* (Baltimore: Johns Hopkins Press, 1979).

_____, and Jerry Fastrup. 1978. "The Regional War for Federal Aid," *The Public Interest*, No. 53 (Fall 1978), pp. 87-99.

McConnell, Grant. 1966. *Private Power and American Democracy*. New York: Alfred Knopf.

Montgomery, Roger. 1979. Personal communication with the authors. Department of City and Regional Planning, University of California, Berkeley, February 26, 1979.

Morss, Elliott. 1966. "Some Thoughts on the Determinants of State and Local Expenditures, " *National Tax Journal,* Volume XIX, pp. 95-103.

Nathan, Richard. 1975A. *The Plot That Fail: Nixon and the Administrative Presidency* (New York: John Wiley and Sons).

——————————, Allen Manvel, Susannah Calkins, and Associates. 1975B. *Monitoring Revenue Sharing* (Washington, D.C.: The Brookings Institution).

——————————, Charles Adams, and Associates, 1977A. *Revenue Sharing: The Second Round* (Washington, D.C.: The Brookings Institution).

Nathan, Richard, Paul Dommel, Sarah Liebshutz, Milton Morris, and Associates. 1977B. *Block Grants for Community Development* (Washington, D.C.: U.S. Department of Housing and Urban Development).

Nathan, Richard, and Paul Dommel. 1977C. "The Cities," in Joseph Pechman, ed., *Setting National Priorities: The 1978 Budget* (Washington D.C.: The Brookings Institution).

Nathan, Richard, Paul Dommel, and James Fossett. July 28, 1977D. "Statement and Testimony," *Financing Municipal Needs.* Joint Economic Committees of Congress (Washington, D.C.: Government Printing Office).

Nathan, Richard, Charles Adams. 1976. "Understanding Central City Hardships," *Political Science Quarterly,* Volume 91, No. 1.

Nathan, Richard. 1978. "The Outlook for Federal Grants to Cities," in Roy Bahl, ed., *The Fiscal Outlook for Cities* (Syracuse: Syracuse University Press).

National Commission on Urban Problems, 1969. *Building the American City* (Washington, D.C.: U.S. Government Printing Office).

Niskanen, William A. 1971. *Bureaucracy and Representative Government* (New York: Aldine-Atherton).

Phillips, Kevin. 1970. *The Emerging Republican Majority* (Garden City, N.Y.: Anchor Books).

Pierce, Neal. 1972. *The Mountain States of America* (New York: Norton and Co.).

——————————. November 27, 1976. "Northeast Governors Map Battle Plan for Fight Over Federal Funds Flow," *National Journal.*

Piven, Frances Fox, and Richard Cloward. 1971. *Regulating the Poor* (New York: Pantheon Books).

Rafuse, Robert W., Jr. April 1977. *The New Regional Debate: A National Overview.* Prepared for the National Governors' Conference, Agenda Setting Series. Washington, D.C.

Schlesinger, Arthur M., Jr. 1960. *The Politics of Upheaval* (Boston: Houghton Mifflin Company).

Schultze, Charles. 1976. "Federal Spending: Past, Present, and Future," in Henry Owen and Charles Schulteze, eds. *Setting National Priorities: The Next Ten Years* (Washington, D.C.: The Brookings Institution).

Singer, James. October 11, 1975. "Employment Report: Congress Confronts Ford Over Bills to Create More Jobs," *National Journal.*

——————————. January 6, 1979. "Big Money at Stake in Redefining Unemployment," *National Journal.*

Stanfield, Rochelle. "Government Seeks the Right Formula for Community Development Funds," *National Journal* (February 12, 1977).

—————————. "Federal Aid for Cities—Is It a Mixed Blessing?," *National Journal* (December 9, 1978B).

—————————. "Playing Computer Politics With Local Aid Formulas," *National Journal* (December 9, 1978B).

Stanley, Dvaid. 1976. *Cities in Trouble* (Columbus: Academy for Contemporary Problems).

U.S. Department of Housing and Urban Development, Office of Policy Development and Research, 1976. *An Evaluation of the Community Block Grant Formula.*

U.S. Department of the Treasury. 1977. *Federal Aid to States.* Washington, D.C.: U.S. Government Printing Office.

U.S. Department of the Treasury, Office of State and Local Finance. January 23, 1978. *Report on the Fiscal Impact of the Economic Stimulus Package on 48 Large Urban Governments.*

Vehorn, Charles L. 1977. *The Regional Distribution of Federal Grants-In-Aid.* Urban and Regional Development Series No. 3 (Columbus, Ohio: Academy for Contemporary Problems).

Wall Street Journal. February 9, 1979. Counting the House," p. 18.

Wamsley, Gary and Mayer Zald. 1973. *The Political Economy of Public Organizations: A Critique and Approach to the Study of Public Administration* (Lexington: Lexington Books).

Weinstein, Bernard L., and Robert E. Firestine. 1978. *Regional Growth and Decline in the United States* (New York: Praeger Publishers).

Wildavsky, Aaron. 1974. *The Politics of the Budgetary Process,* Second Edition (Boston: Little, Brown and Company).

Wilmoth, David. 1978. *Regionalism and the Carter Administration.* Department of City and Regional Planning, (Berkeley: University of California).

Winnick, Louis. 1966. "Place Prosperity vs. People Prosperity: Welfare Considerations in the Geographic Distribution of Economic Activity," in Real Estate Research, *Essays in Urban Land Economics* (Los Angeles: University of California at Los Angeles Press).

Richard D. Gustely and Kenneth P. Ballard - REGIONAL MACRO-ECO-NOMIC IMPACT OF FEDERAL GRANTS: AN EMPIRICAL ANALYSIS

INTRODUCTION

Grants-in-aid payments traditionally have been an important tool of federal government policy. Since the start of this decade, however, numerous changes in the level and distribution of these grants have taken place. First, from 1970 to 1978, the level of grant payments has more than tripled, resulting in a dramatic increase in their share of both federal and state-local budgets.[1] Second, the character of the grants has changed to the point that, currently, about one-quarter of the payments could be classified as broad-based (as opposed to specific-purpose), as compared to only 10 percent in 1972.[2] Third, the regional allocation of federal grants also has changed, with larger fractions of total outlays in 1978 going to states in the New England, Mideast and Great Lakes region and smaller fractions going to states in the other regions.[3]

Accompanying the changes has been increasing research into the economic impacts of these grants. However, while there has been considerable analysis of the impacts of individual federal grant programs,[4] very little research has been undertaken in determining the differential regional impacts caused by combinations of programs.[5] Even fewer studies have analyzed regional impact differentials of the overall grant system. Such impact differentials are likely to occur not only from differences among grants in terms of their allocation formulae but also from regional differences in industry mix.[6] At least two questions concerning regional impact differentials are, therefore, important to consider. First, to what extent do grants have different regional *stimulative effects*? For instance, do the impacts of federal grants on the levels of output, employment and income vary across regions? Second, to what extent do the *distributive effects* of grants redistribute income regionally? For example, do the differences in the amount of aid given to each state contribute to or diminish the existing regional income inequalities?

The purpose of this paper is to make estimates of these regional stimulative and distributional differentials associated with existing grants-in-aid programs. The determination of the extent of stimulative effects is accomplished through an analysis of the regional impacts that would occur if existing grants were doubled. The determination of the extent of redistributive effects is accomplished through an analysis of the impacts of existing grants relative to the impacts generated by a distributionally neutral allocation of grants based upon personal income.

The research results are based upon an application of an interregional econometric model which allows for the analysis of the effects of changes in one region on other regions. This model, the National Regional Impact Evaluation System (NRIES), has been developed at the Bureau of Economic Analysis and is comprised of 51 interactive models (50 states and the District of Columbia) and a model of the national economy.[7] In this application, the state results have been summed to the regional level in order to facilitate analysis. States included in each of the eight study regions are indicated in Exhibit 1.

The remainder of the paper is divided into four sections. In the first section, the structure of NRIES is discussed, with particular emphasis placed upon a delineation of the linkage between grants to state and local governments and the remainder of the model. In the second section, the estimates of regional stimulative effects are discussed, focusing specifically upon the growth (impact) multipliers generated by the model. In the third section, estimates of the regional distributional effects are presented and discussed. Finally, a summary of the results is contained in the fourth section.

EXHIBIT 1

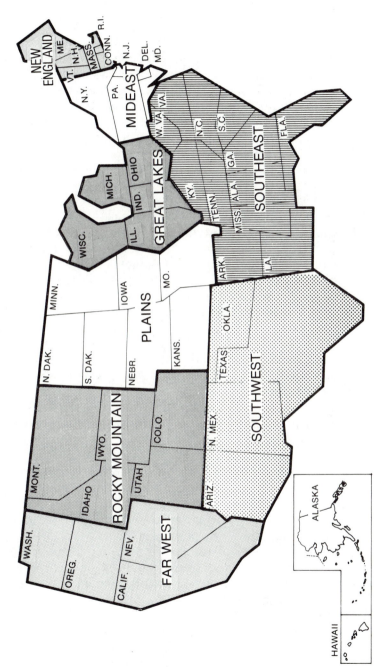

STRUCTURE OF NRIES[8]

Before discussing the results of the modeling analysis, it is first necessary that the reader be briefly acquainted with the structure, advantages and limitations of the modeling system. NRIES is a multistate interactive econometric model of the U.S. economy, developed at the Bureau of Economic Analysis. It is comprised of 51 interrelated state models (50 states and the District of Columbia) which are integrated into a model of the U.S. economy. Its primary uses include medium-range (5 to 10 year) forecasts of regional and national economic trends and estimation of the regional and national impacts of policy alternatives.

As shown in Exhibit 2, the modeling system that forms the basis of NRIES is comprised of regional, national and interregional elements. The regional element includes separate models for each of the states. The national element includes the national aggregates (the sum of the states) and a model of the remaining U.S. economic activity. When linked together, primarily through the interregional element, the model enables the simultaneous consideration of the overall level and regional distribution of economic activity within the U.S.

Since NRIES employs the bottom-up modeling approach, the individual state models form the basic component of the system. In the typical NRIES state model, the level of a particular type of economic activity for one state (e.g., output or employment in an industry) is expressed as a function of three types of variables: the *economic activity in related sectors* in the state, the *economic or demographic "interaction"* with other states and *nationally determined levels of economic activity*.

One set of variables in the typical state model represents *economic activity in related sectors* of the state economy. These variables establish the internal linkages within each of the state models. Such variables include disposable income in an output equation or output in an employment equation for a particular state.

The *interaction variables* of the typical state model are indices of the economic activity in other, surrounding states. These indices are defined as the activity of certain sectors, summed over all other states in the U.S., and deflated by the distance to the particular state in question.[9] These indices establish the explicit interregional linkages among the state models.

The *nationally determined variables* of the typical state model can be divided into two categories. One set of these variables, the

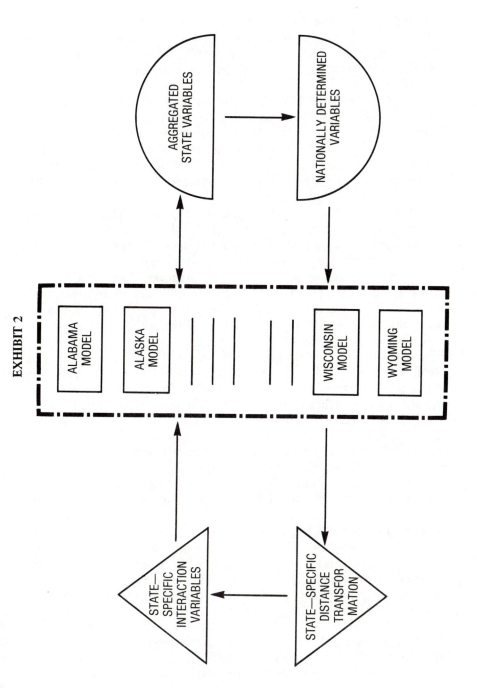

EXHIBIT 2

national totals, are expressed as the sum of an activity in all states. The other set is comprised of certain national variables that typically show little spatial variation (for example, interest rates and sector prices). Accordingly, these variables are modeled as a function of national trends.

As indicated above, NRIES is a highly detailed model of economic and demographic interrelationships within the national economy. Within each of the state models, there are approximately 230 equations, of which 75 are behavioral. In addition, there are approximately 50 national equations in the U.S. model, of which 20 are behavioral. Thus, the full model system has more than 4,000 behavioral and 11,000 total equations.

The model includes a similar range of economic variables included in the typical single-region model.[10] Major categories include industrial output, employment and wages (13 industries each); non-wage income sources (4 components); state and local government revenues and expenditures (10 categories); personal tax and non-tax payments (5 categories); and retail sales (5 outlet types). Demographic variables include population (5 age cohorts); unemployment (total and insured); and labor force.

There are several advantages to the approach employed by NRIES. First, because it is an interregional model, NRIES can be used to analyze the regional or spatial distribution of policy impacts. For example, the model could measure the effects of changes in one region upon all other regions in the economy. Second, the system employs a bottom-up approach in simultaneously determining the level of both national and regional activity, thereby taking account of the effects that changes in regional activity could have on the nation as a whole. Such effects cannot be accounted for in the typical top-down models.[11] Third, by integrating regional and national models, the NRIES structure insures that the sum of regional activity is consistent with forecasts of national activity. In contrast, individual state models often produce overly optimistic forecasts of growth when no national framework is present. Finally, NRIES is able to examine the effects of concurrent national and regional policy changes. This final application is actually a composite of the first three and is the type of application that is emphasized in this paper.

Since the focus of this paper is on an analysis of the effects federal grants-in-aid have on the regional economies, it is useful also to describe the structure of the state and local fiscal sector that has been incorporated into each of the individual state models.[12] Exhibit 3 provides an overview of the basic relation-

EXHIBIT 3

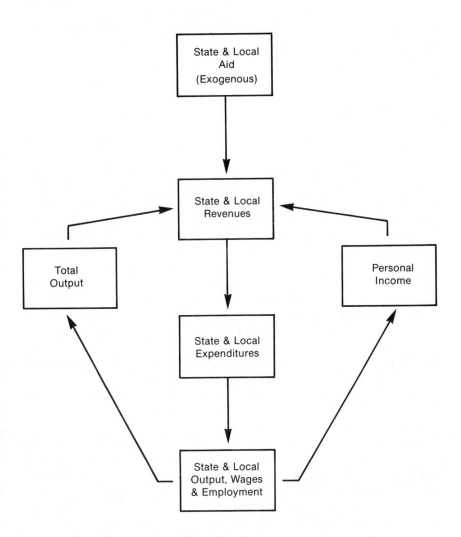

ships included in these models. As indicated in the chart, state and local grants-in-aid are taken as an exogenously determined policy variable. The level of these payments, together with variables reflecting general economic activity (total output or total income) determine state and local revenues.[13] State and local expenditures are then expressed as a function of state and local total revenues, with state and local output, employment and wages being expressed as a function of state and local expenditures. Finally, state and local output, employment and wages, in turn, directly affect total output and income, and indirectly, state and local government revenues.

STIMULATIVE EFFECTS OF GRANTS-IN-AID

The purpose of this section is to provide estimates of regional differentials in the stimulative effects of federal grants-in-aid. The analysis is comprised of an historical simulation of the model employing actual grant-in-aid levels as compared to a simulation over the same period assuming grants for each state to be twice their actual levels. The impacts are thus the direct change in grants-in-aid spending plus any indirect or induced economic stimulus generated by the increased regional and national income. The new growth rates are then computed and regional differentials identified. In addition, expenditure multipliers for gross output, personal income and earnings were calculated for each region.[14] These multipliers were expressed in terms of the change in economic activity (gross output, personal income or earnings) relative to the change in grant-in-aid payments. Alternately, they may be interpreted as the induced economic activity associated with an increase of one dollar in grant payments. The historical period chosen for study is 1969-1977. Exhibits 4-6 summarize the inputs and the results of these simulations.

Exhibit 4 presents data describing the absolute and relative levels of actual grant-in-aid payments over the 1969-1977 period.[15] Several conclusions from these data should be noted here. First, in terms of the absolute level of aid, these data indicate that grants increased nationwide by 223 percent over the period. This is significantly greater than the corresponding increase during the same period of both GNP and state-local expenditures. Generally, total grants grew faster than the national average in the New England, Mideast, Great Lakes and Southeast regions and slower than the average in the remaining regions.[16] These regional differentials in growth rates resulted in a slight increase in the share of total grants going to the New England, Mideast, Great Lakes and Plains regions—from about 49 percent in 1969 to about 52 percent in 1977.

Second, when expressed in per capita terms, grants nationwide grew by about 200 percent, from \$95.2 in 1969 to \$286.1 in 1977. With respect to the regional differentials, these data indicate that per capita grants in three regions—Great Lakes, Plains and Southeast —were below the national average throughout the period. However, while per capita levels in the New England and Mideast regions were also below the national average in 1969, they were well above average in 1977. Similarly, while the Southwest registered per capita grants above the national average in 1969, by 1977 per capita grants to this region had fallen below the national average.

Third, grants nationwide rose faster than personal income and state-local expenditures, rising from 2.5 percent to 4.0 percent of total personal income and from 16.4 percent to 22.7 percent of state and local government current expenditures.[17] Some interesting regional shifts are now evident here. With respect to percent of personal income, grants in 1969 were below the national average in the New England, Mideast, and Great Lakes regions. However, of these three regions in 1977, only in the Great Lakes did grants consistently remain below the national average percent of personal income. The Plains, Southeast and Southwest regions went from above in 1969 to below the national average percent of personal income in 1977. Similar significant shifts in the relative positions of the regions are evident when grants are expressed as a percentage of state and local expenditures.

Exhibit 5 presents a summary of the regional distribution of average annual growth rates before and after the model simulation assuming a doubled level of grant-in-aid payments. Focusing first on the actual historical increases, the data indicate that U.S. income grew at a rate of 9.4 percent, output at 9.2 percent, employment at 2.1 percent and state-local expenditures at 12.1 percent annually between 1969 and 1977. Total income, output and employment in the New England, Mideast, and Great Lakes regions tended to grow at rates consistently below the national average. This is contrasted to their expenditures where the New England and Mideast regions, which had an increasing share of grants, grew faster than the national average, while the Great Lakes, which had a decreasing share of grants, grew more slowly than average. On the other hand, over the historical period, the Southeast, Southwest and Rocky Mountain regions grew at rates greater than the national average for most of the economic indicators shown.

Turning to the change in growth rates induced by a doubling of grants-in-aid, the data indicate national average annual increases of 0.6 percentage points in personal income, 0.8 percentage points

EXHIBIT 4

Distribution of Actual Values of Federal Grants-in-Aid Payments for 1969 Thru 1977*

	1969	1970	1971	1972	1973	1974	1975	1976	1977
FEDERAL GRANTS-IN-AID PAYMENTS TO STATE &LOCAL GOVERNMENTS (millions of dollars)									
United States	19158.0	21863.0	26148.0	31255.0	39264.0	41836.0	47002.0	55587.4	61884.0
New England	1062.0	1218.0	1492.0	1812.0	2205.0	2470.0	2711.0	3330.9	3743.0
Mideast	3864.0	4433.0	5383.0	6801.0	9322.0	9404.0	10524.0	12684.9	13684.0
Great Lakes	3119.0	3336.0	4030.0	5156.0	6362.0	7252.0	7725.0	9351.9	10158.0
Plains	1426.0	1633.0	1906.0	2174.0	2638.0	2915.0	3448.0	4076.0	4468.0
Southeast	3927.0	4405.0	5556.0	6295.0	7723.0	8556.0	10067.0	11396.1	12969.0
Southwest	1587.0	1804.0	2078.0	2421.0	2858.0	3136.0	3587.0	4102.1	4477.0
Rocky Mountain	641.0	740.0	867.0	1024.0	1221.0	1272.0	1460.0	1800.6	1963.0
Far West	3532.0	4294.0	4836.0	5572.0	6935.0	6831.0	7480.0	8844.9	10422.0
FEDERAL GRANTS-IN-AID PAYMENTS: PER CAPITA (DOLLARS)									
United States	95.2	107.3	126.8	150.1	187.1	198.0	220.6	259.0	286.1
New England	90.5	102.5	124.1	149.7	181.6	203.4	222.4	272.6	305.8
Mideast	91.8	104.3	125.5	158.2	217.9	220.5	246.7	297.0	322.4
Great Lakes	78.2	82.8	99.3	126.4	155.8	177.3	188.5	228.5	247.4
Plains	88.0	99.8	115.4	130.8	158.6	175.0	206.6	242.5	264.6
Southeast	90.4	100.2	124.4	138.5	166.8	181.8	210.8	236.6	265.8
Southwest	97.2	108.6	122.7	140.1	161.8	174.5	195.8	219.5	234.1
Rocky Mountain	129.7	146.9	169.0	192.9	222.9	227.5	256.9	311.3	332.1
Far West	132.6	158.6	176.4	201.3	247.6	240.9	260.0	301.6	349.0

EXHIBIT 4 (cont'd)

Distibution of Actual Values of Federal Grants-in-Aid Payments for 1969 to 1977*

FEDERAL GRANTS-IN-AID PAYMENTS: SHOWN AS A PERCENTAGE OF PERSONAL INCOME

	1969	1970	1971	1972	1973	1974	1975	1976	1977
United States	2.5	2.7	3.0	3.3	3.7	3.6	3.7	4.0	4.0
New England	2.2	2.4	2.8	3.1	3.5	3.6	3.7	4.1	4.2
Mideast	2.2	2.3	2.7	3.1	4.0	3.7	3.8	4.3	4.2
Great Lakes	2.0	2.0	2.3	2.7	2.9	3.1	3.1	3.4	3.3
Plains	2.5	2.7	2.9	3.0	3.1	3.3	3.6	4.0	3.8
Southeast	3.0	3.1	3.6	3.6	3.8	3.8	4.2	4.3	4.3
Southwest	3.0	3.1	3.3	3.5	3.5	3.5	3.6	3.6	3.5
Rocky Mountain	3.9	4.1	4.4	4.6	4.7	4.4	4.6	5.1	5.0
Far West	3.2	3.6	3.8	4.1	4.6	4.0	4.0	4.3	4.5

FEDERAL GRANTS-IN-AID PAYMENTS: SHOWN AS A PERCENTAGE OF STATE AND LOCAL EXPENDITURES

	1969	1970	1971	1972	1973	1974	1975	1976	1977
United States	16.4	16.6	17.4	18.7	21.7	21.1	20.5	21.8	22.7
New England	15.4	15.6	16.4	18.0	19.9	20.7	20.2	23.2	24.2
Mideast	13.7	13.9	14.3	16.0	20.3	18.8	18.7	20.7	21.5
Great Lakes	14.3	13.8	14.6	16.7	19.0	20.0	18.5	20.1	20.3
Plains	15.8	16.0	16.8	17.5	20.2	20.4	20.8	21.8	22.1
Southeast	19.5	19.5	21.3	22.1	24.7	24.1	23.8	24.2	25.5
Southwest	20.3	20.3	20.5	21.3	23.1	23.0	22.3	22.1	22.4
Rocky Mountain	21.8	22.6	23.3	24.3	26.7	25.0	23.8	25.2	25.4
Far West	17.7	19.1	19.2	20.6	23.7	21.4	20.4	21.1	23.3

* Total may not add due to rounding

EXHIBIT 5

Growth Characteristics of Selected Variables Due to a Doubling of Federal Grants-in-Aid Payments for 1969-1977*

| | United States | Average Annual Growth Rates Over the Period 1969 Through 1977 | | | | | | | |
		New England	Mideast	Great Lakes	Plains	South East	South West	Rocky Mountain	Far West
Growth Rates Before (GIA) Increase									
Personal Income, Total	9.4	8.4	8.2	9.0	9.6	10.9	11.2	11.2	9.4
Wage Income	8.8	7.4	7.4	8.5	9.2	10.2	10.7	10.8	8.7
Nonwage Income	11.9	11.2	11.1	11.5	11.0	13.5	12.8	12.6	11.9
Gross Output, Total	9.2	8.1	7.9	8.5	9.6	10.4	11.4	11.2	9.4
Manufacturing	7.8	6.2	6.1	7.3	9.4	9.7	10.4	10.3	8.4
Nonmanufacturing (private)	5.8	9.0	8.5	9.1	9.7	11.0	12.1	11.7	9.9
Government	9.2	8.6	9.4	9.7	9.3	9.2	9.1	9.6	8.6
Employment	2.1	1.5	1.1	1.7	2.2	2.7	3.2	3.4	2.6
State & Local government expenditure	12.0	12.2	12.5	11.7	10.8	12.2	12.1	12.2	11.6
Growth Rates After (GIA) Increase									
Personal Income, Total	10.1	8.7	8.9	9.7	10.0	11.5	11.9	11.5	10.0
Wage Income	9.5	7.9	8.2	9.3	9.7	10.9	11.6	11.1	9.5
Nonwage Income	12.0	11.2	11.3	11.5	11.1	13.5	13.0	12.8	12.0
Gross Output, Total	10.0	8.8	8.8	9.2	10.0	11.2	12.2	11.6	10.3
Manufacturing	8.6	6.9	7.0	8.1	10.2	10.5	11.2	10.9	9.3
Nonmanufacturing (private)	10.3	9.4	9.1	9.6	9.7	11.5	12.6	11.8	10.4
Government	11.4	10.8	11.5	12.1	11.2	11.3	11.6	11.5	10.8
Employment	2.8	1.9	1.8	2.5	2.7	3.4	4.1	3.8	3.3
State & Local government expenditure	14.8	15.1	15.4	14.4	13.4	15.3	15.0	15.3	14.4
Change in Growth Rates (After - Before)									
Personal Income, Total	.6	.4	.7	.7	.4	.6	.7	.3	.6
Wage Income	.8	.5	.8	.8	.5	.8	.9	.3	.8
Nonwage Income	.1	.0	.2	.1	.1	.0	.2	.2	.1
Gross Output, Total	.8	.7	.9	.8	.5	.8	.8	.5	.9
Manufacturing	.9	.7	1.0	.9	.8	.8	.9	.6	.9
Nonmanufacturing (private)	.5	.4	.6	.5	.1	.5	.5	.1	.5
Government	2.2	2.2	2.1	2.4	1.9	2.1	2.5	1.9	2.2
Employment	.7	.4	.7	.7	.5	.7	.9	.4	.7
State & Local government expenditures	2.9	2.8	2.9	2.7	2.6	3.1	2.8	3.0	2.9

* Total may not add due to rounding

in gross output, 0.7 percentage points in employment and 2.9 percentage points in expenditures. Lower than average induced growth in most indicators is evident for the New England and Plains regions. On the other hand, somewhat larger than average induced growth is evident for the Mideast, Southeast, and Southwest.

In order to provide further information concerning the regional differentials in stimulative impacts of aid, gross output, personal income and earnings multipliers are presented in Exhibit 6. These data give a clearer picture of net regional impacts because they are standardized across regions, i.e., they represent the total change in economic activity induced per dollar of increased grants-in-aid. Because increases in federal grants most directly affect output, these multipliers are larger than those for personal income and earnings which are less directly affected by federal grants. Nationally, the data indicate that gross output multipliers ranged from 1.3 to 2.1 while personal income (earnings) multipliers ranged from 0.5 to 1.3 (1.2 for earnings). Further, these data indicate that the maximum stimulative impact is not felt until about the sixth year only two-thirds of the impact on output occurs during the first year.[18]

Regionally, a very consistent pattern in stimulative differentials is evident. During the majority of the period, the multipliers in the Mideast, Great Lakes and Southwestern regions are higher than the national average, while those of the remaining regions are smaller than the national average. Further, the multipliers for the Great Lakes region are consistently highest of all the regions, while those of the Rocky Mountain region are consistently lowest.[19]

In summary, the results described above suggest three very important conclusions in regard to the stimulative effects of grants-in-aid. First, the results document the generally accepted notion that federal grants-in-aid produce significant general impacts on the national economy. The multipliers associated with federal grants were found to be approximately 2.0 nationwide for output and about 1.2 for personal income and earnings. Second, the results suggest that the full stimulative impact of grant increases is not at all instantaneous, but rather occurs over an extended period of time. While approximately two-thirds of the impact on output and about one-half the effect on income and earnings is felt in the first year, the maximum economic stimulus associated with grant increases is not felt until the sixth year. Third, this section has identified rather sizable regional differentials in the stimulative effects of federal grants-in-aid. With respect to output, for example, multipliers ranged from about 1.0 for the Rocky Mountain to nearly

EXHIBIT 6

Dynamic Expenditure Multipliers Resulting From a Doubled Federal Grants-in-Aid Payments, 1969-1977

	1969	1970	1971	1972	1973	1974	1975	1976	1977
GROSS OUTPUT MULTIPLIERS									
United States	1.3	1.6	1.7	1.8	1.9	1.8	2.1	1.9	2.1
New England	1.2	1.5	1.5	1.7	1.7	1.6	1.8	1.7	1.6
Mideast	1.4	1.9	1.9	2.1	2.1	2.0	2.5	2.1	2.4
Great Lakes	1.8	1.7	2.3	2.0	2.4	2.1	2.5	2.5	2.6
Plains	1.0	1.4	1.2	1.5	1.4	1.4	1.3	1.4	1.2
Southeast	1.1	1.6	1.4	1.7	1.7	1.7	1.8	1.7	1.9
Southwest	1.6	1.9	2.0	2.1	2.3	2.3	2.5	2.4	2.6
Rocky Mountain	.8	1.1	.9	1.1	1.0	1.0	1.0	1.0	.9
Far West	1.1	1.3	1.3	1.6	1.6	1.6	1.9	1.8	1.9
PERSONAL INCOME MULTIPLIERS									
United States	.5	.8	.9	1.0	1.0	1.1	1.2	1.2	1.3
New England	.4	.6	.6	.7	.7	.8	.8	.8	.7
Mideast	.6	1.0	1.1	1.2	1.2	1.2	1.4	1.2	1.4
Great Lakes	.7	.9	1.2	1.2	1.4	1.5	1.6	1.7	1.8
Plains	.3	.7	.7	.8	.8	.9	.9	1.0	1.0
Southeast	.4	.8	.7	.9	.9	1.0	1.0	1.1	1.1
Southwest	.7	1.0	1.2	1.2	1.4	1.5	1.6	1.6	1.7
Rocky Mountain	.2	.4	.3	.4	.4	.5	.5	.5	.5
Far West	.3	.5	.6	.8	.8	1.0	1.1	1.1	1.1
EARNINGS MULTIPLIERS									
United States	.5	.8	.8	1.0	1.0	1.1	1.2	1.2	1.2
New England	.4	.6	.6	.7	.8	.8	.8	.8	.7
Mideast	.6	1.0	1.0	1.1	1.2	1.1	1.3	1.2	1.3
Great Lakes	.7	.9	1.2	1.2	1.4	1.4	1.6	1.7	1.7
Plains	.3	.6	.6	.8	.8	.9	.9	.9	.9
Southeast	.4	.8	.7	.9	.9	1.0	1.0	1.1	1.1
Southwest	.7	1.0	1.1	1.1	1.3	1.3	1.5	1.5	1.6
Rocky Mountain	.2	.3	.3	.4	.4	.4	.4	.4	.4
Far West	.3	.5	.6	.7	.8	.9	1.0	1.0	1.1

two and one-half times this for the Great Lakes and Southwest regions.

DISTRIBUTIONAL EFFECTS OF GRANTS-IN-AID

The previous section focused upon determining the extent of regional differentials in stimulative impacts of Federal grants. The aim of this section is to analyze the interregional distributional effects of *existing* grants. The specific purpose is to determine the extent to which existing grant-in-aid programs redistribute income regionally. In order to accomplish this, the existing distribution of grants is compared to that which would result if aid were reallocated to each state based upon that state's share of U.S. total personal income, holding the U.S. level of grants set equal to the actual historical values for each year.[20] Since the emphasis here is to characterize the existing allocation of aid relative to a distributionally neutral income-based formula,[21] the solution of the model corresponding to the income-based formula has been adopted as the baseline solution. The basic data inputs as well as the results of this simulation are shown in Exhibits 7-10.

Data relating to the differences between actual grant levels and those based upon a personal income formula are exhibited in Exhibit 7. Several conclusions concerning the differences in aid allocations under these two alternatives are worthy of note here. First, these data indicate that for the entire period, the Southeast, Rocky Mountain and Far West regions consistently receive more and the the Great Lakes and Plains regions receive less aid under the present system than they would have received under a formula based upon personal income. Second, in three regions there are significant relative changes. New England and the Mideast received less under the present system for the early part of the period and more under the present system during the later part of the period.[22] The Southwest, on the other hand, received more under the current system early in the period, but less in later years.

In terms of absolute magnitude of the difference, the Great Lakes region consistently exhibits the largest deficit (less under the present system) amounting to about $2.4 billion in 1977. On the other hand, the Southeast and Far West regions register the largest surplus (more under the present system) amounting to about $1.1 billion and $1.3 billion in 1977, respectively. In relative terms, the Great Lakes region registers the largest deficit associated with the present system, amounting to 23.4 percent or $58 per capita in 1977. On the other

EXHIBIT 7

Distribution of Federal Grants-in-Aid Payments: Comparison of Current versus a Hypothetical Income Based Formula *

	1969	1970	1971	1972	1973	1974	1975	1976	1977
CHANGES IN GIA PAYMENTS: ACTUAL VALUES – PERSONAL INCOME FORMULA (MILLIONS $)									
United States	.0	.0	.0	.0	.0	.0	.0	.0	.0
New England	-152.0	-158.3	-162.4	-158.8	-241.7	-52.0	-121.9	.7	93.1
Mideast	-683.3	-719.4	-794.3	-535.5	273.3	55.5	-14.9	302.5	74.2
Great Lakes	-929.3	-1293.6	-1394.5	-1322.6	-1742.6	-1455.5	-1951.4	-1989.0	-2380.2
Plains	-21.5	-25.0	-81.3	-191.5	-384.5	-513.0	-192.4	-214.6	-120.1
Southeast	622.5	577.4	936.9	705.8	594.9	888.1	1307.6	944.5	1091.6
Southwest	237.8	272.9	197.5	180.7	4.0	6.8	28.7	-224.9	-521.4
Rocky Mountain	232.5	265.0	280.4	313.1	297.1	261.1	310.7	436.3	435.5
Far West	693.2	1081.0	1017.8	1008.8	1199.5	809.0	633.5	744.5	1327.3
PERCENT DIFFERENCE IN GIA PAYMENTS: ACTUAL VALUES – PERSONAL INCOME FORMULA									
United States	.0	.0	.0	.0	.0	.0	.0	.0	.0
New England	-14.3	-13.0	-10.9	-8.8	-11.0	-2.1	-4.5	.0	2.5
Mideast	-17.7	-16.2	-14.8	-7.9	2.9	.6	-.1	.0	.5
Great Lakes	-29.8	-38.8	-34.6	-25.7	-27.4	-20.1	-25.3	-21.3	-23.4
Plains	-1.5	-1.5	-4.3	-8.8	-14.6	-17.6	-5.6	-5.3	-2.7
Southeast	15.9	13.1	16.9	11.2	7.7	10.4	13.0	8.3	8.4
Southwest	15.0	15.1	9.5	7.5	.1	.2	.8	-5.5	-11.6
Rocky Mountain	36.3	35.8	32.3	30.6	24.3	20.5	21.3	24.2	22.2
Far West	19.6	25.2	21.0	18.1	17.3	11.8	8.5	8.4	12.7
CHANGES IN GIA PER CAPITA: ACTUAL VALUES – PERSONAL INCOME FORMULA (DOLLARS)									
United States	.0	.0	.0	.0	.0	.0	.0	.0	.0
New England	-13.0	-13.3	-13.5	-13.1	-19.9	-4.3	-10.0	.1	7.6
Mideast	-16.2	-16.9	-18.5	-12.5	6.4	1.3	-.3	7.1	1.7
Great Lakes	-23.3	-32.1	-34.4	-32.4	-42.7	-35.6	-47.6	-48.6	-58.9
Plains	-1.3	-1.5	-4.9	-11.5	-23.1	-30.8	-11.5	-12.8	-7.1
Southeast	14.3	13.1	21.0	15.5	12.9	18.9	27.4	19.6	22.4
Southwest	14.6	16.4	11.7	10.5	.2	.4	1.6	-12.0	-27.3
Rocky Mountain	47.0	52.6	54.3	59.0	54.2	46.7	54.7	75.4	73.7
Far West	26.0	39.9	37.1	36.4	42.8	28.5	22.0	25.4	44.4

* Total may not add due to rounding

hand, the Rocky Mountain registers the largest surplus associated with the present system, amounting to 22.2 percent or $73.7 per capita in 1977.

Data relating to the differential economic impact of the present system, relative to the hypothetical income-based formula is presented in Exhibit 8. Generally, these results indicate the nationwide effect of the current system of aid relative to an income-based formula is to produce lower levels of economic activity, regardless of the period chosen for study. This finding results from the fact that the current system of aid tends to distribute larger amounts of aid to low multiplier regions of the U.S. than would an aid system based on personal income. For example, in 1977 the Great Lakes region (output multiplier of 2.6) received $2.4 billion less while the Southeast and Far West (output multipliers of 1.9) received a combined total of $2.4 billion more under the current system than according to a system based on personal income. Further, differences in these multipliers can be explained mostly by differences in regional consumption patterns. For example, a dollar of grants spending in a region with a high proportion of imports from outside the U.S. to total consumption will impact the national economy less per dollar spent in a region with a low proportion of import consumption.

Further, the results indicate that, on the average, the current system of aid produces lower levels of economic activity in the New England, Mideast, Great Lakes and Plains regions than would have occurred if aid were allocated based upon income. On the other hand, on the average economic activity in the Southeast, Southwest, Rocky Mountain and Far West regions is higher under the current system than would be the case if aid were allocated based upon personal income. Finally, of all the regions, the Great Lakes, with the lowest per capita aid, registered the largest decrease in economic activity attributable to the current system of aid, with the Far West registered the largest increase.[23]

When comparing the detailed regional economic impacts for the years 1969 and 1977 indicated in Exhibit 8, some interesting regional differences are evident. Specifically, results indicate that, while the direction of the changes between direct and total impacts tend to be the same for the regions, the magnitude of the total changes are usually *lower* than the direct changes. The impacts of the direct grants spending thus tend to be partially evened-out over the entire nation.

In order to shed further light on the timing of economic impacts, results for three key variables—output, personal income and earnings

EXHIBIT 8

Average Impact on Selected Variables Due to a Shift from a Personal Income to the Present GIA Formula (millions of dollars)*

	United States	New England	Mideast	Great Lakes	Plains	South East	South West	Rocky Mountain	Far West
Impacts (Actual − Income Formula) for the year: 1969									
Personal Income, Total	−165.3	3.6	−152.9	−373.2	−1.5	22.6	216.4	17.1	102.4
Wage Income	−206.5	−.1	−155.1	−391.9	−4.4	24.9	199.3	16.0	104.8
Nonwage Income	41.2	3.8	2.2	18.8	3.0	−2.2	17.0	1.1	−2.4
Gross Output, Total	−548.4	−52.1	−325.2	−983.1	−23.1	64.8	359.7	67.2	343.5
Manufacturing	−366.3	−11.2	−87.8	−341.6	−12.6	−17.3	33.7	5.6	64.9
nonmanufacturing (private)	−66.9	−3.6	−70.9	−151.1	−3.9	.0	94.6	9.5	58.3
Government	−115.2	−37.3	−166.6	−490.5	−6.6	82.0	231.5	52.1	220.2
Employment	−12.9	.8	−15.3	−46.4	−.3	4.9	30.1	2.6	10.6
State & Local Government Expenditure	−55.0	−130.2	−633.7	−909.1	−23.9	579.3	225.8	220.6	616.2
Impacts (Actual − Income Formula) for the year: 1977									
Personal Income, Total	−1025.6	50.3	304.7	−1917.4	−116.3	259.3	−87.6	59.8	421.5
Wage Income	−1062.2	46.8	214.6	−1835.8	−109.8	267.9	−81.3	55.6	379.9
Nonwage Income	36.6	3.6	90.2	−81.6	−6.5	−8.7	−6.3	4.2	41.7
Gross Output, Total	−2242.8	110.9	299.5	−3673.6	−182.5	359.3	−59.4	128.4	784.7
Manufacturing	−1170.2	18.6	23.4	−1234.8	−77.2	−41.5	−17.1	8.8	149.7
nonmanufacturing (private)	−413.5	35.4	68.8	−844.1	−86.9	147.9	−57.4	30.8	292.0
Government	−659.2	46.9	207.2	−1594.7	−18.4	252.9	15.2	88.8	342.9
Employment	−64.5	5.3	12.6	−136.8	−7.9	28.5	−.6	6.0	28.4
State & Local Government Expenditure	−11.0	100.3	256.9	−2461.7	−146.2	1067.8	−500.1	421.3	1250.6

EXHIBIT 8 (cont'd)

Average Impact on Selected Variables Due to a Shift from a Personal Income to the Present GIA Formula (millions of dollars)*

	United States	New England	Mideast	Great Lakes	Plains	South East	South West	Rocky Mountain	Far West
Impacts (Actual − Income Formula) for the period 1969-1977 Annual Average									
Personal Income, Total	-463.9	-4.7	-46.4	-765.1	-78.0	118.3	41.2	34.2	236.5
Wage Income	-439.6	.9	-38.6	-744.9	-69.4	130.4	34.4	32.2	215.3
Nonwage Income	-24.3	-5.6	-7.8	-20.2	-8.6	-12.1	6.8	2.0	21.2
Gross Output, Total	-873.1	-9.8	-124.1	-1303.6	-118.0	134.3	65.3	76.0	406.9
Manufacturing	-413.0	-2.8	-54.5	-395.2	-30.3	-9.9	3.2	5.3	71.1
Nonmanufacturing (private)	-140.2	3.3	-43.1	-366.4	-38.0	87.7	34.4	18.3	163.5
Government	-319.8	-10.4	-26.6	-542.0	-49.7	56.5	27.7	52.5	172.3
Employment	-28.4	.8	-4.4	-69.9	-7.0	17.5	10.6	4.2	19.6
State & Local Government Expenditure	-62.3	-97.2	-143.4	-1616.1	-196.8	809.6	22.0	303.5	856.1

* Totals may not add due to rounding

—were investigated over the entire 1969 to 1977 period and are shown in Exhibit 9. Generally, these data indicate that between 1969 and 1972 economic activity in the New England, Mideast, Great Lakes and Plains regions was less under the current system than under the alternative. Conversely, over the same period economic activity in the Southeast, Southwest, Rocky Mountains and Far West regions was greater under the current system of aid than under the alternative system.

Somewhat different conclusions are evident during the 1973-1977 period. While no changes took place in the trends for the Great Lakes, Plains, Southeast, Rocky Mountains and Far West, trends for each of the three remaining regions reversed. Specifically, during the latter part of the study period, the current system produced a differential stimulus to economic activity in the New England and Mideast regions and inhibited growth in the Southwest region. This reversal of economic impact is the direct result of changes that occurred in the geographical allocation of the current aid system over the 1969 to 1977 period as noted in Exhibit 7.[24]

When comparing the distributional effects of the current system of aid with that of a hypothetical income-based system, it is useful to analyze the levels of per capita income that are associated with each of these systems. Data on per capita income relatives under each of these systems is presented in Exhibit 10.[25] First, these data indicate that while incomes are definitely converging over time, under the current system of aid the per capita incomes in the New England, Mideast, Great Lakes and Far West regions remain consistently higher and those of the remaining regions consistently lower than the national average.[26] Second, when the per capita income relatives are compared to those associated with the income-based formula, no net change in relative positions is evident across regions. This result would suggest the general conclusion that, in terms of its effect on regional differentials in per capita income, the current system of aid is *not* substantially different from the hypothetical income-based formula.[27]

While these results suggest there is no overall difference in the effects of the two systems in terms of per capita income levels, the directions of marginal differences in the two systems are useful to note. Focusing specifically on the two regions for which the largest positive (Far West) and negative (Great Lakes) economic impacts were identified, conflicting conclusions regarding the redistributive properties of the current system are evident. At one extreme, while the Far West region gains from the present system

EXHIBIT 9

Economic Impacts Over Time Due to a Shift from a Personal Income to the Present GIA Formula (millions of dollars)*

	1969	1970	1971	1972	1973	1974	1975	1976	1977
IMPACT ON TOTAL GROSS OUTPUT									
United States	−548.4	−372.6	−1088.2	−129.8	−1037.1	−651.2	−1348.8	−438.6	−2242.8
New England	−52.1	−31.2	−81.0	−19.6	−24.8	−25.2	−24.0	−20.5	100.9
Mideast	−325.3	−279.7	−632.7	11.9	99.1	−387.5	309.1	−211.6	299.5
Great Lakes	−983.1	−345.2	−1323.4	−390.0	−2016.6	−104.5	−2815.6	−80.2	−3673.6
Plains	−23.1	−32.6	−43.4	−89.0	−145.6	−202.8	−142.2	−200.7	−188.5
Southeast	64.8	1.8	178.0	−8.7	229.8	−68.4	517.2	−65.5	359.3
Southwest	359.7	43.9	357.2	4.4	184.7	−145.2	204.1	−362.1	−59.4
Rocky Mountain	67.2	29.8	87.6	48.2	98.3	36.9	105.0	83.0	128.4
Far West	343.5	240.6	369.6	313.1	537.9	245.5	449.5	378.1	784.7
IMPACT OF TOTAL PERSONAL INCOME									
United States	−165.3	−400.9	−621.8	−109.8	−330.0	−338.2	−609.1	−574.7	−1025.6
New England	3.6	−31.9	−20.0	−18.4	3.4	−32.2	15.1	−12.2	50.3
Mideast	−152.9	−263.3	−442.5	−.9	208.5	−120.0	259.5	−210.4	304.7
Great Lakes	−373.2	−275.8	−596.4	−359.4	−981.1	−368.9	−1490.5	−523.2	−1917.4
Plains	−1.5	−33.0	−31.9	−53.6	−76.6	−128.9	−95.1	−165.1	−116.3
Southeast	22.6	−16.8	71.1	68.4	131.7	101.9	279.8	145.7	259.3
Southwest	216.4	87.1	195.0	35.7	70.1	−62.0	73.3	−157.1	−87.6
Rocky Mountain	17.1	18.7	30.7	28.9	37.9	27.0	45.6	41.8	59.8
Far West	102.4	113.9	171.5	189.5	275.9	245.0	303.2	305.7	421.5
IMPACT ON EARNINGS									
United States	−206.5	−248.7	−485.9	−177.2	−392.0	−388.5	−633.8	−362.0	−1062.2
New England	−.1	−15.1	−14.0	−18.8	4.8	−24.1	16.3	12.2	46.8
Mideast	−155.1	−152.7	−321.0	−36.3	144.7	−157.1	179.9	−64.4	214.6
Great Lakes	−391.9	−279.2	−601.7	−365.5	−972.0	−361.6	−1409.7	−486.3	−1835.8
Plains	−4.4	−18.7	−20.4	−51.6	−72.6	−121.5	−91.6	−133.9	−109.8
Southeast	24.9	10.9	102.8	67.1	145.6	98.8	295.1	160.6	267.9
Southwest	199.3	75.1	172.1	25.7	60.3	−61.6	65.4	−145.3	−81.3
Rocky Mountain	16.0	17.5	28.5	27.4	36.0	26.2	42.8	40.0	55.6
Far West	104.8	113.7	167.9	174.9	261.2	212.4	268.0	255.2	379.9

* Total may not add due to rounding

EXHIBIT 10

Effects of Relative Grants-in-Aid Allocation Formulas on the Regional Distribution of Per Capita Income*

	1969	1970	1971	1972	1973	1974	1975	1976	1977
PER CAPITA INCOME RATIOS (INCOME FORMULA)	Percentage Ratios of Regional to United States Average Per Capita Personal Income								
United States	100.0	100.0	100.0	100.0	100.0	100.0	100.0	100.0	100.0
New England	108.0	108.6	108.2	107.0	103.9	104.4	104.3	103.2	101.6
Mideast	112.6	113.3	112.9	111.4	108.9	110.1	110.1	109.4	107.2
Great Lakes	106.8	105.0	105.3	105.4	106.7	105.9	105.5	105.3	107.5
Plains	94.9	95.7	95.8	97.7	104.1	98.6	98.5	95.1	98.2
Southeast	80.8	81.3	82.0	82.9	83.3	84.4	84.8	86.1	86.5
Southwest	86.8	88.6	87.7	88.2	89.7	89.7	91.2	93.5	92.7
Rocky Mountain	88.9	91.0	91.9	94.1	95.4	94.8	94.2	93.4	92.0
Far West	111.1	109.7	109.3	109.0	107.2	108.2	107.8	108.2	107.8
PER CAPITA INCOME RATIOS (ACTUAL FORMULA)									
United States	100.0	100.0	100.0	100.0	100.0	100.0	100.0	100.0	100.0
New England	108.0	108.6	108.2	107.0	103.9	104.3	104.4	103.2	101.7
Mideast	112.5	113.2	112.8	111.5	109.0	110.1	110.2	109.3	107.4
Great Lakes	106.6	104.9	105.1	105.3	106.4	105.9	105.1	105.4	107.1
Plains	94.9	95.7	95.8	97.7	104.1	98.5	98.5	95.0	98.2
Southeast	80.8	81.4	82.1	83.0	83.4	84.4	84.9	86.2	86.5
Southwest	87.1	88.7	87.9	88.1	89.7	89.6	91.2	93.3	92.7
Rocky Mountain	89.0	91.1	92.1	94.2	95.5	94.8	94.3	93.5	92.2
Far West	111.2	109.9	109.5	109.2	107.3	108.3	107.9	108.3	107.8
DIFFERENCE IN PER CAPITA INCOME RATIOS (RELATIVE TO INCOME FORMULA)**									
United States	.0	-.0	.0	.0	.0	.0	.0	.0	.0
New England	-.0	.0	-.0	.0	-.0	.0	-.1	.0	-.1
Mideast	.1	.1	.1	-.0	-.1	.0	-.1	.0	-.1
Great Lakes	.2	.1	.2	.1	.3	.0	.4	-.0	.4
Plains	.0	.0	.0	-.0	.3	-.1	.4	-.1	.0
Southeast	.0	.0	.1	.0	.1	.0	.0	.0	.1
Southwest	.3	.1	.2	-.1	.0	-.2	.1	-.2	-.1
Rocky Mountain	.1	.1	.2	.1	.1	.1	.1	.1	.1
Far West	-.1	-.1	-.2	-.1	-.2	-.1	-.1	-.1	-.1

* Totals may not add due to rounding.
** A negative shows movement away from the U.S. average per capita income level.

of aid, its level of per capita income is farther away from the national average than would be the case if aid were distributed according to personal income. At the other extreme, while the Great Lakes loses from the present system of aid, its level of per capita income is closer to the U.S. average than would result if aid were distributed based upon personal income. Similar disparities in the impact of the current system of aid are also evident for several of the other regions.[28]

In summary, the results presented in this section suggest several noteworthy conclusions concerning the distributional effects of existing grants-in-aid. First, when the impact of the current system of aid is compared to that of an hypothetical income-based formula, it is evident that the general level of economic activity nationwide is less under the current system. This conclusion derives from the fact that under the current system, relatively more aid is distributed to regions with low multipliers than under the hypothetical income-based system. Second, sizeable regional differences in economic impact can be associated with the current aid system when compared to an income-based system. At the extremes, the impact of the current system as compared to an income-based system results in a decrease of as much as $3.7 billion in output in the Great Lakes and an increase of $1.1 billion in output in the Far West and Southeast regions combined. In absolute terms, however, the total impact is usually *less* than the direct change in grants spending. Finally, although sizable regional differences in economic impacts can be associated with the current system when compared to an income-based system, the current system does not produce any significant changes in the regional distribution of per capita income from that produced by an income-based formula.

A CONCLUDING NOTE

The purpose of this research has been to analyze the regional differences in the stimulative and distributive impacts of federal grants-in-aid. Estimates of these impacts were derived by employing a state-level interregional econometric model of the U.S. economy. Based upon an analysis of gross output, income and earnings multipliers associated with existing federal grants-in-aid, it was concluded that substantial regional variation in stimulative impacts exist in the U.S. Based upon an analysis of per capita personal income differentials associated with two alternative techniques for regionally allocating federal grants, it was concluded that the existing system of allo-cating grants produces a regional pattern of per capita income nearly identical to that produced by an allocation system governed by the regional distribution of total personal income.

While these results, alone, should provide significant information for those concerned with the formulation of federal grant policy, extensions of this research are currently being undertaken in three areas. First, although the focus of this paper has been upon regions, state-level results can also be generated. The analysis of these state-level impacts has begun, with the aim of determining the extent of impact differentials within regions.

Second, while NRIES as presently constituted is not capable of disaggregating impacts to the substate level, plans are to modify the system to provide for this capability. In this regard, research is currently being undertaken to link NRIES with the Regional Industrial Multiplier System (RIMS).[29] RIMS was designed to estimate industry-specific input-output type multipliers for any combination of U.S. counties and for any of the 478 industries specified in the U.S. input-output table. The linking of these two systems would, in effect, allow the determination of the RIMS-generated substate spatial distribution of the aggregate state impacts generated by NRIES.

Finally, it should be noted that no explicit consideration was given to the existence of regional cost-of-living differences in this paper. This omission results from the fact that such time-series data are presently available at the state level.[30] However, consideration is currently being given to the estimation of state-level differences in cost-of-living with the aim of explicitly including them in the model.

NOTES

1. Gustely (7), p. 3-4.
2. Gustely (7), p. 7.
3. Gustely (7), p. 7.
4. For examples, see Nathan (9), Nathan (10), Ross (12). Numerous other studies of this type are cited in Gustely (7).
5. For one such study on HUD, see Ballard, Glickman, and Wendling (1).
6. See Vaughan (14).
7. See Ballard, Gustely, and Wendling (2) and Ballard and Wendling (3).
8. For a more complete specification of the model, see Ballard, Gustely, and Wendling (2).

9. The interaction indices $\overset{r}{x}\overset{j}{g}\overset{}{t}$ are calculated individually for each state (r) and variable (x^j) based upon the formula shown below:

$$\overset{r}{\underset{x}{g}}\overset{j}{\underset{t}{}} \quad = \quad \sum_{\substack{k=1 \\ k \neq r}}^{n} \frac{k_x{}^j{}_t}{rk_d}$$

To compute the interaction index for a particular variable, the activity levels of the variable x^j in all *other* states are scaled by the distance rk_d from the home state (r) and then summed. In the current NRIES model the distance scalar ^{rk}d originates from a symmetric matrix of geographic distance between the population centers of each region.

10. For examples of single region models see Glickman (5) and Gustely (6).

11. Top-down models allocate given totals to each individual region, thereby disregarding the possible effects of individual regions on the national economy. Such models are described in Harris (8) and Olsen (11).

12. See Gustely (6) Chapter III for a discussion of a similar approach to incorporating a fiscal sector into a model of the State of Tennessee.

13. The model expresses both state and local taxes, and charges and miscellaneous revenues as a function of the general economic activity. The sum of these together with aid, then, determine expenditure levels.

14. Specifically, the multipliers are defined for each state as

(A) $\dfrac{\Delta \text{Output}}{\Delta \text{Grants}}$ (B) $\dfrac{\Delta \text{Personal Income}}{\Delta \text{ Grants}}$ and

(C) $\dfrac{\Delta \text{Earnings}}{\Delta \text{Grants}}$

15. These data were obtained from *Governmental Finances,* Bureau of the Census.

16. This shift is partly attributable to the institution of programs such as the Comprehensive Employment and Training Act (CETA), Anti-Recession Fiscal Assistance (ARFA) and Community Development Block Grants (CDBG) which are targeted on urban areas.

17. It should be noted that aid expressed as a function of local expenditures increased more rapidly than aid as a function of state expenditures. For a discussion of this, see Gustely (7), p. 4.

18. Similar results are evident for personal income and earnings although less of the total impact is felt in the first year for these indicators. This result is due to the fact that these indicators are less directly affected by changes in aid, and so the overall effect takes longer to occur.

19. Several reasons for differences in the size of the multipliers might be

noted here. First, larger regions should be expected to have larger multi-pliers, other things being equal, since larger regions can satisfy more of their demands internally. Second, manufacturing-oriented economies such as the Great Lakes and Mideast tend to have larger multipliers due to the fact that they require a larger local sector to support their manu-facturing export sector.

20. Specifically, the aid under this simulation was allocated according to the following formula:

$$Aid_t^i = Aid_t^{us} \star \frac{PY_{t-1}^i}{PY_{t-1}^{us}}$$

where:
PY = Personal Income
t = time
i = = state

21. The argument here is that since most federal government revenues are derived from the federal personal income tax, the burden of these revenues across regions is distributed as is personal income. An allocation of grants back to states based upon their share of U.S. personal income, then, represents a neutral position with respect to the interregional dis-tribution of personal income.

22. As noted above, this results from the fact that aid programs instituted in the mid-1970s tended to be targeted toward the urbanized areas of the country, many of which are located in the New England and Mideast regions.

23. These extreme results are due to the fact that both regions register large differences in aid under the present system as compared to an income-based system and also because the output multipliers for those regions are among the largest of any regions.

24. These results are due to the fact that programs instituted in the mid-1970s differentially favored urbanized areas including the New England and Mideast regions.

25. These relatives were calculated as follows:

$$\frac{per\ capita\ income_i}{per\ capita\ income_{us}} \times 100$$

where i = state.

26. This represents a continuation of the historical pattern, although the differentials in per capita have narrowed since 1929. See Freidenberg (4).

27. This is an interesting result since there has been an attempt over the 1970s to make the present system of aid more responsive to differences in "need" across jurisdictions, where "need" is sometimes defined in terms of per capita income relatives.

28. The basic conclusion suggested by these mixed results is that the current system of aid when evaluated in terms of distributional effects is a mixed-bag, aiding regional redistribution in some cases and inhibiting it in

others. These results probably are reflective of the sizable differences in program objectives characterizing the existing aid system. Specifically, while some programs seek to be responsive to income differentials, others are not sensitive to this factor whatsoever.

29. See U.S. Water Resources Council (1977).

30. One study estimating state-level cost-of-living differentials for 1977 has recently been released by the National Center for Economic Alternatives, Washington, D.C.

REFERENCES

Ballard, K.P., Glickman, N.J. and R.M. Wendling, "Using a Multi-regional Model to Measure the Spatial Impacts of Federal Policies," in *The Urban Impacts of Federal Policies* (Baltimore: Johns-Hopkins University Press, 1979).

——————,Gustely, R.D., and R.M. Wendling, *The National-Regional Impact Evaluation System: Structure, Performance and Application of a Bottom-up Interregional Econometric Model,* (Washington, D.C.: Bureau of Economic Analysis, forthcoming, 1979).

——————, and R.M.Wendling, "The National-Regional Impact Evaluation System: A Spatial Model of U.S. Economic and Demographic Activity," unpublished manuscript, (1978).

Friedenberg, H.L., "Regional Differences in Personal Income Growth, 1929-77," *Survey of Current Business* (October, 1978). pp. 27-31.

Glickman, N.J., *Econometric Analysis of Regional Systems* (New York: Academic Press, 1977).

Gustely, R.D., *Forecasting Regional Economic Activity: The Tennessee Econometric Model—TEMII* (Knoxville: University of Tennessee, 1978).

——————,"Measuring the Regional Economic Impacts of Federal Grant Programs," in *The Federal Response to the Fiscal Crisis in American Cities,* Kenneth Hubball, ed., (Cambridge: Ballinger, 1979).

Harris, C.C., *The Urban Economies, 1985* (Lexington: Lexington Books, 1973).

Nathan, R.P., R.F. Cook, J.M. Galchick, and R.W. Long, *Monitoring the Public Service Employment Program* (Washington, D.C.: Brookings, 1978).

——————, A.D. Manvel, and S.E. Calkins, *Monitoring Revenue Sharing* (Washington, D.C.: Brookings, 1975).

Olsen, R.J., et al., *Multiregion: A Simulation—Forecasting Model of BEA Economic Area Population and Employment* (Oak Ridge: Oak Ridge National Laboratory, 1977).

Ross, J.P., *Countercyclical Aid and Economic Stabilization, Report A-69* (Washington, D.C.: ACIR, 1978).

U.S. Water Resources Council, *Guideline 5: Regional Multipliers.* Industry-Specific Gross Output Multipliers for BEA Economic Areas prepared by Bureau of Economic Analysis, U.S. Department of Commerce. (Washington, D.C.: U.S. Government Printing Office, 1977).

Vaughan, R.J., *The Urban Impacts of Federal Policies: Vol. 2, Economic Development* (Santa Monica, California: Rand Corporation, 1977).

BIBLIOGRAPHY

Edward Duensing - MUNICIPAL FINANCE EMPHASES - A BIBLIOGRAPHY

---

100. CITIES AND FINANCIAL STRESS–GENERAL

101. Alcaly, Roger E., and David Mermelstein (eds.). *The Fiscal Crisis of American Cities: Essays on the Political Economy of Urban America with Special Reference to New York.* New York: Vintage Books, 1977.
102. Allman, T.D. "The Urban Crisis Leaves Town," *Harpers* (December 1978), pp. 41-56.
103. Anderson, Eric A. "Changing Municipal Finances," *Urban Data Service Report,* Vol. 7, No. 12 (December 1975), pp. 1-14.
104. ———, and John Pazour. "The Fiscal Dilemma of the Cities," *Urban Data Service,* Vol. 3, No. 8 (August 1971), entire issue.
105. Aronson, J. Richard. "Is there a Fiscal Crisis Outside of New York?," *National Tax Journal,* Vol. 31, No. 2 (June 1978), pp. 153-163.
106. Bahl, Roy (ed.). *The Fiscal Outlook for Cities: Implications of a National Urban Policy.* Syracuse, NY: Syracuse University Press, 1978.

695

107. Bahl, Roy. "The Outlook for State and Local Government Finances," *Public Administration Review*, Vol. 36, No. 6 (November/December 1976), pp. 683-687.

108. ———, and David Puryear. *Economic Problems of a Mature Economy*, Occasional Paper No. 27, Syracuse, NY, Syracuse University, Maxwell School, 1976.

109. ———, and Walter Vogt. *Fiscal Centralization and Tax Burdens: State and Regional Finance of City Services.* Cambridge, MA: Ballinger, 1976.

110. Birch, David. *The Process Causing Economic Change in Cities,* prepared for Department of Commerce Roundtable on business retention and expansion in cities, February 22, 1978.

111. Bish, Robert L. *The Public Economy of Metropolitan Areas.* Chicago: Markham, 1971.

112. Black, J. Thomas. *The Changing Economic Role of Central Cities.* Washington, D.C.: Urban Land Institute, 1978.

113. Blair, John P., and David Nachmias (eds.) *Fiscal Retrenchment and Urban Policy.* Beverly Hills, CA: Sage, 1979.

114. *City Financial Emergencies.* Washington, D.C.: Advisory Commission on Intergovernmental Relations, 1973.

115. Cohen, Robert. *The Corporation and the City,* unpublished Paper, Arlington, VA: Analytic Sciences Corporation, 1978.

116. ———. *Urban Effects of the Internationalization of Capital and Labor,* unpublished Paper, New York: Columbia University, Conservation of Human Resources Program, 1977.

117. Colman, William G. *Cities Suburbs, and States: Governing and Financing Urban America.* New York: Free Press, 1975.

118. Conroy, Michael E. *The Challenge of Urban Economic Development: Goals, Possibilities, and Policies for Improving the Economic Structure of Cities.* Lexington, MA: Lexington Books, 1975.

119. *Coordinated Urban Economic Development: A Case Study Analysis.* Washington, D.C.: National Council for Urban Economic Development, 1978.

120. Crider, Robert A. *The Impact of Recession on State and Local Finances.* Columbus, OH: Academy for Contemporary Problems, 1978.

121. Ecker-Racz, L. Laslo. "State/Local Financial Crisis: With Benefit of Hindsight," *National Civic Review.* Vol. 68, No. 11 (December 1979), pp. 605-612.

122. First National Bank of Boston, Economics Department. *Urban Fiscal Stress: A Comparative Analysis of Sixty-Six U.S. Cities.* New York: Touche Ross & Company, 1979.

123. Fischer, Glenn W. "Problems of Financing Local Government in the United States of America," *Local Finance* (September 1973), pp. 8-19.
124. Goldin, Harrison J. "Financial Problems of the Cities," *Bureaucrat*, Vol. 5, No. 4 (January 1977), pp. 377-390.
125. Gordon D. "Capitalist Development and the History of American Cities," in I. Sawers and W. Tabb (eds.) *Marxism and the Megalopolis*. New York: Oxford University Press, 1978.
126. Gorham, William, and Nathan Glazer (eds.) *The Urban Predicament*. Washington, D.C.: Urban Institute, 1976.
127. Greene, Kenneth V., et al. *Fiscal Interactions in a Metropolitan Area*. Washington, D.C.: Urban Institute, 1974.
128. Harris, C. Lowell. "Can Our Cities Survive Financially?" *Mortgage Guaranty Insurance Corporation Newsletter* (March 1976).
129. Hirsch, Werner Z., et al. *Fiscal Pressures on the Central City: The Impact of Commuters, Nonwhites, and Overlapping Governments*. New York: Irvington, 1971.
130. ———. *Urban Economic Analysis*. New York: McGraw Hill, 1973.
131. Hochman, Harold M. (ed.). *The Urban Economy*. New York: Norton, 1976.
132. Hovey, Harold A. *Development Financing for Distressed Areas*. Washington, D.C.: Northeast-Midwest Institute, 1979.
133. Howell, James M., and Charles F. Stamm. *Urban Fiscal Stress: A Comparative Analysis of 66 U.S. Cities*. Lexington, MA: Lexington Books, 1979.
134. Hubbell, L. Kenneth (ed.). *Fiscal Crisis in American Cities: The Federal Response*. Cambridge, MA: Ballinger, 1979.
135. Jones, Benjamin. *Tax Increment Financing of Community Redevelopment*. Lexington, KY: Council of State Governments, 1977.
136. Klaasen, L.H., and L. Van den Berg. "Financing Urban Systems," *Local Finance* (July 1979), pp. 3-15.
137. Kordalewski, John. *Ways of Identifying Cities in Distress*. Washington, D.C.: Urban Institute, 1978.
138. Kraft, Gerald, et al. "On the Definition of a Depressed Area," in John F. Kain, and John R. Meyer (eds) *Essays in Regional Economics*. Cambridge, MA: Harvard University Press, 1971, pp. 58-104.
139. Laird, Melvin R., et al. *The Financial Crisis of Our Cities: A Round Table Held on December 10, 1975*. Washington, D.C.: American Institute for Public Policy Research, 1976.
140. Libassi, Peter, and Victor Hausner. *Revitalizing Central City*

Investment. Columbus, OH: Academy for Contemporary Problems, 1977.

141. Lynch, Lawrence, K., et al. "Comparative Growth and Structures: The South and the Nation," in E. Blain Liner and Lawrence K. Lynch (eds) *The Economics of Southern Growth.* Durham, NC: The Southern Growth Policies Board, 1977.

142. MacManus, Susan A. *Revenue Patterns in U.S. Cities and Suburbs: A Comparative Analysis.* New York: Praeger, 1978.

143. Merget, Astrid E. "The Era of Fiscal Restraint," *Urban Data Service Reports,* Vol. 11, No. 1 (January 1979).

144. ———. and Donna E. Shalala. "Dollars and Cents: The Fiscal Implications of Decentralization in Large City Governments," in Hans B.C. Spiegel, (ed) *Decentralization: Citizen Participation in Urban Development,* Vol. III, Fairfax, VA: Learning Resources Corp./NTL, 1974, pp. 100-119.

145. Mermelstein, David, and Roger Alcoly. *Fiscal Crisis of American Cities: Essays on the Political Economy of Urban America with Special Reference to New York.* New York: Random, 1977.

146. Meyer, John R., and John M. Quigley. *Local Public Finance and the Fiscal Squeeze: A Case Study.* Cambridge, MA: Ballinger, 1977.

147. Miernyk, William H. "The Northeast Isn't What it Used to Be," in *Balanced Growth for the Northeast.* Albany, NY: New York State Senate, 1975.

148. Mieszkowski, Peter, and Mahlon Straszheim (eds.). *Current Issues in Urban Economics.* Baltimore, MD: Johns Hopkins University Press, 1979.

149. Mitchell, George, W. "Is this Where We Came In?," in *Proceedings of the Forty-Ninth Annual Conference on Taxation.* Columbus, OH: National Tax Association, (1956), p. 494.

150. Mollenkopf, J. "The Postwar Politics of Urban Development," *Politics and Society,* Vol. 5, No. 3 (1975).

151. Morris, Richard S. *Bum Rap on America's Cities: The Real Causes of Urban Decay.* Englewood Cliffs, NJ: Prentice Hall, 1978.

152. Moynihan, D.P. "The Politics and Economics of Regional Growth," *Public Interest,* No. 51 (1978), pp. 3-21.

153. Muller, Thomas. "The Declining and Growing Metropolis—A Fiscal Comparison," in George Sternlieb and James W. Hughes (eds.) *Post-Industrial America: Metropolitan Decline and Regional Job Shifts.* New Brunswick, NJ: Rutgers University, CUPR, 1975.

154. ———. "Fiscal Problems of Smaller Growing and Declining

Cities," in *Small Cities in Transition: The Dynamics of Growth and Decline.* Cambridge, MA: Ballinger, 1977.

155. ⸺. *Growing and Declining Urban Areas: A Fiscal Comparison.* Washington, D.C.: Urban Institute, 1975.

156. Nathan, Richard P., et al. "Cities in Crisis: The Impact of Federal Aid," League of Women Voters, *Current Focus.*

157. ⸺. and Charles Adams. "Understanding Central City Hardship," *Political Science Quarterly,* Vol. 91, No. 1 (1976).

158. ⸺. and Paul R. Dommel. "The Strong Sunbelt Cities and the Weak Cold Belt Cities," in U.S. Congress, House Committee on Banking, Finance and Urban Affairs, Subcommittee on the City. *Toward a National Urban Policy.* Washington, D.C.: G.P.O., 1977, pp. 19-26.

159. National League of Cities. *State of the Cities: 1975, A New Urban Crisis?* Washington, D.C.: 1976.

160. Netzer, Dick. "The Public Economy of the Metropolis," in Eli Ginzberg (ed.) *The Future of the Metropolis: People, Jobs, Income.* Salt Lake City: Olympus Publishing Company, 1975, pp. 71-83.

161. Peterson, George E. "The Fiscal and Financial Capacity of City Governments," paper prepared for the Deputy Assistant Secretary of Urban Policy, United States Department of Housing and Urban Development, 1979.

162. ⸺, et al. *Urban Fiscal Monitoring.* Washington, D.C.: Urban Institute, 1978.

163. Petersen, John. *State and Local Fiscal Forecasting.* Washington, D.C.: Government Finance Research Center, 1979.

164. Pettengill, Robert B., and Jogindar S. Uppal. *Can Cities Survive? The Fiscal Plight of American Cities.* New York: St. Martins Press, 1974.

165. Pluta, Joseph E. "The Fiscal Health of Medium-Sized Cities: A Regional Perspective," *Texas Business Review,* Vol. 53, No. 6 (November-December 1979), pp. 192-196.

166. Polensky, A. Mitchell. *Essays in Public Sector Economics: Central and Local.* Washington, D.C.: Urban Institute, 1975.

167. Pred, A. *Advanced City Systems.* New York: John Wiley, 1977.

168. Puryear, David L., et al. "Fiscal Distress: An Imbalance Between Resources and Needs," *Occasional Papers in Housing and Community Affairs,* Vol. 4 (July 1979), pp. 148-168.

169. Quigley, John. *Local Public Finance and The Fiscal Squeeze: A Case Study.* Cambridge, MA: Ballinger, 1977.

170. Research Planning Group on Urban Social Services. "The Political Management of the Urban Fiscal Crisis," *Comparative*

Urban Research, Vol. 5, No. 2/3 (1978), pp. 71-84.

171. Sacks, Seymour, and John Callahan. "Central City-Suburban Fiscal Disparity," appendix to *City Financial Emergencies.* Washington, D.C.: Advisory Commission on Intergovernmental Relations, 1973.

172. Schlosstein, Ralph L. "Older 'Core Cities' Economies Pose Fiscal Problems for State and Local Governments," *Tax Review,* No. 7 (July 1976), pp. 25-28.

173. "The Shame of the Cities," *Forbes* (May 15, 1975), pp. 50-58.

174. Small Cities Financial Management Project. *Is Your City Heading for Financial Difficulty: A Guidebook for Small Cities and Other Governmental Units.* Chicago: Municipal Finance Officers Association, 1978.

175. Stanley, David T. *Cities in Trouble.* Columbus, OH: Academy for Contemporary Problems, 1976.

176. Sternlieb, George, and James W. Hughes (eds.). *Post-Industrial America: Metropolitan Decline and Inter-Regional Job Shifts.* New Brunswick, NJ: Rutgers University, Center for Urban Policy Research, 1975.

177. Swetcky, Joseph J., Jr. *Municipal Finance in Greenwich, Connecticut.* Storrs, CT: University of Connecticut, Institute for Urban Research, 1979.

178. United States Congress, Joint Economic Committee, Subcommittee on Economic Growth and Stabilization, Subcommittee on Fiscal and Intergovernmental Policy. *The Current Fiscal Condition of Cities: A Survey of 67 of the 75 Largest Cities: A Study . . . 95th Congress, 1st Session. July 28, 1977.* Washington, D.C.: G.P.O., 1977.

179. ———. Subcommittee on Fiscal and Intergovernmental Policy. *Central City Business—Plans and Problems.* Washington, D.C.: G.P.O., 1979.

180. ———. House, Committee on Banking, Finance and Urban Affairs, Subcommittee on the City. *Urban Economic Development: Past Lessons and Future Requirements: A National Round Table.* Washington, D.C.: G.P.O. (S/N 052-070-05059-4), 1979.

181. ———. House, Committee on the Budget, Task Force on Community Resources and General Government. *Fiscal Problems Facing Municipalities: Hearings . . . 94th Congress, 2nd Session.* Washington, D.C.: G.P.O., 1976.

182. ———. Senate, Joint Economic Committee. *The Current Fiscal Condition of the Cities: A Survey of 67 of the 75 Largest Cities: A Study Prepared for the Use of the Subcommittee on*

Economic Growth and Stabilization and the Subcommittee on Fiscal and Intergovernmental Policy. Washington, D.C.: G.P.O., 1977.

183. ———. Library of Congress, Congressional Research Service. *The Central City Problem and Urban Renewal Policy: A Study prepared for the Subcommittee on Housing and Urban Affairs, Committee on Banking, Housing and Urban Affairs.* United States Senate. Washington, D.C.: G.P.O., 1973.

184. United States, The President's Urban and Regional Policy Group. *Cities and People in Distress: National Urban Policy Discussion Draft.* Washington, D.C.: U.S. Department of Housing and Urban Development, 1977.

185. "Urban Fiscal Problems," *National Tax Journal* (September 1976), entire issue.

186. Waldo Dwight (ed.). *Public Administration in a Time of Turbulence.* Scranton, PA: Chandler, 1972.

187. Weicher, John C. "The Effect of Political Fragmentation on Central City Budgets," in David C. Sweet (ed.). *Models of Urban Structure.* Lexington, MA: Lexington Books, 1973, pp. 177-203.

200. CITIES IN FISCAL DISTRESS—CASE SAMPLES

201. Auletta, Ken. "An Agenda to Save Our City: 44 Proposals That Could Help Turn This Town Around," *New York,* Vol. 9, No. 12 (March 22, 1976), pp. 39-54.

202. Bahl, Roy W. *Taxes, Expenditures and the Economic Base: A Case Study of New York City.* Syracuse, NY: Syracuse University, Maxwell School of Citizenship and Public Affairs, 1974.

203. Berenyi, John. "Causes and Effects of The New York Financial Crisis," *Local Finance,* Vol. 7, No. 2 (April 1978), pp. 3-11.

204. *Boston's Fiscal Crisis: Origins and Solutions.* Boston: Municipal Research Bureau, 1976.

205. Chinitz, Benjamin. *The Decline of New York in the 1970's: A Demographic, Economic, and Fiscal Analysis.* Springfield, VA: NTIS, 1977.

206. Clark, Terry Nicholas. *How Many New Yorks? The New York Fiscal Crisis in Comparative Perspective.* Chicago: University of Chicago, 1976.

207. Economic Recovery: New York City's Program for 1977-1981. New York: Department of City Planning, 1976.

208. Friedgut, Jac. "Perspectives on New York City's Fiscal Crisis:

The Role of the Banks," *City Almanac,* Vol. 12, No. 1 (June 1977), pp. 1-7.

209. Gramlich, Edward M. "The New York City Fiscal Crisis: What Happened and What is to be Done?" *American Economic Review* (May 1976), pp. 415-428.

210. Haider, Donald, and Thomas Elmore, Jr. "New York at the Crossroads," *City Almanac,* Vol. 9, No. 5 (February 1975).

211. Horton, Raymond D. "People, Jobs, and Public Finance in New York City: Implications of the Fiscal Crisis," *City Almanac,* Vol. 12, No. 2 (August 1977), pp. 1-13.

212. *How Philadelphia can Avoid Following in the Steps of New York City: Findings, Conclusions, and Recommendations of Study Comparing Philadelphia and New York City.* Philadelphia: Pennsylvania Economy League (Eastern Division), 1976.

213. Lewis, Carol W. *Municipal Finance in Connecticut's Five Largest Cities.* Storrs, CT: University of Connecticut, Institute of Urban Research, 1979.

214. Merz, C.M., and David F. Groebner. *Study of Alternatives to the Property Tax for the City of Boise: Final Report.* Boise, ID: Boise Center for Urban Research, 1976.

215. New York (City), Temporary Commission on City Finances. *The City in Transition: Prospects and Policies for New York: The Final Report.* New York: Arno Press, 1978.

216. *New York City's Fiscal Prospects: Forecasts of New York City Revenue and Expenditure Patterns for FY 1979 through 1983.* New York: Citizens Budget Commission, 1978.

217. Pivnicny, Vincent C. *Financial Characteristics of Fiscally Troubled Massachusetts Cities.* Boston: University of Massachusetts, College Professional Studies, 1978.

218. *Preliminary Observations on New York City's Projected Fiscal Year 1980 Expense and Capital Budgets on the Mayor's Management Report.* New York: Citizens Budget Commission, 1979.

219. Reaume, David, and Frank Ripley. *New York City Default: Some Economic Implications.* Washington, D.C.: Congressional Research Service, 1975.

220. Reischauer, R., Peter Clark and Peggy Cuciti. *New York City's Fiscal Problem: Its Origins, Potential Repercussions and Some Alternative Policy Responses.* Washington, D.C.: G.P.O., 1975.

221. Reischauer, Robert D., et al. "The Causes of New York City's Fiscal Crisis," *Political Science Quarterly* (Winter 1975-1976), pp. 659-674.

222. Samuelson, Robert J. "No Funds for Fun City: Bankrupt New York," *New Republic* (May 10, 1975), pp. 17-19.

223. Starr, Roger. "Making New York Smaller," *New York Times Magazine* (November 14, 1977), pp. 32ff.

224. Stein, Rona B. "The New York City Budget: Anatomy of A Fiscal Crisis," *Federal Reserve Bank of New York, Quarterly Review* (Winter 1976), pp. 1-12.

225. Stocker, Frederick D. *Fiscal Options for Older Cities in the Great Lakes Region.* Columbus, OH: Academy for Contemporary Problems, 1978.

226. United States Congress, House, Committee on Banking, Currency, and Housing, Subcommittee on Economic Stabilization. *Debt Financing Problems of State and Local Government; New York City: Hearings. . . 94th Congress, 1st.* Washington, D.C.: G.P.O., 1975.

227. —————. Senate, Committee on Banking, Housing, and Urban Affairs. *New York City: Financial Crisis; Hearings. . . 94th Congress, 1st.* Washington, D.C.: G.P.O., 1975.

228. —————. Senate, Committee on the District of Columbia. *Fiscal Pressures on the District of Columbia. Hearings. . . 94th Congress, 2nd Session.* Washington, D.C.: G.P.O., 1975.

229. United States. Congressional Budget Office. *New York City's Fiscal Problem: Its Origins, Potential Repercussions, and Some Alternative Policy Responses.* Washington, D.C.: Congressional Budget Office, 1975.

230. *Urban Fiscal Stress in Atlanta.* Atlanta, GA: Research Atlanta, 1979.

231. Wade, Richard. "The End of the Self-Sufficient City: New York's Fiscal Crisis in History," *Urbanism Past & Present,* No. 3 (Winter 1976-1977), pp. 1-4.

232. Weiler, Conrad. "The Fiscal Crisis," in *Philadelphia: Neighborhood Authority, and the Urban Crisis.* New York: Praeger, 1974.

233. Yoo, Jang H., and Attiat F. Ott. *New York City's Financial Crisis: Can the Trend be Reversed?* Washington, D.C.: American Enterprise Institute, 1975.

300. MUNICIPAL EXPENDITURES–CAUSE AND CONTROL

301. Adams, Robert F. *Determinants of Local Government Expenditures.* Ph.D. Dissertation, Ann Arbor, University of Michigan, 1963.

302. Akin, John S., and Gerald E. Auten. "City Schools and Suburban

Schools: A Fiscal Comparison," *Land Economics,* Vol. 52, No. 4 (November 1976), pp. 452-466.

303. Anker, Irving. "Urban Bankruptcy and the Schools: A View from the Bottom," *Phi Delta Kappan,* Vol. 58, No. 4 (December 1976), pp. 350-352.

304. Bahl, Roy. "Fiscal Retrenchment in a Declining State: The New York Case," paper presented to a HUD sponsored UCSB Conference on Tax Limitation, Dec. 14-15, 1978, University of California, Santa Barbara, Ca.

305. _____. et al. *The Impact of Economic Base Erosion, Inflation, and Employee Compensation Costs on Local Governments.* Syracuse, NY: Syracuse University, Maxwell School of Citizenship and Public Affairs, 1975.

306. _____. "Studies on Determinants of Public Expenditures: A Review," in Selma J. Mushkin and John Cotton. *Functional Federalism: Grants-in-Aid and PPB Systems.* Washington, D.C.: George Washington University, 1968.

307. _____, and Robert J. Saunders. "Determinants of Changes in State and Local Government Expenditures," *National Tax Journal,* Vol. 18 (1965), pp. 50-57.

308. Baker, David, G., and David P. Colby. *In Search of City Efficient: Economies of Scale in Municipal Services,* paper presented at the Midwest Political Science Association Meeting, April 20-22, 1978.

309. Barr, James L., and Otto A. Davis. "An Elementary Political and Economic Theory of the Expenditures of Local Government," *Southern Economic Journal,* Vol. 33 (1966), pp. 149-165.

310. Beaton, Patrick. "The Determinants of Police Protection Expenditure," *National Tax Journal,* Vol. 29 (1975), pp. 328-335.

311. Bellush, Jewel, and Stephen M. David (eds.). *Race and Politics in New York City.* New York: Praeger, 1971.

312. Bergstrom, T.C., and R.P. Goodman. "Private Demands for Public Goods," *American Economic Review,* Vol. 63, No. 3 (June 1973), pp. 280-297.

313. Berke, Joel S. *Answers to Inequity: An Analysis of the New School Finance.* Berkeley, CA: McCutchan Publishing Corporation, 1974.

314. Block, Peter B. *Equality of Distribution of Police Services: A Case Study of Washington, D.C.* Washington, D.C.: Urban Institute, 1974.

315. Boulding, Kenneth E. "Factors Affecting the Future Demand for

Education," in Roe L. Johns, et al. (eds.) *Economic Factors Affecting the Financing of Education.* Gainesville, FL: National Educational Finance Project, 1979, pp. 1-27.

316. Burchell, Robert, and David Listokin. *Municipal Financial Planning: Techniques to Evaluate the Public Service Costs of Land Development, Federation Planning Information Report,* Vol. 13, No. 1 (Autumn 1978), entire issue.

317. ———. et al. *The Fiscal Impact Handbook.* New Brunswick, NJ: Rutgers University, Center for Urban Policy Research, 1978.

318. Caezza, John F. "Budget Caps—A Short History and a Long Future," *New Jersey Municipalities,* Vol. 55, No. 7 (October 1978), pp. 15-16.

319. Clark, John J., Thomas J. Hindeland and Robert E. Pritchard. *Capital Budgeting: Planning and Control of Capital Expenditures.* Englewood Cliffs, NJ: Prentice-Hall, 1979.

320. Davis, Otto A. "Empirical Evidence of Political Influence Upon the Expenditure Policies of Public Schools," in Julius Margolis, (ed.) *The Public Economy of Urban Communities.* Washington, D.C.: Johns Hopkins Press, 1965.

321. Dougharty, Larry. *Municipal Service Pricing: Impact on Urban Development and Finance Summary and Overview.* Santa Monica, CA: Rand Corporation, 1975.

322. Ehrenberg, R.G. "The Demand for State and Local Government Employees," *American Economic Review,* Vol. 63, No. 3 (June 1973), pp. 366-379.

323. Fisher, Glenn. "Determinants of State and Local Government Expenditures: A Preliminary Analysis," *National Tax Journal,* Vol. 14 (1961), pp. 349-355.

324. Fisk, Donald, and Cynthia A. Lancer. *Equality of Distribution of Recreation Services: A Case Study of Washington, D.C.* Washington, D.C.: Urban Institute, 1974.

325. Friedman, Lewis B. *Budgeting Municipal Expenditures: A Study in Comparative Policy Making.* New York: Praeger, 1975.

326. Gabler, L.R. "Economies and Diseconomies of Scale in Urban Public Sectors," *Land Economics,* Vol. 45, No. 4, November 1979, pp. 425-424.

327. ———. "Population Size as a Determinant of City Expenditure and Employment: Some Further Evidence," *Land Economics,* Vol. 47, No. 2 (May 1971), pp. 130-138.

328. Galambos, Eva C., and Arthur F. Schreiber. *Making Sense Out*

of Dollars: Economic Analysis for Local Government. Washington, D.C.: National League of Cities, 1978.

329. Gardner, John L. "City Size and Municipal Service Costs," *Report on Spatial Alternatives in Growth.* Chicago: University of Chicago, Urban Economics Report, 1973.

330. Greytak, David, Richard Gustely, and Robert Dinlekmeyer. "The Effects of Inflation on Local Government Expenditures," *National Tax Journal,* Vol. 27 (1974), pp. 583-598.

331. Greytak, David, and Bernard Jump. "Inflation and Local Government Expenditures and Revenues: Method and Case Study," *Public Finance Quarterly,* Vol. 5, No. 3 (July 1977), pp. 275-301.

332. Grossman, David A. *The Future of New York City's Capital Plant: A Case Study of Trends and Prospects Affecting the City's Public Infrastructure.* Washington, D.C.: Urban Institute, 1979.

333. Gustely, Richard D. *Municipal Public Employment and Public Expenditure.* Lexington, MA: D.C. Heath and Company, 1974.

334. Guyarati, D. *Pensions and New York City's Fiscal Crisis.* Washington, D.C.: American Enterprise Institute for Public Policy Research, (N.D.).

335. Hallman, Howard W. *Citizen Involvement in the Local Budget Process.* Washington, D.C.: Center for Community Change, 1978.

336. Haskell, Mark. "Toward Equality of Educational Opportunity," *Urban Education,* Vol. 21, No. 3 (October 1977), pp. 313-326.

337. Hill, Richard Child. *Exploring an Urban Contradiction: The Divorce of Municipal Expenditures from Social Needs.* Madison, WI: University of Wisconsin, Institute for Research on Poverty, 1975.

338. Hirsch, Werner Z. "Determinants of Public Education Expenditures," *National Tax Journal,* Vol. 13 (1960), pp. 29-40.

339. _____. "The Supply of Urban Public Services," in Harvey S. Perloff, and Lowden Wingo, Jr. (eds.). *Issues in Urban Economics.* Baltimore, MD: Johns Hopkins University Press, 1968, p. 477.

340. Hu, Teh-wei, and Bernard Booms. "A Simultaneous Equation Model of Public Expenditure Decisions in Large Cities," *The Annals of Regional Science,* Vol. 5 (1971), pp. 73-85.

341. Hufbauer, G.C., and B.W. Severn. "Municipal Costs and Urban Areas," *Journal of Urban Economics,* (July 1975), pp. 6-8.

342. Isard, Walter, and Robert Coughlin. *Municipal Costs and Revenues Resulting from Community Growth.* Wellesley, MA: Chandler-Davis, 1957.

343. Kee, Woo Sik. "Central City Expenditures and Metropolitan Areas," *National Tax Journal,* Vol. 18 (1965), pp. 337-353.

344. Keesling, Frank M., and Charles R. Ajalat. "Proposition 13: The Revolution's Aftermath," *Assessors Journal,* Vol. 14, No. 2 (June 1979), pp. 117-128.
345. Kemp, Roger L. "California's Proposition 13: A One-Year Assessment," *Urban Land,* Vol. 38, No. 7 (July-August 1979), pp. 10-13.
346. Kurnow, Ernest. "Determinants of State and Local Expenditures Re-Examined," *National Tax Journal,* Vol. 16 (1963), pp. 252-255.
347. Levin, Betsy, Thomas Muller, and Corogan Sandoval. *The High Cost of Education in Cities.* Washington, D.C.: The Urban Institute, 1973.
348. Lindholm, Richard W. (ed.). *Property Taxation and the Finance of Education.* Madison, WI: University of Wisconsin Press, 1974.
349. Lineberry, Robert L. "Equality, Public Policy, and Public Services: The Underclass Hypothesis and the Limits to Equality," *Politics and Policy,* Vol. 4 (December 1975).
350. Loewenstein, Louis K. "The Impact of New Industry on Revenues and Expenditures of Suburban Communities," *National Tax Journal,* Vol. 16 (June 1963), pp. 113-137.
351. McMahon, Walter W. "An Economic Analysis of Major Determinants of Expenditures on Public Education," *Review of Economics and Statistics,* Vol. 52 (1970), pp. 242-252.
352. Marini, Frank (ed.). *Toward a New Public Administration.* Scranton, PA: Chandler, 1971.
353. Masten, John T. Jr., and Kenneth E. Quindry. "A Note on City Expenditure Determinants," *Land Economics,* Vol. 46 (1970), pp. 79-81.
354. Merget, Astrid D. "Equalizing Municipal Services: Issues for Policy Analysis," *Policy Studies Journal,* (Spring 1976).
355. ———. and William M. Wolff, Jr. "The Law and Municipal Services: Implementing Equity," *Public Management* (August 1976).
356. Mills, Edwin D., and Wallace E. Oates. *Fiscal Zoning and Land Use Controls.* Lexington, MA: Lexington Books, 1975.
357. Morris, Douglas E. *Economies of City Size.* Ph. D. Dissertation. Stillwater, OK: Oklahoma State University, 1973.
358. Morss, Elliot. "Some Thoughts on the Determinants of State and Local Expenditures," *National Tax Journal,* Vol. 19, pp. 95-103.
359. Muller, Thomas, and Grace Dawson. *An Evaluation of the Subsequent Fiscal Impact of Annexation in Richmond, Virginia.* Washington, D.C.: Urban Institute, 1975.

360. ———. *The Impact of Annexation on City Finances: A Case Study in Richmond, Virginia.* Washington, D.C.: Urban Institute, 1975.

361. Murphy, J.F. "Fiscal Problems of Big City School Systems: Changing Patterns of State and Federal Aid," *Urban Review,* Vol. 1, No. 4 (Winter 1978), pp. 251-265.

362. Murphy, Thomas, and Charles R. Warren (eds.). *Organizing Services in Metropolitan Areas.* Lexington, MA: D.C. Heath, 1974.

363. Mushkin, Selma J. *Public Prices for Public Products.* Washington, D.C.: Urban Institute, 1972.

364. Nathan, Richard P., et al. *Monitoring the Public Service Employment Program: The Second Round.* Washington, D.C.: U.S. National Commission for Employment Policy, 1979.

365. Newton, Kenneth. "American Urban Politics. Social Class, Political Structure, and Public Goods," *Urban Affairs Quarterly,* Vol. 11 (1975).

366. Pattie, Preston S. *Impacts of Urban Growth on Local Government Costs and Revenues.* Oregon State University Extension Service Special Report 423. Corvallis, OR; Oregon State University, November 1974.

367. Pommerehne, Werner W., and Bruno S. Frey. "Two Approaches to Estimating Public Expenditures," *Public Finance Quarterly,* Vol. 4, No. 4 (October 1976), pp. 395-407.

368. Popp, Dean and Walter Vogt. "Alternative Methods of School Finance: An Empirical Analysis of Cities in San Diego County," *American Journal of Economics and Sociology,* Vol. 38, No. 4 (October 1979), pp. 337-348.

369. Rehfuss, John. "Citizen Participation in Urban Fiscal Decisions," *Urban Data Service Report,* Vol. 10, No. 8 (August 1978), entire issue.

370. Sacks, Seymour, and Robert Harris. "The Determinants of State and Local Government Expenditures and Inter-Governmental Flow of Funds," *National Tax Journal,* Vol. 17 (1964), pp. 75-85.

371. Savas, E.S. "How Much do Government Services Really Cost," *Urban Affairs Quarterly,* Vol. 15, No. 1 (September 1979), pp. 23-42.

372. Schroeder, Larry D., and D.L. Sjoquist. *The Property Tax and Alternative Labor Taxes: An Economic Analysis.* New York: Praeger, 1975.

373. Scott, Stanley, and Edward L. Feder. *Factors Associated with Variations in Municipal Expenditure Levels.* Berkeley, CA:

Bureau of Public Administration, University of California at Berkeley, 1957.

374. *Selected Municipal Cost-Cutting Measures.* Knoxville, TN: University of Tennessee, Municipal Technical Advisory Service, 1979.

375. Shalala, Donna, and Astrid E. Merget. "Transition, Problems and Models," in Thomas Murphy and Charles R. Warren (eds.) *Organizing Services in Metropolitan Areas.* Lexington, MA: D.C. Heath, 1974.

376. Shrakansky, Ira. "Some More Thoughts About the Determinants of Government Expenditure," *National Tax Journal,* Vol. 20 (1967), pp. 171-179.

377. Spangler, Richard. "The Effect of Population Growth Upon State and Local Government Expenditures," *National Tax Journal,* Vol. 16 (1963), pp. 193-196.

378. "Stagflation and Municipal Budget." *Public Management.* March 1975, entire issue.

379. Steiss, Alan Walter. *Local Government Finance: Capital Facilities Planning and Debt Administration.* Lexington, MA: Lexington Books, (1975).

380. Sternlieb, George, et al. *Housing Development and Municipal Costs.* New Brunswick, NJ: Rutgers University, Center for Urban Policy Research, 1972.

381. Sternlieb, George, and Robert W. Burchell. "The Numbers Game: Forecasting Household Size," *Urban Land,* Vol. 33 (1974), pp. 3-16.

382. Storm, William J. "Financial Pruning for Cities: Some Tools for Making the Cuts Hurt Less," *Missouri Municipal Review,* Vol. 42, No. 2 (February 1977), pp. 21-22.

383. Sullivan, Patrick J. "Optimality in Municipal Debt: A Comment and Respecification," *Public Finance Quarterly,* Vol. 7, No. 3 (July 1979), pp. 352-363.

384. Sunley, Emile M., Jr. "Some Determinants of Government Expenditures Within Metropolitan Areas," *The American Journal of Economics and Sociology,* Vol. 30 (1971), pp. 345-64.

385. United States Congress, House, Committee on Banking, Finance, and Urban Affairs, Subcommittee on Financial Institutions Supervision, Regulation and Insurance. *The Role of Commercial Banks in the Finances of the City of Cleveland; Staff Study, 96th Congress, 1st. Session, June 1978.* Washington, D.C.: G.P.O., 1979.

386. United States Congressional Budget Office. *Troubled Local*

Economies and the Distribution of Federal Dollars. Washington, D.C.: G.P.O., 1977.
387. Vernez, Georges. *Delivery of Urban Public Services: Production, Cost and Demand Functions and Determinants of Public Expenditures for Fire, Police, Sanitation Services.* Santa Monica, CA: Rand Corporation, 1976.
388. Walzev, Norman, and Peter J. Stratton. *Inflation and Municipal Expenditure Increases in Illinois.* Springfield, IL: Illinois Cities and Villages Municipal Problems Commission, 1977.
389. Weicher, John C. "Determinants of Central City Expenditures: Some Overlooked Factors and Problems," *National Tax Journal,* Vol. 23 (1970), pp. 379-396.
390. ———. "The Effect of Urban Renewal on Municipal Service Expenditures," *Journal of Political Economy,* Vol. 80 (1972), pp. 86-101.
391. Weitzman, Joan. *City Workers and Fiscal Crisis—Cutbacks, Givebacks and Survival: A Study of the New York City Experience.* New Brunswick, NJ: Rutgers University, Institute of Management and Labor Relations, 1979.
392. Wheaton, William L., and Morton J. Schussheim. *The Cost of Municipal Services in Residential Areas.* Washington, D.C.: G.P.O., 1955.
393. *Where Does All the Money Go?* Dayton, OH: Charles F. Kettering Foundation, 1979.
394. Wilenski, Gail. "Determinants of Local Government Expenditures," in John P. Crecine,(ed.) *Financing the Metropolis: Public Policy in Urban Economics.* Beverly Hills, CA: Sage Publications, 1970.

400. TRADITIONAL REVENUE SOURCES–SOLUTIONS TO FISCAL DISPARITY

401. Aaron, Henry J. *Who Pays the Property Tax?* Washington, D.C.: Brookings Institution, 1975.
402. Advisory Commission on Intergovernmental Relations. *Changing Public Attitudes on Government and Taxes.* Washington, D.C.: G.P.O., 1977.
403. Agapos, A.M., and Paul R. Dunlap. "Elimination of Urban Blight Through Inverse Proportional Ad Valorem Property Taxation," *American Journal of Economics and Sociology,* Vol. 32, No. 2 (April 1973), pp. 143-152.
404. Bahl, Roy, and David Puryear. "Regional Tax Base Sharing: Possibilities and Implications," *National Tax Journal,* Vol. 29, No.

3 (September 1976), pp. 328-335.

405. Bish, Robert L. "Fiscal Equalization Through Court Decisions: Policy-Making Without Evidence," in Elinor Ostrom (ed.) *The Delivery of Urban Services: Outcomes of Change.* Beverly Hills, CA: Sage, 1976, pp. 75-102.

406. Booth, Douglas, E., "The Differential Impact of Manufacturing and Mercantile Activity on Local Government Expenditures and Revenues," *National Tax Journal,* Vol. 30, No. 1 (1978), pp. 33-43.

407. Brady, Patrick R., and Thomas P. Murphy. "Should Cities Tax Suburbanites for Working in the Cities?," *Urban Concerns* (May/June 1979), pp. 23-29.

408. Break, George. "The Incidence and Economic Effects of Taxation," in Alan S. Blinder, et al. (eds.) *The Economics of Public Finance.* Washington, D.C.: Brookings Institution, 1974.

409. Breckenfeld, Guerney. "How the Upside-Down Property Tax is Helping to Cripple Our Cities," *Journal of the Institute for Socioeconomic Studies,* Vol. 3, No. 1 (Spring 1978), pp. 32-39.

410. Campbell, Alan K. "Approaches to Defining, Measuring and Achieving Equity in the Public Sector," *Public Administration Review,* Vol. 36 (September/October 1976).

411. Case, Karl E. *Property Taxation: The Need for Reform.* Cambridge, MA: Ballinger, 1978.

412. Cord, Steven. "How to Transform the Property Tax into a Graded Tax," *American Journal of Economics and Sociology,* Vol. 34, No. 2 (April 1975), pp. 127-128.

413. Davidson, Jonathan M. "Tax Increment Financing as a Tool for Community Redevelopment," *Journal of Urban Law,* Vol. 56, No. 2 (Winter 1979), pp. 405-444.

414. Dickstein, Dennis. *Fiscal Controls: A Primer for Local Officials.* Boston, MA: Massachusetts Executive Office of Communities and Development, 1978.

415. Dougharty, L.A. *Forces Shaping Urban Development: The Property Tax.* Santa Monica, CA: Rand Corporation, 1973.

416. Finkelstein, Phillip. *Real Property Taxation in New York City.* New York: Praeger, 1975.

417. Fischel, William. "An Evaluation of Proposals for Metropolitan Sharing of Commercial and Industrial Property Tax Base," *Journal of Urban Economics,* Vol. 3 (1976), pp. 253-263.

418. Fischer, Glenn W. "Property Taxation and the Political System," in Arthur D. Lynn, Jr. *Property Taxation, Land Use, and Public Policy.* Madison, WI: University of Wisconsin Press, 1975, pp. 5-22.

419. Gilbert, D.A. "Property Tax Base Sharing: An Answer to Central City Fiscal Problems?," *Social Science Quarterly,* Vol. 59, No. 4 (March 1979), pp. 681-690.

420 Gilze, Paul. "Recent Developments in Tax Base Sharing," memo to Citizen League Board of Directors, October 19, 1977.

421. Gupta, Dipak K., and Louis M. Rea. *The Investment Decision in the Central City: A Consideration of Property Tax Abatement.* San Diego, CA: San Diego State University, Center for Public Economics, 1978.

422. Harrington, Ray. *Central City Analysis: Final Report.* Washington, D.C.: Dept. of Housing and Urban Development, 1977.

423. Harris, C. Lowell. "Property Taxation After the California Vote." *Tax Review,* Vol. 39, No. 8 (August 1978), entire issue.

424. *The Impact of State School Aid on Property Taxes in 1977: A Report Prepared for the Joint Commission on Public Schools, New Jersey Legislature.* New Brunswick, NJ: Rutgers University: Bureau of Government Research, 1979.

425. Katz, Norman A. *Urban Neighborhoods: An Action Report on the Impact of Tax Assessments and Tax Delinquency Problems.* Chicago, IL: Trust, Inc., 1978.

426. King, Norman R., and Roger L, Kemp. "Proposition 13: The Taxpayer's Revolt," *Management Information Service Report.* Vol. 10, No. 11 (November 1978), entire issue.

427. Ladd, Helen F. "Municipal Expenditures and the Composition of the Local Property Tax Base," in Arthur D. Lynn, Jr. (ed.) *Property Taxation, Land Use and Public Policy.* Madison, WI: University of Wisconsin Press, 1976, pp. 73-98.

428. Lineberry, Robert L. *Equality and Urban Policy.* Beverly Hills, CA: Sage, 1977.

429. Lyall, Katherine C. "Tax Base Sharing: A Fiscal Aid Towards More Rational Land Use Planning," *Journal of the American Institute of Planners,* Vol. 41, No. 2 (March 1975), pp. 90-100.

430. MacManus, Susan A. "Tax Structures in American Cities: Levels, Reliance and Rates," *Western Political Quarterly,* Vol. 30, No. 2 (June 1977), pp. 263-287.

431. Meyers, Edward M., and John J. Musial. *Urban Incentive Tax Credits: A Self-Correcting Strategy to Rebuild Central Cities.* New York: Praeger, 1974.

432. Mushkin, Selma J., and Charles L. Vehorn. "User Fees and Charges," *Governmental Finance,* Vol. 6, No. 4 (November 1977), pp. 42-48.

433. Neenan, William B. "Fiscal Integration of Cities Within One State," in *Political Economy of Urban Areas.* Chicago, IL: Markam, 1972, pp. 140-162.
434. Netzer, Dick. *Impact of Property Tax: Effect on Housing, Urban Land Use, and Local Government Finance.* Washington, D.C.: G.P.O., 1968.
435. Noto, Nonna A., and Donald L. Raiff. "Philadelphia's Fiscal Story: The City and the Schools," *Business Review* (March-April 1977), entire issue.
436. Okun, Bernard. "Factors Affecting Tax Rate Pressure on Central Cities," *American Economist* (1976).
437. Peterson, George. "Finance" in William Gorham and Nathan Glazer (eds.) *The Urban Predicament.* Washington, D.C.: The Urban Institute, 1976.
438. ———, et al. *Property Taxes, Housing and the Cities.* Lexington, MA: D.C. Heath and Company, 1973.
439. Plosila, Walter H. "Metropolitan Tax-Base-Sharing: Its Potential and Limitations," *Public Finance Quarterly,* Vol. 4, No. 2 (April 1976), pp. 205-224.
440. Prentice, P.I. "Urban Financing for Jobs, Profits and Prosperity," *American Journal of Economics and Sociology,* Vol. 35, No. 3 (July 1976), pp. 301-310.
441. *Property Tax Legislation in the United States: 1978.* Chicago: International Association of Assessing Officers, 1978.
442. "Property Tax Limit Legislation: An Evaluation," *Assessors Journal,* Vol. 14, No. 3 (September 1979), pp. 129-154.
443. Rahm, Karen. "Tax Base Sharing: A Fiscal Tool for Land Use Planning in Washington State?" *Washington Public Policy Notes* (Seattle, WA: University of Washington, Institute of Governmental Research) Vol. 5, No. 3 (Summer 1977).
444. Reschovsky, Andrew, and Eugene Knaff. "Tax Base Sharing: An Assessment of the Minnesota Experience," *Journal of the American Institute of Planners,* Vol. 43, No. 4 (October 1977), pp. 361-370.
445. *A Review of Real Estate Tax Incentive Programs in New York City.* New York: Citizens Budget Commission, 1977.
446. Rybeck, Walter. "Can Property Tax Be Made to Work for Rather than Against Urban Development," *American Journal of Economics and Sociology,* Vol. 33, No. 3 (July 1974), pp. 259-271.
447. *School Budgets and Property Taxes in 1978: A Report Prepared for the Joint Committee on the Public Schools, New Jersey*

Legislature. New Brunswick, NJ: Rutgers University, Bureau of Government Research, 1979.

448. Simms, Margaret. *Metropolitan Tax Base Sharing: Is It the Solution to Municipal Fiscal Problems?* Washington, D.C.: Urban Institute, 1977.

449. Stein, Erwin. "Cost Revenue Allocation Model: A Tool for Financial City Planning," *Urban Land,* Vol. 35, No. 1 (January 1976), pp. 13-22.

450. Sternlieb, George, Elizabeth Roistacher, and James W. Hughes. *Tax Subsidies and Housing Investment: A Fiscal Cost-Benefit Analysis.* New Brunswick, NJ: Rutgers University, Center for Urban Policy Research, 1976.

451. Swanson, Austin D., and Richard A. King. "The Impact of the Courts on the Financing of Public Schools in Large Cities," *Urban Education,* Vol. 11, No. 2 (July 1976), pp. 151-166.

452. Vincent, Phillip E. "School Finance Reforms and Big City Fiscal Problems," paper prepared for the United States Committee on Taxation, Resources, and Economic Development Conference, Cambridge, MA, October 1977.

453. Vogt, Walter. "Tax-Base Sharing: Implications from San Diego County," *Journal of the American Planning Association,* Vol. 45, No. 2 (April 1979), pp. 134-142.

454. Walzer, Norman, and Peter J. Stratton. *Financing Township Services.* Macomb, IL: Western Illinois University, Public Policy Research Institute, 1979.

455. Weaver, Charles R. "The Minnesota Approach to Solving Urban Fiscal Disparity," *State Government,* Vol. 45, pp. 100-105.

500-600. INTERGOVERNMENTAL TRANSFERS—TYPES AND EFFECTS OF STATE AND FEDERAL ASSISTANCE

501. Adams, Charles F., and Dan L. Crippen. *The Fiscal Impact of General Revenue Sharing on Local Governments: A Report Prepared for the Office of Revenue Sharing, U.S. Department of the Treasury.* Washington, D.C.: Brookings Institution Monitoring Studies Group, 1978.

502. Advisory Commission on Intergovernmental Relations. *Fiscal Balance in the American Federal System,* Vol. 2, Metropolitan Fiscal Disparities. Washington, D.C.: G.P.O., 1967.

503. Anton, Thomas J. "Outlays Data and the Analysis of Federal Policy Impact," in Norman Glickman (ed.). *The Urban Impact of Federal Policies.* Baltimore, MD: Johns Hopkins University Press, 1979.

504. *An Approach to Federal Urban Policy.* Washington, D.C.: National Committee for Economic Development, 1977.

505. Bahl, Roy, and Walter Vogt. *Fiscal Centralization and Tax Burdens: State and Regional Financing of City Services.* Cambridge, MA: Ballinger, 1975.

506. Banfield, Edward. "Revenue Sharing in Theory and Practice," *Public Interest,* No. 23 (1971), pp. 33-45.

507. Barro, Stephen M. *Equalization and Equity in General Revenue Sharing: An Analysis of Alternative Distribution Formulas: Part I; Alternative Interstate Distribution Formulas.* Santa Monica, CA: Rand Corporation, 1975.

508. ————. *The Impact of Intergovernmental Aid on Public School Spending.* Ph.D. Dissertation, 1974.

509. ————. *The Urban Impacts of Federal Policies: Vol. 3, Fiscal Conditions.* Santa Monica, CA: Rand Corporation, 1978.

510. Beer, Samuel. "The Adoption of General Revenue Sharing: A Case Study in Public Sector Politics," *Public Policy,* Vol. 24, No. 2 (1976).

511. Bennet, Ralph Kinney. "CETA: $11-Billion Boondoggle," *Urban Digest* (August 1978), p. 72.

512. Benson, Charles S. *The Economics of Public Education.* Boston: Houghton Mifflin, 1968, pp. 294-305.

513. *Better Management Needed in Exchanging Federal and State Tax Information, Report by the Comptroller General of the U.S.* Washington, D.C.: U.S. General Accounting Office, 1978.

514. Bilyk, Andrij. "The Federal Budget and the Cities," *Nation's Cities,* Vol. 14, No. 2 (February 1976), pp. 7-13.

515. Blair, Patricia W. *General Revenue Sharing in American Cities: First Impressions.* Washington, D.C.: National Clearinghouse on Revenue Sharing, 1974.

516. Blaydon, Colin C. and Steven R. Gilford. "Financing the Cities: An Issue Agenda," *Duke Law Journal* (January 1976), pp. 1057-1117.

517. Break, George. "Intergovernmental Finance," in John Peterson, et al (eds.) *State and Local Government Finance and Financial Management: A Compendium of Current Research.* Washington, D.C.: Government Finance Center, 1978.

518. Brookings Institution, *Report on the Allocation of Community Development Funds to Small Cities.* Washington, D.C.: G.P.O., 1979.

519. Bunce, Harold. "The Community Development Block Grant Formula: An Evaluation," *Urban Studies Quarterly,* Vol. 14 (June 1979), p. 443.

520. ———. *An Evaluation of the Community Development Block Grant Program.* Washington, D.C.: United States Department of Housing and Urban Development, 1976.

521. ———, and Robert L. Goldberg. *City Need and Community Development Funding.* Washington, D.C.: G.P.O., 1979.

522. Callahan, J.J., and W.H. Wilken (eds.). *School Finance Reform: A Legislator's Handbook.* Washington, D.C.: National Conference of State Legislatures, 1976.

523. Caputo, David A. *Urban Politics and Decentralization: The Case of General Revenue Sharing.* Lexington, MA: Lexington Books, 1974.

524. Caraley, Demetrios. "Congressional Politics and Urban Aid," *Political Science Quarterly,* Vol. 91, No. 1 (Spring 1976), pp. 19-45.

525. *Case Studies of the Impact of Federal Grants in Large Cities,* transcript of working conference proceedings prepared for the Office of Program Evaluation, Employment and Training Administration, U.S. Department of Labor. Washington, D.C.: Brookings Institution, 1978.

526. Cohen, Joel E. "The Limits of State Intervention in a Municipal Fiscal Crisis," *Fordham Urban Law Journal,* Vol. 4, No. 3 (Spring 1976), pp. 545-563.

527. Cole, Richard L., and David A. Caputo. *Urban Politics and Decentralization: The Case of General Revenue Sharing.* Lexington, MA: Heath and Company, 1974.

528. Conant, James B., and James E. Allen, Jr. *State Aid to Local Government.* Washington, D.C.: U.S. Advisory Commission on Intergovernmental Relations, 1969.

529. Congressional Budget Office. *Troubled Local Economies and the Distribution of Federal Dollars.* Washington, D.C.: G.P.O., 1977.

530. Conyers, John, Jr. "The Politics of Revenue Sharing," *Journal of Urban Law* (August 1975), pp. 61-81.

531. *Countercyclical Aid and Economic Stabilization.* Washington, D.C.: U.S. Advisory Commission on Intergovernmental Relations, 1978.

532. Cronin, Joseph M. "School Finance in the Seventies: The Prospect for Reform," *Phi Delta Kappan* (November 1969), p. 117.

533. Cuciti, Peggy L. *Troubled Local Economies and the Distribution of Federal Dollars.* Washington, D.C.: G.P.O., 1977.

534. DeLeon, Richard, and Richard LeGates. *Redistribution Effects of Special Revenue Sharing for Community Development.*

Berkeley, CA: University of California, Institute of Governmental Studies, 1976.

535. Dommel, Paul. *The Politics of Revenue Sharing.* Bloomington, IN: Indiana University Press, 1974.

536. *An Evaluation of the Community Development Block Grant Formula.* Washington, D.C.: U.S. Department of Housing and Urban Development, Office of Policy Development and Research, 1976.

537. *The Federal Budget and the Cities: A Review of the President's Budget in Light of Urban Needs and National Priorities.* Washington, D.C.: U.S. Conference of Mayors, 1979.

538. Frieden, Bernard J., and Marshall Kaplan. *The Politics of Neglect: Urban Aid from Model Cities to Revenue Sharing.* Cambridge, MA: MIT Press, 1975.

539. Friedland, Roger, et al. "Political Conflict, Urban Structure, and the Fiscal Crisis," in Douglas Ashford (ed.) *Comparing Public Policy: New Approaches and Methods.* Beverly Hills, CA: Sage Publications, 1977.

540. Gabler, L. Richard, and Joseph F. Zimmerman. "State Mandating of Local Expenditures," *Urban Data Service Report,* Vol. 10, No. 7 (July 1978), entire issue.

541. General Accounting Office. *Anti-recession Assistance—An Evaluation.* Washington, D.C.: G.P.O., 1977.

542. Glickman, Norman (ed.). *The Urban Impacts of Federal Policies.* Baltimore, MD: Johns Hopkins University Press, 1979.

543. Goldberg, Robert, et al. *CDBG Formula Change.* Washington, D.C.: U.S. Department of Housing and Urban Development, 1977.

544. Gramlich, Edward M. "The Effect of Federal Grants on State-Local Expenditures: A Review of the Economic Literature," in *Proceedings of the Sixty-Second Annual Conference on Taxation.* Columbus, OH: National Tax Association, 1969.

545. ⸺. *Intergovernmental Grants: A Review of the Empirical Literature.* A paper presented at the International Seminar on Public Economics Conference, The Brookings Institution and Cornell University, Berlin, January 1976.

546. Harriss, C. Lowell. "Constructive Opportunities in Property Taxation," *Assessment Digest,* Vol. 1, No. 6 (November-December 1979), pp. 4-9.

547. Havemann, Joel, et al. "Federal Spending: The North's Loss is the Sunbelt's Gain," *National Journal,* Vol. 8, No. 26 (June 1976).

548. Howell, James M., and George D. Brown. "The Revenue Sharing Gauntlet: Fiscal Federalism at the Crossroads," *National Civic Review*, Vol. 68, No. 10 (November 1979), pp. 535-541.

549. Hudnall, Belinda, and Marcus Weiss. "A Special Report on the Expansion of EDA (Economic Development Administration): The Resources Being Considered for Economically Distressed Areas," *Center for Community Economic Development Review*, Special Insert, (Fall 1979).

550. *Impact of Antirecession Assistance on 21 City Governments: Report to Congress by the Comptroller General of the United States.* Washington, D.C.: U.S. General Accounting Office, 1978.

551. *Improving Urban America: A Challenge to Federalism.* Washington, D.C.: Advisory Commission on Intergovernmental Relations, 1976.

552. *Inequality in California School Finances.* Santa Monica, CA: Rand Corp., March 1975.

553. *Intermunicipal Tax Sharing Theory and Operation,* Secaucus, NJ: Hackensack Meadowlands Development Commission, 1972.

554. Isserman, Andrew M., and Karen L. Mayors, "General Revenue Sharing: Federal Incentives to Change Local Government?," *Journal of the American Institute of Planners,* Vol. 44, No. 3 (July 1978), pp. 317-327.

555. Jones, E. Terrence and Donald Phares. "Formula Feedback and Central Cities: The Case of the Comprehensive Employment and Training Act," *Urban Affairs Quarterly,* Vol. 14, September 1978, pp. 31-54.

556. Keating, Dennis, and Richard LeGates. "Who Should Benefit From the Community Development Block Grant Program," *Urban Lawyer,* Vol. 10, No. 4 (1978).

557. Kirk, James E. *Local Government Recovery of Overhead Through Federal Grants.* Columbia, SC: University of South Carolina, Bureau of Governmental Research and Service, 1978.

558. Levin, Betsy, (ed.) *Future Directions in School Finance Reform.* Lexington, MA: Lexington Books, 1974.

559. Levin, Betsy, et al.. *Paying for Public Schools: Issues of School Finance in California.* Washington, D.C.: Urban Institute, 1972.

560. Long, Norton E. "A Marshall Plan for the Cities," *Public Interest,* No. 46 (Winter 1977), pp. 48-58.

561. Lugar, Richard G. "The Federal Government's Role in Relieving Cities of the Fiscal Burden of Low Income Concentration," *National Tax Journal,* Vol. 29, No. 3 (September 1976), pp. 286-292.

562. Lyons, William, and David R. Morgan. "The Impact of Intergovernmental Revenue on City Expenditures: An Analysis Over Time," *Journal of Politics,* Vol. 39 (November 1977), pp. 1088-1097.

563. Manuel, Allen D. "The Fiscal Impact of Revenue Sharing," *Annals of the American Academy of Political and Social Science,* Vol. 419 (May 1975), pp. 36-49.

564. Markusen, Ann. "The Urban Impact Analysis: A Critical Forecast," in Norman Glickman (ed.) *The Urban Impact of Federal Policies.* Baltimore, MD: Johns Hopkins University Press, 1979.

565. _____, and Terry Fastrup. "The Regional War for Federal Aid," *Public Interest,* No. 53 (Fall 1978), pp. 87-99.

566. *Measuring the Fiscal Blood Pressure of the States.* Washington, D.C.: Advisory Commission on Intergovernmental Relations, 1977.

567. Michelson, S. *States and Schools.* Lexington, MA: Lexington, Books, 1974.

568. Michigan. Governor's Commission on Educational Reform. *Report of the Governor's Commission on Educational Reform.* Lansing, MI: Governor's Commission on Educational Reform, September 30, 1969.

569. Molefsky, Burry, and Dennis Zimmerman. "General Revenue Sharing and Alternatives: Economic Rationales Past and Present," *Studies in Taxation, Public Finance and Related Subjects—A Compendium, Vol. 3.* Washington, D.C.: Fund for Policy Research, 1977, p. 33.

570. *Most Federal Assistance to New York City Unlikely to be Affected by City-Initiated Budget Cuts: Report of the Comptroller General.* Washington, D.C.: U.S. General Accounting Office, 1977.

571. Murphy, Josephy H. "State and Local Incentives for Urban Growth: A Concept Whose Time Never Was?," *Fordham Urban Law Journal* (Spring 1978), pp. 457-479.

572. Musgrave, Richard A., and A. Mitchell Polinsky. "Revenue Sharing: A Critical View," *Harvard Journal of Legislation,* Vol. 8 (January 1971), pp. 197-219.

573. Nathan, Richard P. *The Record of the New Federalism: What it Means for the Nation's Cities: Analysis of the Program and Suggestions for Research.* Washington, D.C.: Brookings Institution, 1974.

574. _____. et al. *Block Grants for Community Development.* Washington, D.C.: U.S. Department of Housing and Urban Development, 1976.

575. _____, et al. *Monitoring Revenue Sharing.* Washington, D.C.: Brookings Institution, 1975.

576. _____, et al. "Statement and Testimonies," in U.S. Congress, Joint Economic Committee. *Financing Municipal Needs.* Washington, D.C.: G.P.O., 1977.

577. _____, and Charles Adams, Jr. *Revenue Sharing: The Second Round.* Washington, D.C.: Brookings Institution, 1977.

578. _____, and Paul R. Dommel. *Federal Aid for Cities: A Multiple Strategy.* Washington, D.C.: Brookings Institution, 1976.

579. _____, and Paul R. Dommel. "Federal-Local Relations Under Block Grants," *Political Science Quarterly,* Vol. 3 (Fall 1978), p. 421.

580. _____, and James W. Fossett. *Urban Conditions—The Future of the Federal Role,* paper prepared for presentation to the National Tax Association, Philadelphia, PA., Nov. 13, 1978.

581. National League of Cities and the United States Conference of Mayors. *The Federal Budget and the Cities, A Review of President's FY 77 Budget in Light of Urban Needs and National Priorities.* Washington, D.C.: National League of Cities, 1976.

582. Netzer, Dick. "Federal, State, and Local Finance in a Metropolitan Context," in Harvey S. Perloff and Lowdon Swingo, Jr. (ed.) *Issues in Urban Economics.* Baltimore, MD: Johns Hopkins Press, 1968, pp. 435-476.

583. Oakland, William. *Financial Relief for Troubled Cities: A National Urban Policy Round Table Discussion Policy.* Columbus, OH: Academy for Contemporary Problems, 1978.

584. Olsen, R.J., et al. *Multiregion—A Simulation—Forecasting Model of BEA Economic Area Population and Employment.* Oak Ridge National Laboratory, (1978).

585. Petersen, George. *Federal Tax Policy and Urban Development.* Washington, D.C.: Urban Institute, 1978.

586. Petersen, John E., et al. *State Roles in Local Government Financial Management: A Comparative Analysis.* Washington, D.C.: U.S. Department of Housing and Urban Development, 1979.

587. Pincus, J. (ed.). *School Finance in Transition.* Cambridge, MA: Ballinger, 1974.

588. Puryear, D. et al. *Federal Grants: Their Effect on State and Local Expenditures, Employment Levels, and Wage Rates.* Washington, D.C.: Advisory Commission on Intergovernmental Relations, 1977.

589. *Report on the Fiscal Impact of the Economic Stimulus Package of 48 Large Urban Governments.* Washington, D.C.: U.S. Department of the Treasury, 1978.

590. Rondinelli, Dennis A. "Revenue Sharing and American Cities," *American Institute of Planners Journal* (September 1975), pp. 319-333.
591. Rosentraub, Mark (ed.). *Financing State and Local Governments: New Approaches to Old Problems.* Ann Arbor, MI: Social Science Journal/Xerox Publishing Company, 1977.
592. Ross, J.P. *Countercyclical Aid and Economic Stabilization,* Report A-69. Washington, D.C.: Advisory Council on Intergovernmental Relations, (1978).
593. Ross, John. *Alternative Formulae for General Revenue Sharing: Population Based Measures of Need.* Blacksburg, VA: Virginia Polytechnic Institute and State University, Center for Urban and Regional Study, 1975.
594. Salzstein, Alan L. "Categorical Federal Aid to Cities: Who Needs it Versus Who Wants It." *Western Political Quarterly,* Vol. 30, No. 3 (September 1977), pp. 377-383.
595. Schmidt, Gregory, et al. *An Alternative Approach to General Revenue Sharing: A Needs Based Formula.* Menlo Park, CA: Institute for the Future, 1975.
596. *Significant Features of Fiscal Federalism.* Washington, D.C.: U.S. Advisory Commission on Intergovernmental Relations, 1979.
597. Soule, Don M. *Replacing Local Taxes: Can it be Done?* Lexington, KY: University of Kentucky, Center for Real Estate and Land Use Analysis, 1978.
598. *State and Mandating of Local Expenditures.* Washington, D.C.: U.S. Advisory Commisson on Intergovernmental Relations, 1978.
599. Stulz, Otto. *Revenue Sharing: Legal and Policy Analysis.* New York: Praeger, 1974.
600. Thompson, Richard. *Revenue Sharing—A New Era in Federalism?* Washington, D.C.: Revenue Sharing Advisory Service, 1973.
601. Tron, E.O. (ed.). *Selected Papers in School Finance, 1974.* Washington, D.C.: Office of Education, 1974.
602. United States Comptroller General. *Why the Formula for Allocating Community Development Block Grant Funds Should be Improved.* Washington, D.C.: U.S. General Accounting Office, 1976.
603. United States Congress, House (95-2), Committee on Banking, Finance and Urban Affairs, Subcommittee on the City. *City Need and the Responsiveness of Federal Grants Programs.* Washington, D.C.: G.P.O., 1978.

604. ———. *Report of the Impact of the Federal Budget on the Cities, Together with Additional and Minority Views.* Washington, D.C.: G.P.O., 1977.

605. ———. (96-1). Committee on Banking, Finance, and Urban Affairs, Subcommittee on the City. *Revenue Sharing with the States. Hearings.* Washington, D.C.: G.P.O., 1979.

606. ———, Committee on Banking, Finance, and Urban Affairs, Subcommittee on the City. *Toward a National Urban Policy . . . 95th Congress, 1st Session, April 1977.* Washington, D.C.: G.P.O., 1978.

607. ———, Committee on Government Operations, Commerce, Consumer, and Monetary Affairs Subcommittee. *Federal Response to Financial Emergencies of Cities: Hearings. . .* Washington, D.C.: G.P.O., 1975.

608. ———, Committee on Banking, Housing and Urban Affairs. *New York City Financial Aid: Hearings on S. 2892. . . H.R. 12426.* Washington, D.C.: G.P.O., 1978.

609. ———. Joint Economic Committee (95-1), Subcommittee on Economic Growth and Stabilization and the Subcommittee on Fiscal and Intergovernmental Policy. *Financing Municipal Needs.* Washington, D.C.: G.P.O., 1977.

610. ———, *To Establish a National Development Bank, Hearings . . . August 1 and 2, 1978.* Washington, D.C.: G.P.O., 1978.

611. United States, Department of Housing and Urban Development, Office of Community Planning and Development, Office of Evaluation. *Urban Development Action Grant Program.* Washington, D.C.: G.P.O., 1979.

612. United States General Accounting Office. *Criteria for Participation in the Urban Development Action Grant Program Should be Refined* (Draft). 1980.

613. United States Department of the Treasury. *Federal Aid to States.* Washington, D.C.: G.P.O., 1977.

614. Vaughan, R.J. *The Urban Impacts of Federal Policies: Vol. 2, Economic Development.* Santa Monica, CA: Rand Corporation, 1977.

615. Vehorn, Charles L. *The Regional Distribution of Federal Grants-in-Aid.* Columbus, OH: Academy for Contemporary Problems, 1977.

616. Vernez, Georges, Roger J. Vaughan and Robert K. Yin. *Federal Activities in Urban Economic Development.* Santa Monica, CA: Rand Corporation, 1979.

617. Waltzer, Norman, and David Ward. *General Revenue Sharing in Large Illinois Municipalities.* Macomb, IL: Western Illinois University, Public Policy Research Institute, 1975.
618. Weicher, John C. "The Fiscal Profitability of Urban Renewal Under Matching Grants and Revenue Sharing," *Journal of Urban Economics* (July 1976), pp. 193-208.
619. Wheeler, Gerald R. "New Federalism and the Cities: A Double Cross," *Social Work* (November 1974), pp. 659-664.